Copyright © 2020 by Joel Whitburn

Cover design by Heidi Betz

All photos taken from Joel Whitburn's personal record library

All Rights Reserved

WARNING
No part of this publication may be reproduced, stored in a retrieval system, or transmitted in any form by any means, electronic, mechanical, photocopying, recording or otherwise, without the prior written permission of the author.

ISBN 13: 978-0-89820-235-9
ISBN 10: 0-89820-235-3

Record Research Inc.
P.O. Box 200
Menomonee Falls, Wisconsin 53052-0200 U.S.A.

Phone: 262-251-5408
Email: books@recordresearch.com
Web Site: www.recordresearch.com

AUTHOR'S NOTE

The American public has long had a fascination with Top 10 lists. This is especially true when it comes to popular music.

I began researching the *Billboard* charts in 1965, and published my first Record Research book in 1970. Here it is, the year 2020, and I still eagerly await the new charts each and every week, with special interest in the weekly Top 10.

It's quite an accomplishment for an artist to have their song make the charts in the first place, but it's an even bigger feat to have that song crack the Top 10. Scoring a Top 10 hit means that even casual music fans are probably familiar with both the song and the artist. Because this book covers 1950-2020, every generation will be able to find their favorites, some well-remembered and some long-forgotten, but all certified smash hits in their day.

To make this book even more complete, I've included all the Top 10 hits, from *Billboard*, *Cash Box*, *Music Vendor/Record World* and *Radio & Records*. These highly respected music trade magazines had slightly different methods of compiling their charts, so many artists will get upgraded and/or totally new Top 10 peak positions. For example: Creedence Clearwater Revival never hit #1 in *Billboard*, yet they now are credited with three #1 hits. Also, Led Zeppelin's Top 10 hits total grows from one to four! These are just a couple of the many discoveries that await you in the pages to follow. I've also included lists of artists with the most #1 and most Top 10 hits, along with a full-color photo section, spotlighting many of the diverse artists through the decades.

No matter which particular era is your favorite, you'll find them all here. This book contains an all-encompassing timeline of artists from Eddie Fisher, Patti Page, Elvis Presley, Connie Francis, The Beatles, The Rolling Stones, Elton John, Olivia Newton-John, Prince, Madonna, Mariah Carey, Boyz II Men, Beyoncé, Taylor Swift, Ed Sheeran and Billie Eilish (just to name a select few). These are the most popular songs and artists from the past 70 years of the music that America loves the best. Enjoy!

JOEL WHITBURN

A special note of thanks to my staff ... Brent Olynick, Paul Haney and *Kim Bloxdorf. Thanks, as always, to my wife, Fran, for her continued love and support!*

USER'S GUIDE

EXPLANATION OF CHART DATA

This book contains Pop chart data taken from the following weekly publications:

Billboard [BB] (1950-2020*)
Cash Box [CB] (1950-1996)
Music Vendor [MV] (1954-1964)
Record World [RW] (1964-1982)
Radio & Records [RR] (1973-2009)
*data current through the Billboard Hot 100 chart dated February 29, 2020

The earliest debut date, highest peak position and most weeks charted are shown, no matter which source was utilized. If a song also peaked in the Top 10 in another publication, that peak position is shown to the right of the title. A common practice (especially in the 1950s) was for several different artists to record their own version of a hit record. Billboard always showed each recording at a separate chart position. However, both Cash Box and Music Vendor/Record World showed all versions under one chart position. There could often be several different versions, with only one or two becoming much more popular than the others. We refer to those lesser popular versions as "coat-tail" hits. The data contained in the artist section does not take those "coat-tail" hits into consideration. Please refer to our other Record Research books on those publications to see the designation on those particular song titles.

EXPLANATION OF COLUMNAR HEADINGS

- **DEBUT:** Earliest date song first charted.
- **CHART:** Publication that showed highest peak position.
- **PEAK:** Highest charted position.
- **WEEKS:** Most weeks charted.
- **GOLD:** RIAA certification. Symbols shown in this column:
  - ● Gold - Sales of 1,000,000 (1958-88); 500,000 (1989-on).
  - ▲ Platinum - Sales of 2,000,000 (1976-88); 1,000,000 (1989-on).
  - ○ Digital Gold - Sales of 500,000 (downloads/streams).
  - △ Digital Platinum - Sales of 1,000,000 (downloads/streams).
  - (Each additional level of one million units shown with a superscript number).
  - ⊙ Non-certified million seller - Based on industry sales reports.
- **A-side (Chart Hit):** If the B-side also charted, a slash (/) divides them.
- **Other Charts:** Peak position shown for Top 10 hits on other charts.
- **Label & Number:** Original record label and catalog number of commercial single.

BONUS SECTIONS

In the middle section of this book, you will find a 12 page section containing 420 full-color photos of artists and titles contained in this volume. In the back of the book, you'll find a listing of artists with the most #1 hits and the most Top 10 hits. These artists are the ones that have had the most impact from 1950-2020.

DEBUT	CH	PK	WK	Gold	A-side (Chart Hit) ... Other Charts	Label & Number

A

AALIYAH
04/30/94	BB	5	24	●	1 Back & Forth .... CB 6	Blackground 42174
09/03/94	BB	6	20	●	2 At Your Best (You Are Love)	Blackground 42239
08/24/96	CB	6	20		3 If Your Girl Only Knew	Blackground 98067
10/04/97	BB	9	20	●	4 The One I Gave My Heart To	Blackground 98002
07/04/98	BB	4	30		5 Are You That Somebody? .... RR 4	Blackground
03/18/00	BB	❶¹	32		6 Try Again .... RR 3²	Blackground 38722
11/30/02	BB	3¹	30		7 Miss You	Blackground 000384

ABBA
05/25/74	BB	6	17		1 Waterloo .... RW 9 / CB 10 / RR 10	Atlantic 3035
08/09/75	RW	10	26		2 SOS .... RR 10	Atlantic 3265
08/28/76	CB	10	21		3 Fernando	Atlantic 3346
12/11/76	BB	❶¹	27	●	4 Dancing Queen .... CB ❶¹ / RW ❶¹ / RR 4	Atlantic 3372
04/22/78	BB	3²	19	●	5 Take A Chance On Me .... CB 5 / RR 7 / RW 9	Atlantic 3457
11/22/80	BB	8	26		6 The Winner Takes It All	Atlantic 3776

ABBOTT, Gregory
10/18/86	CB	❶²	25	▲	1 Shake You Down .... BB ❶¹ / RR ❶¹	Columbia 06191

ABC
09/11/82	BB	9	25		1 The Look Of Love (Part One)	Mercury 76168
08/24/85	BB	9	24		2 Be Near Me .... CB 10 / RR 10	Mercury 880626
07/04/87	BB	5	21		3 When Smokey Sings .... RR 5 / CB 8	Mercury 888604

ABDUL, Paula
12/03/88	BB	❶³	25	▲	1 Straight Up .... CB ❶² / RR ❶²	Virgin 99256
03/11/89	BB	❶²	23	●	2 Forever Your Girl .... RR ❶² / CB 2²	Virgin 99230
06/23/89	CB	❶²	23	●	3 Cold Hearted .... BB ❶¹ / RR ❶¹	Virgin 99196
09/23/89	CB	❶¹	22		4 (It's Just) The Way That You Love Me .... RR 2¹ / BB 3¹	Virgin 99282
12/16/89	BB	❶³	23	●	5 Opposites Attract .... RR ❶³ / CB ❶²	Virgin 99158
					PAULA ABDUL (with The Wild Pair) (Marv Gunn & Bruce DeShazer)	
05/03/91	BB	❶⁵	22	●	6 Rush, Rush .... RR ❶⁵ / CB ❶³	Virgin 98828
07/12/91	CB	❶²	19		7 The Promise Of A New Day .... BB ❶¹ / RR ❶¹	Captive/Virgin 98752
10/18/91	RR	2³	27		8 Blowing Kisses In The Wind .... CB 3¹ / BB 6	Captive/Virgin 98683
01/17/92	CB	7	21		9 Vibeology .... RR 9	Captive/Virgin 98737
04/03/92	RR	5	21		10 Will You Marry Me?	Captive/Virgin 98584

ACE
03/01/75	CB	❶¹	22		1 How Long .... RR 3³ / BB 3² / RW 3²	Anchor 21000

ACE, Johnny
02/14/55	MV	8	13		1 Pledging My Love	Duke 136

ACE OF BASE
09/18/93	RR	2⁵	38	▲	1 All That She Wants .... BB 2³ / CB 3⁵	Arista 12614
01/01/94	RR	❶⁹	41	▲	2 The Sign .... BB ❶⁶ / CB ❶³	Arista 12653
04/22/94	RR	❶⁶	39	●	3 Don't Turn Around .... CB ❶³ / BB 4	Arista 12691
10/14/94	RR	7	23		4 Living In Danger .... CB 10	Arista 12754
10/27/95	RR	9	24		5 Beautiful Life .... CB 10	Arista 12889
06/26/98	BB	10	20	●	6 Cruel Summer	Arista 13505

ACKLIN, Barbara
06/29/68	RW	9	15		1 Love Makes A Woman	Brunswick 55379

ADAMS, Bryan
03/12/83	RR	6	19		1 Straight From The Heart .... BB 10	A&M 2536
11/03/84	CB	4	21		2 Run To You .... BB 6 / RR 6	A&M 2686
02/02/85	RR	8	17		3 Somebody .... CB 9	A&M 2701
04/19/85	BB	❶²	20		4 Heaven .... CB ❶¹ / RR ❶¹	A&M 2729
06/29/85	RR	4	18		5 Summer Of '69 .... BB 5 / CB 7	A&M 2739
09/14/85	RR	9	18		6 One Night Love Affair	A&M 2770
03/27/87	BB	6	17		7 Heat Of The Night .... CB 6 / RR 6	A&M 2921
06/28/91	BB	❶⁷	25	▲³	8 (Everything I Do) I Do It For You .... CB ❶⁶ / RR ❶⁶	A&M 1567
09/13/91	CB	❶¹	29	●	9 Can't Stop This Thing We Started .... BB 2¹ / RR 3¹	A&M 1576
12/21/91	CB	8	23		10 There Will Never Be Another Tonight	A&M 1588
03/13/92	RR	4	21		11 Thought I'd Died And Gone To Heaven .... CB 7	A&M 1592
07/31/92	RR	5	20		12 Do I Have To Say The Words? .... CB 8	A&M 1611
10/15/93	RR	2⁴	32		13 Please Forgive Me .... CB 3⁵ / BB 7	A&M 0422
11/19/93	CB	❶⁵	24	▲	14 All For Love .... RR ❶⁴ / BB ❶³	A&M 0476
					BRYAN ADAMS ROD STEWART STING	
04/14/95	BB	❶⁵	27		15 Have You Ever Really Loved A Woman? .... CB ❶¹ / RR 4	A&M 1028
11/15/96	BB	8	20	●	16 I Finally Found Someone	Columbia 78480
					BARBRA STREISAND and BRYAN ADAMS	

DEBUT	CH	PK	WK	Gold	A-side (Chart Hit)	Other Charts	Label & Number
					ADAMS, Oleta		
12/15/90	BB	5	27		1 Get Here	CB 10	Fontana 878476
					ADELE		
12/25/10	BB	❶⁷	65	△⁸	1 Rolling In The Deep		XL/Columbia
03/12/11	BB	❶⁵	39	△⁵	2 Someone Like You		XL/Columbia
03/12/11	BB	❶²	43	△⁴	3 Set Fire To The Rain		XL/Columbia
10/20/12	BB	8	20	△	4 Skyfall		XL/Columbia 42713
11/14/15	BB	❶¹⁰	26	△⁷	5 Hello		XL/Columbia
12/12/15	BB	8	27	△	6 Send My Love (To Your New Lover)		XL/Columbia
					AD LIBS, The		
01/16/65	RW	7	11		1 The Boy From New York City	BB 8 / CB 10	Blue Cat 102
					AEROSMITH		
01/03/76	BB	6	26		1 Dream On	CB 6 / RW 6 / RR 6	Columbia 10278
11/20/76	RW	5	21		2 Walk This Way	RR 5 / CB 7 / BB 10	Columbia 10449
01/30/88	BB	3²	26		3 Angel	CB 3² / RR 4	Geffen 28249
09/01/89	BB	5	21	●	4 Love In An Elevator	CB 6 / RR 7	Geffen 22845
11/25/89	CB	3¹	21		5 Janie's Got A Gun	BB 4 / RR 8	Geffen 22727
03/16/90	CB	8	19		6 What It Takes	BB 9 / RR 10	Geffen 19944
04/09/93	CB	3¹	24		7 Livin' On The Edge	RR 7	Geffen 19149
07/30/93	RR	7	32	●	8 Cryin'		Geffen 19256
11/26/93	RR	7	24		9 Amazing		Geffen 19264
05/20/94	RR	6	26		10 Crazy		Geffen 19267
05/29/98	RR	❶⁸	26	●	11 I Don't Want To Miss A Thing	BB ❶⁴	Columbia 78952
01/19/01	RR	6	20		12 Jaded	BB 7	Columbia 79555
					AFROJACK — see GUETTA, David		
					AFTER 7		
03/31/90	CB	4	23	●	1 Ready Or Not	BB 7 / RR 9	Virgin 98995
07/28/90	RR	5	25	●	2 Can't Stop	BB 6 / CB 7	Virgin 98961
					AFTER THE FIRE		
02/12/83	RR	3¹	22		1 Der Kommissar	BB 5 / CB 5	Epic 03559
					AGUILERA, Christina		
05/21/99	BB	❶⁵	28	▲	1 Genie In A Bottle	RR ❶⁴	RCA 65692
11/12/99	BB	❶²	24	●	2 What A Girl Wants	RR ❶¹	RCA 65960
04/07/00	BB	3²	22		3 I Turn To You	RR 7	RCA 60251
07/21/00	BB	❶⁴	21	●	4 Come On Over Baby (all i want is you)	RR 4	RCA 60341
01/26/01	RR	7	20		5 Nobody Wants To Be Lonely		Columbia 79573
					RICKY MARTIN with CHRISTINA AGUILERA		
04/06/01	RR	❶⁹	20		6 Lady Marmalade	BB ❶⁵	Interscope 497066
					CHRISTINA AGUILERA, LIL' KIM, MYA and PINK		
11/15/02	RR	❶⁴	27	○	7 Beautiful	BB 2¹	RCA 51195
03/21/03	RR	5	20	○	8 Fighter		RCA 50960
07/18/03	RR	3⁴	20		9 Can't Hold Us Down		RCA 54526
					CHRISTINA AGUILERA featuring Lil' Kim		
06/09/06	BB	6	21	○	10 Ain't No Other Man	RR 7	RCA 86851
09/29/06	RR	10	20	○	11 Hurt		RCA 04456
09/19/08	BB	7	18		12 Keeps Gettin' Better		RCA
11/23/13	BB	4	26	△⁶	13 Say Something		Epic
					A GREAT BIG WORLD & CHRISTINA AGUILERA		
					A-HA		
07/13/85	RR	❶³	27		1 Take On Me	CB ❶² / BB ❶¹	Warner 29011
					AIKEN, Clay		
06/28/03	BB	❶²	16	▲	1 This Is The Night		RCA 51785
04/03/04	BB	4	8		2 Solitaire		RCA 60199
					AIR SUPPLY		
02/09/80	CB	2²	25		1 Lost In Love	RR 2¹ / BB 3⁴ / RW 3¹	Arista 0479
06/07/80	RW	❶²	33	●	2 All Out Of Love	RR ❶² / BB 2⁴ / CB 2²	Arista 0520
10/25/80	RW	3²	24		3 Every Woman In The World	RR 4 / BB 5 / CB 9	Arista 0564
05/15/81	RR	❶³	22	●	4 The One That You Love	BB ❶¹ / CB ❶² / RW ❶¹	Arista 0604
09/18/81	RR	2²	21		5 Here I Am (Just When I Thought I Was Over You)	RW 4 / BB 5 / CB 5	Arista 0626
12/12/81	RR	2¹	20		6 Sweet Dreams	BB 5 / RW 7 / CB 8	Arista 0655
06/12/82	BB	5	19		7 Even The Nights Are Better	RR 5 / CB 8	Arista 0692
07/30/83	BB	2³	27	●	8 Making Love Out Of Nothing At All	CB 2² / RR 4	Arista 9056
					AKENS, Jewel		
01/23/65	CB	2²	15		1 The Birds And The Bees	RW 2¹ / BB 3²	Era 3141

6

DEBUT	CH	PK	WK	Gold	A-side (Chart Hit) ... Other Charts	Label & Number
					AKON	
06/12/04	BB	8	27	○	1 Locked Up	SRC 002245
					AKON Feat. Styles P.	
02/26/05	BB	4	20	△²	2 Lonely .... RR 5	SRC 005049
09/29/06	BB	2⁵	30	△²	3 Smack That .... RR 4	SRC 007877
					AKON Featuring Eminem	
10/14/06	BB	❶²	29	△	4 I Wanna Love You .... RR 3¹	SRC
					AKON Featuring Snoop Dogg	
02/03/07	BB	❶²	23	△	5 Don't Matter .... RR 3⁴	SRC
08/04/07	BB	7	19	△	6 Sorry, Blame It On Me	SRC
10/10/08	BB	8	22	△²	7 Right Now (Na Na Na) .... RR 9	SRC 012518
08/15/09	BB	5	40	△³	8 Sexy Chick	Astralwerks
					DAVID GUETTA with AKON	
					ALBERT, Morris	
06/14/75	RW	4	32	●	1 Feelings .... RR 5 / BB 6 / CB 10	RCA Victor 10279
					AL B. SURE!	
04/09/88	BB	7	24		1 Nite And Day .... CB 8 / RR 8	Warner 28192
					ALDEAN, Jason	
04/23/11	BB	7	27	△⁴	1 Dirt Road Anthem	Broken Bow
					ALI, Tatyana	
08/08/98	BB	6	17	●	1 Daydreamin'	MJJ Music 78855
					ALIAS	
09/08/90	CB	2²	24		1 More Than Words Can Say .... BB 2¹ / RR 3¹	EMI 50324
01/18/91	CB	10	18		2 Waiting For Love	EMI 50337
					ALIVE AND KICKING	
05/30/70	RW	3²	16		1 Tighter, Tighter .... CB 5 / BB 7	Roulette 7078
					ALL-AMERICAN REJECTS, The	
08/06/05	RR	5	39	△	1 Dirty Little Secret .... BB 9	Doghouse
02/11/06	RR	7	39		2 Move Along	Doghouse
10/14/06	BB	8	23		3 It Ends Tonight .... RR 8	Doghouse
11/28/08	RR	❶⁴	36	△⁴	4 Gives You Hell .... BB 4	Doghouse
					ALLEN, Rex	
08/01/53	BB	8	15		1 Crying In The Chapel	Decca 28758
					ALL-4-ONE	
01/01/94	RR	2¹	22	●	1 So Much In Love .... CB 3¹ / BB 5	Blitzz/Atlantic 87271
04/15/94	BB	❶¹¹	34	▲	2 I Swear .... CB ❶⁶ / RR ❶²	Blitzz/Atlantic 87243
05/26/95	CB	2¹	37	●	3 I Can Love You Like That .... RR 3² / BB 5	Blitzz/Atlantic 87134
					ALLMAN BROTHERS BAND, The	
08/18/73	CB	❶¹	16		1 Ramblin Man .... BB 2¹ / RW 2¹ / RR 3²	Capricorn 0027
					ALL SAINTS	
05/01/98	BB	4	33		1 Never Ever .... RR 5	London 570178
					ALLURE	
08/22/97	BB	4	28	●	1 All Cried Out .... RR 7	Crave 78678
					ALLURE featuring 112	
					ALPERT, Herb, & The Tijuana Brass	
10/20/62	BB	6	16		1 The Lonely Bull .... CB 6 / MV 7	A&M 703
08/28/65	CB	❶¹	19		2 Taste Of Honey .... RW 3² / BB 7	A&M 775
12/25/65	RW	7	12		3 Zorba The Greek .... CB 8	A&M 787
					HERB ALPERT:	
05/11/68	BB	❶⁴	15	●	4 This Guy's In Love With You .... CB ❶⁴ / RW ❶⁴	A&M 929
07/28/79	BB	❶²	25	●	5 Rise .... CB ❶² / RW ❶¹ / RR ❶¹	A&M 2151
04/11/87	BB	5	20		6 Diamonds .... RR 6 / CB 8	A&M 2929
					AMBROSIA	
09/02/78	CB	2³	21		1 How Much I Feel .... BB 3³ / RR 3² / RW 6	Warner 8640
04/04/80	RR	❶⁴	21		2 Biggest Part Of Me .... CB 2² / RW 2² / BB 3³	Warner 49225
07/12/80	RR	4	18		3 You're The Only Woman (You & I)	Warner 49508
					AMERICA	
02/19/72	BB	❶³	14	●	1 A Horse With No Name .... CB ❶³ / RW ❶³	Warner 7555
05/13/72	CB	8	11		2 I Need You .... RW 8 / BB 9	Warner 7580
10/14/72	RW	7	13		3 Ventura Highway .... BB 8 / CB 8	Warner 7641
08/10/74	BB	2¹	22		4 Tin Man .... BB 4 / CB 6 / RW 6	Warner 8014
12/21/74	BB	5	17		5 Lonely People .... RW 9 / CB 10	Warner 8048
04/05/75	RR	❶²	17		6 Sister Golden Hair .... BB ❶¹ / RW ❶¹ / CB 2¹	Warner 8086
07/31/82	RR	3¹	21		7 You Can Do Magic .... CB 7 / BB 8	Capitol 5142

7

DEBUT	CH	PK	WK	Gold	A-side (Chart Hit) ... Other Charts	Label & Number
					AMERICAN BREED, The	
11/18/67	RW	①¹	17	●	1 Bend Me, Shape Me .... CB 3² / BB 5	Acta 811
					AMERICAN IDOL	
05/03/03	BB	4	8	●	1 God Bless The U.S.A.	RCA 51780
					AMERIE	
02/12/05	BB	8	20	○	1 1 Thing	Rise/Columbia 71958
					AMES, Ed	
01/14/67	BB	8	15		1 My Cup Runneth Over .... CB 8 / RW 8	RCA Victor 9002
					AMES BROTHERS, The	
01/14/50	BB	①²	17	⊙	1 Rag Mop .... CB 2²	Coral 60140
01/28/50	BB	①¹	28	⊙	2 Sentimental Me .... CB 4	Coral 60173
08/12/50	BB	5	23		3 Can Anyone Explain? (No, No, No!) .... CB 5	Coral 60253
09/29/51	BB	2¹	26		4 Undecided .... CB 4	Coral 60566
					AMES BROTHERS And LES BROWN And His Band Of Renown	
06/27/53	BB	①⁸	32	⊙	5 You You You .... CB ①¹	RCA Victor 5325
03/06/54	BB	6	21		6 The Man With The Banjo .... CB 8	RCA Victor 5644
11/08/54	BB	3⁴	19	⊙	7 The Naughty Lady Of Shady Lane .... CB 3³ / MV 3²	RCA Victor 5897
07/01/57	BB	5	24		8 Tammy	RCA Victor 6930
09/09/57	MV	3²	20		9 Melodie D'Amour (Melody Of Love) .... BB 5 / CB 7	RCA Victor 7046
					ANDERSON, Bill	
04/06/63	CB	7	16		1 Still .... BB 8 / MV 10	Decca 31458
					ANDERSON, Carl — see LORING, Gloria	
					ANDERSON, Leroy, And His "Pops" Concert Orchestra	
03/31/51	CB	5	17		1 The Syncopated Clock	Decca 40201
12/29/51	BB	①⁵	42	⊙	2 Blue Tango .... CB ①⁵	Decca 27875
					ANDERSON, Lynn	
11/28/70	CB	①¹	18	●	1 Rose Garden .... RW ①¹ / BB 3²	Columbia 45252
					ANDREWS SISTERS	
10/01/49	CB	①⁶	27	⊙	1 I Can Dream, Can't I? .... BB ①⁴	Decca 24705
01/28/50	BB	6	17		2 Quicksilver	Decca 24827
					BING CROSBY And ANDREWS SISTERS	
05/13/50	BB	①²	24		3 I Wanna Be Loved .... CB 2⁵	Decca 27007
03/10/51	BB	8	15		4 Sparrow In The Tree Top .... CB 8	Decca 27477
					BING CROSBY And ANDREWS SISTERS	
					ANGELS, The	
07/27/63	BB	①³	15	⊙	1 My Boyfriend's Back .... CB ①² / MV ①²	Smash 1834
					ANIMALS, The	
08/08/64	BB	①³	12	⊙	1 The House Of The Rising Sun .... CB ①³ / RW ①³	MGM 13264
09/10/66	BB	10	11		2 See See Rider .... RW 10	MGM 13582
08/05/67	CB	8	11		3 San Franciscan Nights .... RW 8 / BB 9	MGM 13769
12/16/67	CB	10	9		4 Monterey	MGM 13868
					ANIMOTION	
01/26/85	BB	6	25		1 Obsession .... CB 6 / RR 7	Mercury 880266
02/18/89	BB	9	19		2 Room To Move .... RR 9	Polydor 871418
					ANKA, Paul	
06/29/57	MV	①³	29	⊙	1 Diana .... BB ①¹ / CB 2⁴	ABC-Paramount 9831
12/30/57	BB	7	17		2 You Are My Destiny .... CB 9	ABC-Paramount 9880
12/01/58	MV	8	18		3 (All Of A Sudden) My Heart Sings	ABC-Paramount 9987
05/23/59	BB	①⁴	17	⊙	4 Lonely Boy .... MV ①³ / CB ①²	ABC-Paramount 10022
08/24/59	BB	2³	18	⊙	5 Put Your Head On My Shoulder .... CB 2³ / MV 2³	ABC-Paramount 10040
11/09/59	BB	4	16		6 It's Time To Cry .... MV 4 / CB 6	ABC-Paramount 10064
02/20/60	BB	2²	14	⊙	7 Puppy Love .... CB 2² / MV 4	ABC-Paramount 10082
05/09/60	BB	8	15		8 My Home Town .... CB 8 / MV 8	ABC-Paramount 10106
03/06/61	MV	10	12		9 Tonight My Love, Tonight	ABC-Paramount 10194
05/15/61	BB	10	11		10 Dance On Little Girl	ABC-Paramount 10220
02/19/62	MV	8	13		11 Love Me Warm And Tender	RCA Victor 7977
07/06/74	BB	①³	17	●	12 (You're) Having My Baby .... RW ①² / RR ①² / CB ①¹	United Artists 454
11/02/74	BB	7	17		13 One Man Woman/One Woman Man .... CB 7 / RW 8	United Artists 569
03/15/75	CB	5	16		14 I Don't Like To Sleep Alone .... BB 8 / RW 9	United Artists 615
					PAUL ANKA with Odia Coates (above 3)	
11/15/75	BB	7	20		15 Times Of Your Life	United Artists 737
					ANNE-MARIE — see CLEAN BANDIT	
					ANNETTE	
12/29/58	BB	7	16		1 Tall Paul	Disneyland 118
02/08/60	BB	10	14		2 O Dio Mio .... MV 10	Buena Vista 354

DEBUT	CH	PK	WK	Gold	A-side (Chart Hit) ... Other Charts	Label & Number
					ANN-MARGRET	
07/10/61	MV	10	13		1 I Just Don't Understand	RCA Victor 7894
					ANOTHER BAD CREATION	
01/12/91	BB	9	23	●	1 Iesha	Motown 2070
04/27/91	BB	10	17		2 Playground	Motown 2088
					ANTHONY, Marc	
08/20/99	BB	3²	40	●	1 I Need To Know .... RR 5	Columbia 79250
02/25/00	BB	2²	32		2 You Sang To Me	Columbia 79406
					ANTHONY, Ray	
04/15/50	CB	4	26		1 Sentimental Me .... BB 7	Capitol 923
05/27/50	BB	4	21		2 Count Every Star .... CB 6	Capitol 979
09/02/50	BB	5	13		3 Can Anyone Explain	Capitol 1131
09/30/50	BB	4	17		4 Harbor Lights /	
10/21/50	BB	9	14		5 Nevertheless (I'm In Love With You)	Capitol 1190
11/10/51	BB	10	11		6 Undecided	Capitol 1824
02/09/52	BB	2¹	15		7 At Last	Capitol 1912
06/28/52	BB	10	4		8 As Time Goes By	Capitol 2104
08/15/53	BB	2¹	20		9 Dragnet .... CB 4	Capitol 2562
12/29/58	CB	7	18		10 Peter Gunn .... BB 8 / MV 9	Capitol 4041
					APOLLO 100	
12/25/71	BB	6	14		1 Joy .... CB 6 / RW 8	Mega 0050
					AQUA	
08/08/97	BB	7	16		1 Barbie Girl	MCA 55392
					ARCADIA	
10/25/85	BB	6	19		1 Election Day .... RR 6 / CB 7	Capitol 5501
					ARCHIES, The	
09/14/68	RW	6	16		1 Bang-Shang-A-Lang .... CB 9	Calendar 1006
07/19/69	BB	❶⁴	22	●	2 Sugar, Sugar .... CB ❶⁴ / RW ❶³	Calendar 1008
11/29/69	RW	4	13	●	3 Jingle Jangle .... CB 8 / BB 10	Kirshner 5002
					ARCHULETA, David	
08/22/08	BB	2¹	23		1 Crush	19 Records
					ARDEN, Jann	
02/10/96	CB	10	40		1 Insensitive	A&M 1274
					ARDEN, Toni	
04/21/58	MV	7	18		1 Padre	Decca 30628
					ARGENT	
06/03/72	RW	4	17		1 Hold Your Head Up .... BB 5 / CB 5	Epic 10852
					ARMSTRONG, Louis	
09/01/51	BB	10	16		1 (When We Are Dancing) I Get Ideas	Decca 27720
02/15/64	MV	❶³	24	☉	2 Hello, Dolly! .... BB ❶¹ / CB ❶¹	Kapp 573
					ARNOLD, Eddy	
10/16/65	BB	6	15		1 Make The World Go Away .... RW 6	RCA Victor 8679
					ARRESTED DEVELOPMENT	
04/11/92	CB	5	22	●	1 Tennessee .... BB 6	Chrysalis 23829
08/15/92	BB	8	23	●	2 People Everyday .... CB 8	Chrysalis 50397
12/19/92	CB	5	26	●	3 Mr. Wendal .... BB 6 / RR 7	Chrysalis 24810
					ARTISTS FOR HAITI	
02/27/10	BB	2¹	5		1 We Are The World 25: For Haiti	WATW Foundation
					A$AP ROCKY	
11/17/12	BB	8	27	△⁵	1 F**kin Problems	A$AP Worldwide
					A$AP ROCKY Featuring Drake, 2 Chainz & Kendrick Lamar	
					ASHANTI	
02/16/02	BB	❶¹⁰	32		1 Foolish .... RR 2⁵	Murder Inc. 588986
06/01/02	BB	8	23		2 Happy	Murder Inc. 582935
05/10/03	BB	2¹	21		3 Rock Wit U (Awww Baby) .... RR 5	Murder Inc. 000540
08/30/03	BB	7	20		4 Rain On Me	Murder Inc. 001107
					ASIA	
04/17/82	BB	4	18		1 Heat Of The Moment .... RR 4 / CB 6	Geffen 50040
07/24/82	RR	5	15		2 Only Time Will Tell	Geffen 29970
07/22/83	RR	4	15		3 Don't Cry .... CB 9 / BB 10	Geffen 29571

DEBUT	CH	PK	WK	Gold	A-side (Chart Hit)	Other Charts	Label & Number
					ASSOCIATION, The		
05/21/66	BB	7	12		1 Along Comes Mary	CB 9 / RW 10	Valiant 741
08/27/66	BB	❶³	14	●	2 Cherish	CB ❶³ / RW ❶²	Valiant 747
05/27/67	BB	❶⁴	15		3 Windy	CB ❶³ / RW ❶²	Warner 7041
08/26/67	CB	❶¹	14	●	4 Never My Love	BB 2² / RW 2²	Warner 7074
01/27/68	RW	9	11		5 Everything That Touches You	BB 10	Warner 7163
					ASTLEY, Rick		
12/19/87	BB	❶²	26	●	1 Never Gonna Give You Up	CB ❶¹ / RR ❶¹	RCA 5347
04/15/88	BB	❶¹	19		2 Together Forever	CB ❶¹ / RR ❶¹	RCA 8319
07/16/88	RR	9	16		3 It Would Take A Strong Strong Man	BB 10	RCA 8663
12/17/88	BB	6	19		4 She Wants To Dance With Me	CB 6 / RR 7	RCA 8838
02/16/91	BB	7	23		5 Cry For Help	CB 7 / RR 7	RCA 2774
					ATARIS, The		
07/11/03	RR	10	20	○	1 The Boys Of Summer		Columbia
					ATC		
01/12/01	RR	10	20		1 Around The World (La La La La La)		Republic 158610
					ATLANTA RHYTHM SECTION		
01/22/77	RR	4	20		1 So In To You	CB 5 / BB 7 / RW 8	Polydor 14373
02/25/78	BB	7	19		2 Imaginary Lover	RR 8 / CB 9 / RW 9	Polydor 14459
05/26/79	RR	8	15		3 Do It Or Die		Polydor 14568
08/11/79	RR	8	14		4 Spooky		Polydor 2001
					ATLANTIC STARR		
12/28/85	BB	3²	23		1 Secret Lovers	CB 3² / RR 3²	A&M 2788
03/28/87	CB	❶²	23		2 Always	BB ❶¹ / RR ❶¹	Warner 28455
01/24/92	RR	2²	25	●	3 Masterpiece	CB 3² / BB 3¹	Reprise 19076
					AUGUST, Jan		
05/20/50	BB	8	12		1 Bewitched		Mercury 5399
					JAN AUGUST & Jerry Murad's HARMONICATS		
					AUSTIN, Patti		
04/24/82	BB	❶²	37	●	1 Baby, Come To Me	CB 2³ / RR 4	Qwest 50036
					PATTI AUSTIN with JAMES INGRAM		
					AUTRY, Gene		
12/03/49	BB	1¹	7	☉	1 Rudolph, The Red-Nosed Reindeer	CB 3²	Columbia 38610
03/25/50	BB	5	6	☉	2 Peter Cottontail		Columbia 38750
12/02/50	BB	3¹	7		3 Rudolph, The Red-Nosed Reindeer	CB 8	Columbia 38610
12/09/50	BB	7	6	☉	4 Frosty The Snow Man		Columbia 742
12/20/52	BB	9	2		5 The Night Before Christmas Song		Columbia 39876
					ROSEMARY CLOONEY & GENE AUTRY		
					AVALON, Frankie		
01/20/58	BB	7	15	☉	1 DeDe Dinah		Chancellor 1011
07/07/58	BB	9	15		2 Ginger Bread		Chancellor 1021
02/09/59	BB	❶⁵	18		3 Venus	CB ❶⁵ / MV ❶⁴	Chancellor 1031
05/18/59	MV	6	15		4 Bobby Sox To Stockings /	CB 7 / BB 8	
05/25/59	BB	10	14		5 A Boy Without A Girl		Chancellor 1036
08/24/59	BB	7	16		6 Just Ask Your Heart	CB 10	Chancellor 1040
11/16/59	CB	❶³	17	☉	7 Why	BB ❶¹ / MV ❶¹	Chancellor 1045
					AVERAGE WHITE BAND (AWB)		
11/23/74	BB	❶¹	21	●	1 Pick Up The Pieces	CB ❶¹ / RW ❶¹ / RR 4	Atlantic 3229
04/05/75	BB	10	18		2 Cut The Cake		Atlantic 3261
					AVICII		
07/13/13	BB	4	53	△⁶	1 Wake Me Up!		PRMD
					AVICII with ALOE BLACC		
					AZALEA, Iggy		
03/22/14	BB	❶⁷	39	△⁷	1 Fancy		Island
					IGGY AZALEA Featuring Charli XCX		
07/19/14	BB	3²	30	△³	2 Black Widow		Turn First
					IGGY AZALEA with RITA ORA		
					AZ YET		
08/24/96	CB	6	29	●	1 Last Night	BB 9	LaFace 24181
02/22/97	BB	8	34	▲	2 Hard To Say I'm Sorry	RR 10	LaFace 24223
					AZ YET with PETER CETERA		

DEBUT	CH	PK	WK	Gold	A-side (Chart Hit) ... Other Charts	Label & Number

B

BAAUER
| 03/02/13 | BB | ❶⁵ | 20 | △² | 1 Harlem Shake .... | Jeffree's |

BABY BASH
08/23/03	RR	2²	33	○	1 Suga Suga .... BB 7	Universal 001055
					BABY BASH Feat. Frankie J	
08/11/07	BB	7	30	△²	2 Cyclone	Arista
					BABY BASH Featuring T-Pain	

BABYFACE
08/12/89	BB	7	19		1 It's No Crime .... RR 8	Solar 68966
02/24/90	CB	5	20		2 Whip Appeal .... BB 6 / RR 6	Solar 74007
06/04/94	CB	2²	42	●	3 When Can I See You .... BB 4 / RR 4	Epic 77550
04/22/95	CB	5	32	●	4 Someone To Love .... BB 10	Yab Yum 77895
					JON B & BABYFACE	
10/19/96	BB	6	20	▲	5 This Is For The Lover In You .... CB 7	Epic 78443
					BABYFACE Featuring LL Cool J, Howard Hewett, Jody Watley and Jeffrey Daniels	
02/01/97	BB	6	26	●	6 Every Time I Close My Eyes	Epic 78485

BABYS, The
| 10/01/77 | CB | 8 | 19 | | 1 Isn't It Time .... RR 9 | Chrysalis 2173 |
| 12/30/78 | CB | 8 | 21 | | 2 Every Time I Think Of You .... RR 10 | Chrysalis 2279 |

BACHELORS, The
| 04/04/64 | BB | 10 | 16 | | 1 Diane .... CB 10 | London 9639 |

BACHMAN, Tal
| 05/14/99 | RR | 7 | 28 | | 1 She's So High .... | Columbia |

BACHMAN-TURNER OVERDRIVE
05/18/74	CB	6	20		1 Takin' Care Of Business .... RR 8	Mercury 73487
09/14/74	RR	❶³	18	●	2 You Ain't Seen Nothing Yet .... BB ❶¹ / CB ❶¹ / RW ❶¹	Mercury 73622
01/18/75	CB	8	12		3 Roll On Down The Highway	Mercury 73656

BACKSTREET BOYS
05/23/97	RR	2⁴	43	▲	1 Quit Playing Games (With My Heart) .... BB 2²	Jive 42453
10/24/97	RR	3²	56		2 As Long As You Love Me .... BB 4	Jive 42510
03/13/98	BB	4	23	▲	3 Everybody (Backstreet's Back) .... RR 10	Jive 42510
07/10/98	RR	2¹	27		4 I'll Never Break Your Heart .... BB 4	Jive 42528
12/04/98	BB	5	24	▲	5 All I Have To Give .... RR 6	Jive 42562
04/16/99	RR	❶³	31	△³	6 I Want It That Way .... BB 6	Jive 42595
08/20/99	RR	6	22		7 Larger Than Life	Jive 42624
12/17/99	RR	❶¹	24		8 Show Me The Meaning Of Being Lonely .... BB 6	Jive
05/05/00	RR	10	18		9 The One	Jive
10/06/00	RR	7	20		10 Shape Of My Heart .... BB 9	Jive 42758
04/15/05	RR	8	20	○	11 Incomplete	Jive

BAD BUNNY
04/21/18	BB	❶¹	51	△⁷	1 I Like It	KSR Group
					CARDI B, BAD BUNNY & J BALVIN	
10/27/18	BB	5	27		2 MIA	Rimas
					BAD BUNNY Featuring Drake	

BAD COMPANY
| 08/03/74 | CB | ❶¹ | 19 | | 1 Can't Get Enough .... RR 3² / RW 4 / BB 5 | Swan Song 70015 |
| 06/21/75 | BB | 10 | 19 | | 2 Feel Like Makin' Love .... CB 10 | Swan Song 70106 |

BAD ENGLISH
09/16/89	BB	❶²	22	●	1 When I See You Smile .... RR ❶² / CB ❶¹	Epic 69082
12/23/89	CB	4	20		2 Price Of Love .... RR 4 / BB 5	Epic 73094
06/09/90	RR	10	18		3 Possession	Epic 73398

BADFINGER
02/07/70	RW	3¹	15		1 Come And Get It .... CB 6 / BB 7	Apple 1815
10/17/70	RW	4	14		2 No Matter What .... CB 6 / BB 8	Apple 1822
11/27/71	RW	❶²	15	●	3 Day After Day .... CB 3³ / BB 4	Apple 1841
03/18/72	CB	9	11		4 Baby Blue	Apple 1844

BAD MEETS EVIL
| 07/02/11 | BB | 4 | 22 | △² | 1 Lighters .... | Shady |
| | | | | | BAD MEETS EVIL with BRUNO MARS | |

BADU, Erykah
08/19/00	BB	6	20		1 Bag Lady	Motown 158326
09/07/02	BB	9	27		2 Love Of My Life (An Ode To Hip Hop)	Fox/MCA 113987
					ERYKAH BADU Featuring Common	

BAEZ, Joan
| 08/07/71 | RW | ❶¹ | 15 | ● | 1 The Night They Drove Old Dixie Down .... BB 3¹ / CB 3¹ | Vanguard 35138 |

DEBUT	CH	PK	WK	Gold	A-side (Chart Hit)	Other Charts	Label & Number
					BAILEY, Pearl		
09/27/52	BB	7	21		1 Takes Two To Tango	CB 7	Coral 60817
					BAILEY, Philip		
11/24/84	CB	❶¹	24	●	1 Easy Lover	BB 2² / RR 2²	Columbia 04679
					PHILIP BAILEY & PHIL COLLINS		
					BAINBRIDGE, Merril		
08/30/96	RR	2⁴	30	●	1 Mouth	BB 4 / CB 4	Universal 56018
					BAKER, Anita		
08/16/86	BB	8	22		1 Sweet Love	RR 8	Elektra 69557
09/24/88	CB	2²	24		2 Giving You The Best That I Got	RR 3² / BB 3¹	Elektra 69371
01/21/89	RR	10	17		3 Just Because		Elektra 69327
					BAKER, LaVern		
01/03/55	CB	3²	18	☉	1 Tweedlee Dee	MV 5	Atlantic 1047
					LaVERN BAKER and The Gliders		
12/08/58	BB	6	21	☉	2 I Cried A Tear	MV 6 / CB 10	Atlantic 2007
					BALIN, Marty		
05/23/81	RR	4	21		1 Hearts	BB 8 / CB 9 / RW 10	EMI America 8084
					BALL, Kenny, and His Jazzmen		
01/20/62	BB	2¹	17		1 Midnight In Moscow	CB 2¹ / MV 3¹	Kapp 442
					BALLARD, Hank, And The Midnighters		
05/16/60	CB	6	26	☉	1 Finger Poppin' Time	BB 7 / MV 7	King 5341
09/19/60	BB	6	17		2 Let's Go, Let's Go, Let's Go	CB 7	King 5400
					BALVIN, J		
07/22/17	BB	3¹	30	△²	1 Mi Gente		Scorpio
					J BALVIN & WILLY WILLIAM Featuring Beyonce		
04/21/18	BB	❶¹	51	△⁷	2 I Like It		KSR Group
					CARDI B, BAD BUNNY & J BALVIN		
					BANANARAMA		
07/21/84	BB	9	19		1 Cruel Summer	CB 10 / RR 10	London 810127
06/28/86	BB	❶¹	19		2 Venus	CB 3² / RR 3²	London 886056
07/11/87	BB	4	23		3 I Heard A Rumour	CB 4 / RR 6	London 886165
					BAND, Alex — see SANTANA		
					BAND AID		
12/22/84	CB	7	12	●	1 Do They Know It's Christmas?		Columbia 04749
					BANGLES		
01/25/86	BB	2¹	21		1 Manic Monday	CB 3² / RR 5	Columbia 05757
09/27/86	BB	❶⁴	25	●	2 Walk Like An Egyptian	RR ❶³ / CB ❶¹	Columbia 06257
02/14/87	RR	8	19		3 Walking Down Your Street	CB 9	Columbia 06674
11/14/87	BB	2¹	23		4 Hazy Shade Of Winter	CB 3¹ / RR 3¹	Def Jam 07630
10/15/88	BB	5	21		5 In Your Room	RR 9 / CB 10	Columbia 08090
02/03/89	RR	❶²	20	●	6 Eternal Flame	BB ❶¹ / CB ❶¹	Columbia 68533
					BANKS, Lloyd		
05/15/04	BB	8	20	○	1 On Fire		G-Unit 002753
					BANNER, David		
07/23/05	BB	7	20	○	1 Play		SRC 005047
					BARBER('S), Chris, Jazz Band		
01/10/59	MV	3¹	16	☉	1 Petite Fleur (Little Flower)	CB 4 / BB 5	Laurie 3022
					BARE, Bobby		
12/13/58	BB	2¹	16	☉	1 The All American Boy	MV 5 / CB 10	Fraternity 835
					BILL PARSONS		
10/05/63	BB	10	12		2 500 Miles Away From Home	MV 10	RCA Victor 8238
					BAREILLES, Sara		
11/17/07	RR	❶³	41	△³	1 Love Song	BB 4	Epic
					BARENAKED LADIES		
07/24/98	RR	❶⁶	28		1 One Week	BB ❶¹	Reprise 17174
					BARRY, Len		
09/18/65	CB	❶¹	16		1 1-2-3	RW 2² / BB 2¹	Decca 31827
					BARTON, Eileen		
03/11/50	BB	❶¹⁰	18	●	1 If I Knew You Were Comin' (I'd've Baked A Cake)	CB 2⁴	National 9103
12/08/51	BB	10	11		2 Cry		Coral 60592
					BASIL, Toni		
09/04/82	BB	❶¹	29	▲	1 Mickey	CB 2⁴	Chrysalis 2638

DEBUT	CH	PK	WK	Gold	A-side (Chart Hit) ....Other Charts	Label & Number
					BASS, Fontella	
09/18/65	RW	2¹	15		1 Rescue Me ....CB 3¹ / BB 4	Checker 1120
					BASSEY, Shirley	
01/30/65	RW	6	14		1 Goldfinger ....CB 7 / BB 8	United Artists 790
					BASTILLE	
08/31/13	BB	5	53	△⁶	1 Pompeii	Virgin
09/01/18	BB	2¹	52	△⁵	2 Happier	Joytime
					MARSHMELLO & BASTILLE	
					BAXTER, Les, his Chorus and Orchestra	
07/14/51	BB	4	21		1 Because Of You	Capitol 1760
03/15/52	BB	10	17		2 Blue Tango	Capitol 1966
03/21/53	CB	2⁸	27		3 April In Portugal ....BB 2³	Capitol 2374
05/23/53	BB	7	12		4 Ruby	Capitol 2457
07/10/54	BB	4	22		5 The High And The Mighty ....CB 4 / MV 7	Capitol 2845
04/09/55	CB	❶⁷	27	⊙	6 Unchained Melody ....MV ❶³ / BB ❶²	Capitol 3055
07/09/55	MV	4	21		7 Wake The Town And Tell The People ....BB 5 / CB 5	Capitol 3120
01/27/56	BB	❶⁶	24	⊙	8 The Poor People Of Paris ....CB ❶⁴ / MV ❶⁴	Capitol 3336
					BAY CITY ROLLERS	
10/04/75	BB	❶¹	23	●	1 Saturday Night ....CB ❶¹ / RW ❶¹ / RR 3⁴	Arista 0149
02/06/76	CB	7	19		2 Money Honey ....RR 8 / BB 9 / RW 10	Arista 0170
09/04/76	RR	6	19		3 I Only Want To Be With You ....CB 8 / RW 10	Arista 0205
06/04/77	RR	5	18		4 You Made Me Believe In Magic ....CB 7 / RW 9 / BB 8	Arista 0256
					BAZUKA	
04/12/75	BB	10	20		1 Dynomite-Part I ....RW 10	A&M 1666
					Tony Camillo's BAZUKA	
					BBMAK	
04/14/00	RR	8	31		1 Back Here	Hollywood 64040
					BEACH BOYS, The	
07/14/62	CB	10	21		1 Surfin' Safari...	Capitol 4777
03/23/63	MV	2¹	17	⊙	2 Surfin' U.S.A. ....CB 3² / BB 3¹	Capitol 4932
07/20/63	CB	5	16		3 Surfer Girl ....MV 5 / BB 7	Capitol 5009
11/02/63	BB	6	13		4 Be True To Your School ....CB 8 / MV 8	Capitol 5069
02/08/64	BB	5	13	⊙	5 Fun, Fun, Fun ....CB 6 / MV 7	Capitol 5118
05/23/64	BB	❶²	17	●	6 I Get Around ....RW ❶² / CB ❶¹	Capitol 5174
09/05/64	CB	7	10		7 When I Grow Up (To Be A Man) ....RW 8 / BB 9	Capitol 5245
11/07/64	BB	8	11		8 Dance, Dance, Dance ....RW 9 / CB 10	Capitol 5306
04/17/65	BB	❶²	14	⊙	9 Help Me, Rhonda ....RW ❶² / CB ❶¹	Capitol 5395
07/24/65	RW	3³	11	⊙ 10	California Girls ....BB 3² / CB 3¹	Capitol 5464
12/25/65	RW	❶²	12	⊙ 11	Barbara Ann ....CB ❶¹ / BB 2²	Capitol 5561
04/02/66	RW	2¹	11	⊙ 12	Sloop John B ....BB 3¹ / CB 5	Capitol 5602
07/30/66	RW	5	11		13 Wouldn't It Be Nice ....CB 7 / BB 8	Capitol 5706
10/22/66	BB	❶¹	14	▲ 14	Good Vibrations ....CB ❶¹ / RW ❶¹	Capitol 5676
08/05/67	CB	8	8		15 Heroes And Villains ....RW 8	Brother 1001
12/23/67	CB	10	10		16 Darlin'...	Capitol 2068
07/20/68	RW	7	14		17 Do It Again	Capitol 2239
06/05/76	BB	5	24		18 Rock And Roll Music ....RW 7 / RR 10	Brother/Reprise 1354
07/25/81	RW	5	20		19 The Beach Boys Medley ....CB 8	Capitol 5030
09/03/88	CB	❶²	28	▲ 20	Kokomo ....RR ❶² / BB ❶¹	Elektra 69385
					BEASTIE BOYS	
12/20/86	CB	3¹	20		1 (You Gotta) Fight For Your Right (To Party!) ....BB 7	Def Jam 06595
					BEATLES, The	
01/11/64	MV	❶⁹	18	●	1 I Want To Hold Your Hand ....CB ❶⁸ / BB ❶⁷	Capitol 5112
01/25/64	BB	❶²	17	⊙	2 She Loves You ....CB ❶² / MV ❶¹	Swan 4152
02/01/64	BB	3²	14	▲	3 Please Please Me ....CB 3¹ / MV 3¹	Vee-Jay 581
03/07/64	CB	❶¹	13	▲	4 Twist And Shout ....MV ❶¹ / BB 2⁴	Tollie 9001
03/21/64	BB	❶⁵	13	●	5 Can't Buy Me Love ....CB ❶⁵ / MV ❶⁴	Capitol 5150
03/28/64	BB	2¹	12	●	6 Do You Want To Know A Secret ....CB 3³ / MV 3²	Vee-Jay 587
04/04/64	BB	❶¹	16	▲ 7	Love Me Do /	Capitol 5222
					CB ❶¹ / RW ❶¹	
05/02/64	BB	10	10		8 P.S. I Love You ....CB 10	Tollie 9008
07/11/64	CB	❶³	15	●	9 A Hard Day's Night ....RW ❶³ / BB ❶²	Capitol 5222
12/05/64	CB	❶⁴	12	● 10	I Feel Fine /	
					BB ❶³ / RW ❶²	
12/05/64	BB	4	10		11 She's A Woman ....RW 7 / CB 8	Capitol 5327
02/20/65	CB	❶³	11	● 12	Eight Days A Week ....RW ❶³ / BB ❶²	Capitol 5371
04/17/65	BB	❶¹	12		13 Ticket To Ride ....CB ❶¹ / RW ❶¹	Capitol 5407
07/31/65	BB	❶³	14	● 14	Help! ....CB ❶³ / RW ❶¹	Capitol 5476
09/18/65	BB	❶⁴	13	● 15	Yesterday ....CB ❶³ / RW ❶²	Capitol 5498
12/11/65	CB	❶⁴	13	● 16	We Can Work It Out /	
					BB ❶³ / RW ❶²	
12/18/65	BB	5	10		17 Day Tripper ....CB 10	Capitol 5555
03/05/66	RW	❶²	10	● 18	Nowhere Man ....CB 2¹ / BB 3¹	Capitol 5587

DEBUT	CH	PK	WK	Gold	A-side (Chart Hit) .... Other Charts	Label & Number
					BEATLES, The (cont'd)	
06/11/66	BB	❶²	11	● 19	Paperback Writer .... CB ❶² / RW ❶¹	Capitol 5651
08/20/66	CB	❶¹	10	● 20	Yellow Submarine .... RW ❶¹ / BB 2¹	Capitol 5715
02/25/67	CB	❶²	10	● 21	Penny Lane / .... RW ❶² / BB ❶¹	Capitol 5810
02/25/67	BB	8	9	22	Strawberry Fields Forever .... RW 9 / CB ❶¹	
07/22/67	CB	❶²	11	● 23	All You Need Is Love .... RW ❶² / BB ❶¹	Capitol 5964
12/02/67	RW	❶⁴	12	● 24	Hello Goodbye .... BB ❶³ / CB ❶²	Capitol 2056
03/16/68	CB	2³	12	▲ 25	Lady Madonna .... RW 2¹ / BB 4	Capitol 2138
09/07/68	BB	❶⁹	19	▲⁴ 26	Hey Jude / .... CB ❶⁷ / RW ❶⁴	Apple 2276
09/14/68	RW	2¹	11	27	Revolution	
05/03/69	BB	❶⁵	12	▲² 28	Get Back .... CB ❶⁵ / RW ❶⁴	Apple 2490
06/14/69	RW	7	9	● 29	The Ballad Of John And Yoko .... BB 8 / CB 10	Apple 2531
10/18/69	CB	❶³	16	▲² 30	Come Together / .... RW ❶³ / BB 2¹	Apple 2654
10/11/69	RW	❶²	16	31	Something .... CB 2³ / BB 3²	
03/14/70	CB	❶⁴	14	▲² 32	Let It Be .... RW ❶³ / BB ❶²	Apple 2764
05/16/70	BB	❶²	11	▲ 33	The Long And Winding Road .... CB ❶² / RW ❶²	Apple 2832
06/05/76	CB	3¹	23	● 34	Got To Get You Into My Life .... BB 7 / RR 7 / RW 9	Capitol 4274
12/30/95	BB	6	11	● 35	Free As A Bird	Apple 58497
03/23/96	CB	10	7	● 36	Real Love	Apple 58544
					BEAU BRUMMELS, The	
04/17/65	RW	6	12	1	Just A Little .... CB 7 / BB 8	Autumn 10
					BECK	
01/29/94	BB	10	24	● 1	Loser	DGC/Bong Load 19270
					BEDINGFIELD, Daniel	
07/12/02	RR	3⁴	22	1	Gotta Get Thru This .... BB 10	Island 570976
02/28/03	RR	7	20	2	If You're Not The One	Island 000267
					BEDINGFIELD, Natasha	
11/04/05	RR	2⁴	42	△² 1	Unwritten .... BB 5	Epic
10/19/07	RR	10	20	△ 2	Love Like This	Phonogenic 18498
					NATASHA BEDINGFIELD Featuring Sean Kingston	
02/09/08	RR	4	35	△² 3	Pocketful Of Sunshine .... BB 5	Phonogenic
					BEE GEES	
08/10/68	CB	3¹	15	1	I've Gotta Get A Message To You .... RW 7 / BB 8	Atco 6603
12/14/68	RW	5	13	2	I Started A Joke .... BB 6 / CB 6	Atco 6639
11/28/70	CB	❶¹	16	● 3	Lonely Days .... RW ❶¹ / BB 3¹	Atco 6795
06/19/71	BB	❶⁴	15	● 4	How Can You Mend A Broken Heart .... CB ❶³ / RW ❶¹	Atco 6824
07/22/72	RW	9	13	5	Run To Me	Atco 6896
05/24/75	BB	❶⁵	23	● 6	Jive Talkin' .... BB ❶² / RW ❶² / CB ❶¹	RSO 510
10/04/75	CB	4	20	7	Nights On Broadway .... RR 5 / BB 7 / RW 7	RSO 515
12/20/75	RR	8	19	8	Fanny (Be Tender With My Love) .... CB 9 / RW 10	RSO 519
07/02/76	BB	❶¹	22	● 9	You Should Be Dancing .... CB ❶¹ / RR 2¹ / RW 4	RSO 853
09/18/76	BB	3⁴	24	● 10	Love So Right .... CB 3² / RR 6 / RW 10	RSO 859
09/24/77	CB	❶⁴	33	● 11	How Deep Is Your Love .... RR ❶⁴ / BB ❶³ / RW 2²	RSO 882
12/10/77	RW	❶⁶	27	▲ 12	Stayin' Alive .... RR ❶⁶ / BB ❶⁴ / CB ❶⁴	RSO 885
02/03/78	BB	❶⁸	22	● 13	Night Fever .... CB ❶⁸ / RW ❶⁸ / RR ❶⁶	RSO 889
11/10/78	BB	❶²	22	▲ 14	Too Much Heaven .... RR ❶² / RW ❶¹ / CB 2⁵	RSO 913
02/02/79	CB	❶³	20	▲ 15	Tragedy .... BB ❶² / RW ❶² / RR 3²	RSO 918
04/13/79	BB	❶¹	19	● 16	Love You Inside Out .... CB 2² / RR 3² / RW 4	RSO 925
07/29/89	BB	7	16	17	One .... CB 9 / RR 9	Warner 22899
					BEGA, Lou	
08/20/99	RR	❶⁵	22	1	Mambo No. 5 (A Little Bit Of...) .... BB 3²	RCA 65842
					BEGINNING OF THE END, The	
05/01/71	CB	10	15	1	Funky Nassau-Part I	Alston 4595
					BELAFONTE, Harry	
01/12/57	MV	2⁴	20	⊙ 1	Banana Boat (Day-O) .... CB 3¹ / BB 5	RCA Victor 6771
03/16/57	MV	6	20	2	Mama Look At Bubu .... CB 8	RCA Victor 6830
					BELL, Archie, & The Drells	
03/30/68	BB	❶²	15	● 1	Tighten Up .... CB ❶¹ / RW ❶¹	Atlantic 2478
07/20/68	RW	5	10	2	I Can't Stop Dancing .... BB 9	Atlantic 2534
					BELL, William	
02/12/77	RW	7	20	1	Tryin' To Love Two .... CB 8 / BB 10	Mercury 73839
					BELLAMY BROTHERS	
01/31/76	BB	❶¹	24	1	Let Your Love Flow .... CB ❶¹ / RR 3¹ / RW 4	Warner/Curb 8169
					BELL BIV DeVOE	
04/07/90	CB	2¹	22	▲ 1	Poison .... BB 3⁴ / RR 4	MCA 53772
06/30/90	BB	3³	23	2	Do Me! .... CB 5 / RR 7	MCA 53848

DEBUT	CH	PK	WK	Gold	A-side (Chart Hit)	Other Charts	Label & Number
					BELLE, Regina — see BRYSON, Peabo		
					BELL NOTES, The		
01/03/59	BB	6	18		1 I've Had It	CB 8	Time 1004
					BELLS, The		
03/06/71	CB	4	14	●	1 Stay Awhile	RW 4 / BB 7	Polydor 15023
					BELL SISTERS, The		
01/05/52	CB	6	17		1 Bermuda	BB 7	RCA Victor 4422
03/01/52	BB	10	11		2 Wheel Of Fortune		RCA Victor 4520
					BENATAR, Pat		
10/04/80	RW	5	31	●	1 Hit Me With Your Best Shot	CB 7 / BB 9 / RR 9	Chrysalis 2464
01/17/81	CB	10	18		2 Treat Me Right		Chrysalis 2487
10/16/82	BB	8	17		3 Shadows Of The Night		Chrysalis 2647
09/24/83	RR	3²	24	●	4 Love Is A Battlefield	CB 4 / BB 5	Chrysalis 42732
10/26/84	RR	2³	20		5 We Belong	BB 5 / CB 6	Chrysalis 42826
07/06/85	CB	9	18		6 Invincible	BB 10 / RR 10	Chrysalis 42877
					BENNETT, Boyd, And His Rockets		
07/09/55	MV	2¹	21	⊙	1 Seventeen	CB 3² / BB 5	King 1470
					BENNETT, Tony		
06/02/51	BB	❶¹⁰	38	⊙	1 Because Of You	CB ❶⁸	Columbia 39362
07/28/51	BB	❶⁶	30	⊙	2 Cold, Cold Heart	CB 2³	Columbia 39449
09/19/53	BB	❶⁸	25	⊙	3 Rags To Riches	CB ❶⁵	Columbia 40048
11/21/53	CB	❶²	25	⊙	4 Stranger In Paradise	BB 2²	Columbia 40121
03/13/54	BB	7	12		5 There'll Be No Teardrops Tonight		Columbia 40169
07/17/54	BB	8	14		6 Cinnamon Sinner		Columbia 40272
04/06/56	MV	6	22		7 Can You Find It In Your Heart		Columbia 40667
07/20/57	MV	5	21		8 In The Middle Of An Island	CB 8 / BB 9	Columbia 40965
					BENSON, George		
06/05/76	RW	8	26		1 This Masquerade	BB 10	Warner 8209
03/11/78	RW	5	20		2 On Broadway	BB 7	Warner 8542
02/24/79	RR	9	15		3 Love Ballad		Warner 8759
06/28/80	BB	4	25		4 Give Me The Night	RR 5 / CB 6 / RW 6	Warner 49505
10/24/81	RR	3²	23		5 Turn Your Love Around	BB 5 / CB 5 / RW 8	Warner 49846
					BENTON, Brook		
01/19/59	CB	2¹	19	⊙	1 It's Just A Matter Of Time	MV 3³ / BB 3¹	Mercury 71394
07/13/59	MV	9	14		2 Thank You Pretty Baby	CB 10	Mercury 71478
10/05/59	CB	3¹	17	⊙	3 So Many Ways	MV 4 / BB 6	Mercury 71512
01/25/60	CB	2¹	16	⊙	4 Baby (You've Got What It Takes)	BB 5 / MV 5	Mercury 71565
05/21/60	CB	5	15		5 A Rockin' Good Way (To Mess Around And Fall In Love)	BB 7 / MV 8	Mercury 71629
					DINAH WASHINGTON & BROOK BENTON (above 2)		
08/01/60	CB	3¹	18		6 Kiddio	MV 5 / BB 7	Mercury 71652
02/06/61	CB	7	14		7 Think Twice	MV 8	Mercury 71774
05/15/61	BB	2³	16		8 The Boll Weevil Song	CB 2² / MV 2²	Mercury 71820
08/18/62	CB	10	12		9 Lie To Me	MV 10	Mercury 72024
11/24/62	BB	3¹	14		10 Hotel Happiness	MV 5 / CB 6	Mercury 72055
01/03/70	CB	2¹	15	●	11 Rainy Night In Georgia	RW 2¹ / BB 4	Cotillion 44057
					BERLIN		
06/21/86	BB	❶¹	22	●	1 Take My Breath Away	CB ❶¹ / RR 2²	Columbia 05903
					BERNARD, Rod		
03/07/59	MV	8	13		1 This Should Go On Forever		Argo 5327
					BERNSTEIN, Elmer, and Orchestra		
03/23/56	MV	9	15		1 "Main Title" From "The Man With The Golden Arm"		Columbia 05903
					BERRY, Chuck		
08/08/55	MV	4	14	⊙	1 Maybellene	BB 5 / CB 5	Chess 1604
04/06/57	MV	3⁴	26	⊙	2 School Day	BB 3³ / CB 3¹	Chess 1653
11/04/57	BB	8	19		3 Rock & Roll Music		Chess 1671
02/15/58	BB	2³	16		4 Sweet Little Sixteen	CB 2² / MV 4	Chess 1683
04/21/58	BB	8	15	⊙	5 Johnny B. Goode		Chess 1691
05/23/64	BB	6	11		6 No Particular Place To Go	CB 9 / BB 10	Chess 1898
07/29/72	BB	❶²	18	●	7 My Ding-A-Ling	CB ❶² / RW ❶²	Chess 2131
					BEYONCE		
05/24/03	BB	❶⁸	27	○	1 Crazy In Love	RR ❶²	Columbia
					BEYONCE (Featuring Jay-Z)		
08/16/03	BB	❶⁹	29	○	2 Baby Boy	RR ❶⁴	Columbia 76867
					BEYONCE Featuring Sean Paul		
11/15/03	BB	4	24		3 Me, Myself And I		Columbia 76911
03/26/04	RR	2²	22	○	4 Naughty Girl	BB 3²	Columbia 76853

DEBUT	CH	PK	WK	Gold	A-side (Chart Hit) ... Other Charts	Label & Number
					BEYONCE (cont'd)	
11/04/05	RR	❶⁶	28	○	5 Check On It ....BB ❶⁵	Columbia 80277
					BEYONCE Featuring Bun-B & Slim Thug	
07/01/06	BB	4	17	○	6 Deja Vu	Columbia 88435
					BEYONCE Featuring Jay-Z	
11/04/06	BB	❶¹⁰	30	△²	7 Irreplaceable ....RR ❶⁸	Columbia 05024
03/16/07	BB	3¹	18	△	8 Beautiful Liar	Columbia 10320
					BEYONCE & SHAKIRA	
10/24/08	BB	3⁴	20	△²	9 If I Were A Boy ....RR 9	Music World
11/01/08	BB	❶⁴	27	△⁴	10 Single Ladies (Put A Ring On It) ....RR ❶³	Music World
02/07/09	RR	3¹	31	△²	11 Halo ....BB 5	Music World
08/08/09	BB	10	29	△	12 Sweet Dreams	Music World
01/04/14	BB	2¹	20	△³	13 Drunk In Love	Parkwood/Columbia
					BEYONCE Featuring Jay Z	
05/14/16	BB	10	7	△	14 Formation	Parkwood/Columbia
					B-52's, The	
08/26/89	BB	3²	28	●	1 Love Shack ....CB 4 / RR 5	Reprise 22817
12/23/89	RR	2²	22	●	2 Roam ....BB 3² / CB 3²	Reprise 22667
06/19/92	RR	10	16		3 Good Stuff	Reprise 18895
					BICE, Bo	
07/09/05	BB	2¹	7	●	1 Inside Your Heaven	RCA 69495
					BIEBER, Justin	
02/06/10	BB	5	20	△¹²	1 Baby	SchoolBoy
					JUSTIN BIEBER Featuring Ludacris	
06/26/10	BB	8	19	△⁵	2 Never Say Never	SchoolBoy
					JUSTIN BIEBER with JADEN SMITH	
04/14/12	BB	2¹	20	△⁶	3 Boyfriend	SchoolBoy 016817
06/30/12	BB	6	30	△⁴	4 As Long As You Love Me	SchoolBoy
					JUSTIN BIEBER Featuring Big Sean	
07/07/12	BB	5	24	△²	5 Beauty And A Beat	SchoolBoy
					JUSTIN BIEBER Featuring Nicki Minaj	
03/21/15	BB	8	45	△⁴	6 Where Are U Now	Mad Decent
					SKRILLEX & DIPLO with JUSTIN BIEBER	
09/19/15	BB	❶¹	31	△⁶	7 What Do You Mean?	SchoolBoy
11/14/15	BB	❶³	42	△⁸	8 Sorry	SchoolBoy
12/05/15	BB	❶²	41	△⁷	9 Love Yourself	SchoolBoy
08/13/16	BB	2⁴	27	△⁴	10 Cold Water	Mad Decent
					MAJOR LAZER with JUSTIN BIEBER & MO	
05/25/19	BB	2²	38	△²	11 I Don't Care	SchoolBoy
					ED SHEERAN & JUSTIN BIEBER	
10/19/19	BB	4	20	○	12 10,000 Hours	Warner
					DAN + SHAY & JUSTIN BIEBER	
01/18/20	BB	2¹	7		13 Yummy	SchoolBoy
02/22/20	BB	9	2		14 Intentions	SchoolBoy
					JUSTIN BIEBER Featuring Quavo	
					BIG BOPPER	
08/04/58	CB	4	25		1 Chantilly Lace ....MV 4 / BB 6	Mercury 71343
					BIG MOUNTAIN	
02/25/94	CB	2³	30	●	1 Baby, I Love Your Way ....RR 2¹ / BB 6	RCA 62780
					BIG SEAN	
10/22/11	BB	10	24	△⁴	1 Dance (A$$)	G.O.O.D.
					BIG SEAN Featuring Nicki Minaj	
11/26/16	BB	6	28	△⁴	2 Bounce Back	G.O.O.D.
					BILK, Mr. Acker	
03/12/62	MV	❶²	22	●	1 Stranger On The Shore ....BB ❶¹ / CB ❶¹	Atco 6217
					BILLY & LILLIE	
12/28/57	CB	4	13	☉	1 La Dee Dah ....BB 9 / MV 9	Swan 4002
					BILLY JOE & THE CHECKMATES	
01/13/62	BB	10	13		1 Percolator (Twist)	Dore 620
					BISHOP, Elvin	
03/06/76	BB	3²	25	●	1 Fooled Around And Fell In Love ....RW 3² / RR 3² / CB 3¹	Capricorn 0252
					BISHOP, Stephen	
05/07/77	CB	5	28		1 On And On ....RR 8 / RW 10	ABC 12260
					BIZ MARKIE	
01/20/90	BB	9	22	▲	1 Just A Friend ....CB 10	Cold Chillin' 22784
					BLACC, Aloe	
07/13/13	BB	4	53	△⁶	1 Wake Me Up!	PRMD
					AVICII with ALOE BLACC	
12/28/13	BB	8	20	△	2 The Man	Aloe Blacc

DEBUT	CH	PK	WK	Gold	A-side (Chart Hit) .... Other Charts	Label & Number
					BLACK('S), Bill, Combo	
02/22/60	CB	4	19	⊙	1 White Silver Sands .... MV 5 / BB 9	Hi 2021
06/13/60	MV	8	14		2 Josephine .... CB 9	Hi 2022
09/10/60	CB	7	15		3 Don't Be Cruel .... MV 9	Hi 2026
					BLACK, Jeanne	
04/18/60	MV	2¹	14	⊙	1 He'll Have To Stay .... BB 4 / CB 5	Capitol 4368
					BLACK BOX	
08/04/90	CB	7	19		1 Everybody Everybody .... BB 8	RCA 2628
04/06/91	BB	8	22		2 Strike It Up .... RR 9	RCA 2794
					BLACKBYRDS, The	
02/08/75	BB	6	17		1 Walking In Rhythm .... CB 7 / RW 8	Fantasy 736
					BLACK EYED PEAS	
05/23/03	RR	❶⁶	27	○	1 Where Is The Love? .... BB 8	A&M 000714
					BLACK EYED PEAS (Featuring Justin Timberlake)	
01/30/04	RR	9	24	○	2 Hey Mama	A&M 000936
06/25/04	RR	4	24	△³	3 Let's Get It Started	A&M
04/22/05	RR	3⁵	26	○	4 Don't Phunk With My Heart .... BB 3³	A&M 004799
08/05/05	RR	10	20		5 Don't Lie	A&M
08/19/05	BB	3⁶	36		6 My Humps .... RR 4	A&M 005585
03/13/09	BB	❶¹²	33	△⁴	7 Boom Boom Pow .... RR ❶³	Interscope
06/06/09	BB	❶²	27	△²	8 Imma Be	Interscope
06/27/09	BB	❶¹⁴	56	△¹⁰	9 I Gotta Feeling	Interscope
10/03/09	BB	7	24	△²	10 Meet Me Halfway	Interscope
05/15/10	BB	9	18		11 Rock That Body	Interscope
11/27/10	BB	4	20		12 The Time (Dirty Bit)	Interscope
03/05/11	BB	3⁴	31		13 Just Can't Get Enough	Interscope
					BLACKSTREET	
10/22/94	BB	7	29		1 Before I Let You Go	Interscope 98211
10/12/96	BB	❶⁴	31	▲	2 No Diggity .... CB ❶¹	Interscope 97007
					BLACKstreet (Featuring Dr. Dre)	
					BLANC, Mel	
01/27/51	BB	9	11		1 I Taut I Taw A Puddy Tat	Capitol 1360
					BLANCO, Benny	
07/28/18	BB	9	52	△⁴	1 Eastside	Interscope
					BENNY BLANCO, HALSEY & KHALID	
					BLAND, Billy	
02/15/60	BB	7	20		1 Let The Little Girl Dance .... CB 10	Old Town 1076
					BLANE, Marcie	
10/06/62	CB	2¹	19	⊙	1 Bobby's Girl .... MV 2¹ / BB 3⁴	Seville 120
					BLAQUE	
04/17/99	BB	8	20	●	1 808	Track Masters 78857
10/22/99	BB	5	29		2 Bring It All To Me .... RR 5	Track Masters
					BLAQUE (Feat. *NSYNC)	
					BLESSID UNION OF SOULS	
02/17/95	RR	❶²	33		1 I Believe .... CB 4 / BB 8	EMI 58320
07/28/95	RR	10	32		2 Let Me Be The One	EMI 58443
04/02/99	RR	7	24		3 Hey Leonardo (She Likes Me For Me)	Push
					BLEYER, Archie, Orchestra and Chorus	
05/15/54	BB	2²	24		1 Hernando's Hideaway .... CB 2¹	Cadence 1241
					BLIGE, Mary J.	
08/29/92	RR	5	36	●	1 Real Love .... BB 7 / CB 9	Uptown/MCA 54455
05/06/95	BB	3¹	23	▲	2 I'll Be There For You/You're All I Need To Get By .... CB 6	Def Jam 851878
					METHOD MAN and MARY J. BLIGE	
01/27/96	CB	❶²	24	▲	3 Not Gon' Cry .... BB 2²	Arista 12957
07/28/01	BB	❶⁶	41		4 Family Affair .... RR ❶³	MCA 155894
11/26/05	RR	❶⁴	33		5 Be Without You .... BB 3¹	Geffen
					BLIND MELON	
08/21/93	RR	4	30		1 No Rain	Capitol 15994
					BLINK-182	
11/26/99	BB	6	23		1 All The Small Things .... RR 9	MCA 155606
					BLOCBOY JB	
02/24/18	BB	5	25	△⁵	1 Look Alive	OVO Sound
					BLOCBOY JB Featuring Drake	

DEBUT	CH	PK	WK	Gold	A-side (Chart Hit) .... Other Charts	Label & Number

BLONDIE
02/10/79	RR	①²	23	●	1 Heart Of Glass .... BB ①¹ / CB ①¹ / RW ①¹	Chrysalis 2295
02/16/80	CB	①⁷	28	●	2 Call Me .... BB ①⁶ / RW ①⁶ / RR ①⁶	Chrysalis 2414
11/15/80	RR	①³	27	●	3 The Tide Is High .... CB ①² / RW ①² / BB ①¹	Chrysalis 2465
01/30/81	BB	①²	21	●	4 Rapture .... CB ①² / RW ①² / RR 8	Chrysalis 2485

BLOODSTONE
| 04/07/73 | CB | 5 | 20 | ▲ | 1 Natural High .... RW 7 / BB 10 | London 1046 |

BLOOD, SWEAT & TEARS
03/01/69	BB	2³	13	●	1 You've Made Me So Very Happy .... RW 2² / CB 2¹	Columbia 44776
05/31/69	BB	2³	13	●	2 Spinning Wheel .... RW 2³ / CB 3²	Columbia 44871
10/18/69	CB	①¹	13	●	3 And When I Die .... RW 2³ / BB 2¹	Columbia 45008
08/01/70	RW	8	9		4 Hi-De-Ho .... CB 9	Columbia 45204

BLOOM, Bobby
| 09/05/70 | CB | 6 | 16 | | 1 Montego Bay .... BB 8 / RW 8 | L&R/MGM 157 |

BLUE CHEER
| 02/10/68 | RW | 8 | 16 | | 1 Summertime Blues .... CB 9 | Philips 40516 |

BLUEFACE
| 01/26/19 | BB | 8 | 20 | △ | 1 Thotiana .... | Blueface |

BLUE MAGIC
| 05/04/74 | CB | 5 | 22 | ● | 1 Sideshow .... RW 5 / BB 8 / RR 10 | Atco 6961 |

BLUE OYSTER CULT
| 07/31/76 | CB | 7 | 26 | | 1 (Don't Fear) The Reaper .... | Columbia 10384 |

BLUES BROTHERS
| 12/09/78 | RR | 4 | 18 | | 1 Soul Man .... CB 9 | Atlantic 3545 |

BLUES IMAGE
| 04/25/70 | BB | 4 | 16 | ● | 1 Ride Captain Ride .... CB 5 / RW 5 | Atco 6746 |

BLUES MAGOOS
| 11/26/66 | BB | 5 | 17 | | 1 (We Ain't Got) Nothin' Yet .... RW 5 / CB 6 | Mercury 72622 |

BLUES TRAVELER
| 03/17/95 | CB | 4 | 53 | | 1 Run-Around .... RR 5 / BB 8 | A&M 0982 |
| 10/07/95 | RR | 8 | 35 | | 2 Hook .... CB 10 | A&M 1176 |

BLUE SWEDE
| 02/09/74 | RW | ①² | 18 | ● | 1 Hooked On A Feeling .... BB ①¹ / CB ①¹ / RR ①¹ | EMI 3627 |
| 08/24/74 | RW | 6 | 13 | | 2 Never My Love .... BB 7 / CB 10 | EMI 3938 |

BLUNT, James
| 11/12/05 | BB | ①¹ | 38 | △⁴ | 1 You're Beautiful .... RR 5 | Custard/Atlantic |

B.o.B.
02/13/10	BB	①²	28	△³	1 Nothin' On You	RebelRock 524312
					B.o.B. Featuring Bruno Mars	
05/01/10	BB	2¹	30	△⁶	2 Airplanes	RebelRock
					B.o.B. Featuring Hayley Williams of Paramore	
05/15/10	BB	10	20	△²	3 Magic	RebelRock
					B.o.B. Featuring Rivers Cuomo of Weezer	
10/15/11	BB	7	20	△²	4 Strange Clouds	RebelRock
					B.o.B. Featuring Lil Wayne	

BOBBETTES, The
| 08/03/57 | BB | 6 | 24 | | 1 Mr. Lee .... CB 6 / MV 6 | Atlantic 1144 |

BOB B. SOXX And The Blue Jeans
| 11/17/62 | BB | 8 | 14 | | 1 Zip-A-Dee Doo-Dah .... CB 9 | Philles 107 |

BoDEANS
| 01/12/96 | RR | 6 | 23 | | 1 Closer To Free .... | Slash 17674 |

BOLTON, Michael
10/28/89	BB	①³	24		1 How Am I Supposed To Live Without You .... RR ①² / CB 2³	Columbia 73017
03/03/90	BB	3¹	21		2 How Can We Be Lovers .... CB 4 / RR 4	Columbia 73257
05/26/90	RR	5	19		3 When I'm Back On My Feet Again .... BB 7 / CB 8	Columbia 73342
04/12/91	BB	2¹	22		4 Love Is A Wonderful Thing .... CB 3² / BB 4	Columbia 73719
07/12/91	CB	3¹	23		5 Time, Love And Tenderness .... RR 4 / BB 7	Columbia 73889
10/11/91	RR	①³	24		6 When A Man Loves A Woman .... CB ①² / BB ①¹	Columbia 74020
01/24/92	CB	2²	22		7 Missing You Now .... RR 4	Columbia 74184
					MICHAEL BOLTON Featuring Kenny G	
05/08/92	RR	10	20		8 Steel Bars	Columbia
10/17/92	RR	3¹	24		9 To Love Somebody .... CB 9	Columbia 74733
11/05/93	CB	5	25	●	10 Said I Loved You...But I Lied .... BB 6 / RR 6	Columbia 77260

DEBUT	CH	PK	WK	Gold	#	A-side (Chart Hit) .... Other Charts	Label & Number
						BONDS, Gary (U.S.)	
10/17/60	MV	3¹	15		1	New Orleans .... CB 5 / BB 6	Legrand 1003
05/22/61	MV	❶⁴	16	☉	2	Quarter To Three .... CB ❶³ / BB ❶²	Legrand 1008
07/17/61	CB	2²	12		3	School Is Out .... MV 4 / BB 5	Legrand 1009
12/11/61	CB	6	17		4	Dear Lady Twist .... BB 9 / MV 9	Legrand 1015
03/19/62	BB	9	12		5	Twist, Twist Senora	Legrand 1018
04/24/81	CB	7	18		6	This Little Girl .... RR 7	EMI America 8079
						BONE THUGS-N-HARMONY	
05/11/96	BB	❶⁸	23	▲²	1	Tha Crossroads .... CB ❶⁷	Ruthless 6335
06/21/97	BB	4	20	▲	2	Look Into My Eyes	Ruthless 6343
04/14/07	BB	6	18		3	I Tried	Full Surface
						BONE THUGS-N-HARMONY Featuring Akon	
						BON JOVI	
09/06/86	BB	❶¹	26		1	You Give Love A Bad Name .... CB ❶¹ / RR 7	Mercury 884953
12/13/86	BB	❶⁴	23	△³	2	Livin' On A Prayer .... CB ❶⁴ / RR ❶³	Mercury 888184
04/11/87	BB	7	19	△⁴	3	Wanted Dead Or Alive .... CB 7 / RR 8	Mercury 888467
09/23/88	BB	❶²	21		4	Bad Medicine .... CB ❶¹ / RR 2²	Mercury 870657
11/26/88	CB	2¹	22		5	Born To Be My Baby .... RR 2¹ / BB 3¹	Mercury 872156
03/04/89	BB	❶¹	22		6	I'll Be There For You .... CB ❶¹ / RR ❶¹	Mercury 872564
06/03/89	CB	5	21		7	Lay Your Hands On Me .... BB 7 / RR 9	Mercury 874452
10/07/89	BB	9	19		8	Living In Sin .... CB 9 / RR 10	Mercury 876070
07/20/90	CB	❶²	21	▲	9	Blaze Of Glory .... BB ❶¹ / RR 3²	Mercury 875896
						JON BON JOVI	
01/15/93	CB	4	23		10	Bed Of Roses .... RR 4 / BB 10	Jambco 864852
04/30/93	RR	9	21		11	In These Arms	Jambco 862088
09/30/94	RR	2⁸	34	▲	12	Always .... CB 3² / BB 4	Mercury 856227
06/02/95	RR	9	22		13	This Ain't A Love Song	Mercury 856824
						BOOKER T. & THE MG'S	
08/11/62	CB	3²	16	●	1	Green Onions .... MV 3² / BB 3¹	Stax 127
07/06/68	CB	9	12	●	2	Soul-Limbo	Stax 0001
11/09/68	BB	9	18		3	Hang 'Em High .... RW 9	Stax 0013
03/15/69	BB	6	13	●	4	Time Is Tight .... RW 7 / CB 8	Stax 0028
						BOONE, Debby	
08/27/77	RW	❶¹³	28	▲	1	You Light Up My Life .... BB ❶¹⁰ / CB ❶⁸ / RR ❶⁶	Warner/Curb 8455
						BOONE, Pat	
03/07/55	MV	5	14		1	Two Hearts .... CB 9	Dot 15338
06/18/55	BB	❶²	25	☉	2	Ain't That A Shame .... MV ❶² / CB 2⁸	Dot 15377
10/08/55	BB	7	17		3	At My Front Door (Crazy Little Mama) .... MV 7 / CB 8	Dot 15422
01/20/56	BB	4	22	☉	4	I'll Be Home /	Dot 15443
01/20/56	CB	10	17		5	Tutti' Frutti .... MV 10	
03/31/56	MV	5	15		6	Long Tall Sally .... BB 8 / BB 9	Dot 15457
06/01/56	BB	❶⁴	23	☉	7	I Almost Lost My Mind .... CB ❶² / MV 2⁵	Dot 15472
09/15/56	BB	5	24	☉	8	Friendly Persuasion (Thee I Love) /	Dot 15490
						MV 9 / CB 10	
09/08/56	BB	10	14		9	Chains Of Love	
12/08/56	BB	❶¹	22	☉	10	Don't Forbid Me .... CB 3⁵ / MV 3²	Dot 15521
03/09/57	BB	5	21	☉	11	Why Baby Why .... MV 7 / CB 9	Dot 15545
05/04/57	BB	❶⁷	34	☉	12	Love Letters In The Sand .... MV ❶⁷ / CB ❶⁶	Dot 15570
08/03/57	BB	6	21	☉	13	Remember You're Mine /	Dot 15602
08/03/57	MV	8	15		14	There's A Gold Mine In The Sky	
10/26/57	BB	❶⁶	26	☉	15	April Love .... CB 3³ / MV 4	Dot 15660
01/27/58	BB	4	19	☉	16	A Wonderful Time Up There /	Dot 15690
01/27/58	BB	4	17		17	It's Too Soon To Know .... CB 6 / MV 7	
04/28/58	BB	5	14		18	Sugar Moon .... MV 7 / CB 9	Dot 15750
06/30/58	BB	7	14		19	If Dreams Came True	Dot 15785
05/01/61	BB	❶¹	15	☉	20	Moody River .... CB 2¹ / MV 2¹	Dot 16209
06/16/62	BB	6	13		21	Speedy Gonzales .... CB 6 / MV 6	Dot 16368
						BOSTON	
09/11/76	RR	2¹	25	○	1	More Than A Feeling .... CB 4 / RW 4 / BB 5	Epic 50266
08/18/78	BB	4	14		2	Don't Look Back .... RR 4 / CB 7 / RW 8	Epic 50590
09/19/86	CB	❶³	18		3	Amanda .... RR ❶³ / BB ❶²	MCA 52756
12/06/86	RR	7	17		4	We're Ready .... BB 9	MCA 52985
						BOSWELL, Connee	
09/11/54	BB	10	11		1	If I Give My Heart To You	Decca 29148
						BOUNTY KILLER — see NO DOUBT	
						BOWEN, Jimmy, with the Rhythm Orchids	
02/09/57	MV	9	20		1	I'm Stickin' With You	Roulette 4001

DEBUT	CH	PK	WK	Gold	A-side (Chart Hit) .... Other Charts	Label & Number
					BOWIE, David	
01/27/73	RW	10	15		1 Space Oddity	RCA Victor 0876
06/28/75	BB	❶²	26	●	2 Fame .... RW ❶² / RR ❶² / CB ❶¹	RCA Victor 10320
12/13/75	BB	10	23		3 Golden Years	RCA Victor 10441
03/25/83	BB	❶¹	22	●	4 Let's Dance .... CB ❶¹ / RR 2¹	EMI America 8158
06/04/83	CB	9	20		5 China Girl .... BB 10 / RR 10	EMI America 8165
09/15/84	BB	5	18		6 Blue Jean .... BB 8 / RR 10	EMI America 8231
08/30/85	BB	7	16		7 Dancing In The Street .... RR 7 / CB 8	EMI America 8288
					MICK JAGGER/DAVID BOWIE	
					BOWLING FOR SOUP	
08/06/04	RR	10	22	△²	1 1985	Silvertone/Jive
					BOW WOW	
05/28/05	BB	4	24	○	1 Let Me Hold You	Columbia 74625
					BOW WOW Featuring Omarion	
08/06/05	BB	3²	22	○	2 Like You .... RR 9	Columbia 80449
					BOW WOW (feat. Ciara)	
10/21/06	BB	9	21	○	3 Shortie Like Mine	Columbia
					BOW WOW Featuring Chris Brown & Johnta Austin	
					BOX TOPS, The	
08/12/67	BB	❶⁴	17	●	1 The Letter .... RW ❶⁴ / CB ❶³	Mala 565
02/24/68	RW	2³	15	●	2 Cry Like A Baby .... BB 2² / CB 2¹	Mala 593
					BOYCE, Tommy, & Bobby Hart	
12/23/67	RW	6	14		1 I Wonder What She's Doing Tonite .... CB 7 / BB 8	A&M 893
					BOYD, Jimmy	
12/06/52	BB	❶²	6	⊙	1 I Saw Mommy Kissing Santa Claus .... CB ❶¹	Columbia 39871
03/14/53	CB	3¹	16		2 Tell Me A Story .... BB 4	Columbia 39945
					JIMMY BOYD - FRANKIE LAINE	
					BOY GEORGE	
03/19/93	RR	8	18		1 The Crying Game .... CB 10	SBK 50437
					BOY KRAZY	
01/29/93	RR	❶²	24		1 That's What Love Can Do .... CB 9	Next Plateau 857024
					BOY MEETS GIRL	
09/03/88	CB	4	28		1 Waiting For A Star To Fall .... BB 5 / RR 7	RCA 8691
					BOYS CLUB	
10/22/88	CB	4	21		1 I Remember Holding You .... BB 8	MCA 53420
					BOYS LIKE GIRLS	
05/25/07	RR	8	25	△	1 The Great Escape	Columbia
					BOYZ II MEN	
06/15/91	BB	3³	26	▲	1 Motownphilly .... CB 3¹ / RR 5	Motown 2090
09/21/91	CB	❶²	27	●	2 It's So Hard To Say Goodbye To Yesterday .... RR ❶¹ / BB 2⁴	Motown 2136
07/17/92	BB	❶¹³	35	▲	3 End Of The Road .... CB ❶¹⁰ / RR ❶⁶	Motown 2178
11/06/92	RR	2⁷	24	▲	4 In The Still Of The Nite (I'll Remember) .... BB 3³ / CB 3³	Motown 2193
08/05/94	BB	❶¹⁴	34	▲	5 I'll Make Love To You .... CB ❶¹³ / RR ❶⁴	Motown 2257
11/04/94	CB	❶¹¹	28	▲	6 On Bended Knee .... RR ❶⁸ / BB ❶⁶	Motown 0244
04/22/95	CB	❶⁵	30	●	7 Water Runs Dry .... RR 2⁵ / BB 2¹	Motown 0358
10/28/95	BB	❶¹⁶	33	▲²	8 One Sweet Day .... CB ❶¹¹ / RR ❶¹⁰	Columbia 78074
					MARIAH CAREY & BOYZ II MEN	
08/29/97	BB	❶¹	27	▲	9 4 Seasons Of Loneliness .... RR 7	Motown 0684
12/13/97	BB	7	20	▲	10 A Song For Mama	Motown 0720
					BRADLEY, Owen, Quintet	
06/29/57	MV	10	5		1 White Silver Sands	Decca 30363
					BRANCH, Michelle	
07/20/01	RR	7	20		1 Everywhere	Maverick
01/18/02	RR	2²	28		2 All You Wanted .... BB 6	Maverick
10/04/02	BB	5	37		3 The Game Of Love .... RR 5	Arista 15203
					SANTANA with MICHELLE BRANCH	
05/23/03	RR	4	20		4 Are You Happy Now?	Maverick
					BRANDY	
10/01/94	BB	6	28	●	1 I Wanna Be Down .... CB 7	Atlantic 87225
02/04/95	CB	3¹	24	▲	2 Baby .... BB 4	Atlantic 87173
08/19/95	CB	7	25	●	3 Brokenhearted .... BB 9	Atlantic 87150
12/30/95	CB	❶²	33	▲	4 Sittin' Up In My Room .... BB 2²	Arista 12929
05/15/98	BB	❶¹³	27	▲²	5 The Boy Is Mine .... RR 3⁴	Atlantic 84089
					BRANDY & MONICA	
10/23/98	BB	❶²	28		6 Have You Ever? .... RR 2¹	Atlantic 84198
01/26/02	BB	7	18		7 What About Us?	Atlantic 85217

DEBUT	CH	PK	WK	Gold	A-side (Chart Hit)..Other Charts	Label & Number
					BRANIGAN, Laura	
07/03/82	CB	❶¹	36	▲	1 Gloria...BB 2³ / RR 6	Atlantic 4048
03/19/83	RR	5	19		2 Solitaire..BB 7 / CB 8	Atlantic 89868
04/14/84	BB	4	25		3 Self Control...RR 4 / CB 5	Atlantic 89676
					BRAXTON, Toni	
07/03/93	RR	2²	32	●	1 Another Sad Love Song.......................................CB 4 / BB 7	LaFace 24047
10/16/93	CB	2³	38	●	2 Breathe Again..RR 2² / BB 3³	LaFace 24054
04/01/94	CB	2¹	34	●	3 You Mean The World To Me ....RR 4 / CB 5	LaFace 24064
05/24/96	CB	❶⁶	41	▲	4 You're Makin' Me High..BB ❶¹ / RR 5	LaFace 24160
10/18/96	BB	❶¹¹	42	▲	5 Un-Break My Heart..RR 2³ / CB 5	LaFace 24200
03/18/00	BB	2²	37	●	6 He Wasn't Man Enough......................................RR 7	LaFace 24463
					BREAD	
06/13/70	BB	❶¹	17	●	1 Make It With You..CB ❶¹ / RW ❶¹	Elektra 45686
09/26/70	RW	6	11		2 It Don't Matter To Me..CB 7 / BB 10	Elektra 45701
03/20/71	BB	4	13		3 If..CB 6 / RW 6	Elektra 45720
10/16/71	BB	3²	14	●	4 Baby I'm - A Want You..CB 3² / RW 3²	Elektra 45751
01/22/72	BB	5	14		5 Everything I Own...CB 6 / RW 6	Elektra 45765
07/22/72	RW	9	11		6 The Guitar Man...CB 10	Elektra 45803
11/27/76	BB	9	19		7 Lost Without Your Love.......................................RW 10 / RR 10	Elektra 45365
					BREAKFAST CLUB	
03/14/87	BB	7	20		1 Right On Track..	MCA 52954
					BREATHE	
04/16/88	BB	2²	29		1 Hands To Heaven ....CB 2² / RR 3²	A&M 2991
09/10/88	CB	2¹	25		2 How Can I Fall?..BB 3² / RR 3²	A&M 1224
01/14/89	RR	8	18		3 Don't Tell Me Lies...BB 10	A&M 1267
					BRENNAN, Walter	
04/02/62	BB	5	13		1 Old Rivers..MV 6 / CB 8	Liberty 55436
					BREWER, Teresa	
02/04/50	BB	❶⁴	19	◉	1 Music! Music! Music!..CB ❶⁴	London 30023
					TERESA BREWER with THE DIXIELAND ALL STARS	
12/13/52	BB	❶⁷	27	◉	2 Till I Waltz Again With You..................................CB ❶⁶	Coral 60873
10/03/53	CB	2³	25	◉	3 Ricochet (Rick-O-Shay)......................................BB 2²	Coral 61043
04/24/54	BB	6	9		4 Jilted..	Coral 61152
12/18/54	BB	6	12		5 Let Me Go, Lover!..	Coral 61315
					TERESA BREWER with The Lancers	
02/17/56	BB	5	23		6 A Tear Fell...CB 7 / MV 7	Coral 61590
06/01/56	BB	7	20		7 A Sweet Old Fashioned Girl................................MV 9	Coral 61636
11/11/57	BB	8	12		8 You Send Me...	Coral 61898
					BREWER & SHIPLEY	
02/06/71	CB	8	15		1 One Toke Over The Line....................................BB 10 / RW 10	Kama Sutra 516
					BRICK	
10/23/76	BB	3²	23		1 Dazz...RW 3¹ / CB 5 / RR 9	Bang 727
					BRICKELL, Edie, & New Bohemians	
11/26/88	CB	6	21		1 What I Am..BB 7 / RR 10	Geffen 27696
					BRIDGES, Alicia	
07/01/78	BB	5	35	●	1 I Love The Nightlife (Disco 'Round) ....CB 6 / RW 7	Polydor 14483
					BRIGGS, Lillian	
08/15/55	MV	9	11		1 I Want You To Be My Baby.................................	Epic 9115
					BRIGHTER SIDE OF DARKNESS	
11/25/72	RW	8	14	●	1 Love Jones..CB 10	20th Century 2002
					BRISTOL, Johnny	
06/29/74	BB	8	20		1 Hang On In There Baby.....................................CB 8 / RW 9	MGM 14715
					B-ROCK & THE BIZZ	
04/19/97	BB	10	19	●	1 MyBabyDaddy...	Tony Mercedes 24221
					BROOKLYN BRIDGE Featuring Johnny Maestro	
12/07/68	BB	3²	14	●	1 Worst That Could Happen..................................CB 4 / RW 4	Buddah 75
					BROOKLYN DREAMS — see SUMMER, Donna	
					BROOKS, Donnie	
06/13/60	BB	7	21		1 Mission Bell...MV 8	Era 3018
					BROOKS, Garth	
09/11/99	BB	5	10	●	1 Lost In You..	Capitol 58788
					GARTH BROOKS AS CHRIS GAINES	

DEBUT	CH	PK	WK	Gold	A-side (Chart Hit)	Other Charts	Label & Number
					BROOKS, Meredith		
04/26/97	RR	❶³	30	●	1 Bitch	BB 2⁴	Capitol 58634
					BROTHERS FOUR, The		
02/22/60	MV	❶¹	20	☉	1 Greenfields	BB 2⁴ / CB 2²	Columbia 41571
					BROTHERS JOHNSON, The		
05/01/76	BB	3³	23	●	1 I'll Be Good To You	CB 7 / RW 8	A&M 1806
07/02/77	BB	5	19	●	2 Strawberry Letter 23	RR 6 / RW 7 / CB 8	A&M 1949
03/15/80	BB	7	19		3 Stomp!	CB 8	A&M 2216
					BROWN, Arthur [The Crazy World Of]		
09/07/68	CB	2²	13	●	1 Fire	RW 2² / BB 2¹	Atlantic 2556
					BROWN, Bobby		
07/23/88	CB	7	26	●	1 Don't Be Cruel	BB 8	MCA 53327
10/22/88	BB	❶¹	24	●	2 My Prerogative	CB 2³ / RR 2³	MCA 53383
12/10/88	CB	3²	23		3 Roni	BB 3¹ / RR 3¹	MCA 53463
03/25/89	CB	2²	23	●	4 Every Little Step	RR 2¹ / BB 3²	MCA 53618
06/10/89	BB	2³	21	▲	5 On Our Own	CB 2³ / RR 2²	MCA 53662
08/26/89	RR	6	22	●	6 Rock Wit'cha	BB 7 / CB 7	MCA 53652
07/31/92	RR	2⁴	26	●	7 Humpin' Around	BB 3³ / CB 3³	MCA 54342
10/09/92	RR	2²	25	●	8 Good Enough	BB 7 / CB 7	MCA 54517
01/22/93	RR	5	20		9 Get Away		MCA 54511
					BROWN, Chris		
08/27/05	RR	❶⁷	38	△³	1 Run It!	BB ❶⁵	Jive 71831
12/31/05	BB	7	21	△	2 Yo (Excuse Me Miss)		Jive 80865
08/26/06	BB	10	23	△	3 Say Goodbye		Jive
09/29/07	BB	❶³	26	△⁴	4 Kiss Kiss	RR 4	Jive 17392
					CHRIS BROWN Featuring T-Pain		
12/15/07	RR	❶²	29	△⁴	5 With You	BB 2⁶	Jive
01/19/08	RR	2⁶	35	△	6 No Air	BB 3⁴	19 Records
					JORDIN SPARKS & CHRIS BROWN		
05/09/08	RR	❶⁵	33	△⁵	7 Forever	BB 2²	Jive
02/19/11	BB	6	27	△⁷	8 Look At Me Now		Jive
					CHRIS BROWN Featuring Lil Wayne & Busta Rhymes		
03/03/12	BB	10	20	△²	9 Turn Up The Music		RCA
06/09/12	BB	10	28	△²	10 Don't Wake Me Up		RCA
02/01/14	BB	9	36	△⁴	11 Loyal		RCA
					CHRIS BROWN Featuring Lil Wayne & French Montana or Too Short or Tyga		
06/22/19	BB	5	37	△	12 No Guidance		CBE/RCA
					CHRIS BROWN Featuring Drake		
					BROWN, Foxy		
02/15/97	BB	7	20	●	1 I'll Be		Violator 574028
					FOXY BROWN Featuring Jay-Z		
					BROWN, James		
07/17/65	RW	6	14		1 Papa's Got A Brand New Bag (Part I)	BB 8 / CB 8	King 5999
11/06/65	RW	❶¹	13		2 I Got You (I Feel Good)	CB 2² / BB 3³	King 6015
04/30/66	RW	3¹	10		3 It's A Man's Man's Man's World	CB 4 / BB 8	King 6035
07/15/67	RW	4	13		4 Cold Sweat (Part 1)	BB 7 / CB 8	King 6110
03/16/68	RW	5	12		5 I Got The Feelin'	BB 6 / CB 9	King 6155
09/07/68	RW	9	11		6 Say It Loud - I'm Black And I'm Proud (Part 1)	BB 10	King 6187
06/14/69	RW	7	12		7 Mother Popcorn (You Got To Have A Mother For Me) Part 1		King 6245
10/03/70	RW	9	12		8 Super Bad (Part 1 & Part 2)		King 6329
07/03/71	CB	10	11		9 Hot Pants (She Got To Use What She Got To Get What She Wants) (Pt. 1)		People 2501
07/29/72	RW	9	15	●	10 Get On The Good Foot-Part 1	CB 10	Polydor 14139
12/07/85	BB	4	22		11 Living In America	CB 5 / RR 5	Scotti Brothers 05682
					BROWN, Les, And His Orchestra — see AMES BROTHERS		
					BROWN, Peter		
03/04/78	BB	8	28		1 Dance With Me	CB 8	Drive 6269
					PETER BROWN with Betty Wright		
					BROWNE, Jackson		
03/11/72	BB	8	13		1 Doctor My Eyes	RW 10	Asylum 11004
02/11/78	CB	6	17		2 Running On Empty	RR 6	Asylum 45460
07/04/80	RR	4	17		3 Boulevard		Asylum 47003
07/30/82	RR	2¹	21		4 Somebody's Baby	CB 5 / BB 7	Asylum 69982
07/08/83	RR	6	15		5 Lawyers In Love		Asylum 69826
					BROWNS, The		
07/20/59	MV	❶⁵	17	☉	1 The Three Bells	BB ❶⁴ / CB ❶⁴	RCA Victor 7555
10/26/59	MV	10	15		2 Scarlet Ribbons (For Her Hair)		RCA Victor 7614
03/12/60	BB	5	15		3 The Old Lamplighter	CB 8 / MV 9	RCA Victor 7700

DEBUT	CH	PK	WK	Gold	A-side (Chart Hit) ... Other Charts	Label & Number
					BROWNSTONE	
12/10/94	CB	2¹	27	●	1 If You Love Me ..... BB 8	MJJ Music 77732
					BROWNSVILLE STATION	
10/13/73	CB	2¹	22	●	1 Smokin' In The Boy's Room ..... BB 3¹ / RW 4 / RR 5	Big Tree 16011
					BRYANT, Anita	
04/04/60	MV	3²	17		1 Paper Roses ..... BB 5 / CB 7	Carlton 528
07/04/60	BB	10	15		2 In My Little Corner Of The World	Carlton 530
					BRYSON, Peabo	
05/12/84	RR	9	25		1 If Ever You're In My Arms Again ..... BB 10	Elektra 69728
01/18/92	RR	6	24	▲	2 Beauty And The Beast ..... BB 9 / CB 9 CELINE DION and PEABO BRYSON	Epic 74090
12/18/92	RR	❶³	23	●	3 A Whole New World (Aladdin's Theme) ..... BB ❶¹ / CB 2⁴ PEABO BRYSON and REGINA BELLE	Columbia 74751
05/14/93	RR	9	20		4 By The Time This Night Is Over ..... KENNY G with PEABO BRYSON	Arista 12565
					B.T. EXPRESS	
09/21/74	BB	2²	20	●	1 Do It ('Til You're Satisfied) ..... CB 6 / RW 6 / RR 9	Scepter 12395
01/25/75	BB	4	16	●	2 Express ..... RW 8 / CB 9 / RR 9	Roadshow 7001
					BTS	
06/02/18	BB	10	6	○	1 Fake Love	BigHit Entertainment
04/27/19	BB	8	8	△	2 Boy With Luv ..... BTS Featuring Halsey	BigHit Entertainment
					B2K	
11/30/02	BB	❶¹	22		1 Bump, Bump, Bump ..... RR 3¹ B2K & P. DIDDY	Epic 79842
					BUCHANAN & GOODMAN	
08/04/56	CB	3²	13	☉	1 The Flying Saucer (Parts 1 & 2) ..... BB 3¹	Luniverse 101
					BUCKCHERRY	
11/23/07	RR	5	27	△	1 Sorry ..... BB 9	Eleven Seven
					BUCKINGHAM, Lindsey	
10/24/81	RR	3¹	21		1 Trouble ..... CB 8 / RW 8 / BB 9	Asylum 47223
					BUCKINGHAMS, The	
12/24/66	BB	❶²	15	☉	1 Kind Of A Drag ..... RW ❶¹ / CB 3¹	U.S.A. 860
03/11/67	RW	5	14		2 Don't You Care ..... BB 6 / CB 6	Columbia 44053
06/17/67	BB	5	13		3 Mercy, Mercy, Mercy ..... CB 5 / RW 7	Columbia 44182
09/09/67	CB	5	10		4 Hey Baby (They're Playing Our Song) ..... RW 9	Columbia 44254
12/09/67	RW	6	13		5 Susan ..... CB 7	Columbia 44378
					BUCKNER & GARCIA	
12/26/81	RW	3²	23	●	1 Pac-Man Fever ..... CB 7 / BB 9	Columbia 02673
					BUFFALO SPRINGFIELD, The	
01/14/67	BB	7	17		1 For What It's Worth (Stop, Hey What's That Sound) ..... CB 7 / RW 8	Atco 6459
					BUFFETT, Jimmy	
03/26/77	CB	7	24		1 Margaritaville ..... RR 7 / BB 8 / RW 9	ABC 12254
					BURDON, Eric, And War	
05/23/70	CB	❶¹	21	●	1 Spill The Wine ..... RW ❶¹ / BB 3¹	MGM 14118
					BURNETTE, Johnny	
07/09/60	MV	5	19		1 Dreamin' ..... CB 8	Liberty 55258
10/31/60	CB	7	15		2 You're Sixteen ..... MV 7 / BB 8	Liberty 55285
					BURNETTE, Rocky	
05/10/80	CB	6	22		1 Tired Of Toein' The Line ..... RR 6 / BB 8 / RW 8	EMI America 8043
					BUSTA RHYMES	
03/09/96	CB	7	23	▲	1 Woo-Hah!! Got You All In Check ..... BB 8	Elektra 64335
01/10/98	BB	9	19	●	2 Dangerous	Elektra 64131
05/09/98	BB	10	20	●	3 Turn It Up [Remix]/Fire It Up	Elektra 64104
03/13/99	BB	3¹	20	●	4 What's It Gonna Be?! ..... BUSTA RHYMES Featuring Janet Jackson	Elektra 64051
03/08/03	BB	3³	24		5 I Know What You Want ..... RR 4 BUSTA RHYMES AND MARIAH CAREY (feat. The Flipmode Squad)	J Records 21258
					BUTLER, Jerry	
10/15/60	CB	3¹	19		1 He Will Break Your Heart ..... MV 5 / BB 7	Vee-Jay 354
09/25/61	CB	5	17		2 Moon River	Vee-Jay 405
09/05/64	RW	3¹	15		3 Let It Be Me ..... BB 5 / CB 9	Vee-Jay 613
03/01/69	BB	4	13	●	4 Only The Strong Survive ..... CB 5 / RW 6	Mercury 72898

DEBUT	CH	PK	WK	Gold	A-side (Chart Hit) ... Other Charts	Label & Number
					BUTTONS, Red	
05/02/53	CB	8	13		1 The Ho Ho Song .... BB 9	Columbia 39981
					B*WITCHED	
01/29/99	BB	9	17	●	1 C'est La Vie	Epic 79084
					BYRD, Charlie — see GETZ, Stan	
					BYRDS, The	
05/08/65	BB	❶¹	15	⊙	1 Mr. Tambourine Man .... CB ❶¹ / RW ❶¹	Columbia 43271
10/23/65	BB	❶³	15	⊙	2 Turn! Turn! Turn! (To Everything There Is A Season) ... RW ❶² / CB ❶¹	Columbia 43424
					BYRNES, Edd	
04/20/59	CB	3¹	13	⊙	1 Kookie, Kookie (Lend Me Your Comb) .... BB 4 / MV 4	Warner 5047
					EDWARD BYRNES And CONNIE STEVENS	

C

					CABELLO, Camila	
11/05/16	BB	4	23	△³	1 Bad Things	Bad Boy
					MACHINE GUN KELLY & CAMILA CABELLO	
08/26/17	BB	❶¹	46	△⁷	2 Havana	Syco
					CAMILA CABELLO Featuring Young Thug	
12/30/17	BB	6	37	△³	3 Never Be The Same	Syco
07/06/19	BB	❶¹	34	△	4 Senorita	Syco
					SHAWN MENDES & CAMILA CABELLO	
					CABRERA, Ryan	
06/18/04	RR	3¹	27	○	1 On The Way Down	E.V.L.A. 88372
10/29/04	RR	7	22	○	2 True	E.V.L.A.
					CADETS, The	
07/07/56	CB	10	11		1 Stranded In The Jungle	Modern 994
					CAFFERTY, John, And The Beaver Brown Band	
08/18/84	RR	6	21		1 On The Dark Side .... BB 7	Scotti Brothers 04594
					CAILLAT, Colbie	
06/02/07	RR	2⁴	47	△	1 Bubbly .... BB 5	Universal Republic
02/15/08	RR	10	26	△	2 Realize	Universal Republic
					CALDWELL, Bobby	
12/02/78	BB	9	20		1 What You Won't Do For Love .... CB 10	Clouds 11
					CALLING, The	
10/12/01	BB	5	45		1 Wherever You Will Go .... RR 6	RCA 60518
					CALLOWAY	
02/10/90	BB	2¹	24	●	1 I Wanna Be Rich .... CB 2¹ / RR 2¹	Solar 74005
					CALVERT, Eddie	
12/05/53	BB	6	14		1 Oh, Mein Papa	Essex 336
					CAMEO	
09/13/86	BB	6	22		1 Word Up .... CB 7 / RR 10	Atlanta Artists 884933
					CAMPBELL, Glen	
11/02/68	CB	2¹	15	●	1 Wichita Lineman .... RW 3³ / BB 3¹	Capitol 2302
03/01/69	RW	3²	12	●	2 Galveston .... BB 4 / CB 4	Capitol 2428
01/17/70	RW	10	10		3 Honey Come Back	Capitol 2718
09/05/70	RW	8	13		4 It's Only Make Believe .... CB 9 / BB 10	Capitol 2905
05/31/75	BB	❶²	25	●	5 Rhinestone Cowboy .... CB ❶¹ / RW ❶¹ / RR 4	Capitol 4095
02/12/77	BB	❶¹	22	●	6 Southern Nights .... CB ❶¹ / RW ❶¹ / RR 3⁴	Capitol 4376
					CAMPBELL, Tevin	
12/08/90	CB	10	29	●	1 Round And Round	Paisley Park 21740
11/09/91	RR	5	30	●	2 Tell Me What You Want Me To Do .... BB 6	Qwest 19131
10/15/93	RR	4	31	●	3 Can We Talk .... CB 7 / BB 9	Qwest 18346
03/11/94	BB	5	28		4 I'm Ready .... RR 7 / BB 9	Qwest 18264
					CAMP ROCK CAST	
07/05/08	BB	9	7		1 This Is Me	Walt Disney
					CAM'RON	
04/20/02	BB	4	21		1 Oh Boy	Roc-A-Fella 582864
					CAM'RON feat. Juelz Santana	
08/31/02	BB	3¹	22	△	2 Hey Ma .... RR 6	Roc-A-Fella 063958
					CAM'RON (feat. Juelz Santana, Freekey Zekey and Toya)	

24

DEBUT	CH	PK	WK	Gold	A-side (Chart Hit) .... Other Charts	Label & Number
					C & C MUSIC FACTORY Featuring Freedom Williams	
11/17/90	BB	❶²	25	▲	1 Gonna Make You Sweat (Everybody Dance Now) .... CB ❶² / RR 3¹	Columbia 73604
03/02/91	CB	❶¹	25	●	2 Here We Go .... BB 3¹ / RR 5	Columbia 73690
07/19/91	RR	3¹	20	●	3 Things That Make You Go Hmmmm .... BB 4 / CB 5	Columbia 73687
					CANDYMAN	
09/01/90	BB	9	26	▲	1 Knockin' Boots .... CB 10	Epic 73450
					CANNED HEAT	
08/03/68	CB	9	13		1 On The Road Again .... RW 10	Liberty 56038
11/30/68	CB	9	12		2 Going Up The Country .... RW 10	Liberty 56077
					CANNON, Freddy	
05/09/59	MV	5	15	◉	1 Tallahassee Lassie .... BB 6 / CB 6	Swan 4031
11/23/59	BB	3¹	15	◉	2 Way Down Yonder In New Orleans .... CB 3¹ / MV 3¹	Swan 4043
04/30/62	CB	3³	15	◉	3 Palisades Park .... BB 3² / MV 4	Swan 4106
08/14/65	RW	10	10		4 Action	Warner 5645
					CANTRELL, Blu	
05/05/01	RR	❶⁵	34		1 Hit 'Em Up Style (Oops!) .... BB 2²	Arista 13974
					CAPALDI, Lewis	
05/25/19	BB	❶³	41	△	1 Someone You Loved	Vertigo
					CAPITAL CITIES	
05/18/13	BB	8	43	△²	1 Safe And Sound	Lazy Hooks
					CAPITOLS, The	
04/16/66	RW	4	15		1 Cool Jerk .... CB 5 / BB 7	Karen 1524
					CAPRIS, The	
12/26/60	BB	3¹	16		1 There's A Moon Out Tonight .... CB 7 / MV 7	Old Town 1094
					CAPTAIN & TENNILLE	
04/19/75	RR	❶⁶	23	●	1 Love Will Keep Us Together .... BB ❶⁴ / RW ❶³ / CB ❶²	A&M 1672
09/20/75	RR	3³	22	●	2 The Way I Want To Touch You .... CB 3¹ / BB 4 / RW 4	A&M 1725
01/23/76	CB	❶¹	23	●	3 Lonely Night (Angel Face) .... RW ❶¹ / RR 2¹ / BB 3³	A&M 1782
04/24/76	RR	2²	28	●	4 Shop Around .... BB 4 / RW 4 / CB 6	A&M 1817
09/24/76	RR	❶¹	25	●	5 Muskrat Love .... CB 2⁵ / RW 2³ / BB 4	A&M 1870
07/29/78	RW	6	22		6 You Never Done It Like That .... BB 10 / CB 10	A&M 2063
10/20/79	BB	❶¹	27	●	7 Do That To Me One More Time .... CB ❶¹ / RW ❶¹ / RR 4	Casablanca 2215
					CAPTAIN HOLLYWOOD PROJECT	
05/14/93	RR	10	20		1 More And More	Imago 25029
					CARA, Alessia	
08/22/15	BB	5	34	△³	1 Here	EP/Def Jam 0024163
09/17/16	BB	8	43	△²	2 Scars To Your Beautiful	EP/Def Jam
03/18/17	BB	7	31	△²	3 Stay	Interscope
					ZEDD & ALESSIA CARA	
					CARA, Irene	
06/14/80	RW	3³	26		1 Fame .... BB 4 / CB 5	RSO 1034
04/02/83	BB	❶⁶	31	●	2 Flashdance...What A Feeling .... CB ❶⁶ / RR ❶⁵	Casablanca 811440
10/21/83	RR	10	16		3 Why Me?	Geffen 29464
03/24/84	RR	7	20		4 Breakdance .... BB 8 / CB 10	Geffen 29328
					CARAVELLES, The	
11/02/63	BB	3¹	14		1 You Don't Have To Be A Baby To Cry .... MV 3¹ / CB 6	Smash 1852
					CARDI B	
07/22/17	BB	❶³	35	△⁹	1 Bodak Yellow (Money Moves)	KSR Group
11/18/17	BB	6	22	△³	2 MotorSport	Quality Control
					MIGOS, NICKI MINAJ & CARDI B	
01/13/18	BB	3⁸	23	△⁴	3 Finesse	Atlantic
					BRUNO MARS & CARDI B	
04/21/18	BB	❶¹	51	△⁷	4 I Like It	KSR Group
					CARDI B, BAD BUNNY & J BALVIN	
03/02/19	BB	3¹	20	△²	5 Please Me	Atlantic
					CARDI B & BRUNO MARS	
					CARDIGANS, The	
11/22/96	RR	❶⁶	49		1 Lovefool .... BB 2⁸	Mercury
					CAREY, Mariah	
06/02/90	BB	❶⁴	22	●	1 Vision Of Love .... RR ❶³ / CB ❶²	Columbia 73348
09/14/90	BB	❶³	26	●	2 Love Takes Time .... CB ❶² / RR ❶²	Columbia 73455
01/11/91	RR	❶⁴	22	●	3 Someday .... BB ❶² / CB ❶²	Columbia 73561
04/05/91	RR	❶³	24		4 I Don't Wanna Cry .... BB ❶² / CB ❶²	Columbia 73743
08/23/91	BB	❶³	26	●	5 Emotions .... RR ❶³ / CB ❶²	Columbia 73977
11/08/91	RR	❶³	28		6 Can't Let Go .... CB ❶¹ / BB 2¹	Columbia 74088

25

DEBUT	CH	PK	WK	Gold	A-side (Chart Hit)	Other Charts	Label & Number
					CAREY, Mariah (cont'd)		
02/21/92	RR	❶²	24		7 Make It Happen	CB 3¹ / BB 5	Columbia 74239
05/15/92	RR	❶⁶	22		8 I'll Be There	CB ❶³ / BB ❶²	Columbia 74330
07/30/93	RR	❶⁹	33	▲ 9	Dreamlover	BB ❶⁸ / CB ❶⁴	Columbia 77080
10/15/93	RR	❶⁷	32	▲ 10	Hero	BB ❶⁴ / CB 2⁶	Columbia 77224
01/28/94	CB	❶²	24	● 11	Without You	RR 2⁴ / BB 3⁶	Columbia 77358
05/20/94	CB	4	25		12 Anytime You Need A Friend	RR 6	Columbia 77499
09/09/94	BB	2¹	23	● 13	Endless Love	CB 3¹ / RR 6	Columbia 77629
					LUTHER VANDROSS & MARIAH CAREY		
09/01/95	CB	❶⁹	29	▲² 14	Fantasy	BB ❶⁸ / RR ❶⁶	Columbia 78043
10/28/95	BB	❶¹⁶	33	▲² 15	One Sweet Day	CB ❶¹¹ / RR ❶¹⁰	Columbia 78074
					MARIAH CAREY & BOYZ II MEN		
03/01/96	CB	❶⁵	34	▲ 16	Always Be My Baby	BB ❶² / RR 2³	Columbia 78276
06/21/96	RR	6	20		17 Forever	BB 9	Columbia
08/08/97	BB	❶³	20	▲ 18	Honey	RR 10	Columbia 78648
04/03/98	BB	❶¹	20	▲ 19	My All		Columbia 78821
01/22/99	BB	4	20	▲ 20	I Still Believe		Columbia 79093
09/03/99	BB	❶²	21	● 21	Heartbreaker		Columbia 79260
					MARIAH CAREY (Featuring Jay-Z)		
12/10/99	BB	❶¹	20	● 22	Thank God I Found You		Columbia 79338
					MARIAH with Joe & 98°		
06/23/01	BB	2²	14	● 23	Loverboy		Virgin 38791
03/08/03	BB	3³	24		24 I Know What You Want	RR 4	J Records 21258
					BUSTA RHYMES AND MARIAH CAREY (feat. The Flipmode Squad)		
04/15/05	BB	❶¹⁴	43	△⁴ 25	We Belong Together	RR ❶¹¹	Island 005162
07/22/05	RR	❶⁵	26	△ 26	Shake It Off	BB 2⁶	Island
10/14/05	BB	❶²	22	○ 27	Don't Forget About Us	RR 3²	Island 006059
02/22/08	BB	❶²	20	△ 28	Touch My Body	RR 7	Island 011159
07/25/09	BB	7	21	△² 29	Obsessed		Island 013290
12/16/17	BB	9	5	△⁶ 30	All I Want For Christmas Is You		Columbia
12/01/18	BB	3¹	6	△⁶ 31	All I Want For Christmas Is You		Columbia
11/23/19	BB	❶³	7	△⁶ 32	All I Want For Christmas Is You		Columbia
					CARLISLE, Belinda		
05/17/86	BB	3²	22		1 Mad About You	CB 4 / RR 4	I.R.S. 52815
09/26/87	BB	❶¹	23		2 Heaven Is A Place On Earth	CB ❶¹ / RR ❶¹	MCA 53181
01/15/88	BB	2¹	17		3 I Get Weak	CB 3² / RR 3¹	MCA 53242
04/16/88	BB	7	18		4 Circle In The Sand	CB 7 / RR 8	MCA 53308
					CARLISLE, Bob		
05/10/97	BB	10	15	○ 1	Butterfly Kisses		Diadem 1221
					CARLTON, Carl		
09/21/74	BB	6	19		1 Everlasting Love	RR 8 / CB 9 / RW 10	Back Beat 27001
					CARLTON, Larry — see POST, Mike		
					CARLTON, Vanessa		
02/22/02	RR	❶⁵	41		1 A Thousand Miles	BB 5	A&M 497676
07/19/02	RR	9	20		2 Ordinary Day		A&M 497761
					CARMEN, Eric		
12/13/75	CB	❶¹	25	● 1	All By Myself	RW ❶¹ / BB 2³ / RR 2¹	Arista 0165
05/01/76	RR	5	18		2 Never Gonna Fall In Love Again	CB 9 / RW 9	Arista 0184
11/07/87	CB	3²	26		3 Hungry Eyes	BB 4 / RR 6	RCA 5315
05/21/88	BB	3¹	23		4 Make Me Lose Control	CB 4 / RR 5	Arista 9686
					CARMICHAEL, Hoagy		
05/06/50	CB	7	16		1 The Old Piano Roll Blues		Decca 24977
					HOAGY CARMICHAEL and CASS DALEY		
					CARNES, Kim		
03/21/80	RR	2²	21		1 Don't Fall In Love With A Dreamer	BB 4 / CB 4 / RW 4	United Artists 1345
					KENNY ROGERS with KIM CARNES		
05/31/80	RR	6	21		2 More Love	CB 9 / BB 10 / RW 10	EMI America 8045
03/28/81	BB	❶⁹	29	● 3	Bette Davis Eyes	CB ❶⁵ / RW ❶⁵ / RR ❶⁵	EMI America 8077
					CARPENTERS		
06/13/70	BB	❶⁴	17	● 1	(They Long To Be) Close To You	CB ❶² / RW ❶²	A&M 1183
09/12/70	BB	❶¹	17	● 2	We've Only Just Begun	RW ❶¹ / BB 2⁴	A&M 1217
02/06/71	BB	3²	13	● 3	For All We Know	RW 4 / CB 6	A&M 1243
05/08/71	BB	2²	12	● 4	Rainy Days And Mondays	CB 2¹ / RW 1	A&M 1260
08/28/71	RW	❶¹	15	● 5	Superstar	BB 2² / CB 2²	A&M 1289
01/15/72	RW	❶¹	13	● 6	Hurting Each Other	BB 2² / CB 2²	A&M 1322
07/08/72	RW	6	12		7 Goodbye To Love	BB 7 / CB 7	A&M 1367
02/17/73	BB	3²	15	● 8	Sing	RW 4 / CB 5	A&M 1413
06/02/73	CB	❶¹	17	● 9	Yesterday Once More	RW ❶¹ / BB 2¹	A&M 1446
09/29/73	BB	❶²	20	● 10	Top Of The World	CB ❶¹ / RR 2⁴ / RW 3³	A&M 1468
04/06/74	CB	9	12		11 I Won't Last A Day Without You	RW 9 / RR 10	A&M 1521

DEBUT	CH	PK	WK	Gold	A-side (Chart Hit)..Other Charts	Label & Number
					CARPENTERS (cont'd)	
11/23/74	BB	❶¹	17	● 12	Please Mr. Postman............................CB ❶¹ / RW ❶¹ / RR 2³	A&M 1646
03/29/75	BB	4	18	13	Only Yesterday......................................RW 6 / RR 7 / CB 8	A&M 1677
					CARR, Cathy	
03/24/56	MV	2²	24	1	Ivory Tower..BB 2¹ / CB 5	Fraternity 734
					CARR, Joe "Fingers"	
06/17/50	BB	7	13	1	Sam's Song...	Capitol F962
					JOE "FINGERS" CARR And The Carr-Hops	
					CARR, Vikki	
08/26/67	BB	3²	16	1	It Must Be Him..................................CB 5 / RW 5	Liberty 55986
					CARRACK, Paul	
11/14/87	BB	9	25	1	Don't Shed A Tear..............................CB 9 / RR 9	Chrysalis 43164
					CARRADINE, Keith	
05/08/76	CB	10	22	1	I'm Easy...	ABC 12117
					CARROLL, David, And His Orchestra	
01/08/55	BB	8	17	1	Melody Of Love..	Mercury 70516
					CARS, The	
06/30/79	RR	8	16	1	Let's Go..	Elektra 46063
11/20/81	CB	3²	24	2	Shake It Up......................................BB 4 / RW 4 / RR 8	Elektra 47250
03/10/84	RR	4	18	3	You Might Think..............................BB 7 / CB 7	Elektra 69744
05/19/84	RR	6	19	4	Magic..	Elektra 69724
08/03/84	RR	2²	19	5	Drive...BB 3³ / CB 4	Elektra 69706
11/02/85	RR	6	20	6	Tonight She Comes........................BB 7 / CB 10	Elektra 69589
					CARSON, Mindy	
04/15/50	CB	2¹	23	1	My Foolish Heart /	
					BB 6	
03/11/50	CB	8	11	2	Candy And Cake..	RCA Victor 3204
08/01/55	MV	10	4	3	Wake The Town And Tell The People................	Columbia 40537
					CARTER, Clarence	
07/13/68	BB	6	17	● 1	Slip Away..RW 10	Atlantic 2508
11/02/68	RW	7	15	● 2	Too Weak To Fight..	Atlantic 2569
07/18/70	CB	❶¹	15	● 3	Patches..RW 2³ / BB 4	Atlantic 2748
					CARTER, Mel	
06/19/65	BB	8	15	1	Hold Me, Thrill Me, Kiss Me..............................	Imperial 66113
					CASCADA	
12/17/05	RR	7	31	△ 1	Everytime We Touch.................................BB 10	Robbins 72130
					CASCADES, The	
01/12/63	CB	2¹	17	1	Rhythm Of The Rain.....................BB 3¹ / MV 3¹	Valiant 6026
					CASE	
05/11/96	CB	10	23	● 1	Touch Me Tease Me..	Def Jam 854620
12/26/98	BB	10	20	2	Faded Pictures...	Def Jam 566494
					CASE & JOE	
02/10/01	BB	4	22	3	Missing You...	Def Soul 572839
					CASH, Alvin, & The Crawlers	
01/02/65	CB	9	12	1	Twine Time...RW 10	Mar-V-Lus 6002
					CASH, Johnny	
07/26/69	RW	❶¹	12	● 1	A Boy Named Sue........................BB 2³ / CB 2²	Columbia 44944
					CASINOS, The	
01/07/67	RW	2¹	14	1	Then You Can Tell Me Goodbye..........CB 5 / BB 6	Fraternity 977
					CASSIDY	
12/20/03	BB	4	24	1	Hotel..	J Records 56053
					CASSIDY feat. R. Kelly	
					CASSIDY, David	
10/30/71	CB	3²	15	● 1	Cherish...RW 5 / BB 9	Bell 45,150
					CASSIDY, Shaun	
05/14/77	CB	❶²	23	● 1	Da Doo Ron Ron..........................BB ❶¹ / RW ❶¹ / RR ❶¹	Warner/Curb 8365
07/23/77	BB	3²	24	● 2	That's Rock 'N' Roll.......................RW 3² / CB 4 / RR 5	Warner/Curb 8423
11/12/77	BB	7	19	● 3	Hey Deanie...	Warner/Curb 8488
					CASSIE	
04/28/06	BB	3⁴	27	○ 1	Me & U..RR 3²	Bad Boy 94376
					CASTAWAYS, The	
07/10/65	RW	8	21	1	Liar, Liar..	Soma 1433

27

DEBUT	CH	PK	WK	Gold	A-side (Chart Hit)	Other Charts	Label & Number
					CASTOR, Jimmy, Bunch		
05/06/72	CB	2¹	14	●	1 Troglodyte (Cave Man)	RW 5 / BB 6	RCA Victor 1029
					CATES, George, And His Orchestra		
03/30/56	CB	❶²	25		1 Moonglow And Theme From "Picnic"	MV 2¹ / BB 4	Coral 61618
					CATHY JEAN and THE ROOMMATES		
02/06/61	MV	9	15		1 Please Love Me Forever	CB 10	Valmor 007
					CAVALLARO, Carmen, And His Orchestra		
03/11/50	BB	5	9		1 (Put Another Nickel In) Music! Music! Music!		Decca 24881
					CETERA, Peter		
06/07/86	BB	❶²	21		1 Glory Of Love	RR ❶² / CB ❶¹	Full Moon 28662
09/20/86	BB	❶¹	23		2 The Next Time I Fall	RR 2¹ / CB 3²	Full Moon 28597
					PETER CETERA with AMY GRANT		
07/23/88	BB	4	18		3 One Good Woman	RR 4 / CB 6	Full Moon 27824
03/11/89	BB	6	22	●	4 After All	CB 7	Geffen 27529
					CHER and PETER CETERA		
02/22/97	BB	8	34	▲	5 Hard To Say I'm Sorry	RR 10	LaFace 24223
					AZ YET with PETER CETERA		
					CHACKSFIELD, Frank, And His Orch.		
05/30/53	CB	4	21		1 Terry's Theme From "Limelight"	BB 5	London 1342
08/15/53	BB	2⁴	29	◉	2 Ebb Tide	CB 2²	London 1358
					CHAD & JEREMY		
08/15/64	RW	6	14		1 A Summer Song	BB 7 / CB 8	World Artists 1027
					CHAINSMOKERS, The		
11/07/15	BB	6	31	△⁵	1 Roses		Disruptor
					THE CHAINSMOKERS with ROZES		
02/27/16	BB	3²	52	△⁷	2 Don't Let Me Down		Disruptor
					THE CHAINSMOKERS with DAYA		
08/20/16	BB	❶¹²	52	△¹¹	3 Closer		Disruptor
					THE CHAINSMOKERS with HALSEY		
02/04/17	BB	6	20	△³	4 Paris		Disruptor
03/11/17	BB	3¹	39	△⁶	5 Something Just Like This		Disruptor
					THE CHAINSMOKERS & COLDPLAY		
					CHAIRMEN OF THE BOARD		
01/17/70	BB	3¹	15	●	1 Give Me Just A Little More Time	RW 8 / CB 9	Invictus 9074
11/07/70	RW	7	13		2 Pay To The Piper	CB 10	Invictus 9081
					CHAKACHAS, The		
12/25/71	RW	5	19	●	1 Jungle Fever	CB 6 / BB 8	Polydor 15030
					CHAMBERLAIN, Richard		
05/26/62	BB	10	14		1 Theme From Dr. Kildare (Three Stars Will Shine Tonight)		MGM 13075
					CHAMILLIONAIRE		
03/04/06	BB	❶²	31	○	1 Ridin'	RR 3²	Universal 006026
					CHAMILLIONAIRE Featuring Krayzie Bone		
					CHAMPAIGN		
02/07/81	CB	10	24		1 How 'Bout Us		Columbia 11433
					CHAMPS, The		
02/17/58	BB	❶⁵	19	◉	1 Tequila	CB ❶⁵ / MV ❶⁴	Challenge 1016
					CHANDLER, Gene		
01/06/62	CB	❶⁵	17	◉	1 Duke Of Earl	MV ❶⁵ / BB ❶³	Vee-Jay 416
06/27/70	RW	10	18	●	2 Groovy Situation		Mercury 73083
					CHANDLER, Karen		
10/25/52	BB	5	21		1 Hold Me, Thrill Me, Kiss Me	CB 6	Coral 60831
					CHANGING FACES		
07/30/94	BB	3¹	28	▲	1 Stroke You Up	CB 8	Big Beat 98279
05/10/97	BB	8	25	▲	2 G.H.E.T.T.O.U.T.		Big Beat 98026
					CHANNEL, Bruce		
01/20/62	CB	❶⁴	17	◉	1 Hey! Baby	BB ❶³ / MV ❶³	Smash 1731
					CHANTAY'S		
03/02/63	BB	4	17		1 Pipeline	CB 5 / MV 5	Dot 16440
					CHAPIN, Harry		
09/21/74	BB	❶¹	20	●	1 Cat's In The Cradle	CB ❶¹ / RW ❶¹ / RR 3⁴	Elektra 45203
					CHAPMAN, Tracy		
06/04/88	CB	4	21		1 Fast Car	BB 6 / RR 8	Elektra 69412
03/15/96	RR	❶²	39	▲	2 Give Me One Reason	CB 2³ / BB 3⁵	Elektra 64346

DEBUT	CH	PK	WK	Gold	A-side (Chart Hit)	Other Charts	Label & Number
					CHARLENE		
03/06/82	BB	3³	20		1 I've Never Been To Me	CB 3² / RR 4	Motown 1611
					CHARLES, Jimmy		
07/11/60	BB	5	21		1 A Million To One	CB 6 / MV 6	Promo 1002
					CHARLES, Ray		
07/04/59	BB	6	16	☉	1 What'd I Say (Part I & II)	CB 6 / MV 7	Atlantic 2031
09/05/60	BB	❶¹	17	☉	2 Georgia On My Mind	MV 3² / CB 3¹	ABC-Paramount 10135
03/06/61	BB	8	13		3 One Mint Julep	CB 9	Impulse! 200
09/04/61	BB	❶²	15	☉	4 Hit The Road Jack	CB ❶¹ / MV 2⁴	ABC-Paramount 10244
11/20/61	BB	9	13		5 Unchain My Heart	CB 9	ABC-Paramount 10266
04/30/62	BB	❶⁵	18	●	6 I Can't Stop Loving You	CB ❶⁵ / MV ❶⁵	ABC-Paramount 10330
07/21/62	BB	2¹	12		7 You Don't Know Me	MV 3² / CB 5	ABC-Paramount 10345
11/10/62	BB	7	13		8 You Are My Sunshine	MV 8 / CB 8	ABC-Paramount 10375
04/13/63	BB	8	12		9 Take These Chains From My Heart	MV 8	ABC-Paramount 10435
09/07/63	CB	2¹	14		10 Busted	BB 4 / MV 4	ABC-Paramount 10481
12/11/65	RW	5	15		11 Crying Time	BB 6 / CB 6	ABC-Paramount 10739
					CHARLES, Ray, Singers		
04/11/64	BB	3¹	16		1 Love Me With All Your Heart	MV 3¹ / CB 4	Command 4046
					CHARLES, Sonny		
04/26/69	CB	10	16		1 Black Pearl		A&M 1053
					SONNY CHARLES and THE CHECKMATES, LTD.		
					CHARLES & EDDIE		
08/21/92	RR	7	26		1 Would I Lie To You?		Capitol 44809
					CHARLI XCX		
06/21/14	BB	8	25	△³	1 Boom Clap		Neon Gold
					CHEAP TRICK		
04/21/79	CB	3²	24	●	1 I Want You To Want Me	RW 4 / BB 7	Epic 50680
04/09/88	BB	❶²	27		2 The Flame	CB ❶² / RR ❶²	Epic 07745
07/30/88	CB	3¹	19		3 Don't Be Cruel	BB 4 / RR 4	Epic 07965
07/21/90	CB	7	18		4 Can't Stop Fallin' Into Love		Epic 73444
					CHECKER, Chubby		
07/18/60	CB	❶⁴	21	☉	1 The Twist	MV ❶² / BB ❶¹	Parkway 811
10/10/60	MV	10	13		2 The Hucklebuck		Parkway 813
01/23/61	BB	❶³	17	☉	3 Pony Time	CB ❶¹ / MV 2³	Parkway 818
06/19/61	CB	3²	25		4 Let's Twist Again	MV 6 / BB 8	Parkway 824
09/25/61	MV	6	16		5 The Fly	BB 7 / CB 7	Parkway 830
11/13/61	CB	❶⁴	22	☉	6 The Twist	MV ❶³ / BB ❶²	Parkway 811
02/26/62	CB	❶¹	15		7 Slow Twistin'	BB 3¹ / MV 4	Parkway 835
					CHUBBY CHECKER with DEE DEE SHARP		
09/08/62	CB	❶¹	24	☉	8 Limbo Rock /	BB 2² / MV 2¹	
09/08/62	CB	8	17		9 Popeye The Hitchhiker	BB 10	Parkway 849
					CHEECH & CHONG		
08/09/74	CB	4	13		1 Earache My Eye (Featuring Alice Bowie)	RR 8 / BB 9 / RW 9	Ode 66102
					CHEERS, The		
09/12/55	BB	6	13		1 Black Denim Trousers	CB 6 / MV 6	Capitol 3219
					CHER		
07/03/65	CB	9	12		1 All I Really Want To Do	RW 9	Imperial 66114
03/05/66	CB	2²	12		2 Bang Bang (My Baby Shot Me Down)	RW 2² / BB 2¹	Imperial 66160
10/21/67	CB	8	14		3 You Better Sit Down Kids	BB 9 / RW 9	Imperial 66261
09/18/71	BB	❶²	16	●	4 Gypsys, Tramps & Thieves	CB ❶² / RW ❶¹	Kapp 2146
01/22/72	BB	7	14		5 The Way Of Love	CB 9	Kapp 2158
07/21/73	BB	❶²	20	●	6 Half-Breed	CB ❶¹ / RW ❶¹ / RR ❶¹	MCA 40102
01/12/74	BB	❶¹	18	●	7 Dark Lady	CB 2¹ / RR 2¹ / RW 3²	MCA 40161
02/10/79	BB	8	19	●	8 Take Me Home	RW 8 / CB 10	Casablanca 965
11/21/87	BB	10	26		9 I Found Someone		Geffen 28191
04/09/88	RR	10	17		10 We All Sleep Alone		Geffen 27986
03/11/89	BB	6	22	●	11 After All	CB 7	Geffen 27529
					CHER and PETER CETERA		
07/08/89	BB	3²	27	●	12 If I Could Turn Back Time	CB 3² / RR 4	Geffen 22886
10/21/89	BB	4	20		13 Just Like Jesse James	BB 8 / RR 9	Geffen 22844
12/11/98	BB	❶⁴	31	▲	14 Believe	RR 2³	Warner 17119
					CHERISH		
05/20/06	RR	6	21		1 Do It To It		Sho'Nuff 56333
					CHERISH Featuring Sean Paul (of The YoungBloodZ)		

29

DEBUT	CH	PK	WK	Gold	A-side (Chart Hit)	Other Charts	Label & Number
					CHERRY, Don		
07/01/50	BB	7	15		1 Mona Lisa		Decca 27048
09/23/50	CB	2¹	21		2 Thinking Of You	BB 4	Decca 27128
11/26/55	BB	4	22		3 Band Of Gold	CB 4 / MV 4	Columbia 40597
					CHERRY, Eagle-Eye		
07/31/98	RR	❶¹	41		1 Save Tonight	BB 5	Work
					CHERRY, Neneh		
04/01/89	CB	3²	24	●	1 Buffalo Stance	BB 3¹ / RR 4	Virgin 99231
07/22/89	BB	8	14		2 Kisses On The Wind		Virgin 99183
					CHIC		
10/22/77	BB	6	28	●	1 Dance, Dance, Dance (Yowsah, Yowsah, Yowsah)	CB 6 / RW 8 / RR 8	Atlantic 3435
10/28/78	CB	❶⁷	27	▲	2 Le Freak	RW ❶⁷ / BB ❶⁶ / RR ❶⁴	Atlantic 3519
02/10/79	RW	5	20	●	3 I Want Your Love	RR 5 / BB 7 / CB 10	Atlantic 3557
06/16/79	BB	❶¹	21	●	4 Good Times	CB ❶¹ / RW 2³ / RR 3¹	Atlantic 3584
					CHICAGO		
03/28/70	BB	9	16		1 Make Me Smile		Columbia 45127
07/18/70	BB	4	13		2 25 Or 6 To 4	CB 6 / RW 6	Columbia 45194
11/07/70	CB	5	13		3 Does Anybody Really Know What Time It Is?	RW 6 / BB 7	Columbia 45264
06/26/71	BB	7	13		4 Beginnings	RW 7	Columbia 45417
07/29/72	BB	3²	13	●	5 Saturday In The Park	CB 3¹ / RW 3¹	Columbia 45657
06/23/73	CB	8	16		6 Feelin' Stronger Every Day	BB 10	Columbia 45880
09/22/73	CB	❶¹	20	●	7 Just You 'N' Me	RW 2² / BB 4 / RR 4	Columbia 45933
03/16/74	RW	5	16		8 (I've Been) Searchin' So Long	RR 6 / CB 7 / BB 9	Columbia 46020
06/22/74	BB	6	15		9 Call On Me	CB 10	Columbia 46062
10/12/74	CB	9	17		10 Wishing You Were Here		Columbia 10049
04/25/75	BB	5	12		11 Old Days	CB 6 / RR 7 / RW 8	Columbia 10131
08/06/76	RR	❶³	26	▲	12 If You Leave Me Now	BB ❶² / RW ❶² / CB ❶¹	Columbia 10390
09/24/77	RR	3¹	17		13 Baby, What A Big Surprise	BB 4 / CB 4 / RW 8	Columbia 10620
10/13/78	RR	7	13		14 Alive Again		Columbia 10845
12/23/78	RR	9	15		15 No Tell Lover		Columbia 10879
06/05/82	RR	❶⁴	25	●	16 Hard To Say I'm Sorry	BB ❶² / CB 2¹	Full Moon 29979
09/25/82	RR	4	17		17 Love Me Tomorrow		Full Moon 29911
08/04/84	RR	❶¹	25		18 Hard Habit To Break	CB 2² / BB 3²	Warner 29214
11/17/84	RR	❶¹	22		19 You're The Inspiration	BB 3² / CB 4	Warner 29126
02/23/85	RR	7	17		20 Along Comes A Woman		Warner 29082
11/15/86	RR	2²	25		21 Will You Still Love Me?	BB 3¹ / CB 4	Warner 28512
06/04/88	BB	3¹	21		22 I Don't Wanna Live Without Your Love	RR 3¹ / CB 5	Reprise 27855
09/24/88	BB	❶²	24	●	23 Look Away	CB ❶² / RR ❶²	Reprise 27766
01/21/89	CB	9	19		24 You're Not Alone	RR 9 / BB 10	Reprise 27757
12/02/89	RR	4	20		25 What Kind Of Man Would I Be?	BB 5 / CB 5	Reprise 22741
					CHIFFONS, The		
02/23/63	BB	❶⁴	15	☉	1 He's So Fine	CB ❶⁴ / MV ❶³	Laurie 3152
06/01/63	BB	5	10		2 One Fine Day	CB 7 / MV 8	Laurie 3179
05/07/66	RW	9	11		3 Sweet Talkin' Guy	BB 10 / CB 10	Laurie 3340
					CHILD, Jane		
02/10/90	RR	❶²	23	●	1 Don't Wanna Fall In Love	BB 2³ / CB 2³	Warner 19933
					CHILDISH GAMBINO		
05/19/18	BB	❶²	17	△³	1 This Is America		mcDJ
					CHI-LITES, The		
10/23/71	RW	❶²	14		1 Have You Seen Her	BB 3² / CB 5	Brunswick 55462
04/01/72	RW	❶²	15		2 Oh Girl	BB ❶¹ / CB ❶¹	Brunswick 55471
					CHINGY		
05/17/03	BB	2⁵	33		1 Right Thurr	RR 5	Capitol 77995
09/20/03	BB	3³	21	○	2 Holidae In		Capitol 52816
					CHINGY featuring Ludacris & Snoop Dogg		
01/31/04	BB	2⁵	20	○	3 One Call Away	RR 6	Capitol 48595
					CHINGY featuring J. Weav		
07/01/06	BB	9	20		4 Pullin' Me Back		Slot-A-Lot 69129
					CHINGY Featuring Tyrese		
					CHIPMUNKS, The		
12/01/58	BB	❶⁴	13	☉	1 The Chipmunk Song	CB ❶⁴ / MV ❶³	Liberty 55168
02/14/59	CB	3³	12		2 Alvin's Harmonica	BB 3² / MV 4	Liberty 55179
					CHORDETTES, The		
10/11/54	BB	❶⁷	23	☉	1 Mr. Sandman	CB ❶⁷ / MV ❶³	Cadence 1247
05/25/56	MV	4	20		2 Born To Be With You	BB 5 / CB 8	Cadence 1291
08/03/57	BB	8	16		3 Just Between You And Me		Cadence 1330
03/08/58	BB	2²	15		4 Lollipop	CB 2² / MV 3²	Cadence 1345
06/19/61	MV	10	13		5 Never On Sunday		Cadence 1402

DEBUT	CH	PK	WK	Gold	A-side (Chart Hit)	Other Charts	Label & Number
					CHORDS, The		
07/03/54	BB	5	16		1 Sh-Boom		Cat 104
					CHRISTIE, Lou		
03/23/63	CB	3¹	17		1 Two Faces Have I	MV 5 / BB 6	Roulette 4481
12/25/65	CB	❶²	15	●	2 Lightnin' Strikes	BB ❶¹ / RW ❶¹	MGM 13412
08/16/69	RW	5	14		3 I'm Gonna Make You Mine	CB 7 / BB 10	Buddah 116
					CHUMBAWAMBA		
09/13/97	RR	❶⁸	31		1 Tubthumping	BB 6	Republic 56146
					CHURCHILL, Savannah		
10/06/51	BB	5	17		1 (It's No) Sin		RCA Victor 4280
					CIARA		
06/26/04	BB	❶⁷	38	△	1 Goodies	RR 3²	LaFace 57550
					CIARA featuring Petey Pablo		
10/30/04	RR	❶¹	39	△³	2 1,2 Step	BB 2⁷	LaFace 66687
					CIARA featuring Missy Elliott		
03/26/05	BB	2¹	23	△	3 Oh	RR 6	LaFace 68177
					CIARA featuring Ludacris		
07/28/06	BB	7	22	△	4 Get Up		LaFace 88451
					CIARA Featuring Chamillionaire		
03/06/09	BB	10	12	△	5 Love Sex Magic		LaFace
					CIARA Featuring Justin Timberlake		
					CITY HIGH		
03/24/01	RR	2²	28		1 What Would You Do?	BB 8	Booga Basement 497489
					CLANTON, Jimmy		
07/05/58	BB	4	20	⊙	1 Just A Dream	MV 4 / CB 5	Ace 546
11/30/59	BB	5	16		2 Go, Jimmy, Go	CB 7 / MV 7	Ace 575
08/18/62	BB	7	14		3 Venus In Blue Jeans	MV 9 / CB 10	Ace 8001
					CLAPTON, Eric		
07/13/74	RW	❶²	17	●	1 I Shot The Sheriff	BB ❶¹ / CB ❶¹ / RR ❶¹	RSO 409
12/31/77	BB	3³	23	●	2 Lay Down Sally	CB 3² / RR 3² / RW 8	RSO 886
10/14/78	BB	9	20		3 Promises		RSO 910
02/27/81	RR	8	17		4 I Can't Stand It	BB 10	RSO 1060
02/08/92	CB	❶¹	30	▲	5 Tears In Heaven	BB 2⁴ / RR 3⁴	Duck/Reprise 19038
09/26/92	CB	7	26		6 Layla	RR 7	Duck/Reprise 18787
06/14/96	RR	2³	43	●	7 Change The World	CB 4 / BB 5	Reprise 17621
					CLARE, Alex		
04/07/12	BB	7	44	△²	1 Too Close		Universal Republic
					CLARK, Claudine		
06/30/62	BB	5	15		1 Party Lights	CB 6 / MV 8	Chancellor 1113
					CLARK, Dave, Five		
02/15/64	CB	5	16	⊙	1 Glad All Over	BB 6 / MV 8	Epic 9656
03/28/64	MV	3¹	14		2 Bits And Pieces	BB 4 / CB 4	Epic 9671
05/02/64	CB	8	11		3 Do You Love Me		Epic 9678
06/13/64	BB	4	11		4 Can't You See That She's Mine	CB 4 / RW 5	Epic 9692
08/01/64	BB	3¹	12		5 Because	RW 6 / CB 7	Epic 9704
11/14/64	CB	9	12		6 Any Way You Want It	RW 10	Epic 9739
06/19/65	RW	5	12		7 I Like It Like That	CB 6 / BB 7	Epic 9811
08/21/65	BB	4	11		8 Catch Us If You Can	RW 5 / CB 6	Epic 9833
11/06/65	BB	❶¹	12	⊙	9 Over And Over	CB ❶¹ / RW ❶¹	Epic 9863
04/02/66	RW	9	9		10 Try Too Hard	CB 10	Epic 10004
04/01/67	BB	7	10		11 You Got What It Takes	RW 7 / CB 8	Epic 10144
					CLARK, Dee		
05/01/61	BB	2¹	17	⊙	1 Raindrops	CB 2¹ / MV 3²	Vee-Jay 383
					CLARK, Petula		
12/19/64	BB	❶²	16	●	1 Downtown	CB ❶² / RW ❶¹	Warner 5494
03/20/65	CB	2²	12		2 I Know A Place	BB 3¹ / RW 3¹	Warner 5612
12/25/65	BB	❶²	13	⊙	3 My Love	RW ❶¹ / CB 2²	Warner 5684
03/19/66	RW	9	9		4 A Sign Of The Times		Warner 5802
07/16/66	CB	8	10		5 I Couldn't Live Without Your Love	RW 8 / BB 9	Warner 5835
03/04/67	BB	3¹	12		6 This Is My Song	RW 4 / CB 5	Warner 7002
06/03/67	BB	5	11		7 Don't Sleep In The Subway	CB 6 / RW 7	Warner 7049
02/17/68	RW	10	11		8 Kiss Me Goodbye		Warner 7170
					CLARK, Sanford		
07/20/56	BB	7	21		1 The Fool	MV 7 / CB 8	Dot 15481

DEBUT	CH	PK	WK	Gold	A-side (Chart Hit) ... Other Charts	Label & Number

CLARKSON, Kelly
09/13/02	BB	❶²	20	●	1 A Moment Like This .... RR 4	RCA 60622
04/25/03	RR	❶⁶	22	○	2 Miss Independent .... BB 9	RCA 56533
07/30/04	RR	❶¹	46	○	3 Breakaway .... BB 6	RCA 66958
11/26/04	RR	❶⁷	46	△	4 Since U Been Gone .... BB 2¹	RCA 66958
04/08/05	RR	2⁸	34	△	5 Behind These Hazel Eyes .... BB 6	RCA 69520
08/19/05	RR	❶⁴	37	△	6 Because Of You .... BB 7	RCA 76273
12/23/05	RR	5	29	○	7 Walk Away	RCA
04/27/07	BB	8	16	○	8 Never Again	RCA
01/23/09	BB	❶²	24		9 My Life Would Suck Without You .... RR 3²	RCA
04/17/09	RR	8	18		10 I Do Not Hook Up	19 Records
09/24/11	BB	10	23		11 Mr. Know It All	19 Records 97064
11/12/11	BB	❶³	37	△⁴	12 Stronger (What Doesn't Kill You)	19 Records
03/19/16	BB	8	15		13 Piece By Piece	19 Records

CLASH, The
| 10/02/82 | BB | 8 | 24 | | 1 Rock The Casbah | Epic 03245 |

CLASSICS IV
12/09/67	CB	2¹	17		1 Spooky .... BB 3³ / RW 3²	Imperial 66259
10/12/68	CB	2¹	16	●	2 Stormy .... RW 2¹ / BB 5	Imperial 66328
02/01/69	BB	2¹	13		3 Traces .... RW 3² / CB 3¹	Imperial 66352

CLASSICS IV Featuring Dennis Yost (above 2)

CLAY, Tom
| 07/10/71 | CB | 7 | 10 | | 1 What The World Needs Now Is Love/Abraham, Martin and John .... RW 7 / BB 8 | Mowest 5002 |

CLAYTON, Adam, & Larry Mullen
| 05/03/96 | CB | 6 | 23 | ● | 1 Theme From Mission: Impossible .... BB 7 | Mother/Island 576670 |

CLEAN BANDIT
| 06/28/14 | BB | 10 | 31 | △⁴ | 1 Rather Be | Big Beat |

CLEAN BANDIT with JESS GLYNNE

| 12/24/16 | BB | 9 | 27 | △³ | 2 Rockabye | Atlantic |

CLEAN BANDIT with SEAN PAUL & ANNE-MARIE

CLIFF, Jimmy
| 11/05/93 | RR | 8 | 25 | | 1 I Can See Clearly Now | Chaos/Columbia 77207 |

CLIFFORD, Buzz
| 01/07/61 | BB | 6 | 15 | | 1 Baby Sittin' Boogie .... MV 7 / CB 10 | Columbia 41876 |

CLIMAX
| 12/25/71 | CB | ❶¹ | 17 | ● | 1 Precious And Few .... RW ❶¹ / BB 3² | Carousel 30055 |

CLIMAX BLUES BAND
| 02/12/77 | BB | 3¹ | 22 | | 1 Couldn't Get It Right .... RR 6 / CB 7 / RW 9 | Sire 736 |
| 02/14/81 | RR | 7 | 29 | | 2 I Love You .... CB 9 / RW 10 | Warner 49669 |

CLINE, Patsy
02/09/57	MV	7	16		1 Walkin' After Midnight	Decca 30221
10/09/61	BB	9	14		2 Crazy	Decca 31317
01/27/62	MV	6	13		3 She's Got You	Decca 31354

CLOONEY, Rosemary
03/03/51	CB	5	16		1 Beautiful Brown Eyes	Columbia 39212
07/07/51	BB	❶⁸	23	☉	2 Come On-A My House .... CB ❶³	Columbia 39467
05/03/52	BB	❶³	32	☉	3 Half As Much .... CB 2³	Columbia 39710
06/28/52	BB	2³	20		4 Botch-A-Me (Ba-Ba-Baciami Piccina) .... CB 3²	Columbia 39767
12/20/52	BB	9	2		5 The Night Before Christmas Song	Columbia 39876

ROSEMARY CLOONEY & GENE AUTRY

07/03/54	CB	❶⁸	31	☉	6 Hey There / .... BB ❶⁶ / MV ❶³	
08/07/54	BB	❶³	33		7 This Ole House .... MV 2² / CB 3¹	Columbia 40266
10/18/54	MV	8	20		8 Mambo Italiano .... BB 9 / CB 9	Columbia 40361
03/16/57	BB	10	16		9 Mangos	Columbia 40835

CLUB NOUVEAU
| 02/06/87 | BB | ❶² | 17 | ● | 1 Lean On Me .... CB ❶² / RR ❶² | King Jay 28430 |

COASTERS, The
05/13/57	BB	3¹	26	☉	1 Searchin' / .... CB 7 / MV 9	
05/06/57	BB	8	24		2 Young Blood	Atco 6087
05/31/58	BB	❶¹	16	☉	3 Yakety Yak .... CB ❶¹ / MV ❶¹	Atco 6116
02/02/59	MV	2⁴	15	☉	4 Charlie Brown .... BB 2³ / CB 2³	Atco 6132
05/18/59	BB	8	12		5 Along Came Jones .... BB 9	Atco 6141
08/22/59	MV	6	16	☉	6 Poison Ivy .... BB 7 / CB 9	Atco 6146

DEBUT	CH	PK	WK	Gold	A-side (Chart Hit)	Other Charts	Label & Number
					COBRA STARSHIP		
05/30/09	BB	7	25	△	1 Good Girls Go Bad		Decaydance
					COBRA STARSHIP with LEIGHTON MEESTER		
07/30/11	BB	7	29	△²	2 You Make Me Feel...		Decaydance
					COBRA STARSHIP Featuring Sabi		
					COCHRAN, Eddie		
08/04/58	BB	8	16		1 Summertime Blues		Liberty 55144
					COCHRANE, Tom		
05/15/92	RR	5	31	●	1 Life Is A Highway	BB 6 / CB 6	Capitol 44815
					COCKER, Joe		
04/18/70	CB	5	13		1 The Letter	BB 7 / RW 7	A&M 1174
					JOE COCKER with Leon Russell & The Shelter People		
10/03/70	RW	7	10		2 Cry Me A River		A&M 1200
12/28/74	CB	4	19		3 You Are So Beautiful	BB 5 / RW 6 / RW 9	A&M 1641
08/21/82	BB	❶³	25	▲	4 Up Where We Belong	CB ❶³ / RR ❶³	Island 99996
					JOE COCKER and JENNIFER WARNES		
10/28/89	RR	10	21		5 When The Night Comes		Capitol 44437
					COFFEY, Dennis, And The Detroit Guitar Band		
10/30/71	CB	4	17	●	1 Scorpio	BB 6 / RW 6	Sussex 226
					COLDPLAY		
05/07/05	BB	8	20	○	1 Speed Of Sound		Capitol
05/24/08	BB	❶¹	51	△³	2 Viva La Vida		Capitol
05/17/14	BB	10	26	△³	3 A Sky Full Of Stars		Parlophone
03/11/17	BB	3¹	39	△⁶	4 Something Just Like This		Disruptor
					THE CHAINSMOKERS & COLDPLAY		
					COLE, Cozy		
08/25/58	CB	❶¹	21		1 Topsy II	MV 2² / BB 3³	Love 5004
					COLE, J.		
12/31/16	BB	7	20	△²	1 Deja Vu		Dreamville
05/05/18	BB	6	5		2 ATM		Dreamville
05/05/18	BB	8	5		3 Kevin's Heart		Dreamville
05/05/18	BB	10	12		4 KOD		Dreamville
02/02/19	BB	4	27	△⁴	5 Middle Child		Dreamville
					COLE, Jude		
04/13/90	RR	10	20		1 Baby, It's Tonight		Reprise 19869
					COLE, Keyshia		
07/07/07	BB	7	23		1 Let It Go		Imani 009976
					KEYSHIA COLE Featuring Missy Elliott & Lil' Kim		
					COLE, Nat "King"		
06/10/50	BB	❶⁸	33	⊙	1 Mona Lisa	CB ❶⁴	Capitol 1010
09/30/50	BB	5	18		2 Orange Colored Sky	CB 9	Capitol 1184
					NAT "KING" COLE and STAN KENTON		
01/06/51	BB	9	1		3 Frosty The Snow Man		Capitol 1203
04/14/51	CB	❶⁷	37	⊙	4 Too Young	BB ❶⁵	Capitol 1449
05/24/52	BB	8	33		5 Somewhere Along The Way	CB 9	Capitol 2069
07/05/52	BB	8	12		6 Walkin' My Baby Back Home		Capitol 2130
					NAT KING COLE and BILLY MAY and His Orchestra		
02/07/53	BB	2¹	28		7 Pretend	CB 3¹	Capitol 2346
01/23/54	BB	6	28		8 Answer Me, My Love	CB 7	Capitol 2687
10/04/54	BB	10	17		9 Smile	CB 10 / MV 10	Capitol 2897
01/31/55	CB	6	26		10 Darling Je Vous Aime Beaucoup	BB 7	Capitol 3027
04/11/55	BB	2¹	23	⊙	11 A Blossom Fell /	MV 3¹ / CB 5	
04/11/55	BB	8	28		12 If I May		Capitol 3095
06/22/56	MV	7	20		13 That's All There Is To That		Capitol 3456
					NAT "KING" COLE and THE FOUR KNIGHTS (above 2)		
06/17/57	BB	6	27		14 Send For Me	MV 6 / CB 7	Capitol 3737
04/05/58	BB	5	19		15 Looking Back	CB 10 / MV 10	Capitol 3939
09/29/58	MV	6	14		16 Non Dimenticar (Don't Forget)		Capitol 4056
07/28/62	MV	❶¹	18		17 Ramblin' Rose	CB 2³ / BB 2²	Capitol 4804
11/10/62	MV	10	12		18 Dear Lonely Hearts		Capitol 4870
05/04/63	BB	6	13		19 Those Lazy-Hazy-Crazy Days Of Summer	CB 7 / MV 7	Capitol 4965
					COLE, Natalie		
08/09/75	BB	6	27		1 This Will Be	RW 7 / CB 9	Capitol 4109
01/29/77	CB	3¹	24	●	2 I've Got Love On My Mind	BB 5 / RW 5 / RR 9	Capitol 4360
12/24/77	RW	6	21	●	3 Our Love	RR 9 / BB 10	Capitol 4509
03/05/88	BB	5	19		4 Pink Cadillac	CB 5 / RR 7	EMI/Manhattan 50117
04/15/89	BB	7	21		5 Miss You Like Crazy	CB 8 / RR 8	EMI 50185

DEBUT	CH	PK	WK	Gold	A-side (Chart Hit) ... Other Charts	Label & Number
					COLE, Paula	
02/14/97	RR	4	25		1 Where Have All The Cowboys Gone? .... BB 8	Warner 17373
07/18/97	RR	5	56		2 I Don't Want To Wait	Warner 17318
					COLLECTIVE SOUL	
05/07/94	RR	4	31	●	1 Shine .... CB 7	Atlantic 87237
04/25/95	RR	8	38		2 December	Atlantic 87157
11/18/95	RR	8	34		3 The World I Know	Atlantic 87088
					COLLINS, Judy	
11/02/68	BB	8	12		1 Both Sides Now .... CB 8 / RW 8	Elektra 45639
					COLLINS, Phil	
11/06/82	RR	4	21		1 You Can't Hurry Love .... BB 10 / CB 10	Atlantic 89933
02/25/84	RR	❶⁴	24	●	2 Against All Odds (Take A Look At Me Now) .... BB ❶³ / CB ❶³	Atlantic 89700
11/24/84	CB	❶¹	24		3 Easy Lover .... BB 2² / RR 2²	Columbia 04679
					PHILIP BAILEY & PHIL COLLINS	
02/08/85	BB	❶²	20	●	4 One More Night .... CB ❶¹ / RR ❶¹	Atlantic 89588
05/03/85	CB	❶²	18	●	5 Sussudio .... RR ❶² / BB ❶¹	Atlantic 89560
07/19/85	RR	2¹	18		6 Don't Lose My Number .... BB 4 / CB 5	Atlantic 89536
10/04/85	RR	❶²	24		7 Separate Lives .... BB ❶¹ / CB ❶¹	Atlantic 89498
					PHIL COLLINS and MARILYN MARTIN	
03/15/86	RR	3²	18		8 Take Me Home .... BB 7 / CB 7	Atlantic 89472
09/02/88	BB	❶²	25	●	9 Groovy Kind Of Love .... CB ❶² / RR ❶²	Atlantic 89017
11/18/88	RR	❶²	18		10 Two Hearts .... RR ❶² / CB ❶¹	Atlantic 88980
10/27/89	RR	❶⁶	21	●	11 Another Day In Paradise .... CB ❶⁵ / BB ❶⁴	Atlantic 88774
02/02/90	CB	3²	17		12 I Wish It Would Rain Down .... BB 3¹ / RR 4	Atlantic 88738
04/27/90	CB	3²	21		13 Do You Remember? .... BB 4 / RR 5	Atlantic 87955
08/03/90	RR	❶²	22		14 Something Happened On The Way To Heaven ..... CB 3¹ / BB 4	Atlantic 87885
10/29/93	RR	9	22		15 Both Sides Of The Story	Atlantic 87299
					COLLINS, Tyler	
04/28/90	RR	3²	24		1 Girls Nite Out .... BB 6 / CB 7	RCA 2630
					COLOR ME BADD	
04/06/91	BB	2⁴	24	▲²	1 I Wanna Sex You Up .... RR 2³ / CB 2²	Giant 19382
07/26/91	RR	❶³	27	●	2 I Adore Mi Amor .... BB ❶² / CB ❶²	Giant 19204
11/01/91	BB	❶¹	30	●	3 All 4 Love .... CB 2³ / RR 2³	Giant 19236
01/31/92	RR	5	22		4 Thinkin' Back .... CB 7	Giant 19074
05/09/92	RR	6	20		5 Slow Motion .... CB 10	Giant 18908
08/28/92	RR	3²	22		6 Forever Love	Giant 18727
12/17/93	RR	4	17		7 Choose	Giant 18270
04/05/96	RR	4	28		8 The Earth, The Sun, The Rain	Giant 17654
					COLTER, Jessi	
03/29/75	BB	4	21		1 I'm Not Lisa .... CB 5 / RW 6 / RR 10	Capitol 4009
					COLUMBIA TOKYO ORCH.	
03/07/53	CB	9	13		1 Gomen-Nasai (Forgive Me)	Columbia 39954
					COLVIN, Shawn	
02/21/97	RR	2¹	32		1 Sunny Came Home .... BB 7	Columbia 78528
					COMMANDER CODY And His Lost Planet Airmen	
03/25/72	RW	6	14		1 Hot Rod Lincoln .... CB 7 / BB 9	Paramount 0146
					COMMODORES	
12/20/75	BB	5	27		1 Sweet Love .... RW 6 / CB 9	Motown 1381
09/04/76	BB	7	24		2 Just To Be Close To You .... RW 10	Motown 1402
05/28/77	BB	4	23		3 Easy .... CB 4 / RW 5 / RR 6	Motown 1418
08/27/77	BB	5	17	○	4 Brick House .... CB 6 / RW 9 / RR 10	Motown 1425
06/17/78	RR	❶⁶	21		5 Three Times A Lady .... RW ❶⁵ / CB ❶⁴ / BB ❶²	Motown 1443
08/11/79	RR	❶³	20		6 Sail On .... CB ❶¹ / RW ❶¹ / BB 4	Motown 1466
09/29/79	BB	❶¹	21		7 Still .... CB ❶¹ / RR 3³ / RW 3²	Motown 1474
06/20/81	RR	3¹	22		8 Lady (You Bring Me Up) .... RW 7 / BB 8 / CB 8	Motown 1514
09/19/81	RR	3¹	22		9 Oh No .... BB 4 / CB 4 / RW 5	Motown 1527
01/26/85	BB	3¹	23		10 Nightshift .... CB 4 / RR 4	Motown 1773
					COMO, Perry	
10/15/49	BB	3¹	23		1 A Dreamer's Holiday .... CB 4	RCA Victor 3036
01/21/50	CB	7	12		2 Bibbidi-Bobbidi-Boo (The Magic Song) .... CB 4	RCA Victor 3113
04/29/50	BB	❶²	19		3 Hoop-Dee-Doo .... CB 4	RCA Victor 3747
09/30/50	BB	7	17		4 Patricia .... CB 7	RCA Victor 3905
10/21/50	BB	3³	23		5 A Bushel And A Peck .... CB 4	RCA Victor 3930
					PERRY COMO and BETTY HUTTON	
12/09/50	CB	3²	24		6 You're Just In Love .... BB 5	RCA Victor 3945
01/13/51	BB	❶⁸	24		7 If / .... CB ❶²	
01/27/51	CB	10	12		8 Zing Zing—Zoom Zoom	RCA Victor 3997

34

DEBUT	CH	PK	WK	Gold	A-side (Chart Hit)	Other Charts	Label & Number
					COMO, Perry (cont'd)		
06/14/52	BB	3¹	18		9 Maybe	CB 9	RCA Victor 4744
					PERRY COMO and EDDIE FISHER		
12/06/52	BB	❶⁵	26	⊙	10 Don't Let The Stars Get In Your Eyes	CB ❶³	RCA Victor 5064
02/14/53	BB	4	16		11 Wild Horses	BB 6	RCA Victor 5152
04/25/53	BB	3²	22		12 Say You're Mine Again	CB 5	RCA Victor 5277
06/20/53	BB	❶⁴	23		13 No Other Love	CB ❶¹	RCA Victor 5317
10/10/53	CB	8	21		14 You Alone (Solo Tu)	BB 9	RCA Victor 5447
02/27/54	BB	❶⁸	25	⊙	15 Wanted	CB ❶⁸	RCA Victor 5647
10/04/54	MV	❶¹	23	⊙	16 Papa Loves Mambo	CB 2¹ / BB 4	RCA Victor 5857
11/22/54	BB	8	9		17 There's No Place Like Home For The Holidays		RCA Victor 5950
01/17/55	BB	2³	17		18 Ko Ko Mo (I Love You So)	CB 3¹ / MV 4	RCA Victor 5994
07/18/55	MV	4	20		19 Tina Marie	BB 5 / CB 8	RCA Victor 6192
10/24/55	MV	10	19		20 All At Once You Love Her		RCA Victor 6294
03/02/56	BB	❶¹	23	⊙	21 Hot Diggity (Dog Ziggity Boom) /	MV 3⁴ / CB 3²	
03/02/56	CB	8	17		22 Juke Box Baby	BB 10 / MV 10	RCA Victor 6427
06/08/56	BB	4	18		23 More /		
06/08/56	BB	8	17		24 Glendora	CB 7 / MV 7	RCA Victor 6554
02/23/57	BB	❶²	29	⊙	25 Round And Round	CB 2¹ / MV 2¹	RCA Victor 6815
09/30/57	MV	8	17		26 Just Born (To Be Your Baby)		RCA Victor 7050
12/30/57	MV	❶²	23	●	27 Catch A Falling Star /	BB ❶¹ / CB 2¹	
12/30/57	BB	4	17		28 Magic Moments		RCA Victor 7128
04/07/58	BB	6	16		29 Kewpie Doll	MV 7 / CB 9	RCA Victor 7202
10/31/70	RW	7	17		30 It's Impossible	BB 10 / CB 10	RCA Victor 0387
					CONLEY, Arthur		
03/11/67	BB	2¹	15	●	1 Sweet Soul Music	RW 2¹ / CB 4	Atco 6463
					CONNIFF, Ray		
06/11/66	BB	9	15		1 Somewhere, My Love	RW 9	Columbia 43626
					CONTI, Bill		
04/16/77	BB	❶¹	20	●	1 Gonna Fly Now	CB ❶¹ / RW 4 / RR 4	United Artists 940
					CONTOURS, The		
08/11/62	CB	2¹	18	⊙	1 Do You Love Me	MV 2¹ / BB 3³	Gordy 7005
06/04/88	RR	8	16		2 Do You Love Me		Motown Yesteryear 448
					COOK, David		
06/07/08	BB	3¹	20	△	1 The Time Of My Life		Fremantle
					COOK, Lawrence (Piano Roll)		
04/15/50	CB	7	18		1 The Old Piano Roll Blues		Abbey 15003
					COOKE, Sam		
10/14/57	MV	❶⁴	26	⊙	1 You Send Me	BB ❶³ / CB ❶³	Keen 4013
05/07/60	CB	10	16		2 Wonderful World		Keen 2112
08/08/60	MV	2⁴	17	⊙	3 Chain Gang	BB 2² / CB 3³	RCA Victor 7783
01/22/62	MV	5	16		4 Twistin' The Night Away	CB 6 / BB 9	RCA Victor 7983
06/23/62	CB	9	15		5 Bring It On Home To Me		RCA Victor 8036
04/13/63	BB	10	13		6 Another Saturday Night	MV 10	RCA Victor 8164
01/25/64	CB	9	11		7 Good News		RCA Victor 8299
01/09/65	RW	5	12		8 Shake	CB 6 / BB 7	RCA Victor 8486
					COOKIES, The		
03/02/63	BB	7	13		1 Don't Say Nothin' Bad (About My Baby)	CB 8 / MV 8	Dimension 1008
					COOLIDGE, Rita		
05/07/77	CB	❶¹	27	●	1 (Your Love Has Lifted Me) Higher And Higher	RR 2³ / BB 2¹ / RW 3³	A&M 1922
09/10/77	RR	2²	22	●	2 We're All Alone	RW 4 / CB 5 / BB 7	A&M 1965
01/14/78	RR	8	13		3 The Way You Do The Things You Do		A&M 2004
					COOLIO		
06/04/94	BB	3⁵	25	▲	1 Fantastic Voyage	CB 10	Tommy Boy 7617
08/19/95	BB	❶³	41	▲³	2 Gangsta's Paradise	CB ❶³	MCA 55104
					COOLIO featuring L.V.		
03/09/96	CB	4	24	●	3 1,2,3,4 (Sumpin' New)	BB 5	Tommy Boy 7721
					COOPER, Alice		
05/27/72	CB	6	15		1 School's Out	BB 7 / RW 7	Warner 7596
04/05/75	RR	5	19		2 Only Women	RW 9 / CB 10	Atlantic 3254
07/04/76	RW	9	27	●	3 I Never Cry	CB 9 / RR 9	Warner 8228
04/23/77	CB	8	25		4 You And Me	BB 9 / RR 9	Warner 8349
09/09/89	BB	7	22	●	5 Poison	CB 8	Epic 68958
					COOPER, Bradley — see LADY GAGA		
					CORINA		
05/18/91	CB	5	21		1 Temptation	BB 6 / RR 6	Cutting/Atco 98775

DEBUT	CH	PK	WK	Gold	A-side (Chart Hit)	Other Charts	Label & Number
					CORNELIUS BROTHERS & SISTER ROSE		
03/13/71	CB	2¹	23	●	1 Treat Her Like A Lady	BB 3² / RW 3¹	United Artists 50721
05/20/72	CB	❶¹	15	●	2 Too Late To Turn Back Now	RW ❶¹ / BB 2²	United Artists 50910
					CORNELL, Don		
03/22/52	CB	4	26		1 I'll Walk Alone	BB 5	Coral 60659
04/26/52	CB	2⁴	23		2 I'm Yours	BB 3¹	Coral 60690
11/01/52	BB	7	16		3 I	CB 10	Coral 60860
12/05/53	BB	10	10		4 The Gang That Sang "Heart Of My Heart"		Coral 61076
					DON CORNELL, ALAN DALE AND JOHNNY DESMOND		
08/07/54	BB	2¹	23		5 Hold My Hand	MV 3¹ / CB 6	Coral 61206
07/25/55	BB	7	23		6 The Bible Tells Me So	CB 7	Coral 61467
					CORONA		
11/25/94	RR	8	21		1 The Rhythm Of The Night		EastWest 98192
					CORTEZ, Dave 'Baby'		
03/02/59	CB	❶²	20		1 The Happy Organ	BB ❶¹ / MV ❶¹	Clock 1009
07/07/62	MV	9	15		2 Rinky Dink	BB 10	Julia/Chess 1829
					COSBY, Bill		
09/02/67	BB	4	11		1 Little Ole Man (Uptight-Everything's Alright)	RW 4 / CB 5	Warner 7072
					COUGAR, John — see MELLENCAMP, John		
					COUNT FIVE		
09/10/66	CB	4	12		1 Psychotic Reaction	RW 4 / BB 5	Double Shot 104
					COUNTING CROWS		
01/22/94	RR	❶³	47		1 Mr. Jones	BB 5	DGC
06/18/94	RR	9	23		2 Round Here		DGC
11/29/96	BB	6	28		3 A Long December	RR 7	DGC 97216
					COVER GIRLS, The		
12/09/89	CB	5	21		1 We Can't Go Wrong	RR 5 / BB 8	Capitol 44498
05/29/92	CB	2¹	24		2 Wishing On A Star	RR 2¹ / BB 9	Epic 74343
					COWBOY CHURCH SUNDAY SCHOOL, The		
01/01/55	CB	7	21		1 Open Up Your Heart (And Let The Sunshine In)	BB 8	Decca 29367
					COWSILLS, The		
09/30/67	CB	❶¹	16	●	1 The Rain, The Park & Other Things	RW 2³ / BB 2²	MGM 13810
05/25/68	CB	6	13		2 Indian Lake	RW 6 / BB 10	MGM 13944
03/15/69	RW	❶³	15	●	3 Hair	CB ❶² / BB 2²	MGM 14026
					COX, Deborah		
10/03/98	BB	2⁸	29	▲	1 Nobody's Supposed To Be Here		Arista 13550
09/11/99	BB	8	20		2 We Can't Be Friends		Arista 13724
					DEBORAH COX with R.L. from Next		
					CRAMER, Floyd		
10/03/60	MV	❶¹	21	◉	1 Last Date	BB 2⁴ / CB 2²	RCA Victor 7775
03/04/61	BB	4	15		2 On The Rebound	MV 5 / CB 7	RCA Victor 7840
06/05/61	BB	8	12		3 San Antonio Rose		RCA Victor 7893
					CRANBERRIES, The		
10/23/93	RR	5	28	●	1 Linger	BB 8	Island 862800
					CRANE, Les		
10/09/71	BB	8	12		1 Desiderata		Warner 7520
					CRASH TEST DUMMIES		
01/29/94	CB	3¹	25	●	1 Mmm Mmm Mmm Mmm	BB 4 / RR 5	Arista 12654
					CRAWFORD, Johnny		
05/07/62	BB	8	14		1 Cindy's Birthday		Del-Fi 4178
					CRAZY ELEPHANT		
02/22/69	RW	4	15		1 Gimme Gimme Good Lovin'	CB 6	Bell 763
					CRAZY TOWN		
01/06/01	BB	❶²	23		1 Butterfly	RR 2³	Columbia 79549
					CREAM		
01/06/68	RW	4	26	●	1 Sunshine Of Your Love	BB 5 / CB 6	Atco 6544
09/28/68	CB	5	13		2 White Room	BB 6 / RW 7	Atco 6617
					CREED		
09/11/99	RR	3¹	57	○	1 Higher	BB 7	Wind-Up
05/13/00	RR	❶⁵	47	○	2 With Arms Wide Open	BB ❶¹	Wind-Up 18004
10/27/01	BB	4	29		3 My Sacrifice	RR 6	Wind-Up
05/31/02	RR	4	34		4 One Last Breath	BB 6	Wind-Up

DEBUT	CH	PK	WK	Gold	A-side (Chart Hit)	Other Charts	Label & Number
					CREEDENCE CLEARWATER REVIVAL		
09/07/68	CB	9	12	●	1 Suzie Q. (Part One)		Fantasy 616
01/18/69	RW	❶¹	14	▲	2 Proud Mary	BB 2³ / CB 2²	Fantasy 619
05/03/69	RW	❶¹	14	▲	3 Bad Moon Rising	BB 2¹ / CB 2¹	Fantasy 622
07/26/69	RW	2²	15	●	4 Green River	BB 2¹ / CB 3²	Fantasy 625
10/25/69	BB	3¹	15	▲	5 Down On The Corner /	CB 10	
10/25/69	RW	4	14	△²	6 Fortunate Son	CB 6	Fantasy 634
01/24/70	BB	2²	11	▲	7 Travelin' Band	RW 2² / CB 5	Fantasy 637
04/18/70	RW	2²	12	●	8 Up Around The Bend	CB 2¹ / BB 4	Fantasy 641
08/08/70	CB	❶¹	13	▲	9 Lookin' Out My Back Door	RW ❶¹ / BB 2¹	Fantasy 645
01/30/71	CB	3²	10	●	10 Have You Ever Seen The Rain	RW 3² / BB 8	Fantasy 655
07/17/71	RW	3¹	10	●	11 Sweet Hitch-Hiker	CB 5 / BB 6	Fantasy 665
					CRESCENDOS, The		
12/16/57	BB	5	18	⊙	1 Oh Julie	CB 6 / MV 8	Nasco 6005
					CRESTS, The		
11/24/58	BB	2²	21	⊙	1 16 Candles	CB 3³ / MV 3³	Coed 506
					CREW-CUTS, The		
05/08/54	BB	8	22		1 Crazy 'Bout Ya Baby		Mercury 70341
07/10/54	BB	❶⁹	24	⊙	2 Sh-Boom	CB ❶⁷ / MV 3¹	Mercury 70404
01/29/55	CB	2¹	17		3 Earth Angel /	BB 3¹ / MV 7	
01/17/55	BB	6	14		4 Ko Ko Mo (I Love You So)		Mercury 70529
04/11/55	CB	9	20		5 Don't Be Angry		Mercury 70597
07/25/55	BB	10	18		6 Gum Drop	CB 10	Mercury 70668
11/14/55	CB	10	20		7 Angels In The Sky		Mercury 70741
					CREWE, Bob, Generation		
12/31/66	CB	9	11		1 Music To Watch Girls By	RW 9	DynoVoice 229
					CRICKETS, The — see HOLLY, Buddy		
					CROCE, Jim		
06/24/72	CB	7	15		1 You Don't Mess Around With Jim	RW 7 / BB 8	ABC 11328
10/14/72	RW	10	12		2 Operator (That's Not The Way It Feels)		ABC 11335
04/14/73	BB	❶²	22	●	3 Bad, Bad Leroy Brown	CB ❶¹ / RW ❶¹	ABC 11359
09/29/73	CB	3²	17		4 I Got A Name	RW 5 / RR 6 / BB 10	ABC 11389
11/16/73	RR	❶⁴	17	●	5 Time In A Bottle	BB ❶² / CB ❶¹ / RW ❶¹	ABC 11405
02/23/74	RW	6	17		6 I'll Have To Say I Love You In A Song	CB 7 / BB 9 / RR 9	ABC 11424
					CROSBY, Bing		
11/26/49	CB	❶¹	21	⊙	1 Dear Hearts And Gentle People	BB 2⁴	Decca 24798
01/28/50	BB	6	17		2 Quicksilver		Decca 24827
					BING CROSBY And ANDREWS SISTERS		
02/04/50	BB	4	13		3 Chattanoogie Shoe Shine Boy		Decca 24863
07/29/50	BB	2²	20	⊙	4 Play A Simple Melody /	CB 4	
07/22/50	CB	3⁸	20		5 Sam's Song (The Happy Tune)	BB 3⁵	Decca 27112
					GARY CROSBY and FRIEND (above 2)		
11/11/50	BB	8	13		6 Harbor Lights		Decca 27219
03/10/51	BB	8	15		7 Sparrow In The Tree Top	CB 8	Decca 27477
					BING CROSBY and ANDREWS SISTERS		
04/21/51	BB	8	10		8 When You And I Were Young Maggie Blues		Decca 27577
					BING and GARY CROSBY		
12/24/55	BB	7	3	⊙	9 White Christmas		Decca 23778
09/08/56	MV	3²	31	⊙	10 True Love	BB 3¹ / CB 4	Capitol 3507
					BING CROSBY and GRACE KELLY		
					CROSBY, Gary — see CROSBY, Bing		
					CROSBY, STILLS & NASH:		
03/21/70	RW	10	12		1 Woodstock		Atlantic 2723
					CROSBY, STILLS, NASH & YOUNG		
05/28/77	BB	7	21		2 Just A Song Before I Go	CB 8 / RR 10	Atlantic 3401
06/25/82	RR	2¹	17		3 Wasted On The Way	CB 8 / BB 9	Atlantic 4058
09/18/82	RR	7	19		4 Southern Cross		Atlantic 89969
					CROSS, Christopher		
02/09/80	BB	2⁴	23		1 Ride Like The Wind	RR 2² / RW 3⁴ / CB 3³	Warner 49184
06/07/80	RR	❶⁴	24		2 Sailing	CB ❶² / BB ❶¹ / RW ❶¹	Warner 49507
10/10/80	RR	3²	20		3 Never Be The Same	RW 10	Warner 49580
08/14/81	CB	❶⁴	25	●	4 Arthur's Theme (Best That You Can Do)	RR ❶⁴ / BB ❶³ / RW ❶³	Warner 49787
01/21/83	RR	3²	16		5 All Right	CB 9	Warner 29843
12/10/83	CB	6	18		6 Think Of Laura	RR 6 / BB 9	Warner 29658
					CROW, Sheryl		
08/05/94	RR	❶⁶	34	●	1 All I Wanna Do	BB 2⁶ / CB 2⁵	A&M 0702
12/31/94	RR	2⁴	26		2 Strong Enough	CB 4 / BB 5	A&M 0798
07/07/95	RR	10	19		3 Can't Cry Anymore		A&M 0638

DEBUT	CH	PK	WK	Gold	A-side (Chart Hit) ... Other Charts	Label & Number
					CROW, Sheryl (cont'd)	
09/06/96	RR	3¹	27		4 If It Makes You Happy ... BB 10 / CB 10	A&M 1874
01/17/97	RR	4	25		5 Everyday Is A Winding Road	A&M 2032
09/04/98	RR	6	28		6 My Favorite Mistake ... BB 9	A&M 2776
11/01/02	BB	4	34		7 Picture ... RR 5 KID ROCK with SHERYL CROW	Lava
					CROWDED HOUSE	
01/17/87	BB	2¹	26		1 Don't Dream It's Over ... RR 3² / CB 3¹	Capitol 5614
05/02/87	BB	7	21		2 Something So Strong ... CB 8 / RR 8	Capitol 5695
					CRUZ, Taio	
03/13/10	BB	❶¹	29	△³	1 Break Your Heart ... TAIO CRUZ Featuring Ludacris	Mercury 014302
06/19/10	BB	2³	47	△⁸	2 Dynamite	Mercury
					CRYSTALS, The	
03/19/62	CB	10	14		1 Uptown	Philles 102
09/08/62	BB	❶²	18	⊙	2 He's A Rebel ... MV ❶¹ / CB 2²	Philles 106
04/20/63	BB	3¹	15	⊙	3 Da Doo Ron Ron (When He Walked Me Home) ... MV 3¹ / CB 4	Philles 112
08/17/63	MV	4	13		4 Then He Kissed Me ... BB 6 / CB 6	Philles 115
					CUFF LINKS, The	
08/30/69	RW	4	15		1 Tracy ... CB 5 / BB 9	Decca 32533
					CULTURE BEAT	
11/05/93	RR	10	21	●	1 Mr. Vain	550 Music/Epic 77259
					CULTURE CLUB	
12/04/82	CB	❶²	30		1 Do You Really Want To Hurt Me ... RR ❶² / BB 2³	Epic/Virgin 03368
04/16/83	RR	2³	20		2 Time (Clock Of The Heart) ... BB 2² / CB 3²	Epic/Virgin 03796
07/02/83	CB	8	18		3 I'll Tumble 4 Ya ... BB 9 / RR 9	Epic/Virgin 03912
10/21/83	RR	5	17		4 Church Of The Poison Mind ... BB 10 / CB 10	Epic/Virgin 04144
12/03/83	BB	❶³	24	●	5 Karma Chameleon ... CB ❶³ / RR ❶³	Virgin/Epic 04221
03/02/84	RR	3²	18		6 Miss Me Blind ... BB 5 / CB 5	Virgin/Epic 04388
05/11/84	RR	9	13		7 It's A Miracle	Virgin/Epic 04457
					CUMMINGS, Burton	
10/02/76	CB	5	25	●	1 Stand Tall ... RR 6 / RW 9 / BB 10	Portrait 70001
					CURB, Mike, Congregation — see DAVIS, Sammy, Jr.	
					CURE, The	
08/05/89	CB	2²	25		1 Love Song ... BB 2¹ / RR 7	Elektra 69280
06/12/92	RR	4	20		2 Friday I'm In Love	Fiction/Elektra 64742
					CUTTING CREW	
03/06/87	BB	❶²	21		1 (I Just) Died In Your Arms ... CB ❶² / RR ❶²	Virgin 99481
09/05/87	RR	8	23		2 I've Been In Love Before ... BB 9	Virgin 99425
					CYRKLE, The	
05/21/66	BB	2¹	14	⊙	1 Red Rubber Ball ... RW 2¹ / CB 3¹	Columbia 43589
					CYRUS, Billy Ray	
05/09/92	BB	4	29	▲	1 Achy Breaky Heart ... CB 4	Mercury 866522
					CYRUS, Miley	
12/21/07	RR	4	27		1 See You Again ... BB 10	Hollywood
06/06/08	BB	9	15		2 7 Things	Hollywood
02/27/09	BB	4	28	△⁴	3 The Climb ... RR 7	Walt Disney
07/25/09	BB	10	5		4 He Could Be The One ... HANNAH MONTANA	Walt Disney
08/29/09	BB	2³	28	△⁷	5 Party In The U.S.A.	Hollywood
06/05/10	BB	8	10		6 Can't Be Tamed	Hollywood
06/22/13	BB	2³	26	△⁵	7 We Can't Stop	RCA
09/07/13	BB	❶³	32	△⁵	8 Wrecking Ball	RCA
05/27/17	BB	10	15	△²	9 Malibu	RCA

D

DEBUT	CH	PK	WK	Gold	A-side	Label & Number
					DaBABY	
04/13/19	BB	7	37	△²	1 Suge	SouthCoast
					DA BRAT	
06/04/94	BB	6	22	▲	1 Funkdafied	So So Def 77532
					DADDY DEWDROP	
03/06/71	CB	5	16		1 Chick-A-Boom (Don't Ya Jes' Love It) ... BB 9 / RW 9	Sunflower 105

DEBUT	CH	PK	WK	Gold	A-side (Chart Hit) ... Other Charts	Label & Number
					DADDY YANKEE	
02/04/17	BB	❶[16]	52	△[10]	1 Despacito .... LUIS FONSI & DADDY YANKEE Featuring Justin Bieber	Universal Latino
					DAFT PUNK	
05/04/13	BB	2[5]	29	△[4]	1 Get Lucky .... DAFT PUNK with PHARRELL WILLIAMS	Daft Life
					DALE, Alan	
12/05/53	BB	10	10		1 The Gang That Sang "Heart Of My Heart" .... DON CORNELL, ALAN DALE AND JOHNNY DESMOND	Coral 61076
06/06/55	MV	5	16		2 Sweet And Gentle ....CB 8 / BB 10	Coral 61435
					DALE & GRACE	
10/05/63	BB	❶[2]	17	☉	1 I'm Leaving It Up To You .... CB ❶[1] / MV ❶[1]	Montel 921
01/25/64	BB	8	9		2 Stop And Think It Over ....CB 8 / MV 8	Montel 922
					DALEY, Cass — see CARMICHAEL, Hoagy	
					DAMIAN, Michael	
03/18/89	BB	❶[1]	21	●	1 Rock On .... CB ❶[1] / RR ❶[1]	Cypress 1420
					DAMN YANKEES	
09/22/90	CB	2[2]	29	●	1 High Enough .... BB 3[2] / RR 5	Warner 19595
10/09/92	RR	9	23		2 Where You Goin' Now	Warner 18728
					DAMONE, Vic	
07/09/49	CB	❶[5]	28	☉	1 You're Breaking My Heart .... BB ❶[4]	Mercury 5271
07/22/50	BB	7	11		2 Tzena, Tzena, Tzena	Mercury 5454
12/30/50	BB	4	15		3 My Heart Cries For You	Mercury 5563
06/02/51	BB	3[2]	23		4 My Truly, Truly Fair ....BB 4	Mercury 5646
06/14/52	BB	8	9		5 Here In My Heart	Mercury 5858
05/16/53	BB	10	7		6 April In Portugal	Mercury 70128
10/17/53	BB	10	11		7 Ebb Tide	Mercury 70216
04/21/56	BB	4	25	☉	8 On The Street Where You Live .... MV 4 / CB 6	Columbia 40654
					DANA, Vic	
02/06/65	RW	8	12		1 Red Roses For A Blue Lady .... BB 10	Dolton 304
					DAN + SHAY	
10/19/19	BB	4	20	○	1 10,000 Hours .... DAN + SHAY & JUSTIN BIEBER	Warner
					D'ANGELO	
02/24/96	CB	8	23	●	1 Lady .... BB 10	EMI 58543
					DANIELS, Charlie, Band	
06/02/73	BB	9	17		1 Uneasy Rider .... CB 10 / RW 10	Kama Sutra 576
06/23/79	BB	3[2]	23	▲	2 The Devil Went Down To Georgia .... RW 3[2] / CB 4 / RR 9	Epic 50700
05/31/80	CB	10	17		3 In America .... RW 10	Epic 50888
					DANITY KANE	
09/02/06	BB	8	20		1 Show Stopper	Bad Boy
03/29/08	RR	6	22	△	2 Damaged .... BB 10	Bad Boy 512402
					DANLEERS, The	
05/31/58	BB	7	19		1 One Summer Night .... CB 9	Mercury 71322
					DANNY & THE JUNIORS	
11/18/57	BB	❶[7]	21	☉	1 At The Hop .... MV ❶[6] / CB ❶[5]	ABC-Paramount 9871
					D'ARBY, Terence Trent	
01/16/88	BB	❶[1]	28	●	1 Wishing Well .... CB ❶[1] / RR 3[2]	Columbia 07675
05/28/88	CB	3[1]	21		2 Sign Your Name .... RR 3[1] / BB 4	Columbia 07911
					DARIN, Bobby	
06/16/58	MV	2[3]	15	☉	1 Splish Splash .... CB 2[1] / BB 3[1]	Atco 6117
10/04/58	BB	9	19	☉	2 Queen Of The Hop	Atco 6127
04/18/59	BB	2[1]	17	☉	3 Dream Lover .... MV 3[3] / CB 3[1]	Atco 6140
08/24/59	BB	❶[9]	26	☉	4 Mack The Knife .... CB ❶[8] / MV ❶[6]	Atco 6147
01/18/60	BB	6	14		5 Beyond The Sea .... CB 7 / MV 7	Atco 6158
08/21/61	MV	4	12		6 You Must Have Been A Beautiful Baby .... BB 5 / CB 7	Atco 6206
07/07/62	BB	3[1]	12		7 Things .... MV 7 / CB 10	Atco 6229
01/12/63	BB	3[2]	16		8 You're The Reason I'm Living .... MV 4 / CB 5	Capitol 4897
05/04/63	BB	10	11		9 18 Yellow Roses .... MV 10	Capitol 4970
09/24/66	RW	5	11		10 If I Were A Carpenter .... BB 8 / CB 9	Atlantic 2350
					DARREN, James	
10/16/61	CB	2[2]	17		1 Goodbye Cruel World .... BB 3[2] / MV 3[2]	Colpix 609
02/03/62	BB	6	11		2 Her Royal Majesty .... CB 9	Colpix 622

39

DEBUT	CH	PK	WK	Gold	A-side (Chart Hit)	Other Charts	Label & Number

DAUGHTRY
12/09/06	RR	❶²	29	△²	1 It's Not Over	BB 4	RCA
03/17/07	RR	3¹	37	△³	2 Home	BB 5	RCA
08/10/07	RR	4	25	△²	3 Over You		RCA

DAVID, Craig
| 06/09/01 | RR | 6 | 27 | | 1 Fill Me In | | Wildstar 88101 |
| 11/16/01 | RR | 5 | 23 | | 2 7 Days | BB 10 | Wildstar 85232 |

DAVIS, Mac
| 07/01/72 | BB | ❶³ | 19 | ● | 1 Baby Don't Get Hooked On Me | CB ❶¹ / RW ❶¹ | Columbia 45618 |
| 08/17/74 | RW | 5 | 15 | | 2 Stop And Smell The Roses | CB 7 / BB 9 | Columbia 10018 |

DAVIS, Paul
08/27/77	BB	7	40		1 I Go Crazy	CB 7	Bang 733
11/07/81	RR	3¹	21		2 Cool Night		Arista 0645
02/27/82	RR	2²	20		3 '65 Love Affair	BB 6 / CB 10	Arista 0661

DAVIS, Sammy Jr.
05/16/55	CB	4	16		1 Something's Gotta Give	MV 4 / BB 9	Decca 29484
03/11/72	BB	❶³	21	●	2 The Candy Man	RW ❶² / CB ❶¹	MGM 14320
					SAMMY DAVIS, JR. with The Mike Curb Congregation		

DAVIS, Skeeter
| 01/12/63 | MV | ❶¹ | 19 | ☉ | 1 The End Of The World | CB 2³ / BB 2¹ | RCA Victor 8098 |
| 08/24/63 | MV | 5 | 16 | | 2 I Can't Stay Mad At You | CB 6 / BB 7 | RCA Victor 8219 |

DAVIS, Spencer, Group
| 12/31/66 | CB | 5 | 13 | | 1 Gimme Some Lovin' | RW 5 / BB 7 | United Artists 50108 |
| 03/25/67 | RW | 6 | 10 | | 2 I'm A Man | BB 10 / CB 10 | United Artists 50144 |

DAVIS, Tyrone
| 12/21/68 | BB | 5 | 13 | ● | 1 Can I Change My Mind | CB 5 / RW 5 | Dakar 602 |
| 03/07/70 | RW | ❶² | 15 | ● | 2 Turn Back The Hands Of Time | BB 3¹ / CB 4 | Dakar 616 |

DAWN — see ORLANDO, Tony

DAY, Bobby
| 07/26/58 | BB | 2² | 23 | ☉ | 1 Rock-in Robin | CB 4 / MV 5 | Class 229 |

DAY, Dennis
| 12/30/50 | BB | 10 | 3 | | 1 Christmas In Killarney | | RCA Victor 3970 |

DAY, Doris
05/13/50	BB	9	15		1 Bewitched		Columbia 38698
03/10/51	BB	10	10		2 Would I Love You (Love You, Love You)		Columbia 39159
					HARRY JAMES & his ORCH. with DORIS DAY		
06/30/51	BB	7	23		3 (Why Did I Tell You I Was Going To) Shanghai	CB 9	Columbia 39423
03/15/52	BB	❶¹	22	☉	4 A Guy Is A Guy	CB 2¹	Columbia 39673
06/21/52	BB	7	20		5 Sugarbush		Columbia 39693
					DORIS DAY - FRANKIE LAINE		
01/17/53	BB	10	7		6 Mister Tap Toe		Columbia 39906
11/28/53	CB	❶⁵	30	☉	7 Secret Love	BB ❶⁴	Columbia 40108
08/28/54	MV	❶³	24		8 If I Give My Heart To You	CB 2³ / BB 3²	Columbia 40300
06/22/56	BB	2³	27	☉	9 Whatever Will Be, Will Be (Que Sera, Sera)	MV 2² / CB 3³	Columbia 40704
07/07/58	BB	6	18		10 Everybody Loves A Lover	CB 6 / MV 7	Columbia 41195

DAYA — see CHAINSMOKERS, The

DAYNE, Taylor
10/10/87	BB	7	25	●	1 Tell It To My Heart	CB 9 / RR 9	Arista 9612
02/20/88	BB	7	18		2 Prove Your Love	CB 7 / RR 8	Arista 9676
06/11/88	BB	3²	30	●	3 I'll Always Love You	CB 4 / RR 6	Arista 9700
11/05/88	CB	❶¹	21		4 Don't Rush Me	BB 2¹ / RR 2¹	Arista 9722
10/20/89	RR	3²	21		5 With Every Beat Of My Heart	BB 5 / CB 5	Arista 9895
01/26/90	RR	❶²	21	●	6 Love Will Lead You Back	BB ❶¹ / CB ❶¹	Arista 9938
05/04/90	RR	3²	21		7 I'll Be Your Shelter	BB 4 / CB 5	Arista 2005
08/03/90	RR	9	16		8 Heart Of Stone	CB 10	Arista 2057
05/28/93	RR	5	20		9 Can't Get Enough Of Your Love		Arista 12582

DAZZ BAND
| 04/24/82 | BB | 5 | 23 | | 1 Let It Whip | | Motown 1609 |

DEAN, Jimmy
| 10/02/61 | MV | ❶⁶ | 18 | ● | 1 Big Bad John | BB ❶⁵ / CB ❶⁵ | Columbia 42175 |
| 03/31/62 | CB | 7 | 12 | | 2 P.T. 109 | MV 7 / BB 8 | Columbia 42338 |

DeANDA, Paula
| 10/21/06 | RR | 4 | 23 | ○ | 1 Walk Away (Remember Me) | | Arista 02360 |
| | | | | | PAULA DeANDA (feat. The DEY) | | |

DEBUT	CH	PK	WK	Gold	A-side (Chart Hit)	Other Charts	Label & Number
					DeBARGE		
04/16/83	CB	9	21		1 All This Love		Gordy 1660
02/16/85	RR	3³	23		2 Rhythm Of The Night	BB 3² / CB 3²	Gordy 1770
06/01/85	BB	6	19		3 Who's Holding Donna Now	RR 8	Gordy 1793
					DeBARGE, El		
04/26/86	BB	3¹	19		1 Who's Johnny	RR 5 / CB 7	Gordy 1842
					DeBURGH, Chris		
02/14/87	CB	2¹	26		1 The Lady In Red	BB 3² / RR 7	A&M 2848
					DeCASTRO SISTERS, The		
10/04/54	MV	2⁴	23		1 Teach Me Tonight	BB 2¹ / CB 3¹	Abbott 3001
					DEE, Joey, & The Starliters		
11/13/61	BB	❶³	20	⊙	1 Peppermint Twist - Part I	CB 2¹ / MV 2¹	Roulette 4401
03/19/62	BB	6	12		2 Shout - Part I	MV 8 / CB 9	Roulette 4416
					DEE, Kiki — see JOHN, Elton		
					DEEE-LITE		
09/15/90	CB	3²	24	●	1 Groove Is In The Heart	BB 4 / RR 7	Elektra 64934
					DEELE, The		
02/27/88	RR	9	22		1 Two Occasions	BB 10	Solar 70015
					DEEP BLUE SOMETHING		
07/28/95	RR	3⁴	43		1 Breakfast At Tiffany's	CB 3¹ / BB 5	Interscope 98138
					DEEP PURPLE		
08/03/68	BB	4	14		1 Hush	CB 4 / RW 4	Tetragrammaton 1503
05/26/73	RW	2¹	16	●	2 Smoke On The Water	CB 3² / BB 4	Warner 7710
					DEES, Rick, And His Cast Of Idiots		
08/14/76	RW	❶³	28	▲	1 Disco Duck (Part I)	CB ❶² / BB ❶¹ / RR 7	RSO 857
					DEF LEPPARD		
01/23/88	BB	10	17		1 Hysteria	RR 10	Mercury 870004
04/23/88	CB	❶²	25	○	2 Pour Some Sugar On Me	RR ❶¹ / BB 2¹	Mercury 870298
08/12/88	RR	❶²	23		3 Love Bites	BB ❶¹ / CB ❶¹	Mercury 870402
11/19/88	CB	2¹	20		4 Armageddon It	BB 3² / RR 3²	Mercury 870692
04/03/92	CB	7	22		5 Let's Get Rocked	RR 10	Mercury 866568
08/21/92	RR	4	24		6 Have You Ever Needed Someone So Bad		Mercury 864136
12/04/92	RR	10	17		7 Stand Up (Kick Love Into Motion)		Mercury 864604
08/20/93	RR	6	25		8 Two Steps Behind	CB 10	Columbia 77116
					DeFRANCO FAMILY Featuring Tony DeFranco		
08/25/73	CB	❶¹	21	●	1 Heartbeat - It's A Lovebeat	RW ❶¹ / RR 3² / BB 3¹	20th Century 2030
					DeGRAW, Gavin		
04/23/04	RR	❶¹	32	○	1 I Don't Want To Be	BB 10	J Records
03/01/08	RR	10	23		2 In Love With A Girl		J Records
					DeJOHN SISTERS		
12/13/54	BB	6	13		1 (My Baby Don't Love Me) No More	CB 7 / MV 7	Epic 9085
					DEKKER, Desmond, & The Aces		
05/10/69	RW	6	11		1 Israelites	CB 8 / BB 9	Uni 55129
					DEL AMITRI		
06/30/95	RR	6	43		1 Roll To Me	CB 7 / BB 10	A&M 1114
					DELANEY & BONNIE & FRIENDS		
05/22/71	CB	9	16		1 Never Ending Song Of Love		Atco 6804
					DELEGATES, The		
10/21/72	BB	8	8		1 Convention '72	CB 9	Mainstream 5525
					DELFONICS, The		
02/03/68	RW	3¹	15		1 La-La-Means I Love You	BB 4 / CB 4	Philly Groove 150
01/10/70	RW	9	15	●	2 Didn't I (Blow Your Mind This Time)	BB 10	Philly Groove 161
					DELLS, The		
06/29/68	BB	10	13		1 Stay In My Corner		Cadet 5612
08/09/69	BB	10	12		2 Oh, What A Night		Cadet 5649
					DELL-VIKINGS, The		
02/16/57	CB	3³	31	⊙	1 Come Go With Me	BB 4 / MV 5	Dot 15538
06/29/57	BB	9	18		2 Whispering Bells	CB 9	Dot 15592
					THE DELL-VIKINGS Featuring Kripp Johnson		

41

DEBUT	CH	PK	WK	Gold	A-side (Chart Hit)	Other Charts	Label & Number
					DEL REY, Lana		
07/27/13	BB	6	23	△⁴ 1	Summertime Sadness		Polydor
					LANA DEL REY & CEDRIC GERVAIS		
					DEM FRANCHIZE BOYZ		
01/21/06	BB	7	25	1	Lean Wit It, Rock Wit It		So So Def 50656
					DEM FRANCHIZE BOYZ Feat. Lil Peanut & Charlay		
					DENNIS, Cathy		
12/16/89	CB	7	21	1	C'mon And Get My Love	BB 10 / RR 10	FFRR 886798
					D MOB Introducing CATHY DENNIS		
10/27/90	RR	8	24	2	Just Another Dream	BB 9 / CB 10	Polydor 877962
03/02/91	RR	❶¹	27	3	Touch Me (All Night Long)	BB 2² / CB 5	Polydor 879466
06/29/91	RR	6	23	4	Too Many Walls	BB 8	Polydor 867134
					DENNY, Martin (The Exotic Sounds of)		
04/11/59	CB	3²	17	⊙ 1	Quiet Village	BB 4 / MV 5	Liberty 55162
					DENVER, John		
04/10/71	RW	❶²	24	▲ 1	Take Me Home, Country Roads	CB ❶¹ / BB 2¹	RCA Victor 0445
11/25/72	CB	7	20	○ 2	Rocky Mountain High	RW 7 / BB 9	RCA Victor 0829
01/19/74	BB	❶¹	18	3	Sunshine On My Shoulders	CB ❶¹ / RW ❶¹ / RR 3¹	RCA Victor 0213
05/25/74	BB	❶²	17	● 4	Annie's Song	CB ❶¹ / RW ❶¹ / RR 2²	RCA Victor 0295
09/21/74	BB	5	19	● 5	Back Home Again	CB 5 / RW 8 / RR 10	RCA Victor 10065
03/22/75	BB	❶¹	22	● 6	Thank God I'm A Country Boy	CB ❶¹ / RW ❶¹ / RR 3¹	RCA Victor 10239
08/09/75	BB	❶¹	21	● 7	I'm Sorry	CB ❶¹ / RW ❶¹ / RR ❶¹	RCA Victor 10353
12/06/75	CB	6	16	8	Fly Away		RCA Victor 10517
					DEODATO		
02/03/73	BB	2¹	12	1	Also Sprach Zarathustra (2001)	CB 4 / RW 4	CTI 12
					DEPECHE MODE		
05/18/85	RR	10	19	1	People Are People		Sire 29221
04/14/90	CB	2¹	24	● 2	Enjoy The Silence	RR 4 / BB 8	Sire/Reprise 19885
08/11/90	RR	10	16	3	Policy Of Truth		Sire/Reprise 19842
					DEREK		
09/14/68	RW	9	21	1	Cinnamon	CB 10	Bang 558
					DEREK AND THE DOMINOS		
05/13/72	BB	10	15	1	Layla		Atco 6809
					DERULO, Jason		
08/29/09	BB	❶¹	32	△⁵ 1	Whatcha Say		Beluga Heights 522765
12/26/09	BB	5	34	△⁴ 2	In My Head		Beluga Heights
03/20/10	BB	9	28	△⁴ 3	Ridin' Solo		Beluga Heights
01/04/14	BB	3⁵	33	△⁴ 4	Talk Dirty		Beluga Heights
					JASON DERULO Featuring 2 Chainz		
05/17/14	BB	5	21	△³ 5	Wiggle		Beluga Heights
					JASON DERULO Featuring Snoop Dogg		
03/28/15	BB	5	35	△⁴ 6	Want To Want Me		Beluga Heights
					DeSARIO, Teri		
11/17/79	RW	❶¹	25	● 1	Yes, I'm Ready	BB 2² / CB 3² / RR 4	Casablanca 2227
					TERI DeSARIO with K.C.		
					DeSHANNON, Jackie		
05/22/65	BB	7	14	1	What The World Needs Now Is Love	RW 7 / CB 8	Imperial 66110
06/14/69	RW	3¹	16	● 2	Put A Little Love In Your Heart	BB 4 / CB 4	Imperial 66385
					DESIIGNER		
03/12/16	BB	❶²	40	△⁵ 1	Panda		G.O.O.D.
					DESMOND, Johnny		
12/05/53	BB	10	10	1	The Gang That Sang "Heart Of My Heart"		Coral 61076
					DON CORNELL, ALAN DALE AND JOHNNY DESMOND		
12/12/53	CB	6	18	2	Woman	BB 9	Coral 61069
03/14/55	BB	6	13	3	Play Me Hearts And Flowers (I Wanna Cry)	MV 7 / CB 10	Coral 61379
08/01/55	BB	3¹	16	4	The Yellow Rose Of Texas	MV 6	Coral 61476
					DES'REE		
07/23/94	BB	5	51	1	You Gotta Be	CB 5 / RR 7	550 Music/Epic 77551
					DESTINY'S CHILD		
11/29/97	BB	3¹	35	▲ 1	No, No, No Part 2		Columbia 78618
					DESTINY'S CHILD (featuring Wyclef Jean)		
06/19/99	BB	❶¹	20	● 2	Bills, Bills, Bills		Columbia 79175
12/25/99	BB	❶³	32	● 3	Say My Name	RR 3²	Columbia 79342
05/13/00	RR	❶³	32	4	Jumpin', Jumpin'	BB 3⁵	Columbia 79446
09/23/00	BB	❶¹¹	28	5	Independent Women Part I	RR ❶⁹	Columbia 79493
03/09/01	BB	2⁷	20	6	Survivor	RR 2²	Columbia 79566

DEBUT	CH	PK	WK	Gold	A-side (Chart Hit)	Other Charts	Label & Number
					DESTINY'S CHILD (cont'd)		
06/01/01	BB	❶²	19		7 Bootylicious	RR 6	Columbia 79622
09/14/01	RR	8	22		8 Emotion	BB 10	Columbia 79672
09/17/04	BB	3⁴	23	◯	9 Lose My Breath	RR 3¹	Columbia 70096
11/19/04	BB	3¹	22	◯	10 Soldier	RR 5	Columbia 70702
					DESTINY'S CHILD (feat. T.I. and Lil Wayne)		
					DETERGENTS, The		
12/05/64	RW	10	9		1 Leader Of The Laundromat		Roulette 4590
					DeVAUGHN, William		
04/13/74	RW	❶¹	20	●	1 Be Thankful For What You Got	CB 3² / BB 4 / RR 5	Roxbury 0236
					DeVORZON, Barry, and Perry Botkin, Jr.		
08/28/76	CB	5	29	●	1 Nadia's Theme (The Young And The Restless)	RR 5 / RW 7 / BB 8	A&M 1856
					DEXYS MIDNIGHT RUNNERS		
01/22/83	BB	❶¹	24		1 Come On Eileen	CB ❶¹ / RR 3²	Mercury 76189
					DeYOUNG, Dennis		
09/08/84	RR	7	22		1 Desert Moon	BB 10 / CB 10	A&M 2666
					D4L		
10/01/05	BB	❶¹	26	◯	1 Laffy Taffy		DeeMoney 68009
					D.H.T.		
05/27/05	RR	❶¹	27	◯	1 Listen To Your Heart	BB 8	Robbins 72116
					DIAMOND, Neil		
08/20/66	RW	5	13		1 Cherry, Cherry	BB 6 / CB 6	Bang 528
04/08/67	RW	8	12		2 Girl, You'll Be A Woman Soon	CB 9 / BB 10	Bang 542
07/15/67	RW	10	11		3 Thank The Lord For The Night Time		Bang 547
06/14/69	RW	3²	15	▲	4 Sweet Caroline (Good Times Never Seemed So Good)	CB 3¹ / BB 4	Uni 55136
10/25/69	CB	4	14	▲	5 Holly Holy	RW 4 / BB 6	Uni 55175
08/15/70	BB	❶¹	15	▲	6 Cracklin' Rosie	CB ❶¹ / RW ❶¹	Uni 55250
03/20/71	BB	4	11		7 I Am...I Said	CB 4 / RW 4	Uni 55278
11/06/71	RW	10	11		8 Stones		Uni 55310
04/29/72	RW	❶²	14	●	9 Song Sung Blue	BB ❶¹ / CB ❶¹	Uni 55326
10/05/74	CB	4	16		10 Longfellow Serenade	RW 4 / BB 5 / RR 6	Columbia 10043
11/26/77	CB	9	17		11 Desiree	RR 10	Columbia 10657
10/27/78	CB	❶³	18	▲	12 You Don't Bring Me Flowers	RR ❶³ / BB ❶² / RW ❶²	Columbia 10840
					BARBRA & NEIL		
12/22/79	RR	6	18		13 September Morn'	RW 7	Columbia 11175
10/31/80	RR	❶¹	23		14 Love On The Rocks	BB 2³ / RW 3⁴ / CB 4	Capitol 4939
01/23/81	RR	3²	16		15 Hello Again	BB 6 / CB 8 / RW 8	Capitol 4960
04/24/81	RR	5	17		16 America	BB 8 / RW 9 / CB 10	Capitol 4994
11/06/81	RR	9	16		17 Yesterday's Songs		Columbia 02604
09/11/82	RR	4	20		18 Heartlight	BB 5 / CB 10	Columbia 03219
					DIAMONDS, The		
03/02/57	MV	❶¹	26	⊙	1 Little Darlin'	BB 2⁸ / CB 2⁷	Mercury 71060
11/04/57	BB	10	11		2 Silhouettes		Mercury 71197
12/23/57	CB	❶²	21	⊙	3 The Stroll	MV ❶² / BB 4	Mercury 71242
					DICK AND DEEDEE		
07/31/61	BB	2²	15	⊙	1 The Mountain's High	CB 3² / MV 4	Liberty 55350
					DIDO		
01/13/01	RR	3⁴	39	◯	1 Thankyou	BB 3³	Arista 13996
					DINNING, Mark		
12/21/59	BB	❶²	18	⊙	1 Teen Angel	CB ❶² / MV ❶²	MGM 12845
					DINO		
05/13/89	CB	4	25	●	1 I Like It	BB 7 / RR 7	4th & B'way 7483
08/11/90	BB	6	20		2 Romeo	CB 7 / RR 8	Island 878012
07/09/93	RR	10	22		3 Ooh Child		EastWest 98398
					DION		
09/18/61	MV	❶³	17	⊙	1 Runaround Sue	BB ❶² / CB ❶²	Laurie 3110
12/04/61	BB	2¹	18	⊙	2 The Wanderer	MV 3³ / CB 3¹	Laurie 3115
04/21/62	BB	3¹	13		3 Lovers Who Wander	CB 5 / MV 9	Laurie 3123
07/07/62	BB	8	12		4 Little Diane		Laurie 3134
11/10/62	BB	10	12		5 Love Came To Me		Laurie 3145
01/12/63	BB	2³	15	⊙	6 Ruby Baby	MV 2¹ / CB 3⁵	Columbia 42662
09/07/63	BB	6	12		7 Donna The Prima Donna	CB 6 / MV 7	Columbia 42852
11/16/63	CB	5	12		8 Drip Drop	BB 6 / MV 7	Columbia 42917
10/19/68	CB	2¹	15	●	9 Abraham, Martin And John	RW 2¹ / BB 4	Laurie 3464

43

DEBUT	CH	PK	WK	Gold	A-side (Chart Hit) ... Other Charts	Label & Number
					DION and THE BELMONTS	
04/18/59	BB	5	15	⊙	1 A Teenager In Love .... MV 5 / CB 6	Laurie 3027
12/26/59	BB	3¹	16		2 Where Or When .... CB 4 / MV 6	Laurie 3044
					DION, Celine	
12/08/90	BB	4	24		1 Where Does My Heart Beat Now .... CB 4 / RR 4	Epic 73536
01/18/92	RR	6	24	▲	2 Beauty And The Beast .... BB 9 / CB 9	Epic 74090
					CELINE DION and PEABO BRYSON	
04/17/92	RR	2²	29		3 If You Asked Me To .... BB 4 / CB 5	Epic 74277
08/01/92	RR	7	20		4 Nothing Broken But My Heart	Epic 74336
11/27/93	BB	❶⁴	38	▲	5 The Power Of Love .... CB ❶³ / RR 3⁴	550 Music/Epic 77230
04/22/94	CB	9	23		6 Misled	550 Music/Epic 77344
03/01/96	RR	❶⁷	36	▲	7 Because You Loved Me .... BB ❶⁶ / CB ❶³	550 Music/Epic 78237
08/09/96	CB	❶²	30	▲	8 It's All Coming Back To Me Now .... RR 2⁷ / BB 2⁵	550 Music/Epic 78345
01/31/97	BB	4	20		9 All By Myself .... RR 7	550 Music/Epic 78529
12/12/97	RR	❶⁹	27	●	10 My Heart Will Go On (Love Theme From 'Titanic') ..... BB ❶²	550 Music/Epic 78825
10/23/98	BB	❶⁶	18	▲	11 I'm Your Angel	Jive 42557
					R. KELLY & CELINE DION	
10/29/99	RR	3⁴	28		12 That's The Way It Is .... BB 6	550 Music/Epic 79473
					DIPLO — see SKRILLEX	
					DIRE STRAITS	
02/03/79	RR	2²	16		1 Sultans Of Swing .... BB 4 / CB 5	Warner 8736
07/13/85	CB	❶⁴	28		2 Money For Nothing .... BB ❶³ / RR ❶³	Warner 28950
11/02/85	RR	6	22		3 Walk Of Life .... BB 7 / CB 10	Warner 28878
					DIRTY VEGAS	
04/26/02	RR	7	20		1 Days Go By	Capitol 77742
					DISCLOSURE	
03/29/14	BB	7	33	△³	1 Latch	PMR
					DISCLOSURE with SAM SMITH	
					DISCO TEX & THE SEX-O-LETTES	
11/23/74	BB	10	16		1 Get Dancin' .... CB 10	Chelsea 3004
					DISHWALLA	
04/06/96	RR	4	48		1 Counting Blue Cars	A&M 1462
					DIVINE	
09/12/98	BB	❶¹	27	▲	1 Lately	Red Ant 15316
					DIVINYLS	
03/09/91	BB	4	23		1 I Touch Myself .... CB 6 / RR 7	Virgin 98873
					DIXIEBELLES, The	
09/28/63	BB	9	14		1 (Down At) Papa Joe's .... MV 9	Sound Stage 7 2507
					DIXIE CHICKS	
06/22/02	BB	7	20		1 Long Time Gone	Monument 79790
09/21/02	BB	7	29	○	2 Landslide	Monument 79857
05/06/06	BB	4	24	△	3 Not Ready To Make Nice	Columbia 84335
					DIXIE CUPS, The	
05/02/64	RW	❶⁴	14	⊙	1 Chapel Of Love .... BB ❶³ / CB ❶³	Red Bird 001
07/11/64	RW	7	11		2 People Say .... CB 10	Red Bird 006
					D.J. JAZZY JEFF & THE FRESH PRINCE	
06/15/91	BB	4	18	▲	1 Summertime .... RR 7	Jive 1465
					DJ KHALED	
06/04/11	BB	10	23	○	1 I'm On One	We The Best
					DJ KHALED Featuring Drake, Rick Ross & Lil Wayne	
05/20/17	BB	❶¹	22	△⁷	2 I'm The One	We The Best
					DJ KHALED Featuring Justin Bieber, Quavo, Chance The Rapper & Lil Wayne	
07/08/17	BB	2⁷	21	△⁵	3 Wild Thoughts	We The Best
					DJ KHALED Featuring Rihanna & Bryson Tiller	
08/11/18	BB	5	15	△	4 No Brainer	We The Best
					DJ KHALED Featuring Justin Bieber, Chance The Rapper & Quavo	
					DJ SAMMY & YANOU Featuring Do	
05/31/02	RR	4	27	○	1 Heaven .... BB 8	Robbins 72057
					DJ SNAKE	
01/11/14	BB	4	37	△⁶	1 Turn Down For What	Columbia
					DJ SNAKE & LIL JON	
04/25/15	BB	4	48	△⁴	2 Lean On	Mad Decent
					MAJOR LAZER & DJ SNAKE with MO	
08/27/16	BB	4	33	△⁴	3 Let Me Love You	DJ Snake
					DJ SNAKE Featuring Justin Bieber	

DEBUT	CH	PK	WK	Gold	A-side (Chart Hit)	Other Charts	Label & Number
					DNCE		
11/07/15	BB	9	46	△⁴ 1	Cake By The Ocean		Republic
					DOBKINS, Carl Jr.		
04/13/59	MV	❶³	24	⊙ 1	My Heart Is An Open Book	BB 3³ / CB 3¹	Decca 30803
					DR. DRE		
01/30/93	BB	2¹	28	▲ 1	Nuthin' But A "G" Thang	CB 2¹	Death Row 53819
05/15/93	BB	8	24	● 2	Dre Day	CB 8	Death Row 53827
					DR. DRE & SNOOP DOGGY DOGG (above 2)		
03/18/95	BB	10	21	● 3	Keep Their Heads Ringin'		Priority 53188
01/31/09	BB	❶¹	17	△² 4	Crack A Bottle		Web
					EMINEM, DR. DRE & 50 CENT		
02/19/11	BB	4	20	△² 5	I Need A Doctor		Aftermath
					DR. DRE Featuring Eminem & Skylar Grey		
					DR. HOOK		
03/18/72	CB	❶¹	16	● 1	Sylvia's Mother	RW 2² / BB 5	Columbia 45562
11/25/72	RW	4	21	● 2	The Cover Of "Rolling Stone"	CB 5 / BB 6	Columbia 45732
					DR. HOOK AND THE MEDICINE SHOW (above 2)		
01/03/76	CB	5	25	● 3	Only Sixteen	BB 6 / RR 9 / RW 10	Capitol 4171
06/19/76	RR	8	26	4	A Little Bit More	CB 9	Capitol 4280
09/16/78	RR	3¹	23	● 5	Sharing The Night Together	CB 4 / RW 4 / BB 6	Capitol 4621
04/14/79	RR	3²	26	● 6	When You're In Love With A Beautiful Woman	RW 4 / CB 5 / BB 6	Capitol 4705
02/16/80	RW	3²	24	● 7	Sexy Eyes	BB 5 / CB 6 / RR 8	Capitol 4831
					DR. JOHN		
04/14/73	BB	9	20	1	Right Place Wrong Time	RW 10	Atco 6914
					DOGGETT, Bill		
08/18/56	BB	2³	29	⊙ 1	Honky Tonk (Parts 1 & 2)	CB 2¹ / MV 2¹	King 4950
					DOG'S EYE VIEW		
03/01/96	RR	7	32	1	Everything Falls Apart		Columbia
					DOLBY, Thomas		
02/19/83	CB	4	24	1	She Blinded Me With Science	BB 5 / RR 9	Capitol 5204
					DOMINO		
11/27/93	BB	7	20	● 1	Getto Jam		OutBurst 77298
					DOMINO, Fats		
07/16/55	BB	10	13	⊙ 1	Ain't That A Shame		Imperial 5348
04/28/56	BB	3²	23	⊙ 2	I'm In Love Again	CB 3¹ / MV 6	Imperial 5386
09/29/56	BB	2³	27	⊙ 3	Blueberry Hill	MV 3⁴ / CB 4	Imperial 5407
12/22/56	BB	5	18	⊙ 4	Blue Monday	MV 5 / CB 8	Imperial 5417
03/02/57	BB	4	25	⊙ 5	I'm Walkin'	CB 5 / MV 5	Imperial 5428
05/18/57	BB	6	12	⊙ 16	It's You I Love /		
05/13/57	BB	8	18	17	Valley Of Tears		Imperial 5442
11/03/58	BB	6	17	⊙ 8	Whole Lotta Loving	CB 9 / MV 9	Imperial 5553
08/01/59	MV	7	13	9	I Want To Walk You Home	BB 8 / CB 9	Imperial 5606
10/19/59	BB	8	15	10	Be My Guest	CB 8 / MV 8	Imperial 5629
06/20/60	BB	6	14	⊙ 11	Walking To New Orleans	MV 7 / CB 10	Imperial 5675
					DONALDSON, Bo, And The Heywoods		
04/13/74	BB	❶²	19	● 1	Billy, Don't Be A Hero	CB ❶¹ / RW ❶¹ / RR 2¹	ABC 11435
					DON & JUAN		
01/29/62	CB	5	14	1	What's Your Name	BB 7 / MV 8	Big Top 3079
					DONEGAN, Lonnie, And His Skiffle Group		
03/23/56	MV	5	17	1	Rock Island Line	CB 6 / BB 8	London 1650
07/24/61	BB	5	13	2	Does Your Chewing Gum Lose It's Flavor		Dot 15911
					(On The Bedpost Over Night)	CB 6 / MV 6	
					DONNER, Ral		
07/10/61	BB	4	12	1	You Don't Know What You've Got (Until You Lose It)	CB 10	Gone 5108
12/16/61	CB	10	13	2	She's Everything (I Wanted You To Be)		Gone 5121
					DONOVAN		
07/23/66	BB	❶¹	13	⊙ 1	Sunshine Superman	CB ❶¹ / RW ❶¹	Epic 10045
11/12/66	RW	❶²	13	● 2	Mellow Yellow	BB 2³ / CB 3²	Epic 10098
02/04/67	CB	10	9	3	Epistle To Dippy	RW 10	Epic 10127
08/12/67	CB	9	10	4	There Is A Mountain		Epic 10212
06/15/68	RW	3²	13	5	Hurdy Gurdy Man	CB 3¹ / BB 5	Epic 10345
04/05/69	BB	7	13	6	Atlantis	CB 9 / RW 9	Epic 10434
					DOOBIE BROTHERS, The		
09/02/72	CB	9	13	1	Listen To The Music	RW 10	Warner 7619
04/21/73	BB	8	18	2	Long Train Runnin'	CB 9 / RW 9	Warner 7698
08/18/73	CB	8	15	3	China Grove	RW 10	Warner 7728

DEBUT	CH	PK	WK	Gold	A-side (Chart Hit)	Other Charts	Label & Number

DOOBIE BROTHERS, The (cont'd)
12/20/74	RR	❶²	20	●	4 Black Water	BB ❶¹ / RW ❶¹ / CB 3¹	Warner 8062
05/03/75	RW	5	16		5 Take Me In Your Arms (Rock Me)	RR 5 / CB 10	Warner 8092
01/20/79	RR	❶³	21	●	6 What A Fool Believes	CB ❶² / BB ❶¹ / RW ❶¹	Warner 8725
05/05/79	RR	6	14		7 Minute By Minute		Warner 8828
08/29/80	RR	❶²	16		8 Real Love	BB 5 / CB 7 / RW 9	Warner 49503
05/20/89	BB	9	14		9 The Doctor		Capitol 44376

DOORS, The
05/27/67	BB	❶³	23	●	1 Light My Fire	CB ❶¹ / RW ❶¹	Elektra 45615
09/16/67	CB	10	10		2 People Are Strange	RW 10	Elektra 45621
06/29/68	BB	❶²	14	●	3 Hello, I Love You	CB ❶¹ / RW ❶¹	Elektra 45635
12/28/68	CB	❶¹	13	●	4 Touch Me	RW 2² / BB 3¹	Elektra 45646
04/03/71	CB	7	12		5 Love Her Madly	RW 8	Elektra 45726

DORSEY, Jimmy, Orchestra
| 02/23/57 | BB | 2⁴ | 38 | ☉ | 1 So Rare | CB 2¹ / MV 3¹ | Fraternity 755 |

DORSEY, Lee
| 09/02/61 | BB | 7 | 15 | | 1 Ya Ya | CB 8 / MV 9 | Fury 1053 |
| 07/23/66 | BB | 8 | 13 | | 2 Working In The Coal Mine | CB 10 / RW 10 | Amy 958 |

DORSEY, Tommy, Orchestra
| 08/18/58 | CB | 2¹ | 23 | | 1 Tea For Two Cha Cha | MV 2¹ / BB 7 | Decca 30704 |

DOUGLAS, Carl
| 10/12/74 | RR | ❶⁴ | 21 | ● | 1 Kung Fu Fighting | BB ❶² / CB ❶¹ / RW ❶¹ | 20th Century 2140 |

DOUGLAS, Carol
| 11/23/74 | CB | 10 | 16 | | 1 Doctor's Orders | | Midland Int'l. 10113 |

DOUGLAS, Mike
| 12/18/65 | RW | 4 | 10 | | 1 The Men In My Little Girl's Life | BB 6 / CB 7 | Epic 9876 |

DOVE, Ronnie
03/13/65	RW	6	12		1 One Kiss For Old Times' Sake	CB 9	Diamond 179
06/05/65	RW	9	12		2 A Little Bit Of Heaven		Diamond 184
04/09/66	RW	10	9		3 Let's Start All Over Again		Diamond 198

DOVELLS, The
| 09/04/61 | BB | 2² | 17 | ☉ | 1 Bristol Stomp | CB 3² / MV 3¹ | Parkway 827 |
| 04/20/63 | BB | 3¹ | 15 | | 2 You Can't Sit Down | CB 3¹ / MV 5 | Parkway 867 |

DOWELL, Joe
| 06/26/61 | BB | ❶¹ | 17 | ☉ | 1 Wooden Heart | MV 2⁴ / CB 3¹ | Smash 1708 |

DRAKE
05/23/09	BB	2⁴	24	△⁴	1 Best I Ever Had		Young Money
10/03/09	BB	8	24		2 Forever		Young Money
					DRAKE Featuring Kanye West, Lil Wayne & Eminem		
05/22/10	BB	5	21	△³	3 Find Your Love		Young Money
10/29/11	BB	9	20	△	4 Make Me Proud		Young Money
					DRAKE Featuring Nicki Minaj		
12/03/11	BB	7	34	△⁵	5 Take Care		Young Money
					DRAKE Featuring Rihanna		
02/23/13	BB	6	22	△⁶	6 Started From The Bottom		Young Money
08/24/13	BB	4	33	△⁶	7 Hold On, We're Going Home		Young Money
					DRAKE Featuring Majid Jordan		
08/22/15	BB	2⁵	36	△⁸	8 Hotline Bling		Young Money
02/20/16	BB	6	14	△	9 Summer Sixteen		Young Money
04/23/16	BB	❶¹⁰	36	△⁸	10 One Dance		Young Money
					DRAKE Featuring WizKid & Kyla		
11/12/16	BB	8	25	△⁴	11 Fake Love		Young Money
04/08/17	BB	8	20	△³	12 Passionfruit		Young Money
04/08/17	BB	9	16	△²	13 Portland		Young Money
					DRAKE Featuring Quavo & Travis Scott		
02/03/18	BB	❶¹¹	36	△¹¹	14 God's Plan		Young Money
02/03/18	BB	7	3		15 Diplomatic Immunity		Young Money
04/21/18	BB	❶⁸	25	△⁵	16 Nice For What		Young Money
05/26/18	BB	6	29	△³	17 Yes Indeed		Quality Control
					LIL BABY & DRAKE		
06/09/18	BB	7	16		18 I'm Upset		Young Money
07/14/18	BB	❶¹⁰	22	△⁵	19 In My Feelings		Young Money
07/14/18	BB	2¹	22		20 Nonstop		Young Money
07/14/18	BB	8	4		21 Emotionless		Young Money
07/14/18	BB	9	5		22 Don't Matter To Me		Young Money
					DRAKE Featuring Michael Jackson		
06/29/19	BB	7	23		23 Money In The Grave		OVO Sound
					DRAKE Featuring Rick Ross		

DEBUT	CH	PK	WK	Gold	A-side (Chart Hit)	Other Charts	Label & Number

D.R.A.M.
07/02/16	BB	5	37	△⁷	1 Broccoli	#1EpicCheck
					D.R.A.M. Featuring Lil Yachty	

DRAMATICS, The
07/03/71	BB	9	15		1 Whatcha See Is Whatcha Get	RW 10	Volt 4058
02/19/72	CB	3¹	14		2 In The Rain	BB 5 / RW 5	Volt 4075

DRAPER, Rusty
02/28/53	BB	10	8		1 No Help Wanted		Mercury 70077
07/04/53	BB	6	18	⊙	2 Gambler's Guitar		Mercury 70167
09/03/55	BB	3²	22		3 The Shifting, Whispering Sands	CB 5 / MV 6	Mercury 70696
05/18/57	BB	6	18		4 Freight Train		Mercury 71102

DREAM
09/15/00	BB	2²	29	●	1 He Loves U Not	RR 3⁵	Bad Boy 79338

DREAM ACADEMY, The
11/30/85	RR	4	24		1 Life In A Northern Town	CB 6 / BB 7	Warner 28841

DREAMLOVERS, The
07/31/61	BB	10	12		1 When We Get Married		Heritage 102

DREAM WEAVERS, The
10/29/55	CB	6	24		1 It's Almost Tomorrow	BB 7 / MV 7	Decca 29683

DRIFTERS, The
06/01/59	CB	❶²	19	⊙	1 There Goes My Baby	BB 2¹ / MV 5	Atlantic 2025
10/12/59	CB	10	15		2 Dance With Me		Atlantic 2040
02/13/60	CB	9	13		3 This Magic Moment		Atlantic 2050
09/05/60	CB	❶⁶	18	⊙	4 Save The Last Dance For Me	MV ❶⁵ / BB ❶³	Atlantic 2071
11/03/62	BB	5	20		5 Up On The Roof	CB 6 / MV 7	Atlantic 2162
03/16/63	BB	9	11		6 On Broadway		Atlantic 2182
06/27/64	BB	4	15		7 Under The Boardwalk	RW 4 / CB 5	Atlantic 2237

D.R.S.
10/16/93	BB	4	24	▲	1 Gangsta Lean	CB 6	Capitol 44958

DRU HILL
01/11/97	BB	4	25	▲	1 In My Bed		Island 854854
08/09/97	BB	7	20	●	2 Never Make A Promise		Island 572082
10/10/98	BB	3³	20	●	3 How Deep Is Your Love		Island 572424
					DRU HILL Featuring Redman		

D12
03/19/04	RR	3¹	19	○	1 My Band	BB 6	Shady

DUFF, Hilary
01/23/04	RR	9	20	○	1 Come Clean		Buena Vista

DUKE, Patty
06/19/65	RW	5	13		1 Don't Just Stand There	CB 6 / BB 8	United Artists 875

DUPREE, Robbie
04/12/80	RR	4	24		1 Steal Away	CB 5 / RW 5 / BB 6	Elektra 46621
07/19/80	RR	3¹	19		2 Hot Rod Hearts	RW 7	Elektra 47005

DUPREES, The
07/14/62	BB	7	16		1 You Belong To Me	CB 7	Coed 569

DURAN DURAN
12/25/82	BB	3³	23	●	1 Hungry Like The Wolf	CB 4 / RR 5	Harvest 5195
06/04/83	BB	4	19		2 Is There Something I Should Know	RR 4 / CB 7	Capitol 5233
11/04/83	CB	❶³	20		3 Union Of The Snake	RR 2¹ / BB 3³	Capitol 5290
01/14/84	BB	10	17		4 New Moon On Monday	CB 10 / RR 10	Capitol 5309
04/20/84	BB	❶²	21	●	5 The Reflex	CB ❶² / RR ❶¹	Capitol 5345
10/26/84	CB	❶²	19	●	6 The Wild Boys	RR ❶¹ / BB 2⁴	Capitol 5417
02/01/85	RR	10	15		7 Save A Prayer		Capitol 5438
05/17/85	BB	❶²	18		8 A View To A Kill	CB ❶¹ / RR ❶¹	Capitol 5475
10/31/86	BB	2¹	20		9 Notorious	RR 2¹ / CB 4	Capitol 5648
10/14/88	CB	3¹	19		10 I Don't Want Your Love	RR 3¹ / BB 4	Capitol 44237
01/08/93	RR	❶²	25	●	11 Ordinary World	CB ❶¹ / BB 3³	Capitol 44908
04/16/93	RR	2³	27		12 Come Undone	CB 4 / BB 7	Capitol 44918

DYLAN, Bob
07/24/65	CB	❶¹	12		1 Like A Rolling Stone	BB 2² / RW 2²	Columbia 43346
09/25/65	BB	7	10		2 Positively 4th Street	CB 9 / RW 9	Columbia 43389
04/16/66	RW	2¹	11		3 Rainy Day Women #12 & 35	BB 2¹ / CB 2¹	Columbia 43592
07/12/69	BB	7	14		4 Lay Lady Lay	RW 7 / CB 8	Columbia 44926
09/01/73	CB	10	16		5 Knockin' On Heaven's Door	RR 10	Columbia 45913

47

DEBUT	CH	PK	WK	Gold	A-side (Chart Hit) ... Other Charts	Label & Number
					DYSON, Ronnie	
06/13/70	RW	7	15		1 (If You Let Me Make Love To You Then) Why Can't I Touch You?..BB 8 / CB 10	Columbia 45110

E

					EAGLES	
05/20/72	RW	6	13		1 Take It Easy ....CB 9	Asylum 11005
08/26/72	RW	8	16		2 Witchy Woman ....BB 9	Asylum 11008
11/30/74	BB	❶¹	22		3 Best Of My Love ....RR 2² / RW 3¹ / CB 4	Asylum 45218
05/30/75	BB	❶¹	17		4 One Of These Nights ....CB ❶¹ / RW ❶¹ / RR 2²	Asylum 45257
09/13/75	RR	2³	19		5 Lyin' Eyes ....BB 2² / RW 2¹ / CB 3¹	Asylum 45279
12/20/75	BB	4	23		6 Take It To The Limit ....RR 4 / CB 5 / RW 6	Asylum 45293
12/11/76	RR	❶²	19	●	7 New Kid In Town ....BB ❶¹ / CB 2² / RW 3¹	Asylum 45373
02/26/77	RR	❶³	23	●	8 Hotel California ....BB ❶¹ / CB ❶¹ / RW ❶¹	Asylum 45386
05/13/77	RR	7	14		9 Life In The Fast Lane	Asylum 45403
09/28/79	RR	❶⁴	18	●	10 Heartache Tonight ....BB ❶¹ / CB ❶¹ / RW ❶¹	Asylum 46545
11/30/79	RR	❶²	16		11 The Long Run ....RW 4 / BB 8 / CB 10	Asylum 46569
02/22/80	RR	4	16		12 I Can't Tell You Why ....RW 7 / BB 8 / CB 9	Asylum 46608

					EAMON	
10/31/03	RR	9	23	○	1 F**k It (I Don't Want You Back)	Jive 56647

					EARL, Stacy	
02/21/92	RR	7	20		1 Romeo & Juliet	RCA 62192
					STACY EARL (Featuring The Wild Pair)	

					EARTH, WIND & FIRE	
02/08/75	BB	❶¹	24	●	1 Shining Star...CB ❶¹ / RW ❶¹ / RR 2¹	Columbia 10090
07/05/75	RW	6	17		2 That's The Way Of The World	Columbia 10172
11/22/75	BB	5	21	●	3 Sing A Song ....RW 5 / CB 7 / RR 9	Columbia 10251
07/10/76	CB	10	23	●	4 Getaway	Columbia 10373
10/15/77	RW	10	23		5 Serpentine Fire	Columbia 10625
07/22/78	BB	9	14	●	6 Got To Get You Into My Life	Columbia 10796
11/18/78	RW	4	23	●	7 September ....RR 5 / CB 6 / BB 9	ARC 10854
05/12/79	CB	5	19	●	8 Boogie Wonderland ....BB 6 / RR 8	ARC 10956
					EARTH, WIND & FIRE with THE EMOTIONS	
07/07/79	RR	❶¹	17	●	9 After The Love Has Gone ....BB 2² / CB 3² / RW 4	ARC 11033
10/03/81	BB	3⁵	26	●	10 Let's Groove ....CB 3⁵ / RW 3⁵	ARC 02536

					EASTON, Sheena	
02/13/81	CB	❶⁵	27	●	1 Morning Train (Nine To Five) ....RW ❶³ / BB ❶² / RR 3³	EMI America 8071
07/25/81	RW	3⁴	25		2 For Your Eyes Only ....CB 3² / RR 3¹ / BB 4	Liberty 1418
11/28/81	RR	7	19		3 You Could Have Been With Me	EMI America 8101
01/21/83	BB	6	19		4 We've Got Tonight ....CB 10 / RR 10	Liberty 1492
					KENNY ROGERS and SHEENA EASTON	
08/20/83	CB	8	23		5 Telefone (Long Distance Love Affair) ....BB 9 / RR 9	EMI America 8172
08/25/84	CB	4	25		6 Strut ....BB 7 / RR 9	EMI America 8227
12/22/84	CB	5	20		7 Sugar Walls ....BB 9	EMI America 8253
07/25/87	BB	2¹	27		8 U Got The Look ....RR 3² / CB 3¹	Paisley Park 28289
					PRINCE & SHEENA EASTON	
10/29/88	BB	2¹	28		9 The Lover In Me ....CB 2¹ / RR 3¹	MCA 53416

					ECKSTINE, Billy	
03/04/50	CB	2¹	29	☉	1 My Foolish Heart ....BB 6	MGM 10623
06/17/50	BB	7	15		2 I Wanna Be Loved	MGM 10716
02/17/51	BB	10	8		3 If	MGM 10896
02/24/51	BB	6	24	☉	4 I Apologize ....CB 7	MGM 10903

					EDDY, Duane	
06/16/58	BB	6	16	☉	1 Rebel-'Rouser ....CB 7 / MV 7	Jamie 1104
06/13/59	MV	5	16	☉	2 Forty Miles Of Bad Road ....BB 9 / CB 10	Jamie 1126
05/09/60	CB	3¹	18	☉	3 Because They're Young ....MV 3¹ / BB 4	Jamie 1156
09/29/62	MV	9	18		4 (Dance With The) Guitar Man	RCA Victor 8087

					EDEN'S CRUSH	
03/31/01	BB	8	14	●	1 Get Over Yourself	143/London 35063

					EDISON LIGHTHOUSE	
02/14/70	CB	4	13	●	1 Love Grows (Where My Rosemary Goes) ....RW 4 / BB 5	Bell 858

					EDMONDS, Kevon	
11/06/99	BB	10	20	●	1 24/7	RCA 65924

					EDMUNDS, Dave	
12/19/70	RW	3²	14		1 I Hear You Knocking ....BB 4 / CB 5	MAM 3601

DEBUT	CH	PK	WK	Gold	A-side (Chart Hit) .... Other Charts	Label & Number
					EDWARD BEAR	
12/16/72	RW	2¹	18	●	1 Last Song .... CB 3³ / BB 3²	Capitol 3452
					EDWARDS, Bobby	
08/19/61	MV	6	22		1 You're The Reason .... CB 8	Crest 1075
					EDWARDS, Jonathan	
11/13/71	RW	3²	17	●	1 Sunshine .... BB 4 / CB 5	Capricorn 8021
					EDWARDS, Tommy	
08/11/58	BB	❶⁶	24	⊙	1 It's All In The Game .... MV ❶⁶ / CB ❶⁵	MGM 12688
10/20/58	MV	8	16		2 Love Is All We Need	MGM 12722
					EGAN, Walter	
05/20/78	BB	8	23	●	1 Magnet And Steel .... CB 9 / RR 9	Columbia 10719
					EIFFEL 65	
11/26/99	RR	3³	22		1 Blue (Da Ba Dee) .... BB 6	Republic 156638
					8TH DAY, The	
05/08/71	CB	8	13	●	1 She's Not Just Another Woman .... RW 8	Invictus 9087
					EILISH, Billie	
04/13/19	BB	❶¹	47	△	1 Bad Guy	Darkroom
11/23/19	BB	8	15		2 everything i wanted	Darkroom
					ELECTRIC LIGHT ORCHESTRA	
12/07/74	BB	9	20		1 Can't Get It Out Of My Head	United Artists 573
11/15/75	RR	5	19		2 Evil Woman .... CB 9 / RW 9 / BB 10	United Artists/Jet 729
10/30/76	RR	9	22		3 Livin' Thing .... CB 10 / RW 10	United Artists/Jet 888
06/11/77	CB	4	23	●	4 Telephone Line .... RR 4 / BB 7 / RW 7	United Artists/Jet 1000
11/19/77	RR	5	17		5 Turn To Stone	Jet 1099
05/18/79	RR	❶¹	16		6 Shine A Little Love .... CB 7 / BB 8 / RW 8	Jet 5057
07/27/79	RW	3³	18	●	7 Don't Bring Me Down .... BB 4 / CB 4 / RR 5	Jet 5060
07/25/80	RW	8	19		8 All Over The World .... RR 8	MCA 41289
08/09/80	RR	2¹	20		9 Xanadu .... RW 4 / BB 8 / CB 9	MCA 41285
					OLIVIA NEWTON-JOHN/ELECTRIC LIGHT ORCHESTRA	
07/24/81	RR	6	19		10 Hold On Tight .... CB 8 / BB 10 / RW 10	Jet 02408
					ELO	
					ELEGANTS, The	
06/30/58	BB	❶¹	21	⊙	1 Little Star .... CB 2⁵ / MV 2⁴	Apt 25005
					ELLIMAN, Yvonne	
10/02/76	CB	10	21		1 Love Me	RSO 858
01/28/78	RR	❶²	22	●	2 If I Can't Have You .... BB ❶¹ / CB ❶¹ / RW 2²	RSO 884
					ELLIOTT, Missy "Misdemeanor"	
11/27/99	BB	5	21	▲	1 Hot Boyz	Gold Mind 64029
					MISSY "MISDEMEANOR" ELLIOTT (Featuring Nas, Eve & Q-Tip)	
03/24/01	BB	7	24	△	2 Get Ur Freak On	Gold Mind 67190
09/14/02	BB	2¹⁰	25	△	3 Work It .... RR 3¹	Elektra 67340
12/28/02	BB	8	20		4 Gossip Folks .... RR 8	Elektra 67356
					MISSY ELLIOTT Featuring Ludacris	
05/21/05	BB	3¹	28	△²	5 Lose Control .... RR 7	Atlantic 93787
					MISSY ELLIOTT Featuring Ciara & Fat Man Scoop	
					ELLIS, Shirley	
11/09/63	CB	7	16		1 The Nitty Gritty .... BB 8 / MV 10	Congress 202
12/12/64	BB	3²	15		2 The Name Game .... CB 3¹ / RW 3¹	Congress 230
03/20/65	CB	7	10		3 The Clapping Song (Clap Pat Clap Slap) .... BB 8 / RW 10	Congress 234
					EMF	
04/13/91	CB	❶²	26	●	1 Unbelievable .... BB ❶¹ / RR ❶¹	EMI 50350
					EMINEM	
05/06/00	BB	4	19	△⁴	1 The Real Slim Shady	Aftermath 497334
05/10/02	RR	❶¹	20	△⁴	2 Without Me .... BB 2⁵	Aftermath
07/26/02	BB	4	23	△²	3 Cleanin' Out My Closet .... RR 7	Aftermath
09/27/02	BB	❶¹²	23	△¹⁰	4 Lose Yourself .... RR ❶⁸	Shady 497815
01/17/03	RR	10	18	△	5 Superman	Aftermath
03/21/03	RR	5	20	△	6 Sing For The Moment	Aftermath
10/01/04	RR	5	20	△²	7 Just Lose It .... BB 6	Shady 003684
12/10/04	RR	7	22	△⁴	8 Mockingbird	Shady
11/18/05	BB	8	17	△⁴	9 When I'm Gone	Shady 006085
12/23/05	BB	6	21	△³	10 Shake That	Shady
					EMINEM Featuring Nate Dogg	
01/31/09	BB	❶¹	17	△²	11 Crack A Bottle	Web
					EMINEM, DR. DRE & 50 CENT	
04/17/09	BB	9	10	△	12 We Made You	Web
05/22/10	BB	❶¹	25	△¹⁰	13 Not Afraid	Web

49

DEBUT	CH	PK	WK	Gold	A-side (Chart Hit)...Other Charts	Label & Number
					EMINEM (cont'd)	
07/10/10	BB	❶⁷	29	△¹²14	Love The Way You Lie..	Web
					EMINEM Featuring Rihanna	
09/14/13	BB	3¹	20	△³ 15	Berzerk...	Web
11/02/13	BB	7	20	△⁴ 16	Rap God..	Web
11/16/13	BB	❶⁴	29	△⁶ 17	The Monster...	Web
					EMINEM Featuring Rihanna	
09/15/18	BB	6	14	18	Lucky You...	Shady
					EMINEM Featuring Joyner Lucas	
09/15/18	BB	8	4	19	The Ringer..	Shady
09/29/18	BB	3¹	8	20	Killshot...	Shady
02/01/20	BB	3¹	5	21	Godzilla..	Shady
					EMINEM Featuring Juice WRLD	
					EMOTIONS, The	
06/11/77	BB	❶⁵	28	▲ 1	Best Of My Love..CB ❶³ / RW ❶³ / RR ❶²	Columbia 10544
05/12/79	CB	5	19	● 2	Boogie Wonderland.. BB 6 / RR 8	ARC 10956
					EARTH, WIND & FIRE with THE EMOTIONS	
					ENGLAND DAN & JOHN FORD COLEY	
06/12/76	BB	2²	26	● 1	I'd Really Love To See You Tonight.............. RR 2² / CB 4 / RW 5	Big Tree 16069
10/09/76	RW	9	21	2	Nights Are Forever Without You............... RR 9 / BB 10 / CB 10	Big Tree 16079
02/25/78	RR	7	14	3	We'll Never Have To Say Goodbye Again......................... BB 9	Big Tree 16110
03/10/79	RR	8	18	4	Love Is The Answer..BB 10	Big Tree 16131
					ENIGMA	
02/09/91	BB	5	21	● 1	Sadeness Part 1.. CB 6 / RR 7	Charisma 98864
03/05/94	RR	3¹	28	● 2	Return To Innocence.. BB 4 / CB 5	Charisma 38423
					EN VOGUE	
05/05/90	BB	2¹	25	▲ 1	Hold On..CB 3²	Atlantic 87984
03/21/92	RR	❶⁴	30	● 2	My Lovin' (You're Never Gonna Get It)...............CB ❶³ / BB 2³	EastWest 98586
06/06/92	RR	5	31	● 3	Giving Him Something He Can Feel.................... BB 6 / CB 6	EastWest 98560
09/11/92	RR	2²	25	● 4	Free Your Mind...CB 5 / BB 8	EastWest 98487
12/04/92	RR	5	22	5	Give It Up, Turn It Loose...	EastWest 98455
09/03/93	RR	6	10	6	Runaway Love...	EastWest 98354
					EN VOGUE featuring FMob	
01/22/94	BB	3³	31	▲ 7	Whatta Man... RR 4 / CB 5	Next Plateau 857390
					SALT 'N' PEPA with EN VOGUE	
10/04/96	BB	2⁴	35	▲ 8	Don't Let Go (Love)..RR 2⁴ / CB 3¹	EastWest 64231
					ENYA	
07/13/01	BB	10	31	1	Only Time...	Reprise 42420
					ERASURE	
07/30/88	RR	10	20	1	Chains Of Love..	Sire 27844
04/30/94	RR	6	25	2	Always...	Mute/Elektra 64552
					ERIC B. & RAKIM — see WATLEY, Jody	
					ESCAPE CLUB, The	
08/20/88	BB	❶¹	27	● 1	Wild, Wild West..CB ❶¹ / RR ❶¹	Atlantic 89048
05/25/91	BB	8	25	● 2	I'll Be There...RR 8 / CB 9	Atlantic 87683
					ESSEX, The	
06/01/63	BB	❶²	15	◉ 1	Easier Said Than Done......................................CB ❶² / MV ❶²	Roulette 4494
08/24/63	MV	8	11	2	A Walkin' Miracle..CB 10	Roulette 4515
					ESSEX, David	
11/10/73	CB	❶¹	25	● 1	Rock On... RR 2¹ / RW 3¹ / BB 5	Columbia 45940
					ESTEFAN, Gloria / Miami Sound Machine	
					MIAMI SOUND MACHINE:	
10/19/85	BB	10	27	● 1	Conga...	Epic 05457
03/08/86	BB	8	19	● 2	Bad Boy..CB 8 / RR 9	Epic 05805
06/14/86	BB	5	24	3	Words Get In The Way..CB 8 / RR 9	Epic 06120
					GLORIA ESTEFAN and MIAMI SOUND MACHINE:	
05/30/87	BB	5	19	4	Rhythm Is Gonna Get You...................................CB 5 / RR 6	Epic 07059
11/21/87	BB	6	25	5	Can't Stay Away From You................................. RR 6 / CB 10	Epic 07641
03/12/88	BB	❶²	23	● 6	Anything For You..CB ❶² / RR ❶²	Epic 07759
06/04/88	BB	3¹	20	7	1-2-3..CB 3¹ / RR 5	Epic 07921
					GLORIA ESTEFAN:	
07/07/89	CB	❶²	22	● 8	Don't Wanna Lose You...BB ❶¹ / RR ❶¹	Epic 68959
09/29/89	BB	8	19	9	Get On Your Feet..	Epic 69064
12/16/89	BB	6	21	10	Here We Are.. RR 7 / CB 9	Epic 73084
01/25/91	BB	❶²	23	● 11	Coming Out Of The Dark.....................................CB ❶² / RR ❶¹	Epic 73666
08/13/99	BB	2¹	20	● 12	Music Of My Heart..	Miramax/Epic 79245
					*NSYNC and GLORIA ESTEFAN	

50

DEBUT	CH	PK	WK	Gold	A-side (Chart Hit)	Other Charts	Label & Number
					ESTELLE		
05/03/08	BB	9	30	△²	1 American Boy	RR 10	Home School 422972
					ESTELLE Featuring Kanye West		
					ESTUS, Deon		
02/25/89	CB	4	22		1 Heaven Help Me	BB 5 / RR 5	Mika 871538
					DEON ESTUS with GEORGE MICHAEL		
					ETERNAL		
01/15/94	RR	6	20		1 Stay		EMI/1st Avenue 58113
					ETHERIDGE, Melissa		
07/30/94	RR	4	44		1 I'm The Only One	CB 5 / BB 8	Island 854068
01/27/95	RR	6	21		2 If I Wanted To	CB 9	Island 854238
					EUROPE		
01/24/87	RR	7	18		1 The Final Countdown	BB 8 / CB 10	Epic 06416
08/01/87	RR	❶¹	25		2 Carrie	BB 3² / CB 3²	Epic 07282
					EURYTHMICS		
05/14/83	CB	❶²	26	●	1 Sweet Dreams (Are Made of This)	BB ❶¹ / RR 3⁴	RCA 13533
01/28/84	BB	4	20		2 Here Comes The Rain Again	RR 4 / CB 5	RCA 13725
04/27/85	BB	5	20		3 Would I Lie To You?	CB 6 / RR 7	RCA 14078
					EVAN AND JARON		
08/11/00	RR	9	29		1 Crazy For This Girl		Columbia 79484
					EVANESCENCE		
03/07/03	RR	❶¹	32	△³	1 Bring Me To Life	BB 5	Wind-Up
12/12/03	RR	2²	32	△	2 My Immortal	BB 7	Wind-Up
08/25/06	RR	7	22	△	3 Call Me When You're Sober	BB 10	Wind-Up
					EVANS, Faith		
06/14/97	BB	❶¹¹	33	▲³	1 I'll Be Missing You		Bad Boy 79097
					PUFF DADDY & FAITH EVANS (Featuring 112)		
11/14/98	BB	7	20	●	2 Love Like This		Bad Boy 79117
02/06/99	BB	9	19		3 All Night Long		Bad Boy 79203
					FAITH EVANS (feat. Puff Daddy)		
					EVANS, Paul		
09/07/59	CB	5	18		1 (Seven Little Girls) Sitting In The Back Seat	BB 9	Guaranteed 200
05/02/60	MV	8	14		2 Happy-Go-Lucky-Me	BB 10	Guaranteed 208
					EVE		
04/28/01	RR	❶¹	33		1 Let Me Blow Ya Mind	BB 2¹	Ruff Ryders 497562
					EVE Featuring Gwen Stefani		
07/12/02	BB	2⁴	22		2 Gangsta Lovin'	RR 2²	Ruff Ryders 497817
					EVE Feat. Alicia Keys		
					EVERETT, Betty		
02/29/64	MV	5	15		1 The Shoop Shoop Song (It's In His Kiss)	BB 6 / CB 6	Vee-Jay 585
09/05/64	RW	3¹	15		2 Let It Be Me	BB 5 / CB 9	Vee-Jay 613
					BETTY EVERETT & JERRY BUTLER		
					EVERLAST		
12/19/98	RR	5	33		1 What It's Like		Tommy Boy
					EVERLY BROTHERS, The		
05/20/57	CB	❶¹	27	☉	1 Bye Bye Love	MV ❶¹ / BB 2⁴	Cadence 1315
09/16/57	MV	❶⁵	26	☉	2 Wake Up Little Susie	BB ❶⁴ / CB ❶²	Cadence 1337
04/14/58	BB	❶⁵	19	☉	3 All I Have To Do Is Dream	CB ❶⁴ / MV ❶⁴	Cadence 1348
08/04/58	BB	❶¹	19	☉	4 Bird Dog /	CB 2¹ / MV 3¹	
08/04/58	MV	9	16		5 Devoted To You	BB 10	Cadence 1350
11/10/58	BB	2¹	15		6 Problems	MV 5 / CB 7	Cadence 1355
08/15/59	BB	4	18		7 ('Til) I Kissed You	CB 5 / MV 6	Cadence 1369
01/11/60	BB	7	15		8 Let It Be Me	CB 9 / MV 9	Cadence 1376
04/18/60	BB	❶⁵	17	☉	9 Cathy's Clown	CB ❶⁵ / MV ❶⁴	Warner 5151
05/30/60	BB	8	13		10 When Will I Be Loved	CB 9	Cadence 1380
08/29/60	MV	5	14		11 So Sad (To Watch Good Love Go Bad)	BB 7 / CB 9	Warner 5163
01/23/61	MV	6	13	☉	12 Ebony Eyes /	BB 8 / CB 8	
02/04/61	BB	7	15		13 Walk Right Back		Warner 5199
01/08/62	BB	6	13		14 Crying In The Rain	CB 7 / MV 10	Warner 5250
05/12/62	BB	9	11		15 That's Old Fashioned (That's The Way Love Should Be)		Warner 5273
					EVERY MOTHERS' SON		
05/06/67	CB	5	15		1 Come On Down To My Boat	RW 5 / BB 6	MGM 13733
					EVERYTHING BUT THE GIRL		
08/12/95	RR	❶⁴	55	●	1 Missing	CB ❶¹ / BB 2¹	Atlantic 87124
					EVE 6		
08/21/98	RR	9	28		1 Inside Out		RCA

DEBUT	CH	PK	WK	Gold	A-side (Chart Hit) ..... Other Charts	Label & Number
					EXCITERS, The	
11/24/62	BB	4	15		1 Tell Him .... MV 4 / CB 5	United Artists 544
					EXILE	
07/08/78	RR	❶⁵	28	●	1 Kiss You All Over .... BB ❶⁴ / RW ❶³ / CB ❶²	Warner/Curb 8589
					EXPOSÉ	
01/24/87	BB	5	19		1 Come Go With Me .... CB 5 / RR 7	Arista 9555
05/09/87	BB	5	21		2 Point Of No Return .... RR 5 / CB 7	Arista 9579
08/15/87	BB	7	25		3 Let Me Be The One .... CB 8 / RR 8	Arista 9617
11/27/87	BB	❶¹	22		4 Seasons Change .... RR 2¹ / CB 4	Arista 9640
05/19/89	BB	8	19	●	5 What You Don't Know .... CB 8 / RR 8	Arista 9836
08/18/89	RR	6	20		6 When I Looked At Him .... BB 10	Arista 9868
12/09/89	CB	6	19		7 Tell Me Why .... BB 9	Arista 9916
03/30/90	RR	10	17		8 Your Baby Never Looked Good In Blue	Arista 2011
03/26/93	CB	6	31	●	9 I'll Never Get Over You (Getting Over Me) .... RR 7 / BB 8	Arista 12518
					EXTREME	
03/23/91	CB	❶²	27	●	1 More Than Words .... BB ❶¹ / RR 2¹	A&M 1552
08/03/91	BB	4	28		2 Hole Hearted .... CB 4 / RR 5	A&M 1564

F

					FABARES, Shelley	
02/26/62	BB	❶²	16	☉	1 Johnny Angel .... CB ❶¹ / MV ❶¹	Colpix 621
					FABIAN	
03/23/59	CB	8	14		1 Turn Me Loose .... BB 9	Chancellor 1033
06/08/59	BB	3²	13		2 Tiger .... CB 6 / MV 8	Chancellor 1037
11/09/59	BB	9	15		3 Hound Dog Man	Chancellor 1044
					FABOLOUS	
03/08/03	BB	4	23		1 Can't Let You Go	Desert Storm 67428
					FABOLOUS featuring Mike Shorey & Lil' Mo	
06/14/03	BB	4	26		2 Into You	Desert Storm 67452
					FABOLOUS Featuring Tamia or Ashanti	
09/18/04	BB	10	20		3 Breathe	Desert Storm 67616
06/09/07	BB	8	21		4 Make Me Better	Desert Storm 009027
					FABOLOUS Featuring Ne-Yo	
					FABRIC, Bent, and His Piano	
07/14/62	CB	6	20		1 Alley Cat .... BB 7 / MV 8	Atco 6226
					FABULOUS THUNDERBIRDS, The	
04/19/86	BB	10	19		1 Tuff Enuff	CBS Associated 05838
					FACES	
12/25/71	CB	10	12		1 Stay With Me	Warner 7545
					FAGEN, Donald	
10/08/82	RR	6	16		1 I.G.Y. (What A Beautiful World)	Warner 29900
					FAITH, Percy, and his Orchestra	
09/02/50	BB	7	11		1 All My Love	Columbia 38918
05/12/51	BB	10	9		2 On Top Of Old Smoky	Columbia 39328
					PERCY FAITH and his Orchestra and Chorus with BURL IVES	
04/26/52	BB	❶¹	28		3 Delicado .... CB 3²	Columbia 39708
03/28/53	BB	❶¹⁰	31	☉	4 The Song From Moulin Rouge (Where Is Your Heart) .... CB ❶⁹	Columbia 39944
01/11/60	BB	❶⁹	21	●	5 The Theme From "A Summer Place" .... CB ❶⁸ / MV ❶⁵	Columbia 41490
					FAITH NO MORE	
06/09/90	CB	7	21	●	1 Epic .... BB 9	Slash 19813
					FALCO	
02/08/86	BB	❶³	20		1 Rock Me Amadeus .... RR ❶³ / CB ❶²	A&M 2821
					FALL OUT BOY	
07/02/05	RR	5	42	△⁴	1 Sugar, We're Goin' Down .... BB 8	Island
11/05/05	RR	3¹	31	△³	2 Dance, Dance .... BB 9	Island
12/08/06	BB	2²	20	△	3 This Ain't A Scene, It's An Arms Race	Fueled By Ramen
09/27/14	BB	10	34	△⁴	4 Centuries	DCD2
					FALTERMEYER, Harold	
03/30/85	BB	3³	19		1 Axel F .... CB 3³ / RR 3¹	MCA 52536
					FAME, Georgie	
02/10/68	CB	6	16		1 The Ballad Of Bonnie And Clyde .... BB 7 / RW 7	Epic 10283

DEBUT	CH	PK	WK	Gold	A-side (Chart Hit)	Other Charts	Label & Number
					FANCY		
06/01/74	RR	10	18		1 Wild Thing		Big Tree 15004
					FANTASIA		
07/10/04	BB	❶¹	10		1 I Believe		J Records 63091
					FANTASTIC JOHNNY C, The		
10/07/67	BB	7	18		1 Boogaloo Down Broadway	RW 7 / CB 9	Phil-L.A. of Soul 305
					FAR*EAST MOVEMENT		
08/28/10	BB	❶³	26	△⁴	1 Like A G6		CherryTree
					FAR*EAST MOVEMENT Featuring Cataracs & Dev		
12/18/10	BB	7	20		2 Rocketeer		CherryTree
					FAR*EAST MOVEMENT Featuring Ryan Tedder		
					FARGO, Donna		
05/27/72	RW	7	16	●	1 The Happiest Girl In The Whole U.S.A.	CB 8	Dot 17409
09/30/72	BB	5	20	●	2 Funny Face	RW 6 / CB 9	Dot 17429
					FARRIS, Dionne		
01/20/95	RR	❶⁹	39		1 I Know	CB ❶⁶ / BB 4	Columbia 77750
					FASTBALL		
03/07/98	RR	4	39	○	1 The Way	BB 5	Hollywood 5298
04/16/99	RR	8	25		2 Out Of My Head		Hollywood
					FAT JOE		
02/16/02	BB	2⁷	28		1 What's Luv?	RR 3²	Terror Squad 85233
					FAT JOE Featuring Ashanti		
06/03/05	RR	7	20	○	2 Get It Poppin'	BB 9	Terror Squad 93794
					FAT JOE (Feat. Nelly)		
					FEIST		
09/29/07	BB	8	15		1 1234		Cherrytree
					FELICIANO, Jose		
07/20/68	BB	3³	13		1 Light My Fire	CB 3³ / RW 3³	RCA Victor 9550
10/12/68	RW	9	9		2 Hi-Heel Sneakers		RCA Victor 9641
					FENDER, Freddy		
02/01/75	BB	❶¹	25	●	1 Before The Next Teardrop Falls	CB ❶¹ / RW ❶¹	ABC/Dot 17540
06/14/75	RW	3¹	23	●	2 Wasted Days And Wasted Nights	CB 6 / BB 8	ABC/Dot 17558
					FENDERMEN, The		
05/23/60	BB	5	18		1 Mule Skinner Blues	CB 5 / MV 5	Soma 1137
					FERGIE		
07/21/05	BB	❶³	21	△²	1 London Bridge	RR 4	will.i.am 007809
10/07/06	BB	2¹	27	△⁴	2 Fergalicious	RR 2¹	will.i.am
					FERGIE Featuring will.i.am		
01/26/07	BB	❶²	29	△³	3 Glamorous	RR 2¹	will.i.am
					FERGIE Featuring Ludacris		
05/05/07	RR	❶⁸	48	△⁴	4 Big Girls Don't Cry	BB ❶¹	will.i.am
10/12/07	RR	2²	25	△²	5 Clumsy	BB 5	will.i.am
					FERGUSON, Jay		
12/17/77	CB	6	23		1 Thunder Island	RR 8 / BB 9	Asylum 45444
					FERRANTE & TEICHER		
07/09/60	MV	6	24		1 Theme From The Apartment	CB 9 / BB 10	United Artists 231
11/07/60	CB	❶²	22		2 Exodus	MV ❶¹ / BB 2¹	United Artists 274
10/16/61	CB	6	14		3 Tonight	BB 8 / MV 9	United Artists 373
11/01/69	BB	10	15		4 Midnight Cowboy	CB 10 / RW 10	United Artists 50554
					FETTY WAP		
02/07/15	BB	2³	52	△⁷	1 Trap Queen		RGF
07/18/15	BB	4	40	△⁵	2 679		RGF
					FETTY WAP Featuring Remy Boyz		
07/18/15	BB	7	22	△²	3 My Way		RGF
					FETTY WAP Featuring Monty		
					FIASCO, Lupe		
12/29/07	BB	10	20	△	1 Superstar		Atlantic 350844
11/27/10	BB	9	33	△³	2 The Show Goes On		1st & 15th
					FIELD MOB		
04/21/06	BB	10	21		1 So What		DTP 006546
					FIELD MOB featuring Ciara		
					FIELDS, Ernie, Orch.		
09/21/59	MV	3¹	20		1 In The Mood	BB 4 / CB 7	Rendezvous 110

DEBUT	CH	PK	WK	Gold	A-side (Chart Hit)..Other Charts	Label & Number
					5TH DIMENSION, The	
06/03/67	CB	4	12		1 Up — Up And Away .... RW 5 / BB 7	Soul City 756
05/25/68	BB	3³	16	▲	2 Stoned Soul Picnic .... RW 5 / CB 6	Soul City 766
03/08/69	BB	❶⁶	17	▲	3 Aquarius/Let The Sunshine In .... CB ❶⁵ / RW ❶⁴	Soul City 772
09/20/69	BB	❶³	15	▲	4 Wedding Bell Blues .... CB ❶³ / RW ❶¹	Soul City 779
10/17/70	BB	2²	19	▲	5 One Less Bell To Answer .... RW 2² / CB 2¹	Bell 940
03/25/72	CB	6	17	▲	6 (Last Night) I Didn't Get To Sleep At All .... RW 7 / BB 8	Bell 45,195
09/02/72	RW	9	16		7 If I Could Reach You .... BB 10 / CB 10	Bell 45,261
					FIFTH HARMONY	
03/19/16	BB	4	34	△⁵	1 Work From Home	Syco
					FIFTH HARMONY Featuring Ty Dolla $ign	
					50 CENT	
01/11/03	BB	❶⁹	30	◯	1 In Da Club .... RR ❶⁴	Shady 497856
03/22/03	BB	❶⁴	23		2 21 Questions .... RR 6	Shady 080739
					50 CENT Feat. Nate Dogg	
05/31/03	BB	3¹	25	◯	3 P.I.M.P. .... RR 9	Shady 000888
12/11/04	BB	3¹	29	◯	4 Disco Inferno .... RR 8	Shady 004142
02/05/05	BB	❶⁹	23	◯	5 Candy Shop .... RR 5	Shady
					50 CENT Featuring Olivia	
03/26/05	BB	3¹	27		6 Just A Lil Bit .... RR 9	Shady 004726
07/15/05	BB	6	19		7 Outta Control (Remix)	Shady 005439
					50 CENT Featuring Mobb Deep	
08/25/07	BB	5	20		8 Ayo Technology	Shady 009807
					50 CENT Featuring Justin Timberlake & Timbaland	
01/31/09	BB	❶¹	17	△²	9 Crack A Bottle	Web
					EMINEM, DR. DRE & 50 CENT	
					FINE YOUNG CANNIBALS	
01/28/89	BB	❶¹	24	●	1 She Drives Me Crazy .... CB ❶¹ / RR ❶¹	I.R.S./MCA 53483
05/06/89	CB	❶²	20		2 Good Thing .... BB ❶¹ / RR ❶¹	I.R.S./MCA 53639
08/12/89	CB	10	18		3 Don't Look Back	I.R.S./MCA 53695
					FINGER ELEVEN	
05/28/04	RR	10	29		1 One Thing	Wind-Up
06/23/07	RR	5	50	△²	2 Paralyzer .... BB 6	Wind-Up
					FINNEGAN, Larry	
02/24/62	MV	10	14		1 Dear One	Old Town 1113
					FIREBALLS, The	
12/30/67	RW	7	14		1 Bottle Of Wine .... BB 9 / CB 9	Atco 6491
					FIREFALL	
08/14/76	CB	8	29		1 You Are The Woman .... BB 9 / RW 10 / RR 10	Atlantic 3335
08/13/77	RR	7	21		2 Just Remember I Love You .... CB 9	Atlantic 3420
09/30/78	RR	5	19		3 Strange Way	Atlantic 3518
					FIREFLIES	
08/08/59	CB	10	20		1 You Were Mine	Ribbon 6901
					FIREHOUSE	
06/29/91	BB	5	29	●	1 Love Of A Lifetime .... CB 7 / RR 9	Epic 73771
08/07/92	RR	4	27		2 When I Look Into Your Eyes .... CB 7 / BB 8	Epic 74440
02/17/95	RR	7	23		3 I Live My Life For You	Epic 77812
					FIRST CLASS	
07/20/74	CB	3¹	17		1 Beach Baby .... BB 4 / RR 10	UK 49022
					FIRST EDITION — see ROGERS, Kenny	
					FISHER, Eddie	
10/07/50	CB	2¹	21		1 Thinking Of You .... BB 5	RCA Victor 3901
02/03/51	CB	9	16		2 Bring Back The Thrill	RCA Victor 4016
05/05/51	CB	8	16		3 Unless	RCA Victor 4120
09/29/51	BB	8	20		4 Turn Back The Hands Of Time .... CB 9	RCA Victor 4257
12/08/51	BB	2²	33	⊙	5 Any Time .... CB 3¹	RCA Victor 4359
12/15/51	CB	2⁴	29		6 Tell Me Why .... BB 4	RCA Victor 4444
03/29/52	CB	7	22		7 Forgive Me /	
						BB 7	
05/03/52	BB	10	10		8 That's The Chance You Take	RCA Victor 4574
05/03/52	CB	2⁴	23		9 I'm Yours .... BB 3³	RCA Victor 4680
06/14/52	BB	3¹	18		10 Maybe .... CB 9	RCA Victor 4744
07/19/52	BB	❶¹	28		11 Wish You Were Here .... CB 2¹	RCA Victor 4830
09/27/52	BB	6	24		12 Lady Of Spain /	
						CB 6	
10/04/52	BB	8	13		13 Outside Of Heaven	RCA Victor 4953
01/17/53	BB	7	12		14 Even Now .... CB 9	RCA Victor 5106
02/07/53	BB	5	12		15 Downhearted	RCA Victor 5137
05/09/53	BB	❶⁷	26	⊙	16 I'm Walking Behind You .... CB ❶⁵	RCA Victor 5293
07/04/53	BB	7	20		17 With These Hands .... CB 8	RCA Victor 5365

DEBUT	CH	PK	WK	Gold	A-side (Chart Hit) .... Other Charts	Label & Number
					FISHER, Eddie (cont'd)	
09/26/53	BB	4	20		18 Many Times ....CB 8	RCA Victor 5453
11/28/53	BB	❶⁸	23	⊙	19 Oh! My Pa-Pa (O Mein Papa) ....CB ❶⁶	RCA Victor 5552
03/27/54	BB	6	15		20 A Girl, A Girl (Zoom-Ba Di Alli Nella) ....CB 6	RCA Victor 5675
06/12/54	BB	8	8		21 Green Years	RCA Victor 5748
07/03/54	BB	9	11		22 The Little Shoemaker..	RCA Victor 5769
					HUGO WINTERHALTER'S ORCHESTRA and CHORUS and a Friend	
08/21/54	BB	❶³	28	⊙	23 I Need You Now ....CB ❶² / MV ❶¹	RCA Victor 5830
10/04/54	MV	5	22		24 Count Your Blessings (Instead Of Sheep) ....BB 5 / CB 7	RCA Victor 5871
04/25/55	BB	6	17		25 Heart ....MV 7	RCA Victor 6097
07/23/55	CB	10	19		26 Song Of The Dreamer	RCA Victor 6196
12/01/55	BB	7	19		27 Dungaree Doll ....CB 7 / MV 8	RCA Victor 6337
10/06/56	CB	9	20		28 Cindy, Oh Cindy ....BB 10	RCA Victor 6677
					FISHER, Miss Toni	
11/16/59	CB	2¹	17		1 The Big Hurt ....MV 3³ / BB 3²	Signet 275
					FIVE	
05/08/98	BB	10	26	●	1 When The Lights Go Out..	Arista 13495
					FIVE AMERICANS, The	
02/25/67	BB	5	12		1 Western Union ....RW 6 / CB 7	Abnak 118
					FIVE MAN ELECTRICAL BAND	
05/15/71	BB	3¹	20	●	1 Signs ....RW 5 / CB 7	Lionel 3213
					5 SECONDS OF SUMMER	
06/16/18	BB	7	48	△²	1 Youngblood	One Mode
					FIVE STAIRSTEPS, The	
05/02/70	CB	4	16	●	1 O-o-h Child ....RW 4 / BB 8	Buddah 165
					FIXX, The	
08/27/83	RR	3²	22		1 One Thing Leads To Another ....BB 4 / CB 6	MCA 52264
					FLACK, Roberta	
03/04/72	BB	❶⁶	18	●	1 The First Time Ever I Saw Your Face ....RW ❶⁵ / CB ❶⁴	Atlantic 2864
06/03/72	BB	5	14	●	2 Where Is The Love ....RW 5 / CB 7	Atlantic 2879
					ROBERTA FLACK & DONNY HATHAWAY	
01/20/73	BB	❶⁵	16	●	3 Killing Me Softly With His Song ....CB ❶³ / RW ❶³	Atlantic 2940
06/15/74	BB	❶¹	18	●	4 Feel Like Makin' Love ....CB ❶¹ / RW ❶¹ / RR 3²	Atlantic 3025
02/11/78	BB	2²	23	●	5 The Closer I Get To You ....CB 2¹ / RW 3³ / RR 3²	Atlantic 3463
					ROBERTA FLACK with DONNY HATHAWAY	
09/21/91	CB	5	27		6 Set The Night To Music ....BB 6 / RR 6	Atlantic 87607
					ROBERTA FLACK with MAXI PRIEST	
					FLAMINGOS, The	
05/04/59	CB	10	17		1 I Only Have Eyes For You	End 1046
					FLANAGAN, Ralph, and his Orchestra	
02/11/50	BB	3¹	10		1 Rag Mop	RCA Victor 3212
09/23/50	BB	9	14		2 Nevertheless	RCA Victor 3904
10/07/50	BB	5	17		3 Harbor Lights	RCA Victor 3911
12/08/51	BB	6	14		4 Slow Poke	RCA Victor 4373
09/06/52	BB	4	12		5 I Should Care	RCA Victor 4885
01/17/53	BB	7	16		6 Hot Toddy	RCA Victor 5095
					FLEETWOOD MAC	
03/06/76	RR	8	22		1 Rhiannon (Will You Ever Win) ....CB 9 / RW 10	Reprise 1345
07/03/76	RR	8	22		2 Say You Love Me ....BB 10 / CB 10 / RW 10	Reprise 1356
01/01/77	RR	8	20		3 Go Your Own Way	Warner 8304
04/16/77	RR	❶⁴	21	●	4 Dreams ....BB ❶¹ / CB ❶¹ / RW ❶¹	Warner 8371
07/09/77	RR	❶³	20		5 Don't Stop ....CB ❶¹ / BB 3² / RW 3²	Warner 8413
10/14/77	RR	4	15		6 You Make Loving Fun ....CB 7 / RW 8 / BB 9	Warner 8483
09/21/79	RR	5	16		7 Tusk ....BB 8 / CB 8 / RW 8	Warner 49077
12/07/79	RR	❶¹	15		8 Sara ....CB 6 / BB 7 / RW 7	Warner 49150
03/08/80	RR	9	13		9 Think About Me	Warner 49196
06/11/82	RR	2⁴	19		10 Hold Me ....CB 3² / BB 4	Warner 29966
09/03/82	RR	❶¹	14		11 Gypsy	Warner 29918
11/27/82	RR	9	15		12 Love In Store	Warner 29848
03/27/87	RR	4	19		13 Big Love ....BB 5 / CB 7	Warner 28398
08/29/87	BB	4	23		14 Little Lies ....RR 4 / CB 9	Warner 28291
					FLEETWOODS, The	
03/02/59	BB	❶⁴	16	⊙	1 Come Softly To Me ....CB ❶⁴ / MV ❶³	Dolphin 1
09/07/59	CB	❶²	20	⊙	2 Mr. Blue ....MV ❶² / BB ❶¹	Dolton 5
04/17/61	BB	10	12		3 Tragedy	Dolton 40
					FLOATERS, The	
06/25/77	BB	2²	19	●	1 Float On ....CB 3² / RW 4	ABC 12284

55

DEBUT	CH	PK	WK	Gold	A-side (Chart Hit) ... Other Charts	Label & Number
					FLOCK OF SEAGULLS, A	
07/10/82	BB	9	23		1 I Ran (So Far Away) .... RR 9	Jive 102
					FLO RIDA	
11/10/07	BB	❶10	40	△8	1 Low .... RR ❶6	Poe Boy 346620
					FLO RIDA Featuring T-Pain	
07/05/08	BB	9	21	△2	2 In The Ayer	Poe Boy 506684
					FLO RIDA Featuring will.i.am	
01/23/09	BB	❶6	26	△6	3 Right Round .... RR ❶2	Poe Boy 517992
04/03/09	BB	5	18	△	4 Sugar	Poe Boy 519284
					FLO RIDA Featuring Wynter	
07/17/10	BB	9	29	△3	5 Club Can't Handle Me	Poe Boy
					FLO RIDA Featuring David Guetta	
09/17/11	BB	3³	37	△5	6 Good Feeling	Poe Boy
01/07/12	BB	5	36	△5	7 Wild Ones	Poe Boy
					FLO RIDA with SIA	
05/12/12	BB	❶2	29	△5	8 Whistle	Poe Boy
10/13/12	BB	6	21	△2	9 I Cry	Poe Boy
11/08/14	BB	8	35	△4	10 G.D.F.R.	Poe Boy
					FLO RIDA Featuring Sage The Gemini & Lookas	
11/28/15	BB	4	39	△6	11 My House	Poe Boy
					FLORIDA GEORGIA LINE	
04/20/13	BB	4	28		1 Cruise	Republic Nashville
					FLORIDA GEORGIA LINE Featuring Nelly	
11/11/17	BB	2³	52	△8	2 Meant To Be	Warner
					BEBE REXHA & FLORIDA GEORGIA LINE	
					FLOYD, Eddie	
08/27/66	RW	10	21	●	1 Knock On Wood	Stax 194
					FLOYD, King	
10/24/70	CB	4	20	●	1 Groove Me .... RW 4 / BB 6	Chimneyville 435
					FLYING MACHINE, The	
09/20/69	RW	4	16	●	1 Smile A Little Smile For Me .... BB 5 / CB 5	Congress 6000
					FOCUS	
03/03/73	CB	4	19		1 Hocus Pocus .... BB 9 / RW 9	Sire 704
					FOGELBERG, Dan	
12/15/79	RR	❶2	22		1 Longer .... CB ❶1 / BB 2² / RW 2²	Full Moon 50824
12/12/80	CB	7	19		2 Same Old Lang Syne .... BB 9 / RW 9 / RR 9	Full Moon 50961
08/28/81	RR	3⁴	20		3 Hard To Say .... BB 7 / CB 7 / RW 10	Full Moon 02488
11/28/81	RR	2²	20		4 Leader Of The Band .... BB 9 / CB 9 / RW 9	Full Moon 02647
10/09/82	RR	7	16		5 Missing You	Full Moon 03289
02/04/84	RR	9	15		6 The Language Of Love	Full Moon 04314
					FOGERTY, John	
12/02/72	CB	10	16		1 Jambalaya (On The Bayou)	Fantasy 689
					THE BLUE RIDGE RANGERS	
12/22/84	RR	6	18		2 The Old Man Down The Road .... BB 10 / CB 10	Warner 29100
					FOLEY, Red	
01/21/50	BB	❶8	18	☉	1 Chattanoogie Shoe Shine Boy .... CB ❶4	Decca 46205
08/12/50	BB	10	10		2 Goodnight Irene	Decca 46255
					RED FOLEY-ERNEST TUBB	
09/02/50	BB	7	10		3 Cincinnati Dancing Pig .... CB 10	Decca 46261
					FONSI, Luis	
02/04/17	BB	❶16	52	△10	1 Despacito	Universal Latino
					LUIS FONSI & DADDY YANKEE Featuring Justin Bieber	
					FONTANA, Wayne, & The Mindbenders	
03/20/65	BB	❶1	12	☉	1 Game Of Love .... CB ❶1 / RW ❶1	Fontana 1509
					FONTANE SISTERS, The	
11/22/54	MV	❶6	21	☉	1 Hearts Of Stone .... BB ❶3 / CB 2⁴	Dot 15265
01/31/55	MV	9	14		2 Rock Love	Dot 15333
04/04/55	MV	7	11		3 Most Of All	Dot 15352
08/06/55	CB	3²	18		4 Seventeen .... BB 3¹ / MV 3¹	Dot 15386
					FOO FIGHTERS	
02/17/96	RR	10	20		1 Big Me	Roswell
					FORBERT, Steve	
12/01/79	RR	5	19		1 Romeo's Tune .... RW 10	Nemperor 7525
					FORCE M.D.'S	
02/01/86	RR	9	19		1 Tender Love .... BB 10 / CB 10	Warner 28818

56

DEBUT	CH	PK	WK	Gold	A-side (Chart Hit)	Other Charts	Label & Number
					FORD, Lita		
03/04/89	BB	8	25	●	1 Close My Eyes Forever LITA FORD with OZZY OSBOURNE		RCA 8899
					FORD, "Tennessee" Ernie		
08/19/50	BB	3¹	25		1 I'll Never Be Free KAY STARR and TENNESSEE ERNIE	CB 7	Capitol 1124
03/19/55	BB	5	17		2 Ballad Of Davy Crockett		Capitol 3058
10/24/55	BB	❶⁸	23	☉	3 Sixteen Tons	CB ❶⁷ / MV ❶⁷	Capitol 3262
					FOREIGNER		
03/26/77	BB	4	23	○	1 Feels Like The First Time	CB 5 / RR 8 / RW 9	Atlantic 3394
07/23/77	RR	4	21	○	2 Cold As Ice	BB 6 / RW 7 / CB 10	Atlantic 3410
07/01/78	RR	2²	19	▲	3 Hot Blooded	BB 3² / CB 4 / RW 4	Atlantic 3488
09/22/78	BB	2²	20	●	4 Double Vision	RR 2² / CB 5 / RW 8	Atlantic 3514
07/03/81	RW	3²	23		5 Urgent	BB 4 / CB 5 / RR 9	Atlantic 3831
10/02/81	RR	❶⁶	24	▲	6 Waiting For A Girl Like You	BB 2¹⁰ / RW 2⁷ / CB 2⁶	Atlantic 3868
12/07/84	BB	❶²	21	▲	7 I Want To Know What Love Is	RR ❶² / CB ❶¹	Atlantic 89596
03/15/85	CB	10	15		8 That Was Yesterday	RR 10	Atlantic 89571
12/05/87	BB	6	20		9 Say You Will	RR 7 / CB 8	Atlantic 89169
03/19/88	RR	4	19		10 I Don't Want To Live Without You	BB 5 / CB 8	Atlantic 89101
					FORT MINOR		
04/07/06	RR	2⁴	21	△	1 Where'd You Go FORT MINOR Featuring Holly Brook	BB 4	Machine Shop
					FORTUNES, The		
08/21/65	BB	7	11		1 You've Got Your Troubles	CB 7 / RW 8	Press 9773
05/15/71	CB	8	15		2 Here Comes That Rainy Day Feeling Again		Capitol 3086
					FOSTER THE PEOPLE		
05/14/11	BB	3⁸	40	△⁶	1 Pumped Up Kicks		StarTime
					FOUNDATIONS, The		
12/16/67	CB	8	15		1 Baby, Now That I've Found You	RW 9	Uni 55038
12/21/68	CB	❶²	17	●	2 Build Me Up Buttercup	RW ❶² / BB 3³	Uni 55101
					FOUNTAINS OF WAYNE		
09/05/03	RR	3¹	22	○	1 Stacy's Mom		S-Curve/Virgin
					FOUR ACES Featuring Al Alberts		
09/15/51	BB	4	22		1 Sin		Victoria 101
12/08/51	BB	2⁶	29	☉	2 Tell Me Why	CB 2⁴	Decca 27860
02/23/52	BB	7	22		3 Perfidia	CB 7	Decca 27987
08/09/52	BB	9	10		4 Should I		Decca 28323
12/05/53	BB	3¹	16	☉	5 Stranger In Paradise /		
11/14/53	CB	5	23		6 The Gang That Sang "Heart Of My Heart"		Decca 28927
05/15/54	CB	❶²	23	☉	7 Three Coins In The Fountain	BB ❶¹	Decca 29123
11/27/54	BB	5	14		8 Mister Sandman		Decca 29344
01/15/55	MV	2⁴	21		9 Melody Of Love	BB 3¹	Decca 29395
05/28/55	MV	7	6		10 Heart		Decca 29476
08/01/55	BB	❶⁶	29	☉	11 Love Is A Many-Splendored Thing	CB ❶³ / MV ❶²	Decca 29625
11/07/55	MV	7	20		12 A Woman In Love		Decca 29725
					FOUR COINS, The		
11/19/55	MV	9	16		1 Memories Of You		Epic 9129
					FOUR JACKS AND A JILL		
03/16/68	RW	9	16		1 Master Jack	CB 10	RCA Victor 9473
					FOUR KNIGHTS, The		
01/24/53	BB	8	6		1 Oh, Happy Day		Capitol 2315
01/23/54	CB	2³	26		2 I Get So Lonely (When I Dream About You)	BB 2¹	Capitol 2654
					FOUR LADS, The		
10/10/53	CB	5	20		1 Istanbul (Not Constantinople)	BB 10	Columbia 40082
10/04/54	BB	7	12		2 Skokiaan (South African Song)		Columbia 40306
08/27/55	BB	2⁶	28	☉	3 Moments To Remember	MV 2¹ / CB 3³	Columbia 40539
01/20/56	BB	2⁴	24	☉	4 No, Not Much!	MV 3⁵ / CB 3³	Columbia 40629
04/20/56	BB	3³	20	☉	5 Standing On The Corner	MV 3¹ / CB 4	Columbia 40674
01/12/57	BB	9	21		6 Who Needs You	CB 9 / MV 10	Columbia 40811
11/18/57	BB	8	15		7 Put A Light In The Window		Columbia 41058
03/10/58	BB	10	15		8 There's Only One Of You		Columbia 41136
06/14/58	MV	9	15		9 Enchanted Island		Columbia 41194
					4 P.M. (For Positive Music)		
09/17/94	RR	5	33	●	1 Sukiyaki	BB 8 / CB 8	Next Plateau 857736

DEBUT	CH	PK	WK	Gold	A-side (Chart Hit)	Other Charts	Label & Number
					FOUR PREPS, The		
01/18/58	BB	2³	20	⊙ 1	26 Miles (Santa Catalina)	MV 3² / CB 4	Capitol 3845
04/28/58	BB	3²	15	2	Big Man	CB 5 / MV 5	Capitol 3960
					4 SEASONS, The		
08/18/62	CB	❶⁶	16	⊙ 1	Sherry	BB ❶⁵ / MV ❶⁵	Vee-Jay 456
10/20/62	MV	❶⁶	17	⊙ 2	Big Girls Don't Cry	BB ❶⁵ / CB ❶⁵	Vee-Jay 465
01/19/63	BB	❶³	15	⊙ 3	Walk Like A Man	CB ❶² / MV ❶²	Vee-Jay 485
06/29/63	BB	3¹	15	4	Candy Girl	CB 4 / MV 4	Vee-Jay 539
02/01/64	BB	3³	14	5	Dawn (Go Away)	CB 3³ / MV 3³	Philips 40166
04/11/64	BB	6	12	6	Ronnie	CB 6 / MV 6	Philips 40185
06/20/64	BB	❶²	13	● 7	Rag Doll	CB ❶² / RW ❶²	Philips 40211
08/29/64	RW	8	9	8	Save It For Me	CB 9 / BB 10	Philips 40225
01/23/65	RW	6	9	9	Bye, Bye, Baby (Baby, Goodbye)	CB 10	Philips 40260
10/02/65	CB	❶¹	17	10	Let's Hang On!	RW ❶¹ / BB 3¹	Philips 40317
11/06/65	RW	9	11	11	Don't Think Twice	CB 10	Philips 40324
					THE WONDER WHO?		
01/29/66	BB	9	9	12	Working My Way Back To You	RW 9 / CB 10	Philips 40350
05/14/66	CB	9	10	13	Opus 17 (Don't You Worry 'Bout Me)	RW 9	Philips 40370
09/03/66	RW	6	10	14	I've Got You Under My Skin	BB 9 / CB 9	Philips 40393
12/10/66	BB	10	11	15	Tell It To The Rain	RW 10	Philips 40412
06/10/67	BB	9	10	16	C'mon Marianne	CB 9 / RW 9	Philips 40460
08/23/75	BB	3²	24	17	Who Loves You	RW 5 / CB 7 / RR 7	Warner/Curb 8122
12/27/75	BB	❶³	27	● 18	December, 1963 (Oh, What A Night)	RR ❶³ / CB ❶¹ / RW ❶¹	Warner/Curb 8168
08/12/94	RR	7	28	19	December, 1963 (Oh, What A Night)		Curb 76917
					FOUR TOPS		
05/15/65	BB	❶²	15	⊙ 1	I Can't Help Myself	CB ❶² / RW ❶¹	Motown 1076
07/24/65	BB	5	11	2	It's The Same Old Song	RW 5 / CB 6	Motown 1081
09/03/66	BB	❶²	15	● 3	Reach Out I'll Be There	CB ❶¹ / RW 2²	Motown 1098
12/17/66	BB	6	11	4	Standing In The Shadows Of Love	RW 6 / CB 10	Motown 1102
03/04/67	BB	4	11	5	Bernadette	RW 6 / CB 8	Motown 1104
05/20/67	CB	9	9	6	7 Rooms Of Gloom	RW 9	Motown 1110
02/03/68	CB	8	9	7	Walk Away Renee	RW 8	Motown 1119
08/29/70	RW	8	14	8	Still Water (Love)		Motown 1170
11/04/72	CB	9	13	9	Keeper Of The Castle	BB 10 / RW 10	Dunhill/ABC 4330
02/03/73	CB	❶¹	15	● 10	Ain't No Woman (Like The One I've Got)	RW 2¹ / BB 4	Dunhill/ABC 4339
08/22/81	CB	10	22	11	When She Was My Girl		Casablanca 2338
					FOUR TUNES, The		
05/22/54	BB	6	18	⊙ 1	I Understand Just How You Feel	CB 7	Jubilee 5132
					FOX, Samantha		
11/01/86	BB	4	23	1	Touch Me (I Want Your Body)	CB 7 / RR 8	Jive 1006
02/27/88	BB	3¹	27	2	Naughty Girls (Need Love Too)	CB 4 / RR 6	Jive 1089
11/05/88	BB	8	23	● 3	I Wanna Have Some Fun		Jive 1154
					FOXX, Inez, with Charlie Foxx		
06/22/63	BB	7	19	1	Mockingbird	CB 7 / MV 7	Symbol 919
					FOXX, Jamie		
12/03/05	BB	8	22	1	Unpredictable		J Records 75974
					JAMIE FOXX (feat. Ludacris)		
01/31/09	BB	2¹	27	2	Blame It	RR 3²	J Records 46266
					JAMIE FOXX with T-PAIN		
					FOXY		
07/01/78	RW	8	24	1	Get Off	BB 9	Dash 5046
					FRAMPTON, Peter		
02/21/76	CB	4	18	1	Show Me The Way	RR 5 / BB 6 / RW 6	A&M 1795
06/19/76	RR	9	22	2	Baby, I Love Your Way		A&M 1832
09/17/76	RR	5	18	3	Do You Feel Like We Do	BB 10	A&M 1867
05/27/77	RR	❶²	20	4	I'm In You	CB ❶¹ / BB 2³ / RW 3¹	A&M 1941
					FRANCIS, Connie		
02/03/58	MV	2⁴	22	⊙ 1	Who's Sorry Now	CB 3³ / BB 4	MGM 12588
04/21/58	MV	10	13	2	I'm Sorry I Made You Cry		MGM 12647
12/01/58	MV	2³	18	3	My Happiness	BB 2² / CB 2²	MGM 12738
03/02/59	MV	9	11	4	If I Didn't Care		MGM 12769
05/16/59	CB	3¹	17	⊙ 5	Lipstick On Your Collar /	BB 5 / MV 5	MGM 12793
05/04/59	MV	5	16	6	Frankie	BB 9 / CB 9	MGM 12793
11/09/59	CB	5	17	7	Among My Souvenirs	BB 7 / MV 7	MGM 12841
02/22/60	CB	7	14	⊙ 8	Mama	MV 7 / BB 8	MGM 12878
05/09/60	CB	❶³	18	⊙ 9	Everybody's Somebody's Fool	MV ❶³ / BB ❶²	MGM 12899
08/15/60	MV	❶⁴	17	10	My Heart Has A Mind Of Its Own	BB ❶² / CB ❶¹	MGM 12923
10/31/60	MV	6	13	11	Many Tears Ago	BB 7 / CB 7	MGM 12964
01/16/61	MV	2¹	15	12	Where The Boys Are	BB 4 / CB 4	MGM 12971

DEBUT	CH	PK	WK	Gold	A-side (Chart Hit)	Other Charts	Label & Number

FRANCIS, Connie (cont'd)

04/10/61	MV	3¹	12		13 Breakin' In A Brand New Broken Heart	CB 5 / BB 7	MGM 12995
06/26/61	MV	4	12		14 Together	BB 6 / CB 7	MGM 13019
11/20/61	MV	7	12		15 When The Boy In Your Arms (Is The Boy In Your Heart)	CB 8 / BB 10	MGM 13051
02/05/62	BB	❶¹	13		16 Don't Break The Heart That Loves You	CB 2² / MV 2²	MGM 13059
04/30/62	MV	6	10		17 Second Hand Love	BB 7 / CB 7	MGM 13074
07/21/62	BB	9	10		18 Vacation	MV 9 / CB 10	MGM 13087

FRANKE & THE KNOCKOUTS

| 03/07/81 | BB | 10 | 20 | | 1 Sweetheart | | Millennium 11801 |
| 04/03/82 | RR | 10 | 15 | | 2 Without You (Not Another Lonely Night) | | Millennium 13105 |

FRANKIE GOES TO HOLLYWOOD

| 01/19/85 | BB | 10 | 18 | ● | 1 Relax | RR 10 | Island 99805 |

FRANKIE J

| 01/28/05 | RR | 3³ | 21 | ○ | 1 Obsession [No Es Amor] | BB 3¹ | Columbia 70386 |

FRANKIE J featuring Baby Bash

FRANKLIN, Aretha

03/04/67	RW	8	12	●	1 I Never Loved A Man (The Way I Love You)	BB 9 / CB 10	Atlantic 2386
04/29/67	RW	❶³	13	●	2 Respect	BB ❶² / CB ❶²	Atlantic 2403
07/22/67	CB	3³	11	●	3 Baby I Love You	RW 3² / BB 4	Atlantic 2427
09/30/67	BB	8	9		4 (You Make Me Feel Like) A Natural Woman	RW 9	Atlantic 2441
12/09/67	CB	❶¹	12	●	5 Chain Of Fools	BB 2² / RW 2¹	Atlantic 2464
03/02/68	RW	4	12		6 (Sweet Sweet Baby) Since You've Been Gone	BB 5 / CB 5	Atlantic 2486
05/18/68	BB	7	10	●	7 Think	CB 7 / RW 7	Atlantic 2518
08/10/68	BB	6	11	●	8 The House That Jack Built /	RW 6 / CB 9	
08/17/68	BB	10	11		9 I Say A Little Prayer		Atlantic 2546
02/22/69	RW	8	7		10 The Weight	CB 10	Atlantic 2603
08/08/70	RW	7	11	●	11 Don't Play That Song	CB 10	Atlantic 2751

ARETHA FRANKLIN with The Dixie Flyers

04/10/71	RW	2²	12	●	12 Bridge Over Troubled Water	CB 2¹ / BB 6	Atlantic 2796
07/31/71	CB	❶¹	12	●	13 Spanish Harlem	RW ❶¹ / BB 2²	Atlantic 2817
10/23/71	RW	6	10	●	14 Rock Steady	CB 5 / BB 9	Atlantic 2838
03/11/72	BB	5	13	●	15 Day Dreaming	CB 5 / RW 6	Atlantic 2866
11/17/73	BB	3¹	21	●	16 Until You Come Back To Me (That's What I'm Gonna Do)	RW 4 / CB 7	Atlantic 2995
06/22/85	CB	3³	20		17 Freeway Of Love	BB 3¹ / RR 5	Arista 9354
09/27/85	BB	7	20		18 Who's Zoomin' Who	RR 7 / CB 8	Arista 9410
02/20/87	BB	❶²	21		19 I Knew You Were Waiting (For Me)	RR ❶² / CB ❶¹	Arista 9559

ARETHA FRANKLIN AND GEORGE MICHAEL

FRAY, The

02/25/06	RR	5	42	△³	1 Over My Head (Cable Car)	BB 8	Epic
04/15/06	RR	3⁶	58	△³	2 How To Save A Life	BB 3¹	Epic
12/06/08	RR	6	39	△⁴	3 You Found Me	BB 7	Epic

FREBERG, Stan

| 10/03/53 | BB | ❶⁴ | 12 | ⊙ | 1 St. George And The Dragonet / | CB ❶³ | |
| 10/03/53 | BB | 9 | 7 | | 2 Little Blue Riding Hood | CB 10 | Capitol 2596 |

FRED, John, & His Playboy Band

| 11/18/67 | BB | ❶² | 18 | ● | 1 Judy In Disguise (With Glasses) | RW ❶² / CB ❶¹ | Paula 282 |

FREDDIE AND THE DREAMERS

| 03/13/65 | BB | ❶² | 12 | ⊙ | 1 I'm Telling You Now | CB ❶² / RW ❶² | Tower 125 |

FREE

| 08/15/70 | CB | 3¹ | 16 | | 1 All Right Now | BB 4 / RW 4 | A&M 1206 |

FREEMAN, Bobby

| 04/12/58 | BB | 5 | 17 | | 1 Do You Want To Dance | CB 5 / MV 9 | Josie 835 |
| 07/04/64 | BB | 5 | 15 | | 2 C'mon And Swim | CB 6 / RW 8 | Autumn 2 |

FREEMAN, Ernie

| 11/18/57 | BB | 4 | 18 | | 1 Raunchy | | Imperial 5474 |

FREE MOVEMENT, The

| 05/22/71 | BB | 5 | 26 | | 1 I've Found Someone Of My Own | CB 6 / RW 10 | Decca 32818 |

FRENCH, Nicki

| 04/01/95 | BB | 2¹ | 29 | ● | 1 Total Eclipse Of The Heart | CB 3³ / RR 3¹ | Critique 15539 |

FREY, Glenn

08/21/82	RR	2¹	21		1 The One You Love		Asylum 69974
12/08/84	BB	2¹	25		2 The Heat Is On	CB 4 / RR 4	MCA 52512
09/14/85	BB	2²	22		3 You Belong To The City	RR 2² / CB 3²	MCA 52651

FRIDA

| 11/06/82 | RR | 9 | 29 | | 1 I Know There's Something Going On | | Atlantic 89984 |

DEBUT	CH	PK	WK	Gold	A-side (Chart Hit)...Other Charts	Label & Number
					FRIEND AND LOVER	
05/04/68	CB	7	15		1 Reach Out Of The Darkness ....RW 7 / BB 10	Verve Forecast 5069
					FRIENDS OF DISTINCTION, The	
04/05/69	BB	3¹	16	●	1 Grazing In The Grass ....RW 4 / CB 6	RCA Victor 0107
03/07/70	RW	5	13		2 Love Or Let Me Be Lonely ....BB 6 / CB 8	RCA Victor 0319
					FRIJID PINK	
01/24/70	RW	5	16	●	1 House Of The Rising Sun ....CB 6 / BB 7	Parrot 341
					FUGEES	
03/09/96	RR	❶¹	35		1 Killing Me Softly ....BB 2³	Ruffhouse
					FUGEES (feat. Lauryn Hill)	
					FULLER, Bobby, Four	
01/29/66	BB	9	11		1 I Fought The Law ....CB 9 / RW 9	Mustang 3014
					FUN.	
12/24/11	BB	❶⁶	42 △¹⁰		1 We Are Young	Fueled By Ramen
					FUN. Featuring Janelle Monae	
03/10/12	BB	3⁶	56 △⁷		2 Some Nights	Fueled By Ramen
					FUNKADELIC	
09/02/78	RW	7	17	●	1 One Nation Under A Groove - Part I	Warner 8618
					FURTADO, Nelly	
12/15/00	RR	6	33		1 I'm Like A Bird ....BB 9	DreamWorks
07/27/01	RR	4	27		2 Turn Off The Light ....BB 5	DreamWorks 459233
05/05/06	RR	❶⁸	28 △		3 Promiscuous ....BB ❶⁶	Mosley/Geffen 006818
					NELLY FURTADO Featuring Timbaland	
11/17/06	RR	❶⁴	30		4 Say It Right ....BB ❶¹	Mosley/Geffen
					FUTURE	
03/11/17	BB	5	31 △⁶		1 Mask Off	A-1
01/25/20	BB	2⁶	6		2 Life Is Good	Freebandz
					FUTURE Featuring Drake	
					FUZZ, The	
01/23/71	RW	10	20		1 I Love You For All Seasons	Calla 174

G

DEBUT	CH	PK	WK	Gold	A-side	Label & Number
					GABRIEL, Peter	
05/10/86	CB	❶²	22		1 Sledgehammer ....BB ❶¹ / RR ❶¹	Geffen 28718
11/29/86	RR	3¹	24		2 Big Time ....BB 8 / CB 8	Geffen 28503
12/18/92	RR	9	17		3 Steam	Geffen 19145
					GALLERY	
02/26/72	CB	❶¹	22	●	1 Nice To Be With You ....BB 4 / RW 4	Sussex 232
					GAME, The	
11/27/04	BB	4	28	○	1 How We Do	Aftermath 003913
02/12/05	BB	2⁵	23	○	2 Hate It Or Love It	Aftermath
					THE GAME Featuring 50 Cent (above 2)	
					GARFUNKEL, Art	
09/08/73	RR	4	14		1 All I Know ....CB 6 / RW 7 / BB 9	Columbia 45926
					GARFUNKEL	
01/21/78	RR	9	14		2 (What A) Wonderful World	Columbia 10676
					ART GARFUNKEL with JAMES TAYLOR & PAUL SIMON	
					GARNETT, Gale	
08/01/64	CB	❶¹	19		1 We'll Sing In The Sunshine ....BB 4 / RW 4	RCA Victor 8388
					GARRETT, Leif	
11/04/78	BB	10	21		1 I Was Made For Dancin'	Scotti Brothers 403
					GATES, David	
12/10/77	RR	7	25		1 Goodbye Girl ....CB 9	Elektra 45450
					GAYE, Marvin	
05/18/63	MV	9	16		1 Pride And Joy ....BB 10 / CB 10	Tamla 54079
11/21/64	BB	6	16		2 How Sweet It Is To Be Loved By You ....RW 8 / CB 9	Tamla 54107
03/20/65	BB	8	12		3 I'll Be Doggone ....CB 10	Tamla 54112
10/02/65	RW	7	14		4 Ain't That Peculiar ....BB 8 / CB 10	Tamla 54122
09/09/67	BB	5	13		5 Your Precious Love ....CB 6 / RW 6	Tamla 54156
12/02/67	BB	10	12		6 If I Could Build My Whole World Around You	Tamla 54161
04/13/68	RW	7	13		7 Ain't Nothing Like The Real Thing ....BB 8 / CB 9	Tamla 54163
07/27/68	BB	7	12		8 You're All I Need To Get By ....CB 7	Tamla 54169
					MARVIN GAYE & TAMMI TERRELL (above 4)	

60

DEBUT	CH	PK	WK	Gold	A-side (Chart Hit)	Other Charts	Label & Number
					GAYE, Marvin (cont'd)		
11/16/68	BB	❶⁷	15	⊙ 9	I Heard It Through The Grapevine	CB ❶⁵ / RW ❶¹	Tamla 54176
04/19/69	BB	4	15	10	Too Busy Thinking About My Baby	CB 5 / RW 5	Tamla 54181
08/23/69	BB	7	13	11	That's The Way Love Is	CB 10	Tamla 54185
02/20/71	CB	❶¹	15	⊙ 12	What's Going On	BB 2³ / RW 2³	Tamla 54201
06/26/71	RW	2²	13	13	Mercy Mercy Me (The Ecology)	BB 4 / CB 4	Tamla 54207
10/02/71	CB	6	11	14	Inner City Blues (Make Me Wanna Holler)	RW 7 / BB 9	Tamla 54209
12/16/72	RW	6	12	15	Trouble Man	BB 7 / CB 8	Tamla 54228
07/07/73	BB	❶²	21	○ 16	Let's Get It On	RW ❶² / CB ❶¹ / RR 5	Tamla 54234
04/09/77	BB	❶¹	22	17	Got To Give It Up (Pt. I)	CB ❶¹ / RW ❶¹	Tamla 54280
10/30/82	BB	3³	22	▲ 18	Sexual Healing	CB 5 / RR 6	Columbia 03302
					GAYLE, Crystal		
07/30/77	CB	❶²	30	● 1	Don't It Make My Brown Eyes Blue	BB 2³ / RW 2² / RR 2¹	United Artists 1016
10/09/82	BB	7	29	2	You And I		Elektra 69936
					EDDIE RABBITT with CRYSTAL GAYLE		
					GAYLORDS, The		
12/20/52	BB	2¹	23	⊙ 1	Tell Me You're Mine	CB 3³	Mercury 70067
01/30/54	CB	3¹	18	2	From The Vine Came The Grape	BB 7	Mercury 70296
05/01/54	CB	9	20	3	Isle Of Capri		Mercury 70350
06/26/54	CB	2⁴	23	4	The Little Shoemaker	BB 2¹ / MV 9	Mercury 70403
					THE GAYLORDS, Three Friends and a Stranger		
					GAYNOR, Gloria		
11/02/74	CB	8	17	1	Never Can Say Goodbye	BB 9 / RW 9	MGM 14748
12/16/78	BB	❶³	27	▲ 2	I Will Survive	CB ❶¹ / RW ❶¹ / RR 2¹	Polydor 14508
					G-CLEFS, The		
09/11/61	BB	9	18	1	I Understand (Just How You Feel)		Terrace 7500
					G-EAZY		
11/21/15	BB	7	37	△⁵ 1	Me, Myself & I		G-Eazy
					G-EAZY & BEBE REXHA		
09/30/17	BB	4	29	△⁵ 2	No Limit		G-Eazy
					G-EAZY Featuring A$AP Rocky & Cardi B		
					GEDDES, David		
07/26/75	CB	❶¹	21	1	Run Joey Run	BB 4 / RW 4 / RR 6	Big Tree 16044
					GEILS, J., Band		
11/06/81	BB	❶⁶	28	● 1	Centerfold	CB ❶⁶ / RW ❶⁵ / RR 2³	EMI America 8102
02/19/82	RR	3²	19	● 2	Freeze-Frame	BB 4 / CB 4 / RW 5	EMI America 8108
					GENERAL PUBLIC		
04/01/94	RR	10	24	1	I'll Take You There		Epic Soundtrax 77452
					GENESIS		
05/17/80	RR	3¹	20	1	Misunderstanding	RW 9	Atlantic 3662
11/25/83	RR	2²	22	2	That's All!	BB 6 / CB 10	Atlantic 89724
05/30/86	RR	❶²	18	3	Invisible Touch	BB ❶¹ / CB ❶¹	Atlantic 89407
08/15/86	RR	❶¹	18	4	Throwing It All Away	CB 3³ / BB 4	Atlantic 89372
10/31/86	BB	4	21	5	Land Of Confusion	CB 5 / RR 5	Atlantic 89336
02/06/87	RR	3²	16	6	Tonight, Tonight, Tonight	BB 3¹ / CB 3¹	Atlantic 89290
04/24/87	RR	3³	18	7	In Too Deep	BB 3¹ / CB 4	Atlantic 89316
11/01/91	CB	6	26	8	No Son Of Mine	RR 6	Atlantic 87571
01/31/92	RR	3²	23	9	I Can't Dance	RR 5 / BB 7	Atlantic 87532
05/01/92	RR	4	20	10	Hold On My Heart		Atlantic 87481
07/24/92	RR	9	20	11	Jesus He Knows Me		Atlantic 87454
11/06/92	RR	9	24	12	Never A Time		Atlantic 87411
					GENTRY, Bobbie		
08/05/67	BB	❶⁴	15	● 1	Ode To Billie Joe	CB ❶⁴ / RW ❶⁴	Capitol 5950
					GENTRYS, The		
09/04/65	RW	3²	14	1	Keep On Dancing	BB 4 / CB 5	MGM 13379
					GEORGE, Barbara		
11/13/61	BB	3¹	19	1	I Know (You Don't Love Me No More)	CB 3¹ / MV 3¹	A.F.O. 302
					GEORGIA SATELLITES		
11/22/86	BB	2¹	23	1	Keep Your Hands To Yourself	CB 5 / RR 5	Elektra 69502
					GERARDO		
02/02/91	BB	7	19	● 1	Rico Suave		Interscope 98871
					GERRY AND THE PACEMAKERS		
05/23/64	BB	4	12	1	Don't Let The Sun Catch You Crying	CB 6 / RW 6	Laurie 3251
07/11/64	BB	9	12	2	How Do You Do It?	CB 10	Laurie 3261
02/06/65	CB	4	12	3	Ferry Cross The Mersey	BB 6 / RW 7	Laurie 3284

DEBUT	CH	PK	WK	Gold	A-side (Chart Hit) ....Other Charts	Label & Number
					GETZ, Stan	
08/18/62	MV	10	22		1 Desafinado...	Verve 10260
					STAN GETZ/CHARLIE BYRD	
06/06/64	BB	5	13		2 The Girl From Ipanema .... CB 5 / RW 8	Verve 10323
					GETZ/GILBERTO	
					GHOST TOWN DJ'S	
07/06/96	CB	10	31		1 My Boo	So So Def 78358
					GIBB, Andy	
04/23/77	RW	❶⁵	31	●	1 I Just Want To Be Your Everything .... BB ❶⁴ / CB ❶³ / RR ❶³	RSO 872
11/05/77	BB	❶²	29	●	2 (Love Is) Thicker Than Water .... CB ❶¹ / RW ❶¹ / RR 3¹	RSO 883
04/15/78	RW	❶⁸	25	▲	3 Shadow Dancing .... BB ❶⁷ / CB ❶⁶ / RR ❶⁴	RSO 893
07/15/78	BB	5	16	●	4 An Everlasting Love .... CB 5 / RR 6 / RW 9	RSO 904
10/14/78	CB	7	19	●	5 (Our Love) Don't Throw It All Away .... BB 9 / RW 9 / RR 10	RSO 911
01/18/80	BB	4	15		6 Desire .... RW 4 / CB 6 / RR 7	RSO 1019
					GIBB, Barry — see STREISAND, Barbra	
					GIBBS, Georgia	
03/25/50	BB	5	11		1 If I Knew You Were Comin' I'd've Baked A Cake	Coral 60169
08/18/51	BB	6	9		2 While You Danced, Danced, Danced	Mercury 5681
04/19/52	CB	❶⁸	24	☉	3 Kiss Of Fire .... BB ❶⁷	Mercury 5823
03/07/53	BB	5	24		4 Seven Lonely Days .... CB 9	Mercury 70095
01/03/55	BB	2¹	23	☉	5 Tweedle Dee .... CB 3² / MV 5	Mercury 70517
03/07/55	BB	❶³	22	☉	6 Dance With Me Henry (Wallflower)............................MV ❶¹ / CB 3¹	Mercury 70572
06/06/55	MV	5	14		7 Sweet And Gentle .... CB 8	Mercury 70647
08/27/55	MV	10	12		8 I Want You To Be My Baby	Mercury 70685
					GIBBS, Terri	
01/17/81	CB	10	24		1 Somebody's Knockin' .... RW 10	MCA 41309
					GIBSON, Debbie	
05/09/87	RR	3¹	28	●	1 Only In My Dreams .... BB 4 / CB 6	Atlantic 89322
10/03/87	BB	4	22		2 Shake Your Love .... CB 5 / RR 5	Atlantic 89187
01/29/88	RR	3²	20		3 Out Of The Blue .... BB 3¹ / CB 5	Atlantic 89129
04/22/88	BB	❶¹	22		4 Foolish Beat .... CB ❶¹ / RR ❶¹	Atlantic 89109
01/13/89	RR	❶⁴	19	●	5 Lost In Your Eyes .... BB ❶³ / CB ❶³	Atlantic 88970
03/31/89	CB	9	18	●	6 Electric Youth .... RR 9	Atlantic 88919
					GIBSON, Don	
02/22/58	MV	3¹	21	☉	1 Oh Lonesome Me .... BB 7 / CB 10	RCA Victor 7133
					GILBERTO, Astrud — see GETZ, Stan	
					GILDER, Nick	
06/10/78	RW	❶⁴	31	▲	1 Hot Child In The City .... CB ❶³ / BB ❶¹ / RR ❶¹	Chrysalis 2226
					GILKYSON, Terry, and The Easy Riders	
03/31/51	CB	❶²	23	☉	1 On Top Of Old Smoky .... BB 2⁸	Decca 27515
					THE WEAVERS and TERRY GILKYSON	
01/19/57	MV	❶²	19	☉	2 Marianne .... CB 2² / BB 4	Columbia 40817
					GILL, Johnny	
05/12/90	RR	2¹	23	●	1 Rub You The Right Way .... BB 3² / CB 4	Motown 2045
08/04/90	CB	9	19		2 My, My, My .... BB 10	Motown 2033
					GILMER, Jimmy, and The Fireballs	
09/21/63	BB	❶⁵	16	●	1 Sugar Shack.. MV ❶⁵ / CB ❶³	Dot 16487
					GINA G	
11/29/96	RR	5	30		1 Ooh Aah...Just A Little Bit	Eternal/Warner 17455
					GIN BLOSSOMS	
11/20/93	RR	6	36		1 Found Out About You	A&M 0418
09/30/94	RR	8	21		2 Allison Road	A&M 0862
08/04/95	RR	3²	48	☉	3 Til I Hear It From You /	
					CB 7	
02/09/96	RR	5	46		4 Follow You Down .... BB 9	A&M 1380
					GINUWINE	
09/07/96	BB	6	27	▲	1 Pony .... CB 8	550 Music/Epic 78373
07/28/01	BB	4	30		2 Differences	Epic 79711
06/08/02	BB	4	26		3 I Need A Girl (Part Two) .... RR 9	Bad Boy 79441
					P. DIDDY AND GINUWINE Featuring Loon, Mario Winans & Tammy Ruggeri	
06/14/03	BB	8	20		4 In Those Jeans	Epic
					GLAHE, Will, and His Orchestra	
10/14/57	MV	10	23		1 Liechtensteiner Polka	London 1755

DEBUT	CH	PK	WK	Gold	A-side (Chart Hit)	Other Charts	Label & Number
					GLASS TIGER		
07/12/86	BB	2¹	24		1 Don't Forget Me (When I'm Gone)	CB 3¹ / RR 5	Manhattan 50037
11/01/86	BB	7	21		2 Someday	RR 7 / CB 8	Manhattan 50048
					GLEE CAST		
06/06/09	BB	4	6	△	1 Don't Stop Believin'		Fox
11/27/10	BB	8	3	○	2 Teenage Dream		Fox
04/02/11	BB	6	3	○	3 Loser Like Me		Fox
					GLENN, Darrell		
07/18/53	CB	❶³	23		1 Crying In The Chapel	BB 6	Valley 105
					GLITTER, Gary		
07/15/72	CB	3¹	13		1 Rock And Roll Part 2	RW 6 / BB 7	Bell 45,237
					GLYNNE, Jess — see CLEAN BANDIT		
					GNARLS BARKLEY		
05/20/06	BB	2⁷	29	△⁴	1 Crazy	RR 6	Downtown 70002
					GNASH		
05/07/16	BB	10	39	△⁴	1 I Hate U I Love U		gnash
					GNASH with OLIVIA O'BRIEN		
					GODFREY, Arthur		
03/11/50	CB	8	11		1 Candy And Cake		Columbia 38721
03/25/50	BB	8	9		2 Go To Sleep, Go To Sleep, Go To Sleep	CB 10	Columbia 38744
					MARY MARTIN and ARTHUR GODFREY		
12/22/51	BB	6	17		3 Dance Me Loose	CB 7	Columbia 39632
					GODSPELL		
05/13/72	CB	9	16		1 Day By Day		Bell 45,210
					GO-GO'S		
01/23/82	BB	2³	24	●	1 We Got The Beat	CB 2³ / RW 2¹ / RR 5	I.R.S. 9903
07/03/82	CB	6	19		2 Vacation	RR 7 / BB 8	I.R.S. 9907
03/17/84	RR	9	19		3 Head Over Heels	CB 10	I.R.S. 9926
					GOLD, Andrew		
03/19/77	CB	3²	23		1 Lonely Boy	RR 3² / RW 6 / BB 7	Asylum 45384
					GOLDEN EARRING		
05/18/74	RR	7	16		1 Radar Love	RW 9 / CB 10	Track/MCA 40202
11/27/82	BB	10	27		2 Twilight Zone		21 Records 103
					GOLDSBORO, Bobby		
01/11/64	BB	9	13		1 See The Funny Little Clown	CB 10	United Artists 672
01/23/65	RW	9	12		2 Little Things		United Artists 810
03/23/68	BB	❶⁵	15	●	3 Honey	RW ❶⁵ / CB ❶⁴	United Artists 50283
12/19/70	RW	6	14		4 Watching Scotty Grow	CB 8	United Artists 50727
					GOMEZ, Selena		
04/27/13	BB	6	22	△³	1 Come & Get It		Hollywood
11/22/14	BB	6	20	△	2 The Heart Wants What It Wants		Hollywood
07/11/15	BB	5	26	△³	3 Good For You		Interscope
					SELENA GOMEZ Featuring A$AP Rocky		
10/03/15	BB	5	28	△³	4 Same Old Love		Interscope
12/26/15	BB	7	20	△²	5 Hands To Myself		Interscope
03/04/17	BB	10	29	△³	6 It Ain't Me		Ultra
					KYGO & SELENA GOMEZ		
11/02/19	BB	❶¹	18		7 Lose You To Love Me		Interscope
					GOOD CHARLOTTE		
11/15/02	RR	7	22		1 Lifestyles Of The Rich And Famous		Epic/Daylight
					GOODMAN, Dickie		
08/23/75	CB	❶¹	19	●	1 Mr. Jaws	RW ❶¹ / BB 4	Cash 451
					GOO GOO DOLLS		
09/22/95	RR	❶¹	40		1 Name	BB 5 / CB 5	Warner 17758
04/17/98	BB	❶¹⁸	47	△⁴	2 Iris	RR ❶⁴	Warner Sunset
10/02/98	RR	❶²	39	○	3 Slide	BB 8	Warner
					GORDON, Barry		
12/01/55	CB	5	6	⊙	1 Nuttin' For Christmas	BB 6	MGM 12092
					ART MOONEY And His ORCHESTRA with BARRY GORDON		
					GORE, Lesley		
05/04/63	MV	❶³	14	⊙	1 It's My Party	BB ❶² / CB ❶²	Mercury 72119
07/06/63	CB	4	11		2 Judy's Turn To Cry	MV 4 / BB 5	Mercury 72143
09/21/63	MV	3¹	17		3 She's A Fool	BB 5 / CB 6	Mercury 72180
12/28/63	BB	2³	14		4 You Don't Own Me	CB 2² / MV 2²	Mercury 72206

63

DEBUT	CH	PK	WK	Gold	A-side (Chart Hit) .... Other Charts	Label & Number
					GORE, Lesley (cont'd)	
07/25/64	CB	10	11		5 Maybe I Know	Mercury 72309
					GORME, Eydie	
05/05/58	MV	7	16		1 You Need Hands	ABC-Paramount 9925
01/19/63	CB	6	16		2 Blame It On The Bossa Nova .... MV 6 / BB 7	Columbia 42661
					GOTYE	
01/21/12	BB	❶⁸	59	△⁸	1 Somebody That I Used To Know GOTYE Featuring Kimbra	Samples 'n' Seconds
					GOULDING, Ellie	
08/20/11	BB	2²	57	△⁵	1 Lights	Cherrytree
01/24/15	BB	3²	34	△⁵	2 Love Me Like You Do	Cherrytree
					GO WEST	
05/19/90	RR	6	24		1 King Of Wishful Thinking .... BB 8 / CB 8	EMI 50307
11/06/92	RR	6	22		2 Faithful	EMI 50411
					GQ	
03/17/79	CB	10	19	●	1 Disco Nights (Rock-Freak)	Arista 0388
					GRACIE, Charlie	
02/16/57	BB	❶²	17	☉	1 Butterfly .... MV ❶¹ / CB 3¹	Cameo 105
					GRAHAM, Larry	
06/21/80	BB	9	22	●	1 One In A Million You	Warner 49211
					GRAMM, Lou	
01/31/87	BB	5	20		1 Midnight Blue .... RR 7 / CB 8	Atlantic 89304
10/28/89	RR	3¹	22		2 Just Between You And Me .... BB 6 / CB 6	Atlantic 88781
					GRAMMER, Andy	
02/28/15	BB	9	31	△³	1 Honey, I'm Good.	S-Curve
					GRAMMER, Billy	
11/08/58	BB	4	20	☉	1 Gotta Travel On .... MV 4 / CB 6	Monument 400
					GRANDE, Ariana	
04/13/13	BB	9	26	△³	1 The Way	Republic
					ARIANA GRANDE Featuring Mac Miller	
05/17/14	BB	2⁵	25	△⁶	2 Problem	Republic
					ARIANA GRANDE Featuring Iggy Azalea	
07/19/14	BB	4	22	△³	3 Break Free	Republic
					ARIANA GRANDE Featuring Zedd	
08/16/14	BB	3²	31	△⁶	4 Bang Bang	Lava
					JESSIE J, ARIANA GRANDE & NICKI MINAJ	
10/25/14	BB	7	22	△³	5 Love Me Harder	Republic
					ARIANA GRANDE & THE WEEKND	
11/21/15	BB	7	13	△	6 Focus	Republic
04/02/16	BB	8	21	△³	7 Dangerous Woman	Republic
09/17/16	BB	4	28	△⁴	8 Side To Side	Republic
					ARIANA GRANDE Featuring Nicki Minaj	
05/05/18	BB	3¹	27	△³	9 No Tears Left To Cry	Republic
07/28/18	BB	8	22	△²	10 God Is A Woman	Republic
11/17/18	BB	❶⁷	28	△⁵	11 Thank U, Next	Republic
02/02/19	BB	❶⁸	33		12 7 Rings	Republic
02/23/19	BB	2¹	20		13 Break Up With Your Girlfriend, I'm Bored	Republic
08/17/19	BB	8	12		14 Boyfriend	SRV
					ARIANA GRANDE & SOCIAL HOUSE	
					GRAND FUNK	
07/21/73	BB	❶¹	17	●	1 We're An American Band .... CB ❶¹ / RW ❶¹ / RR 4	Capitol 3660
03/09/74	RR	❶⁴	20	●	2 The Loco-Motion .... BB ❶² / CB ❶¹ / RW ❶¹	Capitol 3840
12/14/74	BB	3¹	17		3 Some Kind Of Wonderful .... RW 5 / CB 7 / RR 7	Capitol 4002
04/05/75	BB	4	17		4 Bad Time .... CB 5 / RR 6 / RW 7	Capitol 4046
					GRANT, Amy	
09/20/86	BB	❶¹	23		1 The Next Time I Fall .... RR 2¹ / CB 3²	Full Moon 28597
					PETER CETERA with AMY GRANT	
02/23/91	CB	❶³	27		2 Baby Baby .... RR ❶³ / BB ❶²	A&M 1549
06/14/91	CB	2⁴	22		3 Every Heartbeat .... RR 2² / BB 2¹	A&M 1557
09/27/91	CB	2²	30		4 That's What Love Is For .... RR 4 / BB 7	A&M 1566
01/17/92	RR	3²	25		5 Good For Me .... CB 4 / BB 8	A&M 1573
04/24/92	RR	9	23		6 I Will Remember You	A&M 1600
					GRANT, Earl	
08/25/58	BB	7	19		1 The End .... MV 7 / CB 10	Decca 30719
					GRANT, Eddy	
04/16/83	CB	❶¹	24	▲	1 Electric Avenue .... BB 2⁵ / RR 2²	Portrait 03793

DEBUT	CH	PK	WK	Gold	A-side (Chart Hit) ... Other Charts	Label & Number
					GRANT, Gogi	
09/03/55	MV	7	20		1 Suddenly There's A Valley ... CB 8 / BB 9	Era 1003
04/28/56	BB	❶⁸	28	☉	2 The Wayward Wind ... MV ❶⁸ / CB ❶⁵	Era 1013
					GRASS ROOTS, The	
05/13/67	CB	5	13		1 Let's Live For Today ... RW 5 / BB 8	Dunhill 4084
08/17/68	RW	3¹	18	●	2 Midnight Confessions ... BB 5 / CB 5	Dunhill/ABC 4144
06/05/71	BB	9	12		3 Sooner Or Later ... RW 10	Dunhill/ABC 4279
10/09/71	CB	8	11		4 Two Divided By Love ...	Dunhill/ABC 4289
					GRATEFUL DEAD	
07/25/87	BB	9	16		1 Touch Of Grey ...	Arista 9606
					GRAY, Dobie	
02/17/73	RW	4	21	●	1 Drift Away ... BB 5 / CB 8	Decca 33057
03/29/03	BB	9	35		2 Drift Away ... RR 10	Lava
					UNCLE KRACKER with DOBIE GRAY	
					GRAY, Macy	
01/28/00	RR	❶⁴	27		1 I Try ... BB 5	Epic 79421
					GREAN, Charles Randolph, Sounde	
06/07/69	RW	6	12		1 Quentin's Theme ... CB 8	Ranwood 840
					GREAT BIG WORLD, A	
11/23/13	BB	4	26	△⁶	1 Say Something ...	Epic
					A GREAT BIG WORLD & CHRISTINA AGUILERA	
					GREAT WHITE	
05/13/89	BB	5	26	●	1 Once Bitten Twice Shy ... CB 5 / RR 8	Capitol 44366
					GREAVES, R.B.	
10/04/69	BB	2¹	16	●	1 Take A Letter Maria ... RW 3² / CB 3¹	Atco 6714
					GREEN, Al	
07/24/71	CB	6	19	●	1 Tired Of Being Alone ... BB ❶¹	Hi 2194
11/27/71	CB	❶²	17	●	2 Let's Stay Together ... BB ❶¹ / RW ❶²	Hi 2202
03/25/72	CB	3³	14		3 Look What You Done For Me ... RW 3¹ / BB 4	Hi 2211
07/01/72	CB	❶¹	14		4 I'm Still In Love With You ... RW ❶¹ / BB 3²	Hi 2216
10/21/72	RW	❶¹	15	●	5 You Ought To Be With Me ... CB 2¹ / BB 3²	Hi 2227
02/17/73	RW	8	12	●	6 Call Me (Come Back Home) ... CB 9 / BB 10	Hi 2235
06/30/73	BB	10	16	●	7 Here I Am (Come And Take Me) ... CB 10 / RW 10	Hi 2247
09/28/74	BB	7	19	●	8 Sha-La-La (Make Me Happy) ... CB 7 / RW 10	Hi 2274
02/22/75	CB	10	14		9 L-O-V-E (Love) ...	Hi 2282
11/05/88	CB	5	20		10 Put A Little Love In Your Heart ... RR 6 / BB 9	A&M 1255
					ANNIE LENNOX & AL GREEN	
					GREEN, Cee Lo	
09/11/10	BB	2⁴	48	△⁷	1 F**k You! ...	Elektra 526196
					GREENBAUM, Norman	
02/21/70	CB	❶²	17	●	1 Spirit In The Sky ... RW ❶² / BB 3³	Reprise 0885
					GREEN DAY	
12/10/94	RR	4	40	○	1 When I Come Around ... BB 6	Reprise 17941
11/27/04	RR	❶⁴	36	○	2 Boulevard Of Broken Dreams ... BB 2⁵	Reprise
08/06/05	RR	4	27	△	3 Wake Me Up When September Ends ... BB 6	Reprise
					GREENE, Lorne	
10/31/64	BB	❶¹	13		1 Ringo ... CB ❶¹ / RW 2¹	RCA Victor 8444
					GRIFFITH, Andy	
01/09/54	BB	9	7		1 What It Was, Was Football (Parts I & II) ...	Capitol 2693
					DEACON ANDY GRIFFITH	
					GROCE, Larry	
01/03/76	BB	9	16		1 Junk Food Junkie ...	Warner/Curb 8165
					GROOVE THEORY	
08/26/95	CB	3²	34	●	1 Tell Me ... BB 5	Epic 77961
					GROSS, Henry	
02/21/76	RW	4	30	●	1 Shannon ... RR 4 / CB 5 / BB 6	Lifesong 45002
					GUESS WHO, The	
04/05/69	RW	3²	14	●	1 These Eyes ... CB 4 / BB 6	RCA Victor 0102
07/05/69	RW	5	12	●	2 Laughing ... CB 8 / BB 10	RCA Victor 0195
12/13/69	RW	3¹	16		3 No Time ... CB 4 / BB 5	RCA Victor 0300
03/21/70	BB	❶³	15	●	4 American Woman ... CB ❶² / RW ❶¹	RCA Victor 0325
10/17/70	CB	5	12		5 Share The Land ... RW 9 / BB 10	RCA Victor 0388
07/13/74	BB	6	17		6 Clap For The Wolfman ... CB 10	RCA Victor 0324

DEBUT	CH	PK	WK	Gold	A-side (Chart Hit) .... Other Charts	Label & Number
					GUETTA, David	
08/15/09	BB	5	40	△³	1 Sexy Chick.. DAVID GUETTA with AKON	Astralwerks
09/17/11	BB	4	27	△²	2 Turn Me On.. DAVID GUETTA with NICKI MINAJ	Astralwerks
09/17/11	BB	4	30	△²	3 Without You... DAVID GUETTA with USHER	Astralwerks
05/05/12	BB	7	33	△²	4 Titanium... DAVID GUETTA with SIA	Astralwerks
04/11/15	BB	8	24	△³	5 Hey Mama.. DAVID GUETTA with NICKI MINAJ, BEBE REXHA & AFROJACK	What A Music
					GUIDRY, Greg	
02/13/82	RR	10	16		1 Goin' Down...	Columbia 02691
					GUITAR, Bonnie	
04/13/57	MV	2²	22		1 Dark Moon..CB 5 / BB 6	Dot 15550
					GUNNA — see LIL BABY	
					GUNS N' ROSES	
06/25/88	CB	❶³	24	●	1 Sweet Child O' Mine...BB ❶² / RR ❶²	Geffen 27963
10/21/88	BB	7	19	○	2 Welcome To The Jungle..................................CB 9 / RR 10	Geffen 27759
01/14/89	CB	4	18		3 Paradise City..RR 4 / BB 5	Geffen 27570
04/07/89	BB	4	18	●	4 Patience...CB 4 / RR 6	Geffen 22996
09/21/91	CB	7	27	●	5 Don't Cry...BB 10	Geffen 19027
06/20/92	CB	❶³	32	●	6 November Rain...RR 2¹ / BB 3²	Geffen 19067
					GYM CLASS HEROES	
01/19/07	RR	❶⁵	24	△	1 Cupid's Chokehold...BB 4 GYM CLASS HEROES Featuring Patrick Stump (of Fall Out Boy)	Decaydance
07/02/11	BB	4	37	△⁵	2 Stereo Hearts... GYM CLASS HEROES Featuring Adam Levine	Decaydance

H

					HADDAWAY	
09/03/93	RR	5	27	●	1 What Is Love...CB 9	Arista 12575
					HALEY, Bill, And His Comets	
08/07/54	CB	6	33	☉	1 Shake, Rattle And Roll.....................................MV 6 / BB 7	Decca 29204
05/14/55	BB	❶⁸	24	▲	2 Rock Around The Clock..................................CB ❶⁷ / MV ❶⁴	Decca 29124
10/24/55	BB	9	19		3 Burn That Candle...	Decca 29713
01/13/56	BB	6	19	☉	4 See You Later, Alligator...................................CB 6 / MV 6	Decca 29791
					HALL, Daryl	
08/01/86	RR	3¹	16		1 Dreamtime..BB 5 / CB 5	RCA 14387
					HALL, Daryl, & John Oates	
01/31/76	BB	4	31	●	1 Sara Smile...CB 6 / RR 7 / RW 10	RCA Victor 10530
07/17/76	CB	6	24		2 She's Gone..BB 7 / RR 8 / RW 10	Atlantic 3332
01/22/77	BB	❶²	25	●	3 Rich Girl...CB ❶² / RW ❶² / RR ❶²	RCA 10860
09/26/80	RR	4	21		4 You've Lost That Lovin' Feeling......................CB 10 / RW 10	RCA 12103
01/24/81	BB	❶³	25	●	5 Kiss On My List................................RR ❶² / CB ❶¹ / RW ❶¹	RCA 12142
05/02/81	RR	4	22		6 You Make My Dreams.....................BB 5 / CB 7 / RW 7	RCA 12217
08/28/81	BB	❶²	26	●	7 Private Eyes....................................RW ❶² / RR ❶² / CB ❶¹	RCA 12296
11/13/81	RR	❶⁸	24	●	8 I Can't Go For That (No Can Do).....CB ❶² / BB ❶¹ / RW ❶¹	RCA 12357
03/19/82	RR	3³	16		9 Did It In A Minute..BB 9 / CB 10	RCA 13065
10/15/82	RR	❶⁶	24	●	10 Maneater..CB ❶⁵ / BB ❶⁴	RCA 13354
01/28/83	RR	2¹	21		11 One On One..CB 5 / BB 7	RCA 13421
04/29/83	BB	6	17		12 Family Man..RR 7 / CB 10	RCA 13507
10/28/83	RR	2⁵	19		13 Say It Isn't So...BB 2⁴ / CB 3³	RCA 13654
02/17/84	RR	5	17		14 Adult Education..BB 8	RCA 13714
09/28/84	BB	❶²	23		15 Out Of Touch...RR ❶¹ / CB 3²	RCA 13916
12/14/84	RR	5	19		16 Method Of Modern Love...................................RR 5 / CB 8	RCA 13970
04/15/88	BB	3¹	17		17 Everything Your Heart Desires........................RR 3¹ / CB 5	Arista 9684
09/28/90	RR	9	19		18 So Close..	Arista 2085
					HALSEY	
08/20/16	BB	❶¹²	52	△¹¹	1 Closer... THE CHAINSMOKERS with HALSEY	Disruptor
09/23/17	BB	5	33	△⁴	2 Bad At Love...	Astralwerks
07/28/18	BB	9	52	△⁴	3 Eastside... BENNY BLANCO, HALSEY & KHALID	Interscope
10/20/18	BB	❶²	51	△⁶	4 Without Me..	Capitol

DEBUT	CH	PK	WK	Gold	A-side (Chart Hit)	Other Charts	Label & Number
					HAMILTON, George IV		
10/27/56	BB	6	20	⊙	1 A Rose And A Baby Ruth	CB 6 / MV 6	ABC-Paramount 9765
11/04/57	MV	6	19		2 Why Don't They Understand	CB 9 / BB 10	ABC-Paramount 9862
					HAMILTON, Roy		
04/23/55	BB	6	16		1 Unchained Melody		Epic 9102
					HAMILTON, Russ		
06/17/57	MV	3¹	23	⊙	1 Rainbow	BB 4 / CB 6	Kapp 184
					HAMILTON, JOE FRANK & REYNOLDS		
05/15/71	CB	❶¹	15	●	1 Don't Pull Your Love	RW 3³ / BB 4	Dunhill/ABC 4276
06/21/75	BB	❶¹	19	●	2 Fallin' In Love	CB ❶¹ / RW ❶¹ / RR ❶¹	Playboy 6024
					HAMLISCH, Marvin		
03/16/74	CB	❶¹	17	●	1 The Entertainer	BB 3² / RW 3² / RR 3²	MCA 40174
					HAMMER, Jan		
09/07/85	BB	❶¹	22		1 Miami Vice Theme	CB ❶¹ / RR 2²	MCA 52666
					HAMMOND, Albert		
10/14/72	CB	2¹	16	●	1 It Never Rains In Southern California	RW 3¹ / BB 5	Mums 6011
					HAMPTON, Lionel, And Orchestra		
02/04/50	BB	7	10		1 Rag Mop		Decca 24855
					HANSON		
03/28/97	RR	❶⁹	25	△²	1 MMMBop	BB ❶³	Mercury 574261
07/11/97	RR	6	13		2 Where's The Love		Mercury 574260
10/03/97	BB	9	20	●	3 I Will Come To You		Mercury 568132
					HAPPENINGS, The		
07/09/66	RW	❶¹	15		1 See You In September	BB 3² / CB 4	B.T. Puppy 520
10/01/66	RW	9	9		2 Go Away Little Girl		B.T. Puppy 522
04/08/67	CB	❶¹	14		3 I Got Rhythm	RW 2³ / BB 3³	B.T. Puppy 527
					HARMONICATS		
05/20/50	BB	8	12		1 Bewitched		Mercury 5399
					JAN AUGUST & Jerry Murad's HARMONICATS		
09/05/53	CB	10	16		2 The Story Of Three Loves		Mercury 70202
					JERRY MURAD Of The Harmonicats		
					HARRIS, Calvin		
11/03/12	BB	10	27	△²	1 Sweet Nothing		Ultra
					CALVIN HARRIS with FLORENCE WELCH		
04/05/14	BB	7	26	△³	2 Summer		deConstruction
05/21/16	BB	3³	32	△⁵	3 This Is What You Came For		Westbury Road
					CALVIN HARRIS with RIHANNA		
					HARRIS, Major		
03/29/75	CB	3²	21	●	1 Love Won't Let Me Wait	RW 3² / BB 5 / RR 8	Atlantic 3248
					HARRIS, Phil		
03/11/50	BB	8	6		1 Chattanoogie Shoe-Shine Boy		RCA Victor 3216
11/25/50	BB	❶⁵	16	⊙	2 The Thing	CB ❶¹	RCA Victor 3968
					HARRIS, Richard		
05/04/68	RW	2⁴	14		1 MacArthur Park	BB 2¹ / CB 2¹	Dunhill 4134
					HARRIS, Rolf		
06/08/63	BB	3¹	13		1 Tie Me Kangaroo Down, Sport	CB 4 / MV 4	Epic 9596
					HARRIS, Thurston		
10/12/57	BB	6	17		1 Little Bitty Pretty One	CB 9	Aladdin 3398
					HARRISON, George		
11/28/70	BB	❶⁴	15	●	1 My Sweet Lord	CB ❶⁴ / RW ❶³	Apple 2995
02/20/71	CB	7	11		2 What Is Life	BB 10 / RW 10	Apple 1828
05/12/73	CB	❶²	14		3 Give Me Love - (Give Me Peace On Earth)	BB ❶¹ / RW ❶¹	Apple 1862
02/24/79	RR	4	16		4 Blow Away		Dark Horse 8763
05/15/81	RR	❶²	16		5 All Those Years Ago	BB 2³ / RW 3⁵ / CB 3³	Dark Horse 49725
10/24/87	BB	❶¹	24		6 Got My Mind Set On You	CB ❶¹ / RR ❶¹	Dark Horse 28178
					HARRISON, Wilbert		
04/13/59	BB	❶²	16	⊙	1 Kansas City	MV ❶² / CB ❶¹	Fury 1023
					HART, Corey		
05/26/84	RR	6	24		1 Sunglasses At Night	BB 7 / CB 7	EMI America 8203
06/08/85	BB	3²	20		2 Never Surrender	RR 3² / CB 4	EMI America 8268
					HARTMAN, Dan		
05/05/84	BB	6	25		1 I Can Dream About You	CB 6 / RR 8	MCA 52378

67

DEBUT	CH	PK	WK	Gold	A-side (Chart Hit)...Other Charts	Label & Number
					HATHAWAY, Donny — see FLACK, Roberta	
					HAWKES, Chesney	
08/03/91	BB	10	28		1 The One And Only...	Chrysalis 23730
					HAWKINS, Edwin, Singers	
04/26/69	RW	2¹	10	●	1 Oh Happy Day...CB 3² / BB 4	Pavilion 20,001
					THE EDWIN HAWKINS' SINGERS Featuring Dorothy Combs Morrison	
04/18/70	CB	3¹	17		2 Lay Down (Candles In The Rain)..................................RW 4 / BB 6	Buddah 167
					MELANIE with THE EDWIN HAWKINS SINGERS	
					HAWKINS, Sophie B.	
04/17/92	RR	4	25		1 Damn I Wish I Was Your Lover.....................................BB 5 / CB 5	Columbia 74164
06/03/95	CB	4	44		2 As I Lay Me Down..RR 5 / BB 6	Columbia 77801
					HAYES, Bill	
02/14/55	CB	❶⁸	25	☉	1 The Ballad Of Davy Crockett................................BB ❶⁵ / MV ❶¹	Cadence 1256
					HAYES, Isaac	
10/16/71	BB	❶²	14	●	1 Theme From Shaft..CB ❶² / RW ❶²	Enterprise 9038
					HAYES, Richard	
12/10/49	BB	2¹	16		1 The Old Master Painter..CB 3³	Mercury 5342
09/09/50	CB	5	21		2 Our Lady Of Fatima...BB 10	Mercury 5466
03/03/51	BB	9	10		3 The Aba Daba Honeymoon...	Mercury 5586
					RICHARD HAYES & KITTY KALLEN (above 2)	
10/27/51	BB	9	10		4 Out In The Cold Again..	Mercury 5724
					HAYMAN, Richard	
04/11/53	CB	3³	25		1 Ruby...BB 3²	Mercury 70115
					HAYMES, Dick	
07/22/50	BB	10	11		1 Count Every Star...	Decca 27042
					DICK HAYMES and ARTIE SHAW	
					HEAD, Murray	
12/26/70	CB	8	25		1 Superstar..RW 10	Decca 32603
					MURRAY HEAD With The Trinidad Singers	
02/23/85	BB	3¹	22		2 One Night In Bangkok...CB 4 / RR 5	RCA 13988
					HEAD, Roy	
09/04/65	BB	2²	12		1 Treat Her Right...RW 2² / CB 3¹	Back Beat 546
					HEALEY, Jeff, Band	
06/03/89	BB	5	25		1 Angel Eyes..CB 6 / RR 9	Arista 9808
					HEART	
07/10/76	RR	4	24		1 Magic Man..RW 5 / CB 7 / BB 9	Mushroom 7011
05/28/77	RR	6	21		2 Barracuda...CB 10	Portrait 70004
11/14/80	RR	7	17		3 Tell It Like It Is..BB 8	Epic 50950
06/01/85	BB	10	21		4 What About Love?...	Capitol 5481
09/14/85	BB	4	24		5 Never..RR 4 / CB 6	Capitol 5512
01/17/86	RR	❶²	20		6 These Dreams..BB ❶¹ / CB ❶¹	Capitol 5541
04/19/86	RR	8	16		7 Nothin' At All...BB 10	Capitol 5572
05/15/87	BB	❶³	22		8 Alone..CB ❶² / RR ❶²	Capitol 44002
08/15/87	CB	6	22		9 Who Will You Run To..BB 7 / RR 7	Capitol 44040
03/30/90	CB	❶¹	21	●	10 All I Wanna Do Is Make Love To You..................BB 2² / RR 3²	Capitol 44507
					HEATWAVE	
07/09/77	RW	2⁵	27	▲	1 Boogie Nights...BB 2² / CB 2¹ / RR 3¹	Epic 50370
04/15/78	BB	7	21	▲	2 The Groove Line...RW 7 / CB 10	Epic 50524
					HEBB, Bobby	
06/11/66	CB	❶¹	18	●	1 Sunny..RW ❶¹ / BB 2²	Philips 40365
					HEIGHTS, The	
10/02/92	BB	❶²	22	●	1 How Do You Talk To An Angel.........................CB ❶² / RR ❶²	Capitol 44890
					HELMS, Bobby	
09/09/57	BB	7	23	☉	1 My Special Angel...MV 7 / CB 8	Decca 30423
12/09/57	BB	6	7	☉	2 Jingle Bell Rock...	Decca 30513
12/08/18	BB	8	5		3 Jingle Bell Rock..	Decca
12/07/19	BB	3¹	5		4 Jingle Bell Rock..	Decca
					HENDERSON, Joe	
05/07/62	MV	6	14		1 Snap Your Fingers..CB 7 / BB 8	Todd 1072
					HENLEY, Don	
10/24/81	RR	2⁵	21		1 Leather And Lace..BB 6 / CB 9 / RW 10	Modern 7341
					STEVIE NICKS with DON HENLEY	
10/30/82	BB	3³	20	●	2 Dirty Laundry..CB 5 / RR 5	Asylum 69894
11/10/84	BB	5	24		3 The Boys Of Summer..CB 6 / RR 6	Geffen 29141

DEBUT	CH	PK	WK	Gold	A-side (Chart Hit) ... Other Charts	Label & Number
					HENLEY, Don (cont'd)	
02/23/85	RR	6	20		4 All She Wants To Do Is Dance ... BB 9 / CB 9	Geffen 29065
06/23/89	CB	5	21		5 The End Of The Innocence ... BB 8 / RR 8	Geffen 22925
07/31/92	RR	❶³	34	●	6 Sometimes Love Just Ain't Enough ... BB 2⁶ / CB 2⁶	MCA 54403
					PATTY SMYTH with DON HENLEY	
					HENRY, Clarence	
02/06/61	MV	3¹	16		1 I Don't Know Why [But I Do] ... BB 4 / CB 4	Argo 5378
					HERMAN'S HERMITS	
10/10/64	CB	7	16		1 I'm Into Something Good	MGM 13280
01/30/65	CB	❶¹	15		2 Can't You Hear My Heartbeat ... BB 2² / RW 2¹	MGM 13310
04/03/65	RW	4	13		3 Silhouettes ... BB 5 / CB 5	MGM 13332
04/17/65	CB	❶⁴	12	●	4 Mrs. Brown You've Got A Lovely Daughter ... BB ❶³ / RW ❶³	MGM 13341
05/22/65	World	4	10		5 Wonderful World ... RW 4 / CB 5	MGM 13354
07/03/65	RW	❶³	10	●	6 I'm Henry VIII, I Am ... BB ❶¹ / CB ❶¹	MGM 13367
09/18/65	RW	6	11		7 Just A Little Bit Better ... BB 7 / CB 8	MGM 13398
12/18/65	CB	6	9		8 A Must To Avoid ... RW 6 / BB 8	MGM 13437
02/12/66	BB	3¹	10		9 Listen People ... CB 3¹ / RW 3¹	MGM 13462
04/02/66	RW	7	9		10 Leaning On The Lamp Post ... CB 8 / BB 9	MGM 13500
07/09/66	RW	8	9		11 This Door Swings Both Ways ... CB 10	MGM 13548
10/01/66	BB	5	11		12 Dandy ... RW 6 / CB 8	MGM 13603
02/11/67	CB	3²	12	●	13 There's A Kind Of Hush ... RW 3¹ / BB 4	MGM 13681
					HEYWOOD, Eddie	
06/23/56	MV	❶¹	31	☉	1 Canadian Sunset ... BB 2² / CB 2¹	RCA Victor 6537
					HUGO WINTERHALTER WITH EDDIE HEYWOOD	
06/30/56	MV	7	25		2 Soft Summer Breeze	Mercury 70863
					HIBBLER, Al	
03/21/55	MV	2²	19	☉	1 Unchained Melody ... BB 3¹	Decca 29441
08/29/55	BB	4	29		2 He ... CB 4 / MV 4	Decca 29660
08/03/56	BB	10	20		3 After The Lights Go Down Low	Decca 29982
					HICKS, Taylor	
07/01/06	BB	❶¹	8		1 Do I Make You Proud	J Records 85833
					HI-FIVE	
02/23/91	BB	❶¹	24	●	1 I Like The Way (The Kissing Game) ... RR 2¹ / CB 8	Jive 1424
06/22/91	BB	8	21		2 I Can't Wait Another Minute ... RR 9	Jive 1445
07/31/92	RR	4	22		3 She's Playing Hard To Get ... BB 5 / CB 5	Jive 42067
					HIGGINS, Bertie	
11/07/81	CB	7	32	●	1 Key Largo ... BB 8 / RR 8 / RW 9	Kat Family 02524
					HIGH SCHOOL MUSICAL CAST	
02/04/06	BB	4	11	○	1 Breaking Free	Walt Disney
08/04/07	BB	6	8		2 What Time Is It	Walt Disney 000507
					HIGHWAYMEN, The	
06/24/61	CB	❶⁴	20	☉	1 Michael ... MV ❶⁴ / BB ❶²	United Artists 258
11/27/61	MV	10	18		2 Cotton Fields	United Artists 370
					HILL, Dan	
11/26/77	RR	2²	25	●	1 Sometimes When We Touch ... BB 3² / RW 3² / CB 4	20th Century 2355
06/06/87	BB	6	24		2 Can't We Try ... CB 6 / RR 8	Columbia 07050
					DAN HILL with VONDA SHEPPARD	
					HILL, Faith	
05/17/97	BB	7	20	▲	1 It's Your Love	Curb 73019
					TIM McGRAW with FAITH HILL	
03/21/98	BB	7	48	▲	2 This Kiss	Warner 17247
11/06/99	BB	2⁵	53	●	3 Breathe ... RR 8	Warner 16884
03/11/00	BB	6	56		4 The Way You Love Me	Warner 16818
05/26/01	BB	10	20		5 There You'll Be	Warner 16739
					HILL, Lauryn	
10/30/98	BB	❶²	24	●	1 Doo Wop (That Thing)	Ruffhouse 78868
					HILLSIDE SINGERS, The	
11/27/71	RW	10	12		1 I'd Like To Teach The World To Sing (In Perfect Harmony)	Metromedia 231
					HILLTOPPERS, The	
08/16/52	CB	5	23		1 Trying ... BB 7	Dot 15018
05/30/53	BB	4	24	☉	2 P.S. I Love You / ... CB 5	Dot 15085
06/06/53	BB	8	18		3 I'd Rather Die Young (Than Grow Old Without You)	
10/24/53	BB	8	15		4 Love Walked In /	Dot 15105
10/17/53	BB	8	19		5 To Be Alone	
01/16/54	CB	7	16		6 Till Then ... BB 10	Dot 15132
02/06/54	CB	3¹	17		7 From The Vine Came The Grape ... BB 8	Dot 15127

DEBUT	CH	PK	WK	Gold	A-side (Chart Hit) .... Other Charts	Label & Number
					HILLTOPPERS, The (cont'd)	
11/12/55	BB	8	19		8 Only You (And You Alone)	Dot 15423
01/26/57	MV	❶²	16		9 Marianne .... CB 2² / BB 3¹	Dot 15537
					HILSON, Keri	
04/11/09	BB	3³	31	△²	1 Knock You Down	Mosley
					KERI HILSON Featuring Kanye West & Ne-Yo	
					HINDER	
07/29/06	RR	❶³	33	△⁴	1 Lips Of An Angel .... BB 3⁴	Universal Republic
					HINTON, Joe	
08/08/64	RW	10	15		1 Funny (How Time Slips Away)	Back Beat 541
					HIRT, Al	
01/04/64	BB	4	17		1 Java .... CB 4 / MV 4	RCA Victor 8280
					HODGES, Eddie	
05/27/61	MV	9	19		1 I'm Gonna Knock On Your Door	Cadence 1397
					HOLDEN, Ron	
03/28/60	CB	5	19		1 Love You So .... BB 7	Donna 1315
					RON HOLDEN with The Thunderbirds	
					HOLIDAY, J.	
08/04/07	BB	5	23	○	1 Bed	Music Line 61202
					HOLLIES, The	
07/23/66	RW	3¹	14		1 Bus Stop .... BB 5 / CB 5	Imperial 66186
10/22/66	RW	5	11		2 Stop Stop Stop .... BB 7 / CB 8	Imperial 66214
03/11/67	CB	7	14		3 On A Carousel .... RW 10	Imperial 66231
06/17/67	BB	9	13		4 Carrie-Anne .... CB 10 / RW 10	Epic 10180
12/20/69	BB	7	18		5 He Ain't Heavy, He's My Brother .... CB 8 / RW 8	Epic 10532
06/17/72	CB	❶¹	16	▲	6 Long Cool Woman (In A Black Dress) .... RW ❶¹ / BB 2²	Epic 10871
04/20/74	RW	5	21	●	7 The Air That I Breathe .... RR 5 / BB 6 / CB 7	Epic 11100
					HOLLY, Buddy [THE CRICKETS]	
07/27/57	BB	❶¹	22	●	1 That'll Be The Day .... CB 3⁴ / MV 3²	Brunswick 55009
10/21/57	CB	2¹	22	⊙	2 Peggy Sue .... BB 3³ / MV 3²	Coral 61885
11/16/57	MV	7	20		3 Oh, Boy! .... BB 10	Brunswick 55035
02/17/58	MV	9	14		4 Maybe Baby	Brunswick 55053
					THE CRICKETS (#1, 3 & 4)	
					HOLLYWOOD ARGYLES	
05/23/60	BB	❶¹	16	⊙	1 Alley-Oop .... CB ❶¹ / MV ❶¹	Lute 5905
					HOLMAN, Eddie	
12/20/69	CB	2³	16	●	1 Hey There Lonely Girl .... RW 2² / BB 2¹	ABC 11240
					HOLMES, Clint	
02/17/73	RW	2³	23	●	1 Playground In My Mind .... BB 2² / CB 2¹	Epic 10891
					HOLMES, Leroy, And His Orchestra	
10/04/54	BB	9	14	⊙	1 The High And The Mighty	MGM 11761
					HOLMES, Rupert	
10/20/79	RR	❶⁵	21	●	1 Escape (The Pina Colada Song) .... RW ❶⁴ / BB ❶³ / CB ❶³	Infinity 50,035
01/19/80	RR	2¹	17		2 Him .... BB 6 / CB 6 / RW 7	MCA 41173
					HOMBRES, The	
09/09/67	RW	6	14		1 Let It Out (Let It All Hang Out) .... CB 7	Verve Forecast 5058
					HONDELLS, The	
09/12/64	RW	7	13		1 Little Honda .... BB 9 / CB 10	Mercury 72324
					HONEYCOMBS, The	
09/12/64	CB	4	15		1 Have I The Right? .... RW 4 / BB 5	Interphon 7707
					HONEY CONE, The	
04/10/71	CB	❶²	16	●	1 Want Ads .... RW ❶² / BB ❶¹	Hot Wax 7011
07/31/71	CB	7	14	●	2 Stick-Up .... RW 10	Hot Wax 7106
					HONEYDRIPPERS, The	
10/13/84	BB	3¹	22		1 Sea Of Love .... CB 3¹ / RR 4	Es Paranza 99701
					HOOBASTANK	
03/05/04	RR	❶⁸	38	○	1 The Reason .... BB 2¹	Island 0002875
					HOOTIE & THE BLOWFISH	
10/07/94	RR	2¹	45		1 Hold My Hand .... CB 5 / BB 10	Atlantic 87230
03/11/95	RR	❶¹	35		2 Let Her Cry .... CB 4 / BB 9	Atlantic 87231
07/14/95	RR	❶³	37		3 Only Wanna Be With You .... CB 5 / BB 6	Atlantic 87132
10/27/95	RR	4	28		4 Time	Atlantic 87095

DEBUT	CH	PK	WK	Gold	A-side (Chart Hit) ... Other Charts	Label & Number
					HOOTIE & THE BLOWFISH (cont'd)	
04/12/96	CB	4	22		5 Old Man & Me (When I Get To Heaven) .... RR 5	Atlantic 87074
07/05/96	RR	9	20		6 Tucker's Town	Atlantic 87051
					HOPKIN, Mary	
09/21/68	RW	❶⁴	16	●	1 Those Were The Days .... CB ❶² / BB 2³	Apple 1801
					HORNSBY, Bruce, And The Range	
09/20/86	RR	❶²	25		1 The Way It Is .... BB ❶¹ / CB ❶¹	RCA 5023
01/16/87	BB	4	19		2 Mandolin Rain .... CB 4 / RR 4	RCA 5087
04/29/88	BB	5	17		3 The Valley Road .... CB 5 / RR 6	RCA 7645
					HORTON, Johnny	
04/25/59	CB	❶⁹	21	●	1 The Battle Of New Orleans .... BB ❶⁶ / MV ❶⁶	Columbia 41339
02/15/60	BB	3¹	19		2 Sink The Bismarck .... MV 3¹ / CB 5	Columbia 41568
09/12/60	BB	4	23		3 North To Alaska .... MV 5 / CB 6	Columbia 41782
					HOT	
02/12/77	BB	6	30	●	1 Angel In Your Arms .... CB 6	Big Tree 16085
					HOT BUTTER	
06/17/72	RW	7	21		1 Popcorn .... BB 9	Musicor 1458
					HOT CHELLE RAE	
04/30/11	BB	7	30	△	1 Tonight Tonight	RCA
					HOT CHOCOLATE	
01/25/75	RW	4	18		1 Emma .... CB 6 / RR 6 / BB 8	Big Tree 16031
10/18/75	CB	2¹	26	●	2 You Sexy Thing .... BB 3³ / RW 6 / RR 7	Big Tree 16047
11/11/78	BB	6	19	●	3 Every 1's A Winner .... CB 7 / RW 7 / RR 7	Infinity 50,002
					HOUSE OF PAIN	
06/27/92	BB	3²	30	▲	1 Jump Around .... CB 3²	Tommy Boy 7526
					HOUSTON	
06/19/04	RR	9	20	○	1 I Like That	Capitol 49788
					HOUSTON Featuring Chingy, Nate Dogg & I-20	
					HOUSTON, Thelma	
12/18/76	BB	❶¹	25		1 Don't Leave Me This Way .... CB 3² / RW 4 / RR 7	Tamla 54278
					HOUSTON, Whitney	
05/11/85	CB	3²	22	●	1 You Give Good Love .... BB 3¹ / RR 4	Arista 9274
08/17/85	BB	❶¹	23	●	2 Saving All My Love For You .... RR 3¹ / CB 5	Arista 9381
12/07/85	BB	❶²	26	●	3 How Will I Know .... RR ❶² / CB ❶¹	Arista 9434
03/28/86	BB	❶³	19	●	4 Greatest Love Of All .... CB ❶² / RR ❶²	Arista 9466
05/08/87	RR	❶³	21	▲	5 I Wanna Dance With Somebody (Who Loves Me)... BB ❶² / CB ❶²	Arista 9598
07/31/87	BB	❶²	26		6 Didn't We Almost Have It All .... CB ❶¹ / RR ❶¹	Arista 9616
10/30/87	BB	❶¹	22	●	7 So Emotional .... RR ❶¹ / CB 4	Arista 9642
02/26/88	BB	❶²	21		8 Where Do Broken Hearts Go .... CB ❶¹ / RR ❶¹	Arista 9674
07/01/88	BB	7	16		9 Love Will Save The Day .... BB 9	Arista 9720
09/08/88	BB	5	19	○	10 One Moment In Time .... CB 6 / RR 7	Arista 9743
10/12/90	CB	❶²	23	●	11 I'm Your Baby Tonight .... BB ❶¹ / RR ❶¹	Arista 2108
12/21/90	BB	❶²	24	●	12 All The Man That I Need .... CB ❶² / RR ❶²	Arista 2156
04/12/91	BB	9	22		13 Miracle	Arista 2222
11/13/92	BB	❶¹⁴	30	▲⁴	14 I Will Always Love You .... CB ❶¹³ / RR ❶⁹	Arista 12490
01/09/93	CB	❶¹	26	●	15 I'm Every Woman .... RR ❶¹ / BB 4	Arista 12519
02/13/93	RR	❶⁴	29		16 I Have Nothing .... CB ❶³ / BB 4	Arista 12527
11/03/95	BB	❶¹	24	▲	17 Exhale (Shoop Shoop) .... CB 2⁹ / RR 6	Arista 12885
03/23/96	BB	8	21	●	18 Count On Me .... CB 8	Arista 12976
					WHITNEY HOUSTON & CECE WINANS	
12/28/96	BB	4	20	▲	19 I Believe In You And Me	Arista 13293
12/26/98	BB	2³	28	▲	20 Heartbreak Hotel .... RR 8	Arista 13619
					WHITNEY HOUSTON (Feat. Faith Evans & Kelly Price)	
05/08/99	BB	4	20	●	21 It's Not Right But It's Okay	Arista 13681
09/04/99	BB	4	28	▲	22 My Love Is Your Love .... RR 10	Arista 13730
09/29/01	BB	6	16	▲	23 The Star Spangled Banner	Arista 15054
02/25/12	BB	3¹	3		24 I Will Always Love You	Arista
					HOWARD, Adina	
02/04/95	BB	2²	33	▲	1 Freak Like Me .... CB 3¹	EastWest 64484
					HOWARD, Don	
12/06/52	CB	3¹	20		1 Oh Happy Day .... BB 4	Essex 311
					HOWARD, Eddy, and His Orchestra	
11/04/50	BB	9	18		1 To Think You've Chosen Me .... CB 9	Mercury 5517
09/22/51	CB	❶⁹	29	◉	2 Sin .... BB ❶⁸	Mercury 5711
03/29/52	CB	6	23		3 Be Anything (But Be Mine) .... BB 7	Mercury 5815
06/28/52	BB	4	16		4 Auf Wiederseh'n, Sweetheart	Mercury 5871

DEBUT	CH	PK	WK	Gold	A-side (Chart Hit) .... Other Charts	Label & Number
					HOZIER	
08/30/14	BB	2³	41	△⁶	1 Take Me To Church	Rubyworks
					H-TOWN	
04/10/93	BB	3⁷	26	▲	1 Knockin' Da Boots .... CB 4	Luke 161
					HUES CORPORATION, The	
05/18/74	RR	●⁴	20	●	1 Rock The Boat .... BB ●¹ / CB ●¹ / RW ●¹	RCA Victor 0232
					HUEY	
03/10/07	BB	6	23	△	1 Pop, Lock And Drop It	Jive 00352
					HUMAN BEINZ, The	
11/04/67	CB	5	19		1 Nobody But Me .... RW 5 / BB 8	Capitol 5990
					HUMAN LEAGUE, The	
03/06/82	CB	●⁴	30	●	1 Don't You Want Me .... BB ●³ / RR 3³	A&M/Virgin 2397
05/21/83	CB	7	22		2 (Keep Feeling) Fascination .... BB 8 / RR 8	A&M/Virgin 2547
09/13/86	BB	●¹	21		3 Human .... CB ●¹ / RR 2³	A&M/Virgin 2861
03/17/95	CB	8	12		4 Tell Me When .... RR 8	EastWest 64443
					HUMPERDINCK, Engelbert	
04/08/67	RW	3²	15		1 Release Me (And Let Me Love Again) .... CB 3¹ / BB 4	Parrot 40011
10/16/76	CB	5	24	●	2 After The Lovin' .... BB 8 / RR 8 / RW 10	Epic/MAM 50270
					HUNT, Pee Wee, and His Orchestra	
07/04/53	BB	3¹¹	29	⊙	1 Oh! .... CB 5	Capitol 2442
					HUNT, Sam	
02/18/17	BB	6	41	△⁶	1 Body Like A Back Road	MCA Nashville
					HUNTER, Ivory Joe	
11/17/56	MV	7	22	⊙	1 Since I Met You Baby	Atlantic 1111
					HUNTER, Tab	
01/12/57	MV	●⁷	21	⊙	1 Young Love .... BB ●⁶ / CB ●⁶	Dot 15533
					HURRICANE CHRIS	
06/23/07	BB	7	20	△	1 A Bay Bay	Polo Grounds 11542
					HUSKY, Ferlin	
09/05/53	BB	4	10		1 A Dear John Letter	Capitol 2502
					JEAN SHEPARD with FERLIN HUSKY	
02/23/57	BB	4	27	⊙	2 Gone .... MV 4 / CB 6	Capitol 3628
11/28/60	MV	9	18		3 Wings Of A Dove	Capitol 4406
					HUTTON, Betty — see COMO, Perry	
					HYLAND, Brian	
06/27/60	MV	●²	16	⊙	1 Itsy Bitsy Teenie Weenie Yellow Polkadot Bikini .. BB ●¹ / CB ●¹	Leader 805
06/09/62	BB	3²	15		2 Sealed With A Kiss .... CB 3¹ / MV 3¹	ABC-Paramount 10336
08/29/70	BB	3²	21	●	3 Gypsy Woman .... RW 3² / CB 3¹	Uni 55420
					HYMAN, Dick	
01/06/56	MV	5	20	⊙	1 Moritat (A Theme from "The Three Penny Opera") .... BB 8 / CB 9	MGM 12149

I

					IAN, Janis	
06/14/75	CB	●¹	20		1 At Seventeen .... BB 3² / RW 4 / RR 4	Columbia 10154
					ICEHOUSE	
02/13/88	BB	7	23		1 Electric Blue .... CB 10 / RR 10	Chrysalis 43201
					ICONA POP	
02/16/13	BB	7	29	△⁴	1 I Love It	Record Company Ten
					ICONA POP Featuring Charli XCX	
					IDES OF MARCH, The	
03/21/70	BB	2¹	13		1 Vehicle .... RW 3³ / CB 6	Warner 7378
					IDOL, Billy	
05/05/84	RR	3³	22		1 Eyes Without A Face .... BB 4 / CB 4	Chrysalis 42786
10/04/86	RR	5	18		2 To Be A Lover .... BB 6 / CB 9	Chrysalis 43024
09/05/87	BB	●¹	22		3 Mony Mony "Live" .... CB ●¹ / RR ●¹	Chrysalis 43161
05/05/90	BB	2¹	24	●	4 Cradle Of Love .... CB 2¹ / RR 5	Chrysalis 23509
					IFIELD, Frank	
09/01/62	BB	5	12		1 I Remember You .... MV 7 / CB 9	Vee-Jay 457

DEBUT	CH	PK	WK	Gold	A-side (Chart Hit) ... Other Charts	Label & Number
					IGLESIAS, Enrique	
07/02/99	BB	❶²	20		1 Bailamos .... RR 5	Overbrook 97122
03/10/00	BB	❶³	20		2 Be With You .... RR 5	Interscope 490366
09/14/01	RR	2²	34		3 Hero .... BB 3³	Interscope
02/08/02	RR	7	20		4 Escape	Interscope
05/29/10	BB	4	38	△³	5 I Like It	Universal Republic
					ENRIQUE IGLESIAS Featuring Pitbull	
12/11/10	BB	4	25	△²	6 Tonight (I'm Lovin' You)	Universal Republic
					ENRIQUE IGLESIAS Featuring Ludacris & DJ Frank E	
					IGLESIAS, Julio	
03/03/84	CB	3²	22	▲	1 To All The Girls I've Loved Before .... BB 5	Columbia 04217
					JULIO IGLESIAS & WILLIE NELSON	
					IMAGINE DRAGONS	
08/18/12	BB	3⁴	87	△¹⁰	1 Radioactive	Interscope
01/26/13	BB	6	61	△⁵	2 Demons	Interscope
02/25/17	BB	4	52	△⁵	3 Believer	KIDinaKORNER
05/20/17	BB	4	52	△⁵	4 Thunder	KIDinaKORNER
					IMBRUGLIA, Natalie	
02/13/98	BB	❶¹¹	44		1 Torn .... RR ❶¹¹	RCA
					IMMATURE	
07/30/94	BB	5	26	●	1 Never Lie .... CB 9	MCA 54850
					IMPALAS, The	
03/07/59	BB	2²	18	☉	1 Sorry (I Ran All The Way Home) .... CB 2¹ / MV 3²	Cub 9022
					IMPRESSIONS, The	
09/28/63	BB	4	15		1 It's All Right .... CB 4 / MV 5	ABC-Paramount 10487
06/06/64	BB	10	13		2 Keep On Pushing .... CB 10	ABC-Paramount 10554
11/21/64	RW	6	12		3 Amen .... BB 7 / CB 8	ABC-Paramount 10602
12/23/67	RW	7	15		4 We're A Winner	ABC 11022
					INC., The	
06/22/02	BB	6	20		1 Down 4 U	Murder Inc.
					IRV GOTTI PRESENTS THE INC. Featuring Ja Rule, Ashanti, Charli Baltimore & Vita	
					INCUBUS	
02/17/01	RR	8	39		1 Drive .... BB 9	Immortal/Epic 79627
					INFORMATION SOCIETY	
07/16/88	BB	3¹	25	●	1 What's On Your Mind (Pure Energy) .... CB 3¹ / RR 4	Tommy Boy 27826
11/26/88	RR	6	22		2 Walking Away .... BB 9 / CB 10	Tommy Boy 27736
					INGMANN, Jorgen, & His Guitar	
01/21/61	BB	2²	19	☉	1 Apache .... CB 4 / MV 4	Atco 6184
					INGRAM, James	
08/15/81	RR	10	24		1 Just Once	A&M 2357
					QUINCY JONES with JAMES INGRAM	
04/24/82	BB	❶²	37	●	2 Baby, Come To Me .... CB 2³ / RR 4	Qwest 50036
					PATTI AUSTIN with JAMES INGRAM	
12/20/86	BB	2¹	23	●	3 Somewhere Out There .... CB 4 / RR 9	MCA 52973
					LINDA RONSTADT AND JAMES INGRAM	
08/04/90	BB	❶¹	26		4 I Don't Have The Heart .... CB ❶¹ / RR ❶¹	Warner 19911
					INGRAM, Luther	
05/20/72	BB	3²	18		1 (If Loving You Is Wrong) I Don't Want To Be Right ... CB 3² / RW 3¹	KoKo 2111
					INNER CIRCLE	
05/01/93	RR	5	25	●	1 Bad Boys .... BB 8 / CB 8	Big Beat 98426
08/07/93	RR	8	33		2 Sweat (A La La La La Long)	Big Beat 98429
					INOJ	
07/24/98	BB	6	16	●	1 Time After Time	So So Def 79016
					INTRUDERS, The	
03/23/68	CB	5	14	●	1 Cowboys To Girls .... BB 6 / RW 6	Gamble 214
					INXS	
01/18/86	RR	3²	23		1 What You Need .... CB 4 / BB 5	Atlantic 89460
10/24/87	BB	❶¹	27		2 Need You Tonight .... CB ❶¹ / RR ❶¹	Atlantic 89188
02/13/88	BB	2²	20		3 Devil Inside .... CB 2¹ / RR 3³	Atlantic 89144
05/14/88	RR	2¹	20		4 New Sensation .... BB 3¹ / CB 3¹	Atlantic 89080
08/13/88	RR	6	23		5 Never Tear Us Apart .... BB 7 / CB 8	Atlantic 89038
09/07/90	CB	5	14	●	6 Suicide Blonde .... BB 9 / RR 10	Atlantic 87860
11/24/90	CB	7	24		7 Disappear .... BB 8 / RR 8	Atlantic 87784
					IRISH ROVERS, The	
03/16/68	RW	4	14		1 The Unicorn .... CB 6 / BB 7	Decca 32254

DEBUT	CH	PK	WK	Gold	A-side (Chart Hit) ... Other Charts	Label & Number
					ISAAK, Chris	
12/01/90	BB	6	24	●	1 Wicked Game	Reprise 19704
					ISLEY BROTHERS, The	
06/02/62	CB	7	21		1 Twist And Shout	Wand 124
03/15/69	RW	2²	14	●	2 It's Your Thing .... BB 2¹ / CB 2¹	T-Neck 901
06/19/71	CB	10	12		3 Love The One You're With	T-Neck 930
07/14/73	RR	4	21	●	4 That Lady (Part 1) .... BB 6 / CB 6 / RW 6	T-Neck 2251
06/14/75	BB	4	18	●	5 Fight The Power (Part 1) .... RW 5 / CB 6	T-Neck 2256
					IVES, Burl	
05/12/51	BB	10	9		1 On Top Of Old Smoky	Columbia 39328
					PERCY FAITH and his Orchestra and Chorus with BURL IVES	
12/16/61	CB	7	15		2 A Little Bitty Tear .... MV 7 / BB 9	Decca 31330
03/26/62	MV	9	13		3 Funny Way Of Laughin' .... BB 10	Decca 31371
12/08/18	BB	10	5		4 A Holly Jolly Christmas	Decca
12/07/19	BB	4	5		4 A Holly Jolly Christmas	Decca
					IVY THREE, The	
08/01/60	BB	8	13		1 Yogi .... CB 10 / MV 10	Shell 720
					IYAZ	
09/05/09	BB	2¹	34	△³	1 Replay	Beluga Heights

J

					JACKS, Terry	
01/05/74	RR	❶⁶	22	●	1 Seasons In The Sun .... BB ❶³ / RW ❶³ / CB ❶²	Bell 45,432
					JACKSON, Janet	
02/22/86	BB	4	21	●	1 What Have You Done For Me Lately .... CB 5 / RR 8	A&M 2812
05/17/86	BB	3¹	19	●	2 Nasty .... CB 3¹ / RR 5	A&M 2830
08/09/86	BB	❶²	20	●	3 When I Think Of You .... CB ❶² / RR ❶¹	A&M 2855
11/01/86	BB	5	21	●	4 Control .... CB 5 / RR 5	A&M 2877
01/17/87	BB	2¹	19		5 Let's Wait Awhile .... CB 3² / RR 3²	A&M 2906
08/25/89	BB	❶⁴	22	▲	6 Miss You Much .... CB ❶³ / RR ❶³	A&M 1445
11/10/89	BB	2²	18	●	7 Rhythm Nation .... RR 2² / CB 3³	A&M 1455
01/12/90	RR	❶⁴	19	●	8 Escapade .... BB ❶³ / CB ❶³	A&M 1490
04/06/90	RR	2³	20		9 Alright .... BB 4 / CB 4	A&M 1479
06/29/90	CB	❶¹	18		10 Come Back To Me .... RR ❶¹ / BB 2²	A&M 1475
08/31/90	BB	❶¹	16	●	11 Black Cat .... RR ❶¹ / CB 2²	A&M 1477
11/17/90	RR	❶³	22	●	12 Love Will Never Do (Without You) .... BB ❶¹ / CB ❶¹	A&M 1538
02/08/91	RR	4	13		13 State Of The World .... BB 5 / CB 8	A&M 8694
05/22/92	RR	2²	22		14 The Best Things In Life Are Free .... CB 9 / BB 10	Perspective 0010
					LUTHER VANDROSS and JANET JACKSON with BBD and Ralph Tresvant	
04/23/93	BB	❶⁸	27	▲	15 That's The Way Love Goes .... CB ❶⁸ / RR ❶⁶	Virgin 12650
07/23/93	RR	2⁶	35	●	16 If .... CB 2¹ / BB 4	Virgin 12676
10/01/93	CB	❶⁵	29	▲	17 Again .... RR ❶⁵ / BB 2¹	Virgin 38404
01/14/94	RR	2³	20		18 Because Of Love .... BB 10	Virgin 38422
05/20/94	CB	❶³	24	●	19 Any Time, Any Place .... BB 2¹ / RR 8	Virgin 38435
10/14/94	CB	6	25	●	20 You Want This .... BB 8 / RR 10	Virgin 38455
06/02/95	CB	3¹	20	▲	21 Scream .... BB 5	Epic 78000
					MICHAEL JACKSON & JANET JACKSON	
08/25/95	CB	2¹¹	28	●	22 Runaway .... RR 2⁶ / BB 3⁵	A&M 1194
10/31/97	BB	❶²	46	●	23 Together Again .... RR 5	Virgin 38623
04/17/98	BB	3¹	20	●	24 I Get Lonely	Virgin 38631
					JANET (Featuring BLACKstreet)	
06/16/00	BB	❶³	24	●	25 Doesn't Really Matter .... RR 3¹	Def Jam 562846
03/09/01	BB	❶⁷	22		26 All For You .... RR ❶³	Virgin 97522
06/15/01	BB	3²	20		27 Someone To Call My Lover .... RR 3²	Virgin 38799
					JACKSON, Jermaine	
12/09/72	RW	6	18		1 Daddy's Home .... CB 7 / BB 9	Motown 1216
03/22/80	BB	9	25		2 Let's Get Serious .... CB 9	Motown 1469
05/04/84	RR	6	9		3 Tell Me I'm Not Dreamin' (Too Good To Be True)	Arista
					JERMAINE JACKSON & MICHAEL JACKSON	
					JACKSON, Joe	
08/21/82	RR	2¹	27		1 Steppin' Out .... CB 5 / BB 6	A&M 2428
01/15/83	RR	8	16		2 Breaking Us In Two	A&M 2510
					JACKSON, Michael	
10/30/71	CB	❶¹	14		1 Got To Be There .... BB 4 / RW 4	Motown 1191
03/04/72	CB	❶¹	14		2 Rockin' Robin .... BB 2² / RW 2²	Motown 1197
05/20/72	CB	7	13		3 I Wanna Be Where You Are .... RW 10	Motown 1202
08/05/72	BB	❶¹	16		4 Ben .... CB 2¹ / RW 2¹	Motown 1207

DEBUT	CH	PK	WK	Gold	A-side (Chart Hit)	Other Charts	Label & Number
					JACKSON, Michael (cont'd)		
07/28/79	BB	❶¹	22	▲ 5	Don't Stop 'Til You Get Enough	CB ❶¹ / RW ❶¹ / RR 5	Epic 50742
11/03/79	BB	❶⁴	27	▲ 6	Rock With You	CB ❶³ / RW ❶² / RR 2¹	Epic 50797
02/16/80	RR	9	17	● 7	Off The Wall	BB 10 / RW 10	Epic 50838
04/12/80	RW	7	21	● 8	She's Out Of My Life	BB 10 / RW 10	Epic 50871
11/05/82	BB	2³	18	● 9	The Girl Is Mine	CB 3⁵ / RR 4	Epic 03288
					MICHAEL JACKSON/PAUL McCARTNEY		
01/22/83	BB	❶⁷	27	▲ 10	Billie Jean	CB ❶⁶ / RR ❶²	Epic 03509
02/26/83	BB	❶³	26	▲ 11	Beat It	CB ❶² / RR ❶³	Epic 03759
05/27/83	RR	2¹	17	△ 12	Wanna Be Startin' Somethin'	BB 5 / CB 6	Epic 03914
07/22/83	RR	2¹	16	△ 13	Human Nature	BB 7 / CB 10	Epic 04026
10/07/83	RR	❶⁷	27	▲ 14	Say Say Say	BB ❶⁶ / CB ❶³	Columbia 04168
					PAUL McCARTNEY AND MICHAEL JACKSON		
10/08/83	BB	10	17	△² 15	P.Y.T. (Pretty Young Thing)	RR 10	Epic 04165
01/13/84	RR	❶¹	18	▲ 16	Thriller	BB 4 / CB 4	Epic 04364
05/04/84	RR	6	9	17	Tell Me I'm Not Dreamin' (Too Good To Be True)		Arista
					JERMAINE JACKSON & MICHAEL JACKSON		
07/31/87	CB	❶²	18	● 18	I Just Can't Stop Loving You	RR ❶² / BB ❶¹	Epic 07253
09/11/87	BB	❶²	20	△ 19	Bad	CB ❶² / RR ❶²	Epic 07418
11/13/87	BB	❶¹	21	△² 20	The Way You Make Me Feel	CB ❶¹ / RR ❶¹	Epic 07645
02/05/88	CB	❶³	20	△³ 21	Man In The Mirror	RR ❶³ / BB ❶¹	Epic 07668
05/06/88	BB	❶¹	18	△ 22	Dirty Diana	CB ❶¹ / RR ❶¹	Epic 07739
07/22/88	RR	10	14	23	Another Part Of Me		Epic 07962
11/12/88	BB	7	18	△² 24	Smooth Criminal	CB 7 / RR 8	Epic 08044
11/15/91	BB	❶⁷	22	▲ 25	Black Or White	CB ❶⁴ / RR ❶⁴	Epic 74100
01/17/92	RR	❶³	22	● 26	Remember The Time	CB ❶¹ / BB 3⁴	Epic 74200
04/24/92	RR	2¹	20	● 27	In The Closet	BB 6 / CB 6	Epic 74266
07/10/92	RR	9	14	28	Jam		Epic 74333
03/26/93	RR	4	18	29	Who Is It	CB 5	Epic 74406
07/09/93	RR	5	28	● 30	Will You Be There	CB 6 / BB 7	Epic 77060
06/02/95	CB	3¹	20	▲ 31	Scream	BB 5	Epic 78000
					MICHAEL JACKSON & JANET JACKSON		
08/04/95	CB	❶²	25	▲ 32	You Are Not Alone	BB ❶¹ / RR 4	Epic 78002
08/31/01	BB	10	20	○ 33	You Rock My World		Epic 79656
05/17/14	BB	9	20	△ 34	Love Never Felt So Good		MJJ
					MICHAEL JACKSON & JUSTIN TIMBERLAKE		
					JACKSON, Stonewall		
05/23/59	MV	3⁴	17	☉ 1	Waterloo	CB 3¹ / BB 4	Columbia 41393
					JACKSON 5, The [THE JACKSONS]		
					THE JACKSON 5:		
11/15/69	BB	❶¹	19	▲ 1	I Want You Back	CB ❶¹ / RW 2⁴	Motown 1157
03/14/70	BB	❶²	13	2	ABC	RW ❶² / CB ❶¹	Motown 1163
05/23/70	BB	❶²	14	3	The Love You Save	CB ❶² / RW ❶¹	Motown 1166
09/19/70	BB	❶⁵	16	4	I'll Be There	RW ❶⁴ / CB ❶²	Motown 1171
01/23/71	CB	❶¹	11	5	Mama's Pearl	RW 2³ / BB 2²	Motown 1177
04/03/71	CB	❶¹	12	6	Never Can Say Goodbye	BB 2³ / RW 2³	Motown 1179
12/11/71	CB	6	12	7	Sugar Daddy	RW 7 / BB 10	Motown 1194
04/22/72	CB	5	10	8	Little Bitty Pretty One	RW 7	Motown 1199
03/09/74	CB	❶¹	22	9	Dancing Machine	RW ❶¹ / BB 2² / RR 4	Motown 1286
					THE JACKSONS:		
11/13/76	CB	4	27	▲ 10	Enjoy Yourself	BB 6 / RW 7 / RR 10	Epic 50289
01/20/79	RW	3²	28	▲ 11	Shake Your Body (Down To The Ground)	CB 5 / RR 6 / BB 7	Epic 50656
09/27/80	RW	9	20	12	Lovely One	CB 10	Epic 50938
06/22/84	BB	3³	16	● 13	State Of Shock	CB 3² / RR 3²	Epic 04503
					JACOBS, Dick, And His Orchestra		
03/09/56	MV	9	16	1	"Main Title" And "Molly-O"		Coral 61606
10/13/56	MV	10	15	2	Petticoats Of Portugal		Coral 61724
07/20/57	MV	10	11	3	Fascination		Coral 61864
					JADE		
12/19/92	BB	4	40	● 1	Don't Walk Away	CB 4 / RR 6	Giant 18686
11/04/94	CB	7	26	2	Every Day Of The Week	RR 10	Giant 17988
					JAGGED EDGE		
12/23/00	BB	9	21	1	Promise		So So Def 79545
06/02/01	BB	3⁵	29	2	Where The Party At		So So Def 79626
					JAGGED EDGE featuring Nelly		
09/06/03	BB	6	27	3	Walked Outta Heaven		So So Def 76974
					JAGGER, Mick		
02/08/85	RR	9	15	1	Just Another Night	CB 10	Columbia 04743
08/30/85	BB	7	16	2	Dancing In The Street	RR 7 / CB 8	EMI America 8288
					MICK JAGGER/DAVID BOWIE		

DEBUT	CH	PK	WK	Gold	A-side (Chart Hit) ...... Other Charts	Label & Number
					JAGGERZ, The	
01/24/70	RW	❶²	14	●	1 The Rapper ...... BB 2¹ / CB 2¹	Kama Sutra 502
					JAMES, Harry, and His Orchestra	
03/10/51	BB	10	10		1 Would I Love You (Love You, Love You) ...... HARRY JAMES & his ORCH. with DORIS DAY	Columbia 39159
09/01/51	BB	8	8		2 Castle Rock ...... FRANK SINATRA & HARRY JAMES	Columbia 39527
					JAMES, Joni	
10/18/52	BB	❶⁶	26	⊙	1 Why Don't You Believe Me ...... CB ❶⁴	MGM 11333
12/27/52	CB	3¹	20	⊙	2 Have You Heard ...... BB 4	MGM 11390
02/14/53	BB	2³	22	⊙	3 Your Cheatin' Heart ...... CB 4	MGM 11426
05/02/53	BB	9	9		4 Almost Always	MGM 11470
08/08/53	BB	8	17		5 My Love, My Love	MGM 11543
01/24/55	BB	2¹	19	⊙	6 How Important Can It Be? ...... MV 4 / CB 4	MGM 11919
09/26/55	BB	6	21		7 You Are My Love ...... MV 8	MGM 12066
09/08/58	MV	8	17		8 There Goes My Heart	MGM 12706
					JAMES, Sonny	
12/22/56	MV	❶⁷	22	⊙	1 Young Love ...... CB ❶⁶ / BB ❶¹	Capitol 3602
					JAMES, Tommy	
06/05/71	RW	❶¹	15		1 Draggin' The Line ...... CB 2² / BB 4	Roulette 7103
					JAMES, Tommy, And The Shondells	
05/28/66	BB	❶²	12	●	1 Hanky Panky ...... CB ❶² / RW ❶²	Roulette 4686
02/04/67	CB	3¹	17		2 I Think We're Alone Now ...... BB 4 / RW 4	Roulette 4720
04/29/67	RW	7	10		3 Mirage ...... BB 10 / CB 10	Roulette 4736
03/30/68	RW	3²	17		4 Mony Mony ...... BB 3¹ / CB 3¹	Roulette 7008
12/14/68	BB	❶²	16	⊙	5 Crimson And Clover ...... RW ❶² / CB ❶¹	Roulette 7028
03/22/69	RW	5	11		6 Sweet Cherry Wine ...... BB 7 / CB 10	Roulette 7039
06/07/69	RW	❶¹	15		7 Crystal Blue Persuasion ...... BB 2³ / CB 2²	Roulette 7050
10/04/69	RW	10	8		8 Ball Of Fire	Roulette 7060
					JAN & ARNIE	
05/17/58	CB	3¹	13		1 Jennie Lee ...... MV 6 / BB 8	Arwin 108
					JAN & DEAN	
07/06/59	CB	7	16		1 Baby Talk ...... BB 10	Dore 522
06/08/63	BB	❶²	15	⊙	2 Surf City ...... CB ❶¹ / MV ❶¹	Liberty 55580
09/07/63	MV	9	10		3 Honolulu Lulu ...... CB 10	Liberty 55613
11/30/63	BB	10	12		4 Drag City ...... CB 10	Liberty 55641
03/07/64	BB	8	18		5 Dead Man's Curve ...... CB 9	Liberty 55672
06/27/64	BB	3¹	12		6 The Little Old Lady (From Pasadena) ...... CB 5 / RW 5	Liberty 55704
					JANKOWSKI, Horst	
05/01/65	CB	9	15		1 A Walk In The Black Forest ...... RW 9	Mercury 72425
					JARREAU, Al	
08/01/81	RR	7	24		1 We're In This Love Together	Warner 49746
					JA RULE	
12/23/00	BB	8	27		1 Put It On Me ...... JA RULE (feat. Lil' Mo and Vita)	Murder Inc. 572751
09/01/01	BB	6	25		2 Livin' It Up ...... RR 8 JA RULE (feat. Case)	Murder Inc. 588741
11/17/01	BB	❶²	27		3 Always On Time ...... RR 5 JA RULE (feat. Ashanti)	Murder Inc. 588795
12/28/02	BB	2¹	20		4 Mesmerize ...... RR 3³ JA RULE feat. Ashanti	Murder Inc. 063773
10/16/04	BB	5	20	○	5 Wonderful ...... JA RULE featuring R. Kelly & Ashanti	The Inc. 003482
					JAY & THE AMERICANS	
03/05/62	CB	4	16		1 She Cried ...... MV 4 / BB 5	United Artists 415
09/12/64	BB	3²	15		2 Come A Little Bit Closer ...... RW 3² / CB 4	United Artists 759
12/26/64	CB	10	12		3 Let's Lock The Door (And Throw Away The Key)	United Artists 805
05/29/65	RW	3¹	14		4 Cara, Mia ...... BB 4 / CB 4	United Artists 881
12/14/68	RW	4	17	●	5 This Magic Moment ...... CB 5 / BB 6	United Artists 50475
11/15/69	RW	10	16		6 Walkin' In The Rain	United Artists 50605
					JAY AND THE TECHNIQUES	
07/15/67	RW	3¹	17		1 Apples, Peaches, Pumpkin Pie ...... CB 4 / BB 6	Smash 2086
10/21/67	RW	6	12		2 Keep The Ball Rollin' ...... CB 10	Smash 2124
					JAYHAWKS, The	
07/06/56	CB	10	12		1 Stranded In The Jungle	Flash 109
					JAYNETTS, The	
08/24/63	MV	❶¹	12	⊙	1 Sally, Go 'Round The Roses ...... BB 2² / CB 3²	Tuff 369

DEBUT	CH	PK	WK	Gold	A-side (Chart Hit)	Other Charts	Label & Number
					JAY-Z		
07/28/01	BB	8	20	○ 1	Izzo (H.O.V.A.)		Roc-A-Fella 588701
10/26/02	BB	4	23	○ 2	'03 Bonnie & Clyde	RR 6	Roc-A-Fella 063843
					JAY-Z Featuring Beyonce Knowles		
02/15/03	BB	8	19	○ 3	Excuse Me Miss		Roc-A-Fella 063717
11/15/03	BB	10	18	4	Change Clothes		Roc-A-Fella 001651
01/24/04	BB	5	26	△ 5	Dirt Off Your Shoulder		Roc-A-Fella 001936
10/21/06	BB	8	15	○ 6	Show Me What You Got		Roc-A-Fella
09/27/08	BB	5	20	△ 7	Swagga Like Us		Roc-A-Fella 012284
					JAY-Z & T.I. with KANYE WEST & LIL WAYNE		
08/15/09	BB	2¹	23	△² 8	Run This Town		Roc Nation 521199
					JAY-Z, RIHANNA & KANYE WEST		
09/26/09	BB	❶⁵	30	△³ 9	Empire State Of Mind		Roc Nation 522671
					JAY-Z & ALICIA KEYS		
09/26/09	BB	10	25	10	Young Forever		Roc Nation 523738
					JAY-Z + MR. HUDSON		
08/27/11	BB	5	36	△⁶ 11	Ni**as In Paris		Roc-A-Fella
					JAY-Z & KANYE WEST		
07/27/13	BB	4	27	△⁴ 12	Holy Grail		Roc-A-Fella
					JAY-Z Featuring Justin Timberlake		
					JEAN, Wyclef		
02/07/98	BB	7	20	▲ 1	Gone Till November		Ruffhouse 78752
09/29/07	RR	10	28	△ 2	Sweetest Girl (Dollar Bill)		Columbia 715361
					WYCLEF JEAN Featuring Akon, Lil Wayne & Niia		
					JEFFERSON AIRPLANE		
04/01/67	BB	5	15	○ 1	Somebody To Love	CB 5 / RW 6	RCA Victor 9140
06/24/67	CB	6	11	△ 2	White Rabbit	RW 7 / BB 8	RCA Victor 9248
					JEFFERSON STARSHIP		
08/23/75	RW	2¹	25	1	Miracles	BB 3³ / CB 4 / RR 4	Grunt 10367
07/24/76	RR	9	18	2	With Your Love		Grunt 10746
03/11/78	RR	6	16	3	Count On Me	BB 8 / CB 9 / RW 10	Grunt 11196
05/27/78	RR	8	16	4	Runaway		Grunt 11274
11/03/79	RR	4	17	5	Jane	CB 6	Grunt 11750
					STARSHIP:		
09/07/85	BB	❶²	25	● 6	We Built This City	CB ❶² / RR ❶²	Grunt 14170
12/28/85	BB	❶¹	21	7	Sara	CB ❶¹ / RR 2²	Grunt 14253
01/30/87	CB	❶³	22	● 8	Nothing's Gonna Stop Us Now	BB ❶² / RR ❶²	Grunt 5109
06/27/87	BB	9	16	9	It's Not Over ('Til It's Over)		RCA/Grunt 5225
					JEFFREY, Joe, Group		
05/31/69	RW	9	14	1	My Pledge Of Love		Wand 11200
					JELLY BEANS, The		
06/20/64	BB	9	12	1	I Wanna Love Him So Bad	CB 10	Red Bird 10-003
					JENKINS, Gordon, And His Orchestra		
10/08/49	CB	3¹	21	1	Don't Cry Joe (Let Her Go, Let Her Go, Let Her Go)	BB 3¹	Decca 24720
02/18/50	CB	2¹	29	2	My Foolish Heart	BB 3¹	Decca 24830
04/08/50	CB	❶⁴	26	3	Bewitched	BB 4	Decca 24983
07/08/50	BB	❶¹³	27	⊙ 4	Goodnight Irene /	CB ❶¹⁰	
07/01/50	BB	2¹	20	5	Tzena Tzena Tzena	CB 2¹	Decca 27077
					GORDON JENKINS and his Orchestra and THE WEAVERS (above 2)		
09/16/50	BB	10	10	6	I'm Forever Blowing Bubbles		Decca 27186
					GORDON JENKINS and ARTIE SHAW		
01/13/51	BB	4	16	7	So Long (It's Been Good To Know Yuh)	CB 7	Decca 27376
					GORDON JENKINS and his Orchestra and THE WEAVERS		
06/07/52	BB	3¹	16	8	Lover	CB 10	Decca 28215
					GORDON JENKINS And His Chorus And Orchestra		
					JENNINGS, Waylon		
09/13/80	RW	7	26	● 1	Theme From The Dukes Of Hazzard (Good Ol' Boys)		RCA 12067
					JEPSEN, Carly Rae		
03/10/12	BB	❶⁹	50	△¹⁰ 1	Call Me Maybe		604 Records 016810
07/14/12	BB	8	24	△² 2	Good Time		Universal Republic
					OWL CITY & CARLY RAE JEPSEN		
					JEREMIH		
04/25/09	BB	4	20	△³ 1	Birthday Sex		Mick Schultz
11/27/10	BB	4	33	△⁴ 2	Down On Me		Mick Schultz
					JEREMIH Featuring 50 Cent		
07/12/14	BB	6	31	△³ 3	Don't Tell 'Em		Def Jam
					JEREMIH Featuring YG		
					JESSIE J		
10/29/11	BB	6	29	△ 1	Domino		Lava
08/16/14	BB	3²	31	△⁶ 2	Bang Bang		Lava
					JESSIE J, ARIANA GRANDE & NICKI MINAJ		

DEBUT	CH	PK	WK	Gold	A-side (Chart Hit)	Other Charts	Label & Number
					JESUS JONES		
04/13/91	CB	❶¹	25		1 Right Here, Right Now	RR ❶¹ / BB 2¹	SBK/Food 07345
08/24/91	BB	4	26		2 Real, Real, Real	CB 7 / RR 7	SBK/Food 07364
					JETHRO TULL		
10/26/74	RW	10	16		1 Bungle In The Jungle		Chrysalis 2101
					JETS, The		
04/12/86	BB	3²	20		1 Crush On You	CB 5 / RR 5	MCA 52774
11/15/86	BB	3¹	27		2 You Got It All	RR 3¹ / CB 6	MCA 52968
06/06/87	BB	6	20		3 Cross My Broken Heart	BB 7 / RR 8	MCA 53123
01/23/88	CB	5	24		4 Rocket 2 U	BB 6 / RR 7	MCA 53254
04/16/88	BB	4	20		5 Make It Real	CB 4 / RR 5	MCA 53311
					JETT, Joan, & The Blackhearts		
02/06/82	BB	❶⁷	25	▲	1 I Love Rock 'N Roll	CB ❶⁵ / RW ❶⁵ / RR 4	Boardwalk 135
04/30/82	CB	6	15		2 Crimson And Clover	BB 7 / RR 8	Boardwalk 144
06/25/88	BB	8	26		3 I Hate Myself For Loving You	CB 10	Blackheart/CBS 07919
					JEWEL		
05/10/96	RR	3³	30		1 Who Will Save Your Soul	CB 7	Atlantic 87151
11/01/96	RR	❶⁵	65	▲	2 You Were Meant For Me /	BB 2²	
07/18/97	RR	❶⁴	28		3 Foolish Games	BB 7	Atlantic 87021
10/16/98	RR	3¹	24		4 Hands	BB 6	Atlantic
04/18/03	RR	8	20		5 Intuition		Atlantic 88108
					JIBBS		
08/19/06	BB	7	20	○	1 Chain Hang Low		Geffen 007034
					JIGSAW		
08/30/75	BB	3²	26		1 Sky High	CB 5 / RW 5 / RR 7	Chelsea 3022
					JIMMY EAT WORLD		
03/16/02	RR	4	33		1 The Middle	BB 5	DreamWorks
					JIVE FIVE, The		
07/03/61	BB	3²	19		1 My True Story	CB 6	Beltone 1006
					J-KWON		
01/17/04	BB	2¹	30	○	1 Tipsy	RR 7	So So Def 58460
					JODECI		
04/04/92	CB	9	28	●	1 Come & Talk To Me		Uptown/MCA 54175
06/12/93	BB	4	27	●	2 Lately	RR 6 / CB 7	Uptown/MCA 54652
					JOE		
02/10/96	CB	9	21	●	1 All The Things (Your Man Won't Do)		Island 854530
12/26/98	BB	10	20		2 Faded Pictures		Def Jam 566494
					CASE & JOE		
01/01/00	BB	4	44		3 I Wanna Know	RR 5	Jive
01/06/01	BB	❶⁴	26	●	4 Stutter		Jive 42870
					JOE (Featuring Mystikal)		
					JOEL, Billy		
11/12/77	RR	2²	27	●	1 Just The Way You Are	CB 2¹ / BB 3² / RW 3²	Columbia 10646
11/03/78	RR	2⁶	20	▲	2 My Life	BB 3³ / RW 3³ / CB 3²	Columbia 10853
03/14/80	RR	2²	16	○	3 You May Be Right	BB 7 / RW 7 / CB 8	Columbia 11231
05/16/80	RW	❶⁴	23	▲	4 It's Still Rock And Roll To Me	RR ❶⁴ / CB ❶³ / BB ❶²	Columbia 11276
08/02/80	RR	10	16		5 Don't Ask Me Why		Columbia 11331
11/27/82	RR	3¹	122		6 Allentown		Columbia 03413
07/22/83	RR	❶³	21	●	7 Tell Her About It	BB ❶¹ / CB 3²	Columbia 04012
09/24/83	RR	2⁴	23		8 Uptown Girl	BB 3⁵ / CB 3²	Columbia 04149
12/17/83	RR	7	18		9 An Innocent Man	BB 10	Columbia 04259
03/24/84	CB	10	19	○	10 The Longest Time		Columbia 04400
07/12/85	BB	9	16		11 You're Only Human (Second Wind)	RR 9 / CB 10	Columbia 05417
06/06/86	BB	9	15		12 Modern Woman	BB 10 / CB 10	Epic 06118
08/09/86	BB	10	18		13 A Matter Of Trust		Columbia 06108
10/13/89	BB	❶²	22	●	14 We Didn't Start The Fire	CB ❶¹ / RR 2³	Columbia 73021
01/12/90	BB	6	18		15 I Go To Extremes	CB 6 / RR 7	Columbia 73091
07/30/93	CB	❶¹	32		16 The River Of Dreams	BB 3¹ / RR 3¹	Columbia 77886
					JOE PUBLIC		
03/13/92	RR	2¹	24		1 Live And Learn	BB 4 / CB 5	Columbia 74012
					JOHN, Elton		
11/21/70	RW	6	16	△²	1 Your Song	BB 8 / CB 8	Uni 55265
04/29/72	BB	6	15	△³	2 Rocket Man	RW 6	Uni 55328
08/12/72	RW	7	10		3 Honky Cat	BB 8	Uni 55343
12/09/72	BB	❶³	17	▲	4 Crocodile Rock	CB ❶² / RW ❶²	MCA 40000
04/07/73	CB	2²	15	●	5 Daniel	RW 2² / BB 2¹	MCA 40046

78

DEBUT	CH	PK	WK	Gold	#	A-side (Chart Hit)	Other Charts	Label & Number
						JOHN, Elton (cont'd)		
07/28/73	RW	8	13	○	6	Saturday Night's Alright For Fighting	CB 9	MCA 40105
10/20/73	RR	❶³	17	▲	7	Goodbye Yellow Brick Road	CB ❶¹ / RW ❶¹ / BB 2³	MCA 40148
02/16/74	RR	❶³	18	▲	8	Bennie And The Jets	BB ❶¹ / CB ❶¹ / RW ❶¹	MCA 40198
06/22/74	CB	❶¹	17	●	9	Don't Let The Sun Go Down On Me	RW ❶¹ / BB 2² / RR 2¹	MCA 40259
09/07/74	BB	4	14	●	10	The Bitch Is Back	CB 5 / RR 5 / RW 6	MCA 40297
11/22/74	RR	❶³	14	●	11	Lucy In The Sky With Diamonds	BB ❶² / RW ❶² / CB ❶¹	MCA 40344
03/07/75	RR	❶⁶	21	▲	12	Philadelphia Freedom	RW ❶³ / BB ❶² / CB ❶²	MCA 40364
04/11/75	RR	9	15		13	Pinball Wizard		Polydor
06/06/75	CB	❶¹	17	●	14	Someone Saved My Life Tonight	RW ❶¹ / RR 2² / BB 4	MCA 40421
10/10/75	BB	❶³	20	▲	15	Island Girl	RW ❶³ / RR ❶³ / CB ❶²	MCA 40461
01/24/76	CB	9	11		16	Grow Some Funk Of Your Own		MCA 40505
07/02/76	RR	❶⁷	25	●	17	Don't Go Breaking My Heart	RW ❶⁵ / BB ❶⁴ / CB ❶³	Rocket/MCA 40585
						ELTON JOHN and KIKI DEE		
11/05/76	RR	5	19	●	18	Sorry Seems To Be The Hardest Word	BB 6 / CB 7 / RW 8	MCA/Rocket 40645
06/08/79	RR	4	18	●	19	Mama Can't Buy You Love	RW 7 / BB 9 / CB 10	MCA 41042
05/02/80	RR	2⁴	21	●	20	Little Jeannie	BB 3⁴ / CB 3² / RW 4	MCA 41236
03/20/82	RR	9	18		21	Empty Garden (Hey Hey Johnny)		Geffen 50049
07/10/82	CB	10	18		22	Blue Eyes		Geffen 29954
05/06/83	RR	5	16	○	23	I'm Still Standing		Geffen 29639
10/29/83	BB	4	24	△	24	I Guess That's Why They Call It The Blues	RR 4 / CB 5	Geffen 29460
06/08/84	RR	4	19		25	Sad Songs (Say So Much)	BB 5 / CB 10	Geffen 29292
09/07/84	RR	10	14		26	Who Wears These Shoes?		Geffen 29189
01/18/86	BB	7	19		27	Nikita	RR 7 / CB 9	Geffen 28800
11/07/87	BB	6	22		28	Candle In The Wind	CB 7 / RR 8	MCA 53196
06/17/88	CB	2²	19		29	I Don't Wanna Go On With You Like That	BB 2¹ / RR 2¹	MCA 53345
12/06/91	BB	❶¹	20	●	30	Don't Let The Sun Go Down On Me	CB ❶¹ / RR 2²	Columbia 74086
						GEORGE MICHAEL/ELTON JOHN		
06/26/92	RR	3²	24		31	The One	CB 7 / BB 9	MCA 54423
05/20/94	RR	3⁵	30	●	32	Can You Feel The Love Tonight	BB 4 / CB 4	Hollywood 64543
09/26/97	BB	❶¹⁴	42	▲¹¹	33	Candle In The Wind 1997		Rocket 568108
						JOHN, Robert		
12/25/71	RW	2²	19	●	1	The Lion Sleeps Tonight	CB 2¹ / BB 3³	Atlantic 2846
05/19/79	RW	❶⁵	31	●	2	Sad Eyes	CB ❶² / BB ❶¹ / RR 2¹	EMI America 8015
						JOHNNIE & JOE		
05/11/57	BB	8	22	☉	1	Over The Mountain; Across The Sea		Chess 1654
						JOHNNY AND THE HURRICANES		
07/27/59	BB	5	19		1	Red River Rock	CB 5 / MV 5	Warwick 509
01/25/60	CB	10	14		2	Beatnik Fly	MV 10	Warwick 520
						JOHNNY HATES JAZZ		
03/19/88	BB	2³	21		1	Shattered Dreams	RR 2² / CB 3³	Virgin 99383
						JOHNS, Sammy		
02/01/75	RR	4	20	●	1	Chevy Van	BB 5 / CB 5 / RW 7	GRC 2046
						JOHNSON, Betty		
11/24/56	BB	9	22		1	I Dreamed		Bally 1020
						JOHNSON, Don		
08/22/86	CB	4	17		1	Heartbeat	BB 5 / RR 6	Epic 06285
						JOHNSON, Marv		
10/26/59	CB	5	22		1	You Got What It Takes	MV 8 / BB 10	United Artists 185
02/22/60	CB	8	15		2	I Love The Way You Love	MV 8 / BB 9	United Artists 208
						JOHNSON, Michael		
04/22/78	RR	6	19		1	Bluer Than Blue	CB 10	EMI America 8001
						JOJO		
04/10/04	RR	❶⁶	29	○	1	Leave (Get Out)		Da Family 002062
09/17/04	RR	7	22	○	2	Baby It's You		Da Family
						JOJO (Feat. Bow Wow)		
07/28/06	RR	2¹	27		3	Too Little Too Late	BB 3¹	Da Family
						JONAS, Nick		
09/27/14	BB	7	32	△³	1	Jealous		Safehouse
						JONAS BROTHERS		
07/04/08	BB	5	16	△²	1	Burnin' Up		Hollywood
08/16/08	BB	8	4		2	Tonight		Hollywood
03/16/19	BB	❶¹	46	△²	3	Sucker		Republic
						JON B		
04/22/95	CB	5	32	●	1	Someone To Love	BB 10	Yab Yum 77895
						JON B & BABYFACE		
05/23/98	BB	7	15	▲	2	They Don't Know		Yab Yum 78793

DEBUT	CH	PK	WK	Gold	A-side (Chart Hit) ... Other Charts	Label & Number
					JONES, Donell	
09/25/99	BB	7	24	●	1 U Know What's Up	Untouchables 24420
					JONES, Howard	
03/23/85	RR	4	23		1 Things Can Only Get Better .... BB 5 / CB 7	Elektra 69651
04/05/86	RR	❶[1]	23		2 No One Is To Blame .... CB 3[2] / BB 4	Elektra 69549
10/18/86	RR	8	18		3 You Know I Love You...Don't You?	Elektra 69512
03/18/89	RR	9	21		4 Everlasting Love	Elektra 69308
					JONES, Jim	
10/21/06	BB	5	27	△	1 We Fly High	Diplomats 5964
					JONES, Jimmy	
12/14/59	CB	2[2]	19	⊙	1 Handy Man .... BB 2[1] / MV 4	Cub 9049
04/11/60	CB	3[3]	16	⊙	2 Good Timin' .... CB 3[3] / MV 4	Cub 9067
					JONES, Joe	
09/05/60	CB	2[2]	17		1 You Talk Too Much .... BB 3[1] / MV 5	Roulette 4304
					JONES, Kent	
05/21/16	BB	8	20	△[2]	1 Don't Mind	Epidemic
					JONES, Oran "Juice"	
09/13/86	BB	9	19	●	1 The Rain .... CB 10	Def Jam 06209
					JONES, Quincy	
08/15/81	RR	10	24		1 Just Once	A&M 2357
					QUINCY JONES with JAMES INGRAM	
					JONES, Rickie Lee	
04/28/79	RR	❶[2]	19		1 Chuck E.'s In Love .... BB 4 / CB 4 / RW 7	Warner 8825
					JONES, Spike, & His City Slickers	
12/09/50	BB	7	5		1 Rudolph The Red-Nosed Reindeer .... CB 8	RCA Victor 3934
12/20/52	BB	4	3		2 I Saw Mommy Kissing Santa Claus	RCA Victor 5067
					JONES, Tom	
04/03/65	RW	8	14		1 It's Not Unusual .... BB 10 / CB 10	Parrot 9737
06/12/65	CB	2[2]	13		2 What's New Pussycat? .... RW 2[1] / BB 3[2]	Parrot 9765
12/17/66	CB	10	13		3 Green, Green Grass Of Home	Parrot 40009
05/24/69	CB	7	12		4 Love Me Tonight .... RW 8	Parrot 40038
07/19/69	RW	5	16		5 I'll Never Fall In Love Again .... CB 6 / BB 6	Parrot 40018
12/27/69	RW	3[1]	11	●	6 Without Love (There Is Nothing) .... BB 5 / CB 5	Parrot 40045
04/25/70	CB	10	11		7 Daughter Of Darkness .... RW 10	Parrot 40048
08/15/70	RW	10	10		8 I (Who Have Nothing)	Parrot 40051
01/30/71	CB	❶[1]	16	●	9 She's A Lady .... RW ❶[1] / BB 2[1]	Parrot 40058
					JOPLIN, Janis	
01/30/71	BB	❶[2]	16		1 Me And Bobby McGee .... RW ❶[1] / CB 3[2]	Columbia 45314
					JORDAN, Jeremy	
12/12/92	RR	6	26		1 The Right Kind Of Love	Giant 18718
04/30/93	RR	5	19		2 Wannagirl	Giant 18548
					JORDAN, Montell	
02/25/95	BB	❶[7]	29	▲	1 This Is How We Do It .... CB 2[5]	PMP/RAL 851468
03/07/98	BB	2[2]	21	▲	2 Let's Ride	Def Jam 568475
					MONTELL JORDAN Featuring Master P & Silkk "The Shocker"	
10/23/99	BB	4	32		3 Get It On...Tonite	Def Soul 562622
					JOURNEY	
07/14/79	RR	6	23	●	1 Lovin', Touchin', Squeezin'	Columbia 11036
07/17/81	RR	❶[1]	22	●	2 Who's Crying Now .... RW 3[3] / CB 3[2] / BB 4	Columbia 02241
10/16/81	CB	8	19	●	3 Don't Stop Believin' .... BB 9 / RW 9 / RR 9	Columbia 02567
01/15/82	RR	❶[7]	18	●	4 Open Arms .... CB ❶[1] / RW 2[1] / BB 2[6]	Columbia 02687
02/04/83	RR	❶[2]	17		5 Separate Ways (Worlds Apart) .... BB 8 / CB 9	Columbia 03513
04/16/83	RR	4	16		6 Faithfully	Columbia 03840
01/25/85	RR	6	16		7 Only The Young .... BB 9	Geffen 29090
04/04/86	RR	8	15		8 Be Good To Yourself .... BB 9 / CB 10	Columbia 05869
10/04/96	RR	7	22	●	9 When You Love A Woman	Columbia 78428
					JUICE WRLD	
05/26/18	BB	2[2]	48	△[6]	1 Lucid Dreams	Grade A
10/19/19	BB	10	19	○	2 Bandit	Grade A
					JUICE WRLD & YOUNGBOY NEVER BROKE AGAIN	
					JUMP 'N THE SADDLE	
12/03/83	CB	9	15		1 The Curly Shuffle	Atlantic 89718
					JUSTIS, Bill	
10/28/57	CB	❶[2]	20	⊙	1 Raunchy .... MV ❶[1] / BB 2[1]	Phillips 3519

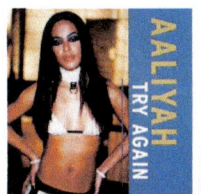

Aaliyah	Abba	Paula Abdul	Ace Of Base	Bryan Adams	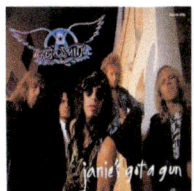
Aerosmith	Christina Aguilera	Air Supply	Herb Alpert	America	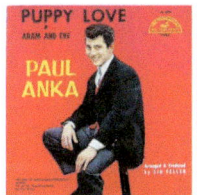
Paul Anka	Annette	Archies	Louis Armstrong	Frankie Avalon	
Backstreet Boys	 Anita Baker	Bananarama	Bangles	Toni Basil	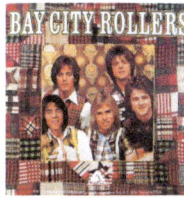
Bay City Rollers	Beach Boys	Beatles	Bee Gees	Lou Bega	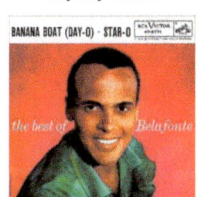
Harry Belafonte	Bell Notes	Pat Benatar	George Benson	Brook Benton	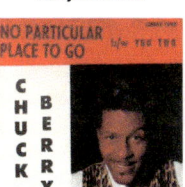
Chuck Berry	Beyonce	Justin Bieber	Biz Markie	Mary J. Blige	

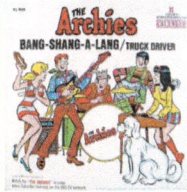

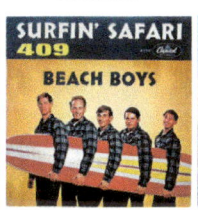

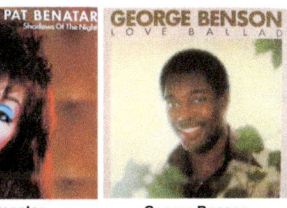

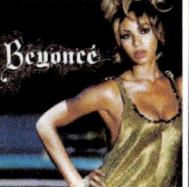

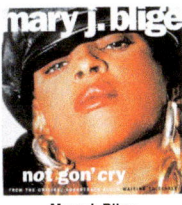

81

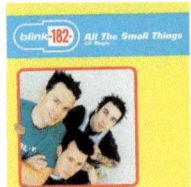

Blink-182	Blondie	B.o.B	Gary U.S. Bonds	Bon Jovi	
Pat Boone	David Bowie	Boyz II Men	Michelle Branch	Brandy	
Toni Braxton	Teresa Brewer	Bobby Brown	Chris Brown	James Brown	
Jackson Browne	Buckinghams	Johnny Burnette	 Byrds	Canned Heat	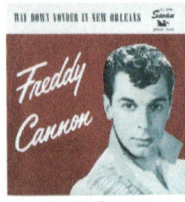
Freddy Cannon	Captain & Tennille	Mariah Carey	Kim Carnes	Carpenters	
Shaun Cassidy	Richard Chamberlain	Champs	Gene Chandler	Ray Charles	
Chubby Checker	Cher	Ciara	Jimmy Clanton	Dave Clark Five	

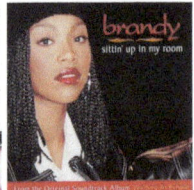

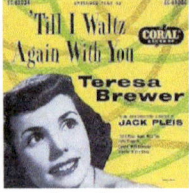

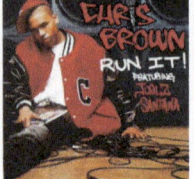

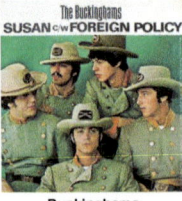

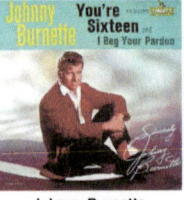

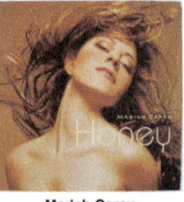

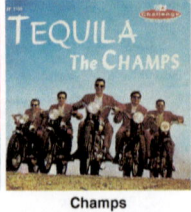

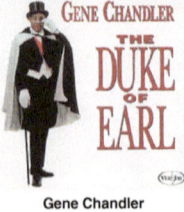

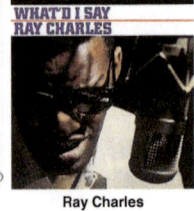

82

Kelly Clarkson	Buzz Clifford	Patsy Cline	Rosemary Clooney		Coasters	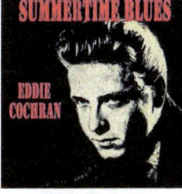
Eddie Cochran	Joe Cocker	Nat "King" Cole	 Phil Collins		Color Me Badd	
Perry Como	Sam Cooke	Rita Coolidge	Alice Cooper	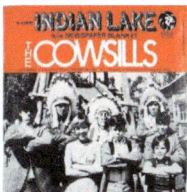	Cowsills	
Floyd Cramer	Johnny Crawford	Creedence Clearwater	Crescendos	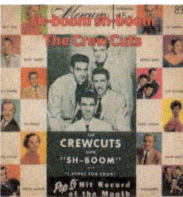	Crew-Cuts	
Bing Crosby	Crosby, Stills & Nash	Sheryl Crow	Crowded House	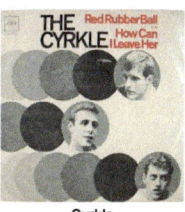	Cyrkle	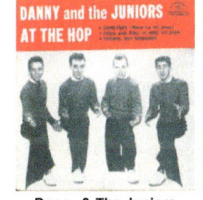
Danny & The Juniors	Bobby Darin	James Darren	Skeeter Davis		Doris Day	
Taylor Dayne	Jimmy Dean	DeBarge	Joey Dee		Deep Purple	

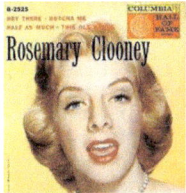

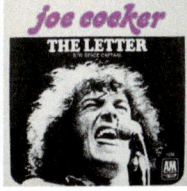

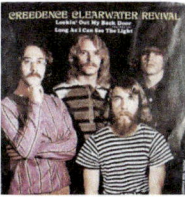

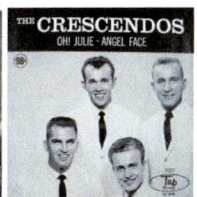

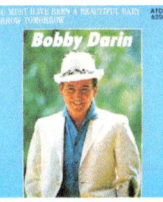

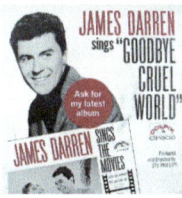

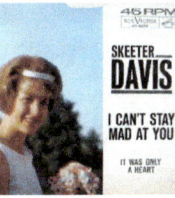

83

DeFranco Family	Dell-Vikings	Dem Franchize Boyz	Destiny's Child		Dexys Midnight Runners
Neil Diamond	Diamonds	Dion & The Belmonts	Celine Dion		Divine
Carl Dobkins Jr.	Fats Domino	Donovan	Doobie Brothers		Doors
Dovells	Drake	Drifters	Patty Duke		Duran Duran
Bob Dylan	Eagles	Earth, Wind & Fire	Sheena Easton	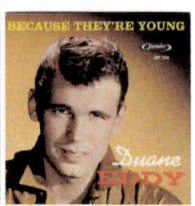	Duane Eddy
Missy Elliott	Eminem	Gloria Estefan	Europe		Faith Evans
Everly Brothers	Expose	Shelley Fabares	Fabian	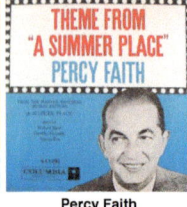	Percy Faith

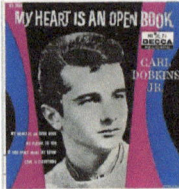

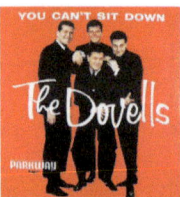

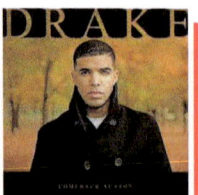

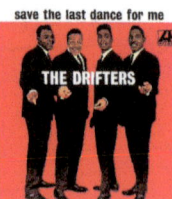

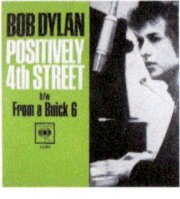

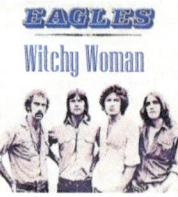

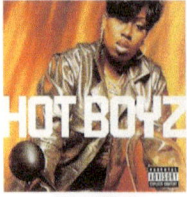

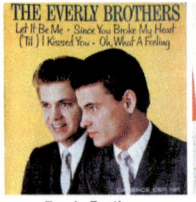

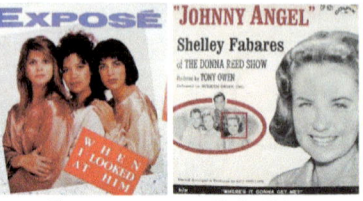

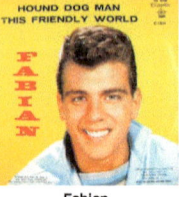

Fantasia	5th Dimension	Firefall	Fixx	Fleetwood Mac
Dan Fogelberg	"Tennessee" Ernie Ford	Four Knights	Four Lads	Four Preps
4 Seasons	Samantha Fox	Peter Frampton	Connie Francis	Aretha Franklin
Stan Freberg	Nelly Furtado	Art Garfunkel	Leif Garrett	Marvin Gaye
Crystal Gayle	Genesis	Georgia Satellites	Andy Gibb	Debbie Gibson
Terry Gilkyson	Glass Tiger	Bobby Goldsboro	Barry Gordon	Lesley Gore
Larry Graham	Ariana Grande	Amy Grant	Earl Grant	Grateful Dead

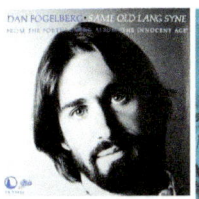

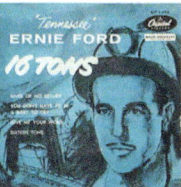

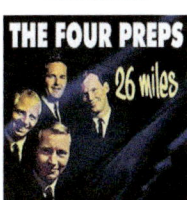

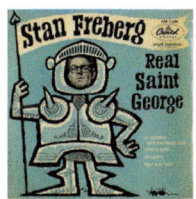

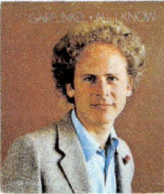

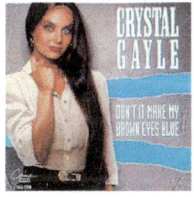

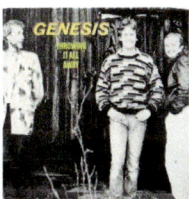

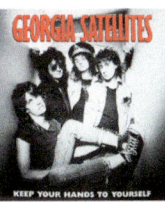

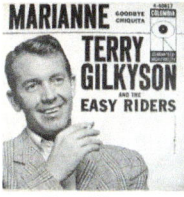

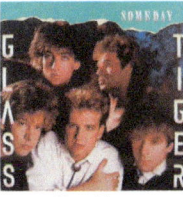

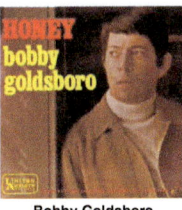

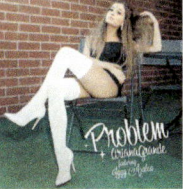

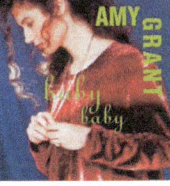

85

Macy Gray	Al Green	Andy Griffith	Guess Who	Guns N' Roses
Bill Haley & His Comets	Daryl Hall & John Oates	Hanson	Rolf Harris	 George Harrison
Corey Hart	Heart	Don Henley	Herman's Hermits	Eddie Hodges
Hollies	Buddy Holly	Bruce Hornsby	Johnny Horton	Whitney Houston
Human League	Brian Hyland	Billy Idol	Enrique Iglesias	Impalas
Impressions	Jorgen Ingmann	INXS	Burl Ives	Janet Jackson
Michael Jackson	Jackson 5	Tommy James	Jan & Arnie	Jan & Dean

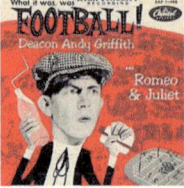

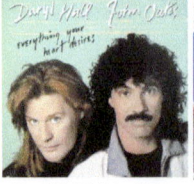

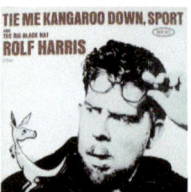

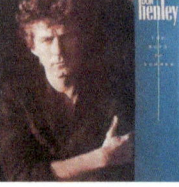

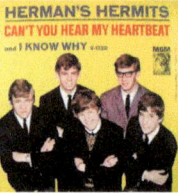

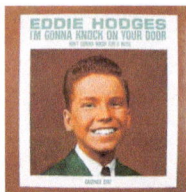

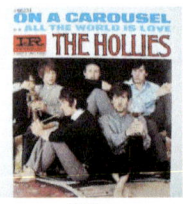

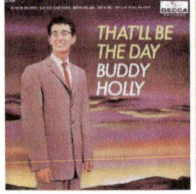

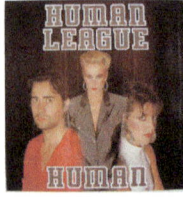

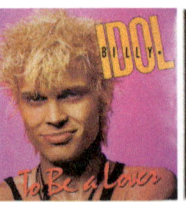

86

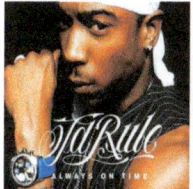

Ja Rule	Jefferson Starship	Jets	Joan Jett	Billy Joel
Elton John	Johnny & The Hurricanes	Marv Johnson	Tom Jones	Journey
Kalin Twins	KC & The Sunshine Band	Alicia Keys	Kingston Trio	Kinks
Gladys Knight & The Pips	Buddy Knox	Kool & The Gang	Lady Gaga	Frankie Laine
Major Lance	Cyndi Lauper	Steve Lawrence	Brenda Lee	John Lennon
Lettermen	Bobby Lewis	Gary Lewis	Huey Lewis & The News	Jerry Lee Lewis
Lisa Lisa & Cult Jam	Little Anthony	Little Eva	Little Richard	Little River Band

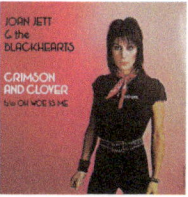

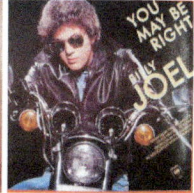

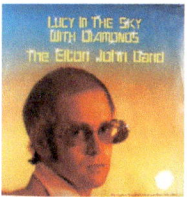

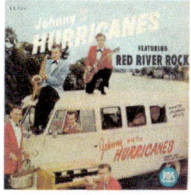

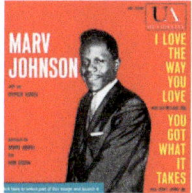

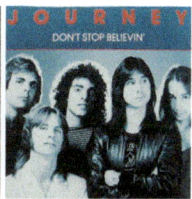

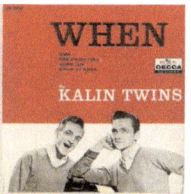

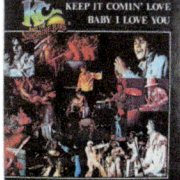

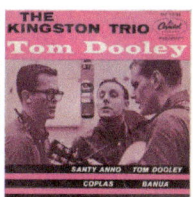

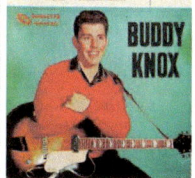

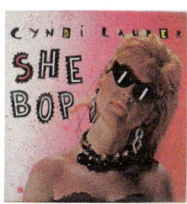

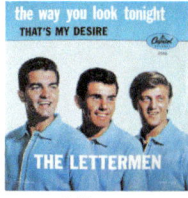

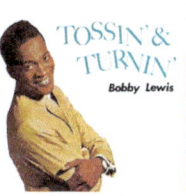

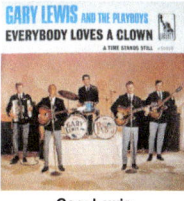

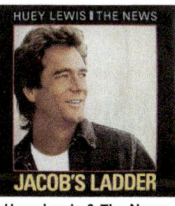

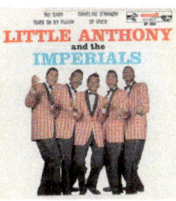

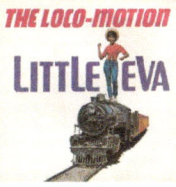

87

Kenny Loggins	Julie London	Jennifer Lopez	Loverboy	Lovin' Spoonful
Robin Luke	Bob Luman	Frankie Lymon	Madness	Madonna
Mamas & Papas	Silvana Mangano	Barry Manilow	Barry Mann	Mantovani
Marcels	Ernie Maresca	Maroon 5	Bruno Mars	Martha & The Vandellas
Ricky Martin	Tony Martin	Wink Martindale	Richard Marx	Matchbox Twenty
Johnny Mathis	Paul McCartney	McGuire Sisters	Clyde McPhatter	John Cougar Mellencamp
 George Michael	Mickey & Sylvia	Steve Miller	Hayley Mills	Nicki Minaj

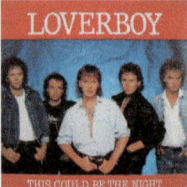

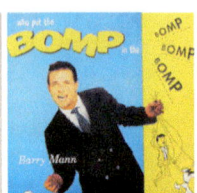

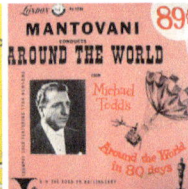

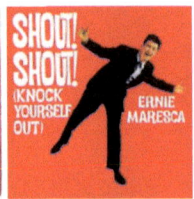

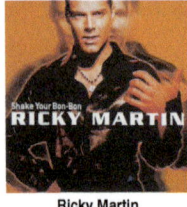

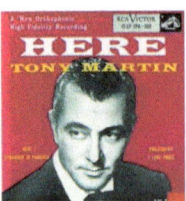

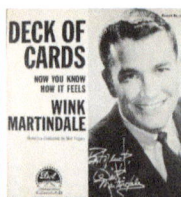

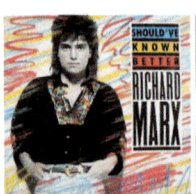

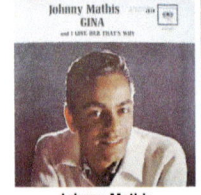

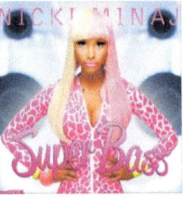

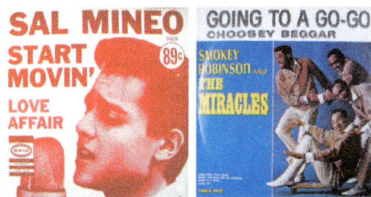

Sal Mineo	Miracles	Guy Mitchell	Eddie Money	Monica	
Monkees	Moody Blues	 Motley Crue	Napoleon XIV	Nelly	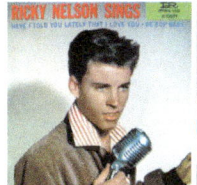
Ricky Nelson	Willie Nelson	New Edition	Juice Newton	Olivia Newton-John	
*NSYNC	O'Jays	Olympics	One Direction	Roy Orbison	
Orlons	Marie Osmond	OutKast	Patti Page	Partridge Family	
Les Paul & Mary Ford	Sean Paul	Carl Perkins	Katy Perry	Peter & Gordon	
Paul Petersen	Ray Peterson	Wilson Pickett	Pink	Gene Pitney	

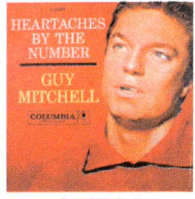

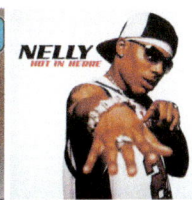

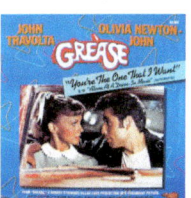

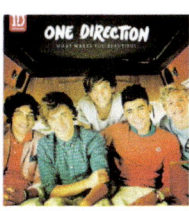

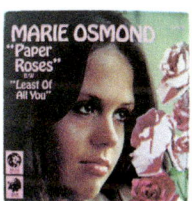

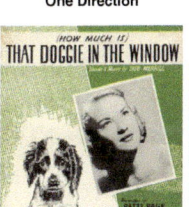

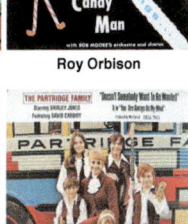

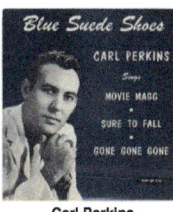

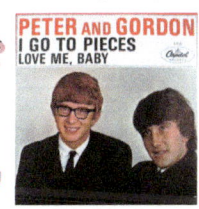

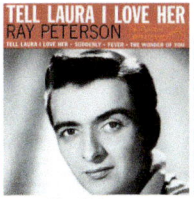

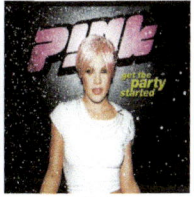

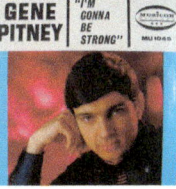

89

Platters	Poison	Police	Perez Prado	Elvis Presley	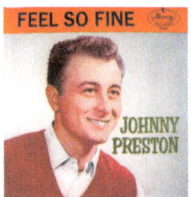
Johnny Preston	Prince	Gary Puckett	Puff Daddy	Queen	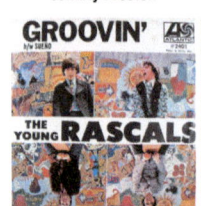
Rascals	Johnnie Ray	Rays	Jim Reeves	Paul Revere & The Raiders	
Debbie Reynolds	Jody Reynolds	Lionel Richie	Righteous Brothers	Rihanna	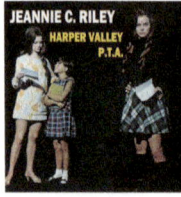
Jeannie C. Riley	Johnny Rivers	Marty Robbins	Jimmie Rodgers	Tommy Roe	
Kenny Rogers	Rolling Stones	Linda Ronstadt	Bobby Rydell	Mitch Ryder	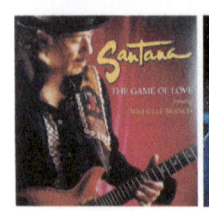
Santana	Savage Garden	Jack Scott	Neil Sedaka	Bob Seger	

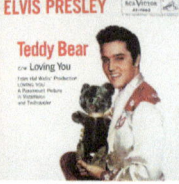

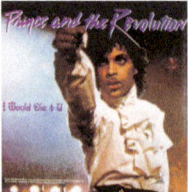

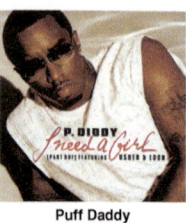

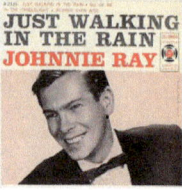

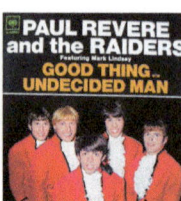

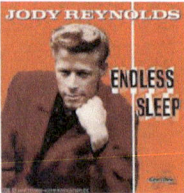

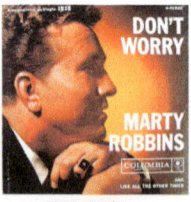

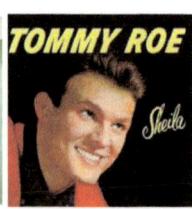

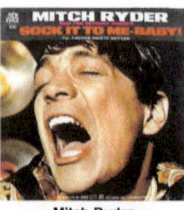

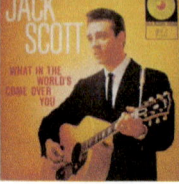

Shaggy	Shakira	Shangri-Las	Del Shannon	Dee Dee Sharp	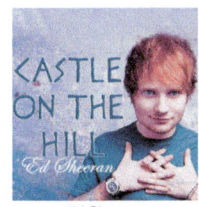
Ed Sheeran	Bobby Sherman	Shirelles	Silhouettes	Carly Simon	
Paul Simon	Simon & Garfunkel	Frank Sinatra	Nancy Sinatra	Percy Sledge	
Will Smith	Britney Spears	Dusty Springfield	Rick Springfield	Bruce Springsteen	
Jo Stafford	Terry Stafford	Ringo Starr	Dodie Stevens	Ray Stevens	
Rod Stewart	Sting	Stray Cats	B. Streisand & D. Summer	Supremes	
Taylor Swift	Tarriers	Temptations	Three Dog Night	Johnny Tillotson	

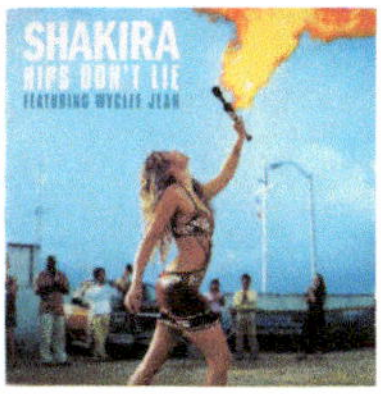

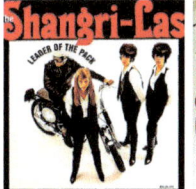

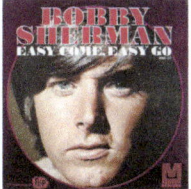

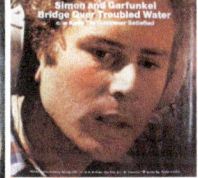

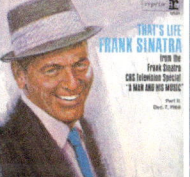

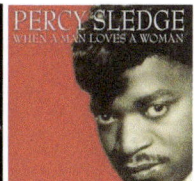

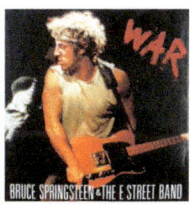

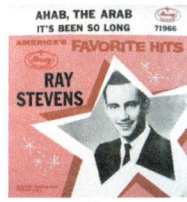

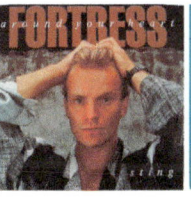

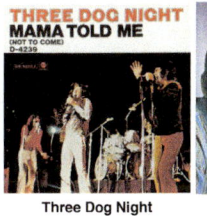

91

TLC	Trashmen	John Travolta	Tina Turner	Turtles
Conway Twitty	Tymes	Carrie Underwood	Usher	Ritchie Valens
Frankie Valli	Van Halen	Bobby Vee	Ventures	Village People
Gene Vincent	Bobby Vinton	Adam Wade	Jerry Wallace	Billy Ward & His Dominoes
Dionne Warwick	Dinah Washington	Mary Wells	Kanye West	Who
Andy Williams	Jackie Wilson	 Steve Winwood	Stevie Wonder	Xscape
Yardbirds	Kathy Young & Innocents	Neil Young	Timi Yuro	Zombies

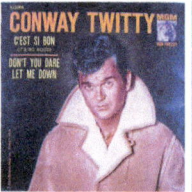

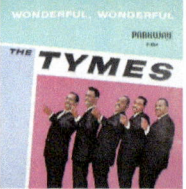

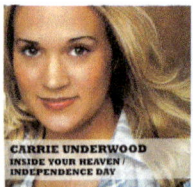

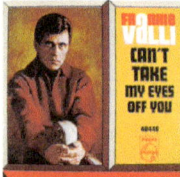

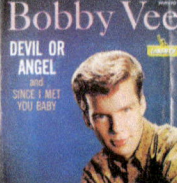

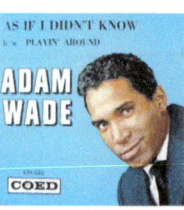

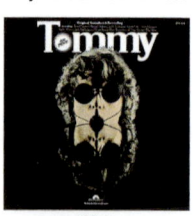

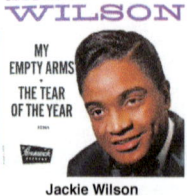

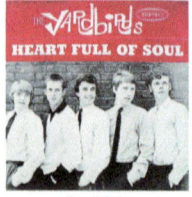

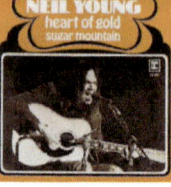

92

DEBUT	CH	PK	WK	Gold		A-side (Chart Hit)	Other Charts	Label & Number
05/01/04	BB	❶²	28	○		**JUVENILE**		
					1	Slow Motion	RR 10	Cash Money
						JUVENILE Featuring Soulja Slim		

K

						KAEMPFERT, Bert, And His Orchestra		
10/31/60	BB	❶³	19	⊙	1	Wonderland By Night	MV ❶³ / CB ❶¹	Decca 31141
01/23/65	RW	8	14		2	Red Roses For A Blue Lady	CB 9	Decca 31722

						KAJAGOOGOO		
04/23/83	RR	4	21		1	Too Shy	BB 5 / CB 5	EMI America 8161

						KALIN TWINS		
05/19/58	MV	4	21	⊙	1	When	BB 5 / CB 5	Decca 30642

						KALLEN, Kitty		
09/09/50	CB	5	21		1	Our Lady Of Fatima	BB 10	Mercury 5466
03/03/51	BB	9	10		2	The Aba Daba Honeymoon		Mercury 5586
04/17/54	BB	❶⁹	28	⊙	3	Little Things Mean A Lot	CB ❶⁷	Decca 29037
						RICHARD HAYES & KITTY KALLEN (above 2)		
10/04/54	BB	4	20		4	In The Chapel In The Moonlight	CB 5 / MV 7	Decca 29130
12/22/62	MV	8	12		5	My Coloring Book		RCA Victor 8124

						KAMOZE, Ini		
09/17/94	BB	❶²	30	▲	1	Here Comes The Hotstepper	CB 2³ / RR 8	Columbia 77614

						KANSAS		
12/11/76	RR	5	25	●	1	Carry On Wayward Son	CB 7 / RW 8	Kirshner 4267
01/28/78	RR	2¹	20	●	2	Dust In The Wind	CB 3² / RW 5 / BB 6	Kirshner 4274

						KARAS, Anton		
02/18/50	BB	❶¹¹	30	⊙	1	"The Third Man" Theme	CB ❶¹¹	London 30005

						KARDINAL OFFISHALL		
05/24/08	RR	3³	27		1	Dangerous	BB 5	KonLive
						KARDINAL OFFISHALL Featuring Akon		

						KATRINA AND THE WAVES		
03/23/85	BB	9	21		1	Walking On Sunshine	CB 9 / RR 10	Capitol 5466

						KAYE, Sammy, And His Orchestra		
02/04/50	BB	2⁶	26		1	It Isn't Fair	CB 3²	RCA Victor 3115
05/06/50	BB	5	15		2	Roses	CB 8	RCA Victor 3754
09/09/50	CB	❶⁶	29		3	Harbor Lights	BB ❶⁴	Columbia 38963

						KC AND THE SUNSHINE BAND		
06/21/75	CB	❶²	24		1	Get Down Tonight	RW ❶² / RR ❶² / BB ❶¹	T.K. 1009
10/17/75	RR	❶⁴	20		2	That's The Way (I Like It)	CB ❶³ / RW ❶³ / BB ❶²	T.K. 1015
07/03/76	BB	❶¹	24		3	(Shake, Shake, Shake) Shake Your Booty	CB ❶¹ / RW ❶¹ / RR ❶¹	T.K. 1019
02/26/77	BB	❶¹	26		4	I'm Your Boogie Man	CB ❶¹ / RW ❶¹ / RR 3¹	T.K. 1022
07/23/77	BB	2³	23		5	Keep It Comin' Love	RW 2³ / CB 2² / RR 2²	T.K. 1023
08/25/79	BB	❶¹	29		6	Please Don't Go	RW 2⁴ / CB 3³ / RR 7	T.K. 1035
11/17/79	RW	❶¹	25	●	7	Yes, I'm Ready	BB 2² / CB 3² / RR 4	Casablanca 2227
						TERI DeSARIO with K.C.		

						K-CI & JOJO		
01/23/98	BB	❶³	36		1	All My Life	RR 2⁷	MCA 55420
05/29/99	BB	2¹	20		2	Tell Me It's Real		MCA 55551
12/08/00	RR	4	25		3	Crazy		MCA

						K-DOE, Ernie		
03/13/61	CB	❶³	16	⊙	1	Mother-In-Law	BB ❶¹ / MV ❶¹	Minit 623

						KEITH		
12/03/66	RW	4	15		1	98.6	BB 7 / CB 7	Mercury 72639

						KELIS		
10/04/03	BB	3⁵	22	○	1	Milkshake	RR 8	Star Trak 61026

						KELLY, R.		
02/05/94	BB	❶⁴	27	▲	1	Bump N' Grind	CB 5	Jive 42207
10/28/95	BB	4	24	▲	2	You Remind Me Of Something	CB 4	Jive 42344
02/24/96	CB	3¹	25	▲	3	Down Low (Nobody Has To Know)	BB 4	Jive 42373
						R. KELLY (featuring Ronald Isley and Ernie Isley)		
07/06/96	CB	4	27	▲	4	I Can't Sleep Baby (If I)	BB 5	Jive 42377
11/08/96	BB	2⁴	34	▲	5	I Believe I Can Fly	RR 8	Jive 42422
06/20/97	BB	9	20	●	6	Gotham City		Jive 42473

DEBUT	CH	PK	WK	Gold	A-side (Chart Hit)	Other Charts	Label & Number
					KELLY, R. (cont'd)		
12/05/98	BB	❶⁶	18	▲⁷	I'm Your Angel		Jive 42557
					R. KELLY & CELINE DION		
03/31/01	BB	6	21	8	Fiesta - Remix		Jive 42904
					R. KELLY (Featuring Jay-Z and Boo & Gotti)		
11/09/02	RR	❶¹	42	9	Ignition	BB 2⁵	Jive 40065
08/23/03	BB	9	27	10	Step In The Name Of Love		Jive 55572
					KEMP, Johnny		
05/14/88	BB	10	22	● 1	Just Got Paid		Columbia 07744
					KEMP, Tara		
01/19/91	RR	2¹	25	● 1	Hold You Tight	BB 3¹ / CB 3¹	Giant 19458
05/11/91	RR	5	20	2	Piece Of My Heart	BB 7 / CB 9	Giant 19364
					KENDRICK, Anna		
01/12/13	BB	6	44	△³ 1	Cups (Pitch Perfect's "When I'm Gone")		UMe
					KENDRICKS, Eddie		
08/18/73	BB	❶²	19	1	Keep On Truckin' (Part 1)	CB ❶¹ / RW ❶¹ / RR 7	Tamla 54238
12/29/73	CB	❶¹	19	2	Boogie Down	RW ❶¹ / BB 2² / RR 6	Tamla 54243
					KENNER, Chris		
05/22/61	BB	2³	17	⊙ 1	I Like It Like That (Part 1)	CB 2² / MV 5	Instant 3229
					KENNY G		
04/04/87	BB	4	23	1	Songbird	CB 4 / RR 6	Arista 9588
12/19/92	RR	9	26	2	Forever In Love		Arista 12482
05/14/93	RR	9	20	3	By The Time This Night Is Over		Arista 12565
					KENNY G with PEABO BRYSON		
12/25/99	BB	7	5	4	Auld Lang Syne (The Millennium Mix)		Arista 13769
					KENTON, Stan — see COLE, Nat "King"		
					KE$HA		
10/24/09	BB	❶⁹	38	△⁸ 1	TiK ToK		Kemosabe
01/23/10	BB	4	28	△⁴ 2	Your Love Is My Drug		Kemosabe
01/23/10	BB	7	20	△² 3	Blah Blah Blah		Kemosabe
					KE$HA Featuring 3OH!3		
01/23/10	BB	8	20	△³ 4	Take It Off		Kemosabe
11/13/10	BB	❶¹	20	△⁵ 5	We R Who We R		Kemosabe
12/04/10	BB	7	26	△⁴ 6	Blow		Kemosabe
10/13/12	BB	2¹	22	△⁴ 7	Die Young		Kemosabe
					KEYS, Alicia		
06/16/01	BB	❶⁶	34	○ 1	Fallin'	RR ❶⁵	J Records 21041
10/27/01	BB	7	20	2	A Woman's Worth		J Records 21112
11/15/03	BB	3¹	20	3	You Don't Know My Name		J Records 56599
03/06/04	BB	4	40	4	If I Ain't Got You	RR 8	J Records 59351
06/19/04	BB	8	28	5	Diary		J Records 59965
					ALICIA KEYS Feat. Tony! Toni! Toné!		
09/10/04	BB	❶⁶	26	○ 6	My Boo	RR 2¹	LaFace 65246
					USHER & ALICIA KEYS		
11/27/04	RR	3¹	29	○ 7	Karma		J Records 62467
09/22/07	BB	❶⁵	39	△³ 8	No One	RR ❶⁵	J Records 20102
09/26/09	BB	❶⁵	30	△³ 9	Empire State Of Mind		Roc Nation 522671
					JAY-Z & ALICIA KEYS		
					KHALID		
03/03/18	BB	9	51	△⁴ 1	Love Lies		RCA
					KHALID & NORMANI		
07/28/18	BB	9	52	△⁴ 2	Eastside		Interscope
					BENNY BLANCO, HALSEY & KHALID		
09/29/18	BB	8	48	△³ 3	Better		Right Hand
02/23/19	BB	3⁴	46	△⁴ 4	Talk		Right Hand
					KHAN, Chaka		
09/08/84	CB	❶¹	26	● 1	I Feel For You	BB 3³ / RR 3¹	Warner 29195
					KID CUDI		
01/31/09	BB	3¹	27	△⁵ 1	Day 'N' Nite		Dream On 013161
					KID ROCK		
02/04/00	RR	7	20	1	Only God Knows Why		Lava/Atlantic 84708
11/01/02	BB	4	34	2	Picture	RR 5	Lava
					KID ROCK with SHERYL CROW		
05/30/08	RR	4	20	3	All Summer Long		Top Dog
					KIHN, Greg, Band		
01/29/83	RR	❶³	23	1	Jeopardy	BB 2¹ / CB 5	Beserkley 69847

DEBUT	CH	PK	WK	Gold	A-side (Chart Hit) .... Other Charts	Label & Number
					KILLERS, The	
02/11/05	BB	10	38	△²	1 Mr. Brightside .... RR 10	Island 004170
					KIM, Andy	
05/17/69	RW	5	17	●	1 Baby, I Love You .... CB 6 / BB 9	Steed 716
06/15/74	BB	❶¹	20	●	2 Rock Me Gently .... CB ❶¹ / RW 5 / RR 6	Capitol 3895
					KING, Ben E.	
12/31/60	CB	9	16	⊙	1 Spanish Harlem .... BB 10	Atco 6185
05/08/61	CB	3¹	14	⊙	2 Stand By Me .... BB 4 / MV 6	Atco 6194
01/25/75	BB	5	17		3 Supernatural Thing - Part I .... RW 5 / CB 9	Atlantic 3241
10/04/86	BB	9	21		4 Stand By Me .... CB 10	Atlantic 89361
					KING, Carole	
05/08/71	BB	❶⁵	17	●	1 It's Too Late .... CB ❶⁴ / RW ❶²	Ode 66015
08/28/71	RW	5	10		2 So Far Away .... CB 10	Ode 66019
01/22/72	CB	8	11		3 Sweet Seasons .... BB 9 / RW 9	Ode 66022
08/31/74	CB	❶¹	17		4 Jazzman .... RW ❶¹ / BB 2¹ / RR 2¹	Ode 66101
12/28/74	BB	9	13		5 Nightingale	Ode 66106
					KING, Claude	
05/19/62	MV	4	17		1 Wolverton Mountain .... CB 5 / BB 6	Columbia 42352
					KING, Elle	
07/25/15	BB	10	38	△³	1 Ex's & Oh's	RCA
					KING, Evelyn "Champagne"	
05/27/78	CB	8	24	●	1 Shame .... BB 9 / RW 9 / RR 10	RCA 11122
					KING, Jonathan	
09/11/65	RW	10	14		1 Everyone's Gone To The Moon	Parrot 9774
					KING, Pee Wee, and His Golden West Cowboys	
11/03/51	BB	❶³	27	⊙	1 Slow Poke .... CB ❶³	RCA Victor 0489
					KING HARVEST	
10/28/72	CB	10	22		1 Dancing In The Moonlight	Perception 515
					KINGSMEN, The	
11/09/63	CB	❶²	17	⊙	1 Louie Louie .... MV ❶¹ / BB 2⁶	Wand 143
01/09/65	BB	4	13		2 The Jolly Green Giant .... RW 6 / CB 8	Wand 172
					KINGS OF LEON	
10/11/08	BB	4	57	△	1 Use Somebody	RCA
					KINGSTON, Sean	
06/01/07	BB	❶⁴	22	△	1 Beautiful Girls .... RR 2³	Beluga Heights 05578
11/09/07	RR	5	25	△	2 Take You There .... BB 7	Beluga Heights
05/08/09	BB	5	21	△²	3 Fire Burning	Beluga Heights
					KINGSTON TRIO, The	
09/27/58	CB	❶³	22	●	1 Tom Dooley .... BB ❶¹ / MV ❶¹	Capitol 4049
04/06/63	MV	4	11		2 Reverend Mr. Black .... CB 7 / BB 8	Capitol 4951
					KINKS, The	
09/26/64	CB	5	15	⊙	1 You Really Got Me .... BB 7 / RW 8	Reprise 0306
12/26/64	CB	6	12		2 All Day And All Of The Night .... BB 7 / RW 8	Reprise 0334
03/13/65	CB	5	12		3 Tired Of Waiting For You .... RW 5 / BB 6	Reprise 0347
11/27/65	CB	9	16		4 A Well Respected Man .... RW 10	Reprise 0420
08/15/70	RW	7	16		5 Lola .... CB 8 / BB 9	Reprise 0930
05/07/83	BB	6	20		6 Come Dancing .... RR 6	Arista 1054
					KISS	
09/04/76	RR	4	22	●	1 Beth .... BB 7 / CB 7 / RW 7	Casablanca 863
03/12/77	CB	10	18		2 Calling Dr. Love	Casablanca 880
05/26/79	RW	5	20		3 I Was Made For Lovin' You .... CB 8	Casablanca 983
02/03/90	BB	8	20		4 Forever .... CB 8 / RR 10	Mercury 876716
					KITT, Eartha	
07/18/53	CB	7	15		1 C'est Si Bon (It's So Good) .... BB 8	RCA Victor 5358
11/21/53	BB	4	8		2 Santa Baby .... CB 8	RCA Victor 5502
					KIX	
10/07/89	CB	9	23	●	1 Don't Close Your Eyes	Atlantic 88902
					KLF, The	
06/22/91	BB	5	20	●	1 3 A.M. Eternal	Arista 2230
01/25/92	CB	8	19		2 Justified & Ancient (Stand By The Jams) .... RR 10 THE KLF with TAMMY WYNETTE	Arista 12401
					KLYMAXX	
09/14/85	BB	5	29		1 I Miss You .... RR 9	Constellation 52606

DEBUT	CH	PK	WK	Gold	A-side (Chart Hit)..Other Charts	Label & Number
					KNACK, The	
06/23/79	BB	❶⁶	26	●	1 My Sharona..CB ❶⁶ / RW ❶⁵ / RR ❶³	Capitol 4731
09/01/79	RW	10	17		2 Good Girls Don't ....RR 10	Capitol 4771
					KNIGHT, Gladys, & The Pips	
05/08/61	BB	6	14		1 Every Beat Of My Heart	Vee-Jay 386
					PIPS	
10/21/67	CB	❶¹	17	⊙	2 I Heard It Through The Grapevine....................BB 2³ / RW 3²	Soul 35039
11/21/70	CB	5	17		3 If I Were Your Woman ....RW 8 / BB 9	Soul 35078
05/22/71	CB	9	13		4 I Don't Want To Do Wrong..RW 9	Soul 35083
01/20/73	CB	❶¹	16		5 Neither One Of Us (Wants To Be The First To Say Goodbye) .RW ❶¹ / BB 2²	Soul 35098
08/25/73	BB	❶²	19	●	6 Midnight Train To Georgia ....CB ❶¹ / RW ❶¹ / RR 2¹	Buddah 383
11/24/73	BB	4	16		7 I've Got To Use My Imagination ....RW 5 / CB 7	Buddah 393
02/09/74	RW	2¹	19	●	8 Best Thing That Ever Happened To Me ....CB 3² / BB 3¹ / RR 6	Buddah 403
05/11/74	BB	5	17	●	9 On And On ....RW 7 / CB 9	Buddah 423
04/26/75	RW	9	20		10 The Way We Were/Try To Remember...............................CB 10	Buddah 463
					KNIGHT, Jean	
05/29/71	RW	❶¹	16	▲²	1 Mr. Big Stuff ....BB 2² / CB 2¹	Stax 0088
					KNIGHT, Jordan	
04/02/99	BB	10	20	●	1 Give It To You..	Interscope 97048
					KNOX, Buddy, With The Rhythm Orchids	
02/09/57	BB	❶¹	23	⊙	1 Party Doll ....CB ❶¹ / MV ❶¹	Roulette 4002
08/24/57	BB	9	23		2 Hula Love ....MV 9	Roulette 4018
					KODAK BLACK	
03/11/17	BB	6	20	△³	1 Tunnel Vision	Dollaz N Dealz
10/27/18	BB	2¹	25	△⁴	2 ZEZE	Atlantic
					KODAK BLACK Featuring Travis Scott & Offset	
					KOKOMO	
01/30/61	BB	8	15		1 Asia Minor	Felsted 8612
					KOOL & THE GANG	
12/08/73	BB	4	22	●	1 Jungle Boogie ....RW 5 / CB 8 / RR 10	De-Lite 559
04/13/74	BB	6	19	●	2 Hollywood Swinging ....CB 7 / RW 7	De-Lite 561
10/06/79	CB	4	27	●	3 Ladies Night...RW 5 / BB 8	De-Lite 801
01/19/80	BB	3¹	20	●	4 Too Hot ....BB 5 / RW 5 / CB 7	De-Lite 802
10/25/80	BB	❶²	33	▲	5 Celebration ....CB ❶¹ / RW ❶¹ / RR 7	De-Lite 807
02/27/82	BB	10	21	●	6 Get Down On It	De-Lite 818
11/05/83	BB	2¹	24	●	7 Joanna ....CB 3² / RR 7	De-Lite 829
11/24/84	BB	10	24		8 Misled ....RR 10	De-Lite 880431
03/23/85	BB	9	19		9 Fresh ....CB 10	De-Lite 880623
07/06/85	BB	2³	25	●	10 Cherish ....CB 3² / RR 5	De-Lite 880869
11/01/86	BB	10	18		11 Victory	Mercury 888074
02/07/87	BB	10	18		12 Stone Love	Mercury 888292
					K.P. & ENVYI	
12/27/97	BB	6	20	●	1 Swing My Way	EastWest 64135
					KRAMER, Billy J., With The Dakotas	
04/18/64	BB	7	16		1 Little Children / ....CB 7 / RW 7	
05/30/64	BB	9	10		2 Bad To Me ....CB 10	Imperial 66027
					KRAVITZ, Lenny	
06/01/91	BB	2¹	22		1 It Ain't Over 'Til It's Over ....RR 3¹ / CB 6	Virgin 98795
12/05/98	RR	6	32		2 Fly Away	Virgin 38668
10/13/00	RR	❶³	33		3 Again ....BB 4	Virgin 38782
					KRIS KROSS	
04/04/92	BB	❶⁸	22	▲²	1 Jump ....CB ❶³ / RR 3¹	Ruffhouse 74197
12/09/95	CB	9	22	●	2 Tonite's Tha Night...	Ruffhouse 78092
					KROEGER, Chad	
05/17/02	RR	2¹	22		1 Hero ....BB 3²	Roadrunner
					CHAD KROEGER Featuring Josey Scott	
					KRUPA, Gene, and his Chicago Jazz	
06/10/50	BB	9	15		1 Bonaparte's Retreat	RCA Victor 3766
					K.W.S.	
06/20/92	BB	6	26	●	1 Please Don't Go ....CB 6 / RR 7	Next Plateau 339
					KYGO	
03/04/17	BB	10	29	△³	1 It Ain't Me...	Ultra
					KYGO & SELENA GOMEZ	

DEBUT	CH	PK	WK	Gold	A-side (Chart Hit)	Other Charts	Label & Number
					KYLE		Indie-Pop
01/14/17	BB	4	30	△⁵	1 iSpy KYLE Featuring Lil Yachty		

L

					LaBELLE		
01/04/75	BB	❶¹	21	●	1 Lady Marmalade	CB ❶¹ / RW ❶¹ / RR 3³	Epic 50048
					LaBELLE, Patti		
03/22/86	BB	❶³	23	●	1 On My Own PATTI LaBELLE AND MICHAEL McDONALD	CB ❶³ / RR ❶¹	MCA 52770
					LA BOUCHE		
11/11/95	RR	4	40	●	1 Be My Lover	CB 5 / BB 6	RCA 64446
03/30/96	RR	5	33		2 Sweet Dreams	CB 8	RCA 64505
					LACHEY, Nick		
03/11/06	RR	5	25	○	1 What's Left Of Me	BB 6	Jive
					LADY ANTEBELLUM		
08/29/09	BB	2²	60	△⁹	1 Need You Now		Capitol
05/21/11	BB	7	42	△²	2 Just A Kiss		Capitol 82752
					LADY GAGA		
08/16/08	BB	❶³	49	△⁸	1 Just Dance LADY GAGA with COLBY O'DONIS	RR ❶²	Streamline 011524
01/03/09	RR	❶⁵	40	△¹⁰	2 Poker Face	BB ❶¹	Streamline 012715
03/21/09	BB	5	22	△³	3 LoveGame		Streamline 013062
09/12/09	BB	6	27	△⁴	4 Paparazzi		Streamline 013571
11/14/09	BB	2⁷	34	△¹¹	5 Bad Romance		Streamline 013969
12/12/09	BB	3¹	33	△³	6 Telephone LADY GAGA Featuring Beyonce		Streamline 014166
04/17/10	BB	5	23	△²	7 Alejandro		Streamline 014501
02/26/11	BB	❶⁶	20	△⁴	8 Born This Way		Streamline 015442
04/30/11	BB	10	8	△²	9 Judas		Streamline
05/28/11	BB	3¹	24	△³	10 The Edge Of Glory		Streamline
06/11/11	BB	6	20	△³	11 You And I		Streamline
08/31/13	BB	4	23	△³	12 Applause		Streamline 58978
11/23/13	BB	8	2		13 Dope		Streamline
10/29/16	BB	4	20	△	14 Million Reasons		Streamline
10/13/18	BB	❶¹	45	△	15 Shallow LADY GAGA & BRADLEY COOPER		Interscope
					LAINE, Frankie		
09/10/49	BB	❶⁸	22		1 That Lucky Old Sun	CB ❶⁶	Mercury 5316
11/19/49	BB	❶⁶	15		2 Mule Train	CB ❶⁵	Mercury 5345
02/11/50	BB	❶²	12	☉	3 The Cry Of The Wild Goose		Mercury 5363
05/05/51	CB	2⁴	26	☉	4 Jezebel /	BB 2²	
05/12/51	BB	3¹	19		5 Rose, Rose, I Love You	CB 5	Columbia 39367
10/20/51	BB	9	15		6 Hey, Good Lookin' FRANKIE LAINE - JO STAFFORD		Columbia 39570
11/10/51	BB	3²	20		7 Jealousy (Jalousie)	CB 6	Columbia 39585
03/08/52	BB	6	14		8 Hambone FRANKIE LAINE & JO STAFFORD	CB 9	Columbia 39672
06/21/52	BB	7	20		9 Sugarbush DORIS DAY - FRANKIE LAINE		Columbia 39693
07/12/52	CB	4	25		10 High Noon (Do Not Forsake Me)	BB 5	Columbia 39770
02/14/53	BB	2³	29	☉	11 I Believe	CB 2³	Columbia 39938
03/14/53	CB	3¹	16		12 Tell Me A Story JIMMY BOYD - FRANKIE LAINE	BB 4	Columbia 39945
08/08/53	BB	6	22		13 Hey Joe!	CB 10	Columbia 40036
12/01/56	BB	3¹	22	☉	14 Moonlight Gambler	MV 3¹ / CB 7	Columbia 40780
03/16/57	BB	10	15		15 Love Is A Golden Ring FRANKIE LAINE with The Easy Riders		Columbia 40856
					LAMAR, Kendrick		
04/22/17	BB	❶¹	37	△⁷	1 Humble		Top Dawg
05/06/17	BB	4	20	△³	2 DNA		Top Dawg
01/20/18	BB	7	21	△²	3 All The Stars KENDRICK LAMAR & SZA		Top Dawg
02/17/18	BB	7	20	△²	4 Pray For Me THE WEEKND & KENDRICK LAMAR		Top Dawg
					LAMBERT, Adam		
01/02/10	BB	10	30		1 Whataya Want From Me		19 Records

DEBUT	CH	PK	WK	Gold	A-side (Chart Hit)	Other Charts	Label & Number
					LANCE, Major		
07/13/63	CB	7	16		1 The Monkey Time	BB 8 / MV 10	Okeh 7175
12/28/63	CB	4	13		2 Um, Um, Um, Um, Um, Um	BB 5 / MV 5	Okeh 7187
					LANZA, Mario		
11/18/50	CB	❶⁵	36	⊙	1 Be My Love	BB ❶¹	RCA Victor 1353
04/14/51	BB	3²	40	⊙	2 The Loveliest Night Of The Year	CB 4	RCA Victor 3300
09/13/52	BB	7	25		3 Because You're Mine	CB 7	RCA Victor 3914
					LARKS, The		
11/07/64	CB	6	16		1 The Jerk	BB 7 / RW 7	Money 106
					LaROSA, Julius		
01/31/53	BB	4	15		1 Anywhere I Wander	CB 7	Cadence 1230
09/05/53	CB	❶¹	25	⊙	2 Eh, Cumpari	BB 2¹	Cadence 1232
06/25/55	MV	7	18		3 Domani (Tomorrow)		Cadence 1265
					LA ROSE, Natalie		
02/07/15	BB	10	26	△²	1 Somebody		Republic
					NATALIE LA ROSE Featuring Jeremih		
					LA ROUX		
03/20/10	BB	8	27	△²	1 Bulletproof		Big Life 013222
					LARSON, Nicolette		
11/25/78	RR	3¹	19		1 Lotta Love	BB 8 / CB 8 / RW 8	Warner 8664
					LaSALLE, Denise		
08/21/71	RW	9	15	●	1 Trapped By A Thing Called Love		Westbound 182
					LAUPER, Cyndi		
12/17/83	CB	❶²	27	▲	1 Girls Just Want To Have Fun	BB 2² / RR 2¹	Portrait 04120
04/13/84	RR	❶³	20	●	2 Time After Time	BB ❶² / CB ❶¹	Portrait 04432
07/21/84	RR	2¹	19	●	3 She Bop	BB 3³ / CB 3¹	Portrait 04516
10/05/84	RR	3¹	19		4 All Through The Night	BB 5 / CB 8	Portrait 04639
05/17/85	BB	10	16		5 The Goonies 'R' Good Enough		Portrait 04918
08/29/86	BB	❶²	21		6 True Colors	CB ❶¹ / RR ❶¹	Portrait 06247
11/29/86	BB	3¹	20		7 Change Of Heart	CB 4 / RR 4	Portrait 06431
05/06/89	CB	5	20		8 I Drove All Night	BB 6 / RR 9	Epic 68759
					LAVIGNE, Avril		
05/24/02	RR	❶⁸	31		1 Complicated	BB 2²	Arista 15185
11/29/02	RR	❶³	27	○	2 I'm With You /	BB 4	
08/30/02	RR	❶²	22	○	3 Sk8er Boi	BB 10	Arista 50972
07/02/04	RR	2⁴	25	○	4 My Happy Ending	BB 9	RCA 62874
03/17/07	BB	❶¹	24	△²	5 Girlfriend	RR ❶¹	RCA
05/05/07	RR	9	20	○	6 When You're Gone		RCA
					LAWRENCE, Joey		
03/06/93	RR	6	22		1 Nothin' My Love Can't Fix		Impact/MCA 54562
					LAWRENCE, Steve		
02/23/57	BB	5	20		1 Party Doll		Coral 61792
11/09/59	MV	5	18		2 Pretty Blue Eyes	CB 7 / BB 9	ABC-Paramount 10058
03/05/60	BB	7	15		3 Footsteps	CB 9 / MV 10	ABC-Paramount 10085
03/06/61	BB	9	16		4 Portrait Of My Love	MV 10	United Artists 291
11/10/62	MV	❶³	19	⊙	5 Go Away Little Girl	BB ❶² / CB ❶²	Columbia 42601
					LAWRENCE, Vicki		
02/03/73	BB	❶²	20	●	1 The Night The Lights Went Out In Georgia	RW ❶² / CB ❶¹	Bell 45,303
					LED ZEPPELIN		
11/15/69	CB	2²	16	●	1 Whole Lotta Love	BB 4 / RW 4	Atlantic 2690
11/14/70	CB	8	14		2 Immigrant Song	RW 10	Atlantic 2777
12/18/71	CB	9	13		3 Black Dog	RW 10	Atlantic 2849
09/21/79	RR	10	10		4 All My Love		Swan Song
					LEE, Brenda		
12/21/59	MV	3²	24		1 Sweet Nothin's	CB 3¹ / BB 4	Decca 30967
05/30/60	BB	❶³	23	⊙	2 I'm Sorry /	MV ❶³ / CB ❶²	
05/23/60	BB	6	14		3 That's All You Gotta Do		Decca 31093
09/12/60	BB	❶¹	15		4 I Want To Be Wanted	MV 2⁴ / CB ❶¹	Decca 31149
12/31/60	MV	3¹	12		5 Emotions	CB 6 / BB 7	Decca 31195
03/27/61	MV	5	12		6 You Can Depend On Me	BB 6 / CB 7	Decca 31231
06/19/61	MV	3²	13		7 Dum Dum	BB 4 / CB 4	Decca 31272
09/25/61	BB	3²	15		8 Fool #1	MV ❶¹ / CB 2	Decca 31309
01/08/62	BB	4	13		9 Break It To Me Gently	CB 6 / MV 6	Decca 31348
04/09/62	MV	5	12		10 Everybody Loves Me But You	BB 6 / CB 7	Decca 31379
09/22/62	CB	3³	16		11 All Alone Am I	MV 3³ / BB 3²	Decca 31424

DEBUT	CH	PK	WK	Gold	A-side (Chart Hit)...Other Charts	Label & Number
					LEE, Brenda (cont'd)	
04/06/63	MV	5	13		12 Losing You...BB 6 / CB 10	Decca 31478
11/30/63	MV	6	12		13 As Usual	Decca 31570
10/01/66	RW	9	13		14 Coming On Strong	Decca 32018
12/08/18	BB	9	5		15 Rockin' Around The Christmas Tree	Decca
12/07/19	BB	2²	5		16 Rockin' Around The Christmas Tree	Decca
					LEE, Curtis	
07/01/61	CB	6	14		1 Pretty Little Angel Eyes..BB 7	Dunes 2007
					LEE, Dickey	
08/18/62	CB	4	16		1 Patches...MV 4 / BB 6	Smash 1758
12/08/62	CB	8	13		2 I Saw Linda Yesterday..MV 10	Smash 1791
					LEE, Johnny	
07/12/80	CB	4	22	●	1 Lookin' For Love...RW 4 / BB 5 / RR 5	Full Moon 47004
					LEE, Murphy — see NELLY	
					LEE, Peggy	
01/07/50	BB	9	7		1 The Old Master Painter..	Capitol 791
					PEGGY LEE and MEL TORMÉ	
06/07/52	BB	3¹	16		2 Lover...CB 10	Decca 28215
					PEGGY LEE and GORDON JENKINS And His Orchestra	
07/07/58	MV	3¹	15		3 Fever..CB 6 / BB 8	Capitol 3998
09/27/69	RW	8	11		4 Is That All There Is...CB 10	Capitol 2602
					LEFT BANKE, The	
09/10/66	CB	2¹	14		1 Walk Away Renee..RW 4 / BB 5	Smash 2041
					LEGEND, John	
09/14/13	BB	❶³	59	△⁸	1 All Of Me	G.O.O.D.
07/25/15	BB	8	39	△⁴	2 Like I'm Gonna Lose You	Epic
					MEGHAN TRAINOR with JOHN LEGEND	
					LEMON PIPERS, The	
12/02/67	BB	❶¹	16	●	1 Green Tambourine...CB ❶¹ / RW ❶¹	Buddah 23
					LEN	
07/23/99	RR	3³	27		1 Steal My Sunshine..BB 9	Work
					LENNON, John	
07/26/69	RW	10	9		1 Give Peace A Chance	Apple 1809
					PLASTIC ONO BAND	
02/21/70	CB	3⁴	14	●	2 Instant Karma (We All Shine On)..............................BB 3³ / RW 3²	Apple 1818
					JOHN ONO LENNON	
03/27/71	RW	8	10		3 Power To The People..CB 10	Apple 1830
					JOHN LENNON/PLASTIC ONO BAND YOKO ONO/PLASTIC ONO BAND	
10/16/71	RW	❶¹	11		4 Imagine...CB 2¹ / BB 3²	Apple 1840
					JOHN LENNON PLASTIC ONO BAND	
11/10/73	CB	10	13		5 Mind Games..RW 10	Apple 1868
09/28/74	BB	❶¹	17		6 Whatever Gets You Thru The Night............CB ❶¹ / RW ❶¹ / RR 6	Apple 1874
					JOHN LENNON With The PLASTIC ONO NUCLEAR BAND	
12/21/74	BB	9	13		7 #9 Dream...CB 10	Apple 1878
10/31/80	BB	❶⁵	25	●	8 (Just Like) Starting Over................................CB ❶⁵ / RW ❶⁵ / RR ❶⁴	Geffen 49604
01/09/81	BB	❶⁴	20		9 Woman..CB ❶² / BB 2³ / RW 2³	Geffen 49644
03/27/81	RR	3²	18		10 Watching The Wheels................................CB 7 / RW 9 / BB 10	Geffen 49695
01/20/84	BB	5	14		11 Nobody Told Me...CB 6 / RR 6	Polydor 817254
					LENNON, Julian	
10/20/84	RR	6	19		1 Valotte..BB 9 / CB 9	Atlantic 89609
01/19/85	RR	4	20		2 Too Late For Goodbyes..................................BB 5 / CB 7	Atlantic 89589
					LENNOX, Annie	
11/05/88	CB	5	20		1 Put A Little Love In Your Heart.......................RR 6 / BB 9	A&M 1255
					ANNIE LENNOX & AL GREEN	
09/04/92	RR	5	31		2 Walking On Broken Glass	Arista 12452
					LESTER, Ketty	
02/17/62	BB	5	17		1 Love Letters..CB 7 / MV 8	Era 3068
					LETTERMEN, The	
08/14/61	CB	8	16		1 The Way You Look Tonight................................MV 10	Capitol 4586
11/20/61	BB	7	14		2 When I Fall In Love	Capitol 4658
12/09/67	RW	6	15		3 Goin' Out Of My Head/Can't Take My Eyes Off You...BB 7 / CB 7	Capitol 2054
					LEVEL 42	
02/15/86	BB	7	27		1 Something About You................................CB 8 / RR 9	Polydor 883362
					LEVERT	
08/15/87	BB	5	23	●	1 Casanova..CB 5 / RR 6	Atlantic 89217

DEBUT	CH	PK	WK	Gold	A-side (Chart Hit)	Other Charts	Label & Number
					LEVINE, Adam — see R. CITY		
					LEWIS, Barbara		
04/20/63	BB	3^2	18		1 Hello Stranger	MV 3^2 / CB 4	Atlantic 2184
06/05/65	CB	10	15		2 Baby, I'm Yours	RW 10	Atlantic 2283
					LEWIS, Bobby		
04/24/61	BB	❶^7	23	☉	1 Tossin' And Turnin'	CB ❶^4 / MV ❶^4	Beltone 1002
08/28/61	BB	9	11		2 One Track Mind		Beltone 1012
					LEWIS, Donna		
06/21/96	RR	❶^{12}	41	●	1 I Love You Always Forever	CB ❶^8 / BB 2^9	Atlantic 87072
					LEWIS, Gary, And The Playboys		
01/09/65	BB	❶^2	14	●	1 This Diamond Ring	RW ❶^2 / CB ❶^1	Liberty 55756
04/03/65	BB	2^2	12		2 Count Me In	RW 3^2 / CB 3^1	Liberty 55778
07/03/65	BB	2^1	12		3 Save Your Heart For Me	RW 3^1 / CB 4	Liberty 55809
09/25/65	BB	4	11		4 Everybody Loves A Clown	RW 5 / CB 6	Liberty 55818
12/04/65	RW	2^1	12		5 She's Just My Style	BB 3^4 / CB 4	Liberty 55846
03/05/66	RW	8	9		6 Sure Gonna Miss Her	BB 9 / CB 10	Liberty 55865
05/07/66	RW	6	9		7 Green Grass	BB 8 / CB 9	Liberty 55880
07/30/66	RW	10	8		8 My Heart's Symphony		Liberty 55898
06/15/68	CB	8	15		9 Sealed With A Kiss		Liberty 56037
					LEWIS, Huey, and The News		
02/06/82	RR	6	17		1 Do You Believe In Love	BB 7	Chrysalis 2589
09/10/83	RR	6	21		2 Heart And Soul	BB 8 / CB 10	Chrysalis 42726
01/14/84	CB	5	21	●	3 I Want A New Drug	RR 5 / BB 6	Chrysalis 42766
04/20/84	RR	2^1	22		4 The Heart Of Rock & Roll	BB 6 / CB 7	Chrysalis 42782
07/20/84	RR	4	18		5 If This Is It	BB 6 / CB 6	Chrysalis 42803
06/28/85	RR	❶^3	20	●	6 The Power Of Love	BB ❶^2 / CB ❶^2	Chrysalis 42876
08/01/86	RR	❶^3	20		7 Stuck With You	CB ❶^3 / RR ❶^3	Chrysalis 43019
10/10/86	RR	❶^1	18		8 Hip To Be Square	BB 3^2 / CB 6	Chrysalis 43065
01/02/87	RR	❶^2	18		9 Jacob's Ladder	BB ❶^1 / CB ❶^1	Chrysalis 43097
04/03/87	RR	8	15		10 I Know What I Like	BB 9 / CB 10	Chrysalis 43108
07/17/87	RR	5	19		11 Doing It All For My Baby	BB 6	Chrysalis 43143
07/15/88	RR	2^3	16		12 Perfect World	BB 3^2 / CB 4	Chrysalis 43265
04/26/91	CB	8	20		13 Couple Days Off	RR 10	EMI 50346
					LEWIS, Jerry		
11/10/56	MV	4	21	☉	1 Rock-A-Bye Your Baby With A Dixie Melody	CB 9 / BB 10	Decca 30124
					LEWIS, Jerry Lee		
06/24/57	BB	3^2	29	☉	1 Whole Lot Of Shakin' Going On	CB 5 / MV 5	Sun 267
11/23/57	BB	2^4	21	☉	2 Great Balls Of Fire	CB 2^1 / MV 2^1	Sun 281
03/01/58	BB	7	15	☉	3 Breathless	CB 10	Sun 288
					LEWIS, Leona		
02/29/08	RR	❶^9	39	△	1 Bleeding Love	BB ❶^4	J Records/SyCo
04/26/08	RR	3^2	31		2 Better In Time		J Records/SyCo
					LEWIS, Ramsey, Trio		
07/31/65	CB	4	17		1 The "In" Crowd	RW 4 / BB 5	Argo 5506
11/13/65	RW	8	9		2 Hang On Sloopy		Cadet 5522
					LFO		
07/02/99	BB	3^4	19	▲	1 Summer Girls		Logic/Arista 13692
10/08/99	BB	10	21	●	2 Girl On TV		Logic/Arista 13756
06/15/01	RR	9	19		3 Every Other Time		J Records 21091
					LIFEHOUSE		
02/10/01	RR	2^8	54		1 Hanging By A Moment	BB 2^4	DreamWorks
02/12/05	RR	4	62	○	2 You And Me	BB 5	Geffen
					LIGHTFOOT, Gordon		
12/26/70	RW	3^1	15		1 If You Could Read My Mind	BB 5 / CB 5	Reprise 0974
04/06/74	RR	❶^3	19	●	2 Sundown	BB ❶^1 / CB ❶^1 / RW ❶^1	Reprise 1194
08/31/74	BB	10	16		3 Carefree Highway		Reprise 1309
08/28/76	CB	❶^1	24		4 The Wreck Of The Edmund Fitzgerald	BB 2^2 / RR 3^2 / RW 5	Reprise 1369
					LIL BABY		
05/26/18	BB	6	29	△^{3}	1 Yes Indeed		Quality Control
					LIL BABY & DRAKE		
09/29/18	BB	4	35	△^{5}	2 Drip Too Hard		Young Stoner Life
					LIL DICKY		
03/31/18	BB	8	20	△^{3}	1 Freaky Friday		Dirty Burd
					LIL DICKY Featuring Chris Brown		

DEBUT	CH	PK	WK	Gold	A-side (Chart Hit) .... Other Charts	Label & Number
					LIL' FLIP	
06/19/04	BB	2²	23	○	1 Sunshine .... RR 6 LIL' FLIP Featuring Lea	Sucka Free 77009
					LIL JON & THE EAST SIDE BOYZ	
05/03/03	BB	2¹	45		1 Get Low .... RR 10 LIL JON & THE EAST SIDE BOYZ Featuring Ying Yang Twins	BME/TVT 2377
11/27/04	BB	3³	22		2 Lovers & Friends .... RR 10 LIL JON & THE EAST SIDE BOYZ Featuring Usher & Ludacris	BME/TVT
04/08/06	BB	7	28		3 Snap Yo Fingers .... LIL JON Feat. E-40 & Sean Paul of YoungBloodZ	BME/TVT 2841
01/11/14	BB	4	37	△⁶	4 Turn Down For What .... DJ SNAKE & LIL JON	Columbia
					LIL' KIM	
07/12/97	BB	6	21	▲	1 Not Tonight .... LIL' KIM Featuring Da Brat, Left Eye, Missy "Misdemenaor" Elliott and Angie Martinez	Undeas 98019
04/06/01	RR	❶¹⁹	20		2 Lady Marmalade .... BB ❶⁵ CHRISTINA AGUILERA, LIL' KIM, MYA and PINK	Interscope 497066
04/26/03	BB	2³	24		3 Magic Stick .... RR 7 LIL' KIM (feat. 50 Cent)	Queen Bee
					LIL MAMA	
06/09/07	BB	10	11	○	1 Lip Gloss	Jive 07519
03/08/08	BB	10	12		2 Shawty Get Loose .... LIL MAMA Featuring Chris Brown & T-Pain	Jive 27082
					LIL NAS X	
03/16/19	BB	❶¹⁹	45	△¹⁰	1 Old Town Road .... LIL NAS X Featuring Billy Ray Cyrus	Lil Nas X
07/06/19	BB	5	32	△²	2 Panini	Columbia
					LIL PUMP	
09/30/17	BB	3²	24	△⁵	1 Gucci Gang	Lyfetime
09/22/18	BB	6	12	△²	2 I Love It .... KANYE WEST & LIL PUMP	G.O.O.D.
					LIL' ROMEO	
05/19/01	BB	3¹	14		1 My Baby	Soulja 50202
					LIL TECCA	
06/15/19	BB	4	31		1 Ran$om	Galactic
					LIL UZI VERT	
04/15/17	BB	7	34	△⁷	1 XO TOUR Llif3	Generation Now
12/28/19	BB	5	9		2 Futsal Shuffle 2020	Generation Now
					LIL WAYNE	
03/29/08	BB	❶⁵	28		1 Lollipop .... RR 5 LIL WAYNE Featuring Static Major	Cash Money 011599
05/10/08	BB	6	23	△²	2 A Milli	Cash Money
06/14/08	BB	10	27	△²	3 Got Money .... LIL WAYNE Featuring T-Pain	Cash Money
09/27/08	BB	5	20	△	4 Swagga Like Us .... JAY-Z & T.I. with KANYE WEST & LIL WAYNE	Roc-A-Fella 012284
09/04/10	BB	6	24	△²	5 Right Above It .... LIL WAYNE Featuring Drake	Cash Money
01/01/11	BB	9	21	△³	6 6 Foot 7 Foot .... LIL WAYNE Featuring Cory Gunz	Cash Money
06/11/11	BB	5	24	△⁴	7 How To Love	Cash Money
09/03/11	BB	3¹	21	△²	8 She Will .... LIL WAYNE Featuring Drake	Cash Money
02/02/13	BB	9	22	△²	9 Love Me .... LIL WAYNE Featuring Drake & Future	Young Money
10/13/18	BB	2¹	8		10 Mona Lisa .... LIL WAYNE Featuring Kendrick Lamar	Young Money
10/13/18	BB	5	3		11 Don't Cry .... LIL WAYNE Featuring XXXTENTACION	Young Money
10/13/18	BB	7	20	△	12 Uproar .... LIL WAYNE Featuring Swizz Beatz	Young Money
10/13/18	BB	10	2		13 Let It Fly .... LIL WAYNE Featuring Travis Scott	Young Money
					LIND, Bob	
01/22/66	BB	5	13		1 Elusive Butterfly .... RW 6 / CB 7	World Pacific 77808
					LINDEN, Kathy	
03/03/58	MV	5	17		1 Billy .... BB 7	Felsted 8510
04/13/59	MV	10	14		2 Goodbye Jimmy, Goodbye	Felsted 8571
					LINDSAY, Mark	
11/29/69	CB	9	16	●	1 Arizona .... RW 9 / BB 10	Columbia 45037

DEBUT	CH	PK	WK	Gold	A-side (Chart Hit) ... Other Charts	Label & Number
					LINEAR	
02/17/90	BB	5	27	●	1 Sending All My Love .... CB 5 / RR 7	Atlantic 87961
					LINKIN PARK	
11/03/01	RR	❶⁶	38	△⁴	1 In The End .... BB 2¹	Warner
11/08/03	RR	5	32		2 Numb	Warner
04/21/07	BB	7	23	△⁵	3 What I've Done	Machine Shop
11/16/07	RR	9	22	△²	4 Shadow Of The Day	Machine Shop
06/06/09	BB	6	20	△³	5 New Divide	Machine Shop
					LIPA, Dua	
08/19/17	BB	6	48	△⁵	1 New Rules	Warner
11/16/19	BB	5	16		2 Don't Start Now	Warner
					LIPPS, INC.	
03/29/80	CB	❶⁵	28	▲	1 Funkytown .... BB ❶⁴ / RW ❶⁴ / RR 7	Casablanca 2233
					LISA LISA AND CULT JAM	
07/26/86	BB	8	26	●	1 All Cried Out .... CB 9 / RR 9	Columbia 05844
					LISA LISA AND CULT JAM WITH FULL FORCE FEATURING PAUL ANTHONY & BOW LEGGED LOU	
04/11/87	CB	❶²	23	●	2 Head To Toe .... BB ❶¹ / RR ❶¹	Columbia 07008
08/01/87	BB	❶¹	26	●	3 Lost In Emotion .... CB ❶¹ / RR ❶¹	Columbia 07267
					LITTLE ANTHONY AND THE IMPERIALS	
08/11/58	BB	4	19	◉	1 Tears On My Pillow .... CB 7 / MV 7	End 1027
11/07/64	RW	4	14		2 Goin' Out Of My Head .... CB 5 / BB 6	DCP 1119
02/06/65	BB	10	11		3 Hurt So Bad	DCP 1128
					LITTLE CAESAR and The Romans	
05/01/61	BB	9	13		1 Those Oldies But Goodies (Remind Me Of You) .... CB 9 / MV 10	Del-Fi 4158
					LITTLE DIPPERS, The	
01/25/60	BB	9	14		1 Forever	University 210
					LITTLE EVA	
06/30/62	CB	❶³	17	◉	1 The Loco-Motion .... MV ❶² / BB ❶¹	Dimension 1000
					LITTLE RICHARD	
01/20/56	CB	10	17	◉	1 Tutti-Frutti .... MV 10	Specialty 561
03/30/56	MV	5	19	◉	2 Long Tall Sally .... BB 6 / CB 8	Specialty 572
06/17/57	BB	10	20		3 Jenny, Jenny	Specialty 606
09/16/57	BB	8	18		4 Keep A Knockin'	Specialty 611
02/15/58	BB	10	15		5 Good Golly, Miss Molly	Specialty 624
					LITTLE RIVER BAND	
07/22/78	RR	2²	21		1 Reminiscing .... BB 3² / CB 3² / RW 5	Harvest 4605
01/06/79	RR	4	21		2 Lady .... RW 7 / BB 10 / CB 10	Harvest 4667
07/14/79	RR	❶³	21		3 Lonesome Loser .... RW 4 / BB 6 / CB 7	Capitol 4748
10/20/79	RR	5	18		4 Cool Change .... BB 10	Capitol 4789
08/21/81	RR	4	23		5 The Night Owls .... BB 6 / CB 7 / RW 8	Capitol 5033
12/05/81	RR	5	19		6 Take It Easy On Me .... BB 10	Capitol 5057
04/03/82	RR	7	16		7 Man On Your Mind	Capitol 5061
11/20/82	RR	5	19		8 The Other Guy .... CB 8	Capitol 5185
					LIVE	
02/04/95	RR	7	33		1 Lightning Crashes	Radioactive
					LIVING COLOUR	
03/11/89	CB	8	21		1 Cult Of Personality	Epic 68611
					LIZZO	
05/18/19	BB	❶⁷	42	△⁴	1 Truth Hurts	Nice Life
09/07/19	BB	3²	26	△	2 Good As Hell	Nice Life
					LL COOL J	
12/01/90	BB	9	26	●	1 Around The Way Girl	Def Jam 73609
11/11/95	BB	3⁸	23	▲	2 Hey Lover .... CB 3⁵	Def Jam 577494
03/02/96	BB	5	24	●	3 Doin It .... BB 9	Def Jam 576120
07/06/96	CB	3⁵	29	▲	4 Loungin .... BB 3¹	Def Jam 575062
08/24/02	BB	4	22		5 Luv U Better	Def Jam 063956
02/24/06	BB	4	11		6 Control Myself	Def Jam 006285
					LL COOL J featuring Jennifer Lopez	
					LLOYD	
11/25/06	BB	9	24		1 You	The Inc.
					LLOYD Featuring Lil Wayne	
					LMFAO	
02/12/11	BB	❶⁶	68	△¹⁰	1 Party Rock Anthem	Party Rock
					LMFAO Featuring Lauren Bennett & GoonRock	
09/17/11	BB	❶²	42	△⁸	2 Sexy And I Know It	Party Rock

DEBUT	CH	PK	WK	Gold	A-side (Chart Hit)	Other Charts	Label & Number
					LOBO		
03/27/71	BB	5	14		1 Me And You And A Dog Named Boo	RW 6 / CB 8	Big Tree 112
09/16/72	CB	❶¹	16	●	2 I'd Love You To Want Me	RW ❶¹ / BB 2²	Big Tree 147
12/30/72	CB	4	14		3 Don't Expect Me To Be Your Friend	RW 6 / BB 8	Big Tree 158
					LOCKLIN, Hank		
05/23/60	MV	5	22	⊙	1 Please Help Me, I'm Falling	CB 6 / BB 8	RCA Victor 7692
					LOEB, Lisa		
04/22/94	RR	❶⁴	42	●	1 Stay (I Missed You)	BB ❶³ / CB ❶²	RCA 62870
					LISA LOEB & NINE STORIES		
10/24/97	RR	10	24		2 I Do		Geffen 19416
					LOGGINS, Dave		
05/11/74	BB	5	21		1 Please Come To Boston	CB 7 / RW 7 / RR 9	Epic 11115
					LOGGINS, Kenny		
07/29/78	RR	❶¹	22		1 Whenever I Call You "Friend"	BB 5 / CB 5 / RW 6	Columbia 10794
					KENNY LOGGINS with STEVIE NICKS		
10/13/79	CB	8	24		2 This Is It	RR 9 / RW 10	Columbia 11109
07/12/80	CB	4	27		3 I'm Alright	BB 7 / RR 7 / RW 10	Columbia 11317
08/28/82	RR	4	15		4 Don't Fight It		Columbia 03192
					KENNY LOGGINS with STEVE PERRY		
11/27/82	RR	3¹	17		5 Heart To Heart		Columbia 03377
01/28/84	BB	❶³	25	▲	6 Footloose	CB ❶³ / RR ❶³	Columbia 04310
05/10/86	BB	2¹	21		7 Danger Zone	RR 3² / CB 4	Columbia 05893
03/07/87	RR	9	26		8 Meet Me Half Way	CB 10	Columbia 06690
07/09/88	RR	6	19		9 Nobody's Fool	BB 8 / CB 9	Columbia 07971
					LOGGINS & MESSINA		
11/04/72	BB	4	17	●	1 Your Mama Don't Dance	CB 5 / RW 5	Columbia 45719
					LOGIC		
05/20/17	BB	3⁴	42	△⁵	1 1-800-273-8255		Def Jam
					LOGIC Featuring Alessia Cara & Khalid		
05/18/19	BB	5	6	△	2 Homicide		Visionary
					LOGIC Featuring Eminem		
					LOLITA		
10/08/60	BB	5	20		1 Sailor (Your Home Is The Sea)	CB 7 / MV 9	Kapp 349
					LOMBARDO, Guy, And His Royal Canadians		
10/01/49	CB	7	18		1 Hop-Scotch Polka (Scotch Hot)		Decca 24704
01/21/50	CB	8	19		2 Enjoy Yourself (It's Later Than You Think)	BB 10	Decca 24825
03/04/50	BB	❶¹¹	30	⊙	3 The 3rd Man Theme	CB ❶¹¹	Decca 24839
03/11/50	CB	4	18		4 Dearie	BB 5	Decca 24899
10/07/50	BB	10	15		5 All My Love ("Bolero")		Decca 27118
09/09/50	CB	❶⁶	29		6 Harbor Lights	BB 2¹	Decca 27208
12/16/50	BB	6	17		7 Tennessee Waltz		Decca 27336
03/29/52	BB	9	19		8 Blue Tango		Decca 28031
					LONDON, Julie		
10/31/55	BB	9	20		1 Cry Me A River		Liberty 55006
					LONDON, Laurie		
03/10/58	BB	❶⁴	19	●	1 He's Got The Whole World (In His Hands)	CB ❶² / MV ❶²	Capitol 3891
					LONDONBEAT		
02/08/91	RR	❶²	24	●	1 I've Been Thinking About You	BB ❶¹ / CB ❶¹	Radioactive 54005
05/11/91	RR	9	19		2 A Better Love		Radioactive 54101
					LONESTAR		
06/05/99	BB	❶²	55	●	1 Amazed	RR 6	BNA 65957
					LONG, Shorty		
06/01/68	BB	8	11		1 Here Comes The Judge	RW 8 / CB 10	Soul 35044
					LOOKING GLASS		
06/10/72	BB	❶¹	16	●	1 Brandy (You're A Fine Girl)	CB ❶¹ / RW 2²	Epic 10874
					LOPEZ, Jennifer		
05/07/99	BB	❶⁵	25	▲	1 If You Had My Love	RR 2³	Epic/WORK 79163
09/24/99	RR	2¹	22		2 Waiting For Tonight	BB 8	Epic/WORK 79292
12/01/00	RR	❶²	22		3 Love Don't Cost A Thing	BB 3²	Epic 79547
03/30/01	RR	6	20		4 Play		Epic
07/06/01	BB	❶⁵	31		5 I'm Real	RR ❶³	Epic 79639
12/29/01	BB	❶⁶	27		6 Ain't It Funny	RR ❶²	Epic
					JENNIFER LOPEZ featuring Ja Rule (above 2)		
04/26/02	RR	7	23		7 I'm Gonna Be Alright	BB 10	Epic 79759
					JENNIFER LOPEZ Featuring Nas		

DEBUT	CH	PK	WK	Gold	A-side (Chart Hit)	Other Charts	Label & Number
					LOPEZ, Jennifer (cont'd)		
10/11/02	RR	2[5]	22		8 Jenny From The Block	BB 3[4]	Epic 79825
					JENNIFER LOPEZ Featuring Jadakiss & Styles		
12/20/02	BB	●[4]	22		9 All I Have	RR ●[4]	Epic
					JENNIFER LOPEZ Featuring LL Cool J		
03/12/11	BB	3[1]	29	△[3] 10	On The Floor		Island
					JENNIFER LOPEZ Featuring Pitbull		
					LOPEZ, Trini		
07/27/63	BB	3[3]	15		1 If I Had A Hammer	CB 3[3] / MV 3[1]	Reprise 20,198
					LOR, Denise		
09/04/54	BB	8	14		1 If I Give My Heart To You		Majar 27
					LORAIN, A'Me		
01/20/90	BB	9	21		1 Whole Wide World	RR 10	RCA 9099
					LORDE		
07/20/13	BB	●[9]	44	△[10] 1	Royals		Lava
10/12/13	BB	6	38	△[4] 2	Team		Lava
					LORD TARIQ & PETER GUNZ		
11/15/97	BB	9	28	▲ 1	Deja Vu (Uptown Baby)		Columbia 78755
					LORENZ, Trey		
09/25/92	RR	6	20		1 Someone To Hold		Epic 74482
					LORING, Gloria		
07/05/86	BB	2[2]	21		1 Friends And Lovers	RR 3[1] / CB 5	USA Carrere 06122
					GLORIA LORING & CARL ANDERSON		
					LOS BRAVOS		
08/13/66	RW	2[1]	13		1 Black Is Black	CB 3[2] / BB 4	Press 60002
					LOS DEL RIO		
09/02/95	BB	●[14]	60	▲[4] 1	Macarena	CB ●[2] / RR 10	RCA 64407
					LOS INDIOS TABAJARAS		
08/10/63	BB	6	21		1 Maria Elena	MV 6 / CB 7	RCA Victor 8216
					LOS LOBOS		
06/27/87	BB	●[3]	23		1 La Bamba	CB ●[2] / RR ●[2]	Slash 28336
					LOST GENERATION, The		
06/06/70	RW	10	14		1 The Sly, Slick, And The Wicked		Brunswick 55436
					LOVATO, Demi		
07/30/11	BB	10	15	△ 1	Skyscraper		Hollywood
03/16/13	BB	10	20	△[2] 2	Heart Attack	BB 10	Hollywood
07/29/17	BB	6	36	△[4] 3	Sorry Not Sorry		Safehouse
					LOVE AND ROCKETS		
05/20/89	BB	3[1]	23		1 So Alive	CB 4 / RR 5	RCA 8956
					LOVERBOY		
06/11/83	RR	10	17		1 Hot Girls In Love		Columbia 03941
08/24/85	BB	9	21		2 Lovin' Every Minute Of It		Columbia 05569
01/18/86	RR	8	18		3 This Could Be The Night	BB 10	Columbia 05765
08/02/86	RR	8	16		4 Heaven In Your Eyes	CB 10	Columbia 06178
					LOVE UNLIMITED		
03/18/72	CB	7	16	● 1	Walkin' In The Rain With The One I Love	RW 9	Uni 55319
					LOVE UNLIMITED ORCHESTRA		
12/01/73	BB	●[1]	22	● 1	Love's Theme	CB ●[1] / RW ●[1] / RR 2[1]	20th Century 2069
					LOVIN' SPOONFUL, The		
08/21/65	RW	4	13		1 Do You Believe In Magic	CB 8 / BB 9	Kama Sutra 201
11/20/65	RW	9	13		2 You Didn't Have To Be So Nice	BB 10	Kama Sutra 205
02/26/66	CB	●[1]	12		3 Daydream	BB 2[2] / RW 2[1]	Kama Sutra 208
05/07/66	BB	2[2]	11		4 Did You Ever Have To Make Up Your Mind?	RW 3[1] / CB 4	Kama Sutra 209
07/09/66	BB	●[3]	12	● 5	Summer In The City	CB ●[2] / RW ●[1]	Kama Sutra 211
10/15/66	RW	6	10		6 Rain On The Roof	CB 9 / BB 10	Kama Sutra 216
12/17/66	BB	8	10		7 Nashville Cats	RW 8 / CB 10	Kama Sutra 219
					LOWE, Jim		
08/25/56	BB	●[3]	29	◉ 1	The Green Door	MV 2[8] / CB 2[4]	Dot 15486
					LOWE, Nick		
07/21/79	RR	6	20		1 Cruel To Be Kind		Columbia 11018
					LSG		
11/01/97	BB	4	20	▲ 1	My Body		EastWest 64132

DEBUT	CH	PK	WK	Gold	A-side (Chart Hit) .... Other Charts	Label & Number
					L.T.D.	
09/17/77	BB	4	24	●	1 (Every Time I Turn Around) Back In Love Again .CB 6 / RW 6 / RR 8	A&M 1974
					LUDACRIS	
06/08/02	BB	10	23		1 Move B***h .... LUDACRIS feat. Mystikal and Infamous 2.0	Def Jam South 063949
09/06/03	BB	❶¹	28	○	2 Stand Up .... RR 9 LUDACRIS featuring Shawnna	Def Jam South 001183
01/03/04	BB	6	21		3 Splash Waterfalls	Def Jam South 001757
06/11/05	BB	9	20		4 Pimpin' All Over The World .... LUDACRIS featuring Bobby Valentino	DTP 004851
08/26/06	BB	❶²	25	○	5 Money Maker .... RR 5 LUDACRIS Featuring Pharrell	DTP 007488
12/02/06	BB	2¹	20		6 Runaway Love .... RR 6 LUDACRIS Featuring Mary J. Blige	DTP
12/26/09	BB	6	21	△	7 How Low	DTP
					LUKAS GRAHAM	
02/06/16	BB	2⁴	36	△⁷	1 7 Years	Warner
					LUKE, Robin	
08/02/58	MV	3³	19		1 Susie Darlin' .... BB 5 / CB 6	Dot 15781
					LULU	
09/02/67	BB	❶⁵	17	●	1 To Sir With Love .... CB ❶³ / RW ❶³	Epic 10187
					LUMAN, Bob	
08/29/60	MV	4	15		1 Let's Think About Living .... CB 5 / BB 7	Warner 5172
					LUMIDEE	
05/31/03	BB	3¹	20		1 Never Leave You - Uh Oooh, Uh Oooh!	Universal 000652
					LUMINEERS, The	
06/23/12	BB	3⁵	62	△	1 Ho Hey	Dualtone
					LUNDBERG, Victor	
11/11/67	CB	6	7		1 An Open Letter To My Teenage Son .... RW 7 / BB 10	Liberty 55996
					LUNIZ	
06/10/95	CB	7	25	▲	1 I Got 5 On It .... BB 8	Noo Trybe 38474
					LYMAN, Arthur, Group	
05/27/61	BB	4	15		1 Yellow Bird .... MV 5 / CB 6	Hi Fi 5024
					LYMON, Frankie, and The Teenagers	
02/04/56	CB	2²	21	☉	1 Why Do Fools Fall In Love .... MV 2¹ / BB 6 THE TEENAGERS Featuring FRANKIE LYMON	Gee 1002
04/20/56	CB	10	19		2 I Want You To Be My Girl .... MV 10	Gee 1012
					LYNN, Barbara	
06/16/62	CB	4	15		1 You'll Lose A Good Thing .... BB 8 / MV 10	Jamie 1220
					LYNN, Cheryl	
11/11/78	RR	6	20	▲	1 Got To Be Real .... RW 9 / CB 10	Columbia 10808
					LYNN, Vera	
06/21/52	BB	❶⁹	26	☉	1 Auf Wiederseh'n Sweetheart .... CB ❶⁹	London 1227
10/25/52	BB	7	12	☉	2 Yours .... CB 10	London 1261
					LYNYRD SKYNYRD	
07/27/74	RR	4	18	○	1 Sweet Home Alabama .... CB 7 / BB 8 / RW 8	MCA 40258
11/26/77	CB	7	22		2 What's Your Name	MCA 40819
					LYTTLE, Kevin	
05/22/04	BB	4	25	○	1 Turn Me On .... RR 4	VP/Atlantic 88374

M

DEBUT	CH	PK	WK	Gold	A-side	Label & Number
					M	
08/11/79	BB	❶¹	26	●	1 Pop Muzik .... RR 3¹ / CB 4 / RW 4	Sire 49033
					MacGREGOR, Byron	
12/29/73	CB	❶¹	13	●	1 Americans .... RW ❶¹ / BB 4 / RR 8	Westbound 222
					MacGREGOR, Mary	
11/13/76	RW	❶⁴	27	●	1 Torn Between Two Lovers .... CB ❶³ / BB ❶² / RR ❶¹	Ariola America 7638
					MACHINE GUN KELLY	
11/05/16	BB	4	23	△³	1 Bad Things .... MACHINE GUN KELLY & CAMILA CABELLO	Bad Boy

105

DEBUT	CH	PK	WK	Gold	A-side (Chart Hit) .... Other Charts	Label & Number
					MACK, Craig	
08/13/94	BB	9	25	▲	1 Flava In Ya Ear	Bad Boy 79001
					MACK, Lonnie	
06/01/63	BB	5	15		1 Memphis .... CB 5 / MV 8	Fraternity 906
					MacKENZIE, Gisele	
06/04/55	MV	2³	22		1 Hard To Get .... BB 4 / CB 4	"X" 0137
					MACKLEMORE & RYAN LEWIS	
09/15/12	BB	❶⁶	49	△¹⁰	1 Thrift Shop	Macklemore
					MACKLEMORE & RYAN LEWIS Featuring Wanz	
02/16/13	BB	❶⁵	39	△⁶	2 Can't Hold Us	Macklemore
					MACKLEMORE & RYAN LEWIS Featuring Ray Dalton	
					MacRAE, Gordon — see STAFFORD, Jo	
					MADDOX, Johnny, and The Rhythmasters	
01/24/55	MV	❶³	22	⊙	1 The Crazy Otto .... BB 2⁷ / CB 2²	Dot 15325
					MADNESS	
04/30/83	CB	5	21		1 Our House .... RR 5 / BB 7	Geffen 29668
					MADONNA	
03/10/84	CB	9	30	●	1 Borderline .... BB 10	Sire 29354
08/18/84	RR	3¹	22		2 Lucky Star .... BB 4 / CB 7	Sire 29177
11/16/84	BB	❶⁶	21	●	3 Like A Virgin .... CB ❶⁵ / RR ❶⁵	Sire 29210
02/08/85	CB	❶¹	19		4 Material Girl .... RR ❶¹ / BB 2²	Sire 29083
03/01/85	RR	❶²	21	●	5 Crazy For You .... BB ❶¹ / CB 2⁴	Geffen 29051
04/26/85	RR	4	18		6 Angel .... BB 5 / CB 7	Sire 29008
05/24/85	RR	6	11	●	7 Into The Groove	Sire 20335
08/09/85	RR	2¹	16		8 Dress You Up .... BB 5 / CB 7	Sire 28919
04/04/86	RR	❶³	18		9 Live To Tell .... BB ❶¹ / CB ❶¹	Sire 28717
06/20/86	BB	❶²	18	●	10 Papa Don't Preach .... CB ❶² / RR ❶²	Sire 28660
09/26/86	BB	3³	18	●	11 True Blue .... RR 3³ / CB 3²	Sire 28591
12/05/86	RR	❶²	21		12 Open Your Heart .... BB ❶¹	Sire 28508
03/20/87	RR	3²	17		13 La Isla Bonita .... BB 4 / CB 4	Sire 28425
07/03/87	RR	❶²	20		14 Who's That Girl .... BB ❶¹ / CB ❶¹	Sire 28341
09/04/87	BB	2³	21		15 Causing A Commotion .... RR 2³ / CB 3¹	Sire 28224
03/10/89	BB	❶³	19	▲	16 Like A Prayer .... CB ❶³ / RR ❶³	Sire 27539
05/26/89	CB	❶¹	17	●	17 Express Yourself .... BB 2² / RR 3⁴	Sire 22948
08/11/89	CB	❶¹	16		18 Cherish .... RR ❶¹ / BB 2²	Sire 22883
02/02/90	RR	4	16	●	19 Keep It Together .... BB 8 / CB 8	Sire 19986
04/06/90	RR	❶⁴	24	▲²	20 Vogue .... BB ❶³ / CB ❶³	Sire 19863
06/22/90	CB	8	15	●	21 Hanky Panky .... BB 10 / RR 10	Sire 19789
11/16/90	CB	❶⁴	20	▲	22 Justify My Love .... RR ❶³ / BB ❶²	Sire 19485
01/18/91	RR	4	14	●	23 Rescue Me .... BB 9	Sire 19490
07/03/92	RR	❶⁴	21	●	24 This Used To Be My Playground .... BB ❶¹ / CB ❶¹	Sire 18822
10/09/92	RR	3²	18	●	25 Erotica .... BB 3¹ / CB 3¹	Maverick/Sire 18782
11/27/92	RR	❶¹	20		26 Deeper And Deeper .... CB 6 / BB 7	Maverick/Sire 18639
07/09/93	RR	4	28		27 Rain	Maverick/Sire 18505
03/25/94	RR	❶⁴	30	●	28 I'll Remember .... BB 2⁴ / CB 3¹	Maverick/Sire 18247
09/30/94	CB	2³	24	●	29 Secret .... RR 2² / BB 3¹	Maverick/Sire 18035
12/09/94	CB	❶⁸	32	●	30 Take A Bow .... BB ❶⁷ / RR ❶⁵	Maverick/Sire 18000
11/03/95	RR	4	26	●	31 You'll See .... CB 5 / BB 6	Maverick/Sire 17719
01/10/97	RR	7	16		32 Don't Cry For Me Argentina .... BB 8	Warner 43809
02/20/98	BB	2¹	20	●	33 Frozen .... RR 4	Maverick 17244
05/08/98	BB	5	20		34 Ray Of Light .... RR 10	Maverick 17206
05/28/99	RR	7	20		35 Beautiful Stranger	Maverick
08/04/00	BB	❶⁴	24	▲	36 Music .... RR 2²	Maverick 16826
12/01/00	BB	4	22	●	37 Don't Tell Me .... RR 4	Maverick 16825
10/11/02	RR	4	17		38 Die Another Day .... BB 8	Warner 42492
10/28/05	BB	7	20	△	39 Hung Up	Warner 42845
03/28/08	BB	3²	20	△²	40 4 Minutes .... RR 5	Warner 463036
					MADONNA with JUSTIN TIMBERLAKE	
02/18/12	BB	10	6	○	41 Give Me All Your Luvin'	Live Nation
					MADONNA Featuring Nicki Minaj & M.I.A.	
					MAGIC!	
05/10/14	BB	❶⁶	41	△³	1 Rude	Latium
					MAI, Ella	
04/14/18	BB	5	35	△⁵	1 Boo'd Up	10 Summers
					MAIN INGREDIENT, The	
07/08/72	CB	❶¹	20	●	1 Everybody Plays The Fool .... RW ❶¹ / BB 3¹	RCA Victor 0731
02/02/74	RW	7	20	●	2 Just Don't Want To Be Lonely .... CB 8 / BB 10	RCA Victor 0205

DEBUT	CH	PK	WK	Gold		A-side (Chart Hit)	Other Charts	Label & Number

MAJOR LAZER
04/25/15	BB	4	48	△⁴	1	Lean On		Mad Decent
						MAJOR LAZER & DJ SNAKE with MO		
08/13/16	BB	2⁴	27	△⁴	2	Cold Water		Mad Decent
						MAJOR LAZER with JUSTIN BIEBER & MO		

MALTBY, Richard, and his Orchestra
03/17/56	MV	9	16		1	Themes From "The Man With The Golden Arm"		Vik 0196

MAMA CASS with The Mamas & The Papas
07/06/68	RW	8	11		1	Dream A Little Dream Of Me	CB 10	Dunhill 4145

MAMAS & THE PAPAS, The
01/01/66	RW	2¹	19	●	1	California Dreamin'	BB 4 / CB 4	Dunhill 4020
04/09/66	BB	❶³	12	●	2	Monday, Monday	CB ❶³ / RW ❶²	Dunhill 4026
07/02/66	RW	4	9		3	I Saw Her Again	BB 5 / CB 6	Dunhill 4031
12/03/66	BB	5	12		4	Words Of Love	RW 5 / CB 5	Dunhill 4057
02/25/67	BB	2³	11		5	Dedicated To The One I Love	CB 2² / RW 2²	Dunhill 4077
04/29/67	RW	4	10		6	Creeque Alley	BB 5 / CB 5	Dunhill 4083

MANCHESTER, Melissa
05/10/75	RW	5	19		1	Midnight Blue	BB 6 / CB 7 / RR 7	Arista 0116
11/11/78	BB	10	23		2	Don't Cry Out Loud	CB 10	Arista 0373
05/22/82	CB	4	25		3	You Should Hear How She Talks About You	BB 5 / RR 5	Arista 0676

MANCINI, Henry, And His Orchestra
10/07/61	CB	5	29		1	Moon River	MV 7	RCA Victor 7916
04/26/69	BB	❶²	15	●	2	Love Theme From Romeo & Juliet	CB ❶² / RW ❶¹	RCA Victor 0131
01/09/71	RW	9	13		3	(Theme From) Love Story		RCA Victor 9927

MANFRED MANN
08/29/64	BB	❶²	15	☉	1	Do Wah Diddy Diddy	CB ❶² / RW ❶²	Ascot 2157
03/02/68	CB	4	12		2	Mighty Quinn (Quinn The Eskimo)	RW 5 / BB 10	Mercury 72770
11/13/76	RR	❶³	29	●	3	Blinded By The Light	BB ❶¹ / CB ❶¹ / RW ❶¹	Warner 8252
						MANFRED MANN'S EARTH BAND		

MANGANO, Silvana
03/28/53	BB	5	23	☉	1	Anna (El N. Zumbon)	CB 6	MGM 11457

MANGIONE, Chuck
01/28/78	BB	4	28		1	Feels So Good	RR 4 / CB 6 / RW 6	A&M 2001

MANHATTANS, The
04/17/76	BB	❶²	29	▲	1	Kiss And Say Goodbye	CB ❶² / RW ❶¹ / RR ❶¹	Columbia 10310
04/26/80	RR	3¹	26	▲	2	Shining Star	RW 4 / BB 5 / CB 7	Columbia 11222

MANHATTAN TRANSFER, The
05/23/81	BB	7	24		1	Boy From New York City	CB 8 / RW 8 / RR 9	Atlantic 3816

MANILOW, Barry
11/16/74	RR	❶⁴	21	●	1	Mandy	BB ❶¹ / CB ❶¹ / RW ❶¹	Bell 45,613
03/01/75	CB	10	16		2	It's A Miracle	RW 10	Arista 0108
06/21/75	BB	6	18		3	Could It Be Magic	CB 7 / RR 7 / RW 8	Arista 0126
11/08/75	BB	❶⁵	24	●	4	I Write The Songs	BB ❶¹ / CB ❶¹ / RW ❶¹	Arista 0157
03/13/76	BB	10	18		5	Tryin' To Get The Feeling Again	CB 10	Arista 0172
11/27/76	RW	6	26		6	Weekend In New England	RR 7 / CB 9 / BB 10	Arista 0212
05/07/77	BB	❶¹	21	●	7	Looks Like We Made It	RR 2³ / CB 3³ / RW 3²	Arista 0244
02/04/78	CB	2⁴	20	●	8	Can't Smile Without You	RW 2⁴ / RR 2² / BB 3³	Arista 0305
06/10/78	RW	6	17	●	9	Copacabana (At The Copa)	RR 7 / BB 8 / CB 10	Arista 0339
09/09/78	RW	5	19		10	Ready To Take A Chance Again	CB 5 / BB 7	Arista 0357
12/16/78	RR	8	15		11	Somewhere In The Night	BB 9	Arista 0382
10/05/79	RR	5	15		12	Ships	BB 9 / RW 9	Arista 0464
11/21/80	BB	10	19		13	I Made It Through The Rain	RW 10 / RR 10	Arista 0566
10/09/81	RR	9	18		14	The Old Songs		Arista 0633

MANN, Barry
07/31/61	MV	5	13		1	Who Put The Bomp (In The Bomp, Bomp, Bomp)	BB 7 / CB 7	ABC-Paramount 10237

MANN, Gloria
12/01/55	MV	9	18		1	Teen Age Prayer		Sound 126

MANTOVANI And His Orchestra
11/17/51	CB	5	25	☉	1	Charmaine	BB 10	London 1020
05/16/53	BB	8	10		2	The Moulin Rouge Theme (Where Is Your Heart)		London 1328
08/14/54	MV	9	18	☉	3	Cara Mia	BB 10	London 1486
						DAVID WHITFIELD with MANTOVANI and his Orchestra and Chorus		
06/15/57	CB	6	23		4	Around The World		London 1746

MARCELS, The
02/27/61	BB	❶³	15	☉	1	Blue Moon	CB ❶³ / MV ❶³	Colpix 186
10/09/61	BB	7	12		2	Heartaches		Colpix 612

DEBUT	CH	PK	WK	Gold	A-side (Chart Hit) ... Other Charts	Label & Number
					MARCH, Little Peggy	
03/16/63	BB	❶³	16	⊙	1 I Will Follow Him .... CB ❶³ / MV ❶³	RCA Victor 8139
					MARCY PLAYGROUND	
02/13/98	RR	3⁴	28		1 Sex And Candy .... BB 8	Capitol 58695
					MARDONES, Benny	
06/07/80	RR	5	22		1 Into The Night .... RW 9 / CB 10	Polydor 2091
					MARESCA, Ernie	
03/17/62	BB	6	17		1 Shout! Shout! (Knock Yourself Out) .... MV 10	Seville 117
					MARIE, Teena	
12/15/84	BB	4	24		1 Lovergirl .... RR 4 / CB 5	Epic 04619
					MARINERS, The	
06/10/50	CB	9	23		1 Sometime	Columbia 38781
					MARIO	
05/25/02	BB	4	21		1 Just A Friend 2002 .... RR 6	J Records 21219
10/23/04	BB	❶⁹	36	○	2 Let Me Love You .... RR ❶	J Records 61888
					MARKETTS, The	
12/07/63	BB	3²	15		1 Out Of Limits .... CB 3¹ / MV 4	Warner 5391
02/05/66	RW	10	9		2 Batman Theme	Warner 5696
					MAR-KEYS	
06/12/61	BB	3²	17		1 Last Night .... CB 3¹ / MV 3¹	Satellite 107
					MARK IV, The	
01/19/59	CB	9	13		1 I Got A Wife .... MV 10	Mercury 71403
					MARKY MARK And The Funky Bunch	
07/20/91	BB	❶¹	27	●	1 Good Vibrations .... CB 4 / RR 4	Interscope 98764
					MARKY MARK And The Funky Bunch Featuring Loleatta Holloway	
11/02/91	RR	7	24	●	2 Wildside .... BB 10	Interscope 98673
					MARMALADE, The	
02/28/70	CB	7	16		1 Reflections Of My Life .... RW 7 / BB 10	London 20058
					MAROON 5	
07/04/03	RR	4	27	△	1 Harder To Breathe	Octone 60635
01/30/04	RR	❶²	43	△²	2 This Love .... BB 5	Octone 63388
07/02/04	RR	❶⁵	41	△⁴	3 She Will Be Loved .... BB 5	Octone 65248
04/06/07	BB	❶³	26	△³	4 Makes Me Wonder .... RR 4	A&M
08/03/07	RR	8	22	△²	5 Wake Up Call	A&M
07/09/11	BB	❶⁴	49	△⁹	6 Moves Like Jagger	A&M
					MAROON 5 Featuring Christina Aguilera	
05/05/12	BB	2⁶	31	△⁷	7 Payphone	A&M 016962
					MAROON 5 Featuring Wiz Khalifa	
07/07/12	BB	❶⁹	42	△⁶	8 One More Night	A&M
12/22/12	BB	7	25	△²	9 Daylight	A&M
06/08/13	BB	10	21	△²	10 Love Somebody	A&M
07/05/14	BB	6	22	△⁴	11 Maps	222 Records
09/06/14	BB	3¹	33		12 Animals	222 Records
01/31/15	BB	2⁴	42	△⁸	13 Sugar	222 Records
10/29/16	BB	6	27	△²	14 Don't Wanna Know	222 Records
					MAROON 5 Featuring Kendrick Lamar	
09/16/17	BB	9	22	△²	15 What Lovers Do	222 Records
					MAROON 5 Featuring SZA	
06/09/18	BB	❶⁷	52	△	16 Girls Like You	222 Records
					MAROON 5 Featuring Cardi B	
10/05/19	BB	2¹	22		17 Memories	222 Records
					MARS, Bruno	
04/17/10	BB	4	27	△⁴	1 Billionaire	Fueled By Ramen
					TRAVIE McCOY with BRUNO MARS	
08/07/10	BB	❶⁴	48	△¹⁰	2 Just The Way You Are	Elektra
10/16/10	BB	❶⁴	36	△⁸	3 Grenade	Elektra
10/23/10	BB	4	27	△⁶	4 The Lazy Song	Elektra
10/15/11	BB	3⁵	29	△⁵	5 It Will Rain	Summit
10/20/12	BB	❶⁶	36	△⁷	6 Locked Out Of Heaven	Atlantic
12/22/12	BB	❶¹	35	△⁸	7 When I Was Your Man	Atlantic
06/01/13	BB	5	23	△⁴	8 Treasure	Atlantic
11/29/14	BB	❶¹⁴	56	△¹¹	9 Uptown Funk!	RCA
					MARK RONSON with BRUNO MARS	
10/29/16	BB	4	41	△⁵	10 24K Magic	Atlantic
12/10/16	BB	❶¹	52	△⁷	11 That's What I Like	Atlantic
01/13/18	BB	3⁸	23	△⁴	12 Finesse	Atlantic
					BRUNO MARS & CARDI B	

DEBUT	CH	PK	WK	Gold	A-side (Chart Hit)	Other Charts	Label & Number
					MARS, Bruno (cont'd)		
03/02/19	BB	3¹	20	△²	13 Please Me		Atlantic
					CARDI B & BRUNO MARS		
					MARSHALL TUCKER BAND, The		
03/12/77	CB	10	22		1 Heard It In A Love Song		Capricorn 0270
					MARSHMELLO		
09/01/18	BB	2¹	52	△⁵	1 Happier		Joytime
					MARSHMELLO & BASTILLE		
					MARTERIE, Ralph, And His Orchestra		
01/10/53	BB	6	10	⊙	1 Pretend		Mercury 70045
03/21/53	BB	6	21	⊙	2 Caravan	CB 10	Mercury 70097
10/04/54	CB	2²	22		3 Skokiaan	BB 3³ / MV 4	Mercury 70432
04/27/57	BB	10	16		4 Shish-Kebab		Mercury 71092
					MARTHA & THE VANDELLAS		
07/27/63	MV	3²	16		1 Heat Wave	BB 4 / CB 4	Gordy 7022
11/23/63	BB	8	12		2 Quicksand	MV 10	Gordy 7025
08/22/64	BB	2²	15	●	3 Dancing In The Street	RW 2¹ / CB 4	Gordy 7033
02/27/65	RW	6	11		4 Nowhere To Run	BB 8 / CB 9	Gordy 7039
10/22/66	RW	8	12		5 I'm Ready For Love	BB 9	Gordy 7056
02/25/67	CB	6	14		6 Jimmy Mack	RW 7 / BB 10	Gordy 7058
					MARTIKA		
05/20/89	BB	❶²	20	●	1 Toy Soldiers	RR ❶¹ / CB 4	Columbia 68747
08/10/91	BB	10	20		2 Love...Thy Will Be Done	CB 10 / RR 10	Columbia 73853
					MARTIN, Bobbi		
03/14/70	RW	8	14		1 For The Love Of Him	CB 9	United Artists 50602
					MARTIN, Dean		
11/07/53	BB	2⁶	24	⊙	1 That's Amore	CB 2¹	Capitol 2589
11/21/55	BB	❶⁶	24	⊙	2 Memories Are Made Of This	MV ❶⁵ / CB ❶³	Capitol 3295
03/17/58	MV	2¹	23		3 Return To Me	CB 3² / BB 4	Capitol 3894
06/27/64	BB	❶¹	16	●	4 Everybody Loves Somebody	CB ❶¹ / RW 2³	Reprise 0281
09/26/64	BB	6	11		5 The Door Is Still Open To My Heart	RW 7 / CB 8	Reprise 0307
10/30/65	RW	9	12		6 I Will	BB 10	Reprise 0415
					MARTIN, Freddy, and his Orchestra		
10/29/49	CB	7	20		1 I've Got A Lovely Bunch Of Coconuts	BB 8	RCA Victor 3047
03/11/50	BB	5	10		2 (Put Another Nickel In) Music! Music! Music!		RCA Victor 3217
					MARTIN, Marilyn — see COLLINS, Phil		
					MARTIN, Mary		
03/25/50	BB	8	9		1 Go To Sleep, Go To Sleep, Go To Sleep	CB 10	Columbia 38744
					MARY MARTIN and ARTHUR GODFREY		
					MARTIN, Ricky		
04/09/99	RR	❶⁷	20	▲	1 Livin' La Vida Loca	BB ❶⁵	C2/Columbia 79124
07/30/99	BB	2²	20	●	2 She's All I Ever Had		C2/Columbia 79259
11/05/99	RR	9	18		3 Shake Your Bon-Bon		C2/Columbia 79333
09/29/00	BB	9	18		4 She Bangs		Columbia 79514
01/26/01	RR	7	20		5 Nobody Wants To Be Lonely		Columbia 79573
					RICKY MARTIN with CHRISTINA AGUILERA		
					MARTIN, Tony		
11/12/49	BB	2¹	29		1 There's No Tomorrow	CB 3²	RCA Victor 3078
01/21/50	CB	3²	14		2 I Said My Pajamas (And Put On My Pray'rs)	BB 3¹	RCA Victor 3119
					TONY MARTIN and FRAN WARREN		
07/08/50	CB	5	25		3 La Vie En Rose	BB 9	RCA Victor 3819
01/20/51	BB	8	19		4 A Penny A Kiss	CB 8	RCA Victor 4019
					TONY MARTIN and DINAH SHORE		
06/02/51	CB	2²	36		5 I Get Ideas	BB 3³	RCA Victor 4141
11/03/51	CB	7	16		6 Domino	BB 9	RCA Victor 4343
05/03/52	BB	6	15		7 Kiss Of Fire		RCA Victor 4671
01/02/54	BB	10	11		8 Stranger In Paradise		RCA Victor 5535
03/20/54	BB	5	21		9 Here	CB 5	RCA Victor 5665
04/21/56	BB	10	20		10 Walk Hand In Hand		RCA Victor 6493
					MARTIN, Vince, with The Tarriers		
10/06/56	BB	9	19		1 Cindy, Oh Cindy	CB 9	Glory 247
					MARTINDALE, Wink		
09/12/59	CB	4	18		1 Deck Of Cards	BB 7 / MV 8	Dot 15968
					MARTINO, Al		
05/17/52	BB	❶³	24		1 Here In My Heart	CB 2⁶	BBS 101
03/16/63	BB	3¹	18		2 I Love You Because	CB 3¹ / MV 3¹	Capitol 4930

DEBUT	CH	PK	WK	Gold	A-side (Chart Hit) .... Other Charts	Label & Number
					MARTINO, Al (cont'd)	
01/25/64	BB	9	13		3 I Love You More And More Every Day	Capitol 5108
05/16/64	RW	9	9		4 Tears And Roses...	Capitol 5183
					MARVELETTES, The	
09/04/61	BB	❶¹	23	●	1 Please Mr. Postman .... MV 2³ / CB 2²	Tamla 54046
04/23/62	BB	7	15		2 Playboy .... CB 8	Tamla 54060
01/01/66	BB	7	13	●	3 Don't Mess With Bill .... RW 7 / CB 9	Tamla 54126
12/16/67	CB	10	11		4 My Baby Must Be A Magician	Tamla 54158
					MARX, Richard	
06/13/87	BB	3¹	21		1 Don't Mean Nothing .... RR 4 / CB 5	Manhattan 50079
09/26/87	BB	3¹	23		2 Should've Known Better .... CB 4 / RR 4	Manhattan 50083
01/22/88	BB	2²	21		3 Endless Summer Nights .... RR 2¹ / CB 4	EMI/Manhattan 50113
05/21/88	BB	❶¹	22		4 Hold On To The Nights.................................... RR 2² / CB 3²	EMI/Manhattan 50106
04/28/89	CB	❶²	19		5 Satisfied .... RR ❶¹ / BB ❶¹	EMI 50189
06/30/89	BB	❶³	21	▲	6 Right Here Waiting .... RR ❶³ / CB ❶²	EMI 50219
10/06/89	CB	2²	19		7 Angelia .... BB 4 / RR 4	EMI 50218
01/12/90	RR	10	14		8 Too Late To Say Goodbye	EMI 50234
04/27/90	RR	8	18		9 Children Of The Night	EMI 50288
11/01/91	CB	5	23		10 Keep Coming Back .... RR 5	Capitol 44753
02/08/92	BB	5	25		11 Hazard .... CB 6 / BB 9	Capitol 44796
06/05/92	RR	7	20		12 Take This Heart	Capitol 44782
01/14/94	CB	3²	29		13 Now And Forever .... BB 7 / RR 7	Capitol 58005
					MARY JANE GIRLS	
03/09/85	CB	5	23		1 In My House .... BB 7 / RR 7	Gordy 1741
					MASE	
11/01/97	BB	5	20	▲	1 Feel So Good..	Bad Boy 79122
01/31/98	BB	6	24	●	2 What You Want...	Bad Boy 79141
					MASE (Featuring Total)	
07/25/98	BB	8	19	●	3 Lookin' At Me	Bad Boy 79176
					MASE featuring Puff Daddy	
					MASEKELA, Hugh	
06/08/68	RW	❶³	13	●	1 Grazing In The Grass .... BB ❶² / CB ❶¹	Uni 55066
					MASON, Barbara	
05/08/65	CB	3¹	16		1 Yes, I'm Ready .... RW 4 / BB 5	Arctic 105
					MATCHBOX TWENTY	
06/07/97	RR	2¹	52		1 Push .... BB 5	Lava/Atlantic 84410
10/25/97	RR	3⁹	58		2 3 AM .... BB 3⁸	Lava/Atlantic
04/11/98	RR	3¹	36		3 Real World .... BB 9	Lava/Atlantic
10/09/98	RR	8	34		4 Back 2 Good	Lava/Atlantic 84410
					MATCHBOX 20 (above 4)	
04/21/00	RR	❶²	39	●	5 Bent .... BB ❶¹	Lava/Atlantic 84704
09/29/00	RR	4	42		6 If You're Gone .... BB 5	Lava/Atlantic
02/28/03	RR	3¹	54	○	7 Unwell .... BB 5	Melisma/Atlantic
					MATHIS, Johnny	
04/27/57	CB	2¹	34	☉	1 It's Not For Me To Say .... MV 3¹ / BB 5	Columbia 40851
09/02/57	CB	❶²	28	☉	2 Chances Are / .... BB ❶¹ / MV 2²	
09/07/57	BB	9	17		3 The Twelfth Of Never	Columbia 40993
09/22/62	BB	6	14		4 Gina .... CB 8 / MV 8	Columbia 42582
01/26/63	MV	8	13		5 What Will My Mary Say .... BB 9 / CB 9	Columbia 42666
03/18/78	BB	❶¹	21	●	6 Too Much, Too Little, Too Late .... RW ❶¹ / CB 2³ / RR 2¹	Columbia 10693
					JOHNNY MATHIS & DENIECE WILLIAMS	
					MATTHEWS, Dave, Band	
03/11/95	RR	7	24		1 What Would You Say	RCA
					MATTHEWS, Ian	
11/25/78	CB	10	20		1 Shake It .... RW 10 / RR 10	Mushroom 7039
					MAURIAT, Paul, and His Orchestra	
12/30/67	CB	❶⁷	19	●	1 Love Is Blue... BB ❶⁵ / RW ❶³	Philips 40495
					MAX, Ava	
12/29/18	BB	10	35	△²	1 Sweet But Psycho	Atlantic
					MAXWELL	
04/10/99	BB	4	25	●	1 Fortunate	Rock Land 79135
					MAXWELL, Robert, His Harp And Orchestra	
03/21/64	CB	9	14		1 Shangri-La .... MV 9	Decca 25622
					MAY, Billy, and His Orchestra — see COLE, Nat "King"	

DEBUT	CH	PK	WK	Gold	A-side (Chart Hit)	Other Charts	Label & Number
					MAYER, John		
05/24/02	RR	9	24	○	1 No Such Thing		Aware
					MAYFIELD, Curtis		
08/19/72	BB	4	17	●	1 Freddie's Dead (Theme From "Superfly")	RW 5 / CB 6	Curtom 1975
11/11/72	CB	6	15	●	2 Superfly	RW 6 / BB 8	Curtom 1978
					MC HAMMER		
03/30/90	RR	❶¹	22	○	1 U Can't Touch This	CB 4 / BB 8	Capitol 15571
06/30/90	RR	3¹	24	●	2 Have You Seen Her	BB 4 / CB 4	Capitol 44573
09/15/90	BB	2²	19	●	3 Pray	CB 3¹ / RR 5	Capitol 44609
11/02/91	BB	5	22	▲	4 2 Legit 2 Quit		Capitol 44785
12/07/91	BB	7	20	●	5 Addams Groove		Capitol 44794
					HAMMER (above 2)		
					MC LYTE		
03/16/96	CB	7	22	●	1 Keep On, Keepin' On	BB 10	Flavor Unit 64302
					MC LYTE with XSCAPE		
					McCAIN, Edwin		
01/30/98	BB	5	45		1 I'll Be	RR 9	Lava/Atlantic 84191
					McCALL, C.W.		
11/22/75	CB	❶³	23	●	1 Convoy	RW ❶³ / BB ❶¹ / RR 2¹	MGM 14839
					McCANN, Peter		
04/23/77	BB	5	23	●	1 Do You Wanna Make Love	RW 7 / RR 8 / CB 9	20th Century 2335
					McCARTNEY, Jesse		
10/22/04	RR	3¹	26	○	1 Beautiful Soul		Hollywood
04/04/08	RR	❶⁵	30	△	2 Leavin'	BB 10	Hollywood
02/06/09	RR	7	20		3 How Do You Sleep?		Hollywood
					JESSE McCARTNEY Featuring Ludacris		
					McCARTNEY, Paul [WINGS]		
02/27/71	BB	5	13		1 Another Day	RW 5 / CB 6	Apple 1829
					PAUL McCARTNEY		
08/14/71	BB	❶¹	13	●	2 Uncle Albert/Admiral Halsey	CB ❶¹ / RW ❶¹	Apple 1837
					PAUL & LINDA McCARTNEY		
12/16/72	CB	6	11		3 Hi, Hi, Hi	RW 7 / BB 10	Apple 1857
					WINGS		
04/14/73	RW	❶⁵	18	●	4 My Love	BB ❶⁴ / CB ❶⁴	Apple 1861
					PAUL McCARTNEY & WINGS		
06/30/73	CB	❶¹	16	●	5 Live And Let Die	RW ❶¹ / BB 2³	Apple 1863
					WINGS		
11/17/73	RW	4	13		6 Helen Wheels	CB 5 / RR 8 / BB 10	Apple 1869
02/02/74	CB	5	15		7 Jet	RW 5 / RR 6 / BB 7	Apple 1871
04/13/74	CB	❶²	18	●	8 Band On The Run	RR ❶² / BB ❶¹ / RW ❶¹	Apple 1873
11/09/74	BB	3¹	17		9 Junior's Farm	CB 4 / RW 5 / RR 6	Apple 1875
					PAUL McCARTNEY & WINGS (above 4)		
05/30/75	RW	❶²	19	● 10	Listen To What The Man Said	BB ❶¹ / CB ❶¹ / RR 2²	Capitol 4091
04/09/76	RR	❶⁶	29	● 11	Silly Love Songs	BB ❶⁵ / RW ❶⁴ / CB ❶²	Capitol 4256
06/19/76	CB	❶¹	24	● 12	Let 'Em In	RR 2³ / BB 3⁴ / RW 4	Capitol 4293
02/12/77	BB	10	15		13 Maybe I'm Amazed	CB 10	Capitol 4385
03/25/78	BB	❶³	19		14 With A Little Luck	BB ❶² / CB ❶² / RW ❶¹	Capitol 4559
03/23/79	RR	2²	16	● 15	Goodnight Tonight	CB 4 / BB 5 / RW 7	Columbia 10939
06/16/79	RR	10	12		16 Getting Closer		Columbia 11020
					WINGS (above 7)		
04/26/80	BB	❶³	21	● 17	Coming Up (Live At Glasgow)	RR ❶¹ / CB 2³ / RW 3⁶	Columbia 11263
					PAUL McCARTNEY & WINGS		
04/02/82	BB	❶⁷	20	● 18	Ebony And Ivory	CB ❶⁶ / RR ❶⁴	Columbia 02860
					PAUL McCARTNEY with STEVIE WONDER		
07/09/82	RR	2¹	16		19 Take It Away	CB 6 / BB 10	Columbia 03018
					PAUL McCARTNEY		
11/05/82	BB	2³	18	● 20	The Girl Is Mine	CB 3⁵ / RR 4	Epic 03288
					MICHAEL JACKSON/PAUL McCARTNEY		
10/07/83	RR	❶⁷	27	▲ 21	Say Say Say	BB ❶⁶ / CB ❶³	Columbia 04168
					PAUL McCARTNEY AND MICHAEL JACKSON		
10/12/84	RR	4	19		22 No More Lonely Nights	BB 6 / CB 10	Columbia 04581
11/22/85	BB	7	22		23 Spies Like Us	RR 9 / CB 10	Capitol 5537
					PAUL McCARTNEY (above 2)		
02/07/15	BB	4	20	△³ 24	FourFiveSeconds		Westbury Road
					RIHANNA & KANYE WEST & PAUL McCARTNEY		
					McCLINTON, Delbert		
12/06/80	BB	8	19		1 Giving It Up For Your Love	RR 9 / CB 10	MSS/Capitol 4948
					McCOO, Marilyn, & Billy Davis, Jr.		
09/11/76	CB	❶²	30	●	1 You Don't Have To Be A Star (To Be In My Show)	BB ❶¹ / RW ❶¹ / RR 3³	ABC 12208

DEBUT	CH	PK	WK	Gold	A-side (Chart Hit) ... Other Charts	Label & Number
					McCOY, Travie	
04/17/10	BB	4	27	△⁴	1 Billionaire .... TRAVIE McCOY with BRUNO MARS	Fueled By Ramen
					McCOY, Van, & The Soul City Symphony	
04/19/75	BB	❶¹	19	●	1 The Hustle .... CB ❶¹ / RW ❶¹ / RR ❶¹	Avco 4653
					McCOYS, The	
08/14/65	RW	❶²	16	⊙	1 Hang On Sloopy .... BB ❶¹ / CB ❶¹	Bang 506
11/06/65	RW	6	13		2 Fever .... BB 7 / CB 9	Bang 511
					McCRACKLIN, Jimmy	
02/17/58	BB	7	16		1 The Walk	Checker 885
					McCRAE, George	
05/25/74	BB	❶²	18		1 Rock Your Baby .... CB ❶¹ / RW ❶¹ / RR ❶¹	T.K. 1004
					McCRAE, Gwen	
04/26/75	BB	9	18		1 Rockin' Chair .... RR 9 / CB 10 / RW 10	Cat 1996
					McDANIELS, Gene	
03/13/61	MV	❶¹	18		1 A Hundred Pounds Of Clay .... CB 3⁴ / BB 3²	Liberty 55308
09/25/61	BB	5	14		2 Tower Of Strength .... MV 7 / CB 9	Liberty 55371
01/15/62	BB	10	11		3 Chip Chip	Liberty 55405
					McDONALD, Michael	
08/06/82	RR	❶³	24		1 I Keep Forgettin' (Every Time You're Near) .... BB 4 / CB 4	Warner 29933
03/22/86	BB	❶³	23	●	2 On My Own .... CB ❶³ / RR ❶¹ PATTI LaBELLE AND MICHAEL McDONALD	MCA 52770
06/14/86	CB	6	21		3 Sweet Freedom .... BB 7 / RR 7	MCA 52857
					McFERRIN, Bobby	
07/30/88	BB	❶²	26	●	1 Don't Worry Be Happy .... CB ❶¹ / RR ❶¹	EMI/Manhattan 50146
					McGOVERN, Maureen	
06/16/73	BB	❶²	19	●	1 The Morning After .... RW ❶¹ / CB 3¹	20th Century 2010
					McGRAW, Tim	
05/17/97	BB	7	20	▲	1 It's Your Love .... TIM McGRAW with FAITH HILL	Curb 73019
04/03/99	BB	10	20		2 Please Remember Me	Curb 73080
10/08/04	RR	❶¹⁰	24	△	3 Over And Over .... BB 3¹ NELLY with TIM McGRAW	Derrty/Curb
					McGUIRE, Barry	
08/14/65	RW	❶²	13	⊙	1 Eve Of Destruction .... BB ❶¹ / CB ❶¹	Dunhill 4009
					McGUIRE SISTERS, The	
06/19/54	BB	7	19		1 Goodnight, Sweetheart, Goodnight .... CB 8	Coral 61187
09/25/54	CB	9	19		2 Muskrat Ramble .... BB 10 / MV 10	Coral 61278
12/20/54	BB	❶¹⁰	24	⊙	3 Sincerely / .... MV ❶⁵ / CB 2³	Coral 61323
01/29/55	MV	9	1		4 No More	
05/16/55	CB	4	19		5 Something's Gotta Give .... MV 4 / BB 5	Coral 61423
10/29/55	BB	10	19		6 He	Coral 61501
12/23/57	BB	❶⁴	23	⊙	7 Sugartime .... MV ❶¹ / CB 7	Coral 61924
					McINTYRE, Joey	
01/29/99	BB	10	15	●	1 Stay The Same	C2/Columbia 79103
					McKENZIE, Bob & Doug	
01/30/82	RW	10	17		1 Take Off .... BOB & DOUG McKENZIE Featuring Geddy Lee	Mercury 76134
					McKENZIE, Scott	
05/27/67	RW	3³	13		1 San Francisco (Be Sure To Wear Flowers In Your Hair) .. BB 4 / CB 4	Ode 103
					McKNIGHT, Brian	
01/23/93	RR	❶¹	38		1 Love Is .... CB 2¹ / BB 3¹ VANESSA WILLIAMS and BRIAN McKNIGHT	Giant 18630
06/11/93	RR	6	23		2 One Last Cry	Mercury 862404
02/07/98	BB	6	40		3 Anytime .... RR 6	Motown 860768
08/28/99	BB	2⁸	37	○	4 Back At One .... RR 3⁵	Motown 156501
					McLACHLAN, Sarah	
03/27/98	BB	3¹	27	●	1 Adia	Arista 13497
11/06/98	RR	3¹	31	○	2 Angel .... BB 4	Arista 13621
05/14/99	RR	10	20	○	3 I Will Remember You	Arista
					McLEAN, Don	
11/27/71	RW	❶⁵	20	●	1 American Pie (Parts I & II) .... BB ❶⁴ / CB ❶⁴	United Artists 50856
01/16/81	BB	5	18		2 Crying .... RR 5 / CB 6 / RW 9	Millennium 11799

DEBUT	CH	PK	WK	Gold	A-side (Chart Hit) .... Other Charts	Label & Number
					McNAMARA, Robin	
05/16/70	RW	6	17		1 Lay A Little Lovin' On Me ....CB 7	Steed 724
					McPHATTER, Clyde	
10/06/58	BB	6	24	⊙	1 A Lover's Question ....CB 10	Atlantic 1199
02/24/62	MV	4	16		2 Lover Please ....BB 7 / CB 7	Mercury 71941
					McVIE, Christine	
01/27/84	RR	7	16		1 Got A Hold On Me ....BB 10	Warner 29372
					MEAD, Sister Janet	
02/09/74	BB	4	18	●	1 The Lord's Prayer ....CB 5 / RW 5 / RR 10	A&M 1491
					MEAT LOAF	
03/18/78	RR	4	25	●	1 Two Out Of Three Ain't Bad ....RW 7 / CB 9	Cleveland I./Epic 50513
09/17/93	CB	❶⁶	29	▲	2 I'd Do Anything For Love (But I Won't Do That) ....BB ❶⁵ / RR 3³	MCA 54626
01/21/94	RR	9	20		3 Rock And Roll Dreams Come Through	MCA 54757
					MECO	
07/30/77	BB	❶²	22	▲	1 Star Wars Theme/Cantina Band ....CB ❶² / RW ❶² / RR ❶²	Millennium 604
06/14/80	RW	9	19		2 Empire Strikes Back (Medley)	RSO 1038
					MEDEIROS, Glenn	
05/18/90	RR	❶³	20	●	1 She Ain't Worth It ....BB ❶² / CB ❶²	MCA 53831
					GLENN MEDEIROS Featuring Bobby Brown	
					MEDLEY, Bill	
09/19/87	BB	❶¹	23	●	1 (I've Had) The Time Of My Life ....CB ❶¹ / RR ❶¹	RCA 5224
					BILL MEDLEY AND JENNIFER WARNES	
					MEEK MILL	
12/15/18	BB	6	37	△²	1 Going Bad	Maybach
					MEEK MILL Featuring Drake	
					MEESTER, Leighton — see COBRA STARSHIP	
					MEL AND TIM	
10/18/69	BB	10	14	●	1 Backfield In Motion	Bamboo 107
					MELANIE	
04/18/70	CB	3¹	17		1 Lay Down (Candles In The Rain) ....RW 4 / BB 6	Buddah 167
					MELANIE with THE EDWIN HAWKINS SINGERS	
10/23/71	BB	❶³	19	●	2 Brand New Key ....CB ❶² / RW ❶¹	Neighborhood 4201
					MELLENCAMP, John Cougar	
04/24/82	CB	❶¹	29	●	1 Hurts So Good ....BB 2⁴ / RR 3³	Riva 209
07/23/82	BB	❶⁴	25	●	2 Jack & Diane ....CB ❶³ / RR ❶³	Riva 210
					JOHN COUGAR (above 2)	
10/07/83	RR	6	17		3 Crumblin' Down ....CB 8 / BB 9	Riva 214
12/02/83	BB	8	16		4 Pink Houses ....RR 9	Riva 215
08/16/85	RR	4	20		5 Lonely Ol' Night ....BB 6 / CB 10	Riva 880984
11/01/85	RR	4	18		6 Small Town ....BB 6 / CB 6	Riva 884202
01/31/86	BB	2¹	18		7 R.O.C.K. In The U.S.A. (A Salute To 60's Rock) ....RR 2¹ / CB 4	Riva 884455
08/14/87	BB	9	17		8 Paper In Fire ....RR 9 / CB 10	Mercury 888763
10/24/87	BB	8	21		9 Cherry Bomb	Mercury 888934
05/21/94	RR	3⁶	45		10 Wild Night ....BB 3² / CB 4	Mercury 858738
					JOHN MELLENCAMP & ME'SHELL NDEGEOCELLO	
08/09/96	RR	9	26		11 Key West Intermezzo (I Saw You First)	Mercury 578398
					JOHN MELLENCAMP	
					MELVIN, Harold, And The Blue Notes	
09/30/72	CB	2¹	17	●	1 If You Don't Know Me By Now ....RW 2¹ / BB 3²	Philadelphia I. 3520
09/22/73	RW	6	18	●	2 The Love I Lost (Part 1) ....BB 7 / CB 9	Philadelphia I. 3533
					MEN AT WORK	
07/10/82	CB	❶²	29		1 Who Can It Be Now? ....BB ❶¹ / RR 4	Columbia 02888
11/06/82	CB	❶⁵	28	▲	2 Down Under ....RR ❶⁵ / BB ❶⁴	Columbia 03303
04/01/83	RR	❶³	16		3 Overkill ....BB 3¹ / CB 5	Columbia 03795
07/01/83	RR	3¹	15		4 It's A Mistake ....BB 6	Columbia 03959
					MENDES, Sergio, & Brasil '66	
05/11/68	BB	4	14		1 The Look Of Love ....CB 5 / RW 6	A&M 924
08/10/68	BB	6	12		2 The Fool On The Hill ....RW 6 / CB 7	A&M 961
04/16/83	CB	3²	26		3 Never Gonna Let You Go ....BB 4 / RR 7	A&M 2540
					SERGIO MENDES	
					MENDES, Shawn	
06/13/15	BB	4	52	△⁷	1 Stitches	Island
06/25/16	BB	6	39	△⁴	2 Treat You Better	Island
05/13/17	BB	6	34	△⁴	3 There's Nothing Holdin' Me Back	Island
05/18/19	BB	2¹	23	△	4 If I Can't Have You	Island

DEBUT	CH	PK	WK	Gold	A-side (Chart Hit) ... Other Charts	Label & Number
					MENDES, Shawn (cont'd)	
07/06/19	BB	❶¹	35	△ 5	Senorita .... SHAWN MENDES & CAMILA CABELLO	Syco
					MEN WITHOUT HATS	
06/25/83	CB	❶¹	26	1	The Safety Dance .... BB 3⁴ / RR 3²	Backstreet 52232
					MENZEL, Idina	
12/14/13	BB	5	33	△⁸ 1	Let It Go	Walt Disney
					MERCHANT, Natalie	
07/28/95	RR	4	38	1	Carnival .... CB 9 / BB 10	Elektra 64413
12/08/95	RR	4	39	2	Wonder	Elektra 64376
05/10/96	RR	5	26	3	Jealousy .... CB 10	Elektra 64301
					MERCY	
04/05/69	CB	2³	14	● 1	Love (Can Make You Happy) .... BB 2² / RW 2²	Sundi 6811
					METALLICA	
06/08/96	BB	10	23	● 1	Until It Sleeps	Elektra 64276
					METHOD MAN	
05/06/95	BB	3¹	23	▲ 1	I'll Be There For You/You're All I Need To Get By ...... CB 6 METHOD MAN and MARY J. BLIGE	Def Jam 851878
					METRO STATION	
04/11/08	RR	4	30	△² 1	Shake It .... BB 10	Red Ink
					MFSB featuring The Three Degrees	
02/23/74	BB	❶²	18	● 1	TSOP (The Sound Of Philadelphia) .... CB ❶² / RW ❶² / RR 3²	Philadelphia I. 3540
					M.I.A.	
08/02/08	BB	4	20	△³ 1	Paper Planes .... RR 10	XL 010912
					MIAMI SOUND MACHINE — see ESTEFAN, Gloria	
					MICHAEL, George [WHAM!]	
					WHAM!:	
09/08/84	BB	❶³	24	▲ 1	Wake Me Up Before You Go-Go .... CB ❶² / RR ❶²	Columbia 04552
12/14/84	CB	❶⁴	22	▲ 2	Careless Whisper .... BB ❶³ / RR ❶²	Columbia 04691
					WHAM! Featuring George Michael	
03/23/85	BB	❶²	20	● 3	Everything She Wants .... CB ❶¹ / RR ❶¹	Columbia 04840
07/26/85	BB	3¹	18	4	Freedom .... RR 6 / CB 10	Columbia 05409
11/29/85	BB	3²	21	5	I'm Your Man .... CB 3² / RR 3¹	Columbia 05721
07/04/86	RR	9	15	6	The Edge Of Heaven .... BB 10 / CB 10	Columbia 06182
					GEORGE MICHAEL:	
04/25/86	BB	7	16	7	A Different Corner .... CB 8 / RR 10	Columbia 05888
02/20/87	BB	❶²	21	8	I Knew You Were Waiting (For Me) .... RR ❶² / CB ❶¹ ARETHA FRANKLIN AND GEORGE MICHAEL	Arista 9559
06/05/87	BB	2¹	22	▲ 9	I Want Your Sex .... CB 2¹ / RR 8	Columbia 07164
10/23/87	CB	❶⁵	23	● 10	Faith .... BB ❶⁴ / RR ❶⁴	Columbia 07623
01/15/88	RR	❶⁴	19	11	Father Figure .... CB ❶³ / BB ❶²	Columbia 07682
04/08/88	RR	❶⁴	19	● 12	One More Try .... BB ❶³ / CB ❶³	Columbia 07773
07/01/88	RR	❶³	17	13	Monkey .... BB ❶² / CB ❶²	Columbia 07941
10/07/88	CB	4	18	14	Kissing A Fool .... BB 5 / RR 6	Columbia 08050
02/25/89	CB	4	22	15	Heaven Help Me .... BB 5 / RR 5 DEON ESTUS with GEORGE MICHAEL	Mika 871538
08/24/90	CB	❶²	15	16	Praying For Time .... RR ❶² / BB ❶¹	Columbia 73512
10/26/90	CB	7	19	● 17	Freedom .... BB 8 / RR 8	Columbia 73559
12/06/91	BB	❶¹	22	● 18	Don't Let The Sun Go Down On Me .... CB ❶¹ / RR 2² GEORGE MICHAEL/ELTON JOHN	Columbia 74086
06/12/92	RR	2¹	20	● 19	Too Funky .... BB 10 / CB 10	Columbia 74353
01/19/96	BB	7	16	● 20	Jesus To A Child .... CB 10	DreamWorks 59000
04/26/96	CB	6	23	● 21	Fastlove .... BB 8 / RR 10	DreamWorks 59001
					MICHAELS, Lee	
07/31/71	CB	4	17	1	Do You Know What I Mean .... RW 5 / BB 6	A&M 1262
					MICHEL'LE	
11/18/89	BB	7	29	● 1	No More Lies .... CB 7	Ruthless 99149
					MICKEY AND SYLVIA	
12/22/56	CB	7	19	1	Love Is Strange .... MV 8	Groove 0175
					MIDLER, Bette	
05/05/73	RW	5	17	1	Boogie Woogie Bugle Boy .... CB 6 / BB 8	Atlantic 2964
03/22/80	RW	❶²	26	● 2	The Rose .... CB ❶¹ / RR / BB 3³	Atlantic 3656
03/04/89	CB	❶²	29	▲ 3	Wind Beneath My Wings .... BB ❶¹ / RR 3¹	Atlantic 88972
10/06/90	BB	2¹	26	▲ 4	From A Distance .... CB 2¹ / RR 4	Atlantic 87820

DEBUT	CH	PK	WK	Gold	A-side (Chart Hit) ... Other Charts	Label & Number
					MIGOS	
12/03/16	BB	❶³	36	△⁴	1 Bad And Boujee	Quality Control
					MIGOS Featuring Lil Uzi Vert	
11/18/17	BB	6	22	△³	2 MotorSport	Quality Control
					MIGOS, NICKI MINAJ & CARDI B	
01/06/18	BB	8	21	△²	3 Stir Fry	Quality Control
02/10/18	BB	10	22	△²	4 Walk It Talk It	Quality Control
					MIGOS Featuring Drake	
					MIKE + THE MECHANICS	
11/23/85	CB	5	24		1 Silent Running (On Dangerous Ground) .... RR 5 / BB 6	Atlantic 89488
03/22/86	RR	3¹	19		2 All I Need Is A Miracle .... BB 5 / CB 9	Atlantic 89450
12/31/88	CB	❶²	23		3 The Living Years .... BB ❶¹ / RR 2³	Atlantic 88964
					MILIAN, Christina	
04/23/04	RR	3⁴	30	○	1 Dip It Low .... BB 5	Island 002034
					MILLER, Chuck	
06/13/55	BB	9	21		1 The House Of Blue Lights	Mercury 70627
					MILLER, Mitch, & his Orch. and Chorus	
07/08/50	CB	2¹	20		1 Tzena Tzena Tzena .... BB 3¹	Columbia 38885
07/25/55	CB	❶⁷	23	⊙	2 The Yellow Rose Of Texas .... MV ❶⁷ / BB ❶⁶	Columbia 40540
07/28/56	BB	8	17		3 Theme Song From "Song For A Summer Night" .... CB 9	Columbia 40730
					MILLER, Ned	
12/15/62	BB	6	17		1 From A Jack To A King .... CB 6 / MV 6	Fabor 114
					MILLER, Roger	
06/06/64	RW	5	13		1 Dang Me .... BB 7 / CB 7	Smash 1881
09/05/64	RW	5	13		2 Chug-A-Lug .... CB 6 / BB 9	Smash 1926
01/30/65	CB	3¹	15	●	3 King Of The Road .... BB 4 / RW 4	Smash 1965
05/08/65	BB	7	10		4 Engine Engine #9 .... RW 7 / CB 9	Smash 1983
10/30/65	RW	5	13		5 England Swings .... BB 8 / CB 8	Smash 2010
					MILLER, Steve, Band	
10/20/73	BB	❶¹	21	●	1 The Joker .... CB ❶¹ / RW ❶¹ / RR 2⁵	Capitol 3732
05/08/76	RR	8	19		2 Take The Money And Run .... CB 9	Capitol 4260
08/14/76	RR	❶³	29		3 Rock'n Me .... BB ❶¹ / CB ❶¹ / RW ❶¹	Capitol 4323
12/11/76	BB	2²	23	●	4 Fly Like An Eagle .... CB 3³ / RR 4 / RW 5	Capitol 4372
					STEVE MILLER (above 3)	
04/30/77	RR	3²	18		5 Jet Airliner .... CB 3¹ / RW 7 / BB 8	Capitol 4424
10/15/77	RR	10	15		6 Swingtown	Capitol 4496
05/29/82	CB	❶⁵	28	●	7 Abracadabra .... BB ❶² / RR 3¹	Capitol 5126
					MILLI VANILLI	
12/31/88	CB	❶¹	26	▲	1 Girl You Know It's True .... BB 2¹ / RR 4	Arista 9781
04/29/89	BB	❶¹	21	●	2 Baby Don't Forget My Number .... CB 2² / RR 3¹	Arista 9832
08/04/89	BB	❶²	22	●	3 Girl I'm Gonna Miss You .... RR ❶² / CB ❶¹	Arista 9870
10/06/89	BB	❶²	23	▲	4 Blame It On The Rain .... RR ❶² / CB ❶¹	Arista 9904
12/30/89	BB	4	17		5 All Or Nothing .... CB 4 / RR 4	Arista 9923
					MILLS, Frank	
01/27/79	RW	❶¹	23	●	1 Music Box Dancer .... CB 2² / BB 3¹ / RR 6	Polydor 14517
					MILLS, Hayley	
09/04/61	CB	5	14		1 Let's Get Together .... BB 8 / MV 8	Buena Vista 385
					MILLS, Stephanie	
08/09/80	BB	6	28	●	1 Never Knew Love Like This Before .... CB 8 / RW 8 / RR 8	20th Century 2460
					MILLS BROTHERS, The	
01/28/50	CB	4	27		1 Daddy's Little Girl .... BB 5	Decca 24872
11/04/50	CB	3²	22		2 Nevertheless (I'm In Love With You) .... BB 4	Decca 27253
01/12/52	BB	7	22		3 Be My Life's Companion	Decca 27889
09/27/52	BB	❶³	26	⊙	4 The Glow-Worm .... CB ❶¹	Decca 28384
					MILSAP, Ronnie	
06/26/81	BB	5	22		1 (There's) No Gettin' Over Me .... RR 6 / RW 8 / CB 9	RCA 12264
					MIMMS, Garnet, & The Enchanters	
08/17/63	BB	4	14		1 Cry Baby .... CB 4 / MV 4	United Artists 629
					MIMS	
02/03/07	BB	❶²	23	△²	1 This Is Why I'm Hot	Capitol 84997
					MINAJ, Nicki	
05/14/11	BB	3²	39	△⁸	1 Super Bass	Young Money 015776
09/17/11	BB	4	27	△²	2 Turn Me On	Astralwerks
					DAVID GUETTA with NICKI MINAJ	
03/03/12	BB	5	31	△⁶	3 Starships	Young Money

115

DEBUT	CH	PK	WK	Gold	A-side (Chart Hit) ... Other Charts	Label & Number
					MINAJ, Nicki (cont'd)	
08/16/14	BB	3²	31	△⁶ 4	Bang Bang JESSIE J, ARIANA GRANDE & NICKI MINAJ	Lava
08/23/14	BB	2¹	22	△² 5	Anaconda	Young Money
04/11/15	BB	8	24	△³ 6	Hey Mama DAVID GUETTA with NICKI MINAJ, BEBE REXHA & AFROJACK	What A Music
11/18/17	BB	6	22	△³ 7	MotorSport MIGOS, NICKI MINAJ & CARDI B	Quality Control
04/21/18	BB	10	16	△ 8	Chun-Li	Young Money
					MINDBENDERS, The	
03/20/65	BB	❶¹	12	⊙ 1	Game Of Love .... CB ❶¹ / RW ❶¹ WAYNE FONTANA & THE MINDBENDERS	Fontana 1509
04/02/66	CB	❶¹	16	⊙ 2	A Groovy Kind Of Love .... RW ❶¹ / BB 2²	Fontana 1541
					MINEO, Sal	
05/11/57	CB	6	19	1	Start Movin' (In My Direction) .... MV 7 / BB 9	Epic 9216
					MINOGUE, Kylie	
08/27/88	BB	3²	27	● 1	The Loco-Motion .... RR 3¹ / CB 4	Geffen 27752
01/11/02	RR	3³	20	○ 2	Can't Get You Out Of My Head .... BB 7	Capitol 77685
					MINT CONDITION	
01/04/92	BB	6	24	● 1	Breakin' My Heart (Pretty Brown Eyes) .... RR 10	Perspective 0004
					MIRACLES, The	
11/28/60	BB	2¹	18	⊙ 1	Shop Around .... CB 2¹ / MV 2¹	Tamla 54034
12/08/62	CB	6	17	2	You've Really Got A Hold On Me .... BB 8 / MV 10	Tamla 54073
08/17/63	MV	7	13	3	Mickey's Monkey .... BB 8 / CB 9	Tamla 54083
12/25/65	RW	9	12	4	Going To A Go-Go .... CB 10	Tamla 54127
11/04/67	CB	3¹	15	5	I Second That Emotion .... RW 3¹ / BB 4	Tamla 54159
01/04/69	RW	7	14	6	Baby, Baby Don't Cry .... BB 8 / CB 9	Tamla 54178
10/10/70	BB	❶²	17	7	The Tears Of A Clown .... CB ❶¹ / RW 2⁴ SMOKEY ROBINSON & THE MIRACLES (above 3)	Tamla 54199
08/03/74	RW	9	17	8	Do It Baby .... CB 10	Tamla 54248
10/25/75	BB	❶¹	28	9	Love Machine (Part 1) .... CB ❶¹ / RW ❶¹	Tamla 54262
					MIS-TEEQ	
04/23/04	RR	10	20	1	Scandalous	Reprise 16435
					MR. BIG	
12/14/91	CB	❶⁵	32	● 1	To Be With You .... BB ❶³ / RR 2²	Atlantic 87580
04/17/92	RR	8	20	2	Just Take My Heart .... CB 9	Atlantic 87509
					MR. HUDSON — see JAY-Z	
					MR. MISTER	
09/21/85	BB	❶²	26	1	Broken Wings .... CB ❶² / RR ❶¹	RCA 14136
12/20/85	BB	❶²	22	2	Kyrie .... CB ❶² / RR ❶²	RCA 14258
03/28/86	RR	7	17	3	Is It Love .... BB 8	RCA 14313
					MITCHELL, Guy	
12/09/50	CB	❶³	22	⊙ 1	My Heart Cries For You /	
12/16/50	BB	4	21	2	The Roving Kind .... CB 6	Columbia 39067
03/03/51	BB	8	15	3	Sparrow In The Tree Top .... CB 8	Columbia 39190
05/05/51	CB	8	16	4	Unless	Columbia 39331
06/02/51	BB	2¹	23	⊙ 5	My Truly, Truly Fair .... CB 3²	Columbia 39415
08/18/51	BB	9	13	6	Belle, Belle, My Liberty Belle .... CB 9	Columbia 39512
03/15/52	BB	4	24	⊙ 7	Pittsburgh, Pennsylvania .... CB 10	Columbia 39663
10/20/56	BB	❶¹⁰	26	⊙ 8	Singing The Blues .... CB ❶⁹ / MV ❶⁷	Columbia 40769
01/19/57	MV	10	13	9	Knee Deep In The Blues	Columbia 40820
03/30/57	MV	7	17	10	Rock-A-Billy .... BB 10	Columbia 40877
10/05/59	MV	❶³	20	11	Heartaches By The Number .... BB ❶² / CB ❶²	Columbia 41476
					MITCHELL, Joni	
03/02/74	BB	7	20	1	Help Me .... RW 7 / CB 8	Asylum 11034
					MO — see MAJOR LAZER	
					MOCEDADES	
12/29/73	BB	9	19	1	Eres Tu (Touch The Wind) .... CB 9 / RW 9	Tara 100
					MODUGNO, Domenico	
07/07/58	CB	❶⁶	21	⊙ 1	Nel Blu Dipinto Di Blu (Volare) .... MV ❶⁶ / BB ❶⁵	Decca 30677
					MOKENSTEF	
06/17/95	BB	7	25	● 1	He's Mine .... CB 8	OutBurst 851704
					MOMENTS, The	
04/04/70	BB	3²	15	● 1	Love On A Two-Way Street .... RW 3¹ / CB 8	Stang 5012

DEBUT	CH	PK	WK	Gold	A-side (Chart Hit)	Other Charts	Label & Number
					MONEY, Eddie		
01/28/78	CB	5	26		1 Baby Hold On	RR 8	Columbia 10663
08/16/86	BB	4	24		2 Take Me Home Tonight	CB 5 / RR 5	Columbia 06231
12/13/86	RR	10	21		3 I Wanna Go Back		Columbia 06569
10/01/88	CB	7	21		4 Walk On Water	BB 9 / RR 9	Columbia 08060
12/02/89	CB	8	19		5 Peace In Our Time	RR 8	Columbia 73047
12/07/91	CB	6	30		6 I'll Get By	RR 10	Columbia 74109
					MONEY, JT		
04/24/99	BB	5	20	●	1 Who Dat		Tony Mercedes 53469
					JT MONEY Featuring Sole		
					MONICA		
04/29/95	BB	2³	29	▲	1 Don't Take It Personal (Just One Of Dem Days)	CB 3²	Rowdy 35040
10/21/95	BB	7	30	▲	2 Before You Walk Out Of My Life	CB 8	Rowdy 35052
06/08/96	CB	6	23	●	3 Why I Love You So Much	BB 9	Rowdy 35072
02/07/97	BB	4	32	▲	4 For You I Will	RR 5	Warner Sunset 87003
05/15/98	BB	❶¹³	27	▲²	5 The Boy Is Mine	RR 3⁴	Atlantic 84089
					BRANDY & MONICA		
08/15/98	BB	❶⁵	23	▲	6 The First Night		Arista 13522
12/05/98	BB	❶⁴	30	▲	7 Angel Of Mine	RR 5	Arista 13590
04/26/03	BB	10	22		8 So Gone		J Records 21260
					MONIFAH		
08/08/98	BB	9	26		1 Touch It		Uptown 56207
					MONKEES, The		
09/03/66	CB	❶²	16	●	1 Last Train To Clarksville	RW ❶² / BB ❶¹	Colgems 1001
12/03/66	CB	❶⁸	17	●	2 I'm A Believer	BB ❶⁷ / RW ❶⁵	Colgems 1002
03/25/67	CB	❶²	11	●	3 A Little Bit Me, A Little Bit You	RW ❶¹ / BB 2¹	Colgems 1004
07/22/67	RW	2¹	11	●	4 Pleasant Valley Sunday /	BB 3² / CB 3¹	
07/22/67	CB	5	10		5 Words		Colgems 1007
11/11/67	BB	❶⁴	13	●	6 Daydream Believer	CB ❶⁴ / RW ❶³	Colgems 1012
03/09/68	CB	❶²	11	●	7 Valleri	RW ❶² / BB 3²	Colgems 1019
06/15/68	CB	10	8		8 D. W. Washburn		Colgems 1023
					MONOTONES, The		
03/22/58	BB	5	18	☉	1 Book Of Love	CB 7	Argo 5290
					MONROE, Vaughn		
01/28/50	BB	4	12		1 Bamboo	CB 10	RCA Victor 3143
04/21/51	BB	3¹	17		2 Sound Off (The Duckworth Chant)	CB 5	RCA Victor 4113
04/21/51	BB	8	16		3 On Top Of Old Smoky		RCA Victor 4114
05/12/51	BB	7	8		4 Old Soldiers Never Die		RCA Victor 4146
07/10/54	BB	7	23		5 They Were Doin' The Mambo	CB 8 / MV 10	RCA Victor 5767
					MONTANA, French		
04/29/17	BB	3²	42	△⁷	1 Unforgettable		Coke Boys
					FRENCH MONTANA Featuring Swae Lee		
					MONTE, Lou		
02/06/54	BB	7	13		1 Darktown Strutters Ball (Italian Style)	CB 9	RCA Victor 5611
02/24/58	MV	7	18		2 Lazy Mary (Luna Mezzo Mare)		RCA Victor 7160
11/24/62	MV	4	13		3 Pepino The Italian Mouse	BB 5 / CB 7	Reprise 20,106
					MONTENEGRO, Hugo, His Orchestra And Chorus		
02/17/68	BB	2¹	22		1 The Good, The Bad And The Ugly	CB 4 / RW 4	RCA Victor 9423
					MONTEZ, Chris		
08/04/62	BB	4	16		1 Let's Dance	MV 5 / CB 6	Monogram 505
					MOODY BLUES, The		
02/13/65	CB	6	16		1 Go Now!	RW 8 / BB 10	London 9726
08/05/72	CB	❶¹	18	●	2 Nights In White Satin	RW ❶² / BB 2²	Deram 85023
01/20/73	CB	8	13		3 I'm Just A Singer (In A Rock And Roll Band)	RW 10	Threshold 67012
06/05/81	RR	6	16		4 Gemini Dream		Threshold 601
08/07/81	RR	6	17		5 The Voice		Threshold 602
04/19/86	BB	9	21		6 Your Wildest Dreams	CB 10	Polydor 883906
					MOONEY, Art, And His Orchestra		
09/03/49	CB	7	22		1 Hop-Scotch Polka (Scotch Hot)		MGM 10500
01/10/55	CB	5	21	☉	2 Honey-Babe	BB 6 / MV 6	MGM 11900
12/10/55	CB	5	6	☉	3 Nuttin' For Christmas	BB 6	MGM 12092
					ART MOONEY And His ORCHESTRA with BARRY GORDON		
					MOORE, Bob, and His Orch.		
08/14/61	MV	5	16		1 Mexico	CB 6 / BB 7	Monument 446
					MOORE, Chante		
05/15/99	BB	10	18	●	1 Chante's Got A Man		Silas/MCA 55544

DEBUT	CH	PK	WK	Gold	A-side (Chart Hit) ... Other Charts	Label & Number
					MOORE, Dorothy	
03/06/76	BB	3[4]	26		1 Misty Blue .... CB 3[2] / RR 4 / RW 6	Malaco 1029
					MORGAN, Al	
09/03/49	CB	3[2]	25		1 Jealous Heart .... BB 4	London 30001
					MORGAN, Debelah	
07/14/00	BB	8	29	●	1 Dance With Me .... RR 8	Atlantic 84783
					MORGAN, Jane	
08/10/57	CB	5	29	◉	1 Fascination .... BB 7 / MV 7	Kapp 191
					JANE MORGAN and The Troubadors	
					MORGAN, Jaye P.	
11/15/54	BB	3[1]	25		1 That's All I Want From You .... MV 4 / CB 6	RCA Victor 5896
02/14/55	MV	10	18		2 Danger! Heartbreak Ahead	RCA Victor 6016
07/04/55	MV	5	17		3 The Longest Walk .... BB 6	RCA Victor 6182
					MORGAN, Russ, And His Orchestra	
04/15/50	CB	4	26		1 Sentimental Me .... BB 7	Decca 24904
					MORISSETTE, Alanis	
06/17/95	RR	9	32		1 You Oughta Know	Maverick
08/19/95	RR	6	28		2 Hand In My Pocket	Maverick
02/16/96	RR	❶[4]	35	●	3 Ironic .... CB 3[6] / BB 4	Maverick 17698
05/24/96	RR	❶[6]	30		4 You Learn .... CB 2[2] / BB 6	Maverick 17644
08/10/96	RR	❶[4]	47		5 Head Over Feet .... BB 3[6]	Maverick
03/28/98	RR	❶[2]	29		6 Uninvited .... BB 4	Warner Sunset
10/02/98	RR	❶[1]	18		7 Thank U .... BB 2[1]	Maverick
					MORRIS, Maren — see ZEDD	
					MORRISON, Mark	
03/01/97	BB	2[1]	40	▲	1 Return Of The Mack .... RR 4	Atlantic 84868
					MORRISON, Van	
06/24/67	RW	7	19	○	1 Brown Eyed Girl .... CB 8 / BB 10	Bang 545
11/07/70	RW	6	12		2 Domino .... BB 9 / CB 9	Warner 7434
					MORROW, Buddy, and His Orchestra	
05/19/51	BB	8	10		1 Rose, Rose, I Love You	RCA Victor 4135
					MORSE, Ella Mae	
02/16/52	BB	3[6]	26	◉	1 The Blacksmith Blues .... CB 3[5]	Capitol F1922
					MOTELS, The	
04/24/82	RR	5	23		1 Only The Lonely .... CB 8 / BB 9	Capitol 5114
09/03/83	RR	5	21		2 Suddenly Last Summer .... BB 9 / CB 10	Capitol 5271
					MOTLEY CRUE	
09/01/89	CB	5	20	●	1 Dr. Feelgood .... BB 6	Elektra 69271
02/24/90	CB	7	18		2 Without You .... BB 8	Elektra 64985
					MOUTH & MACNEAL	
04/29/72	CB	5	19	●	1 How Do You Do? .... BB 8 / RW 8	Philips 40715
					MRAZ, Jason	
04/25/03	RR	7	28		1 The Remedy (I Won't Worry)	Elektra
05/03/08	RR	❶[1]	76	△[10]	2 I'm Yours .... BB 6	Atlantic
01/21/12	BB	8	44	△[6]	3 I Won't Give Up	Atlantic
					MULDAUR, Maria	
02/09/74	CB	4	24		1 Midnight At The Oasis .... RW 5 / BB 6 / RR 8	Reprise 1183
					MULLINS, Shawn	
09/25/98	RR	❶[7]	28		1 Lullaby .... BB 7	Columbia 790847
					MUMBA, Samantha	
08/11/00	BB	4	25		1 Gotta Tell You .... RR 4	Wild Card 497408
					MUNGO JERRY	
07/11/70	RW	❶[1]	13	●	1 In The Summertime .... CB 2[1] / BB 3[1]	Janus 125
					MURMAIDS, The	
11/16/63	MV	❶[1]	15		1 Popsicles And Icicles .... BB 3[2] / CB 3[2]	Chattahoochee 628
					MURPHEY, Michael	
03/22/75	RW	2[2]	22	▲	1 Wildfire .... RR 2[2] / CB 2[1] / BB 3[2]	Epic 50084
					MURPHY, Eddie	
10/05/85	BB	2[3]	26	▲	1 Party All The Time .... CB 2[3] / RR 3[4]	Columbia 05609

DEBUT	CH	PK	WK	Gold	A-side (Chart Hit) ... Other Charts	Label & Number
					MURPHY, Walter, & The Big Apple Band	
05/22/76	BB	❶¹	35	●	1 A Fifth Of Beethoven .... CB ❶¹ / RW ❶¹ / RR 5	Private Stock 45,073
					MURRAY, Anne	
07/18/70	RW	4	18	●	1 Snowbird .... CB 6 / BB 8	Capitol 2738
12/23/72	RW	5	20		2 Danny's Song .... CB 6 / BB 7	Capitol 3481
12/15/73	CB	10	17		3 Love Song	Capitol 3776
04/13/74	BB	8	20		4 You Won't See Me .... CB 8 / RW 9	Capitol 3867
07/08/78	BB	❶¹	28	●	5 You Needed Me .... RW 2³ / CB 4 / RR 4	Capitol 4574
01/20/79	RR	10	18		6 I Just Fall In Love Again	Capitol 4675
12/22/79	RW	10	18		7 Daydream Believer	Capitol 4813
					MUSICAL YOUTH	
12/11/82	BB	10	19		1 Pass The Dutchie	MCA 52149
					MUSIC EXPLOSION, The	
05/06/67	RW	❶¹	17		1 Little Bit O' Soul .... BB 2² / CB 2¹	Laurie 3380
					MYA	
03/14/98	BB	6	20	●	1 It's All About Me	University 97024
					MYA with Sisqo	
08/19/00	BB	2³	30		2 Case Of The Ex (Whatcha Gonna Do) .... RR 2²	University 97457
04/06/01	RR	❶⁹	20		3 Lady Marmalade .... BB ❶⁵	Interscope 497066
					CHRISTINA AGUILERA, LIL' KIM, MYA and PINK	
06/28/03	RR	8	22		4 My Love Is Like...Wo	A&M 000768
					MY CHEMICAL ROMANCE	
09/30/06	BB	9	26	△³	1 Welcome To The Black Parade	Reprise
					MYERS, Billie	
11/08/97	RR	5	31		1 Kiss The Rain	Universal 56140
					MYLES, Alannah	
12/30/89	BB	❶²	25	●	1 Black Velvet .... CB ❶² / RR 2¹	Atlantic 88742

N

DEBUT	CH	PK	WK	Gold	A-side	Label & Number
					NAIM, Yael	
02/16/08	BB	7	19	○	1 New Soul	Tot Ou Tard
					NAKED EYES	
03/12/83	CB	7	23		1 Always Something There To Remind Me .... BB 8 / RR 10	EMI America 8155
07/16/83	RR	8	20		2 Promises, Promises	EMI America 8170
					NAPOLEON XIV	
07/23/66	CB	❶¹	7		1 They're Coming To Take Me Away, Ha-Haaa! .... RW ❶¹ / BB 3¹	Warner 5831
					NASH, Johnny	
09/07/68	RW	4	16		1 Hold Me Tight .... BB 5 / CB 7	JAD 207
08/26/72	BB	❶⁴	21	●	2 I Can See Clearly Now .... CB ❶¹ / RW ❶¹	Epic 10902
					NATALIE	
02/11/05	RR	8	20	○	1 Goin' Crazy	Latium 004381
					NATE DOGG — see WARREN G.	
					NATURAL SELECTION	
08/10/91	BB	2²	28		1 Do Anything .... CB 2¹ / RR 3²	EastWest 98724
					NATURAL SELECTION Featuring Niki Haris	
11/30/91	RR	10	25		2 Hearts Don't Think (They Feel)!	EastWest 98652
					NAUGHTON, David	
03/17/79	BB	5	28	●	1 Makin' It .... CB 5 / RW 9	RSO 916
					NAUGHTY BY NATURE	
09/07/91	BB	6	21	▲²	1 O.P.P.	Tommy Boy 988
01/30/93	CB	7	23	▲	2 Hip Hop Hooray .... BB 8	Tommy Boy 554
07/03/99	BB	10	17	●	3 Jamboree	Arista 13712
					NAUGHTY BY NATURE (Featuring Zhane)	
					NAZARETH	
11/15/75	RR	6	26	●	1 Love Hurts .... BB 8 / RW 8 / CB 9	A&M 1671
					NDEGEOCELLO, Me'Shell — see MELLENCAMP, John	
					NELLY	
04/29/00	BB	7	34	○	1 (Hot S**t) Country Grammar .... RR 9	Fo' Reel 156800
02/24/01	RR	3²	29	○	2 Ride Wit Me .... BB 3¹	Fo' Reel
					NELLY (Featuring City Spud)	
04/26/02	BB	❶⁷	26	△²	3 Hot In Herre .... RR ❶²	Fo' Reel 019279

119

DEBUT	CH	PK	WK	Gold	A-side (Chart Hit) ... Other Charts	Label & Number
					NELLY (cont'd)	
07/12/02	BB	❶¹⁰	29		4 Dilemma ....RR ❶⁵	Fo' Reel 019509
					NELLY with KELLY ROWLAND	
11/09/02	BB	3⁴	22		5 Air Force Ones ....RR 9	Fo' Reel 019509
					NELLY Featuring Kyjuan, Ali and Murphy Lee	
06/27/03	BB	❶⁴	30	○	6 Shake Ya Tailfeather ....RR ❶³	Bad Boy
					NELLY/P. DIDDY/MURPHY LEE	
07/23/04	BB	4	20	○	7 My Place ....RR 10	Derrty 003154
					NELLY Feat. Jaheim	
10/08/04	RR	❶¹⁰	24	△	8 Over And Over ....BB 3¹	Derrty/Curb
					NELLY with TIM McGRAW	
11/19/05	BB	❶²	28	△	9 Grillz ....RR 7	Derrty 005897
					NELLY F/Paul Wall, Ali & Gipp	
09/04/10	BB	3²	28	△³	10 Just A Dream	Derrty
					NELSON	
07/07/90	BB	❶¹	26	●	1 (Can't Live Without Your) Love And Affection............CB ❶¹ / RR 5	DGC 19689
11/03/90	RR	5	24		2 After The Rain ....BB 6 / CB 8	DGC 19667
					NELSON, Ricky	
05/06/57	BB	4	17	☉	1 I'm Walking /	
05/13/57	BB	2¹	19		2 A Teenager's Romance ....CB 8	Verve 10047
10/05/57	BB	3¹	20	☉	3 Be-Bop Baby ....CB 6 / MV 10	Imperial 5463
12/23/57	BB	2³	18	☉	4 Stood Up / CB 3¹ / MV 7	Imperial 5483
12/23/57	CB	6	14		5 Waitin' In School	Imperial 5483
03/29/58	BB	4	12	☉	6 Believe What You Say	Imperial 5503
06/23/58	BB	❶²	17	☉	7 Poor Little Fool ....CB 2² / MV 2¹	Imperial 5528
10/06/58	BB	7	18	☉	8 Lonesome Town / CB 7 / MV 8	Imperial 5545
10/06/58	MV	7	18		9 I Got A Feeling ....CB 10	Imperial 5545
02/23/59	CB	5	16		10 Never Be Anyone Else But You / MV 5 / BB 6	Imperial 5565
03/02/59	CB	6	13		11 It's Late ....MV 8 / BB 9	Imperial 5565
06/29/59	BB	9	13		12 Just A Little Too Much / MV 10	Imperial 5595
06/29/59	BB	9	12		13 Sweeter Than You	Imperial 5595
04/22/61	MV	❶⁴	18	●	14 Travelin' Man / CB ❶³ / BB ❶²	Imperial 5741
04/22/61	BB	9	16		15 Hello Mary Lou ....CB 9	Imperial 5741
					RICK NELSON:	
03/03/62	BB	5	14		16 Young World ....CB 9 / MV 9	Imperial 5805
08/11/62	BB	5	12		17 Teen Age Idol ....MV 8 / CB 9	Imperial 5864
12/15/62	BB	6	13		18 It's Up To You ....CB 7	Imperial 5901
12/28/63	BB	6	12		19 For You ....CB 8 / MV 9	Decca 31574
07/29/72	CB	3¹	19	●	20 Garden Party ....RW 4 / BB 6	Decca 32980
					RICK NELSON & THE STONE CANYON BAND	
					NELSON, Sandy	
09/05/59	MV	3¹	16		1 Teen Beat ....BB 4 / CB 4	Original Sound 5
10/30/61	BB	7	16		2 Let There Be Drums ....MV 7 / CB 9	Imperial 5775
					NELSON, Willie	
03/06/82	CB	4	23	▲	1 Always On My Mind ....BB 5 / RR 8	Columbia 02741
03/03/84	CB	3²	22	▲	2 To All The Girls I've Loved Before ....BB 5	Columbia 04217
					JULIO IGLESIAS & WILLIE NELSON	
					NENA	
12/10/83	CB	❶¹	26	●	1 99 Luftballons ....BB 2¹ / RR 2¹	Epic 04108
					NEON TREES	
03/31/12	BB	6	39	△⁴	1 Everybody Talks	Mercury
					NERVOUS NORVUS	
06/01/56	BB	8	14		1 Transfusion ....CB 10	Dot 15470
					NEVIL, Robbie	
10/11/86	BB	2²	23		1 C'est La Vie ....CB 3² / RR 3¹	Manhattan 50047
05/30/87	BB	10	16		2 Wot's It To Ya	Manhattan 50075
					NEVILLE, Aaron	
11/26/66	BB	2¹	15	☉	1 Tell It Like It Is ....CB 3⁴ / RW 3³	Par-Lo 101
09/30/89	CB	2⁴	26	●	2 Don't Know Much...BB 2² / RR 4	Elektra 69261
					LINDA RONSTADT with AARON NEVILLE	
07/13/91	BB	8	28		3 Everybody Plays The Fool ....RR 9	A&M 1563
					NEWBEATS, The	
08/08/64	RW	❶¹	14	☉	1 Bread And Butter ....BB 2² / CB 2¹	Hickory 1269
09/25/65	RW	10	15		2 Run, Baby Run (Back Into My Arms)	Hickory 1332
					NEW EDITION	
09/22/84	CB	2¹	25	●	1 Cool It Now ....BB 4 / RR 10	MCA 52455
12/22/84	CB	9	18		2 Mr. Telephone Man	MCA 52484
07/02/88	CB	5	21		3 If It Isn't Love ....BB 7 / RR 7	MCA 53264
08/24/96	BB	3¹	20	●	4 Hit Me Off ....CB 4	MCA 55210

DEBUT	CH	PK	WK	Gold	A-side (Chart Hit) ... Other Charts	Label & Number
					NEW EDITION (cont'd)	
11/09/96	BB	7	20	● 5	I'm Still In Love With You	MCA 55264
					NEW KIDS ON THE BLOCK	
06/25/88	BB	10	28	1	Please Don't Go Girl .... RR 10	Columbia 07700
11/19/88	BB	3¹	26	● 2	You Got It (The Right Stuff) .... CB 4 / RR 6	Columbia 08092
04/01/89	RR	❶²	22	● 3	I'll Be Loving You (Forever) .... BB ❶¹ / CB 5	Columbia 68671
07/14/89	BB	❶¹	20	▲ 4	Hangin' Tough / .... RR ❶¹ / CB 2¹	
09/16/89	RR	7	19	5	Didn't I (Blow Your Mind) .... BB 8	Columbia 68960
09/15/89	BB	2¹	20	● 6	Cover Girl .... RR 3² / CB 4	Columbia 69088
11/11/89	BB	7	16	● 7	This One's For The Children .... CB 7 / RR 10	Columbia 73064
05/18/90	CB	❶⁵	18	▲ 8	Step By Step .... BB ❶³ / RR ❶²	Columbia 73343
07/20/90	RR	6	19	9	Tonight .... BB 7 / CB 8	Columbia 73461
					NEWMAN, Randy	
11/12/77	CB	❶¹	22	● 1	Short People .... BB 2³ / RW 3² / RR 3¹	Warner 8492
					NEW ORDER	
05/01/93	RR	5	23	1	Regret	Qwest 18586
					NEW SEEKERS, The	
08/29/70	RW	8	12	1	Look What They've Done To My Song Ma .... CB 10	Elektra 45699
11/27/71	BB	7	12	● 2	I'd Like To Teach The World To Sing (In Perfect Harmony) ... RW 8	Elektra 45762
					NEWTON, Juice	
02/21/81	RW	❶¹	26	● 1	Angel Of The Morning .... CB 2² / BB 4 / RR 4	Capitol 4976
05/30/81	RW	2⁵	29	● 2	Queen Of Hearts .... CB 2³ / BB 2² / RR 5	Capitol 4997
10/17/81	BB	7	24	3	The Sweetest Thing (I've Ever Known) .... CB 7 / RW 10	Capitol 5046
05/07/82	RR	2²	18	4	Love's Been A Little Bit Hard On Me .... CB 5 / BB 7	Capitol 5120
08/21/82	CB	9	16	5	Break It To Me Gently	Capitol 5148
					NEWTON, Wayne	
07/13/63	MV	10	12	1	Danke Schoen	Capitol 4989
04/15/72	RW	❶²	22	● 2	Daddy Don't You Walk So Fast .... CB ❶¹ / BB 4	Chelsea 0100
07/25/92	CB	❶¹	31	3	The Letter	Curb
					NEWTON-JOHN, Olivia	
10/27/73	CB	4	20	● 1	Let Me Be There .... BB 6 / RW 6 / RR 7	MCA 40101
04/06/74	BB	5	20	● 2	If You Love Me (Let Me Know) .... RW 5 / CB 6 / RR 7	MCA 40209
08/16/74	RR	❶⁶	16	● 3	I Honestly Love You .... BB ❶² / CB ❶² / RW ❶²	MCA 40280
01/24/75	RR	❶⁵	16	● 4	Have You Never Been Mellow .... BB ❶¹ / CB ❶¹ / RW ❶¹	MCA 40349
05/30/75	CB	❶¹	15	● 5	Please Mr. Please .... BB 3² / RW 5 / RR 6	MCA 40418
04/01/78	BB	❶¹	25	▲ 6	You're The One That I Want .... RW ❶¹ / CB 3⁴ / RR 3²	RSO 891
					JOHN TRAVOLTA AND OLIVIA NEWTON-JOHN	
07/08/78	RR	3³	19	● 7	Hopelessly Devoted To You .... BB 3² / CB 3¹ / RW 4	RSO 903
08/05/78	CB	3²	17	● 8	Summer Nights .... RW 4 / BB 5 / RR 10	RSO 906
					JOHN TRAVOLTA, OLIVIA NEWTON-JOHN & CAST	
11/25/78	RR	3⁴	21	● 9	A Little More Love .... BB 3² / CB 4 / RW 4	MCA 40975
05/23/80	BB	❶⁴	25	● 10	Magic .... CB ❶³ / RW ❶³ / RR ❶²	MCA 41247
08/09/80	RR	2¹	20	11	Xanadu .... RW 4 / BB 8 / CB 9	MCA 41285
					OLIVIA NEWTON-JOHN/ELECTRIC LIGHT ORCHESTRA	
10/03/81	BB	❶¹⁰	28	▲ 12	Physical .... RW ❶⁹ / CB ❶⁸ / RR 2²	MCA 51182
02/12/82	RR	❶¹	16	13	Make A Move On Me .... RW 4 / BB 5 / CB 5	MCA 52000
09/04/82	CB	2²	21	14	Heart Attack .... BB 3⁴ / RR 5	MCA 52100
11/04/83	RR	4	21	15	Twist Of Fate .... BB 5 / CB 5	MCA 52284
					NEW VAUDEVILLE BAND, The	
10/29/66	BB	❶³	16	● 1	Winchester Cathedral .... CB ❶³ / RW ❶¹	Fontana 1562
					NEXT	
02/14/98	BB	❶⁵	53	▲ 1	Too Close .... RR 6	Arista 13456
05/27/00	BB	7	21	2	Wifey	Arista 13881
					NE-YO	
12/10/05	BB	❶²	25	○ 1	So Sick .... RR ❶¹	Def Jam 006190
06/24/06	BB	7	22	○ 2	Sexy Love	Def Jam 007342
03/16/07	BB	2¹	20	△² 3	Because Of You	Def Jam 008678
05/03/08	BB	2⁴	39	△ 4	Closer .... BB 7	Def Jam 011222
09/06/08	BB	7	28	△ 5	Miss Independent .... RR 10	Def Jam 012111
08/18/12	BB	6	28	△ 6	Let Me Love You (Until You Learn To Love Yourself)	Motown
12/13/14	BB	9	27	7	Time Of Our Lives	Mr. 305
					PITBULL & NE-YO	
					NICHOLAS, Paul	
08/13/77	CB	5	28	● 1	Heaven On The 7th Floor .... BB 6 / RW 8	RSO 878
					NICKELBACK	
09/08/01	RR	❶¹⁰	49	○ 1	How You Remind Me .... BB ❶⁴	Roadrunner 612053
08/23/03	RR	2¹	50	○ 2	Someday .... BB 7	Roadrunner

121

DEBUT	CH	PK	WK	Gold	A-side (Chart Hit)	Other Charts	Label & Number

NICKELBACK (cont'd)
DEBUT	CH	PK	WK	Gold	A-side	Other Charts	Label & Number
08/26/05	BB	2¹	33	△²	3 Photograph	RR 3³	Roadrunner
02/17/06	RR	6	26		4 Savin' Me		Roadrunner
07/21/06	RR	❶²	31		5 Far Away	BB 8	Roadrunner
10/14/06	BB	6	49		6 Rockstar	RR 6	Roadrunner
01/12/07	RR	8	22		7 If Everyone Cared		Roadrunner
10/10/08	BB	10	27		8 Gotta Be Somebody		Roadrunner

NICKS, Stevie
DEBUT	CH	PK	WK	Gold	A-side	Other Charts	Label & Number
07/29/78	RR	❶¹	22		1 Whenever I Call You "Friend"	BB 5 / CB 5 / RW 6	Columbia 10794
					KENNY LOGGINS with STEVIE NICKS		
07/24/81	BB	3⁶	21		2 Stop Draggin' My Heart Around	RR 3² / CB 4 / RW 6	Modern 7336
					STEVIE NICKS with TOM PETTY & THE HEARTBREAKERS		
10/24/81	RR	2⁵	21		3 Leather And Lace	BB 6 / CB 9 / RW 10	Modern 7341
					STEVIE NICKS with DON HENLEY		
06/04/83	RR	2²	21		4 Stand Back	BB 5 / CB 9	Modern 99863
09/09/83	RR	9	15		5 If Anyone Falls		Modern 99832
11/15/85	RR	3²	21		6 Talk To Me	BB 4 / CB 7	Modern 99582

NICO & VINZ
DEBUT	CH	PK	WK	Gold	A-side	Other Charts	Label & Number
05/03/14	BB	4	31	△³	1 Am I Wrong		Warner

NICOLE
DEBUT	CH	PK	WK	Gold	A-side	Other Charts	Label & Number
06/27/98	BB	5	23	●	1 Make It Hot		Gold Mind 64110
					NICOLE Featuring Missy "Misdemeanor" Elliott and Mocha		

NIGHTINGALE, Maxine
DEBUT	CH	PK	WK	Gold	A-side	Other Charts	Label & Number
02/14/76	CB	❶¹	23	●	1 Right Back Where We Started From	RW ❶¹ / RR 2³ / BB 2²	United Artists 752
05/05/79	RR	3¹	29	●	2 Lead Me On	RW 4 / BB 5 / CB 5	Windsong 11530

NIGHT RANGER
DEBUT	CH	PK	WK	Gold	A-side	Other Charts	Label & Number
03/10/84	RR	4	24		1 Sister Christian	BB 5 / CB 6	MCA/Camel 52350
05/24/85	BB	8	17		2 Sentimental Street	RR 9 / CB 10	MCA/Camel 52591

NILSSON
DEBUT	CH	PK	WK	Gold	A-side	Other Charts	Label & Number
08/02/69	BB	6	12		1 Everybody's Talkin'	CB 7 / RW 7	RCA Victor 0161
12/11/71	BB	❶⁴	20	●	2 Without You	CB ❶² / RW ❶²	RCA Victor 0604
06/03/72	BB	8	16		3 Coconut		RCA Victor 0718

NINA SKY
DEBUT	CH	PK	WK	Gold	A-side	Other Charts	Label & Number
05/01/04	BB	4	26	○	1 Move Ya Body	RR 5	J-Time 002570
					NINA SKY feat. Jabba		

NINEDAYS
DEBUT	CH	PK	WK	Gold	A-side	Other Charts	Label & Number
05/05/00	RR	❶²	27		1 Absolutely (Story Of A Girl)	BB 6	550 Music 79532

1910 FRUITGUM CO.
DEBUT	CH	PK	WK	Gold	A-side	Other Charts	Label & Number
01/13/68	RW	❶¹	16	●	1 Simon Says	CB 2² / BB 4	Buddah 24
07/13/68	RW	3³	15		2 1, 2, 3, Red Light	CB 3¹ / BB 5	Buddah 54
01/18/69	RW	3¹	15		3 Indian Giver	CB 4 / BB 5	Buddah 91

98°
DEBUT	CH	PK	WK	Gold	A-side	Other Charts	Label & Number
07/11/97	RR	10	28	●	1 Invisible Man		Motown 860650
08/28/98	BB	3¹	27	▲	2 Because Of You		Motown 860830
03/05/99	RR	4	24		3 The Hardest Thing	BB 5	Universal 156246
07/23/99	RR	5	20		4 I Do (Cherish You)		Universal 158224
08/11/00	BB	2²	20	●	5 Give Me Just One Night (Una Noche)	RR 7	Universal 153296

NIRVANA
DEBUT	CH	PK	WK	Gold	A-side	Other Charts	Label & Number
11/30/91	CB	5	29	▲	1 Smells Like Teen Spirit	BB 6 / RR 9	DGC 19050

NITTY GRITTY DIRT BAND
DEBUT	CH	PK	WK	Gold	A-side	Other Charts	Label & Number
10/31/70	RW	6	23		1 Mr. Bojangles	BB 9 / CB 9	Liberty 56197
12/01/79	RR	9	22		2 An American Dream		United Artists 1330
					THE DIRT BAND		

NIVEA
DEBUT	CH	PK	WK	Gold	A-side	Other Charts	Label & Number
08/10/02	RR	4	36		1 Don't Mess With My Man	BB 8	Jive 40041
					NIVEA Featuring Brian & Brandon Casey Of Jagged Edge		

NOBLES, Cliff, & Co.
DEBUT	CH	PK	WK	Gold	A-side	Other Charts	Label & Number
05/25/68	BB	2³	14	●	1 The Horse	CB 4 / RW 4	Phil-L.A. of Soul 313

NO DOUBT
DEBUT	CH	PK	WK	Gold	A-side	Other Charts	Label & Number
10/19/96	BB	❶¹⁶	63		1 Don't Speak	RR ❶¹¹	Trauma
11/09/01	RR	❶¹	23		2 Hey Baby	BB 5	Interscope
					NO DOUBT with BOUNTY KILLER		
04/05/02	RR	3¹	20		3 Hella Good		Interscope
08/02/02	RR	❶²	30		4 Underneath It All	BB 3²	Interscope 497768
					NO DOUBT featuring Lady Saw		
10/24/03	RR	5	28	○	5 It's My Life	BB 10	Interscope

DEBUT	CH	PK	WK	Gold	A-side (Chart Hit)	Other Charts	Label & Number
					NOLAN, Kenny		
11/06/76	BB	3¹	28	●	1 I Like Dreamin'	CB 3¹ / RW 7	20th Century 2287
					NO MERCY		
06/14/96	RR	3²	39	●	1 Where Do You Go	BB 5 / CB 5	Arista 13225
					N.O.R.E. (Noreaga)		
05/25/02	BB	10	24		1 Nothin'		Def Jam 582914
					NORMAN, Chris — see QUATRO, Suzi		
					NORMANI — see SMITH, Sam		
					NOTORIOUS B.I.G., The		
01/14/95	BB	6	26	▲	1 Big Poppa	CB 7	Bad Boy 79015
06/24/95	BB	2³	21	▲	2 One More Chance/Stay With Me	CB 2³	Bad Boy 79031
04/26/97	BB	❶³	20	▲	3 Hypnotize		Bad Boy 79092
08/02/97	BB	❶²	30	▲	4 Mo Money Mo Problems		Bad Boy 79100
					THE NOTORIOUS B.I.G. Featuring Puff Daddy & Mase		
					***NSYNC**		
01/23/98	RR	5	26	●	1 I Want You Back		RCA 65348
07/03/98	RR	5	28		2 Tearin' Up My Heart		RCA 65469
11/06/98	RR	5	26		3 (God Must Have Spent) A Little More Time On You	BB 8	RCA 65685
08/13/99	BB	2¹	20	●	4 Music Of My Heart		Miramax/Epic 79245
					*NSYNC and GLORIA ESTEFAN		
01/21/00	RR	❶¹⁰	23		5 Bye Bye Bye	BB 4	Jive 42681
04/28/00	RR	❶⁶	25	●	6 It's Gonna Be Me	BB ❶²	Jive 42664
09/08/00	RR	4	26		7 This I Promise You	BB 5	Jive 42746
05/25/01	RR	5	15		8 Pop		Jive 42933
08/24/01	RR	7	24		9 Gone		Jive
01/18/02	BB	5	20		10 Girlfriend	RR 5	Jive 40013
					*NSYNC featuring Nelly		
					NUMAN, Gary		
02/16/80	CB	4	28		1 Cars	RW 5 / BB 9 / RR 9	Atco 7211
					NU SHOOZ		
03/08/86	CB	3²	23	●	1 I Can't Wait	BB 3¹ / RR 4	Atlantic 89446
					NUTTY SQUIRRELS, The		
11/02/59	CB	3¹	13		1 Uh! Oh! Part 2	MV 7	Hanover 4540

O

					OAK RIDGE BOYS		
05/09/81	CB	❶¹	25	▲	1 Elvira	RW 3² / BB 5	MCA 51084
01/16/82	RW	6	16		2 Bobbie Sue		MCA 51231
					OASIS		
12/15/95	CB	6	23	○	1 Wonderwall	BB 8 / RR 9	Epic 78216
02/24/96	RR	9	31	○	2 Champagne Supernova		Epic
					O'BRIEN, Olivia — see GNASH		
					OCEAN		
03/13/71	CB	2³	15	●	1 Put Your Hand In The Hand	BB 2¹ / RW 3²	Kama Sutra 519
					OCEAN, Billy		
08/11/84	BB	❶²	26	●	1 Caribbean Queen (No More Love On The Run)	CB 2¹ / RR 2¹	Jive 9199
12/01/84	BB	2¹	23		2 Loverboy	RR 3¹ / CB 4	Jive 9284
03/23/85	BB	4	22		3 Suddenly	CB 4 / RR 5	Jive 9323
11/30/85	CB	❶¹	23		4 When The Going Gets Tough, The Tough Get Going	RR ❶¹ / BB 2¹	Jive 9432
04/19/86	CB	❶²	21		5 There'll Be Sad Songs (To Make You Cry)	BB ❶¹ / RR ❶¹	Jive 9465
07/26/86	RR	9	17		6 Love Zone	BB 10 / CB 10	Jive 9510
02/12/88	BB	❶²	20		7 Get Outta My Dreams, Get Into My Car	CB ❶² / RR ❶²	Jive 9678
					O'CONNELL, Helen		
12/08/51	BB	8	13		1 Slow Poke		Capitol 1837
					O'CONNOR, Sinead		
03/16/90	BB	❶⁴	21	▲	1 Nothing Compares 2 U	CB ❶³ / RR ❶³	Ensign/Chrysalis 23488
					O'DAY, Alan		
04/02/77	RW	❶⁴	26	●	1 Undercover Angel	RR ❶² / BB ❶¹ / CB ❶¹	Pacific 001

123

DEBUT	CH	PK	WK	Gold	A-side (Chart Hit) .... Other Charts	Label & Number
					O'DONIS, Colby	
04/25/08	RR	8	20		1 What You Got	KonLive
					COLBY O'DONIS Featuring Akon	
08/16/08	BB	❶³	49	△⁸	2 Just Dance .... RR ❶²	Streamline 011524
					LADY GAGA with COLBY O'DONIS	
					OHIO EXPRESS	
04/20/68	BB	4	15	●	1 Yummy Yummy Yummy .... CB 4 / RW 4	Buddah 38
10/19/68	CB	8	14	●	2 Chewy Chewy .... RW 8	Buddah 70
					OHIO PLAYERS	
12/14/74	BB	❶¹	19	●	1 Fire .... CB ❶¹ / RW ❶¹ / RR 3¹	Mercury 73643
11/08/75	BB	❶¹	25	●	2 Love Rollercoaster .... CB 3² / RW 3² / RR 3¹	Mercury 73734
					O'JAYS, The	
07/08/72	CB	❶¹	17	●	1 Back Stabbers .... RW 2⁴ / BB 3¹	Philadelphia I. 3517
01/13/73	BB	❶¹	16	●	2 Love Train .... CB ❶¹ / RW ❶¹	Philadelphia I. 3524
12/22/73	BB	10	17		3 Put Your Hands Together	Philadelphia I. 3535
04/13/74	RR	6	16	●	4 For The Love Of Money .... CB 7 / RW 7 / BB 9	Philadelphia I. 3544
10/25/75	BB	5	19	●	5 I Love Music (Part 1) .... CB 7 / RW 7 / RR 10	Philadelphia I. 3577
04/22/78	RW	3³	20	●	6 Use Ta Be My Girl .... RR 3³ / BB 4 / CB 5	Philadelphia I. 3642
					O'KAYSIONS, The	
08/10/68	RW	4	15	●	1 Girl Watcher .... BB 5 / CB 5	ABC 11094
					O'KEEFE, Danny	
08/26/72	RW	8	14		1 Good Time Charlie's Got The Blues .... BB 9 / CB 10	Signpost 70006
					OLDFIELD, Mike	
02/23/74	RW	5	16		1 Tubular Bells .... CB 6 / BB 7 / RR 10	Virgin 55100
					OLIVER	
05/17/69	BB	3²	13	☉	1 Good Morning Starshine .... RW 3¹ / CB 4	Jubilee 5659
08/09/69	RW	❶¹	15	●	2 Jean .... BB 2² / CB 2¹	Crewe 334
					OLLIE & JERRY	
06/02/84	CB	8	18		1 Breakin'...There's No Stopping Us .... BB 9	Polydor 821708
					OLYMPICS, The	
07/19/58	BB	8	14		1 Western Movies	Demon 1508
					OMARION	
05/28/05	BB	4	24	○	1 Let Me Hold You	Columbia 74625
					OMC	
03/14/97	RR	2⁴	51		1 How Bizarre .... BB 4	Mercury
					OMI	
05/09/15	BB	❶⁶	35	△³	1 Cheerleader	Louder Than Life
					ONE DIRECTION	
03/03/12	BB	4	34	△⁴	1 What Makes You Beautiful	Syco
10/20/12	BB	3¹	16	△	2 Live While We're Young	Syco 887654
08/10/13	BB	2¹	21	△	3 Best Song Ever	Syco 76641
11/16/13	BB	6	32	△³	4 Story Of My Life	Syco
08/22/15	BB	3¹	20		5 Drag Me Down	Syco
11/07/15	BB	10	20		6 Perfect	Syco
					100 PROOF AGED IN SOUL	
08/29/70	CB	6	16	●	1 Somebody's Been Sleeping .... RW 6 / BB 8	Hot Wax 7004
					ONEREPUBLIC	
04/21/07	RR	❶⁸	47	△⁴	1 Apologize .... BB 2⁴	Mosley
					TIMBALAND with ONEREPUBLIC	
12/14/07	RR	6	31		2 Stop And Stare	Mosley
04/23/11	BB	8	35	△³	3 Good Life	Mosley
07/06/13	BB	2²	68	△¹⁰	4 Counting Stars	Mosley
					112	
06/01/96	CB	7	28	●	1 Only You	Bad Boy 79060
					112 Featuring The Notorious B.I.G.	
12/09/00	BB	6	20		2 It's Over Now	Bad Boy 79366
04/14/01	BB	4	29		3 Peaches & Cream	Bad Boy 79387
					ONYX	
05/29/93	BB	4	20	▲	1 Slam .... CB 5	JMJ/RAL 77053
					ORA, Rita — see **AZALEA, Iggy**	

DEBUT	CH	PK	WK	Gold	A-side (Chart Hit)	Other Charts	Label & Number
					ORBISON, Roy		
05/23/60	BB	2¹	21	☉	1 Only The Lonely (Know The Way I Feel)	CB 2¹ / MV 3³	Monument 421
09/05/60	BB	9	14		2 Blue Angel		Monument 425
04/10/61	BB	❶¹	17	☉	3 Running Scared	CB ❶¹ / MV 2³	Monument 438
08/07/61	CB	❶¹	17	☉	4 Crying	MV ❶¹ / BB 2¹	Monument 447
02/05/62	BB	4	12		5 Dream Baby (How Long Must I Dream)	MV 7 / CB 9	Monument 456
02/09/63	MV	5	14		6 In Dreams	BB 7 / CB 10	Monument 806
09/07/63	BB	5	14		7 Mean Woman Blues /	MV 5 / CB 7	
09/07/63	MV	10	12		8 Blue Bayou		Monument 824
04/11/64	MV	8	13		9 It's Over	BB 9 / CB 10	Monument 837
08/29/64	BB	❶³	17	●	10 Oh, Pretty Woman	CB ❶³ / RW ❶¹	Monument 851
					ROY ORBISON And The Candy Men		
01/21/89	BB	9	21		11 You Got It		Virgin 99245
					ORCHESTRAL MANOEUVRES IN THE DARK		
03/08/86	RR	3¹	20		1 If You Leave	BB 4 / CB 8	A&M 2811
					ORLANDO, Tony, & DAWN		
					DAWN:		
07/25/70	CB	❶¹	18	●	1 Candida	RW 2¹ / BB 3²	Bell 903
11/14/70	RW	❶⁴	18	●	2 Knock Three Times	BB ❶³ / CB ❶²	Bell 938
					DAWN Featuring Tony Orlando:		
02/03/73	BB	❶⁴	23	●	3 Tie A Yellow Ribbon Round The Ole Oak Tree	CB ❶³ / RW ❶¹	Bell 45,318
07/14/73	RW	3²	17	●	4 Say, Has Anybody Seen My Sweet Gypsy Rose	BB 3¹ / CB 4	Bell 45,374
					TONY ORLANDO & DAWN:		
08/17/74	BB	7	15		5 Steppin' Out (Gonna Boogie Tonight)		Bell 45,601
03/08/75	BB	❶³	17	●	6 He Don't Love You (Like I Love You)	CB ❶¹ / RW ❶¹ / RR ❶¹	Elektra 45240
					ORLEANS		
07/19/75	RW	4	25	●	1 Dance With Me	RR 4 / CB 5 / BB 6	Asylum 45261
07/24/76	RR	2²	25	●	2 Still The One	BB 5 / CB 6 / RW 7	Asylum 45336
03/24/79	RR	7	15		3 Love Takes Time		Infinity 50,006
					ORLONS, The		
06/09/62	BB	2²	15	☉	1 The Wah Watusi	CB 2² / MV 2¹	Cameo 218
10/13/62	BB	4	16		2 Don't Hang Up	CB 6 / MV 6	Cameo 231
02/09/63	BB	3¹	15		3 South Street	CB 3¹ / MV 4	Cameo 243
					ORRICO, Stacie		
08/01/03	RR	6	24		1 (There's Gotta Be) More To Life		Virgin/ForeFront 52925
					OSBORNE, Joan		
10/27/95	RR	3⁵	30	●	1 One Of Us	CB 3² / BB 4	Blue Gorilla 852368
					OSBOURNE, Ozzy — see FORD, Lita		
					OSMOND, Donny		
03/20/71	RW	5	18	●	1 Sweet And Innocent	BB 7 / CB 7	MGM 14227
08/07/71	BB	❶³	15	●	2 Go Away Little Girl	CB ❶¹ / RW 2²	MGM 14285
11/20/71	BB	9	11		3 Hey Girl	CB 9 / RW 10	MGM 14322
02/19/72	RW	2²	12	●	4 Puppy Love	CB 3³ / BB 3¹	MGM 14367
06/10/72	CB	8	10		5 Too Young		MGM 14407
03/03/73	CB	5	13	●	6 The Twelfth Of Never	RW 6 / BB 8	MGM/Kolob 14503
03/25/89	CB	2²	23		7 Soldier Of Love	BB 2¹ / RR 4	Capitol 44369
06/17/89	CB	10	19		8 Sacred Emotion		Capitol 44379
					OSMOND, Donny And Marie		
07/06/74	BB	4	16	●	1 I'm Leaving It (All) Up To You	RW 4 / CB 7 / RR 8	MGM/Kolob 14735
11/16/74	CB	6	16		2 Morning Side Of The Mountain	BB 8 / RW 10	MGM/Kolob 14765
					OSMOND, Marie		
09/08/73	RW	4	16	●	1 Paper Roses	BB 5 / RR 5 / CB 6	MGM/Kolob 14609
					OSMONDS, The		
12/26/70	BB	❶⁵	16	●	1 One Bad Apple	CB ❶⁴ / RW ❶⁴	MGM 14193
05/15/71	CB	9	10		2 Double Lovin'	RW 10	MGM 14259
09/11/71	RW	❶²	14	●	3 Yo-Yo	CB 2¹ / BB 3³	MGM 14295
01/22/72	CB	3³	14	●	4 Down By The Lazy River	RW 3¹ / BB 4	MGM 14324
06/24/72	RW	10	9		5 Hold Her Tight		MGM 14405
08/31/74	CB	8	15		6 Love Me For A Reason	RR 8 / RW 9 / BB 10	MGM/Kolob 14746
					O'SULLIVAN, Gilbert		
06/17/72	BB	❶⁶	18	●	1 Alone Again (Naturally)	RW ❶⁴ / CB ❶³	MAM 3619
10/21/72	BB	2²	16	●	2 Clair	RW 2¹ / CB 3¹	MAM 3626
06/16/73	CB	4	17	●	3 Get Down	RW 4 / BB 7	MAM 3629
					OTIS, Johnny, Show		
05/19/58	BB	9	21		1 Willie And The Hand Jive		Capitol 3966

DEBUT	CH	PK	WK	Gold	A-side (Chart Hit)	Other Charts	Label & Number
					O-TOWN		
11/24/00	BB	10	16	● 1	Liquid Dreams		J Records 21001
04/13/01	RR	❶⁴	24	2	All Or Nothing	BB 3¹	J Records 21056
					OUTFIELD, The		
02/15/86	RR	5	22	1	Your Love	BB 6 / CB 10	Columbia 05796
					OUTKAST		
11/11/00	BB	❶¹	23	○ 1	Ms. Jackson		LaFace 24525
09/19/03	BB	❶⁹	32	△ 2	Hey Ya! /	RR ❶⁹	
09/27/03	RR	❶³	39	○ 3	The Way You Move	BB ❶¹	Arista 54962
					OUTKAST Featuring Sleepy Brown		
03/13/04	RR	5	21	○ 4	Roses	BB 9	Arista 57551
					OUTSIDERS, The		
02/19/66	BB	5	15	1	Time Won't Let Me	CB 6 / RW 6	Capitol 5573
					OWEN, Reg, And His Orchestra		
12/08/58	BB	10	16	1	Manhattan Spiritual		Palette 5005
					OWL CITY		
09/05/09	BB	❶²	31	△⁷ 1	Fireflies		Universal Republic
07/14/12	BB	8	24	△² 2	Good Time		Universal Republic
					OWL CITY & CARLY RAE JEPSEN		
					OZARK MOUNTAIN DAREDEVILS		
02/08/75	CB	❶²	21	1	Jackie Blue	RW ❶¹ / BB 3² / RR 6	A&M 1654

P

DEBUT	CH	PK	WK	Gold	A-side	Other Charts	Label & Number
					PABLO, Petey		
01/03/04	BB	7	39	○ 1	Freek-A-Leek		Jive 58745
					PABLO CRUISE		
04/09/77	CB	3²	26	1	Whatcha Gonna Do?	RR 4 / RW 5 / BB 6	A&M 1920
05/27/78	RR	4	21	2	Love Will Find A Way	CB 5 / BB 6 / RW 6	A&M 2048
07/04/81	RR	5	17	3	Cool Love		A&M 2349
					PACIFIC GAS & ELECTRIC		
05/23/70	RW	10	13	1	Are You Ready?		Columbia 45158
					PAGE, Jimmy — see PUFF DADDY		
					PAGE, Martin		
12/17/94	RR	8	35	1	In The House Of Stone And Light		Mercury 858940
					PAGE, Patti		
05/20/50	BB	8	14	1	I Don't Care If The Sun Don't Shine		Mercury 5396
08/26/50	BB	❶⁵	27	2	All My Love (Bolero)	CB 2⁴	Mercury 5455
11/18/50	BB	❶¹³	27	◉ 3	The Tennessee Waltz	CB ❶⁶	Mercury 5534
02/10/51	BB	4	20	4	Would I Love You (Love You, Love You)	CB 5	Mercury 5571
02/24/51	CB	❶⁵	25	5	Mockin' Bird Hill	BB 2¹	Mercury 5595
05/19/51	CB	6	15	6	Mister And Mississippi	BB 8	Mercury 5645
08/04/51	BB	5	19	7	Detour		Mercury 5682
09/22/51	BB	4	18	8	And So To Sleep Again	CB 6	Mercury 5706
02/09/52	BB	9	15	9	Come What May		Mercury 5772
06/28/52	BB	9	14	10	Once In Awhile		Mercury 5867
08/30/52	BB	❶¹⁰	28	◉ 11	I Went To Your Wedding /	CB ❶⁶	
08/30/52	BB	4	17	12	You Belong To Me		Mercury 5899
11/29/52	BB	4	13	13	Why Don't You Believe Me		Mercury 70025
01/31/53	BB	❶⁸	26	◉ 14	The Doggie In The Window	CB ❶⁷	Mercury 70070
07/18/53	BB	10	12	15	Butterflies		Mercury 70183
11/21/53	BB	3⁶	23	◉ 16	Changing Partners	CB 4	Mercury 70260
02/20/54	BB	2⁴	21	◉ 17	Cross Over The Bridge	CB 5	Mercury 70302
05/22/54	BB	8	13	18	Steam Heat		Mercury 70380
08/07/54	BB	10	13	19	What A Dream		Mercury 70416
12/18/54	BB	8	7	20	Let Me Go, Lover!		Mercury 70511
06/01/56	BB	2²	29	◉ 21	Allegheny Moon	MV 2² / CB 6	Mercury 70878
05/20/57	BB	3¹	23	22	Old Cape Cod	MV 7 / CB 8	Mercury 71101
06/16/58	MV	5	15	23	Left Right Out Of Your Heart (Hi Lee Hi Lo Hi Lup Up Up)	BB 9 / CB 9	Mercury 71331
04/24/65	BB	8	14	24	Hush, Hush, Sweet Charlotte	RW 8 / CB 10	Columbia 43251
					PAGE, Tommy		
02/16/90	BB	❶¹	20	● 1	I'll Be Your Everything	CB ❶¹ / RR 2¹	Sire 19959
					PAIGE, Jennifer		
06/26/98	RR	2¹	28	● 1	Crush	BB 3⁴	Edel America 64024

126

DEBUT	CH	PK	WK	Gold	A-side (Chart Hit)	Other Charts	Label & Number
					PALMER, Robert		
07/21/79	RR	7	18		1 Bad Case Of Loving You (Doctor, Doctor)	RW 9 / CB 10	Island 49016
02/08/86	CB	❶²	23	●	2 Addicted To Love	BB ❶¹ / RR ❶¹	Island 99570
08/16/86	BB	2¹	23		3 I Didn't Mean To Turn You On	RR 3² / CB 4	Island 99537
07/02/88	BB	2²	20		4 Simply Irresistible	CB 2² / RR 3²	EMI/Manhattan 50133
					PANIC! AT THE DISCO		
03/18/06	RR	2²	37	△⁵	1 I Write Sins Not Tragedies	BB 7	Decaydance
06/09/18	BB	4	52	△⁴	2 High Hopes		DCD2
					PAPA ROACH		
02/25/05	RR	7	38	○	1 Scars		El Tonal
					PAPERBOY		
12/19/92	BB	10	30	▲	1 Ditty		Next Plateau 357012
					PAPER LACE		
06/15/74	RR	❶³	19	●	1 The Night Chicago Died	BB ❶¹ / CB ❶¹ / RW ❶¹	Mercury 73492
					PARAMORE		
03/15/14	BB	10	24	△³	1 Ain't It Fun		Fueled By Ramen
					PARIS SISTERS, The		
09/02/61	BB	5	16		1 I Love How You Love Me	CB 7	Gregmark 6
					PARKER, Fess		
03/12/55	BB	5	17	⊙	1 Ballad Of Davy Crockett		Columbia 40449
					PARKER, Ray Jr. [RAYDIO]		
12/17/77	CB	6	26	●	1 Jack And Jill	RR 6 / RW 7 / BB 8	Arista 0283
04/21/79	RR	5	25		2 You Can't Change That	BB 9 / CB 10	Arista 0399
					RAYDIO (above 2)		
03/07/81	BB	4	27		3 A Woman Needs Love (Just Like You Do)	RW 4 / CB 5 / RR 5	Arista 0592
					RAY PARKER JR. & RAYDIO		
03/20/82	CB	2²	21		4 The Other Woman	BB 4 / RR 4	Arista 0669
11/12/83	RR	10	19		5 I Still Can't Get Over Loving You		Arista 9116
06/16/84	BB	❶³	21	●	6 Ghostbusters	RR ❶³ / CB ❶²	Arista 9212
					RAY PARKER JR. (above 3)		
					PARKER, Robert		
04/23/66	BB	7	14		1 Barefootin'	RW 9	Nola 721
					PARLIAMENT		
05/08/76	RW	8	23	●	1 Tear The Roof Off The Sucker (Give Up The Funk)		Casablanca 856
					PARR, John		
06/22/85	BB	❶²	23		1 St. Elmo's Fire (Man In Motion)	CB ❶² / RR ❶¹	Atlantic 89541
					PARSONS, Alan, Project		
04/18/81	RR	7	23		1 Time		Arista 0598
07/03/82	RR	2¹	25		2 Eye In The Sky	BB 3³ / CB 3²	Arista 0696
03/03/84	RR	10	17		3 Don't Answer Me		Arista 9160
					PARSONS, Bill — see BARE, Bobby		
					PARTON, Dolly		
10/08/77	BB	3²	25	●	1 Here You Come Again	RW 6 / RR 6 / CB 7	RCA 11123
11/29/80	RW	❶⁵	26	▲	2 9 To 5	BB ❶² / CB ❶¹ / RR 2²	RCA 12133
08/27/83	BB	❶²	29	▲	3 Islands In The Stream	CB ❶² / RR 2¹	RCA 13615
					KENNY ROGERS with DOLLY PARTON		
					PARTRIDGE FAMILY, The		
09/26/70	RW	❶⁴	19	●	1 I Think I Love You	BB ❶³ / CB ❶³	Bell 910
02/06/71	CB	❶¹	14	●	2 Doesn't Somebody Want To Be Wanted	RW ❶¹ / BB 6	Bell 963
05/08/71	CB	2¹	11		3 I'll Meet You Halfway	RW 4 / BB 9	Bell 996
08/07/71	CB	9	12		4 I Woke Up In Love This Morning	RW 9	Bell 45,130
					PASSENGER		
08/17/13	BB	5	43	△⁶	1 Let Her Go		Black Crow
					PATIENCE & PRUDENCE		
08/04/56	CB	3¹	25		1 Tonight You Belong To Me	BB 4 / MV 4	Liberty 55022
11/24/56	MV	10	16		2 Gonna Get Along Without Ya Now		Liberty 55040
					PAUL, Billy		
10/21/72	BB	❶³	17	●	1 Me And Mrs. Jones	CB ❶² / RW ❶²	Philadelphia I. 3521
					PAUL, Les, and Mary Ford		
06/24/50	BB	9	21		1 Nola		Capitol 1014
					LES PAUL		
12/30/50	BB	6	14		2 Tennessee Waltz		Capitol 1316
02/17/51	CB	❶⁵	25	⊙	3 Mockin' Bird Hill	BB 2⁵	Capitol 1373

DEBUT	CH	PK	WK	Gold	A-side (Chart Hit) ... Other Charts	Label & Number
					PAUL, Les, and Mary Ford (cont'd)	
03/31/51	BB	❶⁹	27	⊙	4 How High The Moon .... CB ❶²	Capitol 1451
08/18/51	BB	2²	19	¤	5 The World Is Waiting For The Sunrise / .... CB 3¹	
08/18/51	BB	7	22		6 Whispering	Capitol 1748
					LES PAUL	
10/27/51	BB	5	13		7 Just One More Chance	Capitol 1825
12/15/51	BB	10	4		8 Jingle Bells	Capitol 1881
					LES PAUL	
01/19/52	BB	2¹	17		9 Tiger Rag .... CB 8	Capitol 1920
08/30/52	CB	4	21		10 Meet Mister Callaghan .... BB 5	Capitol 2193
					LES PAUL	
11/22/52	BB	7	16		11 My Baby's Coming Home /	
11/08/52	BB	8	8		12 Lady Of Spain	Capitol 2265
					LES PAUL	
01/03/53	BB	5	11		13 Bye Bye Blues	Capitol 2316
03/21/53	CB	8	12		14 I'm Sitting On Top Of The World .... BB 10	Capitol 2400
06/20/53	BB	❶¹¹	35	⊙	15 Vaya Con Dios (May God Be With You) .... CB ❶⁵	Capitol 2486
07/03/54	BB	6	18		16 I'm A Fool To Care	Capitol 2839
10/02/54	BB	10	18		17 Whither Thou Goest .... MV 10	Capitol 2928
06/13/55	CB	6	18		18 Hummingbird .... BB 7 / MV 10	Capitol 3165
					PAUL, Sean	
05/04/02	BB	7	39		1 Gimme The Light	VP 6400
02/22/03	BB	❶³	32	△	2 Get Busy .... RR 3¹	VP/Atlantic 88020
09/17/05	BB	6	28	△	3 We Be Burnin' .... RR 9	VP/Atlantic 93770
01/21/06	RR	❶³	31	△³	4 Temperature .... BB ❶¹	VP/Atlantic 94133
06/09/06	BB	3¹	22		5 (When You Gonna) Give It Up To Me .... RR 8	VP/Atlantic 94413
					SEAN PAUL Featuring Keyshia Cole	
11/10/06	RR	6	22	○	6 Break It Off .... BB 9	Def Jam
					RIHANNA & SEAN PAUL	
12/24/16	BB	9	27	△³	7 Rockabye	Atlantic
					CLEAN BANDIT with SEAN PAUL & ANNE-MARIE	
					PAUL & PAULA	
12/29/62	CB	❶⁴	15	●	1 Hey Paula .... MV ❶⁴ / BB ❶³	Philips 40084
03/16/63	BB	6	11		2 Young Lovers .... CB 7 / MV 7	Philips 40096
					PAYNE, Freda	
04/25/70	RW	❶¹	20	●	1 Band Of Gold .... CB 2¹ / BB 3¹	Invictus 9075
05/22/71	RW	5	15	●	2 Bring The Boys Home .... CB 7	Invictus 9092
					PAYNE, Liam	
06/10/17	BB	10	28	△³	1 Strip That Down	Hampton
					LIAM PAYNE Featuring Quavo	
					PEACHES & HERB	
03/25/67	BB	8	12		1 Close Your Eyes .... RW 9	Date 1549
09/30/67	RW	10	10		2 Love Is Strange	Date 1574
12/09/78	BB	5	25	●	3 Shake Your Groove Thing .... CB 5 / RW 7 / RR 8	Polydor/MVP 14514
03/17/79	BB	❶⁴	23	▲	4 Reunited .... CB ❶⁴ / RW ❶⁴ / RR ❶⁴	Polydor/MVP 14547
					PEARL JAM	
12/23/95	BB	7	20	●	1 I Got Id	Epic 78199
05/29/99	BB	2¹	21	●	2 Last Kiss .... RR 4	Epic 79197
					PEBBLES	
01/30/88	BB	5	21		1 Girlfriend .... CB 6 / RR 6	MCA 53185
05/07/88	BB	2²	20		2 Mercedes Boy .... RR 2¹ / CB 4	MCA 53279
08/18/90	CB	3¹	25		3 Giving You The Benefit .... BB 4 / RR 4	MCA 53891
					PEEPLES, Nia	
10/12/91	RR	7	21		1 Street Of Dreams .... CB 8	Charisma 98690
					PENGUINS, The	
12/25/54	CB	2¹	19	⊙	1 Earth Angel (Will You Be Mine) .... MV 7 / BB 8	DooTone 348
					PENISTON, Ce Ce	
09/28/91	BB	5	33	●	1 Finally .... CB 7 / RR 7	A&M 1586
02/01/92	RR	10	23		2 We Got A Love Thang	A&M 1594
					PEREZ, Amanda	
01/31/03	RR	3¹	20		1 Angel	Virgin 47265
					PERFECT GENTLEMEN	
04/13/90	CB	9	16		1 Ooh La La (I Can't Get Over You) .... BB 10	Columbia 73211
					PERICOLI, Emilio	
05/19/62	BB	6	15		1 Al Di La' .... CB 6 / MV 7	Warner 5259
					PERKINS, Carl	
03/03/56	MV	❶¹	21	⊙	1 Blue Suede Shoes .... BB 2⁴ / CB 2²	Sun 234

DEBUT	CH	PK	WK	Gold	A-side (Chart Hit) ... Other Charts	Label & Number
					PERRY, Katy	
05/23/08	BB	①⁷	23	△⁶	1 I Kissed A Girl ... RR 2³	Capitol
07/05/08	RR	①³	39	△⁸	2 Hot N Cold ... BB 3¹	Capitol
05/01/09	BB	9	23	△²	3 Waking Up In Vegas	Capitol
05/29/10	BB	①⁶	27	△⁸	4 California Gurls	Capitol 41011
					KATY PERRY Featuring Snoop Dogg	
08/07/10	BB	①²	33	△⁷	5 Teenage Dream	Capitol
09/04/10	BB	①⁵	30	△⁸	6 E.T.	Capitol
					KATY PERRY Featuring Kanye West	
11/06/10	BB	①⁴	39	△¹¹	7 Firework	Capitol
06/18/11	BB	①²	24	△⁶	8 Last Friday Night (T.G.I.F.)	Capitol
10/29/11	BB	3²	24	△³	9 The One That Got Away	Capitol
03/03/12	BB	①¹	22	△⁴	10 Part Of Me	Capitol
06/09/12	BB	2¹	26	△⁵	11 Wide Awake	Capitol
08/24/13	BB	①²	35	△¹⁰	12 Roar	Capitol
10/05/13	BB	①⁴	57	△¹¹	13 Dark Horse	Capitol
					KATY PERRY Featuring Juicy J	
03/04/17	BB	4	15	△²	14 Chained To The Rhythm	Capitol
					KATY PERRY Featuring Skip Marley	
					PERRY, Steve	
08/28/82	RR	4	15		1 Don't Fight It	Columbia 03192
					KENNY LOGGINS with STEVE PERRY	
04/06/84	RR	2³	20		2 Oh Sherrie ... BB 3¹ / CB 4	Columbia 04391
11/24/84	RR	10	19		3 Foolish Heart	Columbia 04693
07/15/94	RR	10	19		4 You Better Wait	Columbia 77580
					PERSUADERS, The	
08/14/71	RW	9	15	●	1 Thin Line Between Love & Hate ... CB 10	Atco 6822
					PETER AND GORDON	
05/09/64	BB	①¹	13	☉	1 A World Without Love ... CB ①¹ / RW 2²	Capitol 5175
01/09/65	RW	4	12		2 I Go To Pieces ... CB 6 / BB 9	Capitol 5335
10/08/66	CB	5	15		3 Lady Godiva ... BB 6 / RW 7	Capitol 5740
					PETER, PAUL & MARY	
08/11/62	BB	10	14		1 If I Had A Hammer (The Hammer Song)	Warner 5296
03/16/63	BB	2¹	15		2 Puff The Magic Dragon ... CB 2¹ / MV 2¹	Warner 5348
06/29/63	CB	2²	15		3 Blowin' In The Wind ... BB 2¹ / MV 2¹	Warner 5368
09/14/63	BB	9	10		4 Don't Think Twice, It's All Right	Warner 5385
08/19/67	BB	9	11		5 I Dig Rock And Roll Music	Warner 7067
10/25/69	RW	①²	17	●	6 Leaving On A Jet Plane ... BB ①¹ / CB ①¹	Warner 7340
					PETERSEN, Paul	
11/10/62	BB	6	17		1 My Dad ... CB 6 / MV 6	Colpix 663
					PETERSON, Ray	
06/13/60	CB	5	14		1 Tell Laura I Love Her ... BB 7 / MV 7	RCA Victor 7745
11/21/60	MV	6	15		2 Corinna, Corinna ... CB 7 / BB 9	Dunes 2002
					PET SHOP BOYS	
03/01/86	RR	①²	22		1 West End Girls ... BB ①¹ / CB ①¹	EMI America 8307
05/31/86	CB	9	16		2 Opportunities (Let's Make Lots Of Money) ... BB 10 / RR 10	EMI America 8330
09/05/87	BB	9	23		3 It's A Sin ... RR 10	EMI America 43027
12/12/87	CB	①¹	21		4 What Have I Done To Deserve This? ... BB 2² / RR 2¹	EMI/Manhattan 50107
					PET SHOP BOYS and DUSTY SPRINGFIELD	
03/25/88	BB	4	17		5 Always On My Mind ... RR 5 / CB 7	EMI/Manhattan 50123
					PETTY, Tom, And The Heartbreakers	
11/17/79	RR	4	18		1 Don't Do Me Like That ... CB 7 / RW 8 / BB 10	Backstreet 41138
07/24/81	BB	3⁶	21		2 Stop Draggin' My Heart Around ... RR 3² / CB 4 / RW 6	Modern 7336
					STEVIE NICKS with TOM PETTY & THE HEARTBREAKERS	
11/04/89	CB	6	22		3 Free Fallin' ... BB 7 / RR 9	MCA 53748
					TOM PETTY	
12/25/93	RR	10	20		4 Mary Jane's Last Dance	MCA 54732
12/02/94	RR	4	25		5 You Don't Know How It Feels	Warner 18030
					TOM PETTY	
					PHILLIPS, "Little Esther"	
10/27/62	MV	5	14		1 Release Me ... BB 8 / CB 8	Lenox 5555
					PHILLIPS, Phil, with The Twilights	
06/27/59	MV	2³	19	☉	1 Sea Of Love ... BB 2² / CB 2²	Mercury 71465
					PHILLIPS, Phillip	
06/09/12	BB	6	40	△⁴	1 Home	19 Records
					PICKETT, Bobby "Boris", And The Crypt-Kickers	
09/01/62	CB	①³	16	●	1 Monster Mash ... BB ①² / MV ①²	Garpax 44167
05/05/73	BB	10	20		2 Monster Mash ... CB 10 / RW 10	Parrot 348

DEBUT	CH	PK	WK	Gold		A-side (Chart Hit) .... Other Charts	Label & Number
						PICKETT, Wilson	
02/12/66	RW	6	12		1	634-5789 (Soulsville, U.S.A.) .... CB 9	Atlantic 2320
07/30/66	BB	6	11		2	Land Of 1000 Dances .... RW 6 / CB 9	Atlantic 2348
08/05/67	RW	6	13		3	Funky Broadway .... BB 8 / CB 10	Atlantic 2430
01/16/71	CB	10	12	●	4	Don't Let The Green Grass Fool You	Atlantic 2781
04/24/71	CB	7	14	●	5	Don't Knock My Love - Pt. 1 .... RW 8	Atlantic 2797
						PILOT	
04/05/75	RR	2²	22	●	1	Magic .... BB 5 / CB 5 / RW 5	EMI 3992
						PINETOPPERS, The	
03/03/51	BB	10	17		1	Mockin' Bird Hill	Coral 64061
						P!NK	
03/04/00	RR	2¹	32	●	1	There You Go .... BB 7	LaFace 24456
08/04/00	RR	2³	27		2	Most Girls .... BB 4	LaFace 24490
04/06/01	RR	❶⁹	20		3	Lady Marmalade .... BB ❶⁵	Interscope 497066
						CHRISTINA AGUILERA, LIL' KIM, MYA and PINK	
10/19/01	RR	2⁷	24	○	4	Get The Party Started .... BB 4	Arista 15074
02/15/02	RR	❶⁴	23		5	Don't Let Me Get Me .... BB 8	Arista 50977
06/14/02	RR	2²	21		6	Just Like A Pill .... BB 8	Arista 15186
09/27/02	RR	5	22		7	Family Portrait	Arista 50977
12/08/06	RR	❶⁴	38	△	8	U + Ur Hand .... BB 9	LaFace
04/07/07	RR	❶³	24	△	9	Who Knew .... BB 9	LaFace
08/29/08	RR	❶⁵	31		10	So What .... BB ❶¹	LaFace
12/12/08	RR	3¹	25		11	Sober	LaFace
10/23/10	BB	❶¹	30	△⁵	12	Raise Your Glass	LaFace
01/01/11	BB	2¹	30		13	F**kin' Perfect	LaFace
07/21/12	BB	5	27		14	Blow Me (One Last Kiss)	RCA
10/06/12	BB	9	24		15	Try	RCA
03/02/13	BB	❶³	36	△²	16	Just Give Me A Reason	RCA
						PINK & NATE RUESS	
05/07/16	BB	10	26	△	17	Just Like Fire	Walt Disney
						PINK FLOYD	
05/12/73	CB	10	17		1	Money .... RW 10	Harvest 3609
01/19/80	RW	❶⁵	26	▲	2	Another Brick In The Wall Part II .... BB ❶⁴ / CB ❶³ / RR ❶³	Columbia 11187
						PIPKINS, The	
05/16/70	CB	7	13		1	Gimme Dat Ding .... RW 8 / BB 9	Capitol 2819
						PITBULL	
03/14/09	BB	2¹	35	△²	1	I Know You Want Me (Calle Ocho)	J Records
07/04/09	BB	8	23	△	2	Hotel Room Service	J Records
10/16/10	BB	7	31		3	Hey Baby (Drop It To The Floor)	Mr. 305
						PITBULL Featuring T-Pain	
04/16/11	BB	❶¹	45	△⁶	4	Give Me Everything	Mr. 305
						PITBULL Featuring Ne-Yo, AfroJack & Nayer	
02/09/13	BB	8	24	△	5	Feel This Moment	Mr. 305
						PITBULL Featuring Christina Aguilera	
10/26/13	BB	❶³	39	△⁶	6	Timber	Mr. 305
						PITBULL Featuring Kesha	
12/13/14	BB	9	27		7	Time Of Our Lives	Mr. 305
						PITBULL & NE-YO	
						PITNEY, Gene	
04/09/62	BB	4	15		1	(The Man Who Shot) Liberty Valance .... MV 7 / CB 8	Musicor 1020
09/01/62	BB	2¹	17	⊙	2	Only Love Can Break A Heart .... MV 4 / CB 5	Musicor 1022
07/18/64	RW	6	16		3	It Hurts To Be In Love .... BB 7 / CB 7	Musicor 1040
10/24/64	BB	9	12		4	I'm Gonna Be Strong	Musicor 1045
						PLAIN WHITE T'S	
04/14/07	BB	❶²	35	△³	1	Hey There Delilah .... RR 2³	Hollywood
						PLATTEN, Rachel	
05/02/15	BB	6	31	△⁶	1	Fight Song	Columbia
						PLATTERS, The	
08/01/55	CB	3²	30	⊙	1	Only You (And You Alone) .... MV 4 / BB 5	Mercury 70633
12/09/55	CB	❶³	24	⊙	2	The Great Pretender .... MV ❶³ / BB ❶²	Mercury 70753
03/16/56	CB	3¹	20		3	(You've Got) The Magic Touch .... BB 4 / MV 4	Mercury 70819
06/29/56	BB	❶⁵	23	⊙	4	My Prayer .... MV ❶³ / CB ❶²	Mercury 70893
09/22/56	MV	7	18		5	You'll Never Never Know	Mercury 70948
03/24/58	MV	❶³	20	⊙	6	Twilight Time .... BB ❶¹ / CB ❶¹	Mercury 71289
11/17/58	CB	❶⁴	20		7	Smoke Gets In Your Eyes .... MV ❶⁴ / BB ❶³	Mercury 71383
01/25/60	CB	7	16		8	Harbor Lights .... BB 8 / MV 8	Mercury 71563

DEBUT	CH	PK	WK	Gold	A-side (Chart Hit) ... Other Charts	Label & Number
					PLAYER	
10/01/77	BB	❶³	32	●	1 Baby Come Back ....RR ❶³ / CB ❶² / RW 2⁴	RSO 879
03/11/78	BB	10	17		2 This Time I'm In It For Love	RSO 890
					PLAYMATES, The	
10/27/58	MV	3¹	15	☉	1 Beep Beep ....BB 4 / CB 4	Roulette 4115
					PLIES	
06/30/07	BB	9	22	△	1 Shawty	Slip n Slide 230716
					PLIES (Feat. T-Pain)	
04/12/08	BB	7	22	△	2 Bust It Baby Part 2	Slip n Slide 506620
					PLIES (Feat. Ne-Yo)	
					PM DAWN	
10/11/91	BB	❶¹	22	●	1 Set Adrift On Memory Bliss ....CB 4 / RR 5	Gee Street 866094
09/11/92	RR	❶³	32	●	2 I'd Die Without You..BB 3⁴ / CB 3⁴	Gee Street 24034
03/19/93	CB	❶³	30		3 Looking Through Patient Eyes ....RR ❶² / BB 6	Gee Street 862024
					POCO	
01/13/79	RR	7	19		1 Crazy Love	ABC 12439
					POINTER, Bonnie	
06/16/79	CB	10	23		1 Heaven Must Have Sent You...	Motown 1459
					POINTER SISTERS	
08/18/73	CB	10	16		1 Yes We Can Can..	Blue Thumb 229
07/19/75	RW	7	18		2 How Long (Betcha' Got A Chick On The Side)	ABC/Blue Thumb 265
11/11/78	RR	2³	27	●	3 Fire ....BB 2² / CB 2² / RW 2²	Planet 45901
07/19/80	BB	3³	31	●	4 He's So Shy ....CB 3² / RR 4 / RW 5	Planet 47916
05/30/81	RR	❶²	27	●	5 Slow Hand ....BB 2² / CB 2³ / RW 4	Planet 47929
01/16/82	RR	9	17		6 Should I Do It	Planet 47960
01/28/84	BB	5	22		7 Automatic ....RR 7 / CB 8	Planet 13730
04/28/84	BB	3²	25		8 Jump (For My Love) ....RR 5 / CB 6	Planet 13780
08/04/84	BB	9	24		9 I'm So Excited ....CB 8	Planet 13857
11/24/84	RR	4	23		10 Neutron Dance ....BB 6 / CB 10	Planet 13951
01/16/87	BB	5	16		11 Respect Yourself ....RR 6 / CB 9	Motown 1876
					BRUCE WILLIS with THE POINTER SISTERS	
					POISON	
03/14/87	BB	9	17		1 Talk Dirty To Me	Enigma/Capitol 5686
04/23/88	BB	6	19		2 Nothin' But A Good Time	Enigma/Capitol 44145
10/28/88	CB	❶⁴	21	●	3 Every Rose Has Its Thorn ....BB ❶³ / RR ❶³	Enigma/Capitol 44203
02/18/89	BB	10	19		4 Your Mama Don't Dance	Enigma/Capitol 44293
07/07/90	CB	3²	25	●	5 Unskinny Bop ....BB 3¹ / RR 4	Enigma/Capitol 44584
10/05/90	BB	4	22	●	6 Something To Believe In ....CB 5 / RR 5	Enigma/Capitol 44617
					POLICE, The	
10/25/80	BB	10	23		1 De Do Do Do, De Da Da Da......................................	A&M 2275
02/07/81	CB	9	18		2 Don't Stand So Close To Me..RR 9 / BB 10	A&M 2301
09/25/81	BB	3²	20		3 Every Little Thing She Does Is Magic ....RR 3¹ / CB 6 / RW 8	A&M 2371
01/15/82	RR	9	15		4 Spirits In The Material World	A&M 2390
06/03/83	BB	❶⁸	27	●	5 Every Breath You Take ....RR ❶⁸ / CB ❶⁷	A&M 2542
08/19/83	RR	❶²	20		6 King Of Pain ....BB 3² / CB 5	A&M 2569
11/04/83	RR	9	14		7 Synchronicity II	A&M 2571
01/07/84	RR	4	16		8 Wrapped Around Your Finger ....BB 8	A&M 2614
					PONI-TAILS	
07/07/58	BB	7	18		1 Born Too Late ....CB 10 / MV 10	ABC-Paramount 9934
					POPPY FAMILY, The	
03/14/70	BB	2²	19	●	1 Which Way You Goin' Billy? ....CB 2² / RW 2¹	London 129
					PORTRAIT	
11/14/92	RR	9	27		1 Here We Go Again! ....CB 10	Capitol 44865
					PORTUGAL. THE MAN	
07/08/17	BB	4	45	△⁵	1 Feel It Still	Atlantic
					POSEY, Sandy	
07/23/66	RW	9	15		1 Born A Woman	MGM 13501
11/19/66	RW	10	12		2 Single Girl	MGM 13612
					POSNER, Mike	
05/15/10	BB	6	29	△²	1 Cooler Than Me	J Records
02/06/16	BB	4	37	△⁵	2 I Took A Pill In Ibiza	Island
					POST, Mike	
05/17/75	BB	10	17		1 The Rockford Files ....CB 10	MGM 14772
08/22/81	BB	10	23		2 The Theme From Hill Street Blues	Elektra 47186
					MIKE POST Featuring Larry Carlton	

DEBUT	CH	PK	WK	Gold	#	A-side (Chart Hit) ... Other Charts	Label & Number
						POST MALONE	
12/31/16	BB	8	50	△10	1	Congratulations	Republic
						POST MALONE Featuring Quavo	
10/07/17	BB	●8	41	△8	2	Rockstar	Republic
						POST MALONE Featuring 21 Savage	
03/10/18	BB	●1	39	△5	3	Psycho	Republic
						POST MALONE Featuring Ty Dolla $ign	
05/12/18	BB	3²	52	△4	4	Better Now	Republic
11/03/18	BB	●1	53	△8	5	Sunflower (Spider-Man: Into The Spider-Verse)	Republic
						POST MALONE & SWAE LEE	
01/05/19	BB	2³	44	△	6	Wow.	Republic
07/20/19	BB	3²	21		7	Goodbyes	Republic
						POST MALONE Featuring Young Thug	
09/14/19	BB	●3	25		8	Circles	Republic
09/21/19	BB	8	20		9	Take What You Want	Republic
						POST MALONE Featuring Ozzy Osbourne & Travis Scott	
						POURCEL('S), Franck, French Fiddles	
03/23/59	CB	8	18		1	Only You ... MV 8 / BB 9	Capitol 4165
						POWELL, Jesse	
02/20/99	BB	10	20		1	You	Silas/MCA 55500
						POWERS, Joey	
11/02/63	BB	10	15		1	Midnight Mary ... CB 10	Amy 892
						POWER STATION, The	
03/16/85	BB	6	19		1	Some Like It Hot ... CB 6 / RR 7	Capitol 5444
06/08/85	RR	8	19		2	Get It On ... BB 9 / CB 10	Capitol 5479
						POWTER, Daniel	
02/25/06	BB	●5	32	△3	1	Bad Day ... RR 2¹	Warner
						PRADO, Perez, And His Orchestra	
01/31/55	BB	●10	29	⊙	1	Cherry Pink And Apple Blossom White ... MV ●8 / CB 2⁷	RCA Victor 5965
06/09/58	CB	●4	25	●	2	Patricia ... MV ●4 / BB ●1	RCA Victor 7245
						PRATT & McCLAIN	
04/03/76	BB	5	19		1	Happy Days ... CB 6 / RW 6 / RR 6	Reprise 1351
						PRESIDENTS, The	
10/03/70	RW	6	15		1	5-10-15-20 (25-30 Years Of Love) ... CB 7	Sussex 207
						PRESLEY, Elvis	
03/03/56	BB	●8	27	▲²	1	Heartbreak Hotel ... MV ●7 / CB ●6	RCA Victor 47-6420
05/11/56	BB	●1	24	▲	2	I Want You, I Need You, I Love You ... CB 3¹ / MV 8	RCA Victor 47-6540
07/27/56	BB	●11	28	▲4	3	Don't Be Cruel / ... MV ●8 / CB ●6	RCA Victor 47-6604
07/27/56	BB	●11	28		4	Hound Dog ... CB ●4 / MV 2¹	RCA Victor 47-6604
10/13/56	BB	●5	23	▲³	5	Love Me Tender ... CB ●5 / MV ●1	RCA Victor 47-6643
11/17/56	BB	2²	19		6	Love Me ... CB 10	RCA Victor EPA-992
01/19/57	BB	●3	17	▲	7	Too Much ... CB ●3 / MV 3¹	RCA Victor 47-6800
03/30/57	BB	●9	30	▲²	8	All Shook Up ... CB ●8 / MV ●6	RCA Victor 47-6870
06/24/57	BB	●7	25	▲²	9	(Let Me Be Your) Teddy Bear ... MV ●4 / CB ●3	RCA Victor 47-7000
09/30/57	BB	●7	27	▲²	10	Jailhouse Rock ... CB ●3 / MV 2⁴	RCA Victor 47-7035
01/20/58	BB	●5	20	▲	11	Don't / ... CB ●1 / MV 2¹	RCA Victor 47-7150
01/20/58	MV	7	12		12	I Beg Of You ... BB 8 / CB 9	RCA Victor 47-7150
04/14/58	BB	2¹	15	▲	13	Wear My Ring Around Your Neck ... CB 4 / MV 4	RCA Victor 47-7240
06/23/58	BB	●2	16	▲	14	Hard Headed Woman ... CB 3¹ / MV 4	RCA Victor 47-7280
11/03/58	BB	3¹	17	▲	15	One Night / ... BB 4 / MV 4	RCA Victor 47-7410
11/03/58	CB	5	16		16	I Got Stung ... BB 8 / MV 9	RCA Victor 47-7410
03/23/59	MV	●2	15	▲	17	(Now And Then There's) A Fool Such As I / ... CB 2³ / BB 2¹	RCA Victor 47-7506
03/23/59	MV	3¹	13		18	I Need Your Love Tonight ... BB 4 / CB 6	RCA Victor 47-7506
06/29/59	BB	●2	14	▲	19	A Big Hunk O' Love ... MV 2² / CB 2¹	RCA Victor 47-7600
04/04/60	BB	●4	16	▲	20	Stuck On You ... CB ●4 / MV ●3	RCA Victor 47-7740
07/18/60	BB	●5	20	▲	21	It's Now Or Never ... CB ●4 / MV ●3	RCA Victor 47-7777
11/07/60	BB	●6	16	▲²	22	Are You Lonesome To-night? ... CB ●6 / MV ●4	RCA Victor 47-7810
02/13/61	MV	●3	13	▲	23	Surrender ... BB ●2 / CB ●2	RCA Victor 47-7850
05/15/61	BB	5	10	●	24	I Feel So Bad ... CB 5 / MV 6	RCA Victor 47-7880
08/14/61	MV	3²	11	●	25	Little Sister / ... BB 5 / CB 5	RCA Victor 47-7908
08/21/61	BB	4	11		26	(Marie's The Name) His Latest Flame ... MV 3² / CB 4	RCA Victor 47-7908
12/04/61	BB	2¹	15	▲	27	Can't Help Falling In Love ... CB 4 / MV 4	RCA Victor 47-7968
03/12/62	MV	●3	14	▲	28	Good Luck Charm ... BB ●2 / CB ●1	RCA Victor 47-7992
07/28/62	CB	4	12	●	29	She's Not You ... MV 4 / BB 5	RCA Victor 47-8041
10/13/62	CB	●1	17	▲	30	Return To Sender ... MV ●1 / BB 2⁵	RCA Victor 47-8100
02/09/63	MV	8	10		31	One Broken Heart For Sale ... CB 3¹ / BB 10	RCA Victor 47-8134
06/29/63	BB	3²	12	●	32	(You're The) Devil In Disguise ... CB 3¹ / MV 3¹	RCA Victor 47-8188
10/12/63	MV	7	13	●	33	Bossa Nova Baby ... BB 8 / CB 8	RCA Victor 47-8243
02/08/64	MV	9	12	●	34	Kissin' Cousins ... CB 10	RCA Victor 47-8307

DEBUT	CH	PK	WK	Gold	A-side (Chart Hit) .... Other Charts	Label & Number
					PRESLEY, Elvis (cont'd)	
10/10/64	CB	10	12		35 Ask Me .... RW 10	RCA Victor 47-8440
04/24/65	RW	3²	16	▲	36 Crying In The Chapel .... BB 3¹ / CB 4	RCA Victor 447-0643
06/12/65	RW	10	10		37 (Such An) Easy Question	RCA Victor 47-8585
08/28/65	CB	9	12	●	38 I'm Yours .... RW 9	RCA Victor 47-8657
11/30/68	CB	9	14	●	39 If I Can Dream .... RW 9	RCA Victor 47-9670
05/03/69	CB	❶¹	13	▲	40 In The Ghetto .... RW ❶¹ / BB 3¹	RCA Victor 47-9741
09/13/69	CB	❶²	15	▲	41 Suspicious Minds .... RW ❶² / BB ❶¹	RCA Victor 47-9764
11/29/69	RW	5	13	▲	42 Don't Cry Daddy .... BB 6 / CB 6	RCA Victor 47-9768
02/14/70	CB	10	9	●	43 Kentucky Rain	RCA Victor 47-9791
05/09/70	RW	4	13	●	44 The Wonder Of You .... BB 9 / CB 10	RCA Victor 47-9835
10/24/70	RW	7	10	●	45 You Don't Have To Say You Love Me .... CB 10	RCA Victor 47-9916
08/19/72	CB	❶¹	16	▲	46 Burning Love .... RW 2² / BB 2¹	RCA Victor 74-0769
04/07/73	CB	10	12		47 Steamroller Blues	RCA Victor 74-0910
06/18/77	RW	10	23	▲	48 Way Down	RCA 10998
					PRESTON, Billy	
04/22/72	CB	❶¹	17	●	1 Outa-Space .... RW ❶¹ / BB 2¹	A&M 1320
02/24/73	BB	❶²	25	●	2 Will It Go Round In Circles .... CB ❶¹ / RW 3²	A&M 1411
09/15/73	BB	4	18	●	3 Space Race .... CB 6 / RW 6 / RR 7	A&M 1463
07/13/74	BB	❶¹	20	●	4 Nothing From Nothing .... CB ❶¹ / RW ❶¹ / RR 3¹	A&M 1544
12/08/79	BB	4	29		5 With You I'm Born Again .... CB 5 / RW 5	Motown 1477
					BILLY PRESTON & SYREETA	
					PRESTON, Johnny	
10/12/59	BB	❶³	27	⊙	1 Running Bear .... CB ❶³ / MV ❶³	Mercury 71474
03/19/60	MV	5	16		2 Cradle Of Love .... CB 6 / BB 7	Mercury 71598
06/20/60	CB	9	15		3 Feel So Fine	Mercury 71651
					PRETENDERS, The	
02/16/80	RR	10	22		1 Brass In Pocket (I'm Special)	Sire 49181
12/11/82	BB	5	25		2 Back On The Chain Gang .... CB 5 / RR 8	Sire 29840
10/11/86	RR	5	18		3 Don't Get Me Wrong .... BB 10	Sire 28630
08/13/94	RR	9	33		4 I'll Stand By You	Sire 18160
					PRETTY POISON	
09/26/87	BB	8	24	●	1 Catch Me (I'm Falling) .... CB 8 / RR 9	Virgin 99416
					PRETTY RICKY	
04/16/05	BB	7	22	○	1 Grind With Me	Atlantic 93711
08/19/05	RR	9	22	○	2 Your Body	Atlantic 94131
					PRICE, Lloyd	
11/24/58	BB	❶⁴	21	⊙	1 Stagger Lee .... CB ❶³ / MV ❶³	ABC-Paramount 9972
04/27/59	CB	2⁵	19	⊙	2 Personality .... MV 2⁴ / BB 2³	ABC-Paramount 10018
08/03/59	CB	2¹	14		3 I'm Gonna Get Married .... BB 3² / MV 3¹	ABC-Paramount 10032
					PRIEST, Maxi	
06/30/90	BB	❶¹	30	●	1 Close To You .... RR 3³ / CB 4	Charisma 98951
09/21/91	CB	5	27		2 Set The Night To Music .... BB 6 / RR 6	Atlantic 87607
					ROBERTA FLACK with MAXI PRIEST	
					PRIMA, Louis, And Keely Smith	
10/13/58	MV	9	16		1 That Old Black Magic	Capitol 4063
					PRIMITIVE RADIO GODS	
06/08/96	RR	7	23		1 Standing Outside A Broken Phone Booth With Money In My Hand. BB 10	Ergo
					PRINCE	
11/03/79	RR	9	21	●	1 I Wanna Be Your Lover	Warner 49050
02/26/83	RR	5	23		2 Little Red Corvette .... BB 6 / CB 6	Warner 29746
09/03/83	RR	7	21		3 Delirious .... BB 8 / CB 9	Warner 29503
06/02/84	BB	❶⁵	22	▲	4 When Doves Cry .... CB ❶⁴ / RR ❶⁴	Warner 29286
					PRINCE and The Revolution:	
08/03/84	RR	❶⁴	20	●	5 Let's Go Crazy .... BB ❶² / CB ❶²	Warner 29216
09/21/84	CB	❶²	20	●	6 Purple Rain .... RR ❶² / BB 2²	Warner 29174
12/14/84	RR	7	15		7 I Would Die 4 U .... BB 8 / CB 10	Warner 29121
05/10/85	CB	❶¹	20		8 Raspberry Beret .... RR ❶¹ / BB 2¹	Paisley Park 28972
07/26/85	RR	6	15		9 Pop Life .... BB 7 / CB 7	Paisley Park 28998
02/21/86	BB	❶²	19	●	10 Kiss .... CB ❶² / RR ❶¹	Paisley Park 28751
					PRINCE:	
03/06/87	BB	3¹	17		11 Sign 'O' The Times .... CB 4 / RR 6	Paisley Park 28399
07/25/87	BB	2¹	27		12 U Got The Look .... RR 3² / CB 3¹	Paisley Park 28289
					PRINCE & SHEENA EASTON	
11/14/87	RR	9	20		13 I Could Never Take The Place Of Your Man ...... BB 10 / CB 10	Paisley Park 28288
04/30/88	BB	8	15		14 Alphabet St. .... CB 9 / RR 10	Paisley Park 27900
06/16/89	CB	❶³	19	▲	15 Batdance .... BB ❶¹ / RR ❶¹	Warner 22924
08/03/90	CB	❶²	18	●	16 Thieves In The Temple .... RR 4² / BB 6	Paisley Park 19751

DEBUT	CH	PK	WK	Gold	A-side (Chart Hit)	Other Charts	Label & Number
					PRINCE AND THE NEW POWER GENERATION:		
09/20/91	BB	❶²	27	● 17	Cream	CB ❶² / RR ❶¹	Paisley Park 19175
12/06/91	CB	❶²	28	18	Diamonds And Pearls	RR ❶² / BB 3¹	Paisley Park 19083
03/27/92	RR	6	18	19	Money Don't Matter 2 Night		Paisley Park 19020
11/27/92	RR	2²	28	● 20	7	CB 6 / BB 7	Paisley Park 18824
03/27/93	RR	9	15	21	The Morning Papers		Paisley Park 18583
					PRINCE:		
03/04/94	CB	❶⁵	29	● 22	The Most Beautiful Girl In The World	RR ❶² / BB 3³	NPG 72514
05/07/16	BB	4	2	23	Purple Rain		NPG/Warner
05/07/16	BB	8	2	24	When Doves Cry		NPG/Warner
					PROCLAIMERS, The		
06/12/93	BB	3¹	24	● 1	I'm Gonna Be (500 Miles)	RR 3¹ / CB 4	Chrysalis 24846
					PROCOL HARUM		
06/17/67	RW	3¹	13	1	A Whiter Shade Of Pale	BB 5 / CB 5	Deram 7507
					PRODUCT G&B, The — see SANTANA		
					PSEUDO ECHO		
05/16/87	BB	6	15	1	Funky Town	RR 6	RCA 5217
					PSY		
09/22/12	BB	2⁷	31	△⁵ 1	Gangnam Style		YG
04/27/13	BB	5	15	2	Gentleman		YG
					PUBLIC ANNOUNCEMENT		
02/21/98	BB	5	22	▲ 1	Body Bumpin' Yippie-Yi-Yo		A&M 582444
					PUCKETT, Gary, And The Union Gap		
11/11/67	RW	2¹	18	● 1	Woman, Woman	CB 3² / BB 4	Columbia 44297
03/02/68	CB	❶¹	15	● 2	Young Girl	RW ❶¹ / BB 2³	Columbia 44450
					THE UNION GAP Featuring Gary Puckett (above 2)		
06/08/68	CB	❶¹	13	● 3	Lady Willpower	RW ❶¹ / BB 2²	Columbia 44547
09/14/68	CB	5	12	● 4	Over You	RW 6 / BB 7	Columbia 44644
08/16/69	RW	3¹	12	5	This Girl Is A Woman Now	CB 5 / BB 9	Columbia 44967
					PUDDLE OF MUDD		
12/22/01	RR	4	38	1	Blurry	BB 5	Flawless
10/12/02	RR	7	23	2	She Hates Me		Flawless
					PUFF DADDY / P. DIDDY / DIDDY		
					PUFF DADDY:		
01/25/97	BB	❶⁶	28	▲² 1	Can't Nobody Hold Me Down		Bad Boy 79083
					PUFF DADDY Featuring Mase		
06/14/97	BB	❶¹¹	33	▲³ 2	I'll Be Missing You		Bad Boy 79097
					PUFF DADDY & FAITH EVANS (Featuring 112)		
12/06/97	BB	2²	6	▲ 3	It's All About The Benjamins /		
					PUFF DADDY & THE FAMILY Feat. The Notorious B.I.G./Lil' Kim/The Lox/		
					Dave Grohl/Perfect/FuzzBubble/Rob Zombie		
01/17/98	BB	4	15	4	Been Around The World		Bad Boy 79130
					PUFF DADDY & THE FAMILY Featuring The Notorious B.I.G. & Mase		
06/27/98	BB	4	20	▲ 5	Come With Me		Epic 78954
					PUFF DADDY with JIMMY PAGE		
09/25/99	BB	2³	20	● 6	Satisfy You		Bad Boy 79283
					PUFF DADDY (Featuring R. Kelly)		
					P. DIDDY:		
03/16/02	BB	2⁴	23	7	I Need A Girl (Part One)	RR 3²	Bad Boy 79436
					P. DIDDY Featuring Usher & Loon		
06/08/02	BB	4	26	8	I Need A Girl (Part Two)	RR 9	Bad Boy 79441
					P. DIDDY AND GINUWINE Featuring Loon, Mario Winans & Tammy Ruggeri		
11/30/02	BB	❶¹	22	9	Bump, Bump, Bump	RR 3¹	Epic 79842
					B2K & P. DIDDY		
06/27/03	BB	❶⁴	30	○ 10	Shake Ya Tailfeather	RR ❶³	Bad Boy
					NELLY/P. DIDDY/MURPHY LEE		
					DIDDY:		
09/16/06	BB	9	20	11	Come To Me		Bad Boy 94423
					DIDDY Featuring Nicole Scherzinger		
02/03/07	RR	9	22	12	Last Night	BB 10	Bad Boy 89995
					DIDDY Featuring Keyshia Cole		
					PURE PRAIRIE LEAGUE		
05/09/80	RR	3²	17	1	Let Me Love You Tonight	RW 8 / BB 10	Casablanca 2266
					PURIFY, James & Bobby		
09/24/66	RW	5	15	1	I'm Your Puppet	BB 6 / CB 6	Bell 648
					PURSELL, Bill		
01/26/63	CB	7	15	1	Our Winter Love	BB 9	Columbia 42619

134

DEBUT	CH	PK	WK	Gold	A-side (Chart Hit) ... Other Charts	Label & Number
					PUSSYCAT DOLLS, The	
04/29/05	BB	2³	40	△	1 Don't Cha ... RR 3¹	A&M 004685
					THE PUSSYCAT DOLLS Featuring Busta Rhymes	
10/07/05	RR	●²	26		2 Stickwitu ... BB 5	A&M
05/19/06	RR	●²	30		3 Buttons ... BB 3¹	A&M 006800
					THE PUSSYCAT DOLLS featuring Big Snoop Dogg	
06/14/08	RR	8	20		4 When I Grow Up ... BB 9	Interscope 011750
					PUTH, Charlie	
03/28/15	BB	●¹²	52	△¹¹	1 See You Again ...	Universal Studios
					WIZ KHALIFA with CHARLIE PUTH	
02/20/16	BB	9	24	△⁴	2 We Don't Talk Anymore ...	Atlantic
					CHARLIE PUTH Featuring Selena Gomez	
05/13/17	BB	5	40	△⁴	3 Attention ...	Atlantic

Q

DEBUT	CH	PK	WK	Gold	A-side	Label & Number
					QUAD CITY DJ'S	
03/09/96	BB	3¹	42	▲	1 C'Mon N' Ride It (The Train) ... CB 3¹ / RR 7	Big Beat 98083
					QUARTERFLASH	
10/17/81	BB	3²	25	●	1 Harden My Heart ... CB 4 / RR 4 / RW 5	Geffen 49824
06/17/83	RR	6	16		2 Take Me To Heart ...	Geffen 29603
					QUATRO, Suzi	
01/27/79	BB	4	23	●	1 Stumblin' In ... CB 6 / RR 7 / RW 8	RSO 917
					SUZI QUATRO AND CHRIS NORMAN	
					QUEEN	
02/08/75	RR	10	20		1 Killer Queen	Elektra 45226
12/27/75	RW	4	27	●	2 Bohemian Rhapsody ... CB 6 / RR 8 / BB 9	Elektra 45297
05/28/76	RR	7	20	△	3 You're My Best Friend ... CB 9	Elektra 45318
11/20/76	CB	9	16	△²	4 Somebody To Love ...	Elektra 45362
10/22/77	RW	●³	30	▲	5 We Will Rock You/We Are The Champions ... CB 3² / BB 4 / RR 4	Elektra 45441
12/21/79	BB	●⁴	23	▲	6 Crazy Little Thing Called Love ... CB ●³ / RR ●³ / RW ●²	Elektra 46579
08/16/80	RW	●⁶	34	▲	7 Another One Bites The Dust ... CB ●⁴ / BB ●³ / RR 2¹	Elektra 47031
03/21/92	CB	●¹	27		8 Bohemian Rhapsody ... BB 2¹ / RR 3¹	Hollywood 64794
					QUEENSRYCHE	
03/23/91	BB	9	23		1 Silent Lucidity	EMI 50345
					? (QUESTION MARK) & THE MYSTERIANS	
08/27/66	BB	●¹	16	●	1 96 Tears ... CB ●¹ / RW ●¹	Cameo 428
					QUIET RIOT	
09/17/83	BB	5	25	●	1 Cum On Feel The Noize ... CB 5 / RR 9	Pasha 04005

R

DEBUT	CH	PK	WK	Gold	A-side	Label & Number
					RABBITT, Eddie	
06/21/80	BB	5	31	●	1 Drivin' My Life Away ... CB 5 / RW 5 / RR 9	Elektra 46656
11/08/80	BB	●²	28	●	2 I Love A Rainy Night ... CB ●¹ / RW 3⁴ / RR 5	Elektra 47066
07/24/81	RR	4	25		3 Step By Step ... BB 5 / CB 5 / RW 5	Elektra 47174
11/14/81	RR	10	18		4 Someone Could Lose A Heart Tonight	Elektra 47239
10/09/82	BB	7	29		5 You And I	Elektra 69936
					EDDIE RABBITT with CRYSTAL GAYLE	
					RAE SREMMURD	
10/01/16	BB	●⁷	27	△⁶	1 Black Beatles ...	EarDrummers
					RAE SREMMURD Featuring Gucci Mane	
					RAFFERTY, Gerry	
04/15/78	RR	●⁴	24	●	1 Baker Street ... CB ●² / BB 2⁶ / RW 2⁴	United Artists 1192
08/12/78	RR	7	17		2 Right Down The Line ... CB 8 / RW 9	United Artists 1233
06/02/79	RR	7	11		3 Days Gone Down (Still Got The Light In Your Eyes)	United Artists 1298
					RAITT, Bonnie	
07/13/91	BB	5	29		1 Something To Talk About ... RR 7 / CB 8	Capitol 44724
11/09/91	CB	7	30		2 I Can't Make You Love Me	Capitol 44729
03/11/94	CB	10	24		3 Love Sneakin' Up On You	Capitol 58125
					RANDY & THE RAINBOWS	
06/08/63	BB	10	18		1 Denise	Rust 5059

DEBUT	CH	PK	WK	Gold	A-side (Chart Hit) ... Other Charts	Label & Number
					RARE EARTH	
03/14/70	CB	2[1]	20	●	1 Get Ready .... RW 3[1] / BB 4	Rare Earth 5012
08/01/70	CB	5	15		2 (I Know) I'm Losing You .... RW 6 / BB 7	Rare Earth 5017
07/17/71	BB	7	13		3 I Just Want To Celebrate .... CB 7 / RW 7	Rare Earth 5031
					RASCAL FLATTS	
02/18/06	BB	6	51	△[5]	1 What Hurts The Most	Lyric Street
06/17/06	BB	7	20	△	2 Life Is A Highway	Walt Disney
					RASCALS, The	
03/12/66	RW	❶[2]	15	☉	1 Good Lovin' .... BB ❶[1] / CB ❶[1]	Atlantic 2321
04/22/67	BB	❶[4]	14	●	2 Groovin' .... CB ❶[3] / RW ❶[2]	Atlantic 2401
07/08/67	RW	5	10		3 A Girl Like You .... CB 8 / BB 10	Atlantic 2424
09/09/67	CB	2[2]	12		4 How Can I Be Sure .... RW 3[2] / BB 4	Atlantic 2438
					THE YOUNG RASCALS (all of above)	
04/06/68	RW	2[3]	14	●	5 A Beautiful Morning .... CB 3[3] / BB 3[2]	Atlantic 2493
07/13/68	BB	❶[5]	16	●	6 People Got To Be Free .... CB ❶[3] / RW ❶[2]	Atlantic 2537
08/30/69	RW	10	9		7 Carry Me Back	Atlantic 2664
					RASPBERRIES	
07/01/72	RW	3[1]	18	●	1 Go All The Way .... CB 4 / BB 5	Capitol 3348
11/11/72	RW	7	14		2 I Wanna Be With You .... CB 10	Capitol 3473
					RAWLS, Lou	
05/15/76	BB	2[2]	30		1 You'll Never Find Another Love Like Mine ... RW 2[2] / CB 4 / RR 5	Philadelphia I. 3592
					RAY, Jimmy	
01/23/98	RR	8	18	●	1 Are You Jimmy Ray?	Epic 78816
					RAY, Johnnie	
11/24/51	BB	❶[11]	33	☉	1 Cry / .... CB ❶[8]	
11/24/51	BB	2[2]	26		2 The Little White Cloud That Cried .... CB 4	Okeh 6840
					JOHNNIE RAY & The Four Lads (above 2)	
01/26/52	BB	6	20		3 Please, Mr. Sun / .... CB 6	
01/26/52	BB	8	18		4 Here I Am - Broken Hearted .... CB 10	Columbia 39636
04/12/52	CB	10	12		5 What's The Use?	Columbia 39698
05/24/52	BB	4	23		6 Walkin' My Baby Back Home .... CB 6	Columbia 39750
04/11/53	BB	8	6		7 Somebody Stole My Gal	Columbia 39961
09/01/56	MV	❶[4]	28	☉	8 Just Walking In The Rain .... BB 2[1] / CB 3[2]	Columbia 40729
01/12/57	MV	6	13		9 You Don't Owe Me A Thing .... BB 10 / CB 10	Columbia 40803
					RAYBURN, Margie	
09/23/57	BB	9	19		1 I'm Available	Liberty 55102
					RAYDIO — see PARKER, Ray Jr.	
					RAY, GOODMAN & BROWN	
01/26/80	BB	5	20	●	1 Special Lady .... CB 7 / RW 9	Polydor 2033
					RAY J	
02/16/08	RR	2[1]	26	△	1 Sexy Can I .... BB 3[1]	Koch/Epic
					RAY J & YUNG BERG	
					RAYS, The	
10/07/57	MV	2[3]	20	☉	1 Silhouettes .... CB 3[4] / BB 3[2]	Cameo 117
					R. CITY	
08/08/15	BB	6	27	△	1 Locked Away	Kemosabe
					R. CITY with ADAM LEVINE	
					REA, Chris	
07/01/78	RR	9	16		1 Fool (If You Think It's Over) .... CB 10	United Artists 1198
					READY FOR THE WORLD	
08/03/85	BB	❶[1]	24		1 Oh Sheila .... CB 3[2] / RR 3[1]	MCA 52636
11/29/86	BB	9	19		2 Love You Down .... RR 10	MCA 52947
					REAL McCOY	
08/26/94	RR	❶[4]	54	▲	1 Another Night .... CB 2[7] / BB 3[11]	Arista 12724
02/17/95	BB	3[1]	23	●	2 Run Away .... CB 3[1] / RR 4	Arista 12808
06/02/95	RR	8	23		3 Come And Get Your Love	Arista 12834
					REBELS, The	
12/29/62	BB	8	17		1 Wild Weekend .... CB 8 / MV 9	Swan 4125
					REDBONE	
01/05/74	BB	5	24	●	1 Come And Get Your Love .... CB 5 / RW 8 / RR 9	Epic 11035
					REDDING, Otis	
01/27/68	BB	❶[4]	16	●	1 (Sittin' On) The Dock Of The Bay .... RW 2[1] / CB 3[2]	Volt 157

136

DEBUT	CH	PK	WK	Gold	A-side (Chart Hit) ... Other Charts	Label & Number
					REDDY, Helen	
06/24/72	RW	❶²	24	●	1 I Am Woman ....BB ❶¹ / CB ❶¹	Capitol 3350
06/23/73	CB	❶²	22		2 Delta Dawn ....RW ❶² / BB ❶¹	Capitol 3645
10/27/73	CB	❶¹	16	●	3 Leave Me Alone (Ruby Red Dress)............RW ❶¹ / BB 3² / RR 5	Capitol 3768
03/09/74	RW	9	15		4 Keep On Singing ....CB 10	Capitol 3845
06/08/74	BB	9	20		5 You And Me Against The World ....RW 9 / CB 10	Capitol 3897
10/19/74	BB	❶¹	17	●	6 Angie Baby ....CB ❶¹ / RW ❶¹ / RR 2¹	Capitol 3972
08/09/75	CB	5	19		7 Ain't No Way To Treat A Lady ....RW 7 / BB 8	Capitol 4128
					RED HOT CHILI PEPPERS	
04/04/92	RR	❶²	27	●	1 Under The Bridge ....CB ❶¹ / BB 2¹	Warner 18978
06/05/99	BB	9	29	○	2 Scar Tissue ....RR 10	Warner 16913
04/22/06	BB	6	26	△²	3 Dani California	Warner
					RED JUMPSUIT APPARATUS, The	
08/05/06	RR	10	43		1 Face Down	Virgin
					REED, Jerry	
10/17/70	RW	5	24	●	1 Amos Moses ....BB 8 / CB 8	RCA Victor 9904
04/24/71	RW	8	14		2 When You're Hot, You're Hot ....BB 9 / CB 9	RCA Victor 9976
					REESE, Della	
08/05/57	MV	10	18		1 And That Reminds Me	Jubilee 5292
09/07/59	CB	❶²	21	⊙	2 Don't You Know ....MV ❶² / BB 2¹	RCA Victor 7591
					REEVES, Jim	
04/20/57	MV	7	22		1 Four Walls	RCA Victor 6874
12/21/59	MV	❶³	25	⊙	2 He'll Have To Go ....BB 2³ / CB 2³	RCA Victor 7643
					REFLECTIONS, The	
03/28/64	BB	6	15		1 (Just Like) Romeo & Juliet ....CB 9 / MV 9	Golden World 9
					REGENTS, The	
05/01/61	MV	8	12		1 Barbara-Ann	Gee 1065
					REGINA	
06/21/86	BB	10	21		1 Baby Love ....CB 10 / RR 10	Atlantic 89417
					R.E.M.	
09/19/87	BB	9	22		1 The One I Love ....CB 10	I.R.S. 53171
01/21/89	BB	6	21		2 Stand ....CB 6 / RR 6	Warner 27688
03/30/91	BB	4	25	●	3 Losing My Religion ....RR 4 / CB 6	Warner 19392
07/27/91	CB	8	21		4 Shiny Happy People ....BB 10 / RR 10	Warner 19242
01/29/93	RR	10	17		5 Man On The Moon	Warner 18642
09/11/93	RR	9	25		6 Everybody Hurts	Warner 18638
09/24/94	RR	10	22		7 What's The Frequency, Kenneth?	Warner 18050
01/06/95	RR	8	14		8 Bang And Blame	Warner 17994
					REMBRANDTS, The	
05/19/95	RR	❶⁸	28		1 I'll Be There For You (Theme From "Friends")	EastWest 64384
					RENAY, Diane	
01/18/64	MV	5	14		1 Navy Blue ....BB 6 / CB 6	20th Century 456
					RENE, Henri, and his Orchestra	
06/09/51	BB	6	18		1 I'm In Love Again ....CB 9	RCA Victor 4148
					HENRI RENÉ and his Orchestra featuring April Stevens	
08/11/51	BB	10	5		2 Gimme A Little Kiss, Will Ya Huh?	RCA Victor 4208
					APRIL STEVENS with HENRI RENÉ and his Orchestra	
09/26/53	BB	8	13		3 The Velvet Glove	RCA Victor 5405
					HENRI RENÉ and HUGO WINTERHALTER	
05/08/54	BB	8	15		4 The Happy Wanderer (Val-De Ri, Val-De Ra)	RCA Victor 5715
					HENRI RENÉ'S MUSETTE and CHORUS	
					RENO, Mike	
05/12/84	RR	4	20		1 Almost Paradise...Love Theme From Footloose ....BB 7 / CB 7	Columbia 04418
					MIKE RENO and ANN WILSON	
					REO SPEEDWAGON	
11/29/80	BB	❶¹	29	▲	1 Keep On Loving You ....CB ❶¹ / RW ❶¹ / RR 2¹	Epic 50953
03/20/81	RW	3³	23	●	2 Take It On The Run ....RR 3³ / CB 4 / BB 5	Epic 01054
06/11/82	BB	7	16		3 Keep The Fire Burnin' ....RR 8 / CB 10	Epic 02967
01/18/85	RR	❶⁴	21	●	4 Can't Fight This Feeling ....BB ❶³ / CB ❶²	Epic 04713
					RESTLESS HEART	
11/13/92	RR	5	24		1 When She Cries ....CB 9	RCA 62412
					REUNION	
09/07/74	RR	6	19		1 Life Is A Rock (But The Radio Rolled Me)............CB 7 / BB 8 / RW 9	RCA Victor 10056

DEBUT	CH	PK	WK	Gold	A-side (Chart Hit)	Other Charts	Label & Number

REVERE, Paul, And The Raiders

DEBUT	CH	PK	WK	Gold	#	A-side	Other Charts	Label & Number
03/19/66	CB	3¹	14		1	Kicks	BB 4 / RW 5	Columbia 43556
06/18/66	BB	6	11		2	Hungry	CB 10 / RW 10	Columbia 43678
12/03/66	BB	4	12		3	Good Thing	RW 4 / CB 5	Columbia 43907
04/29/67	BB	5	10		4	Him Or Me - What's It Gonna Be?	RW 6 / CB 9	Columbia 44094
04/10/71	RW	❶³	22	▲	5	Indian Reservation (The Lament Of The Cherokee Reservation Indian)	BB ❶¹ / CB ❶¹	Columbia 45332

RAIDERS

REXHA, Bebe

DEBUT	CH	PK	WK	Gold	#	A-side	Other Charts	Label & Number
04/11/15	BB	8	24	△³	1	Hey Mama		What A Music

DAVID GUETTA with NICKI MINAJ, BEBE REXHA & AFROJACK

| 11/21/15 | BB | 7 | 37 | △⁵ | 2 | Me, Myself & I | | G-Eazy |

G-EAZY & BEBE REXHA

| 11/11/17 | BB | 2³ | 52 | △⁸ | 3 | Meant To Be | | Warner |

BEBE REXHA & FLORIDA GEORGIA LINE

REYNOLDS, Debbie

| 02/03/51 | BB | 3¹ | 17 | ☉ | 1 | Aba Daba Honeymoon | CB 4 | MGM 30282 |

DEBBIE REYNOLDS and CARLETON CARPENTER

| 07/06/57 | CB | ❶⁷ | 31 | ☉ | 2 | Tammy | BB ❶⁵ / MV ❶³ | Coral 61851 |

REYNOLDS, Jody

| 05/03/58 | BB | 5 | 17 | | 1 | Endless Sleep | CB 10 | Demon 1507 |

RHYTHM HERITAGE

| 11/15/75 | RW | ❶² | 27 | ● | 1 | Theme From S.W.A.T. | RR ❶² / BB ❶¹ / CB ❶¹ | ABC 12135 |

RHYTHM SYNDICATE

| 06/01/91 | BB | 2² | 21 | | 1 | P.A.S.S.I.O.N | RR 2² / CB 3³ | Impact 54046 |
| 09/07/91 | RR | 10 | 21 | | 2 | Hey Donna | | Impact 54208 |

RYTHM SYNDICATE (above 2)

RICCH, Roddy

| 12/21/19 | BB | ❶⁷ | 11 | | 1 | The Box | | Bird Visio |

RICH, Charlie

| 09/29/73 | BB | ❶² | 23 | ● | 1 | The Most Beautiful Girl | CB ❶² / RW ❶² / RR 2¹ | Epic 11040 |
| 02/16/74 | CB | 8 | 14 | | 2 | A Very Special Love Song | RW 10 | Epic 11091 |

RICH, Tony, Project

| 12/16/95 | RR | ❶² | 49 | ▲ | 1 | Nobody Knows | BB 2² / CB 2² | LaFace 24115 |

RICHARD, Cliff

06/26/76	RR	3²	28	●	1	Devil Woman	CB 5 / RW 5 / BB 6	Rocket 40574
10/20/79	RR	2⁴	21		2	We Don't Talk Anymore	CB 6 / BB 7 / RW 9	EMI America 8025
09/12/80	RR	3¹	23		3	Dreaming	RW 7 / CB 9 / BB 10	EMI America 8057
12/13/80	RR	5	22		4	A Little In Love		EMI America 8068

RICH BOY

| 12/23/06 | BB | 6 | 21 | | 1 | Throw Some D's | | Zone 4 008391 |

RICH BOY feat. Polow Da Don

RICHIE, Lionel

| 07/04/81 | BB | ❶⁹ | 29 | ▲ | 1 | Endless Love | CB ❶⁹ / RW ❶⁹ / RR ❶⁵ | Motown 1519 |

DIANA ROSS & LIONEL RICHIE

10/09/82	BB	❶²	22	●	2	Truly	CB ❶² / RR ❶¹	Motown 1644
01/14/83	RR	❶¹	22		3	You Are	CB 2² / BB 4	Motown 1657
04/09/83	BB	5	16		4	My Love	RR 6 / CB 9	Motown 1677
09/16/83	BB	❶⁴	27	●	5	All Night Long (All Night)	CB ❶³ / RR ❶³	Motown 1698
11/25/83	RR	4	19		6	Running With The Night	BB 7 / CB 9	Motown 1710
02/25/84	BB	❶²	24	●	7	Hello	CB ❶² / RR 2³	Motown 1722
06/23/84	RR	❶¹	20		8	Stuck On You	BB 3² / CB 3²	Motown 1746
10/06/84	RR	6	18		9	Penny Lover	BB 8	Motown 1762
11/01/85	CB	❶⁵	24	●	10	Say You, Say Me	RR ❶⁵ / BB ❶⁴	Motown 1819
07/11/86	RR	❶¹	17		11	Dancing On The Ceiling	BB 2² / CB 4	Motown 1843
10/03/86	BB	9	20		12	Love Will Conquer All	RR 9 / CB 10	Motown 1866
12/06/86	BB	7	20		13	Ballerina Girl	CB 9 / RR 9	Motown 1873
05/01/92	RR	10	20		14	Do It To Me		Motown 2160

RIDDLE, Nelson, and His Orchestra

| 12/10/55 | BB | ❶⁴ | 29 | ☉ | 1 | Lisbon Antigua | CB ❶² / MV 3⁴ | Capitol 3287 |

RIGHTEOUS BROTHERS, The

12/12/64	CB	❶³	16	☉	1	You've Lost That Lovin' Feelin'	RW ❶³ / BB ❶²	Philles 124
04/10/65	BB	9	11		2	Just Once In My Life	CB 10 / RW 10	Philles 127
07/10/65	BB	4	14	☉	3	Unchained Melody	RW 4 / CB 6	Philles 129
11/27/65	CB	4	10		4	Ebb Tide	RW 4 / BB 5	Philles 130
03/05/66	BB	❶³	13	●	5	(You're My) Soul And Inspiration	CB ❶² / RW ❶²	Verve 10383
05/18/74	BB	3²	20		6	Rock And Roll Heaven	RW 3² / CB 4 / RR 10	Haven 7002
08/25/90	RR	3¹	19		7	Unchained Melody	CB 9	Verve Forecast 871882

DEBUT	CH	PK	WK	Gold	A-side (Chart Hit)	Other Charts	Label & Number
					RIGHT SAID FRED		
12/21/91	BB	❶³	30	▲	1 I'm Too Sexy	CB 4 / RR 4	Charisma 98671
					RIHANNA		
06/10/05	BB	2³	27	△²	1 Pon De Replay	RR 2¹	Def Jam 004809
10/07/05	RR	8	22	○	2 If It's Lovin' That You Want		Def Jam 005342
02/03/06	BB	❶³	28	△²	3 SOS	RR ❶¹	Def Jam 006315
04/28/06	RR	2³	20	△³	4 Unfaithful	BB 6	Def Jam
11/10/06	RR	6	22	○	5 Break It Off	BB 9	Def Jam
					RIHANNA & SEAN PAUL		
04/13/07	BB	❶⁷	33	△⁶	6 Umbrella	RR 2²	SRP/Def Jam 008990
					RIHANNA feat. Jay-Z		
09/14/07	RR	3³	26	△²	7 Hate That I Love You	BB 7	SRP/Def Jam
					RIHANNA Featuring Ne-Yo		
12/08/07	BB	3⁴	30	△⁴	8 Don't Stop The Music	RR 3³	SRP/Def Jam
04/04/08	RR	❶³	27	△⁴	9 Take A Bow	BB ❶¹	SRP/Def Jam
06/27/08	RR	❶³	37	△⁶	10 Disturbia	BB ❶²	SRP/Def Jam 011653
08/15/09	BB	2¹	23	△²	11 Run This Town		Roc Nation 521199
					JAY-Z, RIHANNA & KANYE WEST		
11/07/09	BB	9	14	△²	12 Russian Roulette		SRP/Def Jam
12/05/09	BB	8	20	△²	13 Hard		SRP/Def Jam
					RIHANNA Featuring Jeezy		
02/27/10	BB	❶⁵	22	△⁵	14 Rude Boy		SRP/Def Jam
09/25/10	BB	❶¹	27	△⁶	15 Only Girl (In The World)		SRP/Def Jam
11/06/10	BB	❶¹	22	△⁶	16 What's My Name?		SRP/Def Jam
					RIHANNA Featuring Drake		
12/04/10	BB	❶¹	26	△⁵	17 S&M		SRP/Def Jam
08/13/11	BB	7	18	△²	18 Cheers (Drink To That)		SRP/Def Jam
10/08/11	BB	❶¹⁰	41	△⁹	19 We Found Love		SRP/Def Jam
					RIHANNA Featuring Calvin Harris		
12/10/11	BB	5	26	△⁴	20 Where Have You Been		SRP/Def Jam
10/13/12	BB	❶³	26	△⁶	21 Diamonds		SRP/Def Jam
02/23/13	BB	3²	32	△⁷	22 Stay		SRP
					RIHANNA Featuring Mikky Ekko		
02/07/15	BB	4	20	△³	23 FourFiveSeconds		Westbury Road
					RIHANNA & KANYE WEST & PAUL McCARTNEY		
02/13/16	BB	❶⁹	36	△⁶	24 Work		Westbury Road
					RIHANNA Featuring Drake		
02/20/16	BB	7	45	△⁴	25 Needed Me		Westbury Road
05/21/16	BB	3³	32	△⁵	26 This Is What You Came For		Westbury Road
					CALVIN HARRIS with RIHANNA		
06/11/16	BB	5	31	△³	27 Love On The Brain		Westbury Road
					RILEY, Jeannie C.		
08/24/68	RW	❶³	14	●	1 Harper Valley P.T.A.	BB ❶¹ / CB ❶¹	Plantation 3
					RIMES, LeAnn		
06/21/97	BB	2⁴	69	▲³	1 How Do I Live	RR 4	Curb 73022
11/23/01	RR	9	22	●	2 Can't Fight The Moonlight		Curb 73116
					RIOS, Miguel		
06/06/70	CB	9	10		1 A Song Of Joy (Himno A La Alegria)	RW 10	A&M 1193
					RIP CHORDS, The		
12/14/63	MV	2¹	15	☉	1 Hey Little Cobra	BB 4 / CB 4	Columbia 42921
					RIPERTON, Minnie		
01/18/75	BB	❶¹	21	●	1 Lovin' You	CB ❶¹ / RW ❶¹ / RR ❶¹	Epic 50057
					RITCHIE FAMILY, The		
08/02/75	CB	10	18		1 Brazil		20th Century 2218
					RITENOUR, Lee		
04/18/81	RR	9	19		1 Is It You		Elektra 47124
					RIVERS, Johnny		
05/30/64	BB	2²	14	☉	1 Memphis	CB 2² / RW 3²	Imperial 66032
10/31/64	RW	7	12		2 Mountain Of Love	BB 9 / CB 10	Imperial 66075
05/29/65	BB	7	12		3 Seventh Son	CB 7 / RW 8	Imperial 66112
03/12/66	RW	3²	11		4 Secret Agent Man	BB 3¹ / CB 4	Imperial 66159
09/17/66	BB	❶¹	15	☉	5 Poor Side Of Town	CB ❶¹ / RW ❶¹	Imperial 66205
02/04/67	BB	3²	11		6 Baby I Need Your Lovin'	RW 3¹ / CB 6	Imperial 66227
06/03/67	BB	10	10		7 The Tracks Of My Tears	CB 10 / RW 10	Imperial 66244
11/18/67	CB	10	12		8 Summer Rain		Imperial 66267
10/07/72	RW	4	19	●	9 Rockin' Pneumonia - Boogie Woogie Flu	CB 5 / BB 6	United Artists 50960
06/25/77	CB	6	26	●	10 Swayin' To The Music (Slow Dancin')	RR 7 / BB 10	Big Tree 16094
					RIVIERAS, The		
01/18/64	BB	5	13		1 California Sun	CB 6 / MV 6	Riviera 1401

DEBUT	CH	PK	WK	Gold	A-side (Chart Hit) ... Other Charts	Label & Number
					ROBBINS, Marty	
03/30/57	BB	2¹	26	⊙	1 A White Sport Coat (And A Pink Carnation) .... CB 3² / MV 4	Columbia 40864
11/09/59	BB	❶²	22	⊙	2 El Paso .... MV ❶² / CB 2¹	Columbia 41511
01/21/61	MV	2¹	17		3 Don't Worry .... CB 3² / BB 3¹	Columbia 41922
					ROBERTS, Austin	
09/09/72	RW	9	20		1 Something's Wrong With Me .... CB 10	Chelsea 0101
07/12/75	RW	6	24		2 Rocky .... RR 8 / BB 9	Private Stock 45,020
					ROBERTS, Kenny	
09/24/49	CB	8	18		1 I Never See Maggie Alone .... BB 9	Coral 64012
					ROBERTSON, Don	
04/13/56	MV	5	20		1 The Happy Whistler .... BB 6 / CB 8	Capitol 3391
					ROBIC, Ivo, and The Song-Masters	
08/10/59	MV	9	17		1 Morgen	Laurie 3033
					ROBIN S	
04/03/93	RR	3¹	30	●	1 Show Me Love .... CB 4 / BB 5	Big Beat 10118
					ROBINSON, Smokey	
10/06/79	CB	❶¹	26		1 Cruisin' .... BB 4 / RW 5	Tamla 54306
02/14/81	RR	❶²	25	●	2 Being With You .... CB ❶¹ / RW ❶¹ / BB 2³	Tamla 54321
03/28/87	CB	7	22		3 Just To See Her .... BB 8 / RR 9	Motown 1877
07/18/87	RR	9	20		4 One Heartbeat .... BB 10	Motown 1897
					ROBINSON, Vicki Sue	
04/10/76	BB	10	25	●	1 Turn The Beat Around	RCA Victor 10562
					ROBYN	
05/02/97	RR	2¹	28	●	1 Do You Know (What It Takes) .... BB 7	RCA 64865
09/19/97	RR	3⁷	29	●	2 Show Me Love .... BB 7	RCA 64970
02/27/98	RR	8	18		3 Do You Really Want Me (Show Respect)	RCA 65468
					ROCKWELL	
01/28/84	BB	2³	22	●	1 Somebody's Watching Me .... CB 2³ / RR 2¹	Motown 1702
					RODGERS, Jimmie	
08/03/57	BB	❶⁴	28	⊙	1 Honeycomb .... MV ❶² / CB ❶¹	Roulette 4015
11/04/57	BB	3³	21	⊙	2 Kisses Sweeter Than Wine .... CB 5 / MV 5	Roulette 4031
01/27/58	BB	7	15		3 Oh-Oh, I'm Falling In Love Again .... MV 3	Roulette 4045
04/28/58	MV	2¹	18	⊙	4 Secretly .... BB 3³ / CB 4	Roulette 4070
07/21/58	BB	10	14		5 Are You Really Mine .... MV 10	Roulette 4090
					ROE, Tommy	
07/14/62	BB	❶²	16	●	1 Sheila .... CB 2³ / MV 2¹	ABC-Paramount 10329
10/05/63	BB	3²	16		2 Everybody .... MV 3¹ / CB 5	ABC-Paramount 10478
05/28/66	RW	5	16	●	3 Sweet Pea .... BB 8 / CB 8	ABC-Paramount 10762
09/17/66	RW	4	14		4 Hooray For Hazel .... BB 6 / CB 6	ABC 10852
01/18/69	BB	❶⁴	17	●	5 Dizzy .... CB ❶² / RW ❶²	ABC 11164
11/15/69	RW	4	14		6 Jam Up Jelly Tight .... CB 5 / BB 8	ABC 11247
					ROGER	
11/14/87	BB	3¹	21		1 I Want To Be Your Man .... RR 5 / CB 6	Reprise 28229
					ROGERS, Julie	
11/14/64	RW	7	13		1 The Wedding .... CB 9 / BB 10	Mercury 72332
					ROGERS, Kenny	
03/19/77	BB	5	23	●	1 Lucille .... CB 6 / RW 7	United Artists 929
04/21/79	RR	❶¹	22	●	2 She Believes In Me .... RW 4 / BB 5 / CB 7	United Artists 1273
09/08/79	RR	3²	20		3 You Decorated My Life .... RW 5 / BB 7 / CB 7	United Artists 1315
11/17/79	CB	❶¹	21	●	4 Coward Of The County .... RW ❶¹ / BB 3⁴ / RR 6	United Artists 1327
03/21/80	RR	2²	21		5 Don't Fall In Love With A Dreamer .... BB 4 / CB 4 / RW 4 KENNY ROGERS with KIM CARNES	United Artists 1345
06/14/80	RW	8	16		6 Love The World Away	United Artists 1359
09/26/80	BB	❶⁶	26	●	7 Lady .... RW ❶⁵ / RR ❶⁵ / CB ❶⁴	Liberty 1380
06/05/81	RR	3⁴	23		8 I Don't Need You .... BB 3² / CB 5 / RW 5	Liberty 1415
09/04/81	RR	8	15		9 Share Your Love With Me	Liberty 1430
12/26/81	RR	5	18		10 Through The Years .... RW 10	Liberty 1444
07/03/82	RR	10	17		11 Love Will Turn You Around	Liberty 1471
01/21/83	BB	6	19		12 We've Got Tonight .... CB 10 / RR 10 KENNY ROGERS and SHEENA EASTON	Liberty 1492
08/27/83	BB	❶²	29	▲ 13	Islands In The Stream .... CB ❶² / RR 2¹ KENNY ROGERS with DOLLY PARTON	RCA 13615

DEBUT	CH	PK	WK	Gold	A-side (Chart Hit)	Other Charts	Label & Number
					ROGERS, Kenny, And The First Edition		
02/03/68	RW	3¹	12		1 Just Dropped In (To See What Condition My Condition Was In) THE FIRST EDITION	BB 5 / CB 5	Reprise 0655
06/07/69	BB	6	14		2 Ruby, Don't Take Your Love To Town	CB 7 / RW 9	Reprise 0829
02/07/70	CB	5	19		3 Something's Burning	RW 7	Reprise 0888
					ROLLING STONES, The		
10/10/64	BB	6	15		1 Time Is On My Side	CB 6 / RW 6	London 9708
03/27/65	BB	9	11		2 The Last Time	CB 10 / RW 10	London 9741
06/12/65	BB	❶⁴	14	●	3 (I Can't Get No) Satisfaction	CB ❶⁴ / RW ❶³	London 9766
10/02/65	BB	❶²	12	☉	4 Get Off Of My Cloud	CB ❶² / RW 2¹	London 9792
12/25/65	CB	3²	9		5 As Tears Go By		London 9808
02/26/66	CB	❶¹	11	☉	6 19th Nervous Breakdown	BB 2³ / RW 2²	London 9823
05/14/66	BB	❶²	11	☉	7 Paint It, Black	CB ❶¹ / RW ❶¹	London 901
07/09/66	CB	4	10		8 Mothers Little Helper	RW 4 / BB 8	London 902
10/01/66	RW	3²	8		9 Have You Seen Your Mother, Baby, Standing In The Shadow?	CB 4 / BB 9	London 903
01/21/67	CB	❶²	13	●	10 Ruby Tuesday	BB ❶¹ / RW ❶¹	London 904
09/09/67	CB	6	9		11 Dandelion		London 905
12/30/67	RW	9	8		12 She's A Rainbow	CB 10	London 906
06/08/68	CB	❶¹	12	☉	13 Jumpin' Jack Flash	RW 2³ / BB 3³	London 908
07/19/69	BB	❶⁴	16	●	14 Honky Tonk Women	CB ❶⁴ / RW ❶³	London 910
04/24/71	RW	❶³	12		15 Brown Sugar	BB ❶² / CB 2²	Rolling Stones 19100
04/22/72	RW	4	11		16 Tumbling Dice	BB 7 / CB 10	Rolling Stones 19103
09/08/73	RR	❶⁴	16	●	17 Angie	RW ❶² / BB ❶¹ / CB ❶¹	Rolling Stones 19105
01/12/74	CB	10	11		18 Doo Doo Doo Doo Doo (Heartbreaker)		Rolling Stones 19109
04/24/76	CB	9	16		19 Fool To Cry	BB 10	Rolling Stones 19304
05/27/78	CB	❶²	23	●	20 Miss You	BB ❶¹ / RR ❶¹ / RW 3⁴	Rolling Stones 19307
09/09/78	CB	7	15		21 Beast Of Burden	BB 8	Rolling Stones 19309
07/04/80	RR	2⁴	21		22 Emotional Rescue	CB 3⁴ / BB 3² / RW 5	Rolling Stones 20001
08/21/81	BB	2³	26		23 Start Me Up	CB 4 / RW 5 / RR 9	Rolling Stones 21003
11/27/81	BB	6	17		24 Waiting On A Friend		Rolling Stones 21004
11/11/83	RR	6	15		25 Undercover Of The Night	BB 9	Rolling Stones 99813
03/14/86	BB	5	15		26 Harlem Shuffle	CB 5 / RR 6	Rolling Stones 05802
09/01/89	CB	3²	20		27 Mixed Emotions	BB 5 / RR 9	Rolling Stones 69008
					ROMANTICS, The		
10/08/83	BB	3³	29		1 Talking In Your Sleep	RR 3¹ / CB 4	Nemperor 04135
					ROME		
03/15/97	BB	6	26	▲	1 I Belong To You (Every Time I See Your Face)		RCA 64759
					RONDO, Don		
09/29/56	MV	10	20		1 Two Different Worlds		Jubilee 5256
06/29/57	MV	2²	19		2 White Silver Sands	CB 6 / BB 7	Jubilee 5288
					RONETTES, The		
08/31/63	CB	❶¹	14	☉	1 Be My Baby	BB 2³ / MV 2²	Philles 116
					RONNY & THE DAYTONAS		
08/01/64	BB	4	14	☉	1 G.T.O.	CB 5 / RW 6	Mala 481
					RONSON, Mark		
11/29/14	BB	❶¹⁴	56	△¹¹	1 Uptown Funk! MARK RONSON with BRUNO MARS		RCA
					RONSTADT, Linda		
11/30/74	BB	❶¹	21		1 You're No Good	CB ❶¹ / RW ❶¹ / RR 3¹	Capitol 3990
04/12/75	CB	❶¹	19		2 When Will I Be Loved	BB 2² / RW 4 / RR 4	Capitol 4050
09/20/75	CB	4	21		3 Heat Wave	BB 5 / RR 5 / RW 6	Asylum 45282
09/10/77	RR	2⁶	24	▲	4 Blue Bayou	CB 2² / BB 3⁴ / RW 3²	Asylum 45431
10/08/77	BB	5	18		5 It's So Easy	RR 5 / CB 9	Asylum 45438
11/11/78	BB	7	16		6 Ooh Baby Baby	CB 7 / RR 7	Asylum 45546
02/01/80	CB	6	17		7 How Do I Make You	RW 7 / RR 7 / BB 10	Asylum 46602
04/04/80	RR	3¹	16		8 Hurt So Bad	BB 8 / CB 9 / RW 9	Asylum 46624
12/20/86	BB	2¹	23	●	9 Somewhere Out There LINDA RONSTADT AND JAMES INGRAM	CB 4 / RR 9	MCA 52973
09/30/89	CB	2⁴	26	●	10 Don't Know Much LINDA RONSTADT (featuring Aaron Neville)	BB 2² / RR 4	Elektra 69261
					ROOFTOP SINGERS, The		
12/29/62	BB	❶²	16	☉	1 Walk Right In	CB ❶¹ / MV ❶¹	Vanguard 35017
					ROOMMATES, The — see CATHY JEAN		
					ROS, Edmundo, and His Orchestra		
01/21/50	CB	9	11		1 The Wedding Samba		London 30017
					ROSE, David, and His Orchestra		
04/30/62	CB	❶²	18	☉	1 The Stripper	BB ❶¹ / MV ❶¹	MGM 13064

DEBUT	CH	PK	WK	Gold	A-side (Chart Hit)	Other Charts	Label & Number
					ROSE ROYCE		
10/23/76	CB	❶²	24	▲	1 Car Wash	RW ❶² / BB ❶¹ / RR 2²	MCA 40615
02/26/77	RW	8	17		2 I Wanna Get Next To You	BB 10 / CB 10	MCA 40662
					ROSIE And The Originals		
12/05/60	BB	5	14		1 Angel Baby	CB 6 / MV 8	Highland 1011
					ROSS, Diana		
04/18/70	RW	9	10		1 Reach Out And Touch (Somebody's Hand)	CB 10	Motown 1165
08/08/70	BB	❶³	14		2 Ain't No Mountain High Enough	CB ❶¹ / RW ❶¹	Motown 1169
12/26/70	CB	8	11		3 Remember Me	RW 10	Motown 1176
05/26/73	BB	❶¹	22		4 Touch Me In The Morning	CB ❶¹ / RW ❶¹	Motown 1239
12/22/73	CB	9	15		5 Last Time I Saw Him	RW 9 / RR 10	Motown 1278
11/01/75	BB	❶¹	21		6 Theme From Mahogany (Do You Know Where You're Going To)	CB ❶¹ / RW ❶¹ / RR 2¹	Motown 1377
04/03/76	BB	❶²	23		7 Love Hangover	CB ❶¹ / RW ❶¹ / RR 2²	Motown 1392
07/12/80	BB	❶⁴	30	●	8 Upside Down	CB ❶³ / RW ❶² / RR ❶¹	Motown 1494
09/06/80	BB	5	23		9 I'm Coming Out	CB 6 / RW 9 / RR 10	Motown 1491
10/25/80	BB	9	21		10 It's My Turn		Motown 1496
07/04/81	BB	❶⁹	29	▲	11 Endless Love	CB ❶⁹ / RW ❶⁹ / RR ❶⁵	Motown 1519
					DIANA ROSS & LIONEL RICHIE		
10/16/81	RW	6	20		12 Why Do Fools Fall In Love	RR 6 / BB 7 / CB 7	RCA 12349
01/09/82	CB	7	15		13 Mirror, Mirror	RR 7 / BB 8 / RW 8	RCA 13021
10/02/82	CB	7	18		14 Muscles	BB 10	RCA 13348
12/01/84	BB	10	29		15 Missing You		RCA 13966
					ROSS, Jackie		
07/25/64	RW	9	12		1 Selfish One		Chess 1903
					ROTH, David Lee		
01/11/85	RR	2¹	16		1 California Girls	CB 3³ / BB 3¹	Warner 29102
01/16/88	BB	6	17		2 Just Like Paradise	CB 8 / RR 8	Warner 28119
					ROVER BOYS, The		
05/04/56	MV	9	14		1 Graduation Day		ABC-Paramount 9700
					ROWLAND, Kelly		
09/20/02	RR	10	22		1 Stole		Columbia 79820
07/12/02	BB	❶¹⁰	29		2 Dilemma	RR ❶⁵	Fo' Reel 019509
					NELLY with KELLY ROWLAND		
					ROXETTE		
02/10/89	BB	❶¹	23	●	1 The Look	RR ❶¹ / CB 2²	EMI 50190
08/25/89	BB	❶¹	23		2 Listen To Your Heart	CB ❶¹ / RR ❶¹	EMI 50223
12/16/89	CB	❶¹	21		3 Dangerous	BB 2² / RR 3³	EMI 50233
04/06/90	BB	❶²	25	●	4 It Must Have Been Love	RR ❶¹ / CB 2⁴	EMI 50283
03/01/91	BB	❶¹	24		5 Joyride	CB ❶¹ / RR 2²	EMI 50342
06/14/91	BB	2¹	21		6 Fading Like A Flower (Every Time You Leave)	CB 3¹ / RR 4	EMI 50355
					ROYAL, Billy Joe		
07/03/65	CB	6	13		1 Down In The Boondocks	RW 7 / BB 9	Columbia 43305
					ROYAL GUARDSMEN, The		
12/10/66	RW	❶¹	13	●	1 Snoopy Vs. The Red Baron	BB 2⁴ / CB 2⁴	Laurie 3366
12/09/67	CB	10	5		2 Snoopy's Christmas		Laurie 3416
					ROYAL PHILHARMONIC ORCHESTRA		
10/31/81	RW	9	22		1 Hooked On Classics	BB 10 / CB 10	RCA 12304
					ROYAL SCOTS DRAGOON GUARDS		
05/13/72	CB	10	11		1 Amazing Grace	RW 10	RCA Victor 0709
					THE PIPES AND DRUMS AND THE MILITARY BAND OF THE ROYAL SCOTS DRAGOON GUARDS		
					ROYAL TEENS		
01/13/58	BB	3²	16		1 Short Shorts	CB 3² / MV 5	ABC-Paramount 9882
					RTZ		
01/18/92	CB	5	23		1 Until Your Love Comes Back Around	RR 10	Giant 19051
					RUBY AND THE ROMANTICS		
01/19/63	BB	❶¹	16		1 Our Day Will Come	CB ❶¹ / MV ❶¹	Kapp 501
					RUDOLF, Kevin		
08/29/08	BB	5	35	△⁴	1 Let It Rock	RR 6	Cash Money 012077
					KEVIN RUDOLF Feat. Lil Wayne		
					RUESS, Nate — see PINK		
					RUFF ENDZ		
07/01/00	BB	5	26		1 No More		Epic 79400

DEBUT	CH	PK	WK	Gold	A-side (Chart Hit)	Other Charts	Label & Number
					RUFFIN, David		
02/08/69	BB	9	10		1 My Whole World Ended (The Moment You Left Me)	CB 9 / RW 10	Motown 1140
11/08/75	CB	8	21		2 Walk Away From Love	RW 8 / BB 9	Motown 1376
					RUFFIN, Jimmy		
08/20/66	BB	7	17		1 What Becomes Of The Brokenhearted	RW 7 / CB 9	Soul 35022
03/01/80	BB	10	16		2 Hold On To My Love		RSO 1021
					RUFUS Featuring Chaka Khan		
06/08/74	CB	❶¹	19	●	1 Tell Me Something Good	RR 2¹ / BB 3³ / RW 3²	ABC 11427
					RUFUS		
10/12/74	RW	9	17		2 You Got The Love	CB 10	ABC 12032
02/08/75	CB	6	15		3 Once You Get Started	BB 10 / RW 10	ABC 12066
12/27/75	BB	5	24	●	4 Sweet Thing	CB 5 / RW 5 / RR 5	ABC 12149
					RUNDGREN, Todd		
09/29/73	CB	2¹	20		1 Hello It's Me	RW 4 / BB 5 / RR 8	Bearsville 0009
					RUN-D.M.C.		
07/26/86	BB	4	19	●	1 Walk This Way	CB 9 / RR 10	Profile 5112
					RUSH, Merrilee, & The Turnabouts		
04/27/68	RW	3³	16		1 Angel Of The Morning	CB 3² / BB 7	Bell 705
					RUSSELL, Brenda		
02/13/88	BB	6	25		1 Piano In The Dark	CB 9 / RR 10	A&M 3003
					RUSSELL, Leon		
08/19/72	RW	9	13		1 Tight Rope	CB 10	Shelter 7325
07/26/75	CB	8	23		2 Lady Blue	RW 10	Shelter 40378
					RYDELL, Bobby		
10/12/59	MV	2¹	17		1 We Got Love	CB 4 / BB 6	Cameo 169
01/30/60	BB	2¹	16	◉	2 Wild One	MV 3² / CB 3¹	Cameo 171
04/25/60	BB	5	14	◉	3 Swingin' School	CB 6 / MV 7	Cameo 175
07/11/60	BB	4	16	◉	4 Volare	CB 4 / MV 4	Cameo 179
01/23/61	MV	10	11		5 Good Time Baby		Cameo 186
10/06/62	BB	10	13		6 The Cha-Cha-Cha		Cameo 228
11/02/63	BB	4	18		7 Forget Him	CB 5 / MV 5	Cameo 280
					RYDER, Mitch, And The Detroit Wheels		
12/11/65	BB	10	12		1 Jenny Take A Ride!		New Voice 806
10/08/66	RW	3²	16		2 Devil With A Blue Dress On & Good Golly Miss Molly	BB 4 / CB 4	New Voice 817
02/04/67	CB	4	12		3 Sock It To Me-Baby!	RW 5 / BB 6	New Voice 820

S

					SADE		
03/02/85	BB	5	21		1 Smooth Operator	RR 5 / CB 6	Portrait 04807
11/23/85	BB	5	23		2 The Sweetest Taboo	RR 7 / CB 8	Portrait 05713
					SADLER, SSgt Barry		
01/29/66	BB	❶⁵	15	●	1 The Ballad Of The Green Berets	CB ❶⁴ / RW ❶³	RCA Victor 8739
					SAFARIS		
06/06/60	BB	6	18		1 Image Of A Girl	MV 6 / CB 7	Eldo 101
					SA-FIRE		
02/04/89	RR	7	25		1 Thinking Of You		Cutting 872502
					SAIGON KICK		
09/05/92	RR	8	26	●	1 Love Is On The Way		Third Stone 98530
					ST. PETERS, Crispian		
06/11/66	RW	2²	12		1 The Pied Piper	BB 4 / CB 4	Jamie 1320
					SAKAMOTO, Kyu		
05/04/63	CB	❶⁴	15	◉	1 Sukiyaki	BB ❶³ / MV ❶²	Capitol 4945
					SALT-N-PEPA		
10/09/93	BB	4	31	●	1 Shoop	RR 4 / CB 5	Next Plateau 857314
01/22/94	BB	3³	31	▲	2 Whatta Man	RR 4 / CB 5	Next Plateau 857390
					SALT 'N' PEPA with EN VOGUE		
					SAM & DAVE		
09/09/67	CB	❶¹	15	●	1 Soul Man	RW ❶¹ / BB 2³	Stax 231
01/27/68	CB	8	13		2 I Thank You	BB 9 / RW 9	Stax 242

DEBUT	CH	PK	WK	Gold	A-side (Chart Hit)	Other Charts	Label & Number
					SAM THE SHAM AND THE PHARAOHS		
04/03/65	RW	❶¹	19	●	1 Wooly Bully	BB 2² / CB 2¹	MGM 13322
06/11/66	CB	❶¹	14	●	2 Lil' Red Riding Hood	RW ❶¹ / BB 2²	MGM 13506
					SANDLER, Adam		
12/30/95	BB	10	2	○	1 The Chanukah Song		Warner
					SANDPIPERS, The		
07/23/66	CB	7	13		1 Guantanamera	RW 7 / BB 9	A&M 806
					SANDS, Tommy		
02/16/57	MV	❶¹	17	⊙	1 Teen-Age Crush	BB 2² / CB 2¹	Capitol 3639
					SANFORD/TOWNSEND BAND, The		
06/18/77	RR	8	18		1 Smoke From A Distant Fire	BB 9 / CB 9	Warner 8370
					SANG, Samantha		
11/12/77	CB	❶¹	29	▲	1 Emotion	RR 2¹ / RW 3³ / BB 3²	Private Stock 45,178
					SANTAMARIA, Mongo		
03/09/63	CB	9	13		1 Watermelon Man	MV 9 / BB 10	Battle 45909
					SANTANA		
01/24/70	CB	7	13		1 Evil Ways	BB 9 / RW 10	Columbia 45069
11/07/70	RW	3²	14		2 Black Magic Woman	BB 4 / CB 4	Columbia 45270
02/20/71	CB	10	10		3 Oye Como Va		Columbia 45330
10/09/71	RW	9	11		4 Everybody's Everything	CB 10	Columbia 45472
08/14/82	RR	8	16		5 Hold On	CB 9	Columbia 03160
07/09/99	BB	❶¹²	58	▲	6 Smooth	RR ❶⁹	Arista 13718
					SANTANA with ROB THOMAS		
12/17/99	BB	❶¹⁰	27	▲	7 Maria Maria	RR 2⁴	Arista 13773
					SANTANA with THE PRODUCT G&B		
10/04/02	BB	5	37		8 The Game Of Love	RR 5	Arista 15203
					SANTANA with MICHELLE BRANCH		
07/04/03	RR	3¹	30		9 Why Don't You & I	BB 8	Arista
					SANTANA with ALEX BAND		
					SANTANA, Juelz		
10/15/05	BB	6	24	○	1 There It Go! (The Whistle Song)		Diplomats 005462
					SANTO & JOHNNY		
07/18/59	BB	❶²	18	⊙	1 Sleep Walk	CB 2² / MV 2¹	Canadian American 103
					SAVAGE GARDEN		
02/07/97	RR	❶¹	33	●	1 I Want You	BB 4	Columbia 78503
10/24/97	RR	❶³	52		2 Truly Madly Deeply	BB ❶²	Columbia 78723
10/01/99	RR	❶⁵	33		3 I Knew I Loved You	BB ❶⁴	Columbia 79236
					SAVING ABEL		
06/28/08	RR	7	34	△	1 Addicted		Skiddco
					SAYER, Leo		
02/22/75	RR	5	18		1 Long Tall Glasses (I Can Dance)	CB 6 / RW 8 / BB 9	Warner 8043
10/16/76	RR	❶⁴	26	●	2 You Make Me Feel Like Dancing	BB ❶¹ / CB ❶¹ / RW ❶¹	Warner 8283
02/26/77	RR	❶⁵	24	●	3 When I Need You	CB ❶³ / RW ❶³ / BB ❶¹	Warner 8332
07/09/77	CB	9	15		4 How Much Love	RR 9	Warner 8319
09/27/80	BB	2⁵	27	●	5 More Than I Can Say	RR 2⁴ / CB 3⁵ / RW 3⁴	Warner 49565
					SCAGGS, Boz		
07/03/76	CB	❶¹	27	●	1 Lowdown	BB 3² / RW 4 / RR 4	Columbia 10367
03/12/77	RR	4	18		2 Lido Shuffle	CB 6	Columbia 10491
03/28/80	RR	6	15		3 Breakdown Dead Ahead		Columbia 11241
06/14/80	RR	6	17		4 JoJo		Columbia 11281
08/22/80	RR	6	21		5 Look What You've Done To Me		Columbia 11349
11/29/80	RR	10	17		6 Miss Sun		Columbia 11406
					SCANDAL — see SMYTH, Patty		
05/09/81	RW	❶²	26	●	**SCARBURY, Joey** 1 Theme From "Greatest American Hero" (Believe It Or Not)	CB ❶¹ / RR ❶¹ / BB 2²	Elektra 47147
					SCHILLING, Peter		
09/24/83	CB	10	22		1 Major Tom (Coming Home)	RR 10	Elektra 69811
					S CLUB 7		
02/09/01	RR	6	20		1 Never Had A Dream Come True	BB 10	A&M 7074
					SCORPIONS		
06/01/91	BB	4	25	●	1 Wind Of Change	CB 6 / RR 10	Mercury 868180

144

DEBUT	CH	PK	WK	Gold	A-side (Chart Hit)	Other Charts	Label & Number
					SCOTT, Bobby		
12/30/55	CB	10	15		1 Chain Gang		ABC-Paramount 9658
					SCOTT, Freddie		
07/20/63	MV	9	13		1 Hey, Girl	BB 10 / CB 10	Colpix 692
					SCOTT, Jack		
06/14/58	BB	3[1]	20	☉	1 My True Love	MV 6 / CB 7	Carlton 462
12/01/58	BB	8	16		2 Goodbye Baby	MV 8 / CB 10	Carlton 493
12/28/59	MV	3[1]	17	☉	3 What In The World's Come Over You	BB 5 / CB 5	Top Rank 2028
04/18/60	MV	2[1]	17	☉	4 Burning Bridges	BB 3[2] / CB 4	Top Rank 2041
					SCOTT, Linda		
02/27/61	BB	3[1]	16		1 I've Told Every Little Star	CB 6 / MV 6	Canadian American 123
07/01/61	BB	9	14		2 Don't Bet Money Honey	CB 10	Canadian American 127
					SCOTT, Travis		
08/18/18	BB	❶[1]	52	△[7]	1 Sicko Mode		Cactus Jack
08/18/18	BB	8	8	△	2 Stargazing		Cactus Jack
10/19/19	BB	❶[1]	19	△	3 HIGHEST IN THE ROOM		Cactus Jack
					SCRITTI POLITTI		
09/14/85	CB	10	23		1 Perfect Way	RR 10	Warner 28949
					SEAL		
06/22/91	CB	6	21		1 Crazy	BB 7 / RR 8	ZTT/Sire 19298
06/04/94	CB	9	24		2 Prayer For The Dying	RR 10	ZTT/Sire 18138
06/16/95	RR	❶[8]	39	●	3 Kiss From A Rose	BB ❶[1] / CB ❶[1]	ZTT/Sire 17896
10/25/96	BB	10	20		4 Fly Like An Eagle	RR 10	Warner Sunset 87046
					SEALS & CROFTS		
09/09/72	BB	6	18		1 Summer Breeze	CB 6 / RW 7	Warner 7606
05/12/73	BB	6	18		2 Diamond Girl	RW 6 / CB 8	Warner 7708
04/10/76	RW	4	30		3 Get Closer	RR 4 / BB 6 / CB 7	Warner 8190
					SEALS & CROFTS (Featuring Carolyn Willis)		
					SEAN, Jay		
07/18/09	BB	❶[2]	40	△[6]	1 Down		Cash Money 013306
					JAY SEAN Featuring Lil Wayne		
11/21/09	BB	10	20	△[2]	2 Do You Remember		Cash Money
					JAY SEAN Featuring Sean Paul & Lil Jon		
					SEARCHERS, The		
11/28/64	RW	❶[1]	16		1 Love Potion Number Nine	CB 2[1] / BB 3[2]	Kapp 27
					SEBASTIAN, John		
03/27/76	RR	❶[3]	22	●	1 Welcome Back	CB ❶[2] / RW ❶[2] / BB ❶[1]	Reprise 1349
					SECADA, Jon		
04/04/92	RR	4	43	●	1 Just Another Day	BB 5 / CB 6	SBK/EMI 07383
09/25/92	RR	4	33		2 Do You Believe In Us		SBK/EMI 50408
01/29/93	CB	6	23		3 Angel	RR 7	SBK/EMI 50406
06/25/93	RR	10	21		4 I'm Free		SBK/EMI 50434
05/06/94	CB	5	32		5 If You Go	RR 5 / BB 10	SBK/EMI 58156
					SECONDHAND SERENADE		
06/20/08	RR	6	30	△[2]	1 Fall For You		Glassnote
					SEDAKA, Neil		
12/01/58	MV	8	15		1 The Diary		RCA Victor 7408
09/28/59	CB	5	21		2 Oh! Carol	MV 6 / BB 9	RCA Victor 7595
03/21/60	CB	6	15		3 Stairway To Heaven	MV 7 / BB 9	RCA Victor 7709
12/26/60	BB	4	15		4 Calendar Girl	CB 4 / MV 4	RCA Victor 7829
04/17/61	CB	9	13		5 Little Devil	MV 9	RCA Victor 7874
11/06/61	BB	6	14		6 Happy Birthday, Sweet Sixteen	CB 9 / MV 9	RCA Victor 7957
06/23/62	BB	❶[2]	15	☉	7 Breaking Up Is Hard To Do	CB ❶[1] / MV ❶[1]	RCA Victor 8046
10/06/62	BB	5	11		8 Next Door To An Angel	MV 8 / CB 10	RCA Victor 8086
10/19/74	BB	❶[1]	20		9 Laughter In The Rain	CB ❶[1] / RW ❶[1] / RR 4	Rocket 40313
09/05/75	BB	❶[3]	19	●	10 Bad Blood	RR ❶[3] / CB ❶[2] / RW ❶[1]	Rocket 40460
12/13/75	CB	7	14		11 Breaking Up Is Hard To Do	BB 8 / RR 7 / RW 10	Rocket 40500
					SEDUCTION		
11/11/89	CB	❶[1]	23	●	1 Two To Make It Right	BB 2[2] / RR 2[1]	Vendetta 1464
06/09/90	RR	6	22		2 Could This Be Love		Vendetta 1509
					SEEKERS, The		
03/27/65	BB	4	13		1 I'll Never Find Another You	CB 4 / RW 4	Capitol 5383
12/03/66	CB	❶[1]	16	●	2 Georgy Girl	RW ❶[1] / BB 2[2]	Capitol 5756

DEBUT	CH	PK	WK	Gold	A-side (Chart Hit) .... Other Charts	Label & Number
					SEETHER	
08/13/04	RR	10	22	△	1 Broken.. SEETHER Featuring Amy Lee	Wind-Up
					SEGER, Bob	
12/04/76	BB	4	26		1 Night Moves..RR 4 / RW 5 / CB 6	Capitol 4369
05/12/78	RR	2²	19		2 Still The Same...BB 4 / CB 4 / RW 5	Capitol 4581
08/12/78	RR	10	13		3 Hollywood Nights..	Capitol 4618
10/28/78	RR	9	18		4 We've Got Tonite.. BOB SEGER & The Silver Bullet Band (above 3)	Capitol 4653
02/22/80	RR	2²	17		5 Fire Lake..RW 5 / BB 6 / CB 6	Capitol 4836
05/02/80	RR	3³	18		6 Against The Wind..BB 5 / CB 8 / RW 9	Capitol 4863
07/26/80	RR	8	17		7 You'll Accomp'ny Me...	Capitol 4904
09/11/81	BB	5	21		8 Tryin' To Live My Life Without You ....RR 5 / RW 7 / CB 8	Capitol 5042
12/17/82	RR	●¹	21		9 Shame On The Moon..BB 2⁴ / CB 5	Capitol 5187
03/12/83	BB	8	15		10 Even Now..CB 9 BOB SEGER & The Silver Bullet Band (above 3)	Capitol 5213
05/22/87	BB	●¹	21		11 Shakedown..CB ●¹ / RR ●¹	MCA 53094
					SELENA	
07/08/95	BB	8	23	○	1 I Could Fall In Love..	EMI Latin 18742
					SEMBELLO, Michael	
06/04/83	BB	●²	25		1 Maniac..RR ●¹ / CB 3²	Casablanca 812516
					SEMISONIC	
03/21/98	RR	6	37		1 Closing Time...	MCA
					SENSATIONS, The	
01/06/62	CB	3¹	18		1 Let Me In..BB 4 / MV 4	Argo 5405
					SERENDIPITY SINGERS, The	
02/29/64	CB	5	16		1 Don't Let the Rain Come Down (Crooked Little Man)..MV 5 / BB 6	Philips 40175
					702	
02/15/97	BB	10	20	●	1 Get It Together	Biv 10 0612
05/01/99	BB	4	42	●	2 Where My Girls At?..	Motown 860891
					SEVILLE, David, The Music Of	
04/07/58	BB	●³	19	⊙	1 Witch Doctor ....CB ●¹ / MV 2⁴	Liberty 55132
					SHADES OF BLUE	
04/30/66	RW	8	13		1 Oh How Happy..	Impact 1007
					SHADOWS OF KNIGHT, The	
03/12/66	RW	6	13		1 Gloria..CB 7 / BB 10	Dunwich 116
					SHAGGY	
05/20/95	BB	3²	30	▲	1 Boombastic..CB 3¹	Virgin 38482
10/27/00	BB	●²	25		2 It Wasn't Me..RR 2⁶ SHAGGY (Featuring Ricardo "RikRok" Ducent)	MCA 155782
12/30/00	RR	●⁷	28		3 Angel...BB ●¹ SHAGGY Featuring Rayvon	MCA 155811
					SHAI	
10/17/92	BB	2⁸	31	▲	1 If I Ever Fall In Love.....................................CB 2⁸ / RR 3⁴	Gasoline Alley 54518
01/23/93	BB	10	28	●	2 Comforter..	Gasoline Alley 54596
06/05/93	RR	3¹	27		3 Baby I'm Yours..BB 10	Gasoline Alley 54574
					SHAKESPEAR'S SISTER	
07/04/92	BB	4	20	●	1 Stay..CB 4 / RR 5	London 869730
					SHAKIRA	
10/19/01	RR	4	24		1 Whenever, Wherever...BB 6	Epic 79642
02/22/02	RR	5	20		2 Underneath Your Clothes...BB 9	Epic 79741
03/03/06	RR	●⁷	31	△²	3 Hips Don't Lie...BB ●² SHAKIRA Featuring Wyclef Jean	Epic 84467
03/16/07	BB	3¹	18	△	4 Beautiful Liar... BEYONCE & SHAKIRA	Columbia 10320
					SHALAMAR	
12/08/79	BB	8	23	●	1 The Second Time Around..CB 10	Solar 11709
					SHANGRI-LAS, The	
08/22/64	RW	4	12		1 Remember (Walkin' In The Sand)........................BB 5 / CB 5	Red Bird 10-008
10/10/64	BB	●¹	13	⊙	2 Leader Of The Pack ....CB ●¹ / RW ●¹	Red Bird 10-014
11/06/65	RW	5	11		3 I Can Never Go Home Anymore ....BB 6 / CB 7	Red Bird 10-043
					SHANICE	
11/23/91	RR	●²	27		1 I Love Your Smile..BB 2³ / CB 2²	Motown 2093
10/24/92	CB	3¹	28		2 Saving Forever For You.....................................RR 3¹ / BB 4	Giant 18719

146

DEBUT	CH	PK	WK	Gold	A-side (Chart Hit) ... Other Charts	Label & Number
					SHANNON	
11/12/83	BB	8	25	●	1 Let The Music Play .... CB 8 / RR 9	Mirage 99810
					SHANNON, Del	
03/06/61	BB	❶⁴	17	⊙	1 Runaway .... MV ❶⁴ / CB ❶³	Big Top 3067
06/05/61	CB	2¹	13		2 Hats Off To Larry .... MV 2¹ / BB 5	Big Top 3075
11/21/64	RW	7	15		3 Keep Searchin' (We'll Follow The Sun) .... CB 8 / BB 9	Amy 915
					SHARP, Dee Dee	
02/19/62	CB	❶¹	20	⊙	1 Mashed Potato Time .... MV ❶¹ / BB 2²	Cameo 212
02/26/62	CB	❶¹	15		2 Slow Twistin' .... BB 3¹ / MV 4	Parkway 835
					CHUBBY CHECKER with DEE DEE SHARP	
06/09/62	BB	9	12		3 Gravy (For My Mashed Potatoes) .... CB 9 / MV 10	Cameo 219
10/20/62	BB	5	14		4 Ride! .... CB 9 / MV 9	Cameo 230
02/23/63	BB	10	13		5 Do The Bird	Cameo 244
					SHAW, Artie	
07/22/50	BB	10	11		1 Count Every Star	Decca 27042
					DICK HAYMES and ARTIE SHAW	
09/16/50	BB	10	10		2 I'm Forever Blowing Bubbles	Decca 27186
					GORDON JENKINS and ARTIE SHAW	
					SHAW, Georgie	
01/16/54	BB	7	15		1 Till We Two Are One .... CB 10	Decca 28937
					SHECK WES	
09/08/18	BB	6	28	△³	1 Mo Bamba	Cactus Jack
					SHEERAN, Ed	
06/28/14	BB	9	36	△³	1 Don't	Elektra
10/25/14	BB	2⁸	58	△¹²	2 Thinking Out Loud	Elektra 546349
05/30/15	BB	10	30	△⁴	3 Photograph	Elektra
01/28/17	BB	❶¹²	59	△¹⁰	4 Shape Of You	Atlantic
01/28/17	BB	6	33	△³	5 Castle On The Hill	Atlantic
03/25/17	BB	❶⁶	57	△¹⁰	6 Perfect	Atlantic
05/25/19	BB	2²	38	△²	7 I Don't Care	SchoolBoy
					ED SHEERAN & JUSTIN BIEBER	
					SHEIK, Duncan	
11/30/96	RR	8	55		1 Barely Breathing	Atlantic 87027
					SHEILA E.	
06/16/84	BB	7	26		1 The Glamorous Life .... RR 7 / CB 9	Warner 29285
					SHEP AND THE LIMELITES	
03/27/61	BB	2¹	15	⊙	1 Daddy's Home .... MV 3² / CB 3¹	Hull 740
					SHEPARD, Jean	
09/05/53	BB	4	10		1 A Dear John Letter	Capitol 2502
					JEAN SHEPARD with FERLIN HUSKEY	
					SHEPARD, Vonda — see Hill, Dan	
					SHERIFF	
11/19/88	RR	❶²	21	●	1 When I'm With You .... BB ❶¹ / CB ❶¹	Capitol 44302
					SHERMAN, Allan	
07/27/63	CB	❶¹	11	⊙	1 Hello Mudduh, Hello Fadduh! (A Letter From Camp) ..MV ❶¹ / BB 2³	Warner 5378
					SHERMAN, Bobby	
08/16/69	CB	❶¹	14	●	1 Little Woman .... RW 2¹ / BB 3²	Metromedia 121
11/15/69	RW	8	13	●	2 La La La (If I Had You) .... BB 9	Metromedia 150
02/07/70	RW	5	14	●	3 Easy Come, Easy Go .... CB 7 / BB 9	Metromedia 177
07/25/70	RW	❶¹	15	●	4 Julie, Do Ya Love Me .... CB 3¹ / BB 5	Metromedia 194
02/06/71	CB	10	11		5 Cried Like A Baby	Metromedia 206
					SHINEDOWN	
12/13/08	RR	4	41	△³	1 Second Chance .... BB 7	Atlantic
					SHINER, Mervin	
03/25/50	BB	8	6		1 Peter Cottontail	Decca 46221
					SHIRELLES, The	
11/21/60	BB	❶²	19	⊙	1 Will You Love Me Tomorrow .... CB ❶² / MV 2²	Scepter 1211
01/23/61	BB	3²	16	●	2 Dedicated To The One I Love .... MV 3² / CB 3¹	Scepter 1203
04/10/61	BB	4	13		3 Mama Said .... CB 4 / MV 7	Scepter 1217
12/04/61	BB	8	15		4 Baby It's You .... CB 8 / MV 9	Scepter 1227
03/17/62	BB	❶³	16	⊙	5 Soldier Boy .... CB ❶² / MV ❶²	Scepter 1228
03/16/63	BB	4	15		6 Foolish Little Girl .... CB 6 / MV 9	Scepter 1248
					SHIRLEY (AND COMPANY)	
01/11/75	CB	8	16		1 Shame, Shame, Shame	Vibration 532

DEBUT	CH	PK	WK	Gold	A-side (Chart Hit) ... Other Charts	Label & Number
					SHMURDA, Bobby	
08/16/14	BB	6	25	△	1 Hot Boy	GS9/Epic
					SHOCKING BLUE, The	
12/06/69	CB	❶³	16	●	1 Venus ... RW ❶³ / BB ❶¹	Colossus 108
					SHONDELL, Troy	
08/28/61	CB	5	16		1 This Time ... MV 5 / BB 6	Liberty 55353
					SHOP BOYZ	
05/05/07	BB	2⁶	22	△	1 Party Like A Rock Star ... RR 10	Universal Rep. 009015
					SHORE, Dinah	
11/26/49	CB	❶¹	21		1 Dear Hearts And Gentle People ... BB 2¹	Columbia 38605
12/09/50	CB	❶³	22		2 My Heart Cries For You ... BB 3¹	RCA Victor 3978
01/20/51	BB	8	19		3 A Penny A Kiss ... CB 8	RCA Victor 4019
					TONY MARTIN and DINAH SHORE	
07/07/51	CB	❶¹	24		4 Sweet Violets ... BB 3³	RCA Victor 4174
					SIA	
01/07/12	BB	5	36	△⁵	1 Wild Ones	Poe Boy
					FLO RIDA with SIA	
05/05/12	BB	7	33	△²	2 Titanium	Astralwerks
					DAVID GUETTA with SIA	
05/24/14	BB	8	46	△³	3 Chandelier	Monkey Puzzle
03/05/16	BB	❶⁴	52	△⁴	4 Cheap Thrills	Monkey Puzzle
					SIA Featuring Sean Paul	
					SILENTO	
03/14/15	BB	3⁶	51	△⁶	1 Watch Me	Bolo
					SILHOUETTES, The	
01/06/58	BB	❶²	15	⊙	1 Get A Job ... CB ❶² / MV 2²	Ember 1029
					SILK	
02/20/93	BB	❶²	35	▲	1 Freak Me ... CB 2¹ / RR 3²	Keia/Elektra 64654
					SILKIE, The	
10/09/65	BB	10	12		1 You've Got To Hide Your Love Away	Fontana 1525
					SILVER CONVENTION	
10/04/75	BB	❶³	20	●	1 Fly, Robin, Fly ... CB ❶¹ / RW ❶¹ / RR 2²	Midland Int'l. 10339
03/13/76	CB	❶¹	25	●	2 Get Up And Boogie (That's Right) ... RW ❶¹ / BB 2³ / RR 2¹	Midland Int'l. 10571
					SIMEONE, Harry, Chorale	
12/22/58	CB	10	9		1 The Little Drummer Boy	20th Fox 121
					SIMON, Carly	
04/17/71	RW	7	17		1 That's The Way I've Always Heard It Should Be ... CB 9 / BB 10	Elektra 45724
12/04/71	CB	10	14		2 Anticipation	Elektra 45759
12/02/72	BB	❶³	17	●	3 You're So Vain ... CB ❶² / RW ❶¹	Elektra 45824
03/24/73	CB	10	13		4 The Right Thing To Do	Elektra 45843
02/02/74	CB	3²	16	●	5 Mockingbird ... RW 4 / RR 4 / BB 5	Elektra 45880
					CARLY SIMON & JAMES TAYLOR	
05/04/74	CB	7	12		6 Haven't Got Time For The Pain ... RW 10	Elektra 45887
07/23/77	RR	❶¹	27	●	7 Nobody Does It Better ... CB 2⁴ / BB 2³ / RW 2¹	Elektra 45413
04/15/78	RR	4	19		8 You Belong To Me ... BB 6 / RW 8 / CB 9	Elektra 45477
08/02/80	RW	6	26	●	9 Jesse ... RR 8 / CB 9	Warner 49518
					SIMON, Joe	
11/13/71	RW	6	15	●	1 Drowning In The Sea Of Love ... CB 8	Spring 120
07/01/72	RW	6	16	●	2 Power Of Love ... CB 10	Spring 128
03/29/75	BB	8	18		3 Get Down, Get Down (Get On The Floor) ... CB 9 / RW 9	Spring 156
					SIMON, Paul	
02/05/72	BB	4	14		1 Mother And Child Reunion ... CB 4 / RW 4	Columbia 45547
04/01/72	CB	7	11		2 Me And Julio Down By The Schoolyard ... RW 9	Columbia 45585
05/19/73	RW	❶¹	14		3 Kodachrome ... BB 2² / CB 2¹	Columbia 45859
07/28/73	CB	❶¹	17	●	4 Loves Me Like A Rock ... BB 2¹ / RW 3² / RR 6	Columbia 45907
					PAUL SIMON (with The Dixie Hummingbirds)	
12/13/75	RR	❶⁴	20	●	5 50 Ways To Leave Your Lover ... BB ❶³ / CB ❶² / RW ❶¹	Columbia 10270
10/15/77	BB	5	22	●	6 Slip Slidin' Away ... CB 6	Columbia 10630
01/21/78	RR	9	14		7 (What A) Wonderful World	Columbia 10676
					ART GARFUNKEL with JAMES TAYLOR & PAUL SIMON	
08/01/80	RR	❶²	17		8 Late In The Evening ... BB 6 / CB 9 / RW 9	Warner 49511
					SIMON & GARFUNKEL	
11/20/65	BB	❶²	15	●	1 The Sound Of Silence ... RW ❶² / CB ❶¹	Columbia 43396
02/12/66	BB	5	12		2 Homeward Bound ... CB 5 / RW 5	Columbia 43511
04/30/66	RW	2²	12		3 I Am A Rock ... BB 3² / CB 4	Columbia 43617
04/27/68	CB	❶⁴	14	●	4 Mrs. Robinson ... BB ❶³ / RW ❶³	Columbia 44511

DEBUT	CH	PK	WK	Gold	A-side (Chart Hit) ... Other Charts	Label & Number
					SIMON & GARFUNKEL (cont'd)	
04/05/69	RW	3²	10		5 The Boxer ....CB 4 / BB 7	Columbia 44785
01/31/70	BB	❶⁶	14	●	6 Bridge Over Troubled Water ....CB ❶⁴ / RW ❶³	Columbia 45079
04/11/70	CB	❶¹	13	●	7 Cecilia ....RW ❶¹ / BB 4	Columbia 45133
10/18/75	CB	7	18		8 My Little Town ....BB 9 / RR 9	Columbia 10230
					SIMPLE MINDS	
02/23/85	CB	❶²	22		1 Don't You (Forget About Me) ....RR ❶² / BB ❶¹	A&M 2703
10/18/85	RR	2³	23		2 Alive & Kicking ....CB 3⁵ / BB 3²	A&M 2783
01/25/86	CB	10	16		3 Sanctify Yourself	A&M 2810
					SIMPLE PLAN	
09/19/03	RR	4	24		1 Perfect	Lava
09/24/04	RR	10	22	○	2 Welcome To My Life	Lava
					SIMPLY RED	
04/05/86	BB	❶¹	23		1 Holding Back The Years ....RR 3¹ / CB 4	Elektra 69564
05/06/89	RR	❶²	24	●	2 If You Don't Know Me By Now ....BB ❶¹ / CB 2²	Elektra 69297
					SIMPSON, Ashlee	
05/28/04	RR	❶⁴	24	○	1 Pieces Of Me ....BB 5	Geffen 003019
					SIMPSON, Jessica	
09/17/99	BB	3⁵	22	▲	1 I Wanna Love You Forever	Columbia 79262
06/02/00	RR	4	20		2 I Think I'm In Love With You	Columbia 79467
04/27/01	RR	2¹	20		3 Irresistible	Columbia 79578
11/14/03	BB	❶²	29	○	4 With You	Columbia
03/12/04	RR	8	17	○	5 Take My Breath Away	Columbia 76855
					SIMPSONS, The	
12/07/90	RR	9	9		1 Do The Bartman	Geffen
					SINATRA, Frank	
02/25/50	BB	10	7		1 Chattanoogie Shoe Shine Boy	Columbia 38708
08/05/50	BB	5	12		2 Goodnight Irene	Columbia 38892
11/04/50	BB	9	16		3 One Finger Melody	Columbia 39014
09/01/51	BB	8	8		4 Castle Rock	Columbia 39527
					FRANK SINATRA & HARRY JAMES	
05/16/53	BB	7	10		5 I'm Walking Behind You	Capitol 2450
02/06/54	CB	2³	27	◉	6 Young-At-Heart ....BB 2¹	Capitol 2703
05/29/54	BB	4	9		7 Three Coins In The Fountain	Capitol 2816
04/18/55	BB	❶²	26	◉	8 Learnin' The Blues ....CB 2¹ / MV 2¹	Capitol 3102
10/10/55	BB	5	22		9 Love And Marriage ....MV 5 / CB 6	Capitol 3260
12/01/55	BB	7	15		10 (Love Is) The Tender Trap	Capitol 3290
10/20/56	BB	3¹	20		11 Hey! Jealous Lover ....MV 5 / CB 8	Capitol 3552
09/23/57	BB	2¹	30		12 All The Way ....MV 3¹ / CB 7	Capitol 3793
12/30/57	BB	6	18		13 Witchcraft ....MV 8	Capitol 3859
05/07/66	BB	❶¹	15	●	14 Strangers In The Night ....CB ❶¹ / RW ❶¹	Reprise 0470
11/12/66	RW	❶¹	13		15 That's Life ....BB 4 / CB 5	Reprise 0531
03/18/67	BB	❶⁴	14	●	16 Somethin' Stupid ....RW ❶³ / CB ❶²	Reprise 0561
					NANCY SINATRA & FRANK SINATRA	
					SINATRA, Nancy	
01/22/66	BB	❶¹	14	●	1 These Boots Are Made For Walkin' ....CB ❶¹ / RW ❶¹	Reprise 0432
04/16/66	RW	6	9		2 How Does That Grab You, Darlin'? ....BB 7	Reprise 0461
11/12/66	CB	4	15	●	3 Sugar Town ....RW 4 / BB 5	Reprise 0527
03/18/67	BB	❶⁴	14	●	4 Somethin' Stupid ....RW ❶³ / CB ❶²	Reprise 0561
					NANCY SINATRA & FRANK SINATRA	
					SINGING NUN, The	
11/02/63	CB	❶⁵	16	◉	1 Dominique ....BB ❶⁴ / MV ❶⁴	Philips 40152
					SIR MIX-A-LOT	
04/11/92	BB	❶⁵	36	▲²	1 Baby Got Back ....CB ❶⁴	Def American 18947
					SISQO	
01/29/00	BB	3³	28		1 Thong Song ....RR 4	Dragon 562599
06/24/00	BB	❶²	26	▲	2 Incomplete	Dragon 562854
					SISTER HAZEL	
04/18/97	RR	7	41		1 All For You	Universal 56135
					SISTER SLEDGE	
02/03/79	CB	8	21		1 He's The Greatest Dancer ....BB 9	Cotillion 44245
04/28/79	BB	2²	19	●	2 We Are Family ....CB 2² / RR 3³ / RW 3²	Cotillion 44251
					6IX9INE	
08/04/18	BB	3¹	20	△⁸	1 FEFE	ScumGang
					6IX9INE Featuring Nicki Minaj & Murda Beatz	

149

DEBUT	CH	PK	WK	Gold	A-side (Chart Hit)	Other Charts	Label & Number
					SIXPENCE NONE THE RICHER		
11/28/98	RR	❶²	33	●	1 Kiss Me	BB 2¹	Squint 79101
					69 BOYZ		
07/09/94	BB	8	38	▲	1 Tootsee Roll		Down Low 6911
					SKID ROW		
07/08/89	BB	4	20	●	1 18 And Life	CB 5 / RR 6	Atlantic 88883
11/18/89	BB	6	20		2 I Remember You	CB 7	Atlantic 88886
					SKRILLEX		
03/21/15	BB	8	45	△⁴	1 Where Are U Now		Mad Decent
					SKRILLEX & DIPLO with JUSTIN BIEBER		
					SKYLARK		
02/17/73	RW	8	21		1 Wildflower	BB 9 / CB 9	Capitol 3511
					SKYLINERS, The		
02/14/59	CB	7	19		1 Since I Don't Have You		Calico 103
					SLEDGE, Percy		
04/09/66	BB	❶²	14	●	1 When A Man Loves A Woman	RW ❶² / CB ❶¹	Atlantic 2326
					SLY & THE FAMILY STONE		
02/10/68	RW	5	15		1 Dance To The Music	BB 8 / CB 8	Epic 10256
11/30/68	BB	❶⁴	19	●	2 Everyday People	CB ❶² / RW ❶¹	Epic 10407
08/02/69	BB	2²	16		3 Hot Fun In The Summertime	CB 6 / RW 6	Epic 10497
12/27/69	BB	❶²	15	●	4 Thank You Falettinme Be Mice Elf Agin	RW ❶² / CB ❶¹	Epic 10555
10/30/71	CB	❶⁴	15	●	5 Family Affair	BB ❶³ / RW ❶²	Epic 10805
					SLY FOX		
12/28/85	BB	7	25		1 Let's Go All The Way	RR 8 / CB 9	Capitol 5552
					SMALL, Millie		
05/16/64	BB	2¹	13	⊙	1 My Boy Lollipop	RW 2¹ / CB 4	Smash 1893
					SMASHING PUMPKINS, The		
01/19/96	RR	9	27	●	1 1979		Virgin 38534
					SMASH MOUTH		
07/26/97	BB	2¹	60		1 Walkin' On The Sun	RR 3³	Interscope
05/21/99	RR	❶⁵	30		2 All Star	BB 4	Interscope
10/15/99	RR	4	26		3 Then The Morning Comes		Interscope
					SMITH		
09/06/69	RW	3²	16		1 Baby It's You	CB 4 / BB 5	Dunhill/ABC 4206
					SMITH, Huey (Piano), And The Clowns		
03/15/58	BB	9	13	⊙	1 Don't You Just Know It		Ace 545
					SMITH, Hurricane		
11/18/72	CB	❶¹	17		1 Oh, Babe, What Would You Say?	RW 3² / BB 3¹	Capitol 3383
					SMITH, Jaden - SEE BIEBER, Justin		
					SMITH, Michael W.		
05/04/91	CB	3¹	23		1 Place In This World	BB 6 / RR 7	Reunion 19019
					SMITH, O.C.		
08/17/68	BB	2¹	17	●	1 Little Green Apples	RW 2¹ / CB 3³	Columbia 44616
					SMITH, Patti		
04/08/78	CB	10	18		1 Because The Night		Arista 0318
					SMITH, Rex		
04/21/79	RW	4	23	●	1 You Take My Breath Away	CB 7 / BB 10 / RR 10	Columbia 10908
					SMITH, Sam		
03/29/14	BB	7	33	△³	1 Latch		PMR
					DISCLOSURE with SAM SMITH		
04/19/14	BB	2²	54	△⁸	2 Stay With Me		Capitol
06/21/14	BB	5	37	△⁶	3 I'm Not The Only One		Capitol
02/21/15	BB	8	20	△⁴	4 Lay Me Down		Capitol
09/30/17	BB	4	24	△⁴	5 Too Good At Goodbyes		Capitol
01/26/19	BB	7	45	△²	6 Dancing With A Stranger		Capitol
					SAM SMITH & NORMANI		
					SMITH, Sammi		
01/16/71	RW	7	16	●	1 Help Me Make It Through The Night	BB 8 / CB 9	Mega 0015
					SMITH, Somethin', & The Redheads		
04/02/55	MV	6	26		1 It's A Sin To Tell A Lie	BB 7 / CB 9	Epic 9093

DEBUT	CH	PK	WK	Gold	A-side (Chart Hit) .... Other Charts	Label & Number
					SMITH, Will	
06/20/97	BB	❶⁴	25		1 Men In Black .... RR 5	Columbia
12/12/97	BB	❶³	32	●	2 Gettin' Jiggy Wit It .... RR 6	Columbia 78804
06/05/98	RR	7	25		3 Just The Two Of Us	Columbia 79038
10/30/98	RR	8	28		4 Miami	Columbia
05/14/99	BB	❶¹	20	●	5 Wild Wild West .... RR 4	Overbrook 79157
					WILL SMITH featuring Dru Hill and Kool Moe Dee	
02/25/05	RR	4	28	○	6 Switch .... BB 7	Overbrook 005272
					SMITHEREENS, The	
02/01/92	CB	8	23		1 Too Much Passion	Capitol 44784
					SMYTH, Patty / SCANDAL	
06/30/84	CB	5	21		1 The Warrior .... RR 6 / BB 7	Columbia 04424
					SCANDAL Featuring Patty Smyth	
07/31/92	RR	❶³	34	●	2 Sometimes Love Just Ain't Enough .... BB 2⁶ / CB 2⁶	MCA 54403
					PATTY SMYTH with DON HENLEY	
12/26/92	RR	10	16		3 No Mistakes	MCA 54554
					SNAP!	
05/12/90	BB	2¹	25	▲	1 The Power .... CB 2¹	Arista 2013
08/15/92	BB	5	42	●	2 Rhythm Is A Dancer .... CB 5 / RR 10	Arista 12437
					SNIFF 'N' THE TEARS	
07/21/79	RR	6	17		1 Driver's Seat .... RW 10	Atlantic 3604
					SNOOP DOGG	
01/30/93	BB	2¹	28	▲	1 Nuthin' But A "G" Thang .... CB 2¹	Death Row 53819
05/15/93	BB	8	24	●	2 Dre Day .... CB 8	Death Row 53827
					DR. DRE & SNOOP DOGGY DOGG (above 2)	
12/04/93	BB	8	17	●	3 What's My Name? .... CB 8	Death Row 98340
01/29/94	CB	7	22	●	4 Gin & Juice .... BB 8	Death Row 98318
					SNOOP DOGGY DOGG (above 2)	
02/08/03	BB	6	20		5 Beautiful...	Doggystyle 77887
					SNOOP DOGG featuring Pharrell & Uncle Charlie Wilson	
10/02/04	BB	❶³	30	○	6 Drop It Like It's Hot .... RR 5	Doggystyle 003574
					SNOOP DOGG featuring Pharrell	
12/15/07	BB	7	20		7 Sensual Seduction	Doggystyle 010576
10/29/11	BB	7	32	△⁶	8 Young, Wild & Free	Rostrum
					SNOOP DOGG & WIZ KHALIFA Featuring Bruno Mars	
					SNOW	
01/09/93	BB	❶⁷	26	▲	1 Informer .... CB ❶² / RR 2¹	EastWest 98471
					SNOW, Phoebe	
01/04/75	BB	5	18		1 Poetry Man .... CB 5 / RW 5 / RR 10	Shelter 40353
					SNOW PATROL	
06/03/06	BB	5	45	△⁵	1 Chasing Cars .... RR 10	Polydor
					SNYDER, Bill	
04/08/50	CB	❶⁴	26		1 Bewitched.. BB 3¹	Tower 45-1473
					SOFT CELL	
01/16/82	CB	7	43		1 Tainted Love .... RR 7 / BB 8	Sire 49855
					SOKO	
03/29/14	BB	9	1		1 We Might Be Dead By Tomorrow	Babycat
					SOMETHIN' FOR THE PEOPLE	
08/30/97	BB	4	26	●	1 My Love Is The Shhh!	Warner 17327
					SOMETHIN' FOR THE PEOPLE featuring Trina & Tamara	
					SOMMERS, Joanie	
05/26/62	BB	7	14		1 Johnny Get Angry	Warner 5275
					SONGZ, Trey	
11/28/09	BB	9	29	△²	1 Say Aah	Song Book 523577
					TREY SONGZ Featuring Fabolous	
08/28/10	BB	6	26	△⁴	2 Bottoms Up..	Song Book
					TREY SONGZ Featuring Nicki Minaj	
					SONIQUE	
01/21/00	RR	4	24		1 It Feels So Good .... BB 8	Caffeine 156247
					SONNY	
08/21/65	RW	6	11		1 Laugh At Me.. BB 10	Atco 6369
					SONNY & CHER	
07/10/65	RW	❶⁴	15	●	1 I Got You Babe .... BB ❶³ / CB ❶²	Atco 6359
08/21/65	BB	8	12		2 Baby Don't Go .... CB 10 / RW 10	Reprise 0392
01/14/67	RW	3¹	12		3 The Beat Goes On .... BB 6 / CB 7	Atco 6461
10/16/71	CB	6	15		4 All I Ever Need Is You .... BB 7 / RW 8	Kapp 2151

DEBUT	CH	PK	WK	Gold	A-side (Chart Hit) ... Other Charts	Label & Number
					SONNY & CHER (cont'd)	
02/19/72	CB	6	15		5 A Cowboys Work Is Never Done .... BB 8 / RW 9	Kapp 2163
					S.O.S. BAND, The	
05/24/80	CB	❶¹	24	▲	1 Take Your Time (Do It Right) Part 1 .... BB 3² / RW 3²	Tabu 5522
					SOUL, David	
01/29/77	BB	❶¹	25	●	1 Don't Give Up On Us .... CB ❶¹ / RW ❶¹ / RR 2¹	Private Stock 45,129
					SOUL, Jimmy	
03/23/63	BB	❶²	16	⊙	1 If You Wanna Be Happy .... MV ❶² / CB ❶¹	S.P.Q.R. 3305
					SOUL ASYLUM	
06/11/93	CB	4	33	●	1 Runaway Train .... BB 5 / RR 5	Columbia 74966
					SOULDECISION	
06/16/00	RR	6	30		1 Faded	MCA 156606
					SOULDECISION (Featuring Thrust)	
					SOUL FOR REAL	
01/07/95	BB	2⁴	25	●	1 Candy Rain .... CB 2¹	Uptown/MCA 54906
05/06/95	CB	9	28	●	2 Every Little Thing I Do	Uptown/MCA 55032
					SOULJA BOY TELL'EM	
07/28/07	BB	❶⁷	32		1 Crank That (Soulja Boy) .... RR 9	ColliPark
					SOULJA BOY	
01/10/09	BB	3²	27		2 Kiss Me Thru The Phone .... RR 5	ColliPark
					SOULJA BOY TELL'EM Featuring Sammie	
					SOUL SURVIVORS	
09/02/67	BB	4	15		1 Expressway (To Your Heart) .... RW 5 / CB 7	Crimson 1010
					SOUL II SOUL	
06/24/89	CB	8	20	▲	1 Keep On Movin'	Virgin 99205
09/23/89	CB	3¹	28	▲	2 Back To Life .... BB 4 / RR 5	Virgin 99171
					SOUNDS ORCHESTRAL	
03/20/65	RW	7	14		1 Cast Your Fate To The Wind .... CB 9 / BB 10	Parkway 942
					SOUTH, Joe	
12/28/68	RW	8	13		1 Games People Play .... CB 10	Capitol 2248
					SOUTHER, J.D.	
09/08/79	BB	7	23		1 You're Only Lonely .... CB 7 / RW 8 / RR 8	Columbia 11079
03/06/81	RR	4	15		2 Her Town Too .... CB 8	Columbia 60514
					JAMES TAYLOR AND J.D. SOUTHER	
					SPANDAU BALLET	
07/30/83	RR	3³	25		1 True .... BB 4 / CB 4	Chrysalis 42720
					SPANKY AND OUR GANG	
05/13/67	RW	7	10		1 Sunday Will Never Be The Same .... BB 9 / CB 9	Mercury 72679
					SPARKS, Jordin	
10/05/07	RR	5	31	△	1 Tattoo .... BB 8	19 Records
01/19/08	RR	2⁶	35	△	2 No Air .... BB 3⁴	19 Records
					JORDIN SPARKS & CHRIS BROWN	
07/04/08	RR	3¹	21		3 One Step At A Time	19 Records
05/30/09	BB	10	22		4 Battlefield	19 Records
					SPARXXX, Bubba	
02/04/06	BB	7	24		1 Ms. New Booty .... RR 8	New South 50658
					BUBBA SPARXXX Feat. Ying Yang Twins and Mr. ColliPark	
					SPEARS, Britney	
10/09/98	RR	❶⁵	34	▲	1 ...Baby One More Time .... BB ❶²	Jive 42545
05/07/99	RR	4	20		2 Sometimes	Jive 42576
08/27/99	RR	4	22		3 (You Drive Me) Crazy .... BB 10	Jive 42606
04/14/00	RR	❶³	20		4 Oops!...I Did It Again .... BB 9	Jive 42700
07/28/00	RR	8	14		5 Lucky	Jive 42742
01/09/04	RR	❶⁴	21	○	6 Toxic .... BB 9	Jive 59214
05/07/04	RR	4	20	○	7 Everytime	Jive 62487
09/14/07	BB	3²	20	△	8 Gimme More	Jive 18815
10/10/08	RR	❶²	23		9 Womanizer .... BB ❶¹	Jive
12/19/08	RR	❶¹	22		10 Circus .... BB 3¹	Jive
12/20/08	RR	8	20		11 If U Seek Amy	Jive
10/24/09	BB	❶¹	20		12 3	Jive
01/29/11	BB	❶¹	17		13 Hold It Against Me	Jive
03/19/11	BB	3¹	24		14 Till The World Ends	Jive
04/16/11	BB	7	20		15 I Wanna Go	Jive
12/15/12	BB	3²	24	△³	16 Scream & Shout	will.i.am
					will.i.am & BRITNEY SPEARS	

DEBUT	CH	PK	WK	Gold	A-side (Chart Hit)	Other Charts	Label & Number
					SPENCER, Tracie		
12/22/90	BB	3¹	26		1 This House	CB 4 / RR 7	Capitol 44652
					SPICE GIRLS		
01/10/97	BB	❶⁴	25	▲	1 Wannabe	RR 4	Virgin 38579
04/04/97	RR	2⁵	25	●	2 Say You'll Be There	BB 3³	Virgin 38592
07/04/97	RR	3²	24	●	3 2 Become 1	BB 4	Virgin 38604
01/16/98	BB	9	20		4 Too Much		Virgin 38630
					SPIN DOCTORS		
10/16/92	RR	10	20		1 Little Miss Can't Be Wrong		Epic Associated 74473
01/22/93	RR	2²	29		2 Two Princes	CB 3² / BB 7	Epic Associated 74804
					SPINNERS		
09/02/72	CB	❶¹	17	●	1 I'll Be Around	RW ❶¹ / BB 3²	Atlantic 2904
12/30/72	CB	❶¹	15	●	2 Could It Be I'm Falling In Love	RW ❶¹ / BB 4	Atlantic 2927
04/21/73	CB	8	15	●	3 One Of A Kind (Love Affair)	RW 9	Atlantic 2962
07/20/74	BB	❶¹	19	●	4 Then Came You	CB ❶¹ / RW ❶¹ / RR 6	Atlantic 3202
					DIONNE WARWICKE AND SPINNERS		
08/02/75	RW	❶¹	23	●	5 "They Just Can't Stop It" The (Games People Play)	CB 2¹ / RR 3² / BB 5	Atlantic 3284
09/11/76	BB	2³	27	●	6 The Rubberband Man	RW 2³ / RR 3³ / CB 3¹	Atlantic 3355
12/15/79	BB	2²	26	●	7 Working My Way Back To You/Forgive Me, Girl	RW 2² / CB 3³ / RR 3³	Atlantic 3637
05/16/80	BB	4	20		8 Cupid/I've Loved You For A Long Time	RW 4 / CB 5 / RR 7	Atlantic 3664
					SPIRAL STARECASE		
03/29/69	CB	7	15		1 More Today Than Yesterday	RW 8	Columbia 44741
					SPRINGFIELD, Dusty		
06/20/64	CB	4	14		1 Wishin' And Hopin'	BB 6 / RW 6	Philips 40207
05/14/66	CB	3¹	15	⊙	2 You Don't Have To Say You Love Me	BB 4 / RW 4	Philips 40371
11/23/68	RW	8	14		3 Son-Of-A Preacher Man	BB 10	Atlantic 2580
12/12/87	CB	❶¹	21		4 What Have I Done To Deserve This?	BB 2² / RR 2¹	EMI/Manhattan 50107
					PET SHOP BOYS and DUSTY SPRINGFIELD		
					SPRINGFIELD, Rick		
03/28/81	BB	❶²	32	●	1 Jessie's Girl	RW ❶² / CB ❶¹ / RR 8	RCA 12201
08/22/81	RW	6	25		2 I've Done Everything For You	RR 6 / BB 8 / CB 9	RCA 12166
03/05/82	RR	❶⁵	21		3 Don't Talk To Strangers	BB 2⁴ / CB 2³	RCA 13070
06/04/82	RR	9	12		4 What Kind Of Fool Am I		RCA 13245
04/16/83	RR	5	18		5 Affair Of The Heart	BB 9 / CB 10	RCA 13497
03/10/84	CB	3¹	17		6 Love Somebody	RR 4 / BB 5	RCA 13738
					SPRINGSTEEN, Bruce		
10/24/80	BB	5	21		1 Hungry Heart	RR 5 / CB 6 / RW 10	Columbia 11391
05/25/84	CB	❶²	22	▲	2 Dancing In The Dark	RR ❶¹ / BB 2⁴	Columbia 04463
08/11/84	RR	6	19	●	3 Cover Me	BB 7 / CB 10	Columbia 04561
11/09/84	CB	8	19	●	4 Born In The U.S.A.	BB 9 / RR 10	Columbia 04680
02/16/85	RR	5	20		5 I'm On Fire	BB 6 / CB 8	Columbia 04772
05/31/85	RR	3¹	18		6 Glory Days	BB 5 / RR 9	Columbia 04924
09/06/85	BB	9	14		7 I'm Goin' Down	CB 9 / RR 9	Columbia 05603
12/06/85	BB	6	18	●	8 My Hometown	CB 7 / RR 7	Columbia 05728
11/21/86	BB	8	13		9 War	CB 9	Columbia 06432
					BRUCE SPRINGSTEEN & THE E STREET BAND		
09/25/87	CB	4	19		10 Brilliant Disguise	BB 5 / RR 5	Columbia 07595
12/05/87	BB	9	18		11 Tunnel Of Love		Columbia 07663
03/13/92	RR	8	17		12 Human Touch		Columbia 74273
02/18/94	CB	6	23	●	13 Streets Of Philadelphia	BB 9 / RR 10	Columbia 77384
					SQUIER, Billy		
05/23/81	RW	6	23		1 The Stroke		Capitol 5005
07/07/84	CB	10	16		2 Rock Me Tonite		Capitol 5370
					STACEY Q		
07/12/86	BB	3¹	22		1 Two Of Hearts	CB 7 / RR 10	Atlantic 89381
					STAFFORD, Jim		
11/03/73	CB	3²	25	●	1 Spiders & Snakes	BB 3¹ / RW 4 / RR 4	MGM 14648
04/13/74	CB	10	15		2 My Girl Bill	RW 10	MGM 14718
07/06/74	RW	4	14		3 Wildwood Weed	CB 5 / BB 7 / RR 10	MGM 14737
					STAFFORD, Jo		
09/24/49	BB	4	23		1 Whispering Hope	CB 9	Capitol 690
12/24/49	CB	7	15		2 Bibbidi-Bobbidi-Boo (The Magic Song)		Capitol 782
03/11/50	BB	10	11		3 Dearie		Capitol 858
					JO STAFFORD and GORDON MacRAE (above 3)		
07/22/50	BB	8	21		4 No Other Love		Capitol 1053
08/26/50	BB	9	7		5 Goodnight, Irene		Capitol 1142
12/02/50	BB	7	13		6 Tennessee Waltz		Columbia 39065
01/13/51	BB	8	18		7 If		Columbia 39082

DEBUT	CH	PK	WK	Gold	A-side (Chart Hit)	Other Charts	Label & Number
					STAFFORD, Jo (cont'd)		
10/20/51	BB	9	15		8 Hey, Good Lookin'		Columbia 39570
					FRANKIE LAINE - JO STAFFORD		
11/10/51	BB	2²	24		9 Shrimp Boats	CB 5	Columbia 39581
03/08/52	BB	6	14		10 Hambone	CB 9	Columbia 39672
					FRANKIE LAINE & JO STAFFORD		
03/08/52	BB	9	12		11 Ay-Round The Corner (Bee-hind The Bush)		Columbia 39653
08/09/52	BB	❶¹²	27	◉	12 You Belong To Me	CB ❶⁴	Columbia 39811
08/30/52	BB	3³	25		13 Jambalaya	CB 3¹	Columbia 39838
11/15/52	BB	4	24		14 Keep It A Secret	CB 5	Columbia 39891
01/23/54	BB	❶⁷	24	◉	15 Make Love To Me!	CB 2⁵	Columbia 40143
11/26/55	MV	7	20		16 It's Almost Tomorrow		Columbia 40595
					STAFFORD, Terry		
02/22/64	MV	2¹	15	◉	1 Suspicion	BB 3² / CB 3¹	Crusader 101
					STAIND		
04/14/01	RR	4	46	○	1 It's Been Awhile	BB 5	Flip/Elektra
06/25/05	RR	9	30	○	2 Right Here		Flip/Elektra
					STALLONE, Frank		
07/29/83	RR	8	17		1 Far From Over	BB 10 / CB 10	RSO 815023
					STAMPEDERS		
07/31/71	CB	7	15		1 Sweet City Woman	BB 8 / RW 8	Bell 45,120
					STANDELLS, The		
04/16/66	RW	7	17		1 Dirty Water	CB 8	Tower 185
					STANDLEY, Johnny		
10/04/52	BB	❶²	23	◉	1 It's In The Book (Parts 1 & 2)	CB 3⁴	Capitol 2249
					STANSFIELD, Lisa		
02/03/90	BB	3³	22	▲	1 All Around The World	CB 3² / RR 3²	Arista 9928
					STAPLE SINGERS, The		
10/02/71	RW	9	17	▲	1 Respect Yourself	CB 10	Stax 0104
04/01/72	CB	❶²	15	○	2 I'll Take You There	BB ❶¹ / RW ❶¹	Stax 0125
10/27/73	RW	8	17	●	3 If You're Ready (Come Go With Me)	CB 9	Stax 0179
10/18/75	BB	❶¹	20	●	4 Let's Do It Again	CB ❶¹ / RW 3² / RR 4	Curtom 0109
					STAPLETON, Chris — see TIMBERLAKE, Justin		
					STAPLETON, Cyril, And His Orchestra		
01/05/59	MV	3¹	15		1 The Children's Marching Song (Nick Nack Taddy Whack)	CB 5	London 1851
					STARBUCK		
04/17/76	BB	3²	26		1 Moonlight Feels Right	CB 3¹ / RW 4 / RR 7	Private Stock 45,039
					STARLAND VOCAL BAND		
05/01/76	CB	❶⁴	30	●	1 Afternoon Delight	RR ❶⁴ / BB ❶² / RW ❶²	Windsong 10588
					STARR, Edwin		
02/15/69	RW	5	14		1 Twenty-Five Miles	BB 6 / CB 6	Gordy 7083
07/11/70	BB	❶³	15		2 War	CB ❶² / RW ❶¹	Gordy 7101
					STARR, Kay		
05/06/50	BB	2¹	19		1 Hoop-Dee-Doo	CB 4	Capitol 980
05/27/50	BB	4	27		2 Bonaparte's Retreat	CB 7	Capitol 936
08/19/50	BB	3¹	25		3 I'll Never Be Free	CB 7	Capitol 1124
					KAY STARR and TENNESSEE ERNIE		
11/18/50	BB	7	14		4 Oh, Babe	CB 8	Capitol 1278
08/04/51	BB	8	9		5 Come On-A My House		Capitol 1710
02/16/52	BB	❶¹⁰	26	◉	6 Wheel Of Fortune	CB ❶⁴	Capitol 1964
09/27/52	BB	9	14		7 Comes A-Long A-Love		Capitol 2213
01/31/53	BB	3³	17		8 Side By Side	CB 9	Capitol 2334
06/06/53	CB	7	21		9 Allez-Vous-En /		
06/06/53	BB	7	15		10 Half A Photograph		Capitol 2464
12/05/53	BB	7	13		11 Changing Partners		Capitol 2657
04/17/54	BB	4	20		12 If You Love Me (Really Love Me) /	CB 5	
04/10/54	BB	7	19		13 The Man Upstairs	CB 8	Capitol 2769
12/23/55	BB	❶⁶	25	◉	14 Rock And Roll Waltz	CB ❶² / MV ❶²	RCA Victor 6359
08/05/57	BB	9	17		15 My Heart Reminds Me	MV 10	RCA Victor 6981
					STARR, Ringo		
04/24/71	CB	❶¹	14	●	1 It Don't Come Easy	RW ❶¹ / BB 4	Apple 1831
03/25/72	RW	8	11		2 Back Off Boogaloo	BB 9 / CB 10	Apple 1849
10/06/73	RR	❶³	18	●	3 Photograph	RW ❶² / BB ❶¹ / CB ❶¹	Apple 1865
12/08/73	BB	❶¹	16	●	4 You're Sixteen	CB ❶¹ / RW ❶¹ / RR 2¹	Apple 1870
03/02/74	BB	5	14		5 Oh My My	RW 5 / CB 6 / RR 8	Apple 1872

DEBUT	CH	PK	WK	Gold	A-side (Chart Hit)	Other Charts	Label & Number
					STARR, Ringo (cont'd)		
11/16/74	BB	6	14		6 Only You	CB 6 / RW 9	Apple 1876
02/07/75	CB	❶¹	15		7 No No Song	BB 3² / RW 3¹ / RR 7	Apple 1880
					STARS ON 45		
04/11/81	CB	❶²	24	●	1 Medley	BB ❶¹ / RW ❶¹ / RR 3¹	Radio 3810
					STATLER BROTHERS, The		
11/13/65	BB	4	13		1 Flowers On The Wall	RW 5 / CB 8	Columbia 43315
					STEALERS WHEEL		
03/03/73	CB	3¹	18		1 Stuck In The Middle With You	BB 6 / RW 6	A&M 1416
					STEAM		
09/27/69	BB	❶²	18	●	1 Na Na Hey Hey Kiss Him Goodbye	RW ❶¹ / CB 3²	Fontana 1667
					STEEL BREEZE		
08/28/82	RR	10	20		1 You Don't Want Me Anymore		RCA 13283
					STEELY DAN		
11/18/72	BB	6	17		1 Do It Again	CB 7 / RW 8	ABC 11338
03/10/73	RW	6	16		2 Reeling In The Years	CB 7	ABC 11352
05/04/74	CB	3²	19		3 Rikki Don't Lose That Number	BB 4 / RW 5 / RR 7	ABC 11439
11/19/77	CB	8	20		4 Peg	RR 9	ABC 12320
11/28/80	RR	2²	19		5 Hey Nineteen	BB 10 / CB 10 / RW 10	MCA 51036
					STEFANI, Gwen		
12/10/04	RR	4	27	○	1 Rich Girl	BB 7	Interscope 003978
					GWEN STEFANI featuring Eve		
04/02/05	RR	❶⁶	31	△	2 Hollaback Girl	BB ❶⁴	Interscope 004435
07/01/05	RR	10	20		3 Cool		Interscope 005480
10/21/05	RR	10	22		4 Luxurious		Interscope 005023
11/10/06	BB	6	18		5 Wind It Up		Interscope
12/29/06	RR	2³	40		6 The Sweet Escape	BB 2¹	Interscope 008526
					GWEN STEFANI Featuring Akon		
					STEPPENWOLF		
07/13/68	BB	2³	13	●	1 Born To Be Wild	CB 2³ / RW 2³	Dunhill/ABC 4138
10/05/68	CB	2¹	16	●	2 Magic Carpet Ride	BB 3¹ / RW 3¹	Dunhill/ABC 4161
03/01/69	RW	7	11		3 Rock Me	CB 8 / BB 10	Dunhill/ABC 4182
					STEREO MC'S		
03/27/93	RR	5	25		1 Connected		Gee Street 864744
					STEVENS, April		
06/09/51	BB	6	18		1 I'm In Love Again	CB 9	RCA Victor 4148
					HENRI RENÉ and his Orchestra featuring April Stevens		
08/11/51	BB	10	5		2 Gimme A Little Kiss, Will Ya Huh?		RCA Victor 4208
					APRIL STEVENS with HENRI RENÉ and his Orchestra		
					STEVENS, Cat		
09/25/71	CB	4	13		1 Peace Train	RW 5 / BB 7	A&M 1291
03/25/72	BB	6	15		2 Morning Has Broken	RW 8	A&M 1335
03/16/74	BB	10	17		3 Oh Very Young	CB 10	A&M 1503
08/03/74	BB	6	15		4 Another Saturday Night	CB 9	A&M 1602
					STEVENS, Connie		
04/20/59	CB	3¹	13	⊙	1 Kookie, Kookie (Lend Me Your Comb)	BB 4 / MV 4	Warner 5047
					EDWARD BYRNES And CONNIE STEVENS		
02/01/60	BB	3¹	24	⊙	2 Sixteen Reasons	MV 4 / CB 5	Warner 5137
					STEVENS, Dodie		
02/16/59	CB	3³	19	⊙	1 Pink Shoe Laces	BB 3² / MV 3¹	Crystalette 724
					STEVENS, Ray		
06/23/62	CB	2¹	13		1 Ahab, The Arab	MV 3² / BB 5	Mercury 71966
04/05/69	CB	7	13	●	2 Gitarzan	RW 7 / BB 8	Monument 1131
03/28/70	BB	❶²	15	●	3 Everything Is Beautiful	CB ❶¹ / RW 2¹	Barnaby 2011
04/13/74	BB	❶³	17	●	4 The Streak	RW ❶² / CB ❶¹ / RR ❶¹	Barnaby 600
					STEVENSON, B.W.		
07/28/73	CB	7	16		1 My Maria	RW 8 / BB 9 / RR 10	RCA Victor 0030
					STEVIE B		
10/06/90	BB	❶⁴	25	●	1 Because I Love You (The Postman Song)	CB ❶² / RR ❶²	LMR/RCA 2724
02/02/91	RR	10	20		2 I'll Be By Your Side		LMR/RCA 2758
					STEWART, Al		
12/11/76	RR	2²	21		1 Year Of The Cat	CB 4 / RW 4 / BB 8	Janus 266
09/30/78	RR	6	18		2 Time Passages	BB 7 / CB 9	Arista 0362

155

DEBUT	CH	PK	WK	Gold	A-side (Chart Hit) ... Other Charts	Label & Number
					STEWART, Amii	
01/27/79	BB	❶¹	24	▲	1 Knock On Wood .... CB ❶¹ / RW ❶¹ / RR 3²	Ariola America 7736
					STEWART, Billy	
07/16/66	RW	7	11		1 Summertime .... CB 8 / BB 10	Chess 1966
					STEWART, David A.	
05/18/91	CB	9	20		1 Lily Was Here	Arista 2187
					DAVID A. STEWART Introducing Candy Dulfer	
					STEWART, Jermaine	
05/17/86	BB	5	22		1 We Don't Have To Take Our Clothes Off .... RR 7 / CB 9	Arista 9424
					STEWART, John	
05/19/79	RR	❶²	20		1 Gold .... BB 5 / RW 5 / CB 6	RSO 931
					STEWART, Rod	
08/14/71	BB	❶⁵	18	●	1 Maggie May .... CB ❶³ / RW ❶¹	Mercury 73224
10/02/76	BB	❶⁸	26	●	2 Tonight's The Night (Gonna Be Alright) .... RW ❶⁶ / CB ❶⁵ / RR ❶⁵	Warner 8262
10/22/77	RR	❶²	23	●	3 You're In My Heart (The Final Acclaim) .... CB 3¹ / BB 4 / RW 4	Warner 8475
12/16/78	RR	❶⁶	24	▲	4 Da Ya Think I'm Sexy? .... CB ❶⁵ / RW ❶⁵ / BB ❶⁴	Warner 8724
11/21/80	CB	4	21		5 Passion .... RR 4 / BB 5 / RW 6	Warner 49617
10/16/81	RR	4	22		6 Young Turks .... BB 5 / CB 5 / RW 5	Warner 49843
01/23/82	RR	4	14		7 Tonight I'm Yours (Don't Hurt Me)	Warner 49886
05/28/83	RR	10	16		8 Baby Jane	Warner 29608
05/26/84	RR	5	21		9 Infatuation .... BB 6 / CB 8	Warner 29256
08/25/84	RR	7	17		10 Some Guys Have All The Luck .... BB 10	Warner 29215
05/30/86	RR	5	18		11 Love Touch .... BB 6 / CB 7	Warner 28668
12/03/88	RR	3¹	28		12 My Heart Can't Tell You No .... BB 4 / CB 4	Warner 27729
11/24/89	CB	❶¹	20		13 Downtown Train .... RR ❶¹ / BB 3³	Warner 22685
03/23/90	RR	7	11		14 This Old Heart Of Mine .... BB 10 / CB 10	Warner 19983
					ROD STEWART (with Ronald Isley)	
03/15/91	CB	❶¹	26		15 Rhythm Of My Heart .... RR 3¹ / BB 5	Warner 19366
07/06/91	RR	8	20		16 The Motown Song .... CB 9 / BB 10	Warner 19322
					ROD STEWART with THE TEMPTATIONS	
10/19/91	CB	9	23		17 Broken Arrow .... RR 9	Warner 19274
04/24/93	CB	2³	25	●	18 Have I Told You Lately .... RR 3¹ / BB 5	Warner 18511
08/13/93	CB	10	22		19 Reason To Believe .... RR 10	Warner 18427
					ROD STEWART (with Ronnie Wood)	
11/19/93	CB	❶⁵	24	▲	20 All For Love .... RR ❶⁴ / BB ❶³	A&M 0476
					BRYAN ADAMS ROD STEWART STING	
					STIGERS, Curtis	
09/07/91	BB	9	26		1 I Wonder Why .... CB 9 / RR 10	Arista 12331
					STILLS, Stephen	
12/05/70	RW	10	11		1 Love The One You're With	Atlantic 2778
					STING	
06/07/85	CB	2²	20		1 If You Love Somebody Set Them Free .... BB 3² / RR 3¹	A&M 2738
08/23/85	RR	6	20		2 Fortress Around Your Heart .... BB 8 / CB 10	A&M 2767
10/09/87	BB	7	19		3 We'll Be Together .... CB 7 / RR 8	A&M 2983
01/18/91	CB	5	20		4 All This Time .... CB 5 / RR 9	A&M 1541
02/19/93	CB	5	21		5 If I Ever Lose My Faith In You .... RR 5	A&M 0111
11/19/93	CB	❶⁵	24	▲	6 All For Love .... RR ❶⁴ / BB ❶³	A&M 0476
					BRYAN ADAMS ROD STEWART STING	
					STOLOFF, Morris	
04/13/56	BB	❶³	27	☉	1 Moonglow And Theme From "Picnic" .... CB ❶² / MV 2¹	Decca 29888
					MORRIS STOLOFF Conducting The Columbia Pictures Orchestra	
					STORIES	
06/02/73	BB	❶²	21	●	1 Brother Louie .... CB ❶¹ / RW 2¹	Kama Sutra 577
					STORM, Gale	
10/08/55	BB	2³	21	☉	1 I Hear You Knocking .... CB 3² / MV 3²	Dot 15412
12/24/55	BB	5	16		2 Memories Are Made Of This /	
					MV 8	
12/24/55	BB	6	15		3 Teen Age Prayer .... CB 8	Dot 15436
03/03/56	BB	9	18		4 Why Do Fools Fall In Love	Dot 15448
04/28/56	BB	6	18		5 Ivory Tower	Dot 15458
04/20/57	BB	4	23		6 Dark Moon .... CB 5	Dot 15558
					STRANGELOVES, The	
06/19/65	RW	6	11		1 I Want Candy	Bang 501
					STRAWBERRY ALARM CLOCK	
09/23/67	RW	❶²	16	●	1 Incense And Peppermints .... BB ❶¹ / CB ❶¹	Uni 55018

DEBUT	CH	PK	WK	Gold	A-side (Chart Hit) .... Other Charts	Label & Number
					STRAY CATS	
09/18/82	RR	7	24		1 Rock This Town ....BB 9	EMI America 8132
12/25/82	BB	3³	19		2 Stray Cat Strut ....CB 3³ / RR 5	EMI America 8122
08/05/83	CB	4	19		3 (She's) Sexy + 17 ....BB 5 / RR 9	EMI America 8168
					STREISAND, Barbra	
04/04/64	BB	5	19		1 People ....CB 5 / RW 7	Columbia 42965
10/17/70	BB	6	20		2 Stoney End ....CB 7	Columbia 45236
11/24/73	BB	❶³	23	▲ 3	The Way We Were ....RR ❶³ / CB ❶¹ / RW ❶¹	Columbia 45944
12/11/76	BB	❶³	25	▲ 4	Evergreen (Love Theme From "A Star Is Born") CB ❶³ / RR ❶³ / RW ❶²	Columbia 10450
05/21/77	BB	4	18		5 My Heart Belongs To Me ....CB 5	Columbia 10555
10/27/78	CB	❶³	18	▲ 6	You Don't Bring Me Flowers ....RR ❶³ / BB ❶² / RW ❶²	Columbia 10840
					BARBRA & NEIL	
06/16/79	RR	❶¹	20	● 7	The Main Event/Fight........................BB 3⁴ / CB 3² / RW 3¹	Columbia 11008
10/19/79	RW	❶³	19	▲ 8	No More Tears (Enough Is Enough) ....BB ❶² / CB ❶¹ / RR 3²	Columbia 11125
					BARBRA STREISAND/DONNA SUMMER	
08/29/80	BB	❶³	25	▲ 9	Woman In Love ....RR ❶³ / CB ❶² / RW ❶¹	Columbia 11364
10/31/80	RR	3³	22	● 10	Guilty ....BB 3² / RW 6 / CB 8	Columbia 11390
01/31/81	RR	7	16		11 What Kind Of Fool ....BB 10 / CB 10	Columbia 11430
					BARBRA STREISAND & BARRY GIBB (above 2)	
11/14/81	RR	8	16		12 Comin' In And Out Of Your Life..CB 9	Columbia 02621
11/15/96	BB	8	20	● 13	I Finally Found Someone	Columbia 78480
					BARBRA STREISAND and BRYAN ADAMS	
					STRING-A-LONGS, The	
12/26/60	BB	3²	17	⊙ 1	Wheels ....CB 4 / MV 4	Warwick 603
					STRUNK, Jud	
02/10/73	CB	10	16		1 Daisy A Day	MGM 14463
					STUDDARD, Ruben	
06/28/03	BB	2²	10	● 1	Flying Without Wings	J Records 51786
01/03/04	BB	9	20		2 Sorry 2004	J Records 57204
					STYLES, Harry	
04/29/17	BB	4	13	△² 1	Sign Of The Times	Erskine
					STYLISTICS, The	
10/30/71	BB	9	17	● 1	You Are Everything ....CB 9 / RW 10	Avco 4581
02/19/72	BB	3¹	16	● 2	Betcha By Golly, Wow ....RW 3¹ / CB 4	Avco 4591
10/07/72	BB	9	15	● 3	I'm Stone In Love With You ....BB 10 / RW 10	Avco 4603
02/10/73	BB	5	14	● 4	Break Up To Make Up ....RW 6 / CB 10	Avco 4611
03/16/74	CB	❶¹	25	● 5	You Make Me Feel Brand New...................RW ❶¹ / BB 2² / RR 2¹	Avco 4634
					STYX	
12/07/74	BB	6	22		1 Lady ....CB 6 / RW 7 / RR 7	Wooden Nickel 10102
09/10/77	BB	8	27		2 Come Sail Away ....CB 9 / RW 9 / RR 9	A&M 1977
09/28/79	CB	❶³	21	● 3	Babe ....RR ❶³ / BB ❶² / RW ❶²	A&M 2188
01/16/81	RR	❶³	19		4 The Best Of Times ....BB 3⁴ / CB 5 / RW 6	A&M 2300
03/20/81	RW	7	21		5 Too Much Time On My Hands ....CB 8 / BB 9 / RR 9	A&M 2323
02/11/83	CB	❶¹	20	● 6	Mr. Roboto ....BB 3² / RR 3¹	A&M 2525
04/29/83	RR	3²	17		7 Don't Let It End ....BB 6	A&M 2543
12/08/90	BB	3¹	26		8 Show Me The Way ....CB 6 / RR 7	A&M 1536
					SUGARLOAF	
08/08/70	BB	3²	18		1 Green-Eyed Lady...RW 3² / CB 5	Liberty 56183
12/07/74	BB	9	21		2 Don't Call Us, We'll Call You ....RW 10	Claridge 402
					SUGARLOAF/JERRY CORBETTA	
					SUGAR RAY	
07/05/97	BB	❶⁶	59		1 Fly ....RR ❶⁶	Lava/Atlantic
					SUGAR RAY Featuring Super Cat	
01/08/99	RR	❶⁷	31	● 2	Every Morning...BB 3³	Lava/Atlantic 84462
06/11/99	RR	3⁶	32		3 Someday ....BB 7	Lava/Atlantic 84536
12/10/99	RR	9	22		4 Falls Apart (Run Away)	Lava/Atlantic
05/25/01	RR	9	22		5 When It's Over	Lava/Atlantic
					SUMMER, Donna	
11/08/75	RW	❶¹	22	● 1	Love To Love You Baby ....BB 2² / CB 3² / RR 4	Oasis 401
08/06/77	CB	4	23	● 2	I Feel Love ....RW 4 / RR 4 / BB 6	Casablanca 884
05/13/78	BB	3²	22	● 3	Last Dance ....CB 4 / RW 4 / RR 5	Casablanca 926
09/09/78	BB	❶³	22	● 4	MacArthur Park...................................RR ❶³ / CB ❶² / RW ❶²	Casablanca 939
01/13/79	RR	3¹	19	● 5	Heaven Knows ....BB 4 / CB 4 / RW 5	Casablanca 959
					DONNA SUMMER with BROOKLYN DREAMS	
04/20/79	RW	❶⁵	23	▲ 6	Hot Stuff ....CB ❶⁴ / BB ❶³ / RR ❶²	Casablanca 978
05/26/79	BB	❶⁵	21	▲ 7	Bad Girls ....RW ❶⁴ / CB ❶³ / RR 2¹	Casablanca 988
08/25/79	BB	2²	22	● 8	Dim All The Lights ....RW 2² / CB 3² / RR 6	Casablanca 2201
10/19/79	RW	❶³	19	▲ 9	No More Tears (Enough Is Enough) ....BB ❶² / CB ❶¹ / RR 3²	Columbia 11125
					BARBRA STREISAND/DONNA SUMMER	

157

DEBUT	CH	PK	WK	Gold	A-side (Chart Hit) ... Other Charts	Label & Number
					SUMMER, Donna (cont'd)	
01/12/80	RW	❶[1]	17	● 10	On The Radio .... CB 4 / BB 5 / RR 7	Casablanca 2236
09/12/80	CB	2[2]	24	● 11	The Wanderer .... BB 3[3] / RW 4 / RR 4	Geffen 49563
06/26/82	BB	10	19	12	Love Is In Control (Finger On The Trigger)	Geffen 29982
05/28/83	BB	3[3]	26	13	She Works Hard For The Money .... CB 3[3] / RR 5	Mercury 812370
04/22/89	CB	6	20	● 14	This Time I Know It's For Real .... BB 7 / RR 8	Atlantic 88899
					SUNNY & THE SUNGLOWS	
09/07/63	CB	9	13	1	Talk To Me .... MV 10	Tear Drop 3014
					SUNNYSIDERS, The	
04/11/55	MV	4	16	1	Hey, Mr. Banjo	Kapp 113
					SUPERTRAMP	
03/24/79	RR	❶[1]	23	1	The Logical Song .... CB 4 / BB 6 / RW 6	A&M 2128
07/07/79	RR	7	16	2	Goodbye Stranger	A&M 2162
10/13/79	RR	6	17	3	Take The Long Way Home .... BB 10 / RW 10	A&M 2193
10/29/82	RR	2[2]	18	4	It's Raining Again .... CB 7	A&M 2502
					SUPREMES, The	
07/11/64	BB	❶[2]	15	⊙ 1	Where Did Our Love Go .... CB ❶[2] / RW ❶[2]	Motown 1060
10/03/64	BB	❶[4]	14	● 2	Baby Love .... RW ❶[4] / CB ❶[2]	Motown 1066
11/14/64	BB	❶[2]	15	⊙ 3	Come See About Me .... RW ❶[2] / CB ❶[1]	Motown 1068
02/20/65	BB	❶[2]	13	● 4	Stop! In The Name Of Love .... CB ❶[1] / RW ❶[1]	Motown 1074
05/01/65	BB	❶[1]	12	5	Back In My Arms Again .... CB ❶[1] / RW 2[2]	Motown 1075
07/31/65	CB	8	10	6	Nothing But Heartaches	Motown 1080
10/23/65	RW	❶[3]	12	7	I Hear A Symphony .... BB ❶[2] / CB ❶[1]	Motown 1083
01/15/66	RW	4	11	8	My World Is Empty Without You .... BB 5 / CB 5	Motown 1089
04/23/66	BB	9	10	9	Love Is Like An Itching In My Heart .... CB 9 / RW 9	Motown 1094
08/13/66	BB	❶[2]	13	⊙ 10	You Can't Hurry Love .... RW ❶[2] / CB ❶[1]	Motown 1097
10/29/66	BB	❶[2]	12	⊙ 11	You Keep Me Hangin' On .... RW ❶[2] / CB ❶[1]	Motown 1101
01/28/67	RW	❶[2]	11	12	Love Is Here And Now You're Gone .... BB ❶[1] / CB ❶[1]	Motown 1103
04/08/67	BB	❶[1]	11	13	The Happening .... CB ❶[1] / RW ❶[1]	Motown 1107
					DIANA ROSS AND THE SUPREMES:	
08/05/67	BB	2[2]	13	14	Reflections .... RW 2[2] / CB 2[1]	Motown 1111
11/11/67	RW	8	9	15	In And Out Of Love .... BB 9 / CB 10	Motown 1116
10/19/68	RW	❶[4]	13	⊙ 16	Love Child .... CB ❶[3] / BB ❶[2]	Motown 1135
12/07/68	RW	❶[3]	13	▲ 17	I'm Gonna Make You Love Me .... CB ❶[1] / BB 2[2]	Motown 1137
					DIANA ROSS AND THE SUPREMES & THE TEMPTATIONS	
01/25/69	CB	8	8	18	I'm Livin' In Shame .... RW 8 / BB 10	Motown 1139
11/01/69	CB	❶[2]	16	▲ 19	Someday We'll Be Together .... BB ❶[1] / RW 2[3]	Motown 1156
					THE SUPREMES:	
03/07/70	RW	7	11	20	Up The Ladder To The Roof .... CB 9 / BB 10	Motown 1162
10/31/70	CB	5	15	21	Stoned Love .... RW 5 / BB 7	Motown 1172
05/01/71	RW	8	10	22	Nathan Jones .... CB 10	Motown 1182
					SURFACE	
07/01/89	BB	5	21	● 1	Shower Me With Your Love .... CB 5 / RR 5	Columbia 68746
11/03/90	BB	❶[2]	25	● 2	The First Time .... CB ❶[1] / RR ❶[1]	Columbia 73502
					SURFARIS, The	
06/08/63	MV	2[2]	17	⊙ 1	Wipe Out .... BB 2[1] / CB 5	Dot 16479
07/30/66	CB	9	14	2	Wipe Out	Dot 144
					SURVIVOR	
06/05/82	BB	❶[6]	25	▲[2] 1	Eye Of The Tiger .... RR ❶[5] / CB ❶[4]	Scotti Brothers 02912
09/15/84	RR	10	23	2	I Can't Hold Back	Scotti Brothers 04603
01/26/85	RR	7	17	3	High On You .... BB 8	Scotti Brothers 04685
04/20/85	BB	4	21	4	The Search Is Over .... RR 4	Scotti Brothers 04871
11/02/85	BB	2[2]	25	5	Burning Heart .... CB 2[2] / RR 2[2]	Scotti Brothers 05663
10/25/86	RR	5	20	6	Is This Love .... BB 9	Scotti Brothers 06381
					SWAE LEE — see POST MALONE	
					SWAN, Billy	
09/28/74	BB	❶[2]	21	● 1	I Can Help .... CB ❶[1] / RW ❶[1] / RR ❶[1]	Monument 8621
					SWAYZE, Patrick	
12/19/87	CB	2[2]	21	1	She's Like The Wind .... RR 2[2] / BB 3[3]	RCA 5363
					PATRICK SWAYZE (featuring Wendy Fraser)	
					SWEAT, Keith	
01/16/88	BB	5	20	● 1	I Want Her .... RR 5 / CB 6	Vintertainment 69431
11/30/90	BB	7	20	2	I'll Give All My Love To You	Vintertainment 64915
06/15/96	BB	2[1]	38	▲ 3	Twisted .... CB 2[1] / RR 5	Elektra 64282
10/05/96	BB	3[2]	35	▲ 4	Nobody .... CB 8	Elektra 64245
					KEITH SWEAT featuring Athena Cage	

DEBUT	CH	PK	WK	Gold	A-side (Chart Hit)	Other Charts	Label & Number
					SWEDISH HOUSE MAFIA		
10/06/12	BB	6	33	△³ 1	Don't You Worry Child		Astralwerks
					SWEDISH HOUSE MAFIA Featuring John Martin		
					SWEET		
01/20/73	BB	3³	23	● 1	Little Willy	CB 3² / RW 3²	Bell 45,251
06/14/75	BB	5	25	2	Ballroom Blitz	RR 7 / CB 9	Capitol 4055
11/08/75	RW	4	22	● 3	Fox On The Run	BB 5 / CB 5 / RR 6	Capitol 4157
02/14/76	CB	10	15	4	Action		Capitol 4220
02/18/78	BB	8	25	5	Love Is Like Oxygen	CB 8	Capitol 4549
					SWEET SENSATION		
06/09/90	BB	❶¹	23	1	If Wishes Came True	CB ❶¹ / RR ❶¹	Atco 98953
					SWIFT, Taylor		
03/24/07	RR	7	48	△³ 1	Teardrops On My Guitar		Big Machine 1002
08/30/08	BB	10	3	○ 2	Change		Big Machine
09/27/08	RR	❶¹	49	△⁸ 3	Love Story	BB 4	Big Machine 1015
11/01/08	BB	9	15	△ 4	Fearless		Big Machine
11/22/08	BB	2¹	50	△⁷ 5	You Belong With Me		Big Machine
11/14/09	BB	10	3	○ 6	Jump Then Fall		Big Machine
02/06/10	BB	2¹	18	△ 7	Today Was A Fairytale		Big Machine
08/21/10	BB	3¹	23	△³ 8	Mine		Big Machine
10/23/10	BB	8	3	○ 9	Speak Now		Big Machine
10/30/10	BB	6	20	△² 10	Back To December		Big Machine
11/26/11	BB	10	2	11	If This Was A Movie		Big Machine
08/25/12	BB	❶³	24	△⁶ 12	We Are Never Ever Getting Back Together		Big Machine 401
10/13/12	BB	7	20	△ 13	Begin Again		Big Machine
10/20/12	BB	6	22	△² 14	Red		Big Machine
10/27/12	BB	2¹	36	△⁷ 15	I Knew You Were Trouble		Big Machine
09/06/14	BB	❶⁴	50	△⁹ 16	Shake It Off		Big Machine
11/15/14	BB	❶⁷	36	△⁸ 17	Blank Space		Big Machine
11/15/14	BB	❶¹	25	△⁵ 18	Bad Blood		Big Machine
					TAYLOR SWIFT Featuring Kendrick Lamar		
11/15/14	BB	6	32	△³ 19	Style		Big Machine
09/19/15	BB	5	27	△³ 20	Wildest Dreams		Big Machine
12/31/16	BB	2¹	23	△⁴ 21	I Don't Wanna Live Forever (Fifty Shades Darker)		Universal Studios
					ZAYN & TAYLOR SWIFT		
09/09/17	BB	❶³	20	△⁴ 22	Look What You Made Me Do		Big Machine
09/23/17	BB	4	20	△² 23	...Ready For It?		Big Machine
05/04/19	BB	2¹	20	△ 24	ME!		Republic
					TAYLOR SWIFT & BRENDON URIE		
06/29/19	BB	2¹	21	25	You Need To Calm Down		Republic
08/31/19	BB	10	22	26	Lover		Republic
					SWING OUT SISTER		
08/15/87	CB	5	25	1	Breakout	BB 6 / RR 6	Mercury 888016
					SWITCHFOOT		
01/16/04	RR	5	35	○ 1	Meant To Live		Red Ink/Columbia
08/06/04	RR	6	25	○ 2	Dare You To Move		Red Ink/Columbia
					SWV (Sisters With Voices)		
02/06/93	RR	3¹	33	● 1	I'm So Into You	BB 6 / CB 6	RCA 62451
04/24/93	RR	❶⁴	27	▲ 2	Weak	BB ❶² / CB ❶²	RCA 62521
07/17/93	BB	2³	22	● 3	Right Here/Human Nature	CB 2¹ / RR 3⁵	RCA 62614
04/20/96	CB	3²	23	● 4	You're The One	BB 5	RCA 64516
					SYLK-E. FYNE		
02/14/98	BB	6	20	● 1	Romeo And Juliet		RCA 64973
					SYLK-E. FYNE Featuring Chill		
					SYLVERS, The		
01/24/76	BB	❶¹	32	● 1	Boogie Fever	CB ❶¹ / RW ❶¹ / RR 2¹	Capitol 4179
10/09/76	RW	2²	24	● 2	Hot Line	CB 4 / BB 5 / RR 7	Capitol 4336
					SYLVIA		
03/24/73	CB	2¹	21	● 1	Pillow Talk	BB 3² / RW 3²	Vibration 521
					SYLVIA		
08/21/82	CB	9	26	● 1	Nobody		RCA 13223
					SYNCH		
02/25/89	BB	10	24	1	Where Are You Now?		WTG 68625
					JIMMY HARNEN W/SYNCH		
					SYNDICATE OF SOUND		
05/28/66	BB	8	12	1	Little Girl	CB 8 / RW 9	Bell 640
					SYREETA — see PRESTON, Billy		

159

DEBUT	CH	PK	WK	Gold	A-side (Chart Hit)	Other Charts	Label & Number
04/11/87	BB	4	23		**SYSTEM, The** 1 Don't Disturb This Groove	RR 4 / CB 10	Atlantic 89320
					SZA — see LAMAR, Kendrick		

T

DEBUT	CH	PK	WK	Gold	A-side	Other Charts	Label & Number
06/25/83	CB	❶²	25	●	**TACO** 1 Puttin' On The Ritz	BB 4	RCA 13574
05/29/93	BB	2⁷	49	▲⁴	**TAG TEAM** 1 Whoomp! (There It Is)	CB 2¹	Life 79500
07/28/95	BB	7	30		**TAKE THAT** 1 Back For Good	CB 9 / RR 9	Arista 12848
07/30/83	BB	9	23		**TALKING HEADS** 1 Burning Down The House	CB 10	Sire 29565
01/13/01	BB	10	21		**TAMIA** 1 Stranger In My House		Elektra 67151
12/14/63	BB	9	14		**TAMS, The** 1 What Kind Of Fool (Do You Think I Am)	CB 9 / MV 10	ABC-Paramount 10502
10/06/56	BB	9	19		**TARRIERS, The** 1 Cindy, Oh Cindy	CB 9	Glory 247
12/15/56	MV	2²	19	⊙	VINCE MARTIN with THE TARRIERS 2 The Banana Boat Song	CB 2¹ / BB 4	Glory 249
06/17/78	BB	❶³	27	▲	**TASTE OF HONEY, A** 1 Boogie Oogie Oogie	CB ❶³ / RW ❶¹ / RR 5	Capitol 4565
03/07/81	BB	3³	25	●	2 Sukiyaki	CB 4 / RW 8 / RR 8	Capitol 4953
12/06/02	RR	8	22		**T.A.T.U.** 1 All The Things She Said		Interscope 019354
07/26/75	RW	8	23		**TAVARES** 1 It Only Takes A Minute	BB 10 / CB 10	Capitol 4111
06/05/76	CB	10	24	●	2 Heaven Must Be Missing An Angel (Part 1)		Capitol 4270
09/12/70	BB	3³	16		**TAYLOR, James** 1 Fire And Rain	RW 3³ / CB 4	Warner 7423
05/29/71	BB	❶¹	16	●	2 You've Got A Friend	CB ❶¹ / RW 2¹	Warner 7498
02/02/74	BB	3²	16	●	3 Mockingbird	RW 4 / RR 4 / BB 5	Elektra 45880
					CARLY SIMON & JAMES TAYLOR		
06/21/75	RR	4	17		4 How Sweet It Is (To Be Loved By You)	BB 5 / RW 6 / CB 7	Warner 8109
06/11/77	RR	2²	20		5 Handy Man	CB 2¹ / BB 4 / RW 4	Columbia 10557
01/21/78	RR	9	14		6 (What A) Wonderful World		Columbia 10676
					ART GARFUNKEL with JAMES TAYLOR & PAUL SIMON		
03/06/81	RR	4	15		7 Her Town Too	CB 8	Columbia 60514
					JAMES TAYLOR AND J.D. SOUTHER		
10/19/68	RW	4	14	●	**TAYLOR, Johnnie** 1 Who's Making Love	BB 5 / CB 6	Stax 0009
06/23/73	CB	5	18	●	2 I Believe In You (You Believe In Me)	RW 5	Stax 0161
02/07/76	BB	❶⁴	20	▲	3 Disco Lady	RW ❶³ / CB ❶² / RR ❶²	Columbia 10281
08/29/70	CB	❶¹	15		**TAYLOR, R. Dean** 1 Indiana Wants Me	RW 2² / BB 5	Rare Earth 5013
12/04/65	BB	3¹	14		**T-BONES, The** 1 No Matter What Shape (Your Stomach's In)	CB 3¹ / RW 4	Liberty 55836
03/16/85	BB	❶²	25		**TEARS FOR FEARS** 1 Everybody Wants To Rule The World	CB ❶² / RR ❶²	Mercury 880659
06/15/85	BB	❶³	20	●	2 Shout	RR ❶³ / CB ❶²	Mercury 880294
09/13/85	RR	3³	22		3 Head Over Heels	CB 3² / BB 3¹	Mercury 880899
09/01/89	CB	❶¹	23		4 Sowing The Seeds Of Love	BB 2¹ / RR 4	Fontana 874710
07/10/93	RR	9	33		5 Break It Down Again		Mercury 862330
10/14/89	CB	❶²	24	▲	**TECHNOTRONIC** 1 Pump Up The Jam	BB 2² / RR 7	SBK 07311
					TECHNOTRONIC Featuring FELLY		
01/27/90	BB	7	20	●	2 Get Up! (Before The Night Is Over)	CB 9 / RR 10	SBK 07315
06/13/92	BB	6	23		3 Move This		SBK/EMI 50400
09/22/58	BB	❶³	23	⊙	**TEDDY BEARS, The** 1 To Know Him, Is To Love Him	MV ❶³ / CB ❶¹	Dore 503

160

DEBUT	CH	PK	WK	Gold	A-side (Chart Hit) ... Other Charts	Label & Number
					TEENAGERS — see LYMON, Frankie	
					TEEN QUEENS, The	
02/17/56	MV	4	12		1 Eddie My Love	RPM 453
					TEE SET, The	
01/03/70	RW	4	15		1 Ma Belle Amie ... BB 5 / CB 6	Colossus 107
					TEMPO, Nino, & April Stevens	
09/14/63	CB	❶²	16		1 Deep Purple ... BB ❶¹ / MV ❶¹	Atco 6273
12/21/63	MV	9	9		2 Whispering	Atco 6281
					TEMPTATIONS, The	
02/22/64	CB	10	14		1 The Way You Do The Things You Do	Gordy 7028
01/09/65	BB	❶¹	15	▲	2 My Girl ... CB 2² / RW 3³	Gordy 7038
05/21/66	RW	8	15	●	3 Ain't Too Proud To Beg ... CB 10	Gordy 7054
08/20/66	BB	3¹	12	●	4 Beauty Is Only Skin Deep ... RW 4 / CB 5	Gordy 7055
11/19/66	BB	8	12	●	5 (I Know) I'm Losing You ... RW 10	Gordy 7057
04/29/67	BB	8	11		6 All I Need ... CB 8 / RW 9	Gordy 7061
07/29/67	BB	6	12	●	7 You're My Everything ... RW 6 / CB 7	Gordy 7063
10/07/67	RW	8	10		8 (Loneliness Made Me Realize) It's You That I Need	Gordy 7065
01/06/68	CB	2¹	14	●	9 I Wish It Would Rain ... RW 2¹ / BB 4	Gordy 7068
05/04/68	CB	10	11	● 10	I Could Never Love Another (After Loving You)	Gordy 7072
11/16/68	RW	4	13	● 11	Cloud Nine ... BB 6 / CB 8	Gordy 7081
12/07/68	RW	❶³	13	▲ 12	I'm Gonna Make You Love Me ... CB ❶¹ / BB 2²	Motown 1137
					DIANA ROSS AND THE SUPREMES & THE TEMPTATIONS	
02/15/69	BB	6	12	● 13	Run Away Child, Running Wild ... CB 8 / RW 8	Gordy 7084
08/16/69	BB	❶²	17	▲ 14	I Can't Get Next To You ... RW 2² / CB 3¹	Gordy 7093
01/17/70	CB	4	12	● 15	Psychedelic Shack ... RW 6 / BB 7	Gordy 7096
05/23/70	CB	❶¹	15	▲ 16	Ball Of Confusion (That's What The World Is Today) ... RW 2¹ / BB 3³	Gordy 7099
01/30/71	BB	❶²	16	▲ 17	Just My Imagination (Running Away With Me) ... CB ❶¹ / RW ❶¹	Gordy 7105
10/14/72	BB	❶¹	16	▲ 18	Papa Was A Rollin' Stone ... CB ❶¹ / RW 3¹	Gordy 7121
02/17/73	BB	7	14	● 19	Masterpiece ... RW 8 / CB 9	Gordy 7126
07/06/91	RR	8	20	20	The Motown Song ... CB 9 / BB 10	Warner 19322
					ROD STEWART with THE TEMPTATIONS	
					10cc	
05/10/75	BB	2³	20		1 I'm Not In Love ... CB 3² / RW 3² / RR 5	Mercury 73678
01/01/77	RR	2¹	23	●	2 The Things We Do For Love ... RW 3² / CB 4 / BB 5	Mercury 73875
					10,000 MANIACS	
11/05/93	RR	7	29		1 Because The Night ... CB 9	Elektra 64595
					TERRELL, Tammi — see GAYE, Marvin	
					TERROR SQUAD	
06/26/04	BB	❶³	31	○	1 Lean Back	SRC 002704
					TESLA	
09/30/89	CB	9	27	●	1 Love Song ... BB 10	Geffen 22856
01/05/91	BB	8	27		2 Signs	Geffen 19653
					TETER, Jack, Trio	
11/05/49	CB	3¹	24		1 Johnson Rag ... BB 6	London 30004
					TEX, Joe	
12/19/64	BB	5	12		1 Hold What You've Got ... RW 5 / CB 6	Dial 4001
10/28/67	RW	7	16	●	2 Skinny Legs And All ... CB 9 / BB 10	Dial 4063
01/22/72	BB	2²	21	●	3 I Gotcha ... RW 2² / CB 3²	Dial 1010
03/19/77	RW	10	22		4 Ain't Gonna Bump No More (With No Big Fat Woman)	Epic 50313
					THALIA	
05/30/03	RR	8	20		1 I Want You	Virgin 47305
					THALIA featuring Fat Joe	
					THICKE, Robin	
05/04/13	BB	❶¹²	48	△¹⁰	1 Blurred Lines	Star Trak
					ROBIN THICKE Featuring T.I. + Pharrell	
					THIN LIZZY	
05/15/76	RR	5	26		1 The Boys Are Back In Town ... CB 10	Mercury 73786
					THIRD EYE BLIND	
05/09/97	RR	❶⁶	43	●	1 Semi-Charmed Life ... BB 4	Elektra 64173
11/07/97	BB	9	52		2 How's It Going To Be	Elektra 64130
08/21/98	RR	❶¹	31		3 Jumper ... BB 5	Elektra 64058
01/14/00	RR	4	22		4 Never Let You Go	Elektra
					38 SPECIAL	
05/01/82	RR	6	17		1 Caught Up In You ... CB 9 / BB 10	A&M 2412
02/04/89	BB	6	23		2 Second Chance ... RR 6 / CB 7	A&M 1273

DEBUT	CH	PK	WK	Gold	A-side (Chart Hit) ... Other Charts	Label & Number
					THOMAS, B.J.	
02/19/66	RW	5	14		1 I'm So Lonesome I Could Cry .... BB 8 / CB 9	Scepter 12129
					B.J. THOMAS AND THE TRIUMPHS	
10/26/68	BB	5	19	●	2 Hooked On A Feeling .... CB 5 / RW 5	Scepter 12230
10/25/69	BB	❶⁴	22	●	3 Raindrops Keep Fallin' On My Head .... RW ❶³ / CB ❶²	Scepter 12265
06/13/70	BB	9	13	●	4 I Just Can't Help Believing	Scepter 12283
02/01/75	BB	❶¹	21	●	5 (Hey Won't You Play) Another Somebody Done Somebody Wrong Song .... CB ❶¹ / RW ❶¹ / RR 2¹	ABC 12054
					THOMAS, Carla	
01/21/61	MV	5	15		1 Gee Whiz (Look At His Eyes) .... CB 9 / BB 10	Atlantic 2086
					THOMAS, Rob	
07/09/99	BB	❶¹²	58	▲	1 Smooth .... RR ❶⁹	Arista 13718
					SANTANA with ROB THOMAS	
02/18/05	BB	6	34	△	2 Lonely No More .... RR 9	Melisma 93896
					THOMAS, Rufus	
10/05/63	BB	10	15	●	1 Walking The Dog .... CB 10	Stax 140
					THOMAS, Timmy	
11/25/72	RW	2²	16		1 Why Can't We Live Together .... CB 2¹ / BB 3¹	Glades 1703
					THOMPSON, Sue	
09/02/61	BB	5	16		1 Sad Movies (Make Me Cry) .... CB 5 / MV 6	Hickory 1153
12/04/61	BB	3¹	16		2 Norman .... CB 4 / MV 4	Hickory 1159
					THOMPSON TWINS	
02/11/84	BB	3²	23		1 Hold Me Now .... RR 3² / CB 3¹	Arista 9164
05/26/84	CB	10	18		2 Doctor! Doctor! .... RR 10	Arista 9209
09/21/85	RR	5	20		3 Lay Your Hands On Me .... BB 6 / CB 9	Arista 9396
01/17/86	RR	7	17		4 King For A Day .... BB 8 / CB 9	Arista 9450
					THOMSON, Ali	
06/07/80	RR	8	18		1 Take A Little Rhythm	A&M 2243
					THREE DEGREES, The	
09/21/74	CB	❶¹	22	▲	1 When Will I See You Again .... RW ❶¹ / BB 2¹ / RR 3³	Philadelphia I. 3550
					THREE DOG NIGHT	
04/26/69	RW	❶¹	18	●	1 One .... CB 2³ / BB 5	Dunhill/ABC 4191
08/02/69	RW	❶²	14		2 Easy To Be Hard .... CB 3² / BB 4	Dunhill/ABC 4203
10/18/69	RW	7	15		3 Eli's Coming .... CB 8 / BB 10	Dunhill/ABC 4215
05/23/70	RW	❶³	15	●	4 Mama Told Me (Not To Come) .... BB ❶² / CB ❶²	Dunhill/ABC 4239
08/29/70	CB	9	12		5 Out In The Country	Dunhill/ABC 4250
03/06/71	BB	❶⁶	18	●	6 Joy To The World .... CB ❶⁶ / RW ❶⁵	Dunhill/ABC 4272
07/03/71	RW	6	13		7 Liar .... BB 7 / CB 8	Dunhill/ABC 4282
11/06/71	BB	4	13	●	8 An Old Fashioned Love Song .... CB 4 / RW 4	Dunhill/ABC 4294
12/25/71	RW	3²	12		9 Never Been To Spain .... BB 5 / CB 5	Dunhill/ABC 4299
03/25/72	RW	9	9		10 The Family Of Man .... CB 10	Dunhill/ABC 4306
07/29/72	RW	❶²	14	●	11 Black & White .... BB ❶¹ / CB ❶¹	Dunhill/ABC 4317
05/12/73	CB	❶¹	18	●	12 Shambala .... RW ❶¹ / BB 3¹	Dunhill/ABC 4352
03/16/74	CB	❶¹	19	●	13 The Show Must Go On .... RW ❶¹ / RR 3² / BB 4	Dunhill/ABC 4382
					3 DOORS DOWN	
04/08/00	RR	❶⁵	53	△⁴	1 Kryptonite .... BB 3³	Republic
11/23/02	RR	❶¹	45	○	2 When I'm Gone .... BB 4	Republic 156263
08/08/03	RR	❶³	51	△²	3 Here Without You .... BB 5	Republic
01/14/05	RR	2²	34	○	4 Let Me Go	Republic
04/18/08	RR	9	29	△	5 It's Not My Time	Universal Republic
					3OH!3	
11/15/08	RR	6	37	△³	1 Don't Trust Me .... BB 7	Photo Finish
05/22/10	BB	9	18	○	2 My First Kiss	Photo Finish
					3OH!3 Featuring Kesha	
					THREE SUNS, The	
01/02/54	CB	10	12		1 The Creep	RCA Victor 5553
					3T	
10/07/95	CB	10	35	●	1 Anything	MJJ Music 77913
					THUNDER, Johnny	
12/22/62	BB	4	12		1 Loop De Loop .... MV 7 / CB 9	Diamond 129
					T.I.	
11/27/04	BB	9	21	○	1 Bring Em Out	Grand Hustle 93395
03/18/06	BB	3³	20	○	2 What You Know	Grand Hustle 94251
06/09/07	BB	9	19		3 Big Things Poppin' (Do It)	Grand Hustle 223868
08/23/08	BB	❶⁷	31	△³	4 Whatever You Like .... RR 3⁴	Grand Hustle 514202

162

DEBUT	CH	PK	WK	Gold	A-side (Chart Hit)	Other Charts	Label & Number
					T.I. (cont'd)		
09/27/08	BB	5	20	△ 5	Swagga Like Us		Roc-A-Fella 012284
					JAY-Z & T.I. with KANYE WEST & LIL WAYNE		
10/11/08	BB	❶⁶	28	△³ 6	Live Your Life	RR ❶²	Grand Hustle 516201
					T.I. (Featuring Rihanna)		
10/18/08	BB	2⁵	29	△² 7	Dead And Gone	RR 4	Grand Hustle 519313
					T.I. (Featuring Justin Timberlake)		
					TIFFANY		
08/29/87	BB	❶²	26	1	I Think We're Alone Now	CB ❶² / RR ❶²	MCA 53167
11/28/87	BB	❶²	23	2	Could've Been	CB ❶² / RR ❶²	MCA 53231
02/26/88	BB	7	15	3	I Saw Him Standing There		MCA 53285
11/05/88	BB	6	23	4	All This Time	CB 8	MCA 53371
					TILLOTSON, Johnny		
10/03/60	CB	2²	16	⊙ 1	Poetry In Motion	BB 2¹ / MV 2¹	Cadence 1384
08/07/61	BB	7	13	2	Without You		Cadence 1404
04/30/62	MV	2²	17	3	It Keeps Right On A-Hurtin'	BB 3¹ / CB 5	Cadence 1418
08/11/62	MV	10	9	4	Send Me The Pillow You Dream On		Cadence 1424
11/09/63	BB	7	14	5	Talk Back Trembling Lips	CB 7 / MV 7	MGM 13181
					'TIL TUESDAY		
04/13/85	RR	7	22	1	Voices Carry	BB 8 / CB 8	Epic 04795
					TIMBALAND		
02/09/07	BB	❶²	26	1	Give It To Me	RR 3³	Mosley 008759
					TIMBALAND Featuring Nelly Furtado and Justin Timberlake		
04/21/07	RR	❶⁸	47	△⁴ 2	Apologize	BB 2⁴	Mosley
					TIMBALAND with ONEREPUBLIC		
06/16/07	RR	❶³	38	△³ 3	The Way I Are	BB 3⁴	Mosley
					TIMBALAND Featuring Keri Hilson		
					TIMBERLAKE, Justin		
08/30/02	RR	4	22	1	Like I Love You		Jive 40054
12/06/02	RR	3⁴	22	2	Cry Me A River	BB 3¹	Jive 40073
03/14/03	RR	❶⁵	22	○ 3	Rock Your Body	BB 5	Jive
07/11/03	RR	5	20	4	Senorita		Jive
					JUSTIN TIMBERLAKE featuring Pharrell		
07/14/06	BB	❶⁷	36	△² 5	SexyBack	RR ❶⁵	Jive 88175
					JUSTIN TIMBERLAKE Featuring Timbaland		
09/08/06	BB	❶⁴	29	△ 6	My Love	BB ❶³	Jive 02049
					JUSTIN TIMBERLAKE Featuring T.I.		
12/15/06	BB	❶¹	25	△ 7	What Goes Around...Comes Around	RR ❶¹	Jive
04/13/07	RR	❶⁴	21	△ 8	Summer Love	BB 6	Jive
07/13/07	RR	4	20	○ 9	LoveStoned		Jive 15548
03/28/08	BB	3²	20	△² 10	4 Minutes	RR 5	Warner 463036
					MADONNA with JUSTIN TIMBERLAKE		
01/26/13	BB	3²	26	△² 11	Suit & Tie		RCA
					JUSTIN TIMBERLAKE Featuring Jay-Z		
03/02/13	BB	2¹	42	△² 12	Mirrors		RCA
03/15/14	BB	8	22	○ 13	Not A Bad Thing		RCA
05/17/14	BB	9	20	△ 14	Love Never Felt So Good		MJJ
					MICHAEL JACKSON & JUSTIN TIMBERLAKE		
05/28/16	BB	❶¹	52	△⁴ 15	Can't Stop The Feeling!		DreamWorks
01/20/18	BB	9	6	16	Filthy		RCA
02/10/18	BB	9	16	17	Say Something		RCA
					JUSTIN TIMBERLAKE with CHRIS STAPLETON		
					TIME, The		
06/30/90	CB	5	17	● 1	Jerk-Out	BB 9 / RR 9	Paisley Park 19750
					TIMEX SOCIAL CLUB		
06/14/86	RR	7	20	1	Rumors	BB 8 / CB 8	Jay 7001
					TIMMY -T-		
12/22/90	BB	❶¹	26	▲ 1	One More Try	CB ❶¹ / RR 2³	Quality 15114
					TLC		
02/22/92	BB	6	22	▲ 1	Ain't 2 Proud 2 Beg		LaFace 24008
06/06/92	BB	2⁶	33	▲ 2	Baby-Baby-Baby	RR 2⁴ / CB 2³	LaFace 24028
09/05/92	RR	6	33	● 3	What About Your Friends	BB 7 / CB 7	LaFace 24025
11/05/94	BB	❶⁴	36	▲ 4	Creep	CB 2⁶	LaFace 24082
02/25/95	BB	2³	24	● 5	Red Light Special	CB 2³	LaFace 24097
06/10/95	BB	❶⁷	36	▲ 6	Waterfalls	CB ❶⁷ / RR 2⁵	LaFace 24107
10/13/95	CB	3³	24	● 7	Diggin' On You	BB 5 / RR 5	LaFace 24119
02/19/99	BB	❶⁴	28	● 8	No Scrubs	RR 2⁵	LaFace 24385
06/11/99	BB	❶³	32	● 9	Unpretty	RR 3³	LaFace 24424

163

DEBUT	CH	PK	WK	Gold	A-side (Chart Hit)	Other Charts	Label & Number
					TOAD THE WET SPROCKET		
06/13/92	RR	7	27		1 All I Want	CB 10	Columbia 74355
11/13/92	RR	9	24		2 Walk On The Ocean		Columbia 74706
					TOBY BEAU		
05/13/78	RR	9	19		1 My Angel Baby	CB 10	RCA 11250
					TODD, Art And Dotty		
03/31/58	MV	5	18		1 Chanson D'Amour (Song Of Love)	BB 6 / CB 7	Era 1064
					TOKENS, The		
11/13/61	CB	❶[4]	15	●	1 The Lion Sleeps Tonight	MV ❶[4] / BB ❶[3]	RCA Victor 7954
					TOMMY TUTONE		
01/23/82	BB	4	27	●	1 867-5309/Jenny	CB 5 / RR 7	Columbia 02646
					TONE LOC		
12/03/88	BB	2[1]	25	▲[2]	1 Wild Thing	CB 3[1] / RR 4	Delicious Vinyl 102
03/03/89	CB	3[2]	20	▲	2 Funky Cold Medina	BB 3[1] / RR 5	Delicious Vinyl 104
					TONES AND I		
10/19/19	BB	4	20		1 Dance Monkey		Bad Batch
					TONIC		
05/10/97	RR	10	63		1 If You Could Only See		Polydor
					TONY! TONI! TONE!		
09/01/90	CB	8	25	●	1 Feels Good	BB 9	Wing 877436
06/11/93	RR	2[3]	31	●	2 If I Had No Loot	CB 6 / BB 7	Wing 859056
09/24/93	RR	5	25	●	3 Anniversary	CB 7 / BB 10	Wing 859566
					TORME, Mel		
01/07/50	BB	9	7		1 The Old Master Painter		Capitol 791
					PEGGY LEE and MEL TORMÉ		
05/13/50	BB	8	12		2 Bewitched		Capitol 1000
					TORNADOES, The		
10/27/62	BB	❶[3]	18	☉	1 Telstar	CB ❶[3] / MV ❶[2]	London 9561
					TOTAL		
04/08/95	CB	10	22	●	1 Can't You See		Tommy Boy 7676
					TOTAL featuring The Notorious B.I.G.		
11/07/98	BB	7	20	●	2 Trippin'		Bad Boy 79185
					TOTAL (Feat. Missy Elliott)		
					TOTO		
10/07/78	RR	4	24	●	1 Hold The Line	BB 5 / CB 5 / RW 5	Columbia 10830
12/22/79	RR	5	18		2 99		Columbia 11173
04/17/82	RR	❶[4]	24	●	3 Rosanna	BB 2[5] / CB 2[2]	Columbia 02811
08/07/82	RR	10	13		4 Make Believe		Columbia 03143
10/30/82	BB	❶[1]	26	●	5 Africa	RR 2[2] / CB 3[3]	Columbia 03335
03/12/83	RR	4	17		6 I Won't Hold You Back	BB 10	Columbia 03597
08/30/86	RR	8	23		7 I'll Be Over You		Columbia 06280
					TOVE LO		
06/14/14	BB	3[2]	39	△[5]	1 Habits (Stay High)		Island
					TOWNSEND, Ed		
03/17/58	MV	9	20		1 For Your Love		Capitol 3926
					TOWNSHEND, Pete		
06/14/80	RR	4	19		1 Let My Love Open The Door	BB 9	Atco 7217
					TOYA		
06/02/01	RR	6	39		1 I Do!!		Arista 13972
					TOYS, The		
09/11/65	RW	❶[2]	15	●	1 A Lover's Concerto	CB ❶[1] / BB 2[3]	DynoVoice 209
					T-PAIN		
08/27/05	BB	8	26		1 I'm Sprung		Jive 71697
12/31/05	BB	5	20	○	2 I'm N Luv (Wit A Stripper)		Jive 77102
					T-PAIN Featuring Mike Jones		
03/10/07	BB	❶[1]	35	△	3 Buy U A Drank (Shawty Snappin')	RR 4	Konvict 08718
					T-PAIN Featuring Yung Joc		
06/16/07	BB	5	22	△	4 Bartender	RR 9	Konvict 11814
					T-PAIN Featuring Akon		
08/16/08	BB	7	24		5 Can't Believe It		Konvict 36568
					T-PAIN Featuring Lil Wayne		
01/31/09	BB	2[1]	27		6 Blame It	RR 3[2]	J Records 46266
					JAMIE FOXX with T-PAIN		
10/15/11	BB	10	20		7 5 O'Clock		Nappy Boy
					T-PAIN Featuring Wiz Khalifa & Lily Allen		

DEBUT	CH	PK	WK	Gold	A-side (Chart Hit) ... Other Charts	Label & Number
					T'PAU	
05/02/87	BB	4	27		1 Heart And Soul .... CB 4 / RR 4	Virgin 99466
					TRAIN	
08/06/99	RR	10	29		1 Meet Virginia	Columbia 79565
03/16/01	RR	3¹	53	○	2 Drops Of Jupiter (Tell Me) .... BB 5	Columbia 79565
10/17/09	BB	3⁴	54	△⁶	3 Hey, Soul Sister	Columbia
01/28/12	BB	10	36	△³	4 Drive By	Columbia
					TRAINOR, Meghan	
07/26/14	BB	❶⁸	47	△¹⁰	1 All About That Bass	Epic
11/08/14	BB	4	29	△⁴	2 Lips Are Movin	Epic 53602
07/25/15	BB	8	39	△⁴	3 Like I'm Gonna Lose You	Epic
					MEGHAN TRAINOR with JOHN LEGEND	
03/26/16	BB	3²	20	△²	4 No	Epic
					TRAMMPS, The	
02/11/78	RR	6	21		1 Disco Inferno .... CB 8	Atlantic 3389
					TRAPT	
04/05/03	RR	5	43	△	1 Headstrong	Warner 16534
					TRASHMEN, The	
12/07/63	MV	2¹	13	⊙	1 Surfin' Bird .... BB 4 / CB 4	Garrett 4002
					TRAVIS, Randy — see UNDERWOOD, Carrie	
					TRAVIS & BOB	
03/21/59	BB	8	13		1 Tell Him No .... MV 9	Sandy 1017
					TRAVOLTA, John	
05/01/76	CB	5	22		1 Let Her In .... RR 6 / RR 10	Midland Int'l. 10623
04/01/78	BB	❶¹	25	▲	2 You're The One That I Want .... RW ❶¹ / CB 3⁴ / RR 3²	RSO 891
					JOHN TRAVOLTA AND OLIVIA NEWTON-JOHN	
08/05/78	CB	3²	17	●	3 Summer Nights .... RW 4 / BB 5 / RR 10	RSO 906
					JOHN TRAVOLTA, OLIVIA NEWTON-JOHN & CAST	
					TREMELOES, The	
06/17/67	CB	9	14		1 Silence Is Golden	Epic 10184
					TRESVANT, Ralph	
11/03/90	RR	3²	25	●	1 Sensitivity .... CB 3¹ / BB 4	MCA 53932
					T. REX	
12/18/71	BB	10	17		1 Bang A Gong (Get It On) .... RW 10	Reprise 1032
					TRICK DADDY	
09/18/04	BB	7	22	○	1 Let's Go	Slip n Slide 93348
					TRICK DADDY Featuring Twista and Lil Jon	
01/22/05	RR	4	26	○	2 Sugar (Gimme Some)	Slip n Slide 93644
					TRICK DADDY Featuring Ludacris & Cee-Lo	
					TRIPLETS, The	
03/16/91	CB	9	20		1 You Don't Have To Go Home Tonight .... RR 10	Mercury 878864
					TROCCOLI, Kathy	
02/21/92	RR	4	24		1 Everything Changes .... CB 6	Reunion 19118
					TROGGS, The	
06/18/66	BB	❶²	13	⊙	1 Wild Thing .... RW ❶² / CB ❶¹	Atco 6415
02/17/68	BB	7	17		2 Love Is All Around .... RW 10	Fontana 1607
					TROY, Doris	
06/08/63	CB	9	14		1 Just One Look .... MV 9 / BB 10	Atlantic 2188
					TRUE, Andrea, Connection	
03/13/76	RW	❶¹	34	●	1 More, More, More (Pt. 1) .... CB 3³ / BB 4 / RR 4	Buddah 515
					TRUTH HURTS	
04/20/02	BB	9	20		1 Addictive	Aftermath 497710
					TRUTH HURTS featuring Rakim	
					TUBB, Ernest — see FOLEY, Red	
					TUBES, The	
04/09/83	CB	8	21		1 She's A Beauty .... RR 9 / BB 10	Capitol 5217
					TUCKER, Tommy	
02/08/64	CB	10	13		1 Hi-Heel Sneakers	Checker 1067
					TUNE WEAVERS, The	
09/02/57	BB	5	19		1 Happy, Happy Birthday Baby .... CB 7 / MV 7	Checker 872

DEBUT	CH	PK	WK	Gold	A-side (Chart Hit) .... Other Charts	Label & Number
					TURNER, Ike & Tina	
01/30/71	BB	4	13	●	1 Proud Mary .... CB 5 / RW 6	Liberty 56216
					TURNER, Sammy	
06/22/59	BB	3¹	18		1 Lavender-Blue .... MV 3¹ / CB 4	Big Top 3016
					TURNER, Spyder	
12/10/66	RW	8	12		1 Stand By Me	MGM 13617
					TURNER, Tina	
05/19/84	BB	❶³	28	●	1 What's Love Got To Do With It .... CB ❶³ / RR 2²	Capitol 5354
09/15/84	RR	4	22		2 Better Be Good To Me .... BB 5 / CB 7	Capitol 5387
01/18/85	BB	7	19		3 Private Dancer .... CB 8	Capitol 5433
07/06/85	BB	2¹	21		4 We Don't Need Another Hero (Thunderdome) .... RR 3³ / CB 3²	Capitol 5491
08/29/86	CB	❶¹	21		5 Typical Male .... RR ❶¹ / BB 2³	Capitol 5615
05/28/93	RR	5	29		6 I Don't Wanna Fight .... BB 9 / CB 9	Virgin 12652
					TURTLES, The	
07/31/65	RW	7	13		1 It Ain't Me Babe .... BB 8 / CB 8	White Whale 222
02/11/67	BB	❶³	16	●	2 Happy Together .... CB ❶² / RW ❶²	White Whale 244
05/13/67	RW	❶¹	11		3 She'd Rather Be With Me .... CB 2² / BB 3²	White Whale 249
09/21/68	CB	5	12		4 Elenore .... RW 5 / BB 6	White Whale 276
12/28/68	RW	❶¹	13		5 You Showed Me .... CB 4 / BB 6	White Whale 292
					TWAIN, Shania	
01/30/98	BB	2⁹	42	▲	1 You're Still The One .... RR 3³	Mercury 568452
09/11/98	BB	4	24		2 From This Moment On	Mercury 566450
01/23/99	RR	4	28		3 That Don't Impress Me Much .... BB 7	Mercury 172118
					T-WAYNE	
05/02/15	BB	9	20	△	1 Nasty Freestyle	T-Wayne
					TWEET	
02/09/02	BB	7	20		1 Oops (Oh My)	Gold Mind 67280
					TWENTY ONE PILOTS	
05/16/15	BB	2¹	52	△⁸	1 Stressed Out	Fueled By Ramen
04/02/16	BB	5	39	△⁶	2 Ride	Fueled By Ramen
07/09/16	BB	2⁴	39	△⁷	3 Heathens	Warner
					TWISTA	
12/06/03	BB	❶¹	22		1 Slow Jamz	Atlantic 88288
					TWISTA Featuring Kanye West & Jamie Foxx	
03/27/04	BB	6	20	○	2 Overnight Celebrity	Atlantic 88359
					TWITTY, Conway	
09/08/58	MV	❶³	21	☉	1 It's Only Make Believe .... BB ❶² / CB ❶¹	MGM 12677
09/26/59	CB	7	18		2 Danny Boy .... BB 10	MGM 12826
12/28/59	BB	6	15		3 Lonely Blue Boy .... MV 7 / CB 8	MGM 12857
12/26/60	MV	10	10		4 C'est Si Bon (It's So Good)	MGM 12969
					2PAC	
07/03/93	CB	9	33	●	1 I Get Around	Interscope 98372
03/11/95	BB	9	22	▲	2 Dear Mama .... CB 10	Interscope 98273
06/15/96	BB	❶²	24	▲²	3 How Do U Want It / .... CB 2²	
					2 PAC (featuring KC and JoJo)	
02/23/96	BB	6	24		4 California Love	Death Row 854652
					2 PAC (featuring Dr. Dre nad Roger Troutman)	
					TYGA	
12/10/11	BB	7	25	△⁴	1 Rack City	Young Money
06/09/18	BB	8	29	△⁶	2 Taste	Last Kings
					TYGA Featuring Offset	
					TYLER, Bonnie	
03/25/78	CB	3³	26	●	1 It's A Heartache .... BB 3² / RW 3² / RR 4	RCA 11249
07/16/83	BB	❶⁴	30	▲	2 Total Eclipse Of The Heart .... CB ❶⁴ / RR ❶³	Columbia 03906
					TYMES, The	
06/01/63	BB	❶¹	16	☉	1 So Much In Love .... MV ❶¹ / CB 2³	Parkway 871
08/17/63	BB	7	11		2 Wonderful! Wonderful! .... CB 10	Parkway 884
					TYRESE	
01/04/03	BB	7	25		1 How You Gonna Act Like That	J Records

DEBUT	CH	PK	WK	Gold	A-side (Chart Hit)	Other Charts	Label & Number
					# U		
					UB40		
08/13/88	BB	❶¹	25	●	1 Red Red Wine	CB ❶¹ / RR ❶¹	A&M 1244
09/15/90	CB	4	25	●	2 The Way You Do The Things You Do	BB 6 / RR 9	Virgin 98978
03/23/91	BB	7	27		3 Here I Am (Come And Take Me)	CB 8 / RR 8	Virgin 99141
05/15/93	CB	❶⁸	37	▲	4 Can't Help Falling In Love	BB ❶⁷ / RR ❶³	Virgin 12653
					UGLY KID JOE		
03/14/92	CB	6	28		1 Everything About You	BB 9 / RR 10	Mercury 866632
02/05/93	BB	6	22	●	2 Cats In The Cradle	CB 9 / RR 9	Stardog 864888
					ULLMAN, Tracey		
02/25/84	BB	8	20		1 They Don't Know	RR 8 / CB 10	MCA/Stiff 52347
					UNCLE KRACKER		
12/22/00	RR	3³	35		1 Follow Me	BB 5	Lava/Atlantic 85184
03/29/03	BB	9	35		2 Drift Away	RR 10	Lava
					UNCLE KRACKER with DOBIE GRAY		
					UNCLE SAM		
11/08/97	BB	6	28	▲	1 I Don't Ever Want To See You Again		Stonecreek 78689
					UNDERWOOD, Carrie		
07/02/05	BB	❶¹	12	●	1 Inside Your Heaven		Arista Nashville 70859
09/16/06	BB	8	64	△⁵	2 Before He Cheats	RR 9	Arista Nashville
05/12/07	BB	6	5		3 I'll Stand By You		Fremantle
02/28/09	BB	9	18	△	4 I Told You So		19 Records
					CARRIE UNDERWOOD with RANDY TRAVIS		
					UNDISPUTED TRUTH, The		
06/26/71	CB	❶¹	18		1 Smiling Faces Sometimes	BB 3² / RW 3²	Gordy 7108
					UNK		
09/23/06	BB	10	36	△	1 Walk It Out		Big Oomp
					URIE, Brendon — see SWIFT, Taylor		
					USA FOR AFRICA		
03/15/85	CB	❶⁵	19	▲⁴	1 We Are The World	BB ❶⁴ / RR ❶³	Columbia 04839
					USHER		
08/23/97	BB	2⁷	47	▲	1 You Make Me Wanna...	RR 7	LaFace 24265
01/24/98	BB	❶²	23	▲	2 Nice & Slow		LaFace 24290
06/20/98	BB	2³	24	▲	3 My Way		LaFace 24323
06/16/01	BB	❶⁴	24		4 U Remind Me	RR 6	Arista 13992
09/22/01	BB	❶⁶	32		5 U Got It Bad	RR 3⁴	Arista 15036
02/09/02	BB	3¹	26		6 U Don't Have To Call		Arista
01/10/04	BB	❶¹²	45	△	7 Yeah!	RR ❶⁴	Arista 59149
					USHER Featuring Lil Jon & Ludacris		
03/13/04	BB	❶⁸	30	○	8 Burn	RR 2⁴	Arista 61107
05/01/04	BB	❶²	25		9 Confessions Part II	RR 6	LaFace 64779
09/10/04	BB	❶⁶	26	○	10 My Boo	RR 2¹	LaFace 65246
					USHER & ALICIA KEYS		
12/11/04	RR	2⁴	27		11 Caught Up	BB 8	LaFace 66434
02/29/08	BB	❶³	25	△	12 Love In This Club	RR 2¹	LaFace 30018
					USHER Featuring Young Jeezy		
04/17/10	BB	❶⁴	30		13 OMG		LaFace
					USHER Featuring will.i.am		
07/31/10	BB	4	34		14 DJ Got Us Fallin' In Love		LaFace 76763
					USHER Featuring Pitbull		
09/17/11	BB	4	30	△²	15 Without You		Astralwerks
					DAVID GUETTA with USHER		
05/12/12	BB	9	21	△	16 Scream		RCA
					US3		
11/27/93	RR	6	28	●	1 Cantaloop	CB 7 / BB 9	Blue Note 44945
					U2		
03/20/87	BB	❶³	21		1 With Or Without You	CB ❶³ / RR ❶³	Island 99469
06/12/87	BB	❶²	19		2 I Still Haven't Found What I'm Looking For	CB ❶² / RR ❶¹	Island 99430
09/30/88	CB	2¹	21	●	3 Desire	BB 3¹ / RR 6	Island 99250
11/23/91	CB	3²	27		4 Mysterious Ways	RR 5 / BB 9	Island 866188
03/13/92	RR	2²	24		5 One	CB 3¹ / BB 10	Island 866533
01/24/97	BB	10	11	●	6 Discotheque		Island 854774

V

DEBUT	CH	PK	WK	Gold	A-side (Chart Hit) / Other Charts	Label & Number
					VALE, Jerry	
07/07/56	MV	9	24		1 You Don't Know Me	Columbia 40710
					VALENS, Ritchie	
11/24/58	MV	❶¹	23	◉	1 Donna .... BB 2² / CB 2²	Del-Fi 4110
					VALENTE, Caterina	
03/28/55	MV	6	18		1 The Breeze And I .... BB 8 / CB 9	Decca 29467
					VALENTINO, Bobby	
03/05/05	BB	8	22	○	1 Slow Down	DTP
					VALLI, Frankie	
05/13/67	CB	❶²	17	●	1 Can't Take My Eyes Off You .... RW ❶² / BB 2¹	Philips 40446
11/09/74	BB	❶¹	26	●	2 My Eyes Adored You .... CB ❶¹ / RW ❶¹ / RR 2²	Private Stock 45,003
05/10/75	BB	6	17		3 Swearin' To God .... RW 6 / CB 7 / RR 10	Private Stock 45,021
05/27/78	BB	❶²	23	▲	4 Grease .... RW ❶² / CB ❶¹ / RR ❶¹	RSO 897
					VALLI, June	
08/01/53	BB	4	17		1 Crying In The Chapel	RCA Victor 5368
06/12/54	BB	8	12		2 I Understand	RCA Victor 5740
					VANDROSS, Luther	
12/23/89	BB	6	27	●	1 Here And Now .... CB 7 / RR 7	Epic 73029
04/27/91	BB	4	22		2 Power Of Love/Love Power .... RR 5 / CB 6	Epic 73778
08/03/91	BB	9	29		3 Don't Want To Be A Fool	Epic 73879
05/22/92	RR	2²	22		4 The Best Things In Life Are Free .... CB 9 / BB 10	Perspective 0010
					LUTHER VANDROSS and JANET JACKSON with BBD and Ralph Tresvant	
09/09/94	BB	2¹	23	●	5 Endless Love .... CB 3¹ / RR 6	Columbia 77629
					LUTHER VANDROSS & MARIAH CAREY	
					VAN DYKE, Leroy	
10/28/61	MV	2¹	18		1 Walk On By .... CB 3³ / BB 5	Mercury 71834
					VANGELIS	
12/12/81	CB	❶²	31		1 Chariots Of Fire - Titles .... BB ❶¹ / RR 4 / RW 7	Polydor 2189
					VAN HALEN	
04/28/79	RR	10	16		1 Dance The Night Away	Warner 8823
02/13/82	CB	10	16		2 (Oh) Pretty Woman	Warner 50003
01/13/84	BB	❶⁵	23	●	3 Jump .... RR ❶⁵ / CB ❶²	Warner 29384
04/13/84	RR	8	16		4 I'll Wait	Warner 29307
06/22/84	RR	9	17		5 Panama	Warner 29250
03/14/86	CB	❶¹	19		6 Why Can't This Be Love .... RR 2² / BB 3¹	Warner 28740
07/02/88	BB	5	19		7 When It's Love .... RR 5 / CB 8	Warner 27827
03/10/95	RR	7	22		8 Can't Stop Lovin' You	Warner 17909
					VANILLA FUDGE	
07/13/68	BB	6	12		1 You Keep Me Hangin' On .... CB 7 / RW 7	Atco 6590
					VANILLA ICE	
09/08/90	CB	❶²	22	▲	1 Ice Ice Baby .... RR ❶² / BB ❶¹	SBK 07335
12/08/90	BB	4	22	●	2 Play That Funky Music .... CB 5	SBK 07339
					VANITY FARE	
11/08/69	RW	9	16		1 Early In The Morning .... CB 10	Page One 21,027
03/21/70	RW	3¹	22	●	2 Hitchin' A Ride .... CB 4 / BB 5	Page One 21,029
					VANNELLI, Gino	
09/09/78	CB	2²	21		1 I Just Wanna Stop .... RR 2¹ / BB 4 / RW 8	A&M 2072
03/21/81	RR	2²	20		2 Living Inside Myself .... BB 6 / CB 9 / RW 10	Arista 0588
					VANWARMER, Randy	
03/17/79	BB	4	21	●	1 Just When I Needed You Most .... CB 5 / RW 5 / RR 5	Bearsville 0334
					VAUGHAN, Sarah	
09/16/50	BB	10	7		1 (I Love The Girl) I Love The Guy	Columbia 38925
11/08/54	MV	4	20		2 Make Yourself Comfortable .... BB 6 / CB 8	Mercury 70469
04/16/55	MV	3¹	15		3 Whatever Lola Wants .... BB 6 / CB 6	Mercury 70595
07/18/59	CB	6	19		4 Broken-Hearted Melody .... BB 7 / MV 8	Mercury 71477
					VAUGHN, Billy, and his Orchestra	
12/11/54	CB	❶⁷	28	◉	1 Melody Of Love .... BB 2¹ / MV 4	Dot 15247
08/29/55	MV	4	22		2 The Shifting Whispering Sands (Parts 1 & 2) .... BB 5 / CB 5	Dot 15409
12/02/57	BB	10	22		3 Raunchy /	
12/07/57	CB	4	26	◉	4 Sail Along Silvery Moon .... MV 4 / BB 5	Dot 15661
					VAZQUEZ, Mario	
05/26/06	RR	6	28		1 Gallery	Arista

168

DEBUT	CH	PK	WK	Gold	A-side (Chart Hit) .... Other Charts	Label & Number
					VEE, Bobby	
08/01/60	CB	4	19		1 Devil Or Angel .... BB 6 / MV 7	Liberty 55270
11/28/60	MV	5	14		2 Rubber Ball .... BB 6 / CB 6	Liberty 55287
08/07/61	BB	❶³	15	⊙	3 Take Good Care Of My Baby .... CB ❶³ / MV ❶²	Liberty 55354
11/13/61	MV	2²	15		4 Run To Him .... BB 2¹ / CB 4	Liberty 55388
12/01/62	BB	3²	16		5 The Night Has A Thousand Eyes .... MV 3¹ / CB 4	Liberty 55521
07/08/67	RW	2¹	18	●	6 Come Back When You Grow Up .... BB 3³ / CB 3³	Liberty 55964
					VEGA, Suzanne	
06/06/87	RR	3³	20		1 Luka .... BB 3¹ / CB 4	A&M 2937
10/06/90	CB	4	24	●	2 Tom's Diner .... BB 5 / RR 8	A&M 1529
					D.N.A. Featuring SUZANNE VEGA	
					VENTURES, The	
07/18/60	BB	2¹	18	⊙	1 Walk — Don't Run .... CB 3⁵ / MV 3²	Dolton 25
07/11/64	BB	8	12		2 Walk-Don't Run '64 .... CB 9 / RW 10	Dolton 96
03/08/69	BB	4	14		3 Hawaii Five-O .... RW 4 / CB 6	Liberty 56068
					VERA, Billy, & The Beaters	
11/08/86	BB	❶²	21	●	1 At This Moment .... CB ❶¹ / RR ❶¹	Rhino 74403
					VERNE, Larry	
08/22/60	BB	❶¹	14	⊙	1 Mr. Custer .... MV 3³ / CB 3¹	Era 3024
					VERTICAL HORIZON	
12/03/99	BB	❶¹	41		1 Everything You Want .... RR 2³	RCA 65981
07/28/00	RR	10	21		2 You're A God	RCA 60231
					VERVE PIPE, The	
02/22/97	BB	5	42	●	1 The Freshmen .... RR 5	RCA 64734
					VILLAGE PEOPLE	
10/21/78	BB	2³	32	▲	1 Y.M.C.A. .... RW 2² / CB 3² / RR 6	Casablanca 945
03/17/79	RW	2²	19	●	2 In The Navy .... BB 3² / CB 3¹	Casablanca 973
					VILLAGE STOMPERS, The	
09/21/63	BB	2¹	15		1 Washington Square .... CB 2¹ / MV 3³	Epic 9617
					VINCENT, Gene, and His Blue Caps	
06/15/56	CB	5	20	⊙	1 Be-Bop-A-Lula .... MV 6 / BB 7	Capitol 3450
08/17/57	MV	10	19		2 Lotta Lovin'	Capitol 3763
					VINTON, Bobby	
06/02/62	MV	❶⁵	17	●	1 Roses Are Red (My Love) .... BB ❶⁴ / CB ❶⁴	Epic 9509
05/18/63	MV	❶¹	14		2 Blue On Blue .... BB 3¹ / CB 3¹	Epic 9593
08/10/63	BB	❶³	15	⊙	3 Blue Velvet .... CB ❶³ / MV ❶²	Epic 9614
11/23/63	BB	❶⁴	14	⊙	4 There! I've Said It Again .... MV ❶² / CB ❶¹	Epic 9638
02/29/64	CB	8	11		5 My Heart Belongs To Only You .... MV 8 / BB 9	Epic 9662
05/23/64	RW	8	9		6 Tell Me Why	Epic 9687
10/31/64	RW	❶²	16	⊙	7 Mr. Lonely .... BB ❶¹ / CB 2³	Epic 9730
11/12/66	RW	6	13		8 Coming Home Soldier .... CB 8	Epic 10090
09/23/67	CB	5	14		9 Please Love Me Forever .... RW 5 / BB 6	Epic 10228
10/26/68	CB	4	15	●	10 I Love How You Love Me .... RW 5 / BB 9	Epic 10397
09/21/74	RW	❶¹	20	●	11 My Melody Of Love .... CB 2² / BB 3² / RR 5	ABC 12022
					VIRTUES, The	
03/02/59	BB	5	17		1 Guitar Boogie Shuffle .... CB 5 / MV 5	Hunt 324
					VOGUES, The	
09/11/65	BB	4	14		1 You're The One .... RW 6 / CB 7	Co & Ce 229
11/27/65	CB	3¹	14		2 Five O'Clock World .... RW 3¹ / BB 4	Co & Ce 232
06/08/68	CB	4	15	●	3 Turn Around, Look At Me .... RW 5 / BB 7	Reprise 0686
09/07/68	CB	6	10	●	4 My Special Angel .... RW 6 / BB 7	Reprise 0766
					VOICES OF THEORY	
04/04/98	BB	10	31	●	1 Say It	H.O.L.A. 341032

W

					WADE, Adam	
03/04/61	BB	7	17		1 Take Good Care Of Her .... CB 10	Coed 546
05/15/61	BB	5	11		2 The Writing On The Wall .... CB 10	Coed 550
07/24/61	BB	10	10		3 As If I Didn't Know	Coed 553
					WADSWORTH MANSION	
12/05/70	CB	5	16		1 Sweet Mary .... RW 5 / BB 7	Sussex 209

DEBUT	CH	PK	WK	Gold	A-side (Chart Hit) ... Other Charts	Label & Number
					WAGNER, Jack	
10/20/84	BB	2²	23		1 All I Need .... CB 2² / RR 3³	Qwest 29238
					WAITE, John	
06/23/84	CB	❶²	24		1 Missing You .... RR ❶² / BB ❶¹	EMI America 8212
					WAKELY, Jimmy — see WHITING, Margaret	
					WALKER, Jr., & The All Stars	
02/13/65	RW	3¹	15		1 Shotgun .... BB 4 / CB 4	Soul 35008
05/17/69	BB	4	16		2 What Does It Take (To Win Your Love) .... RW 4 / CB 5	Soul 35062
					WALK THE MOON	
11/22/14	BB	4	53	△³	1 Shut Up And Dance	RCA
					WALLACE, Jerry, with The Jewels	
08/15/59	MV	4	22		1 Primrose Lane .... CB 5 / BB 8	Challenge 59047
					WALLFLOWERS, The	
01/04/97	BB	2⁵	70		1 One Headlight .... RR 2¹	Interscope
					WALSH, Joe	
06/03/78	CB	6	19		1 Life's Been Good .... RR 6 / RW 9	Asylum 45493
					WALTERS, Jamie	
01/27/95	RR	4	30		1 Hold On .... CB 9	Atlantic 87240
					WANG CHUNG	
10/04/86	CB	❶³	22		1 Everybody Have Fun Tonight .... RR ❶¹ / BB 2²	Geffen 28562
01/24/87	RR	5	18		2 Let's Go! .... BB 9 / CB 10	Geffen 28531
					WANTED, The	
01/28/12	BB	3⁴	37	△³	1 Glad You Came	Global Talent 016724
					WAR	
05/23/70	CB	❶¹	21	●	1 Spill The Wine .... RW ❶¹ / BB 3¹	MGM 14118
					ERIC BURDON & WAR	
11/18/72	BB	7	16	●	2 The World Is A Ghetto .... CB 9 / RW 9	United Artists 50975
03/03/73	RW	❶¹	15	●	3 The Cisco Kid .... BB 2² / CB 2¹	United Artists 163
07/14/73	CB	7	15		4 Gypsy Man .... BB 8	United Artists 281
04/26/75	CB	5	21	●	5 Why Can't We Be Friends? .... RW 5 / BB 6 / RR 6	United Artists 629
09/13/75	CB	5	20		6 Low Rider .... BB 7 / RW 7 / RR 10	United Artists 706
07/10/76	BB	7	20	●	7 Summer	United Artists 834
					WARD, Anita	
05/12/79	CB	❶³	21		1 Ring My Bell .... BB ❶² / RW ❶¹ / RR 2¹	Juana 3422
					WARD, Billy, And His Dominoes	
06/17/57	MV	10	24		1 Star Dust	Liberty 55071
					WARNES, Jennifer	
01/29/77	CB	5	22		1 Right Time Of The Night .... RR 5 / BB 6 / RW 10	Arista 0223
08/21/82	BB	❶³	25	▲	2 Up Where We Belong .... CB ❶³ / RR ❶³	Island 99996
					JOE COCKER and JENNIFER WARNES	
09/19/87	BB	❶¹	23	●	3 (I've Had) The Time Of My Life .... CB ❶¹ / RR ❶¹	RCA 5224
					BILL MEDLEY AND JENNIFER WARNES	
					WARRANT	
07/22/89	BB	2²	25	●	1 Heaven .... CB 2² / RR 2²	Columbia 68985
09/08/90	BB	10	19		2 Cherry Pie	Columbia 73510
11/24/90	BB	10	23		3 I Saw Red	Columbia 73597
					WARREN, Fran — see MARTIN, Tony	
					WARREN G	
04/23/94	BB	2³	26	▲	1 Regulate	Death Row 98280
					WARREN G. & NATE DOGG	
07/23/94	BB	9	27	●	2 This DJ	Violator/RAL 853236
					WARWICK, Dionne	
12/07/63	MV	7	14		1 Anyone Who Had A Heart .... BB 8 / CB 8	Scepter 1262
04/18/64	BB	6	15		2 Walk On By .... CB 6 / RW 6	Scepter 1274
04/02/66	RW	7	12		3 Message To Michael .... BB 8 / CB 9	Scepter 12133
10/21/67	BB	4	13	●	4 I Say A Little Prayer /	
					RW 4 / CB 5	
01/20/68	RW	❶²	14		5 (Theme From) Valley Of The Dolls .... BB 2⁴ / CB 3¹	Scepter 12203
04/06/68	RW	8	12		6 Do You Know The Way To San Jose .... BB 10 / CB 10	Scepter 12216
02/01/69	BB	7	12		7 This Girl's In Love With You .... CB 9 / RW 9	Scepter 12241
12/27/69	BB	6	11		8 I'll Never Fall In Love Again .... CB 6 / RW 7	Scepter 12273
07/20/74	BB	❶¹	19	●	9 Then Came You .... CB ❶¹ / RW ❶¹ / RR 6	Atlantic 3202
					DIONNE WARWICKE AND SPINNERS	
06/23/79	RR	3¹	26	●	10 I'll Never Love This Way Again .... BB 5 / CB 5 / RW 5	Arista 0419
11/10/79	RR	10	20		11 Deja Vu	Arista 0459

DEBUT	CH	PK	WK	Gold	A-side (Chart Hit)	Other Charts	Label & Number
					WARWICK, Dionne (cont'd)		
10/09/82	BB	10	22		12 Heartbreaker	RR 10	Arista 1015
11/09/85	BB	❶⁴	26	●	13 That's What Friends Are For	CB ❶³ / RR ❶²	Arista 9422
					DIONNE & FRIENDS (Elton John, Gladys Knight and Stevie Wonder)		
					WASHINGTON, Dinah		
05/09/59	CB	4	24		1 What A Diff'rence A Day Makes	MV 4 / BB 8	Mercury 71435
09/28/59	MV	6	15		2 Unforgettable	CB 8	Mercury 71508
01/25/60	CB	2¹	16	⊙	3 Baby (You've Got What It Takes)	BB 5 / MV 5	Mercury 71565
05/21/60	CB	5	15		4 A Rockin' Good Way (To Mess Around And Fall In Love)	BB 7 / MV 8	Mercury 71629
					DINAH WASHINGTON & BROOK BENTON (above 2)		
					WASHINGTON, Grover Jr.		
02/07/81	RR	❶²	24		1 Just The Two Of Us	BB 2³ / CB 4 / RW 5	Elektra 47103
					GROVER WASHINGTON, JR. with BILL WITHERS		
					WAS (NOT WAS)		
01/28/89	BB	7	18		1 Walk The Dinosaur	CB 7 / RR 8	Chrysalis 43331
					WATERFRONT		
04/08/89	RR	9	20		1 Cry	BB 10 / CB 10	Polydor 871110
					WATERS, Crystal		
05/04/91	BB	8	19	●	1 Gypsy Woman (She's Homeless)		Mercury 868208
06/11/94	CB	5	44	●	2 100% Pure Love	RR 8	Mercury 858485
					WATLEY, Jody		
03/07/87	BB	2⁴	23		1 Looking For A New Love	CB 2³ / RR 2¹	MCA 52956
10/03/87	CB	5	23		2 Don't You Want Me	BB 6 / RR 6	MCA 53162
01/30/88	CB	9	20		3 Some Kind Of Lover	RR 9 / BB 10	MCA 53235
03/18/89	CB	❶²	22	●	4 Real Love	BB 2² / RR 3²	MCA 53484
06/17/89	CB	8	23		5 Friends	BB 9	MCA 53660
					JODY WATLEY with ERIC B. & RAKIM		
10/14/89	BB	4	23		6 Everything	CB 5 / RR 5	MCA 53714
03/07/92	RR	8	22		7 I'm The One You Need		MCA 54276
					WAYNE, Bobby		
02/23/52	BB	6	13		1 Wheel Of Fortune		Mercury 5779
					WAYNE, Thomas		
01/19/59	BB	5	19		1 Tragedy	MV 6 / CB 7	Fernwood 109
					WEAVERS, The		
07/08/50	BB	❶¹³	27	⊙	1 Goodnight Irene /	CB ❶¹⁰	
07/01/50	BB	2¹	20		2 Tzena Tzena Tzena	CB 2¹	Decca 27077
					GORDON JENKINS and his Orchestra and THE WEAVERS (above 2)		
01/13/51	BB	4	16		3 So Long (It's Been Good To Know Yuh)	CB 7	Decca 27376
					GORDON JENKINS and his Orchestra and THE WEAVERS		
03/31/51	CB	❶²	23	⊙	4 On Top Of Old Smoky	BB 2⁸	Decca 27515
					THE WEAVERS and TERRY GILKYSON		
					WEBBIE		
12/08/07	BB	9	25		1 Independent		Trill 511418
					WEBBIE Feat. Lil' Phat & Lil' Boosie		
					WEBER, Joan		
11/22/54	BB	❶⁴	18	⊙	1 Let Me Go Lover	MV ❶³ / CB ❶²	Columbia 40366
					WEEKND, The		
10/25/14	BB	7	22	△³	1 Love Me Harder		Republic
					ARIANA GRANDE & THE WEEKND		
01/10/15	BB	3³	43	△⁶	2 Earned It (Fifty Shades Of Grey)		Universal Studios
06/13/15	BB	❶⁶	48	△¹⁰	3 The Hills		XO
06/27/15	BB	❶³	41	△⁷	4 Can't Feel My Face		XO
10/08/16	BB	❶¹	30	△⁷	5 Starboy		XO
12/10/16	BB	4	26	△³	6 I Feel It Coming		XO
					THE WEEKND Featuring Daft Punk (above 2)		
02/17/18	BB	7	20	△²	7 Pray For Me		Top Dawg
					THE WEEKND & KENDRICK LAMAR		
04/14/18	BB	4	18	△²	8 Call Out My Name		XO
12/07/19	BB	❶¹	13		9 Heartless		XO
12/14/19	BB	10	12		10 Blinding Lights		XO
					WEEZER		
04/16/05	RR	2¹	43	○	1 Beverly Hills	BB 10	Geffen
					WE FIVE		
07/10/65	CB	2²	18		1 You Were On My Mind	RW 2² / BB 3¹	A&M 770
					WEIR, Frank, with his Saxophone, Chorus and Orchestra		
04/24/54	CB	3¹	24		1 The Happy Wanderer	BB 4	London 1448

DEBUT	CH	PK	WK	Gold	A-side (Chart Hit) ... Other Charts	Label & Number
					WEISSBERG, Eric, & Steve Mandell	
01/06/73	RW	❶²	15	●	1 Dueling Banjos .... CB ❶¹ / BB 2⁴	Warner 7659
					WELCH, Bob	
10/08/77	CB	4	20		1 Sentimental Lady .... RR 5 / RW 7 / BB 8	Capitol 4479
01/28/78	RR	5	18		2 Ebony Eyes .... RW 10	Capitol 4543
					WELCH, Lenny	
10/26/63	BB	4	17		1 Since I Fell For You .... CB 4 / MV 5	Cadence 1439
					WELK, Lawrence, And His Orchestra	
01/24/53	BB	5	10		1 Oh Happy Day	Coral 60893
					LAWRENCE WELK And His Champagne Music	
12/12/60	MV	❶⁶	17	●	2 Calcutta .... CB ❶⁴ / BB ❶²	Dot 16161
					WELLS, Mary	
03/05/62	CB	4	20		1 The One Who Really Loves You .... MV 5 / BB 8	Motown 1024
08/11/62	BB	9	13		2 You Beat Me To The Punch .... CB 9	Motown 1032
11/24/62	BB	7	14		3 Two Lovers .... CB 10 / MV 10	Motown 1035
03/28/64	BB	❶²	17	◉	4 My Guy .... CB ❶¹ / MV 2²	Motown 1056
					WEST, Kanye	
03/13/04	BB	7	20	△	1 All Falls Down	Roc-A-Fella 002018
					KANYE WEST featuring Syleena Johnson	
07/30/05	BB	❶¹⁰	39	△⁷	2 Gold Digger .... RR ❶²	Roc-A-Fella 005118
					KANYE WEST featuring Jamie Foxx	
08/03/07	RR	❶³	27	△⁸	3 Stronger .... BB ❶¹	Roc-A-Fella
09/29/07	BB	7	21	△²	4 Good Life	Roc-A-Fella
					KANYE WEST Featuring T-Pain	
09/27/08	BB	5	20	△	5 Swagga Like Us	Roc-A-Fella 012284
					JAY-Z & T.I. with KANYE WEST & LIL WAYNE	
10/04/08	BB	3²	23	△³	6 Love Lockdown .... RR 10	Roc-A-Fella 012384
11/22/08	BB	2¹	30	△⁶	7 Heartless .... RR 4	Roc-A-Fella
08/15/09	BB	2¹	23	△²	8 Run This Town	Roc Nation 521199
					JAY-Z, RIHANNA & KANYE WEST	
08/27/11	BB	5	36	△⁶	9 Ni**as In Paris	Roc-A-Fella
					JAY-Z & KANYE WEST	
02/07/15	BB	4	20	△³	10 FourFiveSeconds	Westbury Road
					RIHANNA & KANYE WEST & PAUL McCARTNEY	
06/16/18	BB	8	5	△	11 Yikes	G.O.O.D.
09/22/18	BB	6	12	△²	12 I Love It	G.O.O.D.
					KANYE WEST & LIL PUMP	
11/09/19	BB	7	6	○	13 Follow God	G.O.O.D.
					WESTON, Paul, And His Orchestra	
10/07/50	BB	2¹	24		1 Nevertheless (I'm In Love With You) .... CB 3²	Columbia 38982
12/29/51	BB	8	6		2 Charmaine	Columbia 39616
					PAUL WESTON & his Orchestra with The Norman Luboff Choir (above 2)	
					WET WILLIE	
05/25/74	BB	10	20		1 Keep On Smilin'	Capricorn 0043
					WHAM! — see MICHAEL, George	
					WHEN IN ROME	
09/03/88	RR	10	25		1 The Promise	Virgin 99323
					WHISPERS, The	
06/06/87	RR	6	23		1 Rock Steady .... BB 7 / CB 10	Solar 70006
					WHITCOMB, Ian, And Bluesville	
05/15/65	RW	6	14		1 You Turn Me On (Turn On Song) ...... BB 8 / CB 10	Tower 134)
					WHITE, Barry	
03/31/73	BB	3¹	18	●	1 I'm Gonna Love You Just A Little More Baby ... CB 4 / RW 4	20th Century 2018
10/27/73	BB	7	18	●	2 Never, Never Gonna Give Ya Up .... CB 9 / RW 9	20th Century 2058
07/27/74	BB	❶¹	15	●	3 Can't Get Enough Of Your Love, Babe ... CB ❶¹ / RW ❶¹ / RR 2³	20th Century 2120
11/02/74	CB	❶¹	17	●	4 You're The First, The Last, My Everything .BB 2² / RW 2¹ / RR 5	20th Century 2133
03/08/75	BB	8	12		5 What Am I Gonna Do With You .... CB 8	20th Century 2177
08/20/77	BB	4	22	●	6 It's Ecstasy When You Lay Down Next To Me ... RW 5 / CB 7	20th Century 2350
					WHITE, Karyn	
10/15/88	CB	5	25	●	1 The Way You Love Me .... RR 6 / BB 7	Warner 27773
01/28/89	BB	8	19	●	2 Superwoman .... CB 8 / RR 9	Warner 27783
05/27/89	BB	6	24		3 Secret Rendezvous .... RR 6 / BB 7	Warner 27863
08/16/91	CB	❶²	28		4 Romantic .... RR ❶² / BB ❶¹	Warner 19319
11/30/91	RR	3²	27		5 The Way I Feel About You .... CB 3¹	Warner 19088
					WHITE, Tony Joe	
07/05/69	BB	8	12		1 Polk Salad Annie .... RW 8 / CB 9	Monument 1104

DEBUT	CH	PK	WK	Gold	A-side (Chart Hit) .... Other Charts	Label & Number
					WHITE LION	
02/27/88	BB	8	21		1 Wait .... CB 10 / RR 10	Atlantic 89126
11/05/88	BB	3¹	23		2 When The Children Cry .... CB 4 / RR 4	Atlantic 89015
					WHITE PLAINS	
04/11/70	CB	10	16		1 My Baby Loves Lovin'	Deram 85058
					WHITESNAKE	
07/04/87	CB	❶²	30		1 Here I Go Again .... BB ❶¹ / RR ❶¹	Geffen 28339
10/23/87	CB	2³	22		2 Is This Love .... RR 2³ / BB 2¹	Geffen 28233
					WHITE TOWN	
03/21/97	RR	5	24		1 Your Woman	Chrysalis/EMI 58638
					WHITFIELD, David	
08/14/54	MV	9	23	⊙	1 Cara Mia .... BB 10	London 1486
					DAVID WHITFIELD with MANTOVANI and His Orchestra and Chorus	
					WHITING, Margaret	
09/10/49	BB	❶³	23		1 Slipping Around .... CB 3³	Capitol 540224
10/28/50	CB	4	23		2 A Bushel And A Peck .... BB 6	Capitol 1234
					MARGARET WHITING and JIMMY WAKELY (above 2)	
					WHITMAN, Slim	
07/26/52	BB	9	16		1 Indian Love Call	Imperial 8156
					WHO, The	
10/07/67	CB	8	13		1 I Can See For Miles .... BB 9 / RW 10	Decca 32206
08/03/68	CB	10	11		2 Magic Bus	Decca 32362
09/19/70	CB	8	14		3 See Me, Feel Me .... RW 9	Decca 32729
07/10/71	RW	8	14		4 Won't Get Fooled Again .... CB 9	Decca 32846
08/26/78	RR	7	16		5 Who Are You .... CB 9 / RW 9	MCA 10948
					WIEDLIN, Jane	
05/07/88	BB	9	21		1 Rush Hour .... CB 10 / RR 10	EMI/Manhattan 50118
					WILD CHERRY	
06/12/76	BB	❶³	33	▲	1 Play That Funky Music .... CB ❶² / RW ❶² / RR 2¹	Epic 50225
					WILDE, Kim	
03/28/87	BB	❶¹	22		1 You Keep Me Hangin' On .... RR ❶¹ / CB 2¹	MCA 53024
					WILDER, Matthew	
09/17/83	CB	2²	32		1 Break My Stride .... BB 5 / RR 9	Private I 04113
					will.i.am	
12/15/12	BB	3²	24	△³	1 Scream & Shout	will.i.am
					will.i.am & BRITNEY SPEARS	
					WILLIAMS, Andy	
08/11/56	BB	7	22		1 Canadian Sunset	Cadence 1297
02/09/57	BB	❶³	20	⊙	2 Butterfly .... MV 2¹ / CB 3¹	Cadence 1308
05/20/57	MV	7	20		3 I Like Your Kind Of Love .... BB 8 / CB 10	Cadence 1323
01/20/58	BB	3¹	18		4 Are You Sincere .... MV 5 / CB 7	Cadence 1340
12/22/58	MV	5	22		5 The Hawaiian Wedding Song (Ke Kali Nei Au) .... CB 6	Cadence 1358
09/07/59	BB	5	16		6 Lonely Street .... MV 5 / CB 7	Cadence 1370
12/07/59	BB	7	14		7 The Village Of St. Bernadette .... MV 7 / CB 9	Cadence 1374
02/23/63	CB	❶¹	17	⊙	8 Can't Get Used To Losing You .... BB 2⁴ / MV 2¹	Columbia 42674
02/06/71	RW	5	14		9 (Where Do I Begin) Love Story .... BB 9 / CB 10	Columbia 45317
12/08/18	BB	10	5		10 It's The Most Wonderful Time Of The Year	Columbia
12/07/19	BB	7	5		11 It's The Most Wonderful Time Of The Year	Columbia
					WILLIAMS, Billy	
06/03/57	MV	2³	23	⊙	1 I'm Gonna Sit Right Down And Write Myself A Letter . CB 2² / BB 3⁴	Coral 61830
					WILLIAMS, Danny	
03/07/64	BB	9	15		1 White On White .... CB 10	United Artists 685
					WILLIAMS, Deniece	
03/18/78	BB	❶¹	21	●	1 Too Much, Too Little, Too Late .... RW ❶¹ / CB 2³ / RR 2¹	Columbia 10693
					JOHNNY MATHIS & DENIECE WILLIAMS	
04/03/82	BB	10	19		2 It's Gonna Take A Miracle	ARC 02812
04/06/84	RR	❶³	22	▲	3 Let's Hear It For The Boy .... BB ❶² / CB ❶²	Columbia 04417
					WILLIAMS, John	
07/09/77	BB	10	17		1 Star Wars (Main Title)	20th Century 2345
12/24/77	RW	10	16		2 Theme From "Close Encounters Of The Third Kind"	Arista 0300
					WILLIAMS, Larry	
06/24/57	BB	5	21	⊙	1 Short Fat Fannie .... MV 9	Specialty 608

DEBUT	CH	PK	WK	Gold	A-side (Chart Hit)	Other Charts	Label & Number
					WILLIAMS, Mason		
06/22/68	CB	❶¹	14		1 Classical Gas	BB 2² / RW 2¹	Warner 7190
					WILLIAMS, Maurice, & The Zodiacs		
09/17/60	BB	❶¹	20	☉	1 Stay	CB 4 / MV 4	Herald 552
					WILLIAMS, Pharrell		
06/14/03	BB	5	23		1 Frontin' PHARRELL Featuring Jay-Z		Star Trak 58647
05/04/13	BB	2⁵	29	△⁴	2 Get Lucky DAFT PUNK with PHARRELL WILLIAMS		Daft Life
01/18/14	BB	❶¹⁰	47	△⁷	3 Happy		Back Lot Music 05363
					WILLIAMS, Roger		
08/01/55	BB	❶⁴	31	☉	1 Autumn Leaves	CB ❶³ / MV ❶³	Kapp 116
08/18/58	MV	9	17		2 Near You	BB 10	Kapp 233
08/27/66	BB	7	22		3 Born Free	CB 7 / RW 7	Kapp 767
					WILLIAMS, Vanessa		
01/07/89	BB	8	20		1 Dreamin'	CB 10 / RR 10	Wing 871078
02/01/92	BB	❶⁵	31	●	2 Save The Best For Last	RR ❶⁴ / CB ❶³	Wing 865136
05/23/92	RR	7	19		3 Just For Tonight		Wing 865888
01/23/93	RR	❶¹	38		4 Love Is VANESSA WILLIAMS and BRIAN McKNIGHT	CB 2¹ / BB 3¹	Giant 18630
06/17/95	BB	4	25	●	5 Colors Of The Wind	CB 6	Hollywood 64001
					WILLIS, Bruce		
01/16/87	BB	5	16		1 Respect Yourself BRUCE WILLIS with THE POINTER SISTERS	RR 6 / CB 9	Motown 1876
					WILLIS, Chuck		
05/12/58	BB	9	19	☉	1 What Am I Living For		Atlantic 1179
					WILLS, Johnnie Lee, And His Boys		
02/04/50	BB	9	11		1 Rag Mop		Bullet 696
					WILL TO POWER		
09/10/88	RR	❶²	25	●	1 Baby, I Love Your Way/Freebird Medley (Free Baby)	BB ❶¹ / CB ❶¹	Epic 08034
11/17/90	RR	4	21		2 I'm Not In Love	BB 7 / CB 7	Epic 73636
					WILSON, Al		
10/06/73	BB	❶¹	22	●	1 Show And Tell	CB ❶¹ / RW ❶¹ / RR 5	Rocky Road 30073
					WILSON, Ann		
05/12/84	RR	4	20		1 Almost Paradise...Love Theme From Footloose MIKE RENO and ANN WILSON	BB 7 / CB 7	Columbia 04418
12/24/88	BB	6	19		2 Surrender To Me ANN WILSON AND ROBIN ZANDER	RR 9	Capitol 44288
					WILSON, J. Frank, and The Cavaliers		
08/08/64	RW	❶²	21	☉	1 Last Kiss	CB ❶¹ / BB 2¹	Josie 923
					WILSON, Jackie		
11/17/58	CB	6	21	☉	1 Lonely Teardrops	MV 6 / BB 7	Brunswick 55105
03/07/60	MV	2¹	20		2 Night	CB 3² / BB 4	Brunswick 55166
07/04/60	CB	8	15		3 (You Were Made For) All My Love		Brunswick 55167
10/10/60	MV	7	15		4 Alone At Last	BB 8 / CB 10	Brunswick 55170
01/02/61	BB	9	10		5 My Empty Arms		Brunswick 55201
03/02/63	CB	4	14		6 Baby Workout	MV 4 / BB 5	Brunswick 55239
10/08/66	RW	10	15		7 Whispers (Gettin' Louder)		Brunswick 55300
08/05/67	BB	6	14		8 (Your Love Keeps Lifting Me) Higher And Higher	CB 6 / RW 6	Brunswick 55336
					WILSON PHILLIPS		
03/17/90	BB	❶¹	25	●	1 Hold On	CB ❶¹ / RR 3¹	SBK 07322
06/30/90	RR	❶³	23	●	2 Release Me	BB ❶² / CB 2¹	SBK 07327
10/12/90	CB	3³	23		3 Impulsive	RR 3² / BB 4	SBK 07337
02/08/91	BB	❶¹	22		4 You're In Love	RR ❶¹ / CB 3¹	SBK 07343
					WINANS, CeCe — see HOUSTON, Whitney		
					WINANS, Mario		
02/21/04	BB	2⁸	30	○	1 I Don't Wanna Know MARIO WINANS Featuring P. Diddy & Enya	RR 4	Bad Boy
					WINDING, Kai		
07/06/63	MV	7	15		1 More	BB 8 / CB 8	Verve 10295
					WINEHOUSE, Amy		
03/31/07	BB	9	20	△	1 Rehab		Universal Rep. 008491
					WINGS — see McCARTNEY, Paul		

174

DEBUT	CH	PK	WK	Gold	A-side (Chart Hit) ... Other Charts	Label & Number
					WINSTONS, The	
05/24/69	RW	6	13	●	1 Color Him Father ... BB 7 / CB 8	Metromedia 117
					WINTER, Edgar, Group	
03/10/73	RW	❶²	20	●	1 Frankenstein ... BB ❶¹ / CB ❶¹	Epic 10967
08/04/73	RW	9	16		2 Free Ride ... CB 10	Epic 11024
					WINTERHALTER, Hugo, and his Orchestra	
04/15/50	BB	10	20		1 Count Every Star ...	RCA Victor 3221
10/07/50	BB	9	7		2 Mr. Touchdown, U. S. A. ...	RCA Victor 3913
01/26/52	BB	10	9		3 A Kiss To Build A Dream On ...	RCA Victor 4455
03/08/52	BB	6	18		4 Blue Tango ...	RCA Victor 4518
06/14/52	BB	9	21		5 Vanessa ... CB 9	RCA Victor 4691
10/03/53	BB	8	5		6 The Velvet Glove ...	RCA Victor 5405
					HENRI RENÉ and HUGO WINTERHALTER	
07/03/54	BB	9	11		7 The Little Shoemaker ...	RCA Victor 5769
					HUGO WINTERHALTER'S ORCHESTRA and CHORUS and a Friend	
06/23/56	MV	❶¹	31	⊙	8 Canadian Sunset ... BB 2² / CB 2¹	RCA Victor 6537
					HUGO WINTERHALTER WITH EDDIE HEYWOOD	
					WINWOOD, Steve	
02/07/81	RR	❶¹	19		1 While You See A Chance ... BB 7 / RW 9 / CB 10	Island 49656
06/14/86	CB	❶²	22		2 Higher Love ... RR ❶² / BB ❶¹	Island 28710
02/07/87	RR	4	23		3 The Finer Things ... CB 7 / BB 8	Island 28498
05/30/87	RR	9	21		4 Back In The High Life Again ...	Island 28472
10/10/87	RR	7	20		5 Valerie ... BB 9 / CB 9	Island 28231
06/10/88	BB	❶⁴	20		6 Roll With It ... CB ❶³ / RR ❶³	Virgin 99326
08/20/88	CB	5	18		7 Don't You Know What The Night Can Do? ... BB 6 / RR 6	Virgin 99290
11/26/88	CB	9	18		8 Holding On ... RR 10	Virgin 99261
					WITHERS, Bill	
07/03/71	BB	3²	18	●	1 Ain't No Sunshine ... RW 3² / CB 4	Sussex 219
04/15/72	BB	❶³	19	●	2 Lean On Me ... CB ❶² / RW ❶¹	Sussex 235
08/19/72	BB	2²	13	●	3 Use Me ... RW 3¹ / CB 5	Sussex 241
02/07/81	RR	❶²	24		4 Just The Two Of Us ... BB 2³ / CB 4 / RW 5	Elektra 47103
					GROVER WASHINGTON, JR. with BILL WITHERS	
					WIZ KHALIFA	
10/02/10	BB	❶¹	25	△⁶	1 Black And Yellow ...	Rostrum 527038
04/09/11	BB	6	15	△²	2 No Sleep ...	Rostrum
10/29/11	BB	7	32	△⁶	3 Young, Wild & Free ...	Rostrum
					SNOOP DOGG & WIZ KHALIFA Featuring Bruno Mars	
03/28/15	BB	❶¹²	52	△¹¹	4 See You Again ...	Universal Studios
					WIZ KHALIFA with CHARLIE PUTH	
					WOLF, Peter	
07/13/84	RR	9	16		1 Lights Out ...	EMI America 8208
					WOMACK, Bobby	
02/02/74	CB	8	19	●	1 Lookin' For A Love ... RW 8 / BB 10	United Artists 375
					WONDER, Stevie	
06/22/63	CB	❶⁴	16	⊙	1 Fingertips - Pt 2 ... BB ❶³ / MV ❶³	Tamla 54080
					LITTLE STEVIE WONDER	
12/11/65	BB	3²	16		2 Uptight (Everything's Alright) ... RW 3² / CB 3¹	Tamla 54124
07/16/66	RW	8	11		3 Blowin In The Wind ... BB 9	Tamla 54136
11/12/66	RW	7	11		4 A Place In The Sun ... BB 9 / CB 10	Tamla 54139
06/03/67	BB	2²	16		5 I Was Made To Love Her ... CB 2¹ / RW 2¹	Tamla 54151
09/30/67	CB	10	9		6 I'm Wondering ...	Tamla 54157
04/06/68	CB	7	13		7 Shoo-Be-Doo-Be-Doo-Da-Day ... BB 9 / RW 9	Tamla 54165
11/02/68	CB	❶¹	14		8 For Once In My Life ... RW ❶¹ / BB 2²	Tamla 54174
05/31/69	RW	3²	15		9 My Cherie Amour ... CB 3¹ / BB 4	Tamla 54180
10/18/69	BB	7	14		10 Yester-Me, Yester-You, Yesterday ... CB 9 / RW 9	Tamla 54188
06/20/70	CB	❶¹	14		11 Signed, Sealed, Delivered I'm Yours ... RW ❶¹ / BB 3²	Tamla 54196
10/17/70	RW	8	11		12 Heaven Help Us All ... BB 9 / CB 9	Tamla 54200
03/13/71	CB	9	12		13 We Can Work It Out ...	Tamla 54202
08/07/71	RW	4	14		14 If You Really Love Me ... BB 8 / CB 9	Tamla 54208
11/11/72	CB	❶²	17		15 Superstition ... RW ❶² / BB ❶¹	Tamla 54226
03/17/73	BB	❶¹	17		16 You Are The Sunshine Of My Life ... CB ❶¹ / RW ❶¹	Tamla 54232
08/18/73	CB	❶¹	16		17 Higher Ground ... RW ❶¹ / BB 4 / RR 8	Tamla 54235
11/10/73	RW	5	18		18 Living For The City ... CB 6 / BB 8 / RR 10	Tamla 54242
03/30/74	CB	10	16		19 Don't You Worry 'Bout A Thing ...	Tamla 54245
08/03/74	BB	❶¹	22		20 You Haven't Done Nothin ... CB ❶¹ / RW ❶¹ / RR 8	Tamla 54252
11/09/74	CB	❶¹	18		21 Boogie On Reggae Woman ... RW ❶¹ / BB 3² / RR 10	Tamla 54254
11/26/76	BB	❶¹	21		22 I Wish ... CB ❶¹ / RW ❶¹ / RR 4	Tamla 54274
04/02/77	BB	❶³	21		23 Sir Duke ... RW ❶² / CB ❶¹ / RR 2²	Tamla 54281
11/03/79	BB	4	18		24 Send One Your Love ... CB 5	Tamla 54303
09/20/80	CB	❶²	24		25 Master Blaster (Jammin') ... BB 5	Tamla 54317

DEBUT	CH	PK	WK	Gold	A-side (Chart Hit)	Other Charts	Label & Number
					WONDER, Stevie (cont'd)		
01/16/82	CB	❶¹	19		26 That Girl	RR 2⁵ / RW 3⁴ / BB 4	Tamla 1602
04/02/82	BB	❶⁷	20	●	27 Ebony And Ivory	CB ❶⁶ / RR ❶⁴	Columbia 02860
					PAUL McCARTNEY with STEVIE WONDER		
08/18/84	CB	❶⁴	26	●	28 I Just Called To Say I Love You	BB ❶³ / RR ❶²	Motown 1745
09/06/85	RR	❶²	21		29 Part-Time Lover	BB ❶¹ / CB ❶¹	Tamla 1808
11/23/85	BB	10	19		30 Go Home	RR 10	Tamla 1817
					WOOD, Brenton		
08/12/67	RW	6	15		1 Gimme Little Sign	CB 7 / BB 9	Double Shot 116
					WOOD, Del		
09/01/51	CB	❶¹	27		1 Down Yonder	BB 4	Tennessee 775
					WOOLEY, Sheb		
05/19/58	BB	❶⁶	14	☉	1 The Purple People Eater	CB ❶⁵ / MV ❶³	MGM 12651
					WRECKX-N-EFFECT		
10/03/92	BB	2³	29	▲²	1 Rump Shaker	CB 2²	MCA 54388
					WRIGHT, Betty		
11/20/71	CB	4	15	●	1 Clean Up Woman	RW 4 / BB 6	Alston 4601
					WRIGHT, Gary		
01/03/76	RR	❶²	25	●	1 Dream Weaver	CB ❶¹ / RW ❶¹ / BB 2³	Warner 8167
04/17/76	BB	2²	29		2 Love Is Alive	RR 2² / CB 3¹ / RW 4	Warner 8143
					WYNETTE, Tammy — see KLF, The		

X

					XSCAPE		
09/18/93	CB	❶¹	29	▲	1 Just Kickin' It	BB 2¹ / RR 8	So So Def 77119
12/17/93	CB	7	20	●	2 Understanding	BB 8	So So Def 77335
10/07/95	BB	8	22	●	3 Who Can I Run To?	CB 8	So So Def 78056
05/02/98	BB	7	20	●	4 The Arms Of The One Who Loves You		So So Def 78788
10/24/98	BB	9	14		5 My Little Secret		So So Def 79036
					XXXTENTACION		
03/17/18	BB	❶¹	38	△⁷	1 Sad!		Bad Vibes Forever

Y

					YAMIN, Elliott		
04/07/07	RR	4	30	△	1 Wait For You		Hickory
					YANKOVIC, "Weird Al"		
03/09/84	CB	4	14	●	1 Eat It		Rock 'n' Roll 04374
10/14/06	BB	9	20	△	2 White & Nerdy		Way Moby
					YARDBIRDS, The		
05/08/65	RW	4	13		1 For Your Love	BB 6 / CB 6	Epic 9790
07/31/65	BB	9	12		2 Heart Full Of Soul	RW 9	Epic 9823
03/12/66	CB	10	13		3 Shapes Of Things	RW 10	Epic 10006
					YES		
02/05/72	CB	10	14		1 Roundabout		Atlantic 2854
11/05/83	BB	❶²	26		2 Owner Of A Lonely Heart	CB ❶² / RR ❶²	Atco 99817
					YING YANG TWINS		
11/15/03	BB	9	26		1 Salt Shaker		TVT 2485
					YING YANG TWINS Feat. Lil Jon & The East Side Boyz		
					YLVIS		
09/21/13	BB	6	18	○	1 The Fox		Concorde
					YO GOTTI		
07/22/17	BB	8	22	△³	1 Rake It Up		Cocaine Muzik
					YO GOTTI Featuring Nicki Minaj		
					YOUNG, Barry		
10/16/65	RW	10	15		1 One Has My Name (The Other Has My Heart)		Dot 16756
					YOUNG, Faron		
03/27/61	MV	7	16		1 Hello Walls	CB 10	Capitol 4533
					YOUNG, John Paul		
07/15/78	BB	7	21		1 Love Is In The Air		Scotti Brothers 402

DEBUT	CH	PK	WK	Gold	A-side (Chart Hit)	Other Charts	Label & Number
					YOUNG, Kathy, with The Innocents		
10/24/60	MV	3³	18	⊙	1 A Thousand Stars	BB 3¹ / CB 4	Indigo 108
					YOUNG, Neil		
01/29/72	BB	❶¹	15	●	1 Heart Of Gold	CB ❶¹ / RW ❶¹	Reprise 1065
					YOUNG, Paul		
05/11/85	CB	❶²	24	●	1 Everytime You Go Away	BB ❶¹ / RR ❶¹	Columbia 04867
09/07/85	CB	10	19		2 I'm Gonna Tear Your Playhouse Down		Columbia 05577
07/14/90	CB	6	23		3 Oh Girl	BB 8 / RR 8	Columbia 73377
01/25/92	CB	8	22		4 What Becomes Of The Brokenhearted		MCA 54331
					YOUNG, Victor, and his Orchestra		
07/01/50	BB	7	15		1 Mona Lisa		Decca 27048
08/07/54	BB	6	15		2 The High And The Mighty	MV 7	Decca 29203
05/20/57	CB	6	34		3 Around The World (Main Theme)	MV 7	Decca 30262
					YOUNGBLOODS, The		
06/28/69	CB	4	18	●	1 Get Together	RW 4 / BB 5	RCA Victor 9752
					YOUNGBLOODZ		
08/09/03	BB	4	32		1 Damn!		So So Def 52215
					YOUNGBLOODZ Featuring Lil' Jon		
					YOUNGBOY NEVER BROKE AGAIN — see JUICE WRLD		
					YOUNG DRO		
06/17/06	BB	10	20		1 Shoulder Lean		Grand Hustle 94282
					YOUNG DRO Featuring T.I.		
					YOUNG-HOLT UNLIMITED		
11/16/68	RW	❶¹	14	●	1 Soulful Strut	BB 3¹ / CB 4	Brunswick 55391
					YOUNG JEEZY		
09/03/05	BB	4	24	△²	1 Soul Survivor	RR 10	Def Jam 005290
					YOUNG JEEZY featuring Akon		
					YOUNG M.C.		
07/29/89	BB	7	39	▲	1 Bust A Move	CB 9	Delicious Vinyl 105
					YOUNG MONEY		
05/23/09	BB	10	20	○	1 Every Girl		Young Money
12/12/09	BB	2¹	25	△³	2 BedRock		Universal Motown
					YOUNG MONEY Featuring Lloyd		
					YOUNG RASCALS — see RASCALS		
					YUNG BERG — see RAY J		
					YUNG JOC		
04/15/06	BB	3¹	28		1 It's Goin' Down		Bad Boy 94249
					YUNG JOC Featuring Nitti		
					YURO, Timi		
07/17/61	MV	3¹	14		1 Hurt	BB 4 / CB 4	Liberty 55343

Z

DEBUT	CH	PK	WK	Gold	A-side	Other Charts	Label & Number
					ZACHARIAS, Helmut, And His Magic Violins		
08/25/56	MV	8	14		1 When The White Lilacs Bloom Again		Decca 30039
					ZACHERLE, John, "The Cool Ghoul"		
03/10/58	BB	6	13		1 Dinner With Drac (Part 1)		Cameo 130
					ZAGER & EVANS		
06/14/69	BB	❶⁶	14	●	1 In The Year 2525	CB ❶⁴ / RW ❶⁴	RCA Victor 0174
					ZANDER, Robin — see WILSON, Ann		
					ZAY HILFIGERRR & ZAYION McCALL		
10/08/16	BB	5	21	△²	1 Juju On That Beat (TZ Anthem)		Atlantic
					ZAYN		
02/20/16	BB	❶¹	24	△³	1 Pillowtalk		RCA
12/31/16	BB	2¹	23	△⁴	2 I Don't Wanna Live Forever (Fifty Shades Darker)		Universal Studios
					ZAYN & TAYLOR SWIFT		

DEBUT	CH	PK	WK	Gold	A-side (Chart Hit) .... Other Charts	Label & Number
					ZEDD	
04/06/13	BB	8	33	△³	1 Clarity	Interscope
					ZEDD with FOXES	
03/18/17	BB	7	31	△²	2 Stay	Interscope
					ZEDD & ALESSIA CARA	
02/10/18	BB	5	40	△³	3 The Middle	Interscope
					ZEDD, MAREN MORRIS & GREY	
					ZERVAS, Arizona	
11/16/19	BB	4	16		1 Roxanne	Arizona Zarvas
					ZHANE	
08/28/93	CB	5	31	●	1 Hey Mr. D.J. .... BB 6 / RR 9	Flavor Unit 77177
					ZOMBIES, The	
10/03/64	CB	❶¹	17	☉	1 She's Not There .... BB 2¹ / RW 4	Parrot 9695
01/09/65	BB	6	12		2 Tell Her No .... CB 6 / RW 8	Parrot 9723
02/08/69	CB	❶¹	14	●	3 Time Of The Season .... BB 3² / RW 4	Date 1628
					ZZ TOP	
05/19/84	RR	5	20		1 Legs .... BB 8	Warner 29272
10/18/85	RR	7	18		2 Sleeping Bag .... BB 8 / CB 9	Warner 28884

ARTISTS WITH THE MOST #1 HITS (1950-2020)

These 60 artists achieved the ultimate prize in the music industry – not only hitting the Top 10, but hitting the coveted #1 spot at least 5 times! Listed to the left of the artist is their #1s total.

24	The Beatles	7	Three Dog Night
23	Mariah Carey	6	Pat Boone
22	Elvis Presley	6	Chicago
17	Michael Jackson	6	Eagles
17	Madonna	6	Eminem
15	Stevie Wonder	6	The 4 Seasons
13	Whitney Houston	6	Daryl Hall & John Oates
13	The Supremes	6	KC & The Sunshine Band
12	Janet Jackson	6	Maroon 5
11	Elton John	6	Bruno Mars
11	Paul McCartney	6	Diana Ross
11	Rihanna	6	Barbra Streisand
10	Bee Gees	6	Donna Summer
10	George Michael	6	Taylor Swift
10	Katy Perry	6	The Temptations
10	Prince	6	Justin Timberlake
10	The Rolling Stones	6	Bobby Vinton
9	Phil Collins	5	Bon Jovi
9	Perry Como	5	Chubby Checker
9	Usher	5	John Denver
8	Lionel Richie	5	Destiny's Child
7	Paula Abdul	5	Celine Dion
7	Boyz II Men	5	Duran Duran
7	Carpenters	5	The Everly Brothers
7	Kelly Clarkson	5	Jennifer Lopez
7	The Jackson 5	5	The Monkees
7	Olivia Newton-John	5	Alanis Morissette
7	Pink	5	Nelly
7	Britney Spears	5	Patti Page
7	Rod Stewart	5	Roxette

ARTISTS WITH THE MOST TOP 10 HITS (1950-2020)

48 Elvis Presley	16 Jo Stafford	12 Jay-Z
41 Madonna	16 Usher	12 Kool & The Gang
36 The Beatles	15 Paul Anka	12 Puff Daddy
34 Michael Jackson	15 Phil Collins	11 Backstreet Boys
33 Elton John	15 The Everly Brothers	11 Brook Benton
32 Mariah Carey	15 Lady Gaga	11 James Brown
30 Perry Como	15 Frankie Laine	11 Ray Charles
30 Stevie Wonder	15 Olivia Newton-John	11 Dave Clark Five
28 Eddie Fisher	15 Diana Ross	11 Creedence (CCR)
27 Janet Jackson	15 Kay Starr	11 Fats Domino
27 Rihanna	14 Beyonce	11 Flo Rida
27 The Rolling Stones	14 Justin Bieber	11 Four Tops
26 Taylor Swift	14 Cher	11 John Lennon
25 Chicago	14 Fleetwood Mac	11 John Mellencamp
24 Whitney Houston	14 Ariana Grande	11 Guy Mitchell
24 Paul McCartney	14 Barry Manilow	11 Roy Orbison
24 Patti Page	14 Katy Perry	11 Pointer Sisters
24 Prince	14 Lionel Richie	11 Neil Sedaka
23 Drake	14 Donna Summer	11 Bob Seger
22 The Supremes	13 Christina Aguilera	11 Bobby Vinton
21 Pat Boone	13 Black Eyed Peas	11 Andy Williams
21 Eminem	13 Bon Jovi	10 Paula Abdul
21 George Michael	13 Carpenters	10 Ray Anthony
20 The Beach Boys	13 Kelly Clarkson	10 Michael Bolton
20 Ricky Nelson	13 Herman's Hermits	10 Boyz II Men
20 Rod Stewart	13 The Jackson 5	10 Commodores
20 The Temptations	13 Huey Lewis	10 Bing Crosby
19 Nat "King" Cole	13 Lil Wayne	10 Bobby Darin
19 The 4 Seasons	13 Bruno Mars	10 Doris Day
19 Aretha Franklin	13 Richard Marx	10 Destiny's Child
18 Neil Diamond	13 Kenny Rogers	10 Earth, Wind & Fire
18 Connie Francis	13 Bruce Springsteen	10 ELO
18 Marvin Gaye	13 Barbra Streisand	10 Foreigner
18 Hall & Oates	13 Three Dog Night	10 Al Green
18 Les Paul & Mary Ford	13 Dionne Warwick	10 Heart
17 Bee Gees	13 Kanye West	10 R. Kelly
17 Maroon 5	12 Aerosmith	10 Gladys Knight
17 Pink	12 Chris Brown	10 Jennifer Lopez
17 Justin Timberlake	12 Celine Dion	10 Tony Martin
16 Bryan Adams	12 Duran Duran	10 Nelly
16 Billy Joel	12 Eagles	10 *NSYNC
16 Brenda Lee	12 Gloria Estefan	10 Johnny Rivers
16 Frank Sinatra	12 Four Aces	10 Linda Ronstadt
16 Britney Spears	12 Genesis	10 The Weeknd

180

Go Beyond the Top 10 Hits ...
Way Beyond

Treat your heart for the charts and dive deep into music history with Joel Whitburn's Record Research collection. Joel created music chart research and then shared his findings with the world when he published his first book based on *Billboard* magazine's Hot 100 chart in 1970. In the decades since, Joel and his Record Researchers have covered singles and album charts spanning multiple genres and various music trade magazines. Below is a sampling from this library, a source of accurate and inexhaustible facts and stats. To view other books, visit recordresearch.com for detailed descriptions, sample pages and more.

Sample Pages From Books Arranged ...

... By Artist

... By Year

... By Week

actual size of pages above: 8.5" x 11"

182